BOTTOM LINE YEAR BOOK 2008

BY THE EDITORS OF

Bottom Line
PERSONAL
www.BottomLineSecrets.com

Contents

PART TWO: YOUR MONEY

7 • MONEYWISE

8 • INSURANCE ADVISER

9 • TAX NEWS

10 • INVESTMENT WISDOM

11 • CONSUMER CONFIDENTIAL

PART THREE: YOUR FINANCIAL FUTURE

12 • RETIREMENT REPORT

PART FOUR: YOUR LEISURE

14 • TRAVEL AND ADVENTURE

16 • ON THE MOVE

PART FIVE: YOUR LIFE

17 • IN THE HOME

18 • WINNING WAYS

1

Health Update

Medical Symptoms Men and Women Should Never Ignore

We all experience troublesome symptoms at different times—such as fatigue or digestive upset. These generally indicate mild conditions, but they can be a sign of dangerous problems. Complicating matters is that some symptoms are more likely to be serious for men, others for women. *Symptoms and what they can mean...*

DANGEROUS SYMPTOMS FOR MEN

Symptom: **Shoulder pain.**

Could be: Coronary artery disease.

A lot of men are sedentary during the week, then overdo it on the weekend—and blame sudden shoulder pain on muscle strain. But shoulder pain that comes on suddenly often is a sign of coronary artery disease. In some cases, this is the only symptom. More often, men also will report that they are experiencing occasional shortness of breath and possibly subtle chest pain.

Important: Call 911 or get to an emergency room immediately if shoulder pain comes on suddenly for no obvious reason—or if it's accompanied by other symptoms. You might be having a heart attack.

Also: Ask your doctor, before an emergency arises, if you should take aspirin if you are having symptoms of a heart attack. Aspirin (chewed and swallowed) can decrease the severity of a heart attack.

Symptom: **Persistent foot and hip pain.**

Could be: Prostate cancer.

Almost everyone experiences joint pain on occasion. It's usually due to overuse injuries or relatively minor "wear and tear" arthritis—joint pain that gets more common with age.

J. Edward Hill, MD, a family physician at North Mississippi Medical Center and a faculty member at Family Medicine Residency Center, both in Tupelo. He is also a past president of the American Medical Association and an adviser for the *American Medical Association Family Medical Guide* (Wiley).

However, a man who experiences joint pain that doesn't improve after a few days with the usual treatments, such as rest and over-the-counter analgesics, should get a complete checkup. This is especially important if the pain starts in the foot or ankle, then extends out to the hip. It could indicate that prostate cancer has started to spread. Any delay could be life-threatening.

Also important: Men should see a doctor if they notice any change in their urine or urinary habits—difficulty urinating, blood in the urine, etc. Men often assume that this is due to normal, age-related changes in the prostate gland—but changes in urinary habits also can indicate early-stage prostate cancer.

DANGEROUS SYMPTOMS FOR WOMEN

Symptoms: **Slight numbness in an arm or leg, transient loss of balance, intermittent blurred vision.**

Could be: Multiple sclerosis (MS).

Numbness, balance difficulties and a change in vision are classic signs of MS, a disease that affects women almost twice as often as men. Women often ignore these symptoms because they tend to come and go quickly—and they may occur so rarely that they don't seem serious. Many patients with MS report having symptoms up to seven years before being diagnosed.

MS symptoms usually get worse over time. Women who have early treatment—with drugs such as beta interferons, for example—usually have a marked reduction in symptoms and retain their ability to live normal lives.

Symptom: **Minor abdominal/pelvic pain that comes and goes.**

Could be: Ovarian cancer.

Most women of child-bearing age experience occasional discomfort in the abdomen or pelvic region. It is usually due to digestive distress or menstruation, but it also can be an early sign of ovarian cancer. The discomfort usually lasts a few days, then goes away for weeks or months. Because the pain tends to be minor and intermittent, most women ignore it—even when it occurs over the course of months or years.

Other possible symptoms of ovarian cancer: Abdominal swelling or bloating…indigestion and/or nausea…and/or urinary urgency.

The discomfort of menstrual or digestive conditions tends to occur in a predictable fashion—for example, at a certain time of the month or after eating certain foods. With ovarian cancer, the discomfort gets more persistent and severe as the cancer grows.

Important: Women experiencing this kind of pain should see a doctor. Ovarian cancer can be successfully treated when it is detected in the early stages. Because it causes only minor symptoms—or no symptoms, in some cases—only about 29% of patients are diagnosed before the cancer has spread. After that point, treatments are much less likely to work.

Symptoms: **Unusual fatigue, shortness of breath.**

Could be: Heart disease.

A woman's symptoms of heart disease or a heart attack are typically different than a man's. Women are unlikely to have crushing chest pain or pain radiating down one or both arms. They are more likely to experience fatigue, difficulty breathing, pressure or pain in the upper abdomen or symptoms resembling indigestion.

A woman with heart disease may get short of breath or feel exhausted all the time. If you suspect you are having a heart attack, call for emergency medical help immediately.

Also: Ask your doctor, before an emergency arises, if you should take aspirin if you are having symptoms of a heart attack. Aspirin (chewed and swallowed) can reduce the severity of a heart attack.

Medical Conditions Doctors Misdiagnose

Vicki Rackner, MD, a board-certified surgeon and clinical instructor at the University of Washington School of Medicine in Seattle. She is founder of Medical Bridges, a patient-advocacy consulting firm and author of *The Biggest Skeleton in Your Doctor's Closet* (Five Star).

Each year, up to 40% of Americans who are seen in an emergency room or intensive care unit are misdiagnosed. In some cases, a patient's condition is later correctly diagnosed, and appropriate treatment is administered. But, in other cases, the time that is lost through a misdiagnosis can be life-threatening.

Important: Listen to your intuition, but don't try to self-diagnose your problem. Get a complete evaluation from your doctor and a second opinion, if desired.

Often-misdiagnosed conditions…

***Wrong diagnosis:* Gastroenteritis.** Gastroenteritis can be triggered by ingesting food or water contaminated with a virus (Norwalk virus, adenovirus)…a bacterium (*Salmonella* or *Escherichia coli)*…a parasite (Giardia)…rare microorganisms (amoebas or parasitic worms)…or a food allergy. Gastroenteritis can result in cramping, vomiting and/or diarrhea.

But all these symptoms also can characterize a bowel obstruction (commonly caused by scar tissue from a previous abdominal or pelvic surgery)…appendicitis…disease of the gallbladder …or antibiotic-associated colitis.

Self-defense: Do not accept a diagnosis of "gastroenteritis" if your symptoms include…

•**Crampy abdominal pain that comes and goes.** This could indicate a bowel obstruction.

•**Pain that begins around the navel and migrates to the lower right abdomen.** This could be appendicitis.

•**Sudden pain in the upper-right abdomen after eating a high-fat meal.** This symptom could be due to a gallbladder attack.

•**Severe diarrhea, abdominal pain and/ or fever.** All these symptoms could be caused from pseudomembranous colitis, an inflammatory condition of the colon that occurs in some people who have used antibiotics. It is usually caused by overgrowth of the bacterium *Clostridium difficile.*

To diagnose your condition correctly, your doctor should take a thorough medical history and perform a physical exam. Tests may include blood work, X-rays, stool tests and an ultrasound or computed tomography (CT) scan.

***Wrong diagnosis:* Migraine.** More than 45 million people seek medical care each year for headaches. Many have a true migraine, a severe headache often accompanied by nausea, vomiting and/or extreme sensitivity to light and sound. Others have a tension or cluster headache.

In rare instances, a headache can indicate a potentially serious condition, such as a stroke… a ruptured brain aneurysm (a weakened blood vessel that has burst)…a contusion (bruising of the brain)…a concussion (a head injury that can cause headache, confusion and amnesia)…a subdural hematoma (bleeding from veins between the outer and middle layers of tissue covering the brain, usually following a head injury)…a brain tumor…meningitis (a bacterial or viral infection of the membrane that surrounds the spinal cord and brain)…or a sinus infection.

Self-defense: Do not accept a diagnosis of "migraine" if your symptoms include…

•**Headache with confusion, weakness on one side of the body, double vision and/or trouble speaking.** This could indicate a stroke.

•**"The worst headache of my life"** or a headache that "hits like a lightning bolt." These are signs of a possible stroke or ruptured brain aneurysm.

•**Headache that gets worse after coughing, exertion, straining or sudden movement.** This can indicate a ruptured brain aneurysm.

•**Headache after a head injury,** especially if the headache gets worse over the next day or two. It could be a brain injury, such as a contusion, concussion or subdural hematoma.

•**New headache pain or changes in headache pattern** (location, intensity or frequency), especially in people age 55 or older. This could signal a brain tumor.

•**Headache with a fever, stiff neck and/or rash.** These are red flags for meningitis.

•**Headache after a recent sore throat, cold or flu.** This could indicate a sinus infection.

Ask your doctor whether you should be seen by a neurologist. Tests may include blood work, a CT or magnetic resonance imaging (MRI) scan, sinus X-rays or a spinal tap, in which a sample of the fluid that surrounds the brain and spinal cord is withdrawn from the lower back with a needle and sent to a lab for analysis.

***Wrong diagnosis:* Muscle strain.** A muscle strain often is diagnosed when a person over-exerts himself/herself and then experiences pain and/or swelling.

Among the more serious conditions characterized by these symptoms are an infection…or an aortic dissection (a potentially fatal condition in which the inner layer of the wall of the aorta, the main artery of the body, tears).

Self-defense: Do not accept a diagnosis of "muscle strain" if your symptoms include…

• **Fever and/or a joint that is red and hot.** These are red flags for infectious arthritis (infection of the tissues of a joint).

• **A "ripping" or "tearing" sensation in the upper back.** This commonly occurs in patients who have suffered an aortic dissection.

An evaluation may include X-rays, a CT or MRI scan, blood tests and/or arthrocentesis (removal of joint fluid that is analyzed for bacteria, other microorganisms or gouty crystals).

Misconceptions That Increase Your Risk For Heart Disease

Barry L. Zaret, MD, the Robert W. Berliner Professor of Medicine and a professor of radiology at Yale University School of Medicine in New Haven, CT. He served as chief of the section of cardiology at Yale from 1978 to 2004. He is coauthor of *Heart Care for Life* (Yale University Press).

One out of every five Americans right now has some type of heart disease. Literally *millions* of cases could be prevented if people had better information about the best prevention and treatment strategies.

Despite the abundance of health information that is reported in the media, many people are endangering their health because they are still ill-informed about key aspects of heart disease. Barry L. Zaret, MD, one of the country's leading specialists in cardiovascular health, discusses the most common of misconceptions regarding heart disease below…

Misconception 1: **High cholesterol is the main risk factor for heart attack.**

Fact: Though high cholesterol does increase risk, recent studies show that elevated levels (3 milligrams per liter [mg/L] or higher) of *C-reactive protein* (CRP), a protein that circulates in the bloodstream, could have an even stronger link than high cholesterol to heart attack and stroke.

Everyone has at least a small amount of CRP in the bloodstream. At higher levels, it indicates the presence of inflammation—possibly caused by an underlying bacterial or viral infection that may harm the linings of blood vessels and promote the development of atherosclerosis.

Every patient with a high risk for cardiovascular disease—smokers and/or those with a family history of heart disease, for example—needs to have a high-sensitivity CRP blood test. This test, not like the standard CRP test, distinguishes between inflammation due to cardiovascular disease and other inflammatory conditions, such as arthritis. The high-sensitivity CRP test is particularly important for patients who have had a previous heart attack or who have unstable angina (angina that worsens). An elevated CRP level in these patients indicates a very high risk for heart attack—even if cholesterol levels are normal.

Misconception 2: **All adults should take a daily aspirin.**

Fact: Daily aspirin therapy is often recommended for patients who have an elevated heart disease risk due to family history, smoking, obesity, diabetes and atherosclerosis. Studies show that it can curb heart attack risk in *men* by more than 40%.

For women, the evidence is less clear. New research indicates that women who take aspirin are more likely to experience gastrointestinal upset or bleeding problems than men. Although research shows that in women age 46 or older aspirin protects against stroke, it does not reduce heart attack risk in all of these women. Aspirin has been shown to lower heart attack risk only in women age 65 or older, whether or not they have risk factors for the disease. Women of any age who smoke or have a family history of heart disease or other risk factors may benefit from aspirin therapy. The standard recommendation for women is 81 milligrams (mg) daily.

There is no evidence to suggest that aspirin helps prevent a heart attack in healthy women who are under age 65. For all these women, not smoking, controlling body weight, getting regular exercise and maintaining a healthful diet are the best ways to guard against the development of heart disease.

This also is true for men age 64 and younger who are healthy and don't have risk factors for heart disease. However, men age 65 or older, even if healthy, should take 81 mg of aspirin daily to protect against heart disease.

Misconception 3: The greatest danger of smoking is lung cancer.

Fact: Lung cancer is obviously a concern for smokers, but the risk for cardiovascular disease is actually higher. Of the approximately 440,000 premature deaths caused annually by smoking, the majority are due to cardiovascular disease, according to the Centers for Disease Control and Prevention.

Smoking increases levels of carbon monoxide in the blood, which damages artery linings and promotes atherosclerosis. It appears to decrease HDL "good" cholesterol and increase blood levels of *fibrinogen*, a substance in the blood that promotes clotting.

Good news: One year after quitting, the risk for heart disease drops to one-half that of current smokers, and within 15 years becomes about the same as for someone who never smoked.

Misconception 4: Exercise is dangerous if you've already had a heart attack.

Fact: Heart attack patients *especially* benefit from regular exercise. An analysis of 22 different studies that followed more than 4,000 patients for three years found that the death rate among patients who participated in a cardiac rehabilitation program that included exercise was 20% to 25% lower than among those who didn't exercise.

Heart patients who exercise have increased endurance, fewer chest or leg pains as well as improved heart function. Regular exercise also lowers blood pressure, increases HDL cholesterol and lowers resting heart rate.

Patients who have heart disease or have had a heart attack, or those who have been sedentary, should get a thorough checkup before starting an exercise program. This should include a treadmill stress test, which evaluates blood flow to the heart. Once your doctor determines that it's safe to exercise, aim for 30 minutes at least three to five days per week. Aerobic exercise—fast walking, swimming, etc.—provides the most benefits for heart patients. If you've had a heart attack or other cardiac event, start your exercise routine at a rehabilitation center, if possible. Ask your cardiologist to recommend one near you.

Misconception 5: The reports saying that chocolate is good for the heart are mostly just hype.

Fact: The cocoa beans used to make chocolate are extremely rich in the *flavonoids*, plant compounds which appear to relax small blood vessels and lower blood pressure. Some of the flavonoids in cocoa also appear to inhibit the ability of platelets to form clots in the arteries.

Harvard researchers recently studied residents of Kuna (an island off Panama), who drink an average of three to four cups of cocoa a day. (They consume even more cocoa in other foods.) Hypertension among these people is almost non-existent—until they leave the island and forgo their cocoa-rich diet. At that point, their rates of hypertension and heart disease rise.

Of course, there is a downside. The high levels of fat and sugar in chocolate can lead to obesity and elevated blood sugar. But one to two small squares daily of dark chocolate that is at least 70% cocoa and low in added sugar does appear to be good for the heart.

Do You Have Silent Heart Disease?

Prediman K. Shah, MD, director of the division of cardiology and the Atherosclerosis Research Center at Cedars–Sinai Heart Center in Los Angeles. He is also a professor of medicine at the David Geffen School of Medicine at the University of California, Los Angeles, and served as leader of the Screening for Heart Attack Prevention and Education (SHAPE) Task Force editorial committee.

Up to 50% of all people who have a first heart attack—which often concludes in sudden death—do not experience prior chest pain, shortness of breath or any other red flags for cardiovascular disease. A heart attack is their first and only symptom.

In the past, cardiologists relied solely on the presence of the risk factors—a family history of heart disease, smoking, diabetes, etc.—to identify "silent" heart disease.

New approach: An international task force of leading cardiologists has just issued new guidelines that could prevent more than 90,000 deaths from cardiovascular disease each year in the US. Most of these patients have *no* prior symptoms.

RISK FACTORS AREN'T ENOUGH

Most heart attacks and many strokes are caused by atherosclerosis, buildup of cholesterol and other substances (plaque) within artery walls.

Over time, increasing accumulations of plaque can compromise circulation—or result in blood clots that block circulation to the heart (heart attack) or brain (stroke).

Plaque can accumulate for decades within the artery walls without causing the arterial narrowing that results in angina (chest pain) or other symptoms. Even patients with massive amounts of plaque may be unaware that they have heart disease until they suffer a heart attack or sudden death.

RECOMMENDED TESTS

Guidelines created by the Screening for Heart Attack Prevention and Education (SHAPE) Task Force advise the noninvasive screening of virtually all asymptomatic males ages 45 to 75 and women ages 55 to 75.* The tests can detect arterial changes that are present in the vast majority of heart attack patients. The SHAPE Task Force highlighted two tests—a computed tomography (CT) scan of the coronary arteries and an ultrasound of the carotid arteries in the neck—that are more accurate than traditional risk-factor assessments in identifying high-risk patients.

Most patients require only one of these tests. Which test is recommended will depend on insurance coverage and/or other underlying health conditions and risk factors. Although these tests are widely available, health insurers do not always cover their cost, which ranges from about $200 to $400 each.**

TREATING SILENT HEART DISEASE

With screening tests, doctors can target high-risk patients more precisely—and recommend appropriate treatment. The aggressiveness of the treatment should be proportionate to the patient's risk level.

It's possible that drugs to reduce levels of existing plaque will be on the market within the next

*Screening for people age 75 or older is not recommended because they are considered to be at high risk for cardiovascular disease based on their age alone.

**Prices subject to change.

five years. *Until then, patients diagnosed with asymptomatic cardiovascular disease (based on one of the above tests) should...*

• **Get a stress test.** Patients who test positive for calcium or plaque in their coronary or carotid arteries should undergo a cardiac stress test. The test, which uses an electrocardiogram, involves walking on a treadmill or riding a bicycle. The test detects impediments in circulation through the coronary arteries and identifies abnormal heart rhythms (arrhythmias) that can occur during exercise in patients with heart disease. Nuclear stress tests (which involve the use of radioactive dye) or echocardiogram (a type of ultrasound) stress tests generally are more reliable than simple electrocardiogram tests.

Patients with significant blockages in the coronary arteries may require invasive procedures, such as angioplasty or bypass surgery, to restore normal circulation to the heart.

• **Control cholesterol and blood pressure.** They're two important risk factors for heart attack and stroke—and both are modifiable with medication and/or lifestyle changes. A patient who tests positive for asymptomatic cardiovascular disease needs to treat these conditions much more aggressively than someone without it. For cardiovascular health, aim for a blood pressure of no more than 110 mmHg to 120 mmHg systolic (top number) and 70 mmHg to 80 mmHg diastolic (bottom number). An ideal LDL "bad" cholesterol level is no more than 70.

Most patients can significantly decrease blood pressure and cholesterol with lifestyle changes —exercising for 30 minutes at least three to four times a week...losing weight, if necessary...eating less saturated fat and/or trans fat...and increasing consumption of fruits, vegetables, whole grains and fish.

The other risk factors to control: Smoking, obesity, diabetes, as well as emotional stress/anger, which may lead to a heart attack or angina. It's important to control all of these risk factors because they can amplify each other—for example, a sedentary lifestyle promotes obesity, which can lead to diabetes—or have a cumulative effect that's much more dangerous than an individual risk factor.

For more on silent heart disease, check with the Association for Eradication of Heart Attack, a nonprofit group that promotes heart disease education and research, 877-742-7311, *www.aeha.org.*

Read This Before Saying "Yes" to Bypass Surgery For Heart Disease

Michael D. Ozner, MD, a clinical assistant professor of both medicine and cardiology for the University of Miami School of Medicine, and medical director of Wellness & Prevention at Baptist Health South Florida, both located in Miami-Dade County. He is also a previous chairman of the American Heart Association of Miami, and author of *The Miami Mediterranean Diet: Lose Weight and Lower Your Risk of Heart Disease* (Cambridge House). Dr. Ozner's Web site is *www.cardiacoz.com.*

About 1.6 million Americans now undergo heart bypass surgery, angioplasty or stent procedures annually, even though there's no evidence that these procedures prolong life or prevent future heart attacks in the majority of patients.

The three-year survival rate for most patients who have had bypass surgery is almost exactly the same as it is for patients with heart disease who don't have surgery.

Good news: With medications and lifestyle changes, the vast majority of patients with heart disease can reduce the risk of a future heart attack by up to 80%—without undergoing expensive and risky procedures.

FLAWED APPROACH

More than half a million Americans die each year from heart disease. The majority suffer from coronary artery disease (CAD).

Many doctors view CAD primarily as a plumbing problem. When imaging tests reveal blockages in the arteries, their first instinct is to clear out the "gunk," whether or not a patient is experiencing troublesome symptoms.

This approach is often flawed. Most bypass and stent procedures are the equivalent of cosmetic cardiology. They make blood vessels appear healthy but do little to reduce heart attack risk. In fact, most heart attacks are caused by tiny blockages that can be hard to detect—and these blockages often are not in the blood vessels that triggered all the concern in the first place.

Surgical procedures are risky. The mortality rate from bypass surgery ranges from 3% to 5%. More than 50% of patients may experience cognitive difficulties after surgery, and patients who have bypass surgery are nearly four times more likely to suffer a subsequent stroke. Those are poor odds for procedures that don't necessarily prolong life or make patients healthier.

MEDICAL BYPASS

Some patients—those with unstable CAD—do require intervention, such as bypass surgery or a stent procedure.

Example: A person with critical blockages in multiple coronary arteries and a weak heart muscle.

Most patients with CAD, however, are stable and unlikely to benefit from a bypass or stent. They are the best candidates for what might be termed a *medical bypass*. With medications and lifestyle changes, most of these patients can eliminate symptoms (if any) and reduce heart attack risk. Only in rare cases, if symptoms get worse, would one of these heart patients need to consider medical intervention.

One key factor in cardiovascular health is to have an ongoing relationship with your doctor—he/she can advise you on the best steps to take to prevent and treat heart disease. *He may recommend that you…*

•**Follow the Mediterranean-style diet.** Eat lots of fruits, vegetables, whole grains and the legumes…olive oil instead of butter or margarine…several servings of fish weekly…and no more than a few weekly servings of lean meats. The landmark Lyon Diet Heart Study showed that people who ate a Mediterranean diet instead of a typical American diet had a 50% to 70% reduction in recurrent cardiovascular disease.

•**Relax with yoga, meditation, exercise, etc.** Doctors do not always ask patients about stress—which is why it is sometimes called the "forgotten" risk factor for heart disease. People who successfully manage stress can significantly lower blood pressure and the risk of heart disease. Stress management also lowers the risk for arrhythmias (heart rate irregularities).

● **Exercise daily for 30 to 45 minutes.** It is one of the best ways to maintain a healthy weight and prevent or control diabetes and high blood pressure. Regular exercise raises levels of HDL "good" cholesterol. It also can contribute to weight control—which can reduce inflammation in the blood vessels, a risk factor for CAD.

All forms of exercise are beneficial. Aerobic exercise, such as brisk walking, is the best choice for most people because it doesn't require a high level of fitness to do it.

● **Get your cholesterol checked annually** —and take cholesterol-lowering medication if necessary. Research indicates that an aggressive lowering of LDL cholesterol helps reduce risk of heart disease and death from CAD.

● **Take a baby aspirin daily.** It helps prevent platelets from clumping together and forming clots that can block blood flow to the heart. The anti-inflammatory effects of aspirin are also beneficial. Since aspirin may cause gastrointestinal upset, talk with your doctor before initiating aspirin therapy for CAD prevention.

● **See your dentist twice per year.** Studies have shown that patients with periodontal disease—gum inflammation that can result in tooth loss—have a higher risk of heart attack as well as stroke.

● **Get more omega-3s.** Most Americans are deficient in omega-3 fatty acids. Omega-3s lower inflammation and triglycerides, a fat that can put you at risk for heart disease. Omega-3s reduce the risk of arrhythmias and heart attack. Sources include cold-water fish, such as salmon, and walnuts and flaxseed. Or ask your doctor about taking a fish oil supplement.

Marital Spats Harm Your Heart

In a new study, 150 healthy married couples discussed a contentious topic for six minutes while being videotaped. Two days later, each spouse had a computed tomography (CT) scan of the chest.

Result: Wives who were hostile and husbands who were controlling had a greater degree of hardening of the arteries than spouses who did not display these behaviors.

Theory: Hostility and dominance can release chemicals that may increase heart disease risk.

Cynthia Berg, PhD, professor of psychology, University of Utah, Salt Lake City.

A Better Measure of Heart Disease Risk

In a study of 14,833 people age 75 and older, those who had the highest waist-to-hip ratios —waist measurement divided by hip measurement—were 40% more likely to die from cardiovascular disease (CVD) over one six-year period than those with the lowest.

Theory: The waist-to-hip ratio is an accurate gauge of excess body fat, since it takes into account abdominal fat, which is one known CVD risk factor.

Astrid E. Fletcher, MD, professor of epidemiology, London School of Hygiene and Tropical Medicine, England.

Coated vs. Uncoated Aspirin

Uncoated aspirin may reduce risk of coronary artery disease (CAD) better than coated aspirin does.

Recent finding: People who took plain aspirin daily for two weeks had levels of thromboxane, a substance that contributes to blood clots, that were 87% lower than in people who took coated aspirin.

Coated aspirin is usually prescribed to prevent stomach upset, but the coating greatly decreases absorption.

Best: Take an 81-mg uncoated aspirin daily.

Dermot Cox, PhD, lecturer on molecular and cellular therapeutics, Royal College of Surgeons, Dublin, Ireland, and leader of a study of 71 people, published in *Stroke*.

Safer Aspirin

Low-dose aspirin can help reduce heart attack risk and may reduce colon cancer risk.

Downsides: Aspirin can deplete the body of folic acid (vitamin B-9), vitamin B-12, vitamin C and zinc. Aspirin can also erode the lining of the stomach, triggering pain and dangerous bleeding.

Consider supplementing with *deglycyrrhizinated licorice* (DGL). One study found that 350 mg of chewable DGL taken together with each daily dose of aspirin decreased gastrointestinal bleeding.

Caution: Aspirin is a blood thinner. If you take it, avoid blood-thinning nutrients, such as vitamin E in doses above 400 IU, fish oil, ginkgo biloba, glucosamine and cayenne (in therapeutic doses). Also check with your doctor before taking aspirin if you are taking blood-thinning medications, such as *warfarin* (Coumadin) and *clopidogrel* (Plavix).

Mark A. Stengler, ND, associate clinical professor, National College of Naturopathic Medicine, Portland, OR, and founder and director of the La Jolla Whole Health Clinic, La Jolla, CA. He is author of the *Bottom Line Natural Healing* newsletter. His Web site is *www.DrStengler.com*.

Blood-Thinner Danger

People who take low-dose aspirin plus *clopidogrel* (Plavix) to prevent a *first* heart attack or stroke are 78% more likely to die from cardiovascular causes than people who take aspirin by itself. Paradoxically, the aspirin/Plavix combination can help to prevent a *second* heart attack or stroke.

Also: Patients who have had a stent should take the aspirin/Plavix combination.

Self-defense: If you use both drugs, consult your physician about the benefits of continuing. Do not stop either drug on your own.

Eric Topol, MD, a heart researcher and professor of genetics, Case Western Reserve University, Cleveland, and coauthor of a study of 15,603 people, published in *The New England Journal of Medicine*.

Blood Test Predicts Heart Attack Risk

A simple blood test can predict risk of heart attack and stroke among patients with cardiovascular disease. The test can measure blood levels of the protein *NT-proBNP* (N-terminal prohormone brain natriuretic peptide)—an indicator of BNP, a hormone that goes up during cardiac stress. The higher the level of this protein, the greater a person's risk of complications.

The test is used in hospitals to diagnose heart failure among patients with difficulty breathing. This test should not be part of routine checkups, but it can be helpful to a cardiologist trying to determine which patients who have known cardiac disease need aggressive treatment.

Kirsten Bibbins-Domingo, MD, assistant professor in residence of medicine, epidemiology and biostatistics at University of California, San Francisco, and coauthor of a study of 987 heart disease patients, published in *The Journal of the American Medical Association*.

Excessive Noise Can Cause a Heart Attack

In recent findings, men who live in noisy areas are 50% more likely to suffer a heart attack than men who live in quiet areas. Women living in noisy areas are 300% more likely to have a heart attack than women who live in quiet areas.

Probable reason: Any prolonged exposure to noise in the 65-to-75-decibel range (such as that in a city street-level apartment) causes your body to release adrenaline, which will drive up blood pressure. Normal conversation levels are at about 60 decibels, so if you have to repeatedly raise your voice to be heard, you're in an unhealthy noise environment.

Mehmet C. Oz, MD, medical director, Integrated Medical Program and director, Cardiovascular Institute, New York–Presbyterian Hospital/Columbia University Medical Center, New York City.

Living with a Partner Is Better for Your Heart

People ages 30 to 69 who live alone are almost twice as likely to develop angina, have a heart attack or suffer sudden cardiac death as people who live with others. The risk is even greater for women over age 60 and men over 50. Living alone itself is not the reason for the increased risk. People who live by themselves eat more fat, are more likely to smoke and are less likely to exercise.

Kirsten Melgaard Nielsen, MD, internist, Aarhus Sygehus University Hospital, Aarhus, Denmark.

Psoriasis Is Linked to Heart Attack Risk

In a recent study of patients ages 20 to 90, a patient who is 30 years old with severe psoriasis has more than three times the risk of heart attack as a person the same age without psoriasis. Risk also is elevated—but not as much—in older patients and people with mild psoriasis.

Likely link: Both psoriasis and heart disease are associated with high levels of inflammation.

If you have psoriasis, ask your doctor to evaluate your risk factors.

Joel M. Gelfand, MD, medical director of the clinical studies unit and assistant professor of dermatology, University of Pennsylvania School of Medicine, Philadelphia. His study of 130,976 people was published in *The Journal of the American Medical Association*.

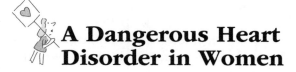 # A Dangerous Heart Disorder in Women

A dangerous heart disorder frequently doesn't show up on women's angiograms.

Recent study: At least half of women with chest pain who showed no evidence of blocked arteries on an angiogram had cholesterol buildup that restricted blood flow to the heart. This disorder, *coronary microvascular syndrome,* which affects women 80% of the time, can more than triple heart attack risk.

Self-defense: If you have recurrent chest pain and an angiogram shows no blockage, ask your physician about further testing.

C. Noel Bairey Merz, MD, director of the women's heart program, Cedars–Sinai Medical Center in Los Angeles, and coleader of a study of more than 1,000 women, published in the *Journal of the American College of Cardiology*.

Heart Attack Detector

Heart attacks can now be detected with a 15-second scan in the emergency room. *Multidetector computed tomography* (MDCT) helps doctors see plaque in arteries. Chest pain from heart attacks and angina rarely occurs without plaque buildup. A few hospitals can do MDCT now, and more are expected to in the future.

Udo Hoffman, MD, director of cardiac CT research, department of radiology, Massachusetts General Hospital... assistant professor of radiology, Harvard Medical School, both in Boston...and leader of a study of 103 people with acute chest pain, published in *Circulation*.

Better Heart Attack Therapy

In a two-year study of 37,233 heart attack patients, those who underwent angioplasty in a hospital that used that treatment most often had a 36% lower risk of dying in the hospital than patients who were treated in hospitals that use angioplasty or drug treatment interchangeably.

Reason: Hospitals that specialize in angioplasty (inserting a catheter and then expanding a balloon where a blood vessel has narrowed) restored blood flow to patients' hearts with this procedure an average of 19 minutes faster than hospitals that performed angioplasty less often.

If you're at risk for heart attack: Ask your doctor which hospitals in your area specialize in angioplasty.

Brahmajee K. Nallamothu, MD, MPH, assistant professor of internal medicine, University of Michigan, Ann Arbor.

Statins to the Rescue

Heart attack patients treated with statins within 24 hours of the attack were 54% less likely to die than those not given the drugs.

Reason: Statins increase the release of nitric oxide, which reduces heart damage.

If you are diagnosed as having a heart attack: Ask your physician about starting with a statin immediately.

Gregg C. Fonarow, MD, professor of cardiovascular medicine and science, David Geffen School of Medicine, UCLA, director of the Ahmanson-UCLA Cardiomyopathy Center and the leader of a study of 170,000 patients, published in *The American Journal of Cardiology*.

The Latest Thinking on Cholesterol Ratios

Daniel Rader, MD, director, Preventive Cardiovascular Medicine and Lipid Clinic, University of Pennsylvania School of Medicine, Philadelphia.

Don't focus on the cholesterol ratio by itself. Instead, target high-density lipoprotein (HDL) and low-density lipoprotein (LDL) independently. Look first at LDL ("bad") cholesterol. People with heart disease or anyone at risk because of diabetes, family history or multiple risk factors, such as weight, age, diet and overall health, should aim for LDL of less than 70. If better diet, weight loss and exercise don't work, this may require statins, sometimes supplemented with *ezetimibe* (Zetia), which inhibits cholesterol absorption. Men over age 40 and postmenopausal women should aim for LDL of less than 100 if they are not at high risk. For younger, low-risk people, 130 is acceptable.

After LDL is under control, focus on increasing HDL ("good") cholesterol. This often can be achieved through better diet, weight loss and exercise. High-risk people with HDL under 40 may need drug therapy, usually with niacin or fibrates, a class of drug used to reduce triglycerides and raise HDL modestly. The HDL target for people with no risk factors is 60 or above.

Get a Better Blood Pressure Reading

In a recent finding, systolic (the top number) blood pressure averaged 14 points higher if taken shortly after a patient arrived in the exam room and sat on an exam table than if he/she sat in a chair for five minutes.

Theory: Foot and back support induce a relaxed state, which helps allow for more accurate blood pressure readings.

Self-defense: The next time you have your blood pressure taken, ask if you could sit in a chair with your back supported and feet flat on the floor for five minutes. Remain in this position (instead of sitting on an exam table) while the reading is taken.

Melanie F. Turner, RN, cardiology clinic practice nurse, University of Virginia Health System, Charlottesville.

Acetaminophen May Cause Hypertension

In a recent finding, women who took a daily dose of more than 500 mg of acetaminophen —the equivalent of one extra-strength Tylenol tablet—had double the risk of developing high blood pressure within three years.

Both *ibuprofen* (Advil or Motrin) and *naproxen* (Aleve) have been linked with hypertension, but until recently, acetaminophen was thought safe.

Best: Monitor blood pressure if you are taking these drugs.

Christie Ballantyne, MD, cardiologist, Methodist DeBakey Heart Center, Houston.

 # Too Much Coffee May Cause Heart Trouble

In a recent finding, people who drank three or more cups of coffee per day had twice as many signs of abnormal arterial pressure and stiffening of the arteries as people who drank less coffee.

Possible reason: Caffeine may interfere with the metabolism of adenosine, a substance that relaxes arteries.

Self-defense: Drink no more than two cups of regular coffee a day, especially if you have high blood pressure.

Charalambos Vlachopoulos, MD, staff cardiologist, first department of cardiology, Athens Medical School, Hippokration Hospital, University of Athens, Greece, and leader of a study of 228 participants, published in *The American Journal of Clinical Nutrition*.

High Blood Pressure/ Glaucoma Link

In a study among people with glaucoma, 29% also had high blood pressure—a significantly higher percentage than is in the population as a whole. If you have hypertension, watch your weight, eat healthful foods, exercise on a regular basis and ask your doctor about medication.

Michael J. S. Langman, MD, professor of medicine at the University of Birmingham, Queen Elizabeth Hospital, Birmingham, England.

Hypertension Danger

In a new study, more than 300 men who had normal or high blood pressure (above 140/90) were given tests for verbal fluency (generating words) and short-term memory (word recall).

Result: The people who were hypertensive despite taking medication performed 2.4 times worse on verbal fluency and 1.3 times worse on short-term memory.

Theory: Chronic hypertension damages small blood vessels, which interferes with blood flow to the brain.

Self-defense: Maintain a blood pressure of 140/90 or below (ideally, below 120/80) through diet and exercise and/or medication.

Christopher B. Brady, PhD, instructor in medicine at Harvard Medical School, Boston.

New Blood Pressure Therapy

An experimental device that stimulates nerves in the carotid arteries can significantly lower blood pressure. The device could eventually give patients with hypertension better control— or even eliminate the need for medications.

Virginia Commonwealth University, Richmond, *www.vcu.edu*.

Are You Headed for A Stroke? "Ministrokes" Often Are a Signal

James F. Toole, MD, Walter C. Teagle Professor of Neurology and director of the Stroke Research Center at Wake Forest University Baptist Medical Center in Winston-Salem, NC. He is immediate past president of the International Stroke Society, *www.internationalstroke.org*.

What if people received warnings about coming strokes one week or even a full month before they occurred? You might assume that such an alert would cause people to seek medical attention so that the patient and his/her doctor could take measures to prevent a stroke. Usually, that's not the case.

Each year, an estimated quarter-million Americans receive a warning in the form of a transient ischemic attack (TIA), commonly known as a "ministroke." Unfortunately, the majority of patients who experience a TIA don't recognize its importance—and fail to get prompt medical care that likely could prevent a full-blown stroke. About 11% to 20% of patients who experience a TIA go on to suffer a stroke within three months.

Good news: Patients who experience a TIA and then take preventive steps can greatly reduce their risk for further problems.

Important: A TIA is an *emergency*, and everyone should know the symptoms. If you experience one of the symptoms described below for at least five minutes, see a doctor the same day—go to the emergency room, if necessary.

KNOW THE SYMPTOMS

Like the majority of strokes, a TIA is usually caused by a blood clot and/or material that breaks free from artery walls and temporarily blocks off blood flow to parts of the brain. The blockage of the artery lasts long enough to stop blood flow and cause stroke-like symptoms, but not long enough to kill brain cells.

What to watch for…

•**A dizzy spell that occurs for no obvious reason,** such as standing too quickly…or dizziness from a middle ear disease.

•**Weakness and/or numbness on one side of the body**—usually in the face or an arm or leg.

•**The sensation that there is something in the eye,** causing blurriness, double vision or even temporary blindness.

•**Difficulty speaking** or difficulty in understanding what others are saying.

People should *not* panic if they experience one or more of these symptoms—they are not always caused by a TIA. A dizzy spell can be caused by something as simple as a plug of earwax. The only way to know for sure whether you've suffered a TIA is to see a doctor.

DIAGNOSING TIAs

Researchers are in the process of identifying brain enzymes that are released during a TIA. Blood tests that diagnose TIAs based on the presence of these enzymes are being developed.

In the meantime, doctors diagnose most TIAs by taking a medical history of the event—what the patient felt, how long the symptoms lasted and whether the person has stroke risk factors, such as high blood pressure, family history, diabetes or smoking.

Physical findings: Atherosclerosis (a hardening of the arteries) is the underlying trigger of most TIAs (and the majority of strokes). Patients who have atherosclerosis elsewhere in the body, such as in the arteries leading to the legs, kidneys, heart, etc., are very likely to also have damaged carotid arteries—blood vessels in the neck that carry blood to the brain.

In some cases, a doctor can detect problems in the carotid artery by listening carefully with a stethoscope. There are characteristic sounds (bruits) that indicate atherosclerosis.

In other cases, additional tests are required…

•**Carotid ultrasonography** utilizes sound waves to detect blood-vessel narrowing and/or clots in the carotid arteries. This is a good test for patients with stroke risk factors or a family history of strokes or TIAs.

•**Magnetic resonance imaging** (MRI) also measures blockages in the carotid arteries.

If atherosclerotic blockages of 50% to 70% are found from either test, further evaluation and additional treatment may be necessary.

TREATMENT APPROACHES

Patients with carotid artery blockages of 50% or more are usually advised to take strict steps, including the use of medication, to reduce risk. *If their disease progresses to 70% blockage, surgery is typically recommended…*

•**Carotid endarterectomy** is an in-patient procedure in which an incision is made to expose the carotid artery, and plaques are removed from the artery. When performed by a skilled surgeon, the risk for stroke or death is less than 1%, and the patient recovers within a week.

•**Stenting** is an inpatient procedure in which an expandable metal net is threaded into the carotid artery. The net presses against the artery walls…dilates the opening for better circulation …and helps prevent the artery from "shedding" any more clots. Stenting, however, hasn't been performed long enough for its long-term effectiveness and durability to be known. One possible risk is that a dislodged blood clot could get carried in the bloodstream to the brain.

TIA patients who don't require surgery are almost always treated with drugs to prevent blood from clotting. *Main drug therapies…*

•**Aspirin is most often used.** Taking a regular aspirin (three times weekly) or baby aspirin (daily), depending on the patient, can decrease stroke risk by up to 20%.

•**Aspirin plus an anticlotting drug.** Adding other active ingredients to aspirin can reduce stroke risk by an additional 3% to 5%.

Example: Aspirin plus the drug *dipyridamole* (Aggrenox).

•**Aspirin alternatives,** including *clopidogrel* (Plavix) and *ticlopidine* (Ticlid), can prevent excessively sticky platelets from clumping together and forming clots. These drugs are a good choice for patients who are allergic to aspirin or who have an ulcer or acid reflux disease, which can be aggravated by aspirin.

STROKE PREVENTION

Most stroke risk factors can be reduced with lifestyle modifications. *Most important…*

- **Not smoking.**
- **Limiting dietary fat.**
- **Eating fruits and vegetables.**
- **Exercising regularly.**

Patients who maintain healthy blood pressure readings and total cholesterol levels…avoid (or reverse) obesity…and control underlying diseases, such as diabetes, are far less likely to develop hardening of the arteries, thereby reducing their risk for TIAs and stroke.

Stroke Danger

In a recent study, among 10,405 adults ages 49 to 73, people with early-stage age-related macular degeneration (AMD), an eye disorder that gradually destroys central vision, were 87% more likely to suffer a stroke over a 10-year period than those without AMD.

Theory: AMD risk factors, such as hypertension and smoking, also increase stroke risk.

If you're diagnosed with AMD: Ask your doctor whether you should be monitored for stroke risk factors, including hypertension and diabetes.

Tien Yin Wong, MD, PhD, MPH, professor of ophthalmology at the University of Melbourne located in East Melbourne, Australia.

Don't Ignore Stroke Symptoms

Strokes that affect the right side of the brain are not always accurately diagnosed by emergency room doctors soon enough—even though these strokes are as common as those that affect the left side of the brain.

Reason: Right-sided stroke symptoms—such as vision problems, memory loss, skipping food on the left side of the plate—often are overlooked by the patient and don't appear critical to family members and doctors.

Result: Patients get to the hospital later and often don't get the treatment they need.

Self-defense: If you or a loved one experiences any stroke symptoms, be sure to seek immediate care.

Vladimir Hachinski, MD, Hon. Dr. Med, University of Western Canada, London, Ontario, and part of a study of emergency care given to more than 750 right-brain stroke victims, published in *Neurology.*

Stroke Detector

If you think someone is having a stroke, ask him/her three questions—Can you smile? Can you raise both arms? Can you say a simple sentence, such as "It is sunny out today"? If he has trouble carrying out these three tasks, call 911 immediately.

American Stroke Association, Dallas, *www.strokeasso ciation.org.*

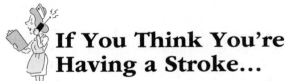 # If You Think You're Having a Stroke…

Call an ambulance if you think you are having a stroke, even if you live close to a hospital.

Recent finding: Stroke sufferers who were transported by an ambulance to the emergency room were seen and evaluated by a physician within 30 minutes, compared with 34 minutes for the patients who drove themselves or were brought by friends or loved ones and 55 minutes for those who arrived by other means.

With stroke, even four minutes can make a huge difference in outcome.

Yousef Mohammad, MD, an assistant professor, department of neurology, college of medicine and public health, Ohio State University, Columbus, and leader of a study of 630,000 stroke patients, presented at the annual American Stroke Association's International Stroke Conference 2006.

Surprising Diabetes Link

A study of 4,572 men and women found that 17% of nonsmokers exposed to second-hand smoke developed glucose intolerance, the precursor to diabetes. Fewer than 12% of those not exposed developed the condition.

Theory: All the toxins in secondhand smoke may affect the pancreas, which produces blood sugar–regulating insulin.

BMJ (British Medical Journal), London, on the Web at *www.bmj.com*.

New Diabetes Drug

The new diabetes drug Januvia blocks the enzyme that suppresses the release of insulin after blood sugar rises—for instance, after a meal. This lets the body release insulin longer. Januvia—chemical name *sitagliptin phosphate*—works like the injected drug *exenatide* (Byetta), but Januvia is taken by mouth. It is best for people with type 2 diabetes who cannot keep their blood sugar levels low enough with older diabetes medications, such as *metformin*.

Carol Levy, MD, a diabetes specialist and an assistant attending physician at New York–Presbyterian Hospital/Weill–Cornell Medical Center, New York City.

Can Drugs Really Increase Cancer Risk?

Eric L. Matteson, MD, consultant, division of rheumatology, Mayo Clinic, Rochester, MN.

Researchers have discovered that there is a cancer risk associated with some types of medications.

Background: Many rheumatoid arthritis patients take *infliximab* (Remicade) or *adalimumab* (Humira), tumor necrosis factor (TNF)–blocking antibodies, usually after all other treatments have failed to help arthritis symptoms.

New finding: Scientists reviewed studies involving 3,493 patients who took one of these drugs and 1,512 patients who took a placebo.

Result: Those who took TNF-blocking antibodies had 3.3 times the risk of developing cancer, and 2.2 times the risk for serious infections, like pneumonia, as those who took a placebo.

Theory: The drugs interfere with the body's infection-fighting mechanisms and its ability to defend itself against cancerous cells.

Self-defense: Patients who take these drugs should watch for symptoms of infection, such as fever and chills…get their vaccinations, such as those for flu and pneumonia…and ask their doctors about appropriate cancer screenings for their situation.

Deadly Hazards of Secondhand Smoke

Frank T. Leone, MD, pulmonologist and tobacco specialist at Thomas Jefferson University in Philadelphia.

Smoking is the main cause of lung cancer, but *everyone* is vulnerable to the effects of secondhand smoke. Although Dana Reeve, the widow of *Superman* star Christopher Reeve, was a nonsmoker, secondhand smoke she was exposed to as a cabaret singer may have played a role in the development of her lung cancer and death.

Secondhand smoke is responsible for about 3,000 cases of lung cancer annually—and an estimated 38,000 cases of smoke-related diseases, including stroke and heart disease.

Even if you're a nonsmoker, the risk of dying from lung cancer is 30% higher if you live with a smoker. Similarly, the nonsmoking wives of men who smoke are 30% to 35% more likely to die from cardiovascular disease than the wives of nonsmokers.

There's *no* safe level of secondhand smoke. Living with a pack-a-day smoker involves the same risks as living in a home with a level of radon (another known lung cancer risk factor) that exceeds the EPA's recommended limit.

To protect yourself and your family…

•**Keep your house smoke-free.** Ask family or guests to smoke outside.

•**Avoid clusters of smokers outside office doors…**and only patronize smoke-free bars and restaurants.

Also: If you use a fireplace or woodstove, have it inspected by a professional for proper ventilation. Exposure to soot particles can contribute to the development emphysema.

A New Way to Quit Smoking: Log on to the Web

The on-line stop-smoking programs provide round-the-clock help for people wanting to kick the habit. Smokeclinic.com has a free step-by-step program. QuitNet.com provides an active chat community with expert advice, a directory of local support programs and self-assessment tools among other benefits at no cost. The American Lung Association offers the quit-smoking action plan through its Freedom from Smoking Online cessation clinic (*www.ffsonline.org*).

A New Blood Test For Lung Cancer

A new blood test for lung cancer is 90% accurate—and can detect tumors years earlier than a computed tomography (CT) scan. Lung cancer is the leading cause of cancer deaths, mainly because 85% of cases are detected too late for effective treatments.

The test, still in development, could greatly improve survival in high-risk patients.

University of Kentucky, Lexington, *www.uky.edu.*

Surprising Sign of Cancer

In a recent finding, 27% of esophageal cancer patients had experienced persistent hiccups prior to diagnosis. People who have hiccups for more than 48 hours—especially if accompanied by swallowing problems and/or weight loss—should see their physicians. The incidence of this very serious cancer is on the rise.

Thomas Noel Walsh, MD, associate professor of surgery, Royal College of Surgeons in Ireland (RCSI), Dublin, and leader of a study of 99 esophageal cancer patients, presented at a recent RCSI conference.

Skin Cancer Alert

Persistent itching may be a sign of skin cancer. Any skin irritation that persists for weeks may be early-stage skin cancer, especially if it increases in size, changes color or bleeds. See a dermatologist. He/she usually can tell quickly if an irritation is benign or cancerous.

Perry Robins, MD, a dermatologist and professor of dermatology at New York University Medical Center, New York City, and president of The Skin Cancer Foundation.

More from Dr. Perry Robins…

Are You Using Enough Sunscreen?

The average adult needs at least one ounce (the amount held by a shot glass) of sunscreen to adequately coat the body.

Also important: If you plan to be in the sun for more than 20 minutes (no matter what your skin type), use broad-spectrum sunscreen with a sun-protection factor (SPF) of 15 or higher that blocks both ultraviolet A (UVA) and ultraviolet B (UVB) rays…reapply it every two hours (even on cloudy days, year-round) to all exposed areas, including your ears, hands—and even your fingernails. Skin cancer also can occur on the scalp, so wear a wide-brimmed hat.

Meat Lovers Beware

Beef and pork are linked to pancreatic cancer. In a seven-year study, people who reported eating the most beef or pork were 50% more likely to develop pancreatic cancer than those who reported eating the least.

Possible reasons: Carcinogens caused from cooking red meat at high temperatures...or nitrites used as preservatives in processed meats.

Further research is needed to confirm a link between meat and pancreatic cancer.

Bonnie Liebman, MS, director of nutrition, *Nutrition Action Healthletter*, 1875 Connecticut Ave. NW, Washington, DC 20009.

Cancer Care Varies by Region

More than twice as many patients with stomach cancer survive for five years in Hawaii—where doctors remove an average of 15 lymph nodes when treating the disease—as in Utah, where the average removed is six. Cancer researchers are developing standard care recommendations in hopes of getting all patients the best available care.

Ezekiel J. Emanuel, MD, PhD, chair of the department of clinical bioethics, Magnuson Clinical Center, National Institutes of Health, Bethesda, MD, and liaison between the American Society of Clinical Oncologists and a Rand Corporation–Harvard team that studied US cancer care by geographic area.

New Cancer Treatment Is Much More Effective

Proton-beam therapy is best for tumors that can't be controlled with low doses of radiation and that are in or near sensitive areas, such as the prostate, chest, lungs and brain. There are proton-beam facilities in California, Florida, Indiana, Massachusetts, Texas and other states. This treatment costs more than standard radiation but is covered by most insurers.

James D. Cox, MD, professor and head of the division of radiation oncology at the M.D. Anderson Cancer Center, Houston, TX.

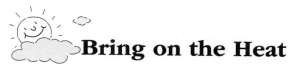

Bring on the Heat

Heat may kill some cancer cells directly and make others more responsive to radiation treatment.

Recent finding: Treating superficial (or "contained") tumors in tissue of the breast, cervix, head, neck and skin with hyperthermia—gradually increasing the temperature of the cancerous tissue to between 105°F and 113°F—decreased the risk of recurrence by 68%.

Ellen Jones, MD, PhD, associate professor, department of radiation oncology, Duke University Medical Center, Durham, NC, and leader of a study of 109 patients with recurrent, superficial cancers, published in the *Journal of Clinical Oncology*.

Better Cancer Pain Relief

In one recent study, cancer patients who ordinarily used oral morphine for "breakthrough" pain (sudden moderate to severe pain that is not controlled by regular drug therapy) experienced 33% greater relief within 15 minutes of dissolving a lozenge containing the painkiller *fentanyl* (Actiq) in their mouths.

Theory: The fentanyl lozenge dissolves quickly, allowing it to pass into the central nervous system faster than oral pain medication, such as morphine.

Giovambattista Zeppetella, MD, medical director of St. Clare Hospice, Hastingwood, England. His study of 393 cancer patients was published in *The Cochrane Library*, 111 River St., Hoboken, NJ 07030.

Silent Kidney Disease: Many Doctors Don't Recognize the Symptoms

L. Ebony Boulware, MD, MPH, an internist as well as assistant professor of medicine and epidemiology at the Welch Center for Prevention, Epidemiology and Clinical Research at Johns Hopkins University School of Medicine in Baltimore. She was the lead author of a study on physicians' recognition of the signs and symptoms of kidney disease, which was published in the August 2006 issue of the *American Journal of Kidney Diseases*.

It's widely known that diseases such as high blood pressure (hypertension) and diabetes can go undetected for quite some time. But so few patients, and a relatively small percentage of physicians, realize that chronic kidney disease (CKD) is equally threatening and often remains hidden.

Danger: CKD—and the subsequent kidney damage—can be markedly slowed with medications and also by controlling the underlying causes. Yet many primary care physicians don't fully understand how to diagnose this condition or how to assess the main risk factors.

Result: So many of the estimated 20 million Americans with CKD aren't diagnosed as early as they could be. By the time symptoms appear, the kidneys could have lost more than 75% of their normal function. At that point, the damage may be so extensive that patients will eventually require dialysis or a kidney transplant—or they die waiting.

Simple blood and urine tests can detect most cases of early CKD. Patients who are diagnosed and referred to a nephrologist (kidney specialist) early are often able to delay dialysis or transplant, or even avoid them altogether.

WHAT'S GETTING MISSED

One of the main functions of the kidneys is to eliminate wastes, such as urea, from the body. In CKD, damage to the filtering units (nephrons) in the kidneys is typically caused by hypertension or diabetes, typically over a period of decades. About 45% of all CKD cases are caused by diabetes, while 27% are caused by hypertension. Because CKD causes no symptoms, laboratory tests are the only way to detect it early.

That is why patients with hypertension, diabetes or other risk factors for CKD should have tests for kidney function during annual exams. But even that might not be sufficient. A new study reports that many doctors miss the signs of early CKD even when those signs should be apparent to them.

The study: Researchers from Johns Hopkins University School of Medicine asked 304 randomly picked US physicians, including kidney specialists, internists and family physicians, to evaluate the medical files of a fictitious patient.

These doctors also were given the raw data needed to calculate the glomerular filtration rate, an important measure of kidney function. They were asked to calculate this number themselves using accepted equations.

Result: Of all the kidney specialists surveyed, 97% did accurately diagnose CKD, and 99% of those said they would have recommended that the primary care physician refer the patient to a kidney specialist. Among all the internists, only 78% made the accurate diagnosis of CKD, and 81% of those recommended a referral to a kidney specialist. Even worse, only 59% of the family physicians offered the accurate diagnosis of CKD, and merely 76% of those recommended a specialist referral.

The implications of this study are troublesome. Delays in diagnosing CKD greatly increase the risk for complications, including heart disease.

New finding: CKD promotes atherosclerosis and is an independent risk factor (like smoking, diabetes or hypertension) for cardiovascular disease.

SELF-PROTECTION

Blood and/or urine testing, when interpreted properly, can easily detect early CKD, but doctors don't order these tests as often as they should. Patients who have been diagnosed with diabetes or hypertension should insist on getting tested for CKD. This is particularly important for African-Americans. They are six times more likely than Caucasians to develop hypertension-related kidney failure. People age 60 or older—even if they don't have diabetes or hypertension—also may want to be tested, because they are at higher risk for CKD. The testing can be done by a primary care physician.

TREATING CKD

Apart from a transplant operation, there isn't a cure for CKD. The most important strategy is to control (or prevent) hypertension and diabetes through medication and lifestyle changes, such as following a low-fat, low-salt diet. These conditions can double or triple the risk of CKD—and accelerate the damage in patients who already have it.

Because many patients with CKD also have hypertension, doctors will often prescribe blood pressure medication. Lowering blood pressure to below 120/80 mmHg can significantly slow the progression of CKD. These drugs also are helpful for patients with CKD caused by diabetes.

Important: Studies have shown that using an angiotensin converting enzyme (ACE) inhibitor or angiotensin II receptor blocker can slow the progression of CKD by as much as 30%. The drugs are effective even in CKD patients who do not have hypertension or diabetes.

Weight and Kidney Disease Link

In a review of the health data of 320,252 adults, those with a body mass index (BMI) of 25 to 29.9 (moderately overweight) were nearly 90% more likely than those of normal weight to develop end-stage renal disease (ESRD), which typically requires a kidney transplant or dialysis.

Theory: Excess body weight puts more demand on the kidneys, and people who are overweight are more likely to develop diabetes and high blood pressure, two risk factors for ESRD.

Chi-yuan Hsu, MD, associate professor in residence, division of nephrology at the University of California in San Francisco.

Alzheimer's Vaccine

A new vaccine tested in animals decreased brain protein deposits, an underlying cause of Alzheimer's, by up to 38.5%. If further tests of the vaccine are promising, it could be tested in humans within three years.

The Wall Street Journal, 200 Liberty St., New York City 10281, *online.wsj.com.*

Cognitive Decline Linked To Dietary Copper

In a six-year study of 3,718 people ages 65 or older, those who ate a diet high in the saturated fats and trans fats and who also consumed an average of 2.75 mg of copper daily suffered greater declines in mental capacity than those who ate a high-fat diet but who consumed only 0.88 mg of copper daily. The recommended dietary allowance of copper (found in shellfish and liver) is 0.9 mg.

Theory: High levels of copper may prevent the body from ridding itself of brain-damaging proteins.

Martha Clare Morris, ScD, associate professor, department of internal medicine, Rush University Medical Center, Chicago.

Botox May Relieve Depression

In a recent finding, two months after receiving Botox injections in their foreheads, nine out of 10 women previously diagnosed with depression were no longer depressed.

Theory: Injections prevented these patients from frowning. Researchers believe that there may be direct feedback between the facial frown muscles and the depression center of the brain.

Eric Finzi, MD, PhD, dermatologic surgeon and president at Chevy Chase Cosmetic Center, Chevy Chase, MD, *www.chevychasecosmeticcenter.com,* and lead author of a study of depressed patients, published in *Dermatologic Surgery.*

Antidepressants May Increase Risk Of Broken Bones

Everyday use of selective serotonin reuptake inhibitors (or SSRIs), including Paxil (*paroxetine*), Prozac (*fluoxetine*) and Zoloft (*sertraline*), doubles the risk of fractures in adults age 50 and older. SSRIs decrease bone mineral density at the hip.

Self-defense: People using SSRIs should have annual bone-density tests.

David Goltzman, MD, professor of medicine and director, Metabolic Bone Disease Centre at McGill University, and physician-in-chief, Royal Victoria Hospital, both in Montreal, Quebec. He is senior author of a study of fracture rates in 5,008 adults, published in the *Archives of Internal Medicine*.

Arthritis May Be Tied to Different Leg Lengths

A long-term study suggested that even a slight difference in the length of a person's legs may play a role in arthritis. People with different leg lengths were more likely to have arthritis in the hip and especially the knee.

Help: Using orthotic devices or shoe lifts to equalize leg length may prevent the disease or keep it from getting worse.

Joanne M. Jordan, MD, MPH, associate professor of medicine and orthopedics, Thurston Arthritis Research Center, University of North Carolina, Chapel Hill.

Better Arthritis Treatment

In an 18-month study of 110 people with an undetermined form of arthritis characterized by painful and stiff joints, those who took weekly doses of *methotrexate* (Rheumatrex) over 12 months were less likely to develop rheumatoid arthritis, one of the most debilitating forms of the disease—and more likely to go into remission—than those who took a placebo.

Theory: Methotrexate, a drug used to treat some cancers and severe psoriasis, works, in part, by curbing activation of white blood cells, which may play a role in causing rheumatoid arthritis.

Caution: For treatment of rheumatoid arthritis, methotrexate is taken once a week, not once a day, as it is for the treatment of cancer.

Thomas W. J. Huizinga, MD, PhD, professor and chairman, department of rheumatology, Leiden University Medical Center, The Netherlands.

Do You Really Need Back Surgery for Sciatica?

Eugene Carragee, MD, professor of orthopedic surgery and director of the Orthopedic Spine Center at Stanford University School of Medicine in Stanford, CA. He is also author of an editorial on the new sciatica studies, published in *The Journal of the American Medical Association*.

Sciatica is a common form of lower back pain that radiates along one of the two sciatic nerves, each of which runs down the back of the thigh and calf and into the foot. About 1 million Americans suffer from sciatica, and up to 300,000 a year have surgery to relieve the pain.

For decades, physicians have recommended back surgery for people who have a damaged spinal disk that triggers sciatica (pain that radiates from the low back down the leg). Sciatica can cause shooting pains that some people describe as being as excruciating as childbirth.

The surgery, which involves the partial removal of the damaged disk, is the most common operation in the US for people who have back and leg pain due to sciatica. In at least 80% of cases, the operation relieves symptoms and prevents nerve damage that could potentially cause permanent pain and disability, including paralysis and incontinence.

A new finding: In a pair of recent studies comparing the results for back pain sufferers who received surgery versus those who waited, patients in both groups did equally well in the long run. Not one of the patients who delayed surgery—or didn't get it at all—experienced serious complications. Meanwhile, less than 5% of the patients in the surgery groups had complications, such as a tear in the membrane covering the spinal cord.

The research, which included 1,244 patients and was published in *The Journal of the American Medical Association*, showed that the only major difference between the back patients who underwent surgery and those who did not was the speed with which backs got better. In the surgery groups, a significant number of patients had regained all (or most) of their normal function within three months. A similar number of patients in the nonsurgical group also regained near-normal function, but it took much longer —up to two years, in some instances. Based on these findings, many doctors are now advising some sciatica sufferers to put off or even forgo surgery if their pain is not severe.

TO WAIT OR NOT

Even when sciatica causes severe pain initially, people usually get better on their own within weeks or months as the body secretes *collagenases*, enzymes that break down disk collagen. Once the disk material breaks down—or when a disk protrusion retreats back into its normal space—the pain and inflammation may gradually decrease.

Important: Prompt surgery may be needed when a large disk bulge or fragment compromises bowel or bladder control, or leads to leg paralysis. If you suffer from back pain that occurs suddenly, see your physician—especially if you have fever and the chills, which could indicate an infection near the spine, or if you are taking a blood thinner (internal bleeding might be occurring).

When deciding whether to have surgery, the following points should be considered...

• **Size of herniation.** Disk fragments/protrusions that are smaller than 5 mm (about one-fifth of an inch) are less likely than larger ones to cause serious sciatica.

• **Pain severity.** Some patients with sciatica are unable to sit or lie down—or even move— without excruciating pain, so surgery is a reasonable decision for them. Others experience only minor discomfort, or are able to tolerate the pain for longer periods, so they may be able to forgo having surgery.

• **Job/family requirements.** Some patients can't afford to wait six months—or two years— for their condition to improve on its own.

Example: A self-employed plumber or carpenter probably can't afford to wait months or years before going back to work.

NONSURGICAL ALTERNATIVES

Patients who decide not to have surgery can try to control pain/inflammation with a variety of nonsurgical treatments, such as physical therapy.

Other important therapies...

• **Anti-inflammatory analgesics,** including *ibuprofen* (Advil), *naproxen* (Aleve) and *indomethacin* (Indocin). These drugs can make a difference for patients with relatively mild sciatica, but they aren't very helpful for severe pain.

• **Daily exercise.** Those with sciatica who exercise may recover more quickly than patients who are sedentary since exercise helps to keep them physically fit.

• **Cold/heat applications** can help to block pain signals as they travel to the brain.

What to do: Apply an ice pack to the painful area for about 20 minutes, followed by 20 minutes with a heating pad. Do this up to three times a day.

Caution: Do not use heat therapy within the first 48 hours of experiencing the pain, as this may increase the inflammation.

• **Steroid injections,** given into the open space that surrounds the spinal nerves, may reduce inflammation. Steroids can safely be given up to three times a year.

• **Oral steroids,** usually taken for one week, also decrease inflammation and may make the pain more tolerable. However, oral steroids are more likely to cause side effects (such as a worsening of diabetes or hypertension in patients with these conditions) than injections.

Statins May Help Prevent Osteoporosis

In one study of more than 91,000 men, those who took a cholesterol-lowering statin had an overall 36% lower risk for fractures.

Theory: Statins improve the function of small blood vessels, which may promote bone growth and remodeling.

If you have high cholesterol: Ask your doctor about taking a statin to decrease cholesterol—and to help prevent osteoporosis.

Richard E. Scranton, MD, MPH, director of projects, Massachusetts Veterans Epidemiology Research and Information Center, Boston.

Corticosteroid Alert

Corticosteroids can cause bone loss if taken for long periods and in high doses. High doses are used to treat lung disease, arthritis and other severe conditions. Patients taking corticosteroids daily for three months or longer also should take calcium and vitamin D supplements to prevent bone loss. Your doctor should arrange a bone-density test if you have been, or will be, taking high doses of these drugs or inhaled steroid drugs for asthma for longer than three months. Topical corticosteroids are usually safe.

Harris H. McIlwain, MD, Tampa Medical Group and adjunct professor, University of South Florida College of Public Health, both in Tampa.

Is It Shingles?

Shingles is a painful rash caused by the reactivation of the varicella virus that causes chicken pox. Typically, shingles start as vesicles (small blisters) that may look like small pimples. Oftentimes, the patient will experience an itching, tingling or burning sensation. Shingles is usually unilateral, meaning that it follows a nerve and therefore will not cross the midline of the body. The rash will always be either on the left or right side.

Self-defense: The best treatment is an oral antiviral, such as *acyclovir* (Zovirax), *valacyclovir* (Valtrex) or *famciclovir* (Famvir). It is important to take one of these medications within 48 to 72 hours of the onset of symptoms for it to be effective. After 72 hours, use a warm compress to relieve symptoms and a topical antibiotic ointment, such as *mupirocin* (Bactroban), to prevent infection.

Leon Kircik, MD, clinical associate professor of dermatology at the Indiana University School of Medicine in Indianapolis.

Carbohydrates And Cataracts

In a recent study, people who consumed 200 grams or more per day of any kind of carbohydrate for more than 14 years had more than twice the risk of developing cataracts as people who consumed the USDA-recommended 130 grams per day. Carbohydrates are found in such foods as bread, cookies, white potatoes and rice.

Theory: The excess glucose liberated within the body from the digestion of dietary carbohydrates may damage proteins in the lens of the eye and lead to cataracts.

Allen Taylor, PhD, professor of nutrition, biochemistry and ophthalmology, USDA Human Nutrition Research Center on Aging, Tufts University, Boston, and leader of a study of 417 women, published in *The American Journal of Clinical Nutrition*.

New Drug Fights Vision Loss

The wet form of age-related macular degeneration (AMD)—a primary cause of blindness—is characterized by growth of abnormal leaky blood vessels in the retina. The drug *ranibizumab* (Lucentis) helps to block off blood vessel growth, preventing further deterioration in AMD patients. The medication is injected inside the eye monthly for three months. Anesthetizing eyedrops prevent pain.

George A. Williams, MD, director of Beaumont Eye Institute, Royal Oak, MI, and spokesperson for the American Academy of Ophthalmology, *www.aao.org.*

Common Bacteria May Cause Blindness

In a recent study, the bacteria that causes respiratory infections, *Chlamydia pneumoniae,* was found in six of nine samples from patients who had age-related macular degeneration, the leading cause of blindness in people over age 55 in the US. *C. pneumoniae* also has been linked to coronary artery disease, heart attack and cerebrovascular disease (related to the blood supply to the brain).

Theory: The bacteria cause inflammation, a factor that can contribute to the development of macular degeneration.

Self-defense: Eat a heart-healthy diet, and do not smoke.

Joan W. Miller, MD, professor and chair, department of ophthalmology, Harvard Medical School, Boston, and senior author of a study, published in the *Archive for Clinical and Experimental Ophthalmology.*

New Tinnitus Therapy

In a three-month study of 50 people with tinnitus (ringing in the ears), half the group took *acamprosate* (Campral), a drug that reduces alcohol cravings, three times a day, while the rest took a placebo.

Result: An overall improvement in tinnitus symptoms occurred in 87% of the patients who took acamprosate, while the placebo group experienced no significant improvement.

Theory: Acamprosate promotes brain activity that may also be involved in the prevention of tinnitus.

If you have tinnitus: Ask your physician whether acamprosate is right for you.

Andreia Aparécida de Azevedo, MD, otolaryngologist, South Fluminense Otolaryngology, Volta Redonda, Brazil.

Better Gum Disease Treatment

In a study, patients with severe gum disease, who seemed to require periodontal surgery or tooth extraction of nine to 10 teeth, instead took 500 mg of the antibiotic *metronidazole* (Flagyl) twice a day for two weeks and received regular cleanings for five years.

Result: On average, these patients ended up needing extraction of only two to three teeth after taking the antibiotic and receiving regular cleanings.

If you have gum disease due to anaerobic infection (one caused by germs that grow in the absence of oxygen), ask your doctor about trying metronidazole.

Walter Loesche, DMD, PhD, emeritus professor of dentistry at the University of Michigan School of Dentistry, Ann Arbor.

Mercury Fillings Are Not Safe

Studies at University of Calgary have found that mercury vapor from fillings enters the body and may cause brain-cell degeneration and immune suppression, among other problems.

Self-defense: Have your dentist use mercury-free white composite fillings, and also try to have existing amalgam ones replaced over time by a "biological dentist."

Mark A. Stengler, ND, associate clinical professor, National College of Naturopathic Medicine, Portland, OR, and founder and director of the La Jolla Whole Health Clinic, La Jolla, CA. He is author of the *Bottom Line Natural Healing* newsletter. His Web site is *www.DrStengler.com.*

Sinusitis: Surprising New Findings

Jordan S. Josephson, MD, director of the New York Nasal and Sinus Center, which treats people who suffer from sinus disease and related conditions, in New York City. He is the author of *Sinus Relief Now: The Groundbreaking 5-Step Program for Sinus, Allergy and Asthma Sufferers* (Penguin).

Chronic sinusitis is often part of a cluster of health problems that includes asthma and bronchitis as well as serious digestive problems, such as chronic heartburn. Sinusitis also is a cause of sleep apnea (a temporary cessation of breathing while at sleep), which can indirectly lead to a heart attack and stroke. Knowing that these conditions can be connected helps sinusitis sufferers to protect themselves from seemingly unrelated health problems.

SINUSITIS DANGERS

When the sinuses become inflamed from infection or allergy, the tissues swell, closing off the flow of air and making it difficult to breathe through the nose. As a result of inflammation, mucus turns thick and sticky and can become yellow, green, brown or tan.

The inflammation and/or infection associated with sinusitis can spread to the respiratory tract and affect the digestive system as well, causing a broad set of health problems called chronic airway-digestive inflammatory disease, which results in…

• **Lung problems.** When the sinuses no longer cleanse the air properly, inflammation of the large and medium airways can result. This can lead to bronchitis, causing congestion, coughing and shortness of breath. Inflammation of the small airways can cause asthma.

• **Digestive disorders.** Infectious mucus dripping down the back of the throat may inflame the stomach, causing acid to back up into the esophagus, leading to chronic heartburn, a symptom of gastroesophageal reflux disease (GERD).

• **Sleep apnea.** Many people who snore also suffer from sleep apnea. Besides the stress of extreme fatigue caused by the cessation of breathing and subsequent repeated awakenings, sleep apnea reduces oxygen levels in the blood, increasing heart attack and stroke risk.

BEST TREATMENT APPROACHES

Mild sinus symptoms should be treated the same way you would treat any cold—with lots of fluids to keep mucus thin and flowing, and plenty of rest (ideally, 12 or more hours each night). An over-the-counter decongestant, such as *pseudoephedrine* (Sudafed), can relieve stuffiness and pain. Decongestants do have stimulant effects and should be used for no more than two days without the guidance of a physician. If used for longer than a few days, decongestants can have a rebound effect, leading to more congestion. Avoid antihistamines unless sinusitis is caused by an allergy.

If sinus symptoms last for more than 48 to 72 hours or are accompanied by even a mild fever or nausea, diarrhea, facial swelling or swollen neck glands, or if the pain is severe, see your doctor. You may have a bacterial infection and need to take an antibiotic.

Important: Some sinusitis symptoms are often overlooked—headache, typically around the eyes and forehead…persistent cough…hearing loss (caused by fluid buildup in the middle ear), resulting in ringing in the ears (tinnitus)…and toothache (the roots of some teeth are close to the sinuses).

To prevent sinusitis or if it recurs twice per month or more, or if symptoms linger despite treatment, follow my program of self-care which includes…

• **Irrigation.** Washing out the sinuses maintains healthy mucous membranes and keeps air passages open. When symptoms are acute, irrigate the sinuses twice a day. Daily irrigation will keep problems from returning, especially in the winter and during allergy attacks.

What to do: Use "normal saline"—a solution of salt water diluted to the same concentration as bodily fluids. Good sterile saline preparations, which are available at drugstores, include Ayr…Breathe-ease XL…or Goldberger's Ultra Saline Nasal Mist (available at 800-228-5382, *www.goldbergerspharmacy.com*).

• **Environmental control.** The airborne allergens…other irritants, including cleaning chemicals and smoke…and microorganisms, such as mold, trigger and exacerbate sinusitis. Household dust is a common allergen and irritant.

To minimize dust exposure: Wash bedding weekly in hot water, and place plastic covers or allergen-resistant fabric covers on the mattress and pillows…vacuum at least weekly, using a vacuum cleaner that has a high-efficiency particulate air (HEPA) filter…shampoo area rugs once or twice a year…use sealed wood, plastic and metal furniture…and replace drapes with venetian blinds.

To prevent mold exposure: Clean mold-prone areas (in and around the shower, kitchen sink and washing machine) with a solution of bleach and water. Because mold thrives in damp places, do not let kitchen and bathroom walls and floors remain wet, and don't let water accumulate around the washer, sink or refrigerator. Leave the washer door open after use, to let it dry out inside. Repair roof and basement leaks promptly.

To keep sinus membranes from drying out, use a humidifier in the winter to add moisture to the air. Be sure to clean the humidifier at least weekly to prevent the growth of mold and other microorganisms.

SURGICAL OPTIONS

When sinusitis persists despite medical treatment and self-help, surgery may be necessary…

• **Debridement** gets rid of scar tissue, scabs and infectious matter from the sinuses. It is usually performed in the doctor's office with a topical anesthetic.

• **Functional endoscopic sinus surgery,** or FESS, involves opening passages and removing small growths and other blockages to promote better movement of air and drainage of mucus. FESS is usually outpatient surgery that is performed in a hospital under local or general anesthesia. Bleeding and postoperative pain are generally minimal.

Aspirin Lowers Adult-Onset Asthma Risk

In one 4.9-year, randomized study of 22,071 healthy male physicians ages 40 to 84, half the participants took 325 mg of aspirin every other day, while the other half took a placebo. Among participants who took aspirin, the relative risk for adult-onset asthma was 22% lower than in the placebo group, regardless of age, weight or tobacco use.

Theory: Aspirin may decrease inflammatory processes involved in asthma occurrence.

Caution: Aspirin should not be used to treat asthma symptoms—it can trigger attacks in some asthma sufferers.

Tobias Kurth, MD, ScD, assistant professor of medicine, Harvard Medical School, Boston.

Killer Pneumonia Is on the Rise: How to Protect Yourself

Donald M. Yealy, MD, a professor and vice-chair of emergency medicine at the University of Pittsburgh Medical Center/Presbyterian University Hospital. He has written more than 150 articles, reviews and book chapters on various aspects of pneumonia.

An estimated 30 million Americans will come down with influenza during flu season. That's bad enough—but many of these patients go on to develop *secondary pneumonia,* a much more serious condition.

Pneumonia, whether it follows another infection or occurs on its own (primary pneumonia), is the sixth leading cause of death in the US. More than 60,000 Americans die from it annually, and many more require hospitalization.

New danger: A rare—but particularly lethal —form of pneumonia is resistant to all standard antibiotics. It is caused by the bacterium *methicillin-resistant Staphylococcus aureus* (MRSA), which has appeared in recent years in hospitals and increasingly in the wider community. The death rate from MRSA pneumonia is roughly double that of other pneumonias.

What you need to know…

WHO GETS PNEUMONIA

Pneumonia is an illness of the lungs and respiratory system in which the *alveoli* (tiny sacs in the lungs) become inflamed and flooded with fluid. Pneumonia can be caused by bacteria, viruses or fungi. The viral form is the most common.

People get pneumonia in the same ways that they get the flu—by touching their eyes, nose or mouth after shaking hands, for example, with someone who has the virus on his/her hands—or through airborne droplets from coughs or sneezes.

Bacterial pneumonia is usually the most serious form. It is most commonly acquired by inhaling or aspirating bacteria into the lungs. Hospital patients have a high risk of contracting bacterial pneumonia since their immune systems tend to be weakened, and germs are so prevalent in the hospital. Other vulnerable people include those who have diabetes, heart or lung disease…adults age 65 and older…young children…and anyone who abuses alcohol or smokes.

Surprising new risk factor: People who take acid-suppressing heartburn drugs, such as *cimetidine* (Tagamet), *ranitidine* (Zantac), *omeprazole* (Prilosec) and *esomeprazole* (Nexium), have been found to be 27% more likely to develop pneumonia—especially hospital-acquired pneumonia—than those not taking such medication.

Researchers theorize that these drugs might increase a person's vulnerability to infection by reducing stomach acid, a major defense mechanism against pathogens ingested through your mouth. People should not use over-the-counter acid-reducing drugs for more than a few weeks unless these medications are prescribed by their physicians.

HOW IT'S DIAGNOSED

It can sometimes be difficult for a patient to distinguish the symptoms of pneumonia from those caused from a cold or the flu. Therefore, anyone who has a high fever (102°F or higher)…chills…a persistent cough…shortness of breath …and/or pain when inhaling should see a doctor right away.

What the doctor will look for…

●**Abnormal chest sounds heard through a stethoscope.** The doctor will listen for crackling sounds (rales) or rumblings (rhonchi), caused by air passing through mucus and/or other fluids in the lungs.

●**X-ray showing a cloudy area,** caused by fluid in the lungs.

Caution: An X-ray often will look normal in patients with early-stage pneumonia. A second X-ray is typically taken if symptoms do not improve in two to three days or worsen, especially if the first X-ray looked normal.

A sputum test is also recommended to identify the cause of the pneumonia—and help the doctor choose the best treatment. After an X-ray, it's the best test for diagnosing pneumonia, but only 20% to 25% of patients are able to bring up sputum (by coughing) for analysis.

TREATMENT

An antiviral drug, such as *oseltamivir* (Tamiflu), is sometimes prescribed for a viral pneumonia. In the viral pneumonia patients who are otherwise healthy, doctors may recommend the same therapy as for the flu—rest, plenty of liquids (up to one gallon daily) and medication to reduce fever and/or pain.

Because a bacterial and viral pneumonia can appear quite similar, doctors typically err on the side of caution and assume that it's bacterial in origin when uncertain and prescribe antibiotics.

Studies show that older patients as well as those with underlying health problems do better when they're given antibiotics promptly—preferably within four to eight hours of the initial diagnosis. Most bacterial pneumonias are treated (orally or intravenously) with a penicillin antibiotic, such as Augmentin…a cephalosporin antibiotic, such as *cefaclor* (Ceclor) or *ceftriaxone* (Rocephin)…and/or *azithromycin* (Zithromax).

In-the-home treatment: Patients with pneumonia are sometimes advised to use an incentive spirometer (a tubelike device that patients breathe into, as hard as they can, at least two to three times a day). It helps maintain open breathing passages.

Preventive: An incentive spirometer also can be used by patients who don't have pneumonia but who have underlying lung disease, such as chronic bronchitis, emphysema or some other obstructive lung disease. It helps keep the airways open and less vulnerable to pneumonia.

AN EMERGING THREAT

MRSA is primarily a skin infection that can enter your body through cuts and scrapes. MRSA was originally found only in health-care settings. In the 1990s, it began showing up in the general community. This form of infection has the prefix CA, denoting community-acquired.

CA-MRSA pneumonia is not as dangerous as the hospital-acquired form. It is usually treated with the antibiotics *sulfamethoxazole* and *trimethoprim* (Bactrim). Those in the hospital with MRSA-related pneumonia require a much stronger antibiotic—*vancomycin* (Vancocin), which is given intravenously.

Self-protection: CA-MRSA is spread by airborne droplets. It also can be present on drinking glasses, toothbrushes, etc. In community settings, such as health clubs, people should never share their personal items.

In the hospital: Patients should wash their hands after touching any object, as MRSA can survive on doorknobs, faucet handles, bedrails, remote controls, telephones, food trays, etc. Patients also should wash after using the bathroom and prior to eating. For convenience, any 62% alcohol hand sanitizer gel can be used. Patients should require that all medical personnel wash their hands before and after performing any procedure, and even before and after touching any object in the room.

PREVENTION

Not smoking and frequent hand-washing help prevent pneumonia. *Also important...*

•**Annual flu vaccine.** People who do not get the flu are far less likely to get pneumonia. The Centers for Disease Control and Prevention (CDC) recommends the flu vaccine for all adults age 50 and older...children ages six months to five years old...women who are pregnant during flu season (typically October to as late as May)...people of any age with certain chronic medical conditions...people who live in nursing homes...and health-care workers or others who have close contact with people in a high-risk group. However, flu vaccine, if available, can help most people reduce risk.

Important: The FluMist nasal vaccine, which has been approved for healthy people ages five to 49, may be more effective than conventional flu shots. There appears to be a greater immune response in the nose, where the vaccine is administered. This can make it harder for an inhaled flu virus to cause infection.

Caution: FluMist isn't recommended for anyone with asthma or lung disease.

•**Pneumococcal vaccine.** It's recommended for adults age 65 and older as well as for those with pneumonia risk factors, such as cardiovascular or lung disease, cancer or a previous illness with pneumonia. People with certain illnesses, such as kidney or severe lung disease, may need a second dose after five or more years.

Legionnaires' Disease Warning

This respiratory infection is caused by a bacteria most often found in the water-distribution and air-conditioning systems of large buildings and cruise ships. More than 20,000 cases occur nationwide each year. And, about one-quarter of those afflicted die. Symptoms—high fever, cough, headache and diarrhea—are similar to those of other illnesses, so the disease may go untreated until it is too late for antibiotics to work.

Self-defense: If you do experience symptoms and recently have been in a hospital or hotel or on a cruise, ask to be tested for the disease.

Janet E. Stout, PhD, a microbiologist at Pittsburgh VA Healthcare System, and research assistant professor in the School of Medicine at University of Pittsburgh.

Update on Rocky Mountain Spotted Fever

Rocky Mountain spotted fever can be spread by the common brown dog tick. Until recently, it was thought that only two less common ticks could transmit the disease, which is found across the country and has a fatality rate as high as 20% when untreated. Rocky Mountain spotted fever is especially severe in children. Symptoms, including fever, nausea, vomiting, muscle pain, lack of appetite, severe headache and a rash, appear one to two weeks after infection.

Good news: Antibiotics are effective when given early.

Linda J. Demma, PhD, senior epidemiologist, Foodborne & Diarrheal Diseases Branch, Division of Viral and Rickettsial Diseases, Centers for Disease Control and Prevention, Atlanta, and leader of a study of tick transmission of Rocky Mountain spotted fever, published in *The New England Journal of Medicine.*

Adult Vaccinations

William Schaffner, MD, chairman, department of preventive medicine, Vanderbilt University School of Medicine, Nashville.

There are a variety of vaccinations adults should get, including the *Tdap vaccination* every 10 years. This protects against tetanus, diphtheria and pertussis (or whooping cough). This is especially important now because of recent outbreaks of whooping cough among adolescents and young adults.

If you are not in a monogamous long-term relationship, get the *Hepatitis B vaccine* to protect against this sexually transmitted liver disease.

Also, the new *shingles vaccine* (Zostavax) has been approved by the FDA. Shingles is caused by the chickenpox virus. The vaccine is recommended for everyone age 60 and above who had chicken pox—except those with weakened immune systems. The vaccine reduces shingles incidence by half.

The *pneumococcal vaccine* prevents pneumococcal pneumonia. Anyone who is age 65 or older, as well as younger people with heart or lung disease or compromised immune systems, should get this vaccination.

An annual *flu shot* is recommended for people over age 50 and younger adults with diabetes, asthma, kidney disease, heart or lung disease, or a weakened immune system. See page 27 for complete details.

Germ-Fighting Secrets

Philip M. Tierno, Jr., PhD, director of clinical microbiology and immunology at New York University Medical Center, and associate professor, department of microbiology and pathology at New York University School of Medicine, both in New York City. He is the author of *The Secret Life of Germs* (Atria).

Everyone already knows about the disease-causing potential of germs. Yet very few people realize that these microorganisms are essential for human health.

Of the 65,000 known species of germs, only about 1,400 cause disease. The rest are "good" germs, which establish our immune response, help us digest food and protect our bodies from pathogens. But, the germs that do promote disease can be deadly. Infectious diseases, such as pneumonia and septicemia (or blood infection), are leading causes of death in the US.

A surprising number of people are still not aware of the best ways to guard against infection through proper hygiene. Fortunately, most infections—everything from colds and the flu to life-threatening Legionnaires' disease—usually can be prevented. *My germ-fighting secrets…*

• **Wash thoroughly.** The Centers for Disease Control and Prevention (CDC) now claims that proper hand-washing could prevent thousands of deaths annually, but studies show that less than 10% of people wash their hands as long or as thoroughly as they should.

To effectively remove germs: Wash with warm water and soap for about 20 to 30 seconds (roughly the time it takes to sing "Happy Birthday" twice) and rinse. Warmer water dissolves soap more readily and makes it easier to remove germs. Rub the soapy water all over your hands—including the wrists, between the fingers and under the fingernails.

Best: Wash your hands several times a day—always before eating…after using the bathroom …after coughing or sneezing, especially when you use your hands or a tissue…after shaking hands…and after handling anything touched by many people, such as door handles and automatic teller machines (ATMs). If soap and water aren't available, use an alcohol gel containing at least 62% alcohol.

• **Use antibacterial products when necessary.** Our hands pick up *millions* of potentially harmful organisms during daily activities—handling raw meats, poultry and/or fish…changing diapers…picking up pet wastes in the yard, etc. Washing with soap and water removes (rather than kills) most germs, but some are left behind—potentially causing illness.

Interesting: Some experts believe that the regular use of antibacterial soaps will promote the emergence of antibiotic-resistant organisms, but there is no evidence that links these products to resistance. More study is needed to determine the long-term effects of antibacterial soaps.

Best: After washing your hands with soap, use an antibacterial cleaner if you've handled materials such as those described above. Some antibacterial products (including Dial Complete hand wash) contain *triclosan*, a germicide that kills virtually all harmful bacteria.

Also important: Never permit a pet to lick your mouth, nose, eyes or an open wound. Many people believe that the mouths of dogs and cats are relatively germ-free—however, dogs and cats can carry *Pasteurella*, a bacterium that can cause skin infection in humans. And turtles, frogs and snakes can harbor *Salmonella*, a bacterium that causes gastroenteritis and other illnesses.

• **Limit kissing to close friends and family.** Mouth-to-mouth kissing obviously spreads germs, but even face kissing (kissing anywhere on the face, except the lips) can be dangerous if someone is ill. Flu viruses, for example, can be spread by an infected person during face kissing up to three days before full-blown symptoms develop and five days after they subside.

Here's how: Before the kiss, the infected person may have touched his/her mouth or nose, then touched his face, contaminating it with infected saliva or mucus.

Best: Instead of kissing someone who may be sick, hug him.

• **Air-dry toothbrushes and razors.** Bacteria grow on toothbrushes and razors that stay damp. Bacteria on a razor could cause a staphylococcal infection of the skin, while a contaminated toothbrush can spread cold or flu viruses. Rinse and let them air-dry after every use—and store them upright so that they'll dry completely. To sanitize a toothbrush, put it in a cup of antiseptic mouthwash or 3% hydrogen peroxide (enough to cover the brush head), leave for one minute, then rinse and air-dry. Replace razors after two or three uses…toothbrushes should be replaced when the bristles are worn.

• **Clean the showerhead.** The *Legionella* bacterium causes a potentially fatal, pneumonia-like condition called Legionnaires' disease, which is contracted by inhaling infected water droplets. This organism thrives on *cysteine*, a substance produced by a wide variety of waterborne organisms and by bacteria found in potable water. The Legionella can thrive in tap water for many months, and showerheads provide a hospitable environment.

Best: Remove showerheads once a year. Disassemble and clean them thoroughly with a wire brush to remove any organisms that might be present. Use a solution of one ounce of bleach mixed with one quart of water.

Also important: Replace the water in humidifiers with fresh water at least once a week. Before adding fresh water, clean the filters/trays according to the manufacturer's directions.

• **Close the toilet lid.** Flushing an older toilet with the lid up can hurl droplets of water that contain fecal matter (and potentially other disease-causing organisms) up to 20 feet. The droplets can contaminate toothbrushes, combs, faucets, etc. The risk for disease is even higher if the toilet bowl isn't cleaned regularly. Among those diseases that can be transmitted by fecal matter from an infected person are stomach flu and hepatitis A.

Best: In addition to closing the toilet lid, sanitize the bowl weekly with a commercial cleaner or a mixture of one ounce of bleach added to one quart of water.

• **Launder with hot water.** Bath towels can harbor fecal bacteria, including E. coli, along with hepatitis A and other harmful viruses—and these germs aren't necessarily killed by running them through a cold- or warm-water wash.

Warning: Because washing in cold or warm water doesn't kill germs, it's possible to get infected just by removing wet clothes from the washer if you then touch your nose, mouth or eyes.

Best: Use the "hot" washer setting (150°F or hotter) to kill most germs. Another option is to add bleach to the wash, which is effective even in cold or warm water. If you live in a sunny climate, consider line-drying clothes rather than using the dryer. Like the hottest cycle of a clothes dryer, the sun's ultraviolet rays kill most germs.

Also important: Launder underwear separately in hot water to avoid contaminating other clothes. For added safety, use bleach to ensure that germs are killed when washing underwear.

More from Dr. Philip Tierno, Jr....

How to Combat Germs In a Public Bathroom

To avoid germs in public bathrooms, use the first stall—it tends to be the least popular. Flush the toilet with your foot, then leave the stall quickly to avoid airborne bacteria. To be sure you are washing your hands long enough, see full details on page 28. Use a paper towel to turn off the faucet and pull the door open.

Dirty Ice

A 12-year-old middle-school student got national attention when her science project revealed that the ice in some fast-food restaurants harbored more *E. coli* bacteria than toilet water from the same restaurants. Beware, ice machines are rarely cleaned and people use unwashed hands to scoop the ice.

ABCnews.com.

 # Chicken Safety Alert

Rebecca Shannonhouse, editor of *Bottom Line/Health*, Boardroom Inc., 281 Tresser Blvd., Stamford, CT 06901.

Chicken has been touted as an alternative to red meat because it has less saturated fat. However, a new study shows that some chicken may be less healthful than once believed.

Arsenic (a known carcinogen) was found in 55% of 155 samples of raw chicken purchased in Minnesota and California supermarkets, according to research commissioned by the nonprofit Institute for Agriculture and Trade Policy (IATP).* All of the 90 samples purchased from fast-food restaurants contained arsenic.

Many poultry producers feed animals an organic form of arsenic, which is believed to be harmless, to control intestinal parasites. But there is evidence suggesting that some of this arsenic is converted in the birds into a toxic, inorganic form of arsenic. Questions remain about what happens to it in the human body.

The US Department of Agriculture tests chicken livers for arsenic (residues are almost always found to be under the legal standard), but the IATP report is the first extensive data on other chicken meat.

"You don't want to have any more arsenic in your body than what you absolutely cannot avoid," says toxicologist Paul Mushak, PhD, of Durham, North Carolina, an expert on arsenic and other toxic metals.

To decrease exposure: Call the customer-service line of the producer whose poultry you buy and ask if the birds are given arsenic.

Another option: Buy only organic chicken —these birds cannot legally be given arsenic. Use of arsenic is not prohibited in chicken labeled only as kosher or "free range."

*To read the 2006 IATP report, go to *www.iatp.org*.

Multivitamin Problems

Half the multivitamins brands recently tested by ConsumerLab had too little or too much of some nutrients...did not break down properly...or were contaminated with lead.

There was no relationship between price and quality—some brands that cost $3 a day failed, while some costing five cents a day passed.

Among the multivitamins that passed the test: Centrum Silver...One-A-Day Women's... and Puritan's Pride ABC Plus Senior.

Tod Cooperman, MD, president of ConsumerLab.com, an independent evaluator of health products, White Plains, NY, *www.consumerlab.com*.

2

The Best Medical Care

How a Dental Visit Can Save Your Life

If you believe that regular dental exams are just for your teeth and gums and aren't very important, you could be putting yourself in danger. Dentists are able to identify signs of a variety of serious conditions that affect other parts of the body.

Recent finding: About 78% of periodontists (a dentist who specializes in the diagnosis and treatment of gum disease) have referred patients age 60 or beyond to be evaluated for diabetes, and 21% have made referrals for osteoporosis, according to a poll conducted by the American Academy of Periodontology. All dentists have been trained to identify these diseases and other illnesses.

How can a dental exam yield such crucial health information? While you're sitting in the dentist's chair to be treated for tooth or gum problems, your dentist is also checking for signs of cancer and other diseases. By monitoring the changes in your gum tissue, your dentist can look for oral manifestations of diseases or other serious health problems.

Adults should get dental exams at least twice a year, or three to four times if they have gum (periodontal) disease. During a thorough exam, a dentist inspects all of the soft tissues, including the gums, tongue, palate and throat, as well as feels (palpates) the patient's neck and under the chin.

Signs of possible health problems include ulcerations, thickened tissue, pigmentation changes and abnormal color or consistency of gums and other soft tissues.

No one should consider their dental exam an adequate screening of overall physical health. However, your dentist can serve as a valuable adjunct to your other doctors in helping to spot signs of serious medical conditions.

Alan Winter, DDS, a periodontist in private practice and associate professor of implant dentistry at the New York University College of Dentistry, both in New York City. He has published more than a dozen medical journal articles on gum disease.

31

CANCER

Dentists can spot possible malignancies that form in the gums, palate, cheek or other soft tissues. They also can identify tumors in the jawbone, which either originated there or metastasized (spread) from the breasts, bones, lungs or elsewhere in the body.

Warning signs: A newly formed lesion (open sore) or bump anywhere in the mouth that doesn't go away after seven to 10 days…swelling of the gums…teeth that suddenly become loose…and/or nonspecific mouth pain that doesn't seem to be related to a tooth problem. Less commonly, a cancerous lesion in the jawbone may be seen on an X-ray, but many people who have cancer that has spread to the jaw are already being treated by an oncologist or surgeon. On rare occasions, a dentist may be the first to identify such a cancer.

Self-defense: If you have a bump or lesion that has not healed in seven to 10 days without treatment, see your dentist. He/she will decide whether you should see a specialist, such as a periodontist, oral surgeon or ear, nose and throat specialist.

Important: Although some bumps and lesions are cancerous, most are benign and due to canker sores, routine gum problems, root canal problems—or they are the result of trauma, such as hitting your gum with the head of your toothbrush. To reach a proper diagnosis, your dentist will do a thorough examination, get a detailed medical history and may even take a biopsy.

DIABETES

Periodontal disease develops over a period of years. If a dentist sees gum breakdown that is more rapid than expected or there has been extreme bone loss that can't be explained, diabetes should be suspected.

Warning signs: Poor healing after having oral surgery, inflammation in the gums and other periodontal problems. These may be signs of diabetes or diabetes that is not well controlled. Such problems can occur because diabetes suppresses the immune system, which impairs the infection-fighting function of white blood cells.

Self-defense: If your dentist suspects diabetes, you should see your primary care doctor or an endocrinologist for a glucose tolerance test.

OSTEOPOROSIS

Most people associate osteoporosis with bone loss in the spine or hips, but it also can occur in the jawbone.

Warning sign: On an X-ray, the jawbone will look less dense than it should.

Self-defense: Follow up with your primary care doctor. A bone-density test may be needed.

Caution: Bisphosphonate drugs, such as *alendronate* (Fosamax), have been linked to *osteonecrosis* of the jaw—death of areas of jawbone. Most reports of this side effect are associated with bisphosphonates taken intravenously by cancer patients whose malignancy has spread to their bones, but a handful of cases have involved people who took the oral form of the medication.

A LINK TO HEART DISEASE

Contrary to what many people believe, dentists cannot *diagnose* heart disease based on the appearance of a person's gums. Much has been written about a possible link between gum disease and heart disease. However, the research that showed a connection was retrospective—that is, it reviewed the characteristics of a particular group.

One such study was conducted by Robert Genco, PhD, of the State University of New York at Buffalo, and colleagues at the University of North Carolina at Chapel Hill. The researchers noted that cumulative evidence supports—but does not prove—an association between periodontal infection and cardiovascular disease. In a recent Finnish study, people with gum disease were found to be 1.6 times more likely to suffer a stroke.

Additional research is required to determine whether gum disease is, in fact, a risk factor for cardiovascular disease. In the meantime, it makes good sense to keep your gums healthy to help minimize the possible risk for heart disease. Studies have shown that people with heart disease are more likely to smoke, not exercise regularly and/or have poor diets.

Dentists often send patients with diagnosed heart disease for a cardiovascular evaluation.

Reason: These patients need to get medical clearance for dental surgery. During these evaluations, a cardiologist checks the patient's blood pressure, use of blood thinners and overall risk for heart attack and stroke. The cardiovascular evaluation also helps to determine which anesthetic to use—adrenaline (*epinephrine*) used in some anesthesia can stimulate the heart.

Afraid of the Dentist?

Try out these helpful relaxation techniques to calm yourself at the dentist…

- **Progressive muscle relaxation**—tense and relax each muscle one by one until every body part is relaxed.
- **Guided imagery**—imagine a happy scene.
- **Paced breathing**—breathe very slowly and evenly.
- **Meditation**—focus on a soothing thought and repeat it to yourself.

More information: *www.dentalgentlecare.com*, *www.saveyoursmile.com* and *www.colgate.com*.

Robert F. Kroeger, DDS, a dentist in private practice, Cincinnati, *cincinnatismiles.com.*

Get Better Care From Your Doctor

Mehmet C. Oz, MD, medical director of the Integrated Medical Program and director of the Cardiovascular Institute at New York–Presbyterian Hospital/Columbia University Medical Center and professor and vice chairman of surgery at Columbia University, both in New York City. He is coauthor, with Michael F. Roizen, MD, of *You: The Smart Patient: An Insider's Handbook for Getting the Best Treatment* (Free Press).

Even the people who are ordinarily savvy consumers forget their normal assertiveness at the examining room door—just when it's needed most.

The average internist sees 22 to 28 patients a day. In hectic medical environments, doctors barely have time to discuss their patients' major symptoms and complaints, much less minor health problems.

Traps to avoid…

- **Trap 1.** Wasting time during the exam. Most patients can provide a doctor with all the pertinent information in about 90 seconds—if they're mentally organized and make sure the doctor actually hears what they're saying.

Research indicates that doctors interrupt patients, on average, after 23 seconds—and only 2% of patients get a chance to finish their opening statements.

Many people know to write down their symptoms and/or complaints ahead of time. But they make long, complicated lists that aren't much help during a short exam.

Helpful: Limit your written list to three main points—and keep the sentences short.

Example: "I've been having pain in my lower back," "I haven't been sleeping well" and "I'm having trouble with urination."

Hand a copy of the list to your doctor when he/she comes into the examining room. Reading a list while you're talking makes it easier for the doctor to process the information…and it ensures that you don't forget key points.

- **Trap 2.** Not getting a second opinion. Even though most people agree that second opinions are a good idea, only 20% of patients actually seek them out—often because they are afraid of offending their doctors.

Getting a second opinion doesn't mean that you don't trust your doctor, or that his recommendations aren't valid. It just means that you're wisely exploring other treatment choices. One study found that 33% of second opinions resulted in a significant change in treatment. Health insurers will typically pay for second opinions, especially for important procedures. It's a good idea to submit your request in writing to your insurer.

When to seek a second opinion…

- If your physician recommends *any* kind of surgery.
- If you have a condition that's uncommon or that is outside of your doctor's main area of expertise.
- If a treatment doesn't seem to be working. A patient with high blood pressure, for example, should show improvement within a few weeks. If

that doesn't occur, a drug combination suggested by a different doctor might work better.

Useful: Use the Internet to look for scientific papers that have been written about your health problem. When you find a relevant study, write down the *first* author and *last* author listed at the end. The first author will be the doctor who did most of the research. The last author is usually the supervising physician. Either is a good choice for a second opinion. Doctors who write papers for medical journals are usually among the country's top experts. Even if these doctors are not based in your area, they can probably provide a second opinion by phone if your doctor sends reports, test results, X-rays, etc.

• **Trap 3.** Not educating yourself on your condition. Patients who do their research have basic knowledge which allows them to use their appointment time much more productively. Rather than wasting time discussing, say, the anatomy of the heart, you can inquire about the specifics of various treatments—for example, whether one class of drugs is better than another, different types of surgery, etc.

Important: When conducting research, Internet sites with URLs that end with ".edu" (educational institutions) or ".gov" (US government agencies) are among the most reliable. My favorite is *www.pubmed.gov*, sponsored by the National Library of Medicine and the National Institutes of Health.

Other research strategies…

• Check when the information was updated. Medical information that's more than two years old is *ancient*. Anything newer than that generally is timely.

• Use Web sites that don't include advertising.

• Don't trust information that suggests only one treatment plan. That's often a tip-off that the information is biased and unreliable.

If you do not have time to do your own research, consider using a fee-based medical research service, such as The Health Resource, Inc. (800-949-0090, *www.thehealthresource.com*).

• **Trap 4.** Not understanding how to take your medication. Only about half of all prescriptions are filled or taken correctly. In addition, medication errors—especially not identifying dangerous

drug interactions—are among the most common preventable mistakes.

Smart idea: Go to the same pharmacy every time—and get to know the pharmacists. Someone who knows your health history is more likely to catch potential problems. The pharmacist might look at a new prescription and say something like, "You have never taken anything like this before. Let me call the doctor and check."

Other advice…

• Choose a pharmacy that uses cross-checking software and medication-monitoring technology, which checks for any potential drug interactions. (Just ask the staff if they use this technology.)

• Ask your doctor to write detailed notes for you on the drug(s) you are taking. Make sure you know the dose, when you are supposed to take it and how to take it (on an empty stomach, for example) and whether there are possible interactions with other drugs.

• Inquire about the age-related side effects. A large study at Duke University found that more than 20% of older patients were given prescriptions for drugs that could cause serious side effects in people age 65 or older.

Keep Your Medical Records At an On-Line Site

The free iHealthRecord service lets you set up and modify your history of health conditions, allergies, medications, etc. Doctors anywhere in the world can access the information with your permission. Or you can print out data before going to a new doctor. You can update information and set up secure records for people you care for, such as children and aging parents. The system also can alert you to problems.

Example: An FDA warning about a previously unknown risk of a drug you use.

Details: *www.ihealthrecord.org*.

James Rohack, MD, past chair, American Medical Association (AMA), Chicago. The AMA and other medical societies formed Medem, which offers the iHealthRecord service.

How to Make Your Lab Tests More Accurate

Kandice Kottke-Marchant, MD, PHD, Clinical Pathologist, Cleveland Clinic.

A colleague who had recently had her annual physical exam decided to get her cholesterol levels checked out again at an employer-sponsored health fair. To her surprise—and dismay—the reading on the second cholesterol test was nearly 20% higher than the first. Which results should she believe?

Many factors can influence test results. These can include diet, medications, differences among laboratories, even season (cholesterol counts tend to increase in winter). Patients can't control all of these factors—but there are ways to increase lab test accuracy. *Steps to take in advance...*

• **Make sure the lab is accredited.** The physician and the insurance carrier dictate where a test is performed. Labs are typically accredited by reputable organizations, but it is a good idea to check that the lab has accreditation.

• **Use the same lab every time,** if possible, since there can be significant testing differences between laboratories. In the case above, only the first test actually involved a lab. The health-fair test was the "instant" kind—so disparate results were more likely.

• **Follow all instructions**—for example, eating a meal exactly two hours before a two-hour postprandial blood sugar test or abstaining from ejaculation for two days prior to a prostate-specific antigen (PSA) test.

• **Review your medications, dietary supplements and herbal treatments** with your doctor. These can affect lab test results. For example, high amounts of vitamin C interfere with different tests...birth control pills could increase blood sugar...some antidepressants and blood pressure medications can decrease blood sugar. All these factors can be taken into account when interpreting the test results, but your doctor may advise a change in your regimen prior to the test.

• **Tell your doctor if you've experienced significant stress recently or have exercised strenuously.** Those factors can increase blood levels of *C-reactive protein* (CRP), an inflammation indicator associated with heart disease.

• **To avoid bacterial contamination, clean yourself with soap and water** before giving a urine sample, or particularly for women, use the special wipes available at testing facilities.

Patients need to keep a watchful eye *during* a test, as well...

• **If blood flows too slowly as it is drawn,** clots may form, invalidating the results for some tests, in particular hematology and coagulation tests (drawn in tubes with purple or light blue tops). A simple tilt of the tube back and forth may detect a clotted sample.

• **Check that the sample is labeled accurately.** Confirm your name, type of test, date drawn and, if at a hospital, patient ID number.

Treatment decisions generally should not be made on the basis of a single out-of-range reading. A second test, drawn from a new sample, helps to confirm whether an out-of-range result is in line with prior results.

Sometimes trends can be more important than absolute numbers. A Johns Hopkins University finding, for example, indicates that the annual rate of increase in PSA may be more significant than simply looking at whether the numbers are within the normal range.

No More Needles?

The British company PowderMed has created a device that delivers vaccines without needles. The PMED is a flashlight-sized device that uses pressurized helium to shoot powdered vaccine just below the skin surface rather than into the muscle, as with needles. This results in less pain and better absorption. PowderMed is working on powdered vaccines for influenza, other viral diseases and cancer.

Popular Science, 2 Park Ave., New York City 10016.

Dangerous Medication Risks For Seniors

Robert N. Butler, MD, professor of geriatrics at Mount Sinai School of Medicine, and the president of the International Longevity Center (*www.ilcusa.org*), both in New York City. He won the Pulitzer Prize for his book *Why Survive? Being Old in America* (Johns Hopkins University) and is coauthor of *Aging and Mental Health* (Allyn & Bacon) and *The New Love and Sex After 60* (Ballantine).

M odern medications are now so powerful that they both save lives and endanger them. After age 50, just when people are most likely to take several medications prescribed by multiple health professionals who often don't communicate with each other, they become increasingly vulnerable to adverse drug reactions.

Reasons: Aging slows recovery...diminished liver and kidney functions result in altered metabolism and excretion. Also, a generally higher level of fat and changes in lean body tissue alter drug distribution.

Surprising: The drugs most commonly implicated in adverse drug reactions are time-honored medications prescribed for chronic conditions.

Examples: Diuretics (or water pills), such as *hydrochlorothiazide* (HydroDiuril) and furosemide (Lasix), to reduce fluid retention and blood pressure...oral anticoagulants (blood thinners), such as warfarin (Coumadin), to restrict clotting after a heart attack or stroke.

DANGEROUS INTERACTIONS

A frequently-quoted 1998 study published in *The Journal of the American Medical Association* found that in the US, more than 2.2 million people a year have serious adverse reactions to prescribed drugs and 100,000 of them die, making drug interactions one of the leading causes of hospitalization and death. *Watch out for these...*

●**Drug–food interactions.** Some labels say, "Take with food." Which food? Grapefruit juice often triggers a drug–food interaction that can increase drug absorption *or* deactivate certain drugs like blood pressure drugs and cholesterol-lowering drugs. Oat bran can make blood pressure drugs less effective.

Solution: Ask your physician or pharmacist which foods might affect the actions of your medications and how.

Although taking drugs with a meal may reduce stomach upset, food may delay the drug's absorption, change its characteristics or make its actions less predictable. Speak up—ask whether this applies to any medication you take.

●**Drug–alcohol interactions.** Reduced body mass and increased fat make older people more sensitive to alcohol, which interacts with many commonly prescribed drugs and many of the commonly prescribed sleep aids, such as sedatives and hypnotics. Discuss with your doctor or pharmacist.

Danger: Alcohol is a primary ingredient in many liquid medications, such as cough syrup.

●**Drug–drug interactions.** Prescription drugs known for interacting with other drugs include cholesterol-lowering statins, such as *atorvastatin* (Lipitor) and *pravastatin* (Pravachol), and blood pressure–lowering antihypertensives, such as *furosemide, propranolol* (Inderal) and *clonidine* (Catapres).

Self-defense: Find out which potential interactions apply to each medication you take now ...and whenever a new drug is prescribed, ask your doctor and/or pharmacist which drugs or foods not to take with it. Just separating the food and drug by two or three hours might be safer.

Over-the-counter (OTC) drugs can wreak as much havoc as prescription drugs.

Examples: Antacids, antihistamines as well as heavy use of nonsteroidal anti-inflammatory drugs (NSAIDs), such as aspirin and *ibuprofen* (Advil, Motrin). According to an estimate by James Fries, MD, of the Stanford University School of Medicine, NSAID-induced gastrointestinal bleeding sends about 76,000 Americans to the hospital each year...and kills about 10% of them.

Antacids (Milk of Magnesia, Tums, Amphojel) can reduce the effectiveness of antibiotics, such as *tetracycline* and *ciprofloxacin* (Cipro)...antihypertensive drugs, including *propranolol* and *captopril* (Capoten)...and heartburn drugs, such as *ranitidine* (Zantac) and *famotidine* (Pepcid AC). But antacids can also increase the potency of *valproic acid* (Depakote/Depakene), for seizures and bipolar disorder...*sulfonylurea* (Glucotrol), for diabetes...*quinidine* (Quin-Release), for arrhythmias…and *levodopa* (Larodopa), for Parkinson's disease.

The older (or first-generation) antihistamines, taken widely for allergies, colds and flu, may have dangerous interactions when taken with other drugs that cause drowsiness, such as antidepressants, alcohol, pain relievers, muscle relaxants and medications for seizures or anxiety.

Examples: *Brompheniramine* (in Robitussin Allergy & Cough) and *doxylamine* (which is in NyQuil).

The examples above are just a small sampling. Check your own medications.

PERILOUS FALSE ALARM

Some drugs can deplete certain vitamins from the body. If these vitamins aren't replaced, resulting symptoms may mimic those of dementia or other age-related conditions.

Examples: Tuberculosis drugs can deplete vitamin B-6, leading to amnesia, and vitamin-B complex, leading to apparent senility. Seizure drugs (anticonvulsants) can deplete vitamin D, leading to hearing and walking problems and general weakness. An elderly person displaying symptoms that are associated with dementia may just have an easily corrected vitamin deficiency.

MEDICATION ERRORS

More than 7,000 deaths in US hospitals were caused by medication errors in a single year, according to a major report published in 1999 by the Institute of Medicine. As it happens, the drugs found by the United States Pharmacopoeia* to be most frequently implicated in medication errors are commonly taken by seniors.

Examples: *Insulin* (for diabetes)…*warfarin* and *heparin* (to control clotting, such as in cardiovascular disease)…*albuterol* (Proventil, for asthma or bronchitis).

The Joint Commission on Accreditation of Healthcare Organizations (or JCAHO) has asked hospitals to start providing every hospital patient with a list of all his/her prescribed drugs and instructions for taking new ones. Patients should show the list to everyone providing care in the hospital, at any follow-up facility and after going home.

*The not-for-profit public standards–setting authority for prescription and OTC medicines, dietary supplements and other health-care products made and sold in the US.

Have a family member or a friend with you when in the hospital. Anyone hospitalized in my family is attended by a relative night and day.

Potentially fatal danger: Poor communication about meds when a patient is moved, such as from a critical care unit to a general medical unit or when nurses change shifts.

Self-defense: If you don't get a list from the hospital, maintain and hand out a list of your own. A free form is available on the Web from JCAHO at *http://store.tribost.com/jcaho/assets/pdf/spkwc.pdf*. Also, question every drug you're given by anyone, anywhere, anytime.

New Prescription Alert

Derjung Mimi Tarn, MD, PhD, assistant professor of family medicine at the University of California, Los Angeles, and the lead author of the study.

Nearly half of all Americans take one or more prescription drugs. You may assume that doctors would routinely explain the basics—what a drug does, how long to take it, etc. Don't count on it.

A new study based on audiotapes of 185 patient–doctor visits and published in the *Archives of Internal Medicine* found that physicians do a poor job of explaining critical information related to medication. Doctors discussed drug side effects in only 35% of cases…told patients how long to take a drug just 34% of the time…and were remiss in telling how many pills to take in 45% of the taped visits.

Prescription drug misuse accounts for thousands of deaths annually—and poor communication from doctors may be a factor.

Patients can get some information from pharmacists, medication labels, package inserts and/or the Internet.* But doctors are more likely to understand the patient's individual needs—and know what other drugs a patient is taking.

Before leaving your doctor's office, make sure that you understand…

- **Why the drug is being prescribed.**
- **The generic and brand names.**

*Consult the Physicians' Desk Reference Web site at *www.pdrhealth.com*.

- **How and when to take it.**
- **How long to take it.**
- **Whether it's likely to cause side effects or interact with other drugs.**

Don't settle for any less from your doctor!

No More Side Effects

To help guard against potentially dangerous side effects, follow these steps when your doctor prescribes medication...

• **Review the dosage.** Medication dosages are usually determined by studies based on young, healthy volunteers or patients with uncomplicated diseases. People who have less body mass (under 120 pounds) don't need the same dose as someone who tops 200 pounds.

• **Mention your age.** As we age, our kidneys and liver are less efficient at metabolizing drugs.

What to do: Ask your doctor whether he/she is prescribing the lowest possible dose for a person of your age and weight.

Jack E. Fincham, PhD, RPh, A.W. Jowdy professor of pharmacy care, department of clinical and administrative pharmacy at the College of Pharmacy and adjunct professor of public health, Institute of Gerontology, both at the University of Georgia, Athens, GA. He is also editor of the *Journal of Public Health Pharmacy* and associate editor of *The American Journal of Pharmaceutical Education*.

Spice Eases Nausea

In a review of studies involving a total of 363 people, those who were given at least 1 g of powdered gingerroot capsules one hour prior to surgery were one-third less likely to suffer nausea and vomiting during the first 24 hours after the operation than those who got a placebo capsule.

Theory: Ginger might suppress the neurotransmitter serotonin, which plays a role in triggering nausea and vomiting.

Nathorn Chaiyakunapruk, PhD, assistant professor in the department of pharmacy practice, Naresuan University, Phitsanulok, Thailand.

How to Avoid Dangerous Herb–Drug Interactions

Catherine Ulbricht, PharmD, a senior attending pharmacist at Massachusetts General Hospital in Boston. She is editor in chief of the *Journal of Herbal Pharmacotherapy* and cofounder of Natural Standard (*www.naturalstandard.com*), a Web site dedicated to the scientific study of integrated medicine. She is coeditor of *Natural Standard Herb & Supplement Handbook: The Clinical Bottom Line* (C.V. Mosby).

An increasing number of American adults now take herbs and/or nutritional supplements for a wide range of ailments, including arthritis, depression and nausea.

Problem: Unlike prescription drugs, herbal supplements are not regulated by the FDA, so there are no labeling requirements regarding the potential interactions with prescription or over-the-counter (OTC) drugs.

Whether they are used in capsules, extracts, liquid, cream or tea, many herbal products can be harmful when combined with prescription or OTC medication.

What happens: Various herbs will interact with medications by affecting their absorption, metabolism or by other mechanisms. As a result, drug levels may become too high or too low.

Below, Catherine Ulbricht, PharmD, one of the country's leading authorities on herb–drug interactions, gives her advice on commonly used herbs...*

CAYENNE

Cayenne is also known as chili or red pepper. Cayenne's active component, *capsaicin*, which is used as a spice in food, is commonly used as a pain reliever in prescription medicine, often for osteoarthritis, rheumatoid arthritis and diabetic neuropathy (nerve pain resulting from diabetes).

Possible interactions: When combined with aspirin, *ibuprofen* (Advil) or any other nonsteroidal anti-inflammatory drug (NSAID), cayenne may increase these drugs' side effects, especially gastrointestinal (GI) upset. In some people, cayenne also may enhance the pain-relieving action of NSAIDs.

*Check with your doctor or pharmacist before taking any herbal product.

Like the NSAIDs, cayenne can have a blood-thinning effect, increasing the risk for bleeding. (When used topically, this risk is lessened because smaller doses of cayenne are absorbed.) Do not use cayenne if you take a monoamine oxidase (MAO) inhibitor antidepressant, such as *phenelzine* (Nardil).

Caution: Avoid getting cayenne (in any form) in your eyes, nose, etc., where it can cause burning or stinging.

GINGER

Ginger is a popular antidote for nausea and/or vomiting. Research suggests that ginger also may help prevent blood clotting and decrease blood sugar levels.

Possible interactions: If you take an NSAID or antiplatelet drug, such as *clopidogrel* (Plavix), ginger may further increase bleeding risk.

Caution: Although there is strong evidence that it is particularly effective for nausea and/or vomiting in pregnant women, high-dose supplemental ginger (more than 1 g daily) is not recommended during pregnancy because of possible fetal damage and/or increased bleeding risk. Because of the lack of long-term studies on ginger, consult your doctor before taking it for an extended period of time.

GREEN TEA

As more scientific evidence has revealed the disease-fighting power of antioxidant-rich green tea, increasing numbers of Americans have begun drinking it—or in some instances, taking it in capsules or extracts. Though some studies do question the health benefits of green tea, other studies have found that it may help to prevent cancer, especially malignancies of the GI tract, breast and lung. More investigation is needed to confirm these findings. To read more about trials on green tea, go to the National Institutes of Health's Web site, *www.clinicaltrials.gov*.

Possible interactions: Most forms of green tea contain caffeine, which may intensify the effect of any medication that increases blood pressure and/or heart rate, such as the decongestant *pseudoephedrine* (Sudafed). Decaffeinated green tea is available, but this form still contains some caffeine and may not have the same health benefits.

Caution: People with arrhythmia (abnormal heart rhythm) should consume no more than moderate amounts of green tea, determined by their personal sensitivity to caffeine.

LICORICE

Licorice contains a compound known as *glycyrrhizin*, which has antiviral properties. For this reason, licorice is often used to treat the common cold and herpes infections (including cold sores). However, some studies have shown that topical licorice cream does not help genital herpes.

Possible interactions: Licorice can interact with diuretics, such as *chlorothiazide* (Diuril) and *furosemide* (Lasix), and any medication that affects hormone levels, such as birth control pills.

Caution: It also may increase blood pressure and bleeding risk.

MILK THISTLE

This popular herb is used for liver problems, including cirrhosis and hepatitis. These benefits are well documented by research.

Possible interactions: Milk thistle may interfere with how the liver breaks down certain drugs, such as antibiotics and antifungals. Milk thistle also may interact with the anticonvulsant *phenytoin* (Dilantin). The herb may lower blood sugar and cause heartburn, nausea and vomiting or other GI upset.

Caution: If you take diabetes medication, do not use milk thistle unless you are supervised by a health-care professional.

ST. JOHN'S WORT

St. John's wort is commonly used for depression. Several studies show that it may work as well as a prescription antidepressant, like *paroxetine* (Paxil), for mild to moderate depressive disorders. More research is needed before it can be recommended for severe depression.

Possible interactions: St. John's wort may interact with drugs that are broken down by the liver, including birth control pills, the blood thinner *warfarin* (Coumadin) and the migraine medications. People who take St. John's wort may experience stomach upset, fatigue, sexual dysfunction, dizziness or headaches.

Caution: St. John's wort should not be taken with prescription antidepressant medication.

Popular Drugs That Steal Nutrients

Frederic Vagnini, MD, medical director for the Heart, Diabetes and Weight-Loss Centers of New York and an assistant clinical professor of surgery at Weill Cornell Medical College, both in New York City. Dr. Vagnini is coauthor of *The Side Effects Bible: The Dietary Solution to Unwanted Side Effects of Common Medications* (Broadway).

Depletion of nutrients is among the most common—and most overlooked—side effect of both over-the-counter (OTC) and prescription drugs.

Here's what happens: The medications can cause improper absorption of vitamins and minerals—or they can accelerate the elimination of nutrients from the body. The consequences may range from bothersome symptoms, such as fatigue or stomach upset, to serious heart, muscle or nerve damage.

Most physicians are aware of some minerals that are depleted through the use of diuretics (water-excreting drugs). However, few doctors are aware of the dangers of nutrient depletion caused by many other types of medication, because the problem is not widely reported.

Popular drugs that deplete nutrients…

ANTIBIOTICS

The most commonly prescribed antibiotics include *azithromycin* (Zithromax), *amoxicillin* (Amoxil), *ampicillin* (Omnipen), *ciprofloxacin* (Cipro), *ofloxacin* (Floxin) as well as *erythromycin* (Eryc).

Nutrients depleted…

• **B vitamins.** The B vitamins are essential for normal metabolism as well as immune and nervous system functioning.

• **Vitamin K.** This vitamin is critical for blood clotting and bone strength.

• **The "friendly" intestinal bacteria** known as *Bifidobacterium bifidum* and *Lactobacillus acidophilus*. Antibiotics kill not only dangerous bacteria but also "good" bacteria that promote gastrointestinal health and help to balance immune response.

If you are prescribed an antibiotic: Ask your doctor about also taking a B-complex vitamin—50 milligrams (mg)…vitamin K supplement—60 micrograms (mcg) to 80 mcg…and

probiotic supplements providing 15 billion live B. bifidum and 15 billion live L. acidophilus organisms daily.*

In addition, eat more vitamin B–rich foods, such as beef liver, chicken, pork, fortified breads and cereals, whole-grain pastas, legumes, nuts and dark, leafy greens.

To increase your intake of vitamin K, eat kale …collard, turnip or mustard greens…spinach… broccoli…and Swiss chard.

Caution: Do not take vitamin K supplements or eat excessive amounts of vitamin K–rich foods if you take *warfarin* (Coumadin) or another type of blood-thinning drug.

For additional B. bifidum, eat more asparagus, garlic and/or onions, which stimulate growth of this friendly bacteria. For L. acidophilus, yogurt containing live cultures is your best food source.

HIGH-CHOLESTEROL DRUGS

The most widely prescribed cholesterol-lowering "statins" include *atorvastatin* (Lipitor), *simvastatin* (Zocor), *fluvastatin* (Lescol), *lovastatin* (Mevacor) and *pravastatin* (Pravachol).

Nutrient depleted…

• **Coenzyme Q10 (CoQ10).** All cells require CoQ10 for the proper function of mitochondria (small energy-producing structures within the cells). The more energy a cell must produce, the more it depends on CoQ10. That's why cells of the heart, in particular—because it is constantly beating—require an abundance of CoQ10.

Unfortunately, statin drugs, which effectively prevent the production of harmful cholesterol, also prevent CoQ10 production.

Some doctors worry that long-term use of statins may worsen heart failure. Studies have found that patients with chronic heart failure have lower CoQ10 levels, and that CoQ10 supplements may improve their heart condition. Signs of CoQ10 deficiency include fatigue and muscle weakness.

If you are prescribed a statin: Ask your doctor about taking 30 mg to 100 mg of a CoQ10 supplement daily. This nutrient also is available in some foods, including beef, chicken, salmon, oranges and broccoli.

*If you're taking any medications, consult your doctor before changing your diet or beginning a supplement. In rare cases, increasing a nutrient may interfere with a drug's potency or worsen your condition.

PAINKILLERS

Millions of Americans take nonsteroidal anti-inflammatory drugs (NSAIDs), such as *ibuprofen* (Motrin or Advil), *naproxen* (Aleve), *celecoxib* (Celebrex) and *nabumetone* (Relafen), to help relieve arthritis and other inflammatory pain.

Nutrient depleted…

• **Folic acid.** Your body needs this water-soluble B vitamin to produce new cells and DNA and to synthesize and utilize proteins.

Several large epidemiological studies associate lower folic acid levels to increased risk for colon, breast and pancreatic cancers.

Heart health is also affected by folic acid. As folic acid levels decline, levels of the amino acid homocysteine rise. Studies suggest that elevated homocysteine can raise the risks for blood clots, heart attack and stroke.

Low folic acid levels may cause loss of appetite, irritability, weakness, shortness of breath, diarrhea, anemia, headaches, heart palpitations and a sore tongue.

If you take an NSAID regularly (daily for at least one to two weeks): Talk to your physician about also taking 400 mcg to 800 mcg of folic acid daily.

You also can get more folic acid by consuming fortified breakfast cereals, orange juice, spinach and other leafy greens, peas and beans.

BETA-BLOCKERS

Beta-blockers, such as *propranolol* (Inderal), *atenolol* (Tenormin), *betaxolol* (Betoptic S), *carteolol* (Cartrol) and *labetalol* (Normodyne), are commonly prescribed for high blood pressure or glaucoma.

Nutrients depleted…

• **CoQ10.** Not only does CoQ10 appear to improve cardiac function in patients with chronic heart failure, studies suggest that it also may prevent second heart attacks and possibly protect against Parkinson's disease.

• **Melatonin.** The hormone melatonin is essential for healthy sleep-wake cycles, and there's some early evidence that it may slow aging.

If you take a beta-blocker: Ask your physician about taking 30 mg to 100 mg of CoQ10 daily…and 1 mg to 3 mg of melatonin nightly, just before bed, if you have trouble sleeping.

DIABETES DRUGS

Patients with type 2 diabetes are often prescribed *tolazamide* (Tolinase), *acetohexamide* (Dymelor), *glimepiride* (Amaryl) or *glipizide* (Glucotrol)—all sulfonylurea drugs. These medications stimulate the pancreas to produce more insulin, which lowers blood sugar.

Nutrient depleted…

• **CoQ10.** Diabetes more than doubles your chances of dying from heart disease or stroke—and low CoQ10 levels exacerbate those risks.

If you're taking a sulfonylurea drug: Ask your doctor about supplementing with 30 mg to 100 mg of CoQ10 daily.

REFLUX DRUGS

Proton pump inhibitors, such as *esomeprazole* (Nexium), *lansoprazole* (Prevacid), *omeprazole* (Prilosec) and *rabeprazole* (AcipHex), are prescribed for chronic heartburn—also known as gastroesophageal reflux disease (or GERD)—as well as for ulcers.

Nutrients depleted…

• **Vitamin B-12.** Vitamin B-12 is essential for producing red blood cells and for maintaining a healthy nervous system. Deficiency may trigger fatigue, dizziness, shortness of breath, diarrhea, tingling in the hands or feet, unsteady gait, nervousness, cognitive changes and even dementia.

Vitamin B-12 is found in red meat, fish, eggs and dairy foods, but our bodies require stomach acid to release the vitamin from these foods. Proton pump inhibitors reduce the production of stomach acid, inhibiting the release and absorption of vitamin B-12.

• **Iron.** Low iron reduces the amount of oxygen your red blood cells can transport to body tissues, leaving you feeling weak and fatigued. A serious iron deficiency results in anemia.

If you take a proton pump inhibitor: Ask your doctor about taking 500 mcg to 1,000 mcg of vitamin B-12 daily and for advice on the best way to increase your iron intake.

Caution: Never take a supplement for iron without consulting your physician—excess iron can accumulate in your major organs and cause severe damage. Most individuals, however, can safely eat more iron-rich foods, including liver, beef, dark-meat chicken or turkey, legumes and fortified cereals.

Counterfeit Drug Watch

Katherine Eban, investigative journalist who has documented counterfeit drugs in her book *Dangerous Doses* (Harcourt).

Most people know that there is a risk of purchasing counterfeit drugs over the Internet.

Problem: Even drugs that are purchased from US pharmacies might be fake.

According to an FDA estimate, about 1% of the nation's drug supply—about 35 million prescriptions annually—is believed to be counterfeit.

What happens: Drugs are typically sold by manufacturers to wholesalers, who then sell them to pharmacies. However, some dishonest wholesalers tamper with drugs before selling them. Often, they buy cut-rate—sometimes phony—drugs from unlicensed or suspicious sources.

The drugs most vulnerable to counterfeiting are commonly used and/or expensive.

Examples: The cholesterol-lowering drug *atorvastatin* (Lipitor) and the anemia drug *epoetin* (Procrit). Even some antibiotics have been faked.

How to protect yourself…

• **Sign up for free e-mail alerts on bogus drugs at *www.safemedicines.org,*** the site of the nonprofit Partnership for Safe Medicines.

• **Become familiar with the shape, color and, if applicable, taste of the drugs that you take.** Some counterfeits will appear and/or taste slightly different from the real drug.

• **Note if your medicine appears to stop working or causes new side effects.**

If you suspect that a drug may be a counterfeit, tell your pharmacist and physician immediately—and report it on the FDA Web site (*www.fda.gov/medwatch/how.htm*).

What Nurses Know About Medications That Doctors Don't Tell You

Patricia Carroll, RN, quality-management coordinator, Franciscan Home Care and Hospice Care in Meriden, CT. She also is the author of *What Nurses Know and Doctors Don't Have Time to Tell You: Practical Wisdom for Everyday Home Health Care* (Perigee) and *The Surgical Nurse's Managed Care Manual* (Total Learning Concepts).

Medical doctors are trained to treat most illness, injury and disease with a medication, surgery and/or hospitalization—but they seldom have the time to give detailed self-care advice.

Nurses are generally the best people to provide this type of advice and help patients avoid dangerous medical mistakes.

Common mistakes…

• **Using silverware to measure liquid medicines.** Daily doses of certain medications—for example, the heart drug *digoxin* (Lanoxin) and anticonvulsant drugs, such as *phenytoin* (Dilantin)—must be measured precisely because there is a narrow range between optimal and toxic doses. Liquid drug doses are prescribed in milliliters (ml) but often are translated into teaspoons and tablespoons for convenience. However, the sizing of silverware teaspoons and tablespoons varies widely.

Ask that your health-care provider skip this translation. Measure out your prescribed dose in ml in a needleless syringe or a dosing spoon (a plastic device with a spoon on one end and measurements along the handle).

Check with your health-care provider to get a needleless syringe. Or buy a dosing spoon, available at a drugstore for about $2.* If you're not sure how to use these devices, ask a pharmacist or nurse for a demonstration.

• **Storing medicine in the bathroom medicine cabinet.** The humidity that commonly develops in a bathroom with a shower or bathtub increases the chances that your prescription or over-the-counter (OTC) drugs will break down quickly, losing efficacy and possibly triggering

*Price subject to change.

unwanted side effects, such as stomach upset or skin rash.

A box, placed in a linen closet near the bathroom, is the best place for your drugs because it keeps the medication cool and dry. (If you have children in your home, place the box on the top shelf, where it is out of reach.)

•**Taking pain relievers that contain caffeine instead of getting it from coffee.** The OTC pain reliever Excedrin contains *acetaminophen*, aspirin and caffeine. Anacin, another OTC pain reliever, contains buffered aspirin and caffeine. These drugs cost up to three times more than plain aspirin or acetaminophen.

Caffeine is added because aspirin and acetaminophen are absorbed up to 40% faster when taken with caffeine. However, a cup of caffeinated coffee contains about 135 milligrams (mg) of caffeine—compared with 64 mg to 130 mg per dose of pain reliever—and works just as well. Black tea, which contains 40 mg to 70 mg of caffeine per cup, also can be used.

If you use aspirin or acetaminophen, take it with a cup of coffee or tea in the morning to boost the drug's absorption. To avoid unwanted side effects, such as restlessness, do *not* drink coffee or tea at night.

Many people with arthritis suffer the most severe pain when they wake in the morning. Taking a pain reliever without caffeine allows you to take it at bedtime so it lasts until morning, without keeping you up at night.

Can Pills Be Crushed To Make Them Easier To Swallow?

Crushing a pill makes it easier to swallow when mixed with food or liquid but may reduce its effectiveness. A crushed pill releases its active ingredients immediately, which may not be appropriate for some extended-release drugs. Also, some tablets contain a coating for easier swallowing and to help mask the taste. If the pill is crushed, it may be more difficult to swallow due to the bitter taste.

If your pill has a small line called a score etched in it, this indicates that you can split the tablet, and it is probably safe to crush. Ask your pharmacist first to be sure.

Susan C. Winckler, RPh, vice president of policy and communications and staff counsel, American Pharmacists Association, Washington, DC.

Medical Emergency? Why Calling 911 May Not Be Wise

Charles B. Inlander, a Fogelsville, PA–based consumer advocate and health-care consultant. He was the founding president of the nonprofit People's Medical Society, a consumer advocacy organization credited with key improvements in the quality of US health care in the 1980s and 1990s, and is the author of 20 books, including Take This Book to the Hospital with You: A Consumer Guide to Surviving Your Hospital Stay (St. Martin's).

When faced with a medical emergency, our initial instinct is to dial 911. But calling 911 may not be your only—or even your best—choice. The 911 emergency response program began in the US about 35 years ago. Most people assume that if they call 911 in response to a medical emergency, an ambulance and medical personnel will arrive in a matter of minutes. That's not necessarily true.

Operators at 911 call centers are trained to assess the situation by asking the caller about the person in need, his/her symptoms, whether he is conscious, the nature of the injury and any other pertinent information that is necessary to provide the appropriate response. In some cases, such as a severe sprain or a nonlife-threatening broken bone, the 911 operator may suggest that the caller take the person to a hospital emergency room. In other instances, such as a possible heart attack, a stroke, a severe injury from a fall or a sudden severe fever in a child (above 104°F), the operator will almost always dispatch an ambulance.

Most emergency medical services units consist of an ambulance with two or more emergency medical technicians (EMTs) and, in some cases, a paramedic. EMTs receive 110 to 400 hours of training from programs typically conducted at community colleges. A paramedic receives 1,000 to 1,300 hours of training, typically culminating in a two-year college degree. Paramedics are allowed to start intravenous lines, give shots and insert airway devices to assist breathing. EMTs are usually restricted to using oxygen masks and performing other noninvasive procedures, such as applying bandages or compresses.

As you can see, it's preferable to have a paramedic on the team, so check with local emergency medical services to see if the emergency response units in your area are staffed by both EMTs and paramedics. The emergency response units are required to take their patients to the nearest or most appropriate emergency facility. The patient and family have no say in this. Each unit is in constant contact with the local hospital emergency room, notifying the nurses and physicians of the patient's status.

In some cases, medical care might start sooner if you take the patient to an emergency room on your own, particularly if the patient is able to move and/or you live more than 30 minutes from an ambulance service.

Important: Arriving at a hospital in an ambulance does not *necessarily* mean that you will get quicker care. Most emergency rooms make an immediate assessment of each patient and quickly move the most severe into care units, no matter how they arrived.

In many areas of the country, "urgicare" and "emergicare" centers—freestanding facilities that usually are not affiliated with any hospital—are available for minor medical emergencies, such as ankle sprains, minor rashes and sore throats. These facilities, which are typically staffed with doctors and nurse practitioners, are usually less crowded than hospital emergency rooms. The centers accept most types of insurance and are usually open 12 to 24 hours a day.

Danger of TV Sports

Up to 50% of men will not seek out emergency treatment until a televised sporting event is completed.

Best: Go to the emergency room immediately if you think you need medical attention. Waiting

even a few minutes greatly increases your risk of complications.

David Jerrard, MD, director of emergency department, Baltimore VA Medical Center, and the leader of a study of emergency department records following nearly 800 sporting events, presented at a recent meeting of the American College of Emergency Physicians.

How to Survive A Trip to the ER

Joel Cohen, MD, medical director, MD Room-Service/DoctorCare, a house call practice in Scottsdale, AZ, *www.mdroomservice.com* He has practiced emergency care, urgent care and internal medicine for 15 years and is also author of *ER: Enter at Your Own Risk—How to Avoid Dangers Inside Emergency Rooms* (New Horizon).

To experience some real chaos, just visit an emergency room. Through those metal doors is a busy, often disorganized place that can be hazardous to your health.

ERs are overcrowded and understaffed. You may be treated by an overworked medical student, an exhausted intern or a doctor trained in a field unrelated to your problem.

Obtaining high-quality emergency care quickly can be vital after an accident or when a chronic illness, such as heart disease or asthma, suddenly becomes life threatening. But in a surprising number of situations, you'll have enough leeway to *choose* your ER.

Key: Know how to go to the right place at the right time for the right reasons—and be treated by the right caregiver. *Here's how...*

PREPARATION IS IMPORTANT

Get ready for the ER visit that you hope you'll never need. *Do your homework...*

• **Visit all ERs within 30 minutes of your home.** If your condition demands exceptional treatment, arriving in a half hour may be better than being transferred from another hospital later.

Look around. Would you feel well cared for?

Snowbird alert: If you have multiple homes or travel to the same places frequently, also do this exercise in these locations.

• **Identify facilities geared to your health problems.**

Example: If you have a heart condition, locate the ER with the best cardiac service. Your ultimate plan will be to ask an ambulance driver to take you there if your condition, such as symptoms of a mild heart attack, permits.

It surprises many people to learn that you often can get an ambulance crew to take you to the hospital of your choosing. If the ambulance must go elsewhere or your condition demands faster treatment, the paramedic will say so.

Find the best ERs: Ask your primary care doctor, pulmonologist, cardiologist or other specialist where to find local high-level trauma or teaching hospitals. Ask the public relations departments at nearby hospitals for brochures promoting the hospitals' areas of expertise. Check hospital Internet sites. Consult Castle Connolly Medical Ltd., a guide to top doctors and hospitals (212-367-8400, ext. 16, *www.castleconnolly. com*).

Cost: $24.95 for a one-year membership.*

• **Wear a tag, necklace or bracelet identifying your medical status.**

Examples: Diabetes, medication allergies, need for dialysis. Wearing this information on a medical alert tag will help ensure that you receive appropriate care. Also, medical personnel will be able to retrieve your health information by calling the tag sponsor.

Information: MedicAlert (888-633-4298, *www. medicalert.org*)...Bodyguard Medical I.D. Tags (800-383-7790, *www.medicalidtags.com*).

• **Research your health insurance plan's emergency coverage.** Must you report an ER visit within 24 hours? What if you're out of town or taken to an out-of-plan hospital? Having this information handy will save precious time when admitted to an ER.

• **Maintain a relationship with a trusted physician.** In an emergency, your doctor may help you decide whether an ER visit is warranted...meet you there or consult by phone...recommend a specialist if you need one...find you a local doctor if you're out of town.

*Price and offer subject to change.

KNOW WHEN TO GO

For flu, a twisted ankle, longtime bad back or repeat kidney stone pain, phone your doctor for an appointment. Consider going to a good walk-in urgent-care center (their quality varies tremendously) if your doctor isn't available and your insurance covers it. If you can, avoid ERs on Mondays and on Friday and Saturday nights, the busiest times.

Do head for the ER if you are experiencing unbearable or worst-ever pain...profuse bleeding...unfamiliar or severe chest pain, shortness of breath or abdominal pain...sudden arm or leg numbness or weakness...any other signs of a stroke or heart attack (see below).

STEALTH SYMPTOMS

If you are having a stroke or heart attack, the sooner you reach an ER that has the appropriate technology and expertise, the better. When given within about three hours for stroke, six hours for a heart attack, clot-busting drugs may save your life or decrease disability. Optimal stroke treatment can make the difference between paralysis and a little weakness.

Little-known symptom: In an older woman, shortness of breath is a more common primary heart attack symptom than chest pain.

Other subtle heart symptoms: Weakness... fatigue...unfamiliar indigestion...jaw or upper back pain.

Information: American Heart Association (800-242-8721 or *www.americanheart.org*)...National Heart, Lung, and Blood Institute (301-592-8573 or *www.nhlbi.nih.gov/actintime*).

Subtle stroke symptoms: Severe headache... facial tingling...drooping mouth...unexplained dizziness.

Information: American Stroke Association (888-478-7653 or *www.strokeassociation.org*).

THE BEST CARE ONCE THERE

At the ER, contribute to the quality of your care. *Be sure to...*

• **Enter riding.** In my experience, patients arriving by ambulance get much faster attention than walk-ins. Don't let a friend drive you unless waiting for an ambulance would take too long.

- **Focus on one or two chief complaints.** The more vague you are, the less seriously your problem will be taken.

Example: Mention the new sharp pain in your side, not your arthritic hip.

- **Help the staff to help you.** Don't accept every test or treatment suggested without a discussion. Ask the doctor treating you in the ER to help you decide whether the potential gains of any proposed intervention justify possible risks.

- **Identify yourself and your circumstances often.** Ask what you're being given and why. To a nurse adding medication to your IV line, say, "Do you know about my drug allergies?" Don't assume that everyone has read your chart.

- **Be wary.** Reject medications and prescriptions proposed without logical, compelling reasons. Refuse any risky or unnecessary test or treatment.

Reasons: Older people are particularly vulnerable to complications from invasive procedures...standard adult drug dosages can be too strong for older people.

If you are sensitive to drugs or you have kidney or liver problems, tell every ER staff member who treats you.

- **Don't leave too soon.** An ER staff eager to "clear the board" may want to send you home although you feel the same as or worse than when you arrived. Explain that you still feel bad. Ask the person discharging you, "Are you an attending physician here? Will you discuss my case with my family doctor?" You can also ask to speak to the attending physician yourself, but he/she may not be available.

TAKE AN ADVOCATE

It's hard to advocate for yourself in the middle of a health emergency. A relative, friend or neighbor can make sure your needs are met... scrutinize your care...discuss alternatives...make phone calls...take detailed notes. Staff are more vigilant when someone is watching.

Your advocate can request the business card of every doctor who sees you...the name of every nurse who treats you...the name of every test that you're given. You may need these details later in the day or for your records.

Self-defense: With an "ER buddy," visit ERs together and compare notes. Show each other

where your relevant medical papers are kept, such as health-care proxies naming the person who can make health decisions for you. Agree to accompany each other to the ER if needed.

More from Dr. Joel Cohen...

Keep These ER Aids In Your Wallet

Regularly update information that could be lifesaving in the ER. *Don't leave home without a...*

- **List of your drug allergies (or the statement "no known drug allergies").**

- **List of all current medications,** prescription and nonprescription (herbs, vitamins, antacids), including dose and reason.

- **Health insurance and/or Medicare card.**

- **Miniature copy of your baseline electrocardiogram (ECG),** laminated. Take your ECG readout to a copy place, reduce it to wallet size and cover it with self-stick clear plastic sheets, sold at stationery and office supply stores.

Why: Comparing a new ECG with an older one can increase accuracy in diagnosing heart problems.

Deadly Errors in the Hospital Can Be Avoided

Michael F. Roizen, MD, chair of the division of anesthesiology, critical care management and comprehensive pain management at the Cleveland Clinic, OH. He is the author of *RealAge* (Collins) and coauthor, with Mehmet C. Oz, MD, of *You: The Smart Patient* (Free Press).

The hospital is one of the most dangerous places you'll ever go. Patients are exposed to bacteria and viruses...subjected to tests and procedures that have high risks...and given medications that need to be closely monitored—but sometimes aren't.

Between 44,000 and 98,000 Americans die annually from hospital errors. Although patients can't control everything that happens in the hospital, they can lower their risks more than they realize.

Example: Use only a hospital that's accredited by the Joint Commission on Accreditation of Healthcare Organizations. Accreditation means that a hospital is evaluated every three years to ensure that it meets the best standards in cleanliness, infection control, drug administration guidelines, etc. Nearly 15,000 health-care facilities are accredited—but many are not. To check, go to *www.qualitycheck.org*, or call 630-792-5800. *Other ways to stay safe...*

PICK THE BEST HOSPITAL

Teaching hospitals affiliated with major medical universities tend to have the latest technology and best-trained staff. If you require major surgery (such as a transplant operation) or have a life-threatening condition (such as an aortic aneurysm or pancreatic cancer), a teaching hospital is your best option. Smaller hospitals are fine for patients with "routine" health problems, such as pneumonia or a broken leg.

Warning: In the summer months, teaching hospitals are largely staffed with new residents and interns. Their dearth of experience can adversely affect care of patients. If you can, avoid teaching hospitals during the first two weeks of July, when the new school year begins. *Other points to consider...*

• **Is it a "magnet" hospital?** Medical centers with outstanding nursing programs receive this designation from the American Nurses Credentialing Center (800-284-2378, *www.nursecredentialing.org*). Patients in these hospitals benefit from improved care...less staff turnover...and high-quality physicians, who are more likely to work at a hospital with magnet status.

• **Are there full-time intensivists and hospitalists?** Intensivists are doctors who specialize in treating critically ill patients. Hospitalists are doctors who advise only hospital patients. Both types of specialists provide superior hospital care and don't maintain private practices "on the side."

• **How often does the hospital perform the procedure you're undergoing?** The best outcomes usually occur at the hospitals where a given procedure is performed most often, on average.

Examples: A top-flight hospital will perform at least 500 open-heart procedures annually ...100 carotid-artery grafts or surgeries...and 25 mastectomies.

CHOOSE THE BEST SURGEON

Only use a surgeon who is board certified in the specialty related to your operation—neurosurgery, cardiac surgery, etc. Look for the letters "FACS" (Fellow, American College of Surgeons) after his/her name. This means that the surgeon has been evaluated for competence and ethical standards.

Helpful: Call the hospital anesthesiology department, and ask one of the anesthesiologists which surgeon he would pick. (Anesthesiologists often are free between 3 pm and 5 pm.) They know all the surgeons and have no reason not to give a straight answer.

Once you compile some recommendations, choose a surgeon who does only a few types of procedures. Research has shown that surgeons who specialize—in nerve-sparing prostate surgery, for example—have better results and fewer complications than the national average.

Caution: Don't shave your surgical site before surgery. You'll wind up with thousands of invisible nicks that increase the risk for infection. Let the operating room staff do it. They use special creams that prevent nicks.

Important: Ask the anesthesiologist to provide a blanket (if it will not get in the way) to keep you warm during surgery. Patients who maintain *normothermia* (normal body temperature) have a lower risk for infection and other complications.

PREVENT HOSPITAL INFECTIONS

Each year, an estimated 2 million hospital patients develop an infection. With the emergence of antibiotic-resistant bacteria, even a minor initial infection can be fatal.

We all know the importance of hand washing, so insist that all visitors (including nurses and doctors) wash their hands before touching you. A quick rinse doesn't help. Studies show that you must wash vigorously with soap and warm water for at least 15 seconds to remove all bacteria.

As an alternative, hand-sanitizing gel, which is now provided outside many hospital rooms, may be used by visitors.

Other self-defense strategies…

● **Keep a bottle of hand-sanitizing gel at your bedside.** Use this hand cleanser yourself before eating.

● **Beware of the TV remote control.** One study found that remote controls in hospitals have three times more bacteria than doorknobs or nurse call buttons. To protect yourself, cover the TV remote with a new hospital glove. You'll still be able to change the channels.

● **Ask about the stethoscope.** Doctors and nurses are supposed to clean their stethoscopes with alcohol between patients, but some get too busy and simply forget. Uncleaned stethoscopes have been linked to hospital infections.

DRUG PROTECTION

Drug mistakes—giving the wrong drug, a dangerous drug combination or the wrong dose—often occur in hospitals. Ask your primary care doctor to supervise *all* of your health care, including drug prescriptions. If that isn't possible, ask one of the hospitalists to do it. Patients with one supervising doctor face fewer risks.

To ensure that you're getting the right drug (medical test or procedure), ask your nurse to check your ID wrist bracelet every time.

Also, ask the nurse to tell you what each drug is and why you're taking it. Don't take a drug unless you're sure it's the one that you're supposed to be taking. If you're receiving a medical test or procedure, confirm that it's the correct one.

Finally, ask a family member or friend to help monitor your daily care. This is especially important when the patient is not able to do so for himself/herself.

More from Dr. Michael Roizen…

Don't Wait for the Doctor to Call You with Test Results

When tests are performed, ask the nurse when the results will be in. Call the office that day to get them—and if they are not yet available, call again every day until they are. Taking active control of your health is better than waiting at home for a call that office personnel may forget to make.

Little-Known Hospital Risk

Patients who have had a heart attack or stroke and who have even slightly elevated blood sugar—as little as one point beyond the normal range—are more likely to die in intensive care.

Self-defense: Make sure doctors monitor a loved one's blood glucose level before and after surgery. And, get diabetes under control before any surgery.

Mercedes Falciglia, MD, assistant professor of medicine, University of Cincinnati College of Medicine, and lead author of a study of 216,000 patients, presented at a recent meeting of the American Diabetes Association.

Best Time for Surgery

Patients who have early surgery are less likely to develop complications of anesthesia than those who have surgery at 4 pm or later.

Possible reasons: Fatigue of doctors and other health-care workers by late afternoon…shift changes…less staff available later in the day.

Good news: Even when postsurgical problems do develop, they are usually minor ones involving nausea or pain management.

Melanie C. Wright, PhD, assistant professor of anesthesiology, Duke University Medical Center, Durham, NC.

Portable Pain Pumps

Portable pain pumps help a surgical patient recover at home. These systems, commonly used after orthopedic surgery, provide a preset amount of painkiller to the treatment area.

Advantage: Patients can avoid the dizziness, lethargy, nausea and other side effects of oral pain medications.

Frank C. Detterbeck, MD, professor and chief of thoracic surgery, Yale University School of Medicine, New Haven, CT.

3

Common Health Problems

Foods Fight Headaches: What's Good to Eat And What's Bad

More than 45 million individuals in the US annually seek medical treatment for either frequent or severe headaches. Doctors have identified dozens of headache triggers, including stress, air pollution and weather changes, but one of the primary triggers—especially for migraines—is diet.

At least 30% of migraine patients have one or more food triggers. In some cases, a single food may be responsible. Most patients have combination triggers—for example, red wine plus a high level of stress plus an extra cup of coffee in the morning.

Everyone who experiences migraines and/or other types of headaches should keep a food and lifestyle diary. Write down all the foods and beverages you consume. Also note patterns that precede headaches—exercise activities, changes in sleep, stress level, menstrual cycle, etc. After a few weeks, review your diary and identify likely connections.

WHAT TO AVOID

• **Caffeine** is one of the main headache triggers. Some patients get headaches when they consume any caffeine. And others get headaches when they consume less than they usually do and then need caffeine to relieve the headache.

If you drink coffee or other caffeinated beverages regularly, blood vessels in the brain become sensitized to the caffeine's effects. Eliminating or cutting back on caffeine causes rebound headaches in about half of patients.

People who have chronic headaches often are advised to eliminate caffeine completely. Instead of quitting abruptly, gradually taper off. If you're used to drinking three cups of coffee a day, drink only two cups daily for a week. For

Elaine Magee, MPH, RD, registered dietitian, Pleasant Hill, CA, and author of 25 books on nutrition, including *Tell Me What to Eat If I Have Headaches and Migraines* (New Page).

49

several days after that, substitute decaf for one of your daily servings. Then dilute your regular coffee with decaf until you quit entirely.

●**High-fat foods.** Significantly reducing dietary fat decreases the frequency and intensity of headaches. Try to limit total fat intake to 20% of total calories. In particular, avoid saturated fats (mainly found in meats, fast food and full-fat dairy products) and trans fats (often called "partially hydrogenated oils" on product labels and found in margarines, snack foods and packaged baked goods).

●**Tyramine** is a natural by-product of the amino acid *tyrosine.* Foods that are aged or fermented tend to be high in tyramine, which can cause vascular spasms that result in migraines.

Main offenders: Red wine, aged cheeses including blue and cheddar, deli meats and over-ripe bananas.

Stick with the fresh meats and cheeses such as cottage cheese, ricotta and fresh mozzarella. White wine and beer have less tyramine than red wine—but any alcohol can trigger headaches.

●**Food additives,** such as *monosodium glutamate* (MSG), nitrates and nitrites, dilate blood vessels and trigger migraines in people who are sensitive to these additives. Nitrates and nitrites are found mainly in processed meats, such as hot dogs, bacon and salami. MSG is added to literally thousands of processed foods. Check food labels, and avoid products that contain any of these additives.

FOODS THAT HELP

●**Omega-3 fatty acids.** The healthful fats in fish, flaxseeds and olive oil can reduce migraines by stimulating the production of body chemicals that inhibit inflammation in blood vessels located in the brain.

Recommended: Two to three fish servings every week. Also, have one tablespoon daily of ground flaxseed (you can add it to your cereal or smoothies or sprinkle on salads or yogurt). Cook with olive oil or canola oil, which contain more omega-3s than other vegetable oils.

●**Magnesium.** There is some evidence that adequate magnesium intake can help women prevent headaches (including migraines) associated with menstruation. The recommended daily intake for most women is 320 milligrams

(mg). Foods high in magnesium include whole grains, nuts, seeds, soy foods, legumes and dark green vegetables.

Examples: Almonds, two tablespoons (86 mg of magnesium)…artichoke, one medium (180 mg)…brown rice, two-thirds cup (57 mg)…peanut butter, two tablespoons (51 mg)…pumpkin seeds, two tablespoons (152 mg)…cooked spinach, one-half cup (78 mg)…tofu, one-half cup (118 mg).

●**Water** helps prevent dehydration—a common cause of headaches. Try to drink eight eight-ounce glasses every day.

Exercise Fights Colds

Researchers studied 160 overweight, sedentary women ages 18 to 85. Half walked for 45 minutes five days a week for 12 to 15 weeks, while the other half remained sedentary.

Result: The walkers who got colds had 40% to 50% fewer days of illness than nonwalkers who got colds.

Theory: Thirty to 60 minutes a day of moderate exercise, such as walking at a 15-minute-per-mile pace, spurs production of germ-killing cells called neutrophils.

Caution: Ninety minutes or more of high-intensity daily exercise, such as long-distance running, has just the opposite effect, increasing stress hormones and immune dysfunction.

David C. Nieman, MD, DrPH, professor of health and exercise science at Appalachian State University, Boone, NC.

 # Wear Your Slippers

Researchers asked 90 participants to place their bare feet in cold (50°F) water for 20 minutes, while 90 others kept their feet in an empty bowl. Thirteen people from the chilled group developed a cold within five days, compared with five people from the other group.

Theory: Chilling the body constricts blood vessels in the nose, reducing the supply of infection-fighting white blood cells to the nasal passages. This sets the stage for cold viruses to multiply and trigger cold symptoms.

Self-defense: Wear waterproof, insulated footwear during the winter to keep your feet warm and dry.

Ronald Eccles, PhD, director, Common Cold Centre and Healthcare Clinical Trials, Cardiff University, Cardiff, Wales.

Natural Cures for Nasal Congestion

Jamison Starbuck, ND, a naturopathic physician in family practice and a lecturer at the University of Montana, both in Missoula. She is past president of the American Association of Naturopathic Physicians and a contributing editor to *The Alternative Advisor: The Complete Guide to Natural Therapies and Alternative Treatments* (Time Life).

When cold weather arrives, decongestants and boxes of tissue are familiar standbys for people with stuffy, runny noses. The common cold is often the culprit. With a cold, the nose can become congested as the body tries to eliminate the virus that is causing the illness. But there are other irritants that also cause nasal congestion. Fortunately, you can get at the root cause of your nasal congestion and avoid taking decongestants, which only temporarily mask symptoms. *Just follow these steps…*

• **Identify the respiratory irritants.** One of my patients recently complained of congestion when she vacuumed her house. Although she has a cat, she claimed to not be allergic since she does not sneeze or get congested when she spends time with her pet. As an experiment, I asked her to visit a friend who doesn't have pets and spend a little time vacuuming. When she did not become congested, my patient agreed that the cat dander released in the air from the vacuum could be the problem.

A simple dust mask worn while vacuuming prevented any other bouts of congestion. Dust masks made from paper (about $1 each*) work

*Prices subject to change.

nicely for relieving sneezing and/or runny noses triggered by dust, pollen, pet dander, smoke, grass, hay or fallen leaves. If potentially harmful vapors, such as fumes from paint, varnish or cleaning compounds, bother your nose, use a carbon-filtration mask, available in paint stores for about $35. They trap vapors, removing them from the air breathed.

• **Test for food allergies.** If you're chronically congested, or regularly get a stuffy nose after eating, ask your doctor for a food allergy blood test to check for IgG mediated—or delayed sensitivity—food allergens. These allergies cause generalized inflammation, leading to congestion.

Most common food allergens: Dairy, wheat, peanuts and soy.

• **Eat the right foods.** To soothe and strengthen the mucous membranes of your nose and upper-respiratory tract, eat lots of proanthocyanidins, a type of plant pigment with anti-inflammatory, antiviral and antiallergenic properties. Blueberries, blackberries, Marion berries or raspberries (fresh or frozen) are great sources of proanthocyanidins. If you suffer from chronic nasal congestion, eat one-half cup daily.

• **Drink hot tea.** For a gentle decongestant, try a tea made from equal parts dried linden, elder and chamomile flowers. Combine all the herbs and use three teaspoons of the mix per 10 ounces of boiling water. Steep, covered, for 10 minutes. Strain and flavor the tea with honey and lemon, if desired. Drink one cup twice daily until congestion is eliminated.

• **Use a neti pot.** In Ayurvedic (Indian) medicine, neti pots, which cost about $20 and resemble small watering cans, are used to pour a saline solution through each nostril, to reduce congestion. You can buy saline solution at drugstores or make your own (follow the instructions that accompany the pot). Use it once or twice daily—upon waking and/or at bedtime, when congested or exposed to allergens.

Congested? Try This…

Relieve a stuffy nose by alternately thrusting your tongue against the roof of your mouth, then pressing a finger between your eyebrows. This will cause the vomer and ethmoid bones to move up and down, which helps loosen congestion. After 20 seconds or so, your sinuses will start to drain.

Lisa DeStefano, DO, assistant professor, college of osteopathic medicine, Michigan State University, East Lansing.

Best Way to Blow Your Nose

When blowing your nose, use a paper facial tissue, not a handkerchief, in which bacteria can grow. Also, use a tissue once, then throw it away. Blow gently—too much pressure could push infectious fluid into ears and sinuses. Press a finger outside one nostril, then blow through the open nostril. Repeat on the other side and wash your hands after blowing. Wait 10 minutes after waking in the morning before blowing your nose—congestion decreases after you get up from a prone position.

Murray Grossan, MD, otolaryngologist, Towers Ear, Nose and Throat Clinic, Cedars-Sinai Medical Center, Los Angeles.

Better Cough Relief

Allergy medications can soothe coughs due to colds better than over-the-counter (OTC) cough remedies, such as *dextromethorphan* and *guaifenesin*. OTC allergy medications, such as those that contain *diphenhydramine, chlorpheniramine* and *brompheniramine*, help to quiet a cough due to the common cold by drying the secretions in the back of the throat.

Downside: These allergy medications may cause drowsiness as well.

Also helpful for a cough: Pain relievers, such as Advil and Aleve—they may lessen the severity and frequency of the cough by inhibiting chemicals that cause inflammation.

Richard Irwin, MD, professor of medicine, University of Massachusetts Medical School in Worcester, and editor in chief of the American College of Chest Physicians guidelines for treatment of cough.

Before You Insist On Antibiotics

In a recent finding, bronchitis sufferers who were otherwise healthy did not get better any faster by taking antibiotics.

Possible reason: Most bronchitis infections are caused by viruses, which antibiotics do not fight off.

Best treatment: Drink lots of fluids, and take pain and fever relievers, such as acetaminophen.

Paul Little, MD, professor of primary care research at the University of Southampton, Highfield, England, and author of a study of 640 bronchitis patients, published in *The Journal of the American Medical Association*.

Sick? How to Know Whether to Stay Home Or Go to Work

Susan Rehm, MD, vice-chair, department of infectious disease, Cleveland Clinic, OH, and medical director, National Foundation for Infectious Diseases, Bethesda, MD, *www.nfid.org*.

A recent national survey found that 35% of US workers feel pressured to go to work when they are sick with the flu. This is usually because they feel guilty and are worried that their work won't get done. Some even fear that they will lose their jobs. However, employees who do go to work sick risk infecting their coworkers.

Although both the common cold and flu can be transmitted in the workplace, the flu is the more serious illness. If you have the common cold, you will probably experience a stuffy and runny nose and a sore throat. The flu is typically accompanied by a sudden high fever, intense headache, muscle and body aches, extreme tiredness and a dry cough. A fever over 100° F is a sign that an illness is significant. If you think you have the flu, see your doctor right away. He/she may prescribe an antiviral medication, such as *oseltamivir* (Tamiflu) or *zanamivir* (Relenza), to help reduce the duration and severity of your illness.

A Quick Flu Diagnosis

A new test diagnoses flu the same day. That is especially important for older individuals and those with compromised immune systems or chronic diseases, and it could help prevent complications.

Cost for the test: About $30.*

Antiviral medicines generally shorten the course of the flu by one day if taken within 48 hours of initial symptoms. The best defense against flu is vaccination.

Katherine A. Poehling, MD, assistant professor of pediatrics at Monroe Carell Jr. Children's Hospital, Vanderbilt University, Nashville, and leader of a study of influenza in more than 4,500 preschoolers, published in *The New England Journal of Medicine.*

*Price subject to change.

An Herbal Defense Against Hay Fever

Ara DerMarderosian, PhD, professor of pharmacognosy (the study of natural products used in medicine) and Roth chair of natural products at the University of the Sciences in Philadelphia.

O ver-the-counter (OTC) and prescription antihistamines and decongestants are heavily advertised and are a mainstay of treatment for most of the 20 million to 40 million Americans who suffer from hay fever. The fact that an herbal therapy also can be effective as a treatment for hay fever is much less well known.

Stinging nettle (*Urtica dioica)* is a flowering plant found in most temperate regions of the world. In a clinical double-blind trial of 69 hay fever sufferers, 58% taking freeze-dried stinging nettle leaf daily for one week experienced a reduction of symptoms, such as sneezing and itchy eyes, compared with 37% of those receiving a placebo. The mechanism for stinging nettles' beneficial effect is unknown.

Typical dose: 450 mg in freeze-dried stinging nettle leaf capsules two to three times daily …or 2 ml to 4 ml of tincture three times daily. Take at the onset of symptoms and continue to take as needed.

Side effects are rare, but some patients taking oral stinging nettle formulations experience mild gastrointestinal upset.

Stinging nettle should be avoided by people taking blood-thinning medication, such as *warfarin* (Coumadin). Stinging nettle has a diuretic (water-excreting) effect, so it should not be used by people with kidney disease.

Because herbs can interact with medication, consult with an allergist or herbalist before trying stinging nettle.

Do You Need a Prescription for Hay Fever Relief?

I n a new finding, ragweed sufferers who took either the over-the-counter (OTC) decongestant *pseudoephedrine* (Sudafed) or the prescription allergy medication *montelukast* (Singulair) for two weeks indicated equal relief of symptoms that included congestion, runny noses and sneezing. Neither of these medicines brought on significant side effects.

Self-defense: Hay fever sufferers can try pseudoephedrine or other OTC decongestants before considering a prescription allergy medication.

Samantha Mucha, MD, resident in otolaryngology, University of Chicago.

Dry-Eye Care

P eople with dry eyes may not need drops, gels or ointments if they use a warm compress.

What to do: Soak a clean washcloth in warm water, then gently press it against the eyelids for five minutes daily. Reheat the washcloth as soon as it starts to cool.

A warm-water compress melts oils from the meibomian gland (an oil-producing gland in the eyelid)…removes blockages…and helps the oil flow more freely.

J. Daniel Nelson, MD, professor of ophthalmology, University of Minnesota, Minneapolis.

Relief for Eczema: Steps to Prevent And Treat Chronic Dry Skin

Marianne N. O'Donoghue, MD, associate professor of dermatology at Rush University Medical Center, Chicago, and dermatologist in private practice for more than 30 years in Oak Brook, IL. She is past president of the Women's Dermatologic Society and a member of the American Academy of Dermatology.

Eczema, a chronic, dry skin condition that afflicts 15 million Americans, accounts for at least 20% of my practice, especially in winter, when the humidity is low. Both men and women of all ethnic groups are equally vulnerable to the disease, but children under the age of six are slightly more likely to develop it.

The term *eczema* is broadly used to describe a variety of noncontagious conditions characterized by dry, red, scaly, itchy patches on the skin. It most often targets the arms and legs.

There are many different types of eczema, and the disorder can have many causes and occur in many forms. The most common variety of eczema—*atopic dermatitis*—is caused by an allergic reaction. It usually occurs in people who have a family history of hay fever, asthma or other allergies. I recently treated a little girl whose eczema was made worse because she was allergic to the nickel snaps on the front of her pants.

Eczema cannot be cured—but it can be controlled. *Here's how...*

PREVENTION

If you are prone to eczema, do not wait for a flare-up to take these steps, especially in the winter months...

•**Use mild cleansers.** Use bar soaps that are meant for the face on your entire body. They are gentler on the skin. Better brands include Dove, Aveeno, Basis, Oil of Olay and Camay. Avoid antibacterial soaps and deodorant soaps, all of which aggravate eczema.

•**Lubricate skin twice a day.** Emollients are necessary to decrease the loss of water from the skin and prevent it from becoming too dry. Lotions won't do the trick. They are too watery and won't seal in moisture as ointments will. I recommend Vaseline Petroleum Jelly and Aquaphor to my patients.

•**Take no more than one shower a day.** People who shower at home, then go to the health club and take a second shower, particularly during the winter, are going to have more trouble with eczema than people who shower just once a day. It's even better not to shower daily—three or four times per week is optimal. And when you shower or bathe, make sure the water is lukewarm, not hot. Hot water dries out the skin more than cooler water.

If you swim in a pool for exercise, be sure not to shower before getting in the pool. After getting out, rinse only long enough to get the chlorine off—and don't use soap.

•**Avoid animals.** Many people are allergic to the shed skin—the dander—of animals, such as cats, dogs and rabbits. Animal dander floats in the air and gets on furniture and clothes. Without even touching an animal, you still can come in contact with its dander.

•**Watch what children eat.** Children under the age of six who have eczema should avoid orange juice, egg whites and peanuts—including peanut products, such as peanut butter and foods that contain even traces of peanuts. Children usually outgrow these allergies, and adults usually don't have to worry that something they eat will trigger their eczema.

TREATMENT

If you have a flare-up, patches of skin may become itchy. Avoid scratching. You will likely complicate the eczema by infecting it with bacteria and germs from your fingernails.

To relieve the itching, you may need medication. *The most effective medications include...*

•**Oral antihistamines.** I encourage my patients to use an oral antihistamine to help break the itch/scratch cycle. The topical antihistamines don't make the grade. They contain ingredients that may irritate your skin. Stick with oral antihistamines, and follow the directions on the label.

There are many over-the-counter oral antihistamines. They include *chlorpheniramine maleate* (Chlor-Trimeton) and *diphenhydramine hydrochloride* (Benadryl), both of which can make you drowsy. Another oral antihistamine is *loratadine* (Claritin), which doesn't have this particular side effect. Or you can ask your doctor to prescribe an antihistamine for you.

Children who are prone to being itchy and have a habit of scratching should take an oral antihistamine when they take a nap or go to bed at night, so they don't scratch themselves while they sleep.

• **Cortisone ointment** has been used since the 1950s to help relieve symptoms of eczema. Over-the-counter steroids often are not strong enough, and you may need prescription-strength.

Downside: Skin can get thin if cortisone is used too often.

• **Calcineurin inhibitors.** Patients who don't want to use topical steroids or who have used them without success can try the effective, new prescription drugs called calcineurin inhibitors. These are applied topically and may sting slightly. They can be given to people over the age of two to control eczema. If you don't have insurance, be aware that calcineurin inhibitors are a lot more expensive than cortisone.

OTC Acne Creams Work

Over-the-counter (OTC) acne creams are just as effective for mild to moderate acne as prescription oral antibiotics.

Bonus: Use of the topical creams—such as Clearasil and Oxyderm—does not lead to antibiotic resistance.

Hywel C. Williams, PhD, professor of dermatology, University of Nottingham, England, and leader of a study comparing commonly used acne treatments, published in *The Lancet*.

Natural Acne Control

In one recent finding, patients with moderate to severe acne showed significant improvement after applying a specially formulated 3%

green tea solution to their skin twice daily for 12 weeks. The solution cleared skin as effectively as the conventional acne medication benzoyl peroxide but with less itching, peeling and other side effects. Green tea cream is available at health-food stores.

Jennifer Gan-Wong, MD, dermatologist, Chinese General Hospital and Medical Center, located in Manila, the Philippines.

How to Keep Hands Looking Young

Neal Schultz, MD, dermatologist in private practice at Park Avenue Skin Care, New York City, and author of *It's Not Just About Wrinkles* (Stewart, Tabori & Chang).

You work hard to keep the skin on your face young and smooth, so don't let your hands give away your age. *A dermatologist's tips for younger-looking hands...*

• **Apply sunscreen** of SPF 30 or higher on hands every day. Use products with Z-Cote, a microfine zinc oxide. Always reapply sunscreen after washing, swimming or perspiring.

• **Use a bleaching product** to fade brown spots (age, sun or liver spots). Your dermatologist can give you a prescription for one, or you can try one of the milder over-the-counter products, such as Porcelana.

• **Wear gloves** whenever possible.

• **Have bulging blue veins removed** by a dermatologist with a laser, or have a dermatologist inject a sclerosing agent, which causes veins to collapse and fade.

Cost: $3,000 or more.*

• **Remove fine lines** and improve the paper-like quality of aging skin with laser treatments that generate collagen, also available from your dermatologist.

Cost: $2,000 to $4,000.

*Prices subject to change.

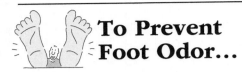

To Prevent Foot Odor...

Do not be embarrassed by foot odor. *Some simple things you can do to prevent it...*

• **Apply a natural antiperspirant** that has buffered aluminum or aluminum chloride, such as Certain Dri Antiperspirant Roll-On, to the bottom of your feet.

• **Wear natural fibers**—socks made of cotton, which wicks away the moisture and allows greater circulation, and shoes made from cotton canvas or leather.

• **Don't wear the same pair of shoes two days in a row.**

• **Go barefoot** whenever possible.

• **Cut back on all caffeinated beverages**—sweating can sometimes be caused by consuming too much caffeine.

Natural Health, Box 37474, Boone, IA 50037.

How to Prevent Nighttime Leg Cramps

Jacqueline Jacques, ND, a naturopathic physician and specialist in pain management, Irvine, CA.

Nocturnal leg cramping can have many causes, such as deficiencies of some vitamins or minerals (including B-1, B-12, vitamin E, magnesium, calcium or potassium), anemia, circulatory problems, dehydration and, less commonly, the metabolic disorders (such as thyroid disease and diabetes) and spinal stenosis (narrowing of the space around the spinal cord). Being overweight or obese also increases your chances of having leg cramps. Or, they can result from simple overexertion or be a side effect of a prescription medication.

Self-defense: To prevent leg cramps, take a multivitamin/mineral supplement and drink six to eight glasses of water throughout the day—or consider an electrolyte drink, such as Gatorade, which provides both sodium and potassium

to increase the amount of water your body absorbs. Stretch your muscles several times during the day and before bed to release tension. You also might massage your feet, calves and legs. When cramps occur, try the "tense and release" technique—tighten up your muscles as much as you can, hold for 30 seconds, then release. Repeat several times if required. Another option is to take a hot bath with two cups of Epsom salts, which relaxes muscles, before going to bed.

Bottom line: If simple steps like these do not work, consult your doctor for advice.

Don't Use Quinine For Leg Cramps

The Food and Drug Administration (FDA) has concluded that quinine drugs for leg cramps can't be sold over the counter because of serious side effects. Quinine has a narrow margin between effective and toxic doses.

Alternative treatments for leg cramps: The remedies described above as well as certain prescription drugs, Botox and biofeedback.

The best treatment depends on the cause of the cramps—tests may be necessary.

Norman Marcus, MD, medical director of the Norman Marcus Pain Institute, 30 E. 40 St., New York City 10016.

Drink Water to Prevent Back Pain

Depending on your age and spinal health, the shock-absorbing discs in your spine are 70% to 90% water. If a person is not adequately hydrated, increased back stiffness may result.

Self-defense: Drink about one-half ounce of water per pound of body weight.

Also: Use proper lifting techniques (bend with your knees and keep the object as close to you as possible)...and maintain a healthy weight.

If back pain is severe or accompanied by leg weakness, numbness or fever, seek immediate attention. This could be a sign of a disc herniation, circulatory problems, infection or cancer.

Daniel A. Shaye, DC, certified chiropractic rehabilitation doctor, Williamsburg, VA.

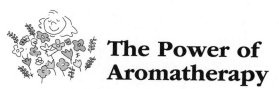

The Power of Aromatherapy

Alan Hirsch, MD, founder and neurological director of the Smell & Taste Treatment and Research Foundation in Chicago, www.scienceofsmell.com. He is a neurologist and psychiatrist, and is author of Life's a Smelling Success *(Authors of Unity) and* What's Your Food Sign?: How to Use Food Cues to Find True Love *(Stewart, Tabori & Chang).*

Aromatherapy can be a remarkable remedy. When a patient smells a particular odor, scent molecules bind to the surface of cell walls at the top of the nose, which will trigger the release of neurotransmitters, as well as other chemicals that stimulate different parts of the brain.

Scents that patients enjoy are more effective remedies than those that they find unpleasant.

Example: One study found that patients with claustrophobia who enjoyed the smell of green apple felt less anxious when they smelled it, but patients who didn't like the smell had no improvement.

Intermittent bursts of a particular aroma are more therapeutic than smelling it continuously. Patients who use aromatherapy are advised to limit their scent exposure to about three minutes or less at a time—by putting an essential oil on a handkerchief and smelling it briefly, for example, or by walking in and out of a room where an aromatherapy candle is burning. Essential oils and aromatherapy candles are available at most health-food stores and many grocery stores. Or you can sniff the actual food or flower, such as green apple or jasmine.

Many health conditions can be improved with aromatherapy. Whether or not these problems can be *prevented* with aromatherapy is still being researched.

ANXIETY

Some scents appear to calm the limbic system, the "emotional" part of the brain involved in anxiety. Also, patients who smell a pleasing odor feel happy—and this crowds out feelings of anxiety and stress.

Proven effective: Green apple and/or cucumber have been shown to reduce anxiety by about 18%. Also, patients who sniff lavender have an increase in their alpha waves, a sign of heightened relaxation.

MIGRAINE HEADACHE

Most migraines are caused in part from inflammation and alternating cycles of dilation/constriction of blood vessels in the brain. Aromatherapy changes the electrical activity in the brain, which can help relieve migraines. Aromatherapy appears to be effective for other types of headaches as well, such as muscle contraction headaches. It also promotes feelings of relaxation, which can reduce both the frequency of headaches and a patient's sensitivity to pain.

Proven effective: Green apple. It has effects similar to that of *sumatriptan* (Imitrex), a leading migraine drug, and can reduce the severity and duration of migraines by about 16%.

Caution: About 15% of all migraine sufferers have *osmophobia*, the hypersensitivity to odors that can make migraines worse. Also, about 18% of migraine patients have a decreased sense of smell and don't respond to aromatherapy.

CIGARETTE ADDICTION

A number of studies have shown that smokers given cigarettes infused with a pepperlike smell have reduced cravings. More recently, smokers who were exposed to both pleasant and unpleasant odors found it easier to quit smoking, but the pleasant odors were somewhat more effective.

Proven effective: Any odor that you find particularly pleasant—lavender, mint, etc. Smell the scent whenever you feel an urge to light up a cigarette.

Also helpful: People who were born prior to 1930 tend to respond better to natural smells—citrus, the odor of baking bread, etc. Younger patients often respond better to artificial smells, such as Play-Doh or Pez candy, that evoke strong positive memories.

LOW ENERGY

The odors that stimulate the trigeminal nerve (which has receptors in the nose and eyes and is the same nerve that makes people cry when they cut an onion) cause increased activity in the part of the brain that is involved in wakefulness.

Proven effective: Peppermint. People who smell a peppermint scent or chew a piece of peppermint gum or candy experience a sudden burst of energy.

Also helpful: The smell of strawberries or buttered popcorn. Both cause an increase in energy as well as metabolism.

OBESITY

A number of studies have shown that particular odors can help people lose weight. Some scents stimulate the part of the hypothalamus that controls appetite. Odors also may act as a displacement mechanism—a reminder to eat less.

Proven effective: Peppermint and green apple. One large study found that people who sniffed either one of these scents when they felt hungry lost an average of 30 pounds over a six-month period.

Also helpful: Take frequent deep sniffs of food while eating. Odor molecules, regardless of the food they come from, can fool the brain into thinking that more has been consumed, which helps suppress the appetite.

REDUCED MEMORY/ CONCENTRATION

Most adults find that they do not remember new information—telephone numbers, the plot twists in a novel, etc.—as well as they used to. Aromatherapy can be used to accelerate learning speed and to promote better concentration and memory.

Proven effective: Floral scents. Sniffing any floral essential oil triggers the release of *norepinephrine* and *adrenocorticotropic hormone* (ACTH), hormones that increase attention. Floral scents have been shown to improve memory and learning speed by about 17%.

In one study, people were exposed to different scents prior to bowling. Those who smelled jasmine knocked down 28% more pins, probably because it improved their concentration and hand/eye coordination.

Strategy: Sniff a floral scent when the material to be learned is initially presented, and repeat exposure to the same odor when the material must be recalled.

Folk Remedies That Really Work...for Fatigue, Insomnia And More

Joan Wilen and Lydia Wilen, folk-remedy experts located in New York City. The sisters are the coauthors of many books, including *Bottom Line's Secret Food Cures & Doctor-Approved Folk Remedies*, from which this article is adapted (Bottom Line Books, 800-678-5835, *www.bottomlinesecrets.com*).

Expensive medications aren't the only solution for certain health conditions. The following folk remedies have stood the test of time—and many have received a measure of acceptance from the scientific community. They are much cheaper than prescription medications, are available without a prescription and typically involve familiar ingredients known to be safe, reducing the odds of side effects. Consult with your doctor if a health condition persists or seems potentially serious.

FATIGUE

If you've lost some of your get-up-and-go and your doctor can't find an underlying medical explanation, try...

- **Figs.** Dried figs contain slow-burning natural sugars for a lasting energy boost. They are also full of potassium and calcium and low in fat, cholesterol and sodium.

- **Cayenne pepper.** Mix ⅛ teaspoon of cayenne pepper into a cup of water and drink it down for a spicy eye-opener.

- **Chia seeds.** Chia seeds, a staple of Native American cultures, are high in beneficial omega-3 fatty acids, and they seem to aid the circulatory system, even reducing high blood pressure. Available at all health food stores, they can be ground and sprinkled on salads or soups.

INSOMNIA

Pharmaceutical sleep aids often leave users feeling drowsy or drugged the following day. *Consider these natural cures instead…*

•**Socks.** Keep your bedroom cool, but wear warm socks to bed, or rest your feet on a hot-water bottle when you climb into bed. A Swiss sleep experiment conducted in 1999 confirmed that while most people prefer to sleep in cool rooms, we fall asleep faster when our feet are kept warm.

•**Chamomile tea.** Drink a cup of chamomile tea next time you can't sleep. Recent experiments on mice indicate that this herb is indeed a mild sedative.

•**Nutmeg.** The oil in nutmeg can act as a sedative. Steep half of a crushed nutmeg (no more) in hot water 10 minutes, strain and drink a half hour before bedtime. Or, stir a half teaspoon of powdered nutmeg into a glass of warm milk. Milk contains the amino acid *tryptophan*, which encourages sleep by increasing serotonin levels in the brain.

ARTHRITIS

There are many types of arthritis, and no one treatment can improve them all. *But the following are worth trying…*

•**Cherries.** Cherries are rich in anthocyanins, a class of chemical known to suppress the production of inflammation-related compounds in the body. Eat fresh, canned or frozen cherries daily, or drink 100% pure cherry juice. A dozen cherries a day and a glass of cherry juice is a good starting point, but feel free to eat more if your body doesn't protest.

Note: Excessive cherry consumption causes diarrhea in some individuals.

•**Cod-liver oil.** Cod-liver oil acts as an anti-inflammatory, and studies suggest that it might limit cartilage damage caused by osteoarthritis. Cod-liver oil is also rich in vitamin D. People who consume diets rich in vitamin D have been shown to be less likely to develop rheumatoid arthritis.

Take one tablespoon daily with a meal. Emulsified Norwegian cod-liver oil is less fishy-tasting than other cod liver oils.

Important: If you take supplements that contain vitamin D, adding a daily tablespoon of cod-liver oil is not likely to push you beyond the maximum recommended intake. However, it's best to check with your doctor.

•**Avoid all nightshade foods.** Eliminate the nightshade family of plants—white potatoes… eggplant…all peppers (including table pepper and cayenne pepper)…and tomatoes—from your diet for a few weeks. If your arthritis improves, give them all up permanently. Consumption of these foods might create a buildup in the body of the inflammation-causing enzyme known as *cholinesterase*.

CARPAL TUNNEL SYNDROME

This swelling of tendons in the wrist can compress the median nerve, causing pain, numbness or other unpleasant sensations in the hands. The problem is most common among people who regularly use their hands in rapid, repeated motions, such as for typing. Proper ergonomics can reduce the risk of carpal tunnel syndrome, while prescription drugs can lessen the pain and surgery can correct very serious cases. *Some home remedies that also might ease the discomfort…*

•**Willow bark.** Willow tree bark contains *salicylates* that reduce pain *and* inflammation and was the original source of aspirin. Steep one to two teaspoons of dried, powdered willow bark (or five teaspoons of fresh bark) in hot water for 10 minutes, then strain out the plant material. Drink three cups a day. If it is too bitter, mix it with lemonade.

Warning: Don't take willow bark if you are using blood-thinning medications or are allergic to aspirin.

•**Chamomile tea.** The herb chamomile contains the anti-inflammatories *alphabisabolol* and *chamazulene* and has long been used to treat ailments that involve swelling. Consume several cups daily.

•**Pineapple, ginger and papaya.** Pineapple and papaya contain enzymes that serve as anti-inflammatories. Compounds in ginger known as *gingerols* have a similar effect. Eat at least one of these daily.

URINARY PROBLEMS

Bladder and kidney ailments can be serious, so always consult a doctor. *With your doctor's permission, also try the following…*

• **Parsley.** This diuretic can help treat urinary tract infections and kidney and bladder stones. Drink parsley tea or juice three or four times daily until the condition improves, or sprinkle fresh parsley flakes on your food. Parsley tea bags can be found in health food stores, or you can steep fresh parsley leaves in hot water. Combine fresh parsley and water in a food processor to make parsley juice (add carrot juice to dilute the taste).

• **Cranberry juice.** Cranberries contain a compound called *proanthocyanidin* that makes it difficult for the strains of bacteria responsible for certain urinary tract infections, kidney infections and bladder infections to adhere to cells in the body. Drink two ounces of pure cranberry juice (no sugar or preservatives added) diluted in six ounces of water at room temperature three times a day as long as urinary discomfort persists.

• **Buchu leaves.** Used for centuries to treat incontinence, painful urination and bladder inflammation, Buchu's effectiveness has not been scientifically proven. It's available in health food stores if you would like to give it a try. Steep three to four tablespoons of dried buchu leaves in hot water, strain and drink three times a day until the condition improves.

VARICOSE VEINS

Surgery isn't the only way to minimize varicose veins…

• **Apple cider vinegar.** Twice a day, soak a cheesecloth bandage in apple cider vinegar and use it to wrap the affected area for 30 minutes. After wrapping, recline with your legs at heart level or above. Vinegar is believed to encourage varicose veins to contract. Some folk remedies suggest drinking two teaspoons of apple cider vinegar in a cup of warm water at the end of each session.

• **Bromelain.** This collection of enzymes in pineapples has anti-inflammatory properties believed to inhibit the uncomfortable and unattractive swelling that often occurs around varicose veins. It's available at health food stores in pill form. Take 500 mg to 1,000 mg with each meal.

Note: Check with your doctor before drinking vinegar or taking bromelain if you have ulcers or gastritis.

• **Sit with uncrossed legs.** Crossing the legs puts unnecessary strain on the veins. Also avoid high heels, knee-high stockings and tight socks.

Is It True That We Need Less Sleep As We Age?

James B. Maas, PhD, Weiss presidential fellow and professor of psychology, Cornell University, Ithaca, NY.

As we age, we need almost as much sleep as we did during our midlife years. Most adults need 7.5 to 8.5 hours of sleep to be fully alert during the day. However, changes in the brain due to aging (such as hardening of the arteries) and side effects from medications we might be taking for other medical problems (such as heart disease, hypertension, type 2 diabetes or arthritis) often make it difficult to sustain adequate sleep. If you can't get to sleep, or you wake up during the night or very early in the morning, you are probably among the 75% of the adult population who have insomnia at least one night a week.

What to do: Avoid caffeine after 2 pm…avoid alcohol within three hours of your bedtime…get plenty of exercise and mental stimulation (do not exercise vigorously within two hours of bedtime)…and don't nap during the day.

Caution: If you have a problem getting adequate sleep for more than three weeks, ask your doctor whether you should make an appointment at an accredited sleep disorders center.

Better Insomnia Relief

In a study of 46 people with chronic insomnia, one group was trained in cognitive-behavior therapy (CBT) techniques, including relaxation practices and stimulus (noise and light) control. Two other groups took either the sleeping pill *zopiclone* (Imovane) or a placebo every night.

Result: After six weeks, time spent awake dropped 52% in the CBT group compared with

4% in the zopiclone group and 16% in people taking a placebo.

Theory: CBT helps patients to identify and change negative thoughts, which can be an underlying cause of insomnia.

Borge Sivertsen, PhD, researcher and psychologist, University of Bergen, Norway.

Sleeping Pills Can Cause More Risks Than Benefits

Researchers analyzed studies involving 2,417 people who took either a placebo or a prescription sleep aid, such as *zolpidem* (Ambien), or over-the-counter medication, such as *diphenhydramine* (Benadryl), for five or more consecutive nights.

Result: People who took the sedatives were more than twice as likely to report daytime fatigue, headache, dizziness, nausea and falls as they were to gain a better quality of sleep.

If you have trouble sleeping: Ask your doctor about nondrug strategies, such as cognitive behavioral therapy and/or exercise.

Nathan Herrmann, MD, head, division of geriatric psychiatry, Sunnybrook Health Sciences Centre, University of Toronto, Canada.

Recipe for a Great Power Nap

For a nice nap, find a quiet place where you can fall asleep easily…set an alarm if you are worried about oversleeping—a nap should last 30 to 40 minutes…nap at the time of the afternoon when you normally feel sleepiest…and be sure to give yourself time to wake up—be fully alert before driving or doing any demanding task.

If you find it hard to get going after a nap, shorten nap time. If you find that you are having trouble falling asleep or staying asleep at night, try other afternoon pick-me-ups (some people are nappers and some are not).

Examples: A well-balanced snack, exposure to bright light, 10 to 20 minutes of moderate exercise.

Scott Campbell, PhD, sleep expert, department of psychiatry, Weill Medical College of Cornell University, White Plains, NY.

Stay Alert with Self-Applied Acupressure

To give yourself an energy boost, use your index and middle fingers to massage stimulation points in a circular motion—90 seconds in one direction, then 90 seconds the other way. Be sure to use a very firm touch—slight discomfort is normal.

Best places to massage: Back of the head at the hairline, on left and right sides at the same time…area between thumb and forefinger, just beyond the webbing on the hand…front of the leg, between kneecap and knee bone…just below the ball of the foot, toward the arch.

Richard Harris, PhD, division of rheumatology, University of Michigan Medical School, Ann Arbor.

Hiccup Cures That Work

Hiccups can drive you batty. *Here is how to stop them at once…*

• **Stick a finger into each ear**—this stimulates the vagus nerve, which runs from the brain to the abdomen and controls hiccups.

• **Use a cotton swab to draw a line gently down the roof of your mouth**—the tickling stops the throat spasm that causes hiccups.

• **Breathe into a paper bag** to produce carbon dioxide, which helps calm the diaphragm—but do this only if someone is with you, in case you get light-headed.

• **Get distracted**—have someone ask you a nonsensical question or try to make you hiccup at an exact moment.

Health, 2 Embarcadero Center, San Francisco 94111.

A Natural Insect Repellent

A new herbal insect repellent—oil of lemon eucalyptus—now is on the Centers for Disease Control and Prevention's recommended list. But it must be reapplied more often than DEET or *picaridin* (frequency depends on the concentration).

Warning: Just one mosquito bite can transmit West Nile virus or other infections.

Be sure to apply repellent to exposed skin whenever you are outdoors, especially between dusk and dawn.

Emily Zielinski-Gutierrez, DrPH, a behavioral scientist, Division of Vector-Borne Diseases, Centers for Disease Control and Prevention, Fort Collins, CO.

Anger Increases Risk of Injury

In a recent finding, people who feel hostile are twice as likely to get injured as people who don't feel hostile.

Also: Men are more likely than women to get injured while angry.

Daniel C. Vinson, MD, professor of family and community medicine, University of Missouri–Columbia, and leader of a study of 2,446 emergency room patients, published in *Annals of Family Medicine*.

Speedier Healing

To prevent scarring after an injury, wash the affected area with soap and water, not peroxide—which slows healing by preventing new cells from forming. Then, put a protective film, such as Aquaphor or petroleum jelly, over the wound—keeping the area moist speeds healing. Instead of an adhesive bandage, apply an Adaptic bandage—the plastic coating prevents gauze from sticking to the wound. Or try a liquid bandage, which seals the cut like a scab for faster healing.

Jeffrey Dover, MD, dermatologist, SkinCare Physicians, Chestnut Hill, MA, *www.skincarephysicians.net*.

No More Bleeding with Paint-On Bandages

Scientists have developed a liquid composed of protein fragments that forms a gel when applied to wounds. The clear liquid stops bleeding almost immediately, and could eventually replace adhesive strips, and be used during surgery to stop internal bleeding.

LiveScience.com.

Home Remedies for Common Pains

No need to suffer with these minor aches and pains. *Try these natural remedies…*

•**For muscle soreness,** drink ginger tea—grate a two-inch piece of fresh gingerroot and steep for three to five minutes in a cup of boiling water, then strain and drink at least twice a day.

•**For headache,** rub Tiger Balm ointment, available at drugstores, onto your temples.

•**To dull tooth pain,** rub an ice cube in the V-shaped area where the bones of your thumb and forefinger meet.

•**For canker sores,** place a wet, tepid bag of black tea against the sore for three to five minutes, as needed—the tannins in the tea relieve pain and help speed healing.

AARP Magazine, 601 E St. NW, Washington, DC 20049.

4

Fitness Now

Secrets of Thin People

Do you know people who never put on any weight and yet do not seem to have to watch what they eat? Good genes play a role—if your parents were thin, more than likely you will be, too. But in helping thousands of patients slim down, Stephen Gullo, PhD, author of *The Thin Commandments Diet*, has found that though most of us assume thin people never give their weight a second thought, they actually do rely on a number of strategies to keep the pounds from accumulating. *Here, the secrets of thin people, which can help anyone who is trying to lose weight or maintain a healthy weight...*

• **Thin people don't skip meals.** They don't allow themselves to get so hungry that they become compulsive eaters rather than selective eaters. Thin people have structured eating habits. They eat three meals and one to two healthful snacks a day to keep blood sugar stable and

prevent the body from secreting large amounts of *insulin*, the hunger hormone. Stable blood sugar levels also help the body metabolize calories efficiently and prevent cravings for sweets.

• **Thin people eat the right breakfast.** The National Weight Control Registry, which monitors people who have lost weight and successfully kept it off, found that 78% of those who have maintained their weight loss eat breakfast every day. But the wrong breakfast isn't helpful. A breakfast high in simple carbohydrates, such as a sugary cereal, stimulates appetite. That's because blood sugar is low in the morning. If you eat a sugary breakfast, blood sugar levels rise and then crash rapidly, making you hungry. A breakfast that contains protein and fiber—such as oatmeal and skim milk or low-fat yogurt with

Stephen Gullo, PhD, health psychologist and president of the Center for Healthful Living at the Institute for Health and Weight Sciences in New York City. He is previous chairman of the National Obesity and Weight Control Education Program of the American Institute for Life-Threatening Illness at Columbia-Presbyterian Medical Center and author of *The Thin Commandments Diet* (Rodale).

fresh fruit—is better. It satisfies your appetite, keeps blood sugar levels on an even keel and helps you feel full longer.

- **Thin people act quickly.** If they gain a few pounds, they immediately cut back on portion sizes and exercise more. I tell my patients that a mark of a winner at weight control is to own only one size of clothing. When thin people think their clothing is getting too tight, they don't buy larger clothes. They change the habits that are creating the problem. It's far easier to lose three or four pounds than it is to lose 20.

- **Thin people weigh themselves regularly.** Most people who have lost weight and kept it off weigh themselves at least once a week. A gain of even two to three pounds motivates them to shift into a more restricted eating plan for a few days. I weigh myself on Monday, right after the weekend, when my eating habits tend to be more liberal, and again on Friday. If I don't like what I see on Monday, I make changes in my diet. I eat lighter meals, such as broiled fish and chicken, egg white omelets and steamed vegetables without oil or butter, and I don't eat sweets. I weigh myself again on Wednesday to see if my weight is coming down.

- **Thin people don't deprive themselves.** They devise creative strategies to limit consumption of high-calorie foods. They don't stock the house with them. When they do buy them, they select individual portions or serve them only when they have company or on weekends. A patient of mine only buys her children cookies containing peanuts because she doesn't like peanuts. Other people eat desserts only in restaurants.

- **Thin people get sufficient sleep.** Being sleep-deprived can stimulate the appetite, especially carbohydrate cravings. Researchers at the University of Chicago studied young men who got only four hours of sleep per night for two nights. The researchers measured levels of the hormone *leptin*. An increase in leptin signals the brain that no more food is required...a *decrease* brings on hunger. The sleep-deprived men had an 18% decrease in leptin. The researchers also found that amounts of *ghrelin*, a hormone that causes hunger, increased by 28%.

The sleep-deprived men were not only hungrier, they also all craved carbohydrates, such as sweets, and salty foods, such as chips. They may have wanted sweets because of lower blood sugar levels. The salt cravings may have been because sleep-deprivation decreases blood pressure. Salty foods raise blood pressure and may have temporarily made the young men feel more energetic.

- **Thin people move a lot.** Studies show that people who lose weight and keep it off exercise regularly. They may not work out in a gym or have a structured program, but they walk a lot, garden or take the stairs instead of the elevator. The National Weight Control Registry found that people who keep off weight burn about 11,830 calories per week through physical activity—the equivalent of walking more than 20 miles.

Researchers at the Mayo Clinic have reported that lean people expend about 350 more calories per day, on average, than sedentary obese people—and not just through exercise, such as walking. They fidget, tap their toes and so on.

- **Thin people exercise portion control.** They know which foods they can eat in generous amounts, such as lean protein, fruits and vegetables. If they overeat, they do it at a special restaurant or on a holiday. There is nothing wrong with overeating during Thanksgiving, but there is something destructive about consuming a pint of ice cream every night. Thin people also consider how food is prepared. They know that a healthy, low-calorie filet of sole, for example, is neither healthy nor low-calorie if it's fried in oil or sautéed in butter.

- **Thin people don't use food to deal with emotion.** Many of my patients don't really enjoy the foods that are making them heavy. They use food to cope with anger, depression and stress. People who stay trim over a lifetime don't use food as therapy. They also don't eat because of boredom or out of habit, such as when they go to the movies or they're watching TV.

Instead, they have other ways to deal with their emotions. They may go for a walk, take a bath, play a computer game or browse in a store. Mental diversion turns off the food switch. If they associate watching television with food, they chew on a stick of gum or eat cut-up vegetables. Or they allow themselves a sensible portion of a low-cal snack, such as a small bag of low-fat popcorn.

"The Less You Eat, the More You Lose"…and Other Diet Myths

Mark Hyman, MD, editor in chief of the medical journal *Alternative Therapies in Health and Medicine*. He is also author of *Ultrametabolism: The Simple Plan for Automatic Weight Loss* (Scribner) and coauthor of the best-seller *Ultraprevention: The Six-Week Plan That Will Make You Healthy for Life* (Atria). Formerly co-medical director of Canyon Ranch, a health spa resort in the Berkshires, MA, he's now in private practice in Lenox, MA.

Losing weight can be hard work. People feel they have to count calories, endure hunger pangs and work up a sweat. It is no wonder so many give up and regain their hard-lost pounds. It does not have to be that way. The reason we are losing the battle of the bulge is that we have bought into some common myths about weight loss. *Here, six of those myths and what to do instead…*

Myth 1: The less you eat, the more weight you'll lose.

Our bodies are made up of hundreds of genes that protect us from starvation. That's why we end up gaining weight if we start out eating too few calories. You can starve yourself for only so long before your body engages a primitive response that compensates for starvation by making you overeat. In my experience, the average person who goes on a diet actually gains five pounds instead of losing weight.

What to do: Never go on a "diet." Instead, eat foods that turn on your metabolism. These are whole foods that come from nature, such as vegetables, fruits, whole grains, nuts, seeds, beans and lean animal protein. If you eat only these foods, you won't have trouble with your appetite—it will self-regulate, and the triggers that drive overeating will be under control.

Myth 2: It doesn't matter what kind of exercise you do, as long as you exercise.

It's true that any kind of exercise is better than no exercise, but interval training is the most effective for weight loss. Interval training consists of short bursts of intense activity followed by longer periods of lighter activity. This kind of training tunes up your metabolism so you burn more calories all day and while you sleep, not just when you are exercising.

What to do: Aim for 20 to 30 minutes of interval training two to three days a week. Exercise as vigorously as you can for 30 to 60 seconds, and then slow your pace for three minutes, repeating this pattern for about a half hour.

If you are over 30, have a physical before you start interval training. If you are out of shape, ease into a regular exercise routine first—you might start by walking for 30 minutes five times a week.

Myth 3: You can control your weight by counting calories.

Many people believe that all calories are the same when it comes to weight control—that if you substitute 100 calories' worth of, say, cookies for 100 calories of carrots, you'll come out even. But food isn't just about calories. Everything that you eat contains "instructions" for your DNA, your hormones and your metabolism. Different foods contain different information.

For instance, the sugar in soda enters your blood rapidly, increasing insulin levels. Insulin is a hormone that promotes more fat storage around the middle and raises inflammation levels in the body, which in turn promotes more weight gain.

On the other hand, the same amount of sugar from kidney beans enters your blood slowly. Because the sugar is absorbed over time, your insulin levels remain stable and more of the calories are burned and fewer are stored.

What to do: Don't focus on the number of calories you are consuming. Losing weight is not about counting calories—it's about eating the right calories.

Myth 4: Eating fat makes you fat.

Fat in the diet does not correlate with excess body fat. Any weight-loss resulting from a low-fat diet is usually modest and temporary. The amount of fat Americans eat has dropped from 42% to 34% of total calories on average, but we still are getting fatter. That's because all fats are not created equal. There are good fats, bad fats and ugly fats. Good fats actually can help you lose weight, but many of us have nearly eliminated them from our diet.

Two examples of good fats are omega-3s and monounsaturated fats. Omega-3s are found in fish, flaxseed and flax oil, and nuts and seeds, such as walnuts and pumpkin seeds. Monounsaturated fats are found in olive oil, avocados and nuts.

Bad fats include refined polyunsaturated vegetable oils—such as corn and safflower—and most saturated fat, found in meat and animal products, such as butter.

The ugly fats are trans fats, often found in snack foods and packaged baked goods. Trans fat comes from adding hydrogen to vegetable oil through a process called hydrogenation.

What to do: Eat the good fats. They improve your metabolism by activating genes that help you to burn fats. Saturated and trans fats turn off fat-burning genes. The Inuit people of Greenland used to eat a diet that was very high in fat—primarily omega-3 and monounsaturated fats—and they were thin and healthy. Now they have shifted to a diet that is lower in fat and high in carbohydrates from junk food, and many are obese, with higher rates of heart disease and other types of illnesses.

Myth 5: **Going low-carbohydrate makes you thin.**

Carbohydrates are the single most important food that you can eat for long-term health and weight loss. They are the source of most of the vitamins, minerals and fiber in our diet—and all the phytonutrients, plant compounds that are key regulators of our health. Phytonutrients turn on the genes that help us burn fat and age slowly. They offer key disease-fighting nutrients. Some examples are the *isoflavones* in soy foods, *polyphenols* in cocoa and *glucosinolates* in broccoli.

However, just as there are different fats, there are different types of carbohydrates.

What to do: Eat the complex carbohydrates—vegetables, fruits, nuts, seeds, beans and whole grains. These tend to have low glycemic loads, which means they are absorbed slowly and don't raise blood sugar quickly, so you feel full longer. Refined carbs, such as white flour, rice and pasta, along with sugary foods, make your blood sugar spike so that you feel hungry sooner.

Myth 6: **It doesn't matter what time you eat.**

Sumo wrestlers look the way they do because they fast during the day, then overeat at night and go to bed. Like Sumo wrestlers, we eat most of our calories late in the day. When you eat later in the day, those calories are stored instead of burned off.

What to do: Don't eat within two to three hours of going to sleep, because you need to give your body time to digest and to burn off your food. Also, eat throughout the day to keep blood sugar levels stable. Breakfast is important. I can't tell you how many people I have helped to lose weight by having them eat breakfast. The National Weight Control Registry, which is tracking long-term weight-loss maintenance in more than 5,000 people, has found that 96% of those who have maintained weight loss for six years eat breakfast regularly.

Surprising Reasons Why We Overeat

Brian Wansink, PhD, professor of marketing and nutritional science, and director of the Food and Brand Lab at Cornell University, Ithaca, NY. He is author of *Mindless Eating: Why We Eat More Than We Think* (Bantam). His Web site is *www.mindlesseating.org.*

Our brains, not our stomachs, determine our eating habits—but our minds don't always do a good job of making food decisions. Most people put on weight because their minds don't accurately keep track of how much they have eaten, not because they don't have the willpower to put down their forks.

Surprisingly, when our minds tell us which foods we enjoy, it's often for reasons that have little to do with how they taste.

Example: Approximately one-third of the World War II veterans who served in the South Pacific love Chinese food 50 years later. A similar percentage hate it. It turns out that almost all the veterans who love Chinese food did not experience frequent heavy combat when in Asia, but those who hate it did.

Brian Wansink, PhD, a noted food psychologist, has done extensive research on how our minds trick us into unhealthy eating habits. *Here are some of the ways...*

• **If it looks like a small meal, it feels like a small meal.** Our eyes, not our stomachs, tell us when we are full. In a study conducted by our research team, when we replaced eight-inch dinner plates with 12-inch plates, diners consumed 20% to 35% more because their portions looked smaller on the larger plates. After the meal, they were certain that they hadn't eaten any more than usual.

What to do: Use smaller plates, bowls and spoons if you want to eat less. Drink from tall, thin glasses—not short, fat ones—so you will think you are drinking more. When it's possible, serve food over a bed of lettuce so that the plate looks full.

• **We feel full when there's visual evidence that we have had a lot to eat.** In one study, we gave chicken wings to graduate students while they watched the Super Bowl. When we left the bones in front of the students, they ate an average of four wings apiece. When we cleared the bones away frequently—removing the visual evidence of earlier consumption—each student ate an average of six wings. After the game, students in both groups estimated that they had only four wings each.

What to do: When you are eating—particularly when you are snacking—leave out candy wrappers, peanut shells and other evidence of snacking so that your eyes can warn you about how much you have eaten.

• **When there's no distance to the food, there's no thinking prior to eating.** Office workers consumed an average of nine Hershey's Kisses per day when we put bowls of the chocolate candies on their desks. Their consumption dropped by more than 50% when these bowls were positioned just six feet away. Six feet is only two steps, but even a short distance forces us to think twice before we eat.

What to do: At home, fill individual plates at the stove, and leave the leftovers on the stove or a sideboard. The more hassle it is to eat, the less we eat. You will have fewer additional helpings if you must stand up to get them. A bowl of salad or vegetables can be brought to the dinner table because second helpings of these foods won't add many calories.

With snack foods, pour a serving into a bowl rather than eating straight from the bag. Then if you want more, you have to go to the kitchen to get it.

• **"Comfort foods" trigger overconsumption.** Comfort foods improve our moods. These foods pick us up when we're feeling stressed or unhappy and serve as rewards when we're feeling good.

Women's comfort foods tend to be unhealthy dessert or snack items, however men's comfort foods are more likely to be hot meals. Why the difference? Men tend to associate home-cooked meals with someone taking care of them, because men's meals often are prepared by their wives. Women associate a home-cooked meal with the chore of cooking, so they prefer prepared snack foods and desserts.

What to do: We get nearly as much emotional benefit from a small serving of a comfort food as from a large one—for example, a single scoop of ice cream instead of a pint.

Also, we get nearly as much emotional benefit from our second- or third-favorite comfort food as from our absolute favorite. If your top comfort food is chocolate ice cream but tomato soup is a close second, keep plenty of microwavable tomato soup in the house so that low-calorie comfort is just seconds away.

• **We underestimate calories in beverages.** When people are asked to gauge the calories in a drink, they typically undershoot by 30% or more. Beverages don't seem to be filling, so we don't assume that they have as many calories as they actually do.

What to do: As a rule of thumb, estimate that you are consuming 10 calories an ounce for the "thin" beverages, such as juice, soda and milk… and 20 calories per ounce for "thick" beverages, such as smoothies and meal-replacement shakes. That adds up quickly when you're drinking a 32-ounce soda—to an estimated 320 calories.

Interestingly, if you load that drink with ice, you'll actually burn off a few of those calories. Since your body has to use energy to heat up an iced beverage, you actually burn about one calorie for every ice-cold ounce you drink. If you drink the recommended eight eight-ounce glasses of water a day and if you fill those 64 ounces with ice, you'll burn about 70 extra calories a day, the equivalent of about seven pounds a year.

• **Exercise might make you fatter.** You've forced yourself to jog three miles every day for months—yet you weigh just as much as when you started. What are you doing wrong?

Most exercisers overestimate the calories their exercise burns and then reward themselves with high-calorie foods after their workouts because they think they've earned it. They don't realize that the six Oreo cookies they treat themselves to as a reward have more calories (around 320) than the number of calories they burned while running three miles (around 300).

What to do: If you need a reward, opt for nonfood treats, perhaps a half-hour doing something you enjoy, such as reading a good book or watching a favorite TV show.

• **Birth order might affect your eating habits.** Oldest children and only children tend to save their favorite foods for last. Give them a chocolate chip cookie, and it might become a special treat for after dinner.

The youngest children and middle children in large families are more likely to polish off favorite foods as soon as they receive them—probably to ensure that older siblings won't snatch the food away. These birth-order eating patterns tend to continue into adulthood.

For adults who are the youngest or middle children, the result can be unnecessary pounds. Favorite foods tend to be unhealthy foods, and people who eat unhealthy foods as soon as they get them may be inclined to eat larger quantities in the long run.

What to do: Don't bring favorite snacks into the house in large quantities, especially if you are a youngest or middle child. You might polish off a box in a single sitting.

Quick and Healthy Snacks

All the snacks listed here are healthier than the 100-calorie packaged snacks that are so popular now...

• **One hard-boiled egg** with half a slice of toasted wheat bread—total 109 calories.

• **One-half cup of ice milk or sherbet—**100 calories.

• **One large rectangular graham cracker spread with about one-and-a-half teaspoons of peanut butter—**105 calories.

• **One-ounce slice of angel-food cake** with half a cup of fresh strawberries—95 calories.

• **One cup of chicken noodle soup with two saltine crackers—**100 calories.

Woman's Day, 1633 Broadway, New York City 10019.

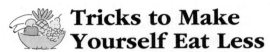 # Tricks to Make Yourself Eat Less

Lisa R. Young, PhD, RD, adjunct professor of nutrition at New York University and a nutritionist in private practice, both in New York City. She is the author of *The Portion Teller Plan: The No-Diet Reality Guide to Eating, Cheating and Losing Weight Permanently* (Morgan Road).

The "supersized" portion phenomenon is fooling you into eating more than you think—even when at home. Here is how to beat it.

The food industry knows the powerful truth about one of your human weaknesses: The more food that is put in front of you, the more you will eat. This is generally true even for people who are weight-conscious, or who just feel better when they eat less.

It's easy to see the "supersized" portion trend at a restaurant when you receive a giant bowl of pasta or a six-inch-high pile of onion rings—less easy to escape the same mindset when you eat at home.

Problem: Because Americans are consuming more food than ever before, 66% of them are overweight or obese.* Being overweight or obese increases risk for diabetes, heart disease, high blood pressure, joint problems and even some types of cancer.

Childhood admonitions to "clean your plate!" ...the desire to get what you pay for...and the

*Overweight is defined as a body mass index, or BMI, above 25...obesity is a BMI above 30. To determine your BMI, multiply your weight in pounds by 704.5. Divide that figure by your height in inches squared. For a BMI calculator, visit the National Heart, Lung and Blood Institute Web site (*http://nhlbisupport.com/bmi*).

time lapse between eating and feeling full (about 20 minutes) are simply a few of the factors that make most people eat whatever food is in front of them.

What's worse: The degree to which typical portion sizes have increased over the years is astounding. For example, fountain sodas during the 1950s and 1960s were about seven ounces, compared with 12 to 64 ounces these days. A typical bag of popcorn at the movies was once about five to six cups. Now a large bucket with butter flavor contains up to 20 cups and 1,640 calories. A pasta entrée at a restaurant? Double what it used to be. Eating at home? Standard plates, bowls and glasses are bigger, too—so we fill them up with more food.

HOW MUCH ARE YOU EATING?

The first step toward eating sensibly is to know just how much you're consuming. This is much harder than it sounds. In one informal experiment conducted by a food writer in New York City, four expert nutritionists were given heaping plates of food (including pasta, risotto and sandwiches) and asked to estimate calorie and fat content. No one came even remotely close.

Nutritional guidelines generally suggest eating a set number of "servings" of meats, vegetables and other food groups. But one serving, which is usually defined in ounces, tablespoons or cups, is not the same as a portion, which is the actual amount of food served—at home or at a restaurant.

Examples: For grain products, a "serving" equals one slice of bread, one cup of ready-to-eat cold cereal or one-half cup of pasta. A restaurant order of linguine is likely to be three cups—nearly a whole day's recommended intake of grain! And a single bagel, in today's standard size of five ounces, equals *five* slices of bread.

DEVELOP PORTION AWARENESS

The problem with dietary guidelines is that measurements, such as cups, ounces and tablespoons, aren't easy to eyeball.

Helpful: Measure out the portion you ordinarily take. Then measure out a standard serving of meat, vegetables, pasta, etc. to see what each looks like in comparison.

Important: If your usual portion of meat is actually two servings, you don't necessarily have to cut back during that meal—just know that you have consumed nearly a day's allocation of meat and then adjust the rest of the day's intake accordingly.

RESTAURANT SMARTS

Portion inflation is most out of control in restaurants—where the average American eats four times a week. *To defend yourself against today's supersized restaurant meals, follow these steps...*

• **Have a snack at home.** About one hour before eating out, eat some fruit, low-fat yogurt or vegetable-based soup (made without milk or cream), so that you won't arrive at the restaurant famished.

• **Have the right appetizer.** Many people skip the appetizer in an attempt to cut down on the size of their meal. That's a mistake. Order a soup, salad or a vegetable appetizer to fill up, and tell the waiter not to bring the bread basket. A Pennsylvania State University study found that starting lunch with a low-calorie salad cuts the total caloric intake of the meal by as much as 12% because the fiber that is contained in the salad is filling.

• **Order small entrées.** Or order a half-sized portion, if available. Or share a full-sized entrée with your dining companion—in most restaurants, it will be enough (especially if you add a salad or a side order of vegetables).

• **Eat only half of the meal.** When you order an entrée for yourself, eat half and ask the waiter to wrap up the rest to take home. This way, you'll be eating about as much as restaurant-goers did 20 years ago.

Helpful: Do not rely on willpower alone—when the entrée first arrives, set aside what you plan to eat and ask the waiter to wrap up the rest of the meal.

• **Slow down!** Eat at a leisurely pace to give your body time to catch up with your appetite, and stop before you're full—no matter how much is left. If you're tempted to finish off the plate or go back for seconds, stop and wait 20 minutes. That's usually all it takes to feel satiated.

PORTION CONTROL AT HOME

Portion sizes are set not only by restaurants, but also by food and even dinnerware manufacturers. *Here's how to protect yourself...*

• **Choose smaller dinnerware.** We're conditioned to think that a meal-sized portion is what fills a plate. That's why you should set your table with eight- to 10-ounce (not 20-ounce) glasses…10-inch (rather than 12-inch) dinner plates… and bowls that hold two cups rather than four.

Helpful: One woman I know found a simple way to downsize her portions—she bought a charming set of 1950s dishes at a flea market.

• **Divide your plate.** Allocate space on your plate to meet healthful dietary recommendations —fill half with vegetables and fruit…one-fourth with meat, fish or another protein source…and one-fourth with grains or starchy vegetables.

Helpful: Plates marked with portion reminders for adults and children are available from Be-Better Networks, 304-345-6800, *www.theportion plate.com.*

Cost: About $11 per plate.*

• **Create your own snack portions.** To control your consumption of pretzels, chips and other snack foods, read the label to see how many servings the package contains—and portion it out into that number of plastic, resealable bags. Do this with three-ounce portions of deli meats, as well.

• **Substitute foods.** Three cups of popcorn is just as filling as three-quarters cup of pretzels —and popcorn is a healthful whole grain, while pretzels are typically refined. Three cups of puffed wheat go a lot further than one-quarter cup of granola. Fresh fruits typically leave you feeling more satisfied and with fewer calories than juices or dried fruit.

*Price subject to change.

A Drink a Day May Keep the Pounds Away

In a recent study, people who drank one alcoholic drink a day, including wine, beer and mixed drinks, were 54% less likely to be obese than those who didn't drink at all. Those who had two drinks were 41% less likely to be obese.

But: Don't overdo it—people who drink four or more drinks per day are 46% *more* likely to be obese than nondrinkers. And, binge drinkers, who sometimes have five or more drinks per day, are 80% more likely to be obese.

Ahmed Arif, MD, PhD, assistant professor of family and community medicine, Texas Tech University Health Sciences Center, Lubbock, and leader of a study of the link between obesity and alcohol consumption in 8,236 nonsmokers, published in BMC Public Health.

Natural Supplements That Help You Drop Pounds

Harry G. Preuss, MD, CNS, FACN, professor of physiology, medicine and pathology at Georgetown University Medical Center, Washington, DC. He is a certified nutrition specialist, fellow of the American College of Nutrition and author of more than 300 scientific studies. He is coauthor of The Natural Fat-Loss Pharmacy *(Broadway).*

Weight-loss "pills" often are looked at with skepticism and for good reason. Many are ineffective…and some even are dangerous. But a few nutritional and herbal supplements do work. Some offer bonus health benefits, as well. These natural substances have been scientifically shown to aid weight loss by helping the body burn more calories and fat… decreasing appetite…improving how the body handles blood sugar…and blocking absorption of fat and carbohydrates.

Laboratory, toxicological and clinical studies —and years of everyday use by millions of people—all demonstrate that these supplements are safe. However, it is prudent to take any supplement under the guidance of a qualified health professional. All of the following are available in health-food stores unless otherwise noted.

GREEN TEA EXTRACT

Green tea contains *catechins,* a class of powerful antioxidants. *Epigallocatechin gallate* (EGCG) is the most abundant catechin in green tea.

In a study published in the *British Journal of Nutrition* in 2005, Canadian researchers gave one group of men a supplement that contained EGCG and caffeine and a second group a placebo. Those who took the supplement burned 180 more calories a day—a level that could help a person shed 22 pounds in one year. For those already at their normal weight, studies show an EGCG/caffeine supplement can help maintain weight. (Previous research had shown that an EGCG/caffeine combination burns off more calories than either EGCG or caffeine alone.)

This combination works by stimulating the sympathetic nervous system, which helps regulate appetite, temperature and many other metabolic processes, including calorie-burning and fat-burning. However, unlike potentially heart-damaging weight-loss herbs, such as ephedra, which also stimulate the sympathetic nervous system, a therapeutic dosage of EGCG/caffeine doesn't increase heart rate or significantly boost blood pressure.

Dose: 575 milligrams (mg) of green tea catechins (with 325 mg from EGCG) and 100 mg of caffeine a day. Supplements with this mixture include Schiff-Natural Green Tea Diet and Universal Nutrition-Thermo Green Tea Caps.

Bonus: EGCG may be neuroprotective in humans—it has reduced the severity of Alzheimer's disease in various laboratory animals genetically programmed to develop the disease.

CLA

Conjugated linoleic acid (CLA) is one type of fatty acid—a building block of fat. It is found in small quantities in meat and milk. CLA can help the body lose fat and build muscle.

In a study conducted in Norway and published in *The American Journal of Clinical Nutrition*, 149 women and 31 men received either the CLA or a placebo daily. Within three months, the CLA group lost an average of five pounds of body fat and gained two pounds of firming muscle—without dieting or exercise. The placebo group had no change in body composition.

In a study published in the *International Journal of Obesity* in 2006, people who took CLA for six months—from August 2004 through February 2005—experienced no weight gain throughout the November to December holiday period. People who didn't take CLA gained an average of 1.5 pounds during the holidays.

Researchers don't yet know exactly how CLA works, but it may stop dietary fat from entering fat cells.

Dose: 3.4 grams a day.

Bonus: In one study conducted at the University of British Columbia, people with mild-to-moderate asthma experienced normalization of their airways when they took CLA, which decreases inflammation.

MCTs

The *medium-chain triglycerides* (MCTs) are a type of fat. Triglyceride molecules are typically arranged in chains, with carbon atoms as the links. Most triglycerides you eat are long-chain triglycerides, with up to 24 carbon links. MCTs possess only six to 12 carbon links. During digestion, long-chain triglycerides combine with transport molecules and travel in the circulatory system, where they're deposited in fat cells. Because of their unique length, MCTs don't require transport molecules—they move directly from the stomach to the liver, where most are instantly incinerated for fuel (and very few are stored as fat). This unusual digestive process increases calorie burning.

In a study conducted at the University of Manitoba in Canada and published in *The American Journal of Clinical Nutrition*, 24 men who took MCT supplements burned off an average of 100 more calories per day, compared with men who took a placebo.

Dose: MCT is derived from coconut oil, a saturated fat. There have been concerns that MCT supplements could increase cholesterol levels. The MCT formulation used in the study above includes cholesterol-lowering plant sterols—and lowered total cholesterol by 13% and LDL (bad) cholesterol by 14%. This supplement, Slim Smart (*www.nfb.ca*), is available for sale only through health professionals.

CHROMIUM

The trace mineral chromium increases the number of insulin receptors on muscle and fat cells, helping those cells to utilize blood sugar more effectively. The body uses blood sugar to build muscle, storing less of it as fat.

In a study of overweight women, those who took a chromium supplement while on a diet and exercise program lost weight in a healthy way—84% as fat, 16% as muscle. Those who didn't take chromium lost weight but 8% as fat and 92% as muscle.

Losing muscle rather than fat is the sad fate of many dieters. (Evolutionarily, your hunter-gatherer body is programmed to lose muscle, to preserve fat stores in case of famine.) Muscle burns many more calories a day than fat, so you end up with a body that burns fewer calories. Postdiet, you return to a normal level of eating but gain weight. Chromium can help prevent this common metabolic problem.

Dose: 600 micrograms (mcg) daily, until you reach your weight-loss goal. The maintenance dose—for lifelong blood sugar balance—is 200 mcg a day.

Caution: Too much chromium can bring on major side effects, such as anemia, kidney failure and liver damage. Ask your doctor if chromium is right for you.

Bonus: Because chromium regulates blood sugar, it can help prevent or normalize type 2 diabetes.

STARCH-BLOCKER

An extract of white kidney beans, a starch-blocker limits the action of *alpha-amylase*, the digestive enzyme that breaks down starches in the intestines. In a study conducted in Italy, 60 overweight but healthy people received either a starch-blocker or a placebo for 30 days while on a diet of 2,000 to 2,200 calories per day that included lots of starch, such as bread and pasta. Those taking the starch-blocker lost an average of seven pounds…those taking the placebo didn't lose weight.

Dose: A dose of 300 mg, taken right before each meal, with eight ounces of water. Look for a product with Phase 2 as the starch-blocker. It's the most widely studied starch-blocker.

HOW TO CHOOSE

With a health professional's guidance, choose one or two supplements that fit your weight-loss goals and lifestyle.

Example: A person eating a lot of carbohydrates might take a starch-blocker to cut absorption and chromium to balance blood sugar.

If after two months or so the selection doesn't seem to be working, stop taking those and try another one or two supplements.

Weight Gain May Be Controlled by a Vaccine Someday

Researchers are working on a vaccine that targets the appetite-control hormone *ghrelin*. Rats given the vaccine did not gain weight, even when they were allowed free access to food.

Kim D. Janda, PhD, professor of chemistry, Skaggs Institute for Chemical Biology, Scripps Research Institute, La Jolla, CA, and leader of the vaccine study, published in *Proceedings of the National Academy of Sciences*.

Eggs for Weight Loss

In a new study, overweight women ages 24 to 60 ate either eggs or a bagel-based breakfast of equal calories followed by a lunch of pasta with marinara sauce and sliced apples.

Result: The women who ate eggs at breakfast reported feeling more satisfied and consumed an average of 420 fewer calories than the bagel group over the next 28 hours.

Theory: High-protein foods, such as eggs, tend to induce feelings of fullness better than foods rich in simple sugars, carbohydrates and fats.

Caution: Eggs should be thoroughly cooked.

Jillon S. Vander Wal, PhD, assistant professor, department of psychology, St. Louis University, St. Louis, MO.

Fish Curbs Appetite

In one study of 23 men ages 20 to 32, those who ate fish (salmon) for lunch consumed 11% fewer calories at dinner than those who ate beef for lunch. The lunches contained the same number of calories and the same ratio of proteins, carbohydrates and fats.

Theory: Fish protein takes longer to digest than beef (or chicken) protein, so eating fish may help you feel full longer.

Stephan Rossner, PhD, obesity unit, Karolinska University Hospital, Stockholm, Sweden.

Sweetener Alert

Rebecca Shannonhouse, editor of *Bottom Line/Health*, Boardroom Inc., 281 Tresser Blvd., Stamford, CT 06901.

Splenda, which has been in use in the US for almost 10 years, is the nation's best-selling artificial sweetener, and it's one of the most controversial. Some consumer groups argue that Splenda was given an FDA approval without adequate studies for toxicity and that it may increase the risk for cancer.

Sucralose (the main ingredient in Splenda) is an amalgam of sugar molecules spliced together with chlorine—and chlorine can potentially damage cellular DNA. Yet there's no evidence—either from case reports or scientific studies—that sucralose poses any real increased risk for cancer.

"When you consider the number of people who are consuming Splenda, the fact that cancer hasn't appeared suggests that the risk, if any, would likely be very modest," explains David L. Katz, MD, director of the Yale Preventive Research Center in New Haven, Connecticut.

But there are other reasons to be concerned about—and to avoid—any artificial sweetener, Dr. Katz says. For example, some studies indicate that people who use an artificial sweetener (or products that contain them) consume even more—rather than fewer—calories.

Possible reason: Artificial sweeteners are 300 to 600 times sweeter than sugar. People who consume them can develop a higher "threshold for satisfaction"—and wind up consuming excess amounts of regular sugar-rich foods.

If you're trying to lose weight: Avoid artificial sweeteners and curtail your intake of regular sugar.

"Sugar-Free" vs. "No Added Sugar"

According to FDA regulations, the claim of "sugar-free" on a label means that one serving of the food contains only a small amount of sugar (less than 0.5 g). "No added sugars" or "no sugar added" means that no sugar and no ingredients containing sugar, such as jelly, honey or fruit juice concentrate, are added.

Suzanne Havala Hobbs, DrPH, RD, clinical assistant professor, School of Public Health, University of North Carolina, Chapel Hill.

The Amazing No Sweat Exercise Plan

Harvey B. Simon, MD, associate professor of medicine at Harvard Medical School and a founding member of the Harvard Cardiovascular Health Center, both in Boston. Dr. Simon is the author of various books on health and fitness, including *The No Sweat Exercise Plan* (McGraw-Hill).

During the past two decades, as "no pain, no gain" has reigned as a fitness mantra, most experts have told us that physical activity won't significantly improve our health unless we perform intense aerobic exercise.

Now, it turns out that this was only half the story. Intense exercise that makes you perspire does reduce your risk for heart disease, diabetes, some types of cancer and other serious illnesses. But, until recently, it was not clear that moderate and gentle exercise—everything from sex to yard work—also can help guard against serious illness.

RESEARCHERS IDENTIFY BENEFITS

A study published in the August 2000 *American Journal of Medicine* followed 110 healthy but sedentary men, ages 48 to 64. One group went about their normal routines without adding any exercise. The second group performed their normal routines but also played 18 holes of golf (and walked the course) two to three times a week. By the end of the 20-week study, the golfers lost weight, reduced their waist sizes and improved their cholesterol levels. The nongolfers experienced no changes.

Since then, more than 22 studies, involving about 320,000 individuals, have examined how moderate exercise affects cardiovascular health and longevity. The results are stunning. Moderate physical activity can decrease the risks for heart disease (by 18% to 84%)...stroke (by 21%

to 34%)…diabetes (by 16% to 50%)…colon malignancies (by 30% to 40%)…and dementia (by 15% to 50%).

How did the experts miss all these benefits? In assessing a fitness program's efficacy, most researchers have traditionally only measured the aerobic capacity—which is, how much oxygen your lungs can hold and how efficiently you use it. To improve that particular measure of fitness, known as "maximum volume of oxygen," or as VO_2 max, you do need to work out hard.

But when researchers began investigating measures of good health based on everyday activities, they found that even small doses of moderate exercise really do add up. Health benefits can be obtained by climbing 55 flights of stairs per week or even by gardening for one hour per week.

The point is to just get moving. In one study, healthy 20-year-old men were asked to spend three weeks in bed. The men developed many physiological characteristics of men twice their age. The same group of men then worked out regularly for eight weeks. They experienced an improvement in weight, resting heart rate, blood pressure and VO_2 max.

HOW TO MEASURE EXERTION

With all this evidence confirming the benefits of moderate exercise, I felt that a system was required to measure the exercise value of various everyday physical activities. That is why I created cardiometabolic exercise (CME) points, which assign values to physical activities based on the degree of exertion that's required to perform them.

You can significantly improve your health by accruing a total of 150 CME points every day (or about 1,000 CME points per week). Even if you're a couch potato, you can work up to the target level of about 1,000 points a week over the course of nine weeks. Gradually building up to your target level helps prevent injury.

Recommended: Carry a pocket-sized notebook to record your daily activities. Then tally up your CME points at the end of the day. (See the table on the next page for the CME points of selected activities.)

Important: If weight loss is your goal, you may need to work harder or longer, doubling the target number of CME points to approximately 2,000 per week.

Caution: Before starting a new exercise program, consult your doctor. If you have heart disease or are at risk (due to family history, high blood pressure, etc.), you should have a stress test. For this test, you will receive an electrocardiogram (ECG), a painless procedure that measures electrical impulses circulating through the heart, during exercise.

For healthy people, a simple 12-minute self-test devised by Kenneth H. Cooper, MD, a renowned fitness expert, can help to assess your fitness level.

What to do: See how far you can go by walking, jogging or running for 12 minutes. To measure the distance accurately, do this on a track or use a pedometer. If you are out of shape, do not push yourself too hard. Your fitness level is considered poor to fair if you cover less than ¾ of a mile…good if you can cover ¾ to one mile…very good for 1 to 1¼ miles…and excellent for more than 1¼ miles. Take your fitness rating into account when choosing activities.

CREATING A PROGRAM

For people who use everyday physical activity as the core of their exercise program, it is a good idea to add some strength exercises, such as weight training…some exercises for flexibility, such as yoga and stretching…and balance exercises, such as tai chi or even standing on one foot while brushing your teeth. Strength training improves muscle mass and bone density. Flexibility exercises help prevent injury and reduce stress. Balance exercises help protect you from falls.

Over the nine-week period, aim to work up to 15 to 20 minutes of strength training two to three times a week…flexibility exercises for 10 to 15 minutes three to four times a week…and balance exercises for five minutes three to four times a week.

Because walking is so convenient, it's an ideal exercise for most people to include in their regimen. The number of CME points for this activity depends on your body weight and speed, but typically a 160-pound man or woman can chalk up about 125 CME points for every 30 minutes.

Each hour of moderate exercise that you perform will extend your life by two hours, according to my analysis of the Harvard Alumni study. This goes to show that exercise may be the best antiaging medicine we have.

FITNESS POINTS FOR PHYSICAL ACTIVITIES

Cardiometabolic exercise (CME) points rate everyday and recreational activities according to the degree of physical exertion required to complete them. You can achieve significant health benefits by accruing a total of 150 points per day. Use the chart below to determine the CME points for various activities. The point values are based on a moderate level of exertion for 30 minutes, unless noted otherwise.

ACTIVITY	CME POINTS
Swimming	230
Aerobics	200
Jogging (12-minute mile)	200
Mowing lawn (pushing hand mower)	200
Tennis (singles)	200
Golfing (carrying clubs)	165
Ballroom dancing	150
Gardening	150
Mowing lawn (pushing power mower)	145
Raking leaves	130
Yoga	130
Vacuuming	115
Bowling	100
Walking up stairs (10 minutes)	100
Washing car by hand	100
Cooking	60
Washing dishes	60
Laundering or ironing (15 minutes)	35
Walking down stairs (10 minutes)	30
Sexual activity (15 minutes)	25

From *The No Sweat Exercise Plan* (McGraw-Hill).

Burn More Calories By Walking *Slower*

A new study has discovered that obese individuals who walked one mile at a leisurely pace burned more calories than if they walked a mile at their normal pace. In addition, those who walked at two miles per hour rather than three miles per hour reduced the load on their knee joints by up to 25%. The message is that by walking more slowly, obese individuals can burn more calories per mile and may reduce the risk of arthritis or joint injury.

Ray Browning, PhD, department of integrative physiology, University of Colorado at Boulder.

Running Backward

Running backward works the lungs more efficiently than running forward, burns more calories and lets bones absorb shock more effectively. Backward running also helps recovery from sprained ankles, pulled hamstrings and other types of leg and knee injuries, because it puts less impact on joints.

Best: Start slowly, until you build confidence.

Dean Karnazes, San Francisco–based ultra-marathoner and author of *Ultra-Marathon Man: Confessions of an All-Night Runner* (Tarcher).

Better Weight Control With Yoga

In a new finding, overweight men and women who practiced yoga regularly (at least once a week) for four or more years lost about five pounds between ages 45 and 55, while subjects who did not do yoga gained an average of 14 pounds during the same period.

Theory: Yoga usually does not burn enough calories to account for this weight loss, but it does increase body awareness and self-control—factors that can contribute to sensible eating.

Alan R. Kristal, DrPH, professor of epidemiology, University of Washington, Seattle.

A Vitamin That Helps You Burn More Fat

In a recent study, people who took 500 mg of vitamin C daily burned 39% more fat while exercising than people who took less. Since it is difficult to get enough vitamin C just from fruits and vegetables, take a vitamin C supplement to be sure you get at least 500 mg per day.

Carol Johnston, PhD, RD, professor and chair, department of nutrition, Arizona State University, Mesa, and the leader of a study published in the *Journal of the American College of Nutrition*.

What Not to Drink Before a Workout

Drinking coffee prior to exercise could prove dangerous.

New finding: The equivalent of two cups of coffee 50 minutes before exercise reduces by 22% the body's ability to boost blood flow to heart muscles.

Theory: Caffeine blocks the release of adenosine, a compound produced during exercise that opens the arteries.

This finding is especially important if you have coronary artery disease or other conditions that reduce blood flow to the heart.

Philipp Kaufmann, MD, professor of nuclear medicine and cardiology, University Hospital, Zurich, Switzerland.

Best Time to Exercise

Exercise in the late afternoon to achieve the best results.

New finding: Lung performance, which is governed by circadian (24-hour) rhythms, drops in the early morning and again at about noon. In the late afternoon (4 pm to 5 pm), lung function is about 15% to 20% more effective than at noontime.

Important: Although your lungs may function most effectively in the late afternoon, it is still advisable to exercise whenever you can fit it in.

Rubin Cohen, MD, codirector of the Asthma Center at Long Island Jewish Medical Center, New Hyde Park, NY.

The Latest on Cellulite Removal

Clinical experiments have found that anticellulite formulations are no more successful than placebos at reducing cellulite, those fatty dimples that make skin on the hips and thighs appear lumpy.

The only treatment that has been proven to temporarily reduce cellulite is *endermologie*—a somewhat painful procedure in which a suction device squeezes and kneads skin that's affected between two rollers. A course of 15 to 20 treatments over several months produces a temporary visible reduction in cellulite. Monthly sessions are required to maintain results. Each treatment costs $50 to $70.*

Some physicians are testing a new procedure called *thermage*, which attempts to eliminate cellulite by the application of heat.

Barney J. Kenet, MD, assistant attending dermatologist, Weill Medical College of Cornell University in New York City.

*Prices subject to change.

5

Natural Health

Add Healthy Years to Your Life: Seven Steps That Really Work

We are constantly hearing of new antiaging treatments, including products intended to promote a longer life. Yet despite heavy advertising and high prices, there's no scientific evidence that the treatments such as human growth hormone and testosterone injections will increase your life span by so much as a day.

There are, however, proven ways to lengthen our lives...or at least lengthen our "quality life span," when we can still walk without assistance, take care of ourselves and enjoy the activities that make life worth living. *Here are seven things you can do that really make a difference...*

• **Cardiovascular exercise.** Most people do know exercise is good for you, but it's worth repeating here because it's the single best way

to improve health. People who exercise 30 to 60 minutes per day can add five to 10 years to their quality life span. Exercise measurably reduces the risk of heart disease, stroke, obesity, diabetes, insomnia, depression and certain cancers.

Exercise need not be too strenuous. Walking briskly is sufficient.

Important: Do not exceed 60 minutes of strenuous exercise per day. After an hour, the damage your body absorbs from the prolonged strain outweighs the health benefits. Moderate exercise for more than 60 minutes is okay—for example, walking longer than an hour will not cause harmful effects.

• **Lifting weights** for just five minutes each day will strengthen your bones and the surrounding muscles, making broken bones less likely. For seniors, broken bones can mean shorter lives

---

Edward L. Schneider, MD, professor of gerontology and medicine at University of Southern California in Los Angeles, and former deputy director of the National Institutes of Health's Institute on Aging. He is author of *What Your Doctor Hasn't Told You and the Health Store Clerk Doesn't Know: The Truth About Alternative Treatments and What Works* (Avery).

—one of every four people who suffers a hip fracture after age 65 will die within 12 months. Building stronger muscles and bones also will keep you active and independent longer, so you can better enjoy the years you have.

Ask a physical therapist or personal trainer to develop a low-impact weight-lifting regimen to tone the muscles of your arms, shoulders, abdomen, back and legs for a few minutes each day. Do not use the heaviest weights you can pick up—choose weights you can lift 20 to 30 times in a row. Increase the weight only when this becomes easy.

●**A Mediterranean-style diet.** Heart disease and cancer are two of the most imposing obstacles standing in the way of long life. The vitamins, antioxidants and monounsaturated fats found in the Mediterranean-style diet have been found to reduce these risks. The diet incorporates lots of fruits, vegetables, whole grains, legumes, garlic, nuts, tomato sauce, berries and fish. You can also consume one or two alcoholic drinks a day but no more—women do have an increased risk of breast cancer if they have more than one drink a day. Multivitamins are not a suitable substitute for a healthful diet.

Minimize consumption of meat, saturated fats and fatty dairy products—these all help increase heart disease risk.

Important: Not all fat is bad. Olive oil is full of monounsaturated fats, which are wonderful for the heart. The residents of the Greek island of Crete consume more olive oil per capita than any other area in Europe. They have the lowest rate of heart disease and are 20% less likely to die of coronary artery disease than Americans.

●**Sufficient sleep.** Your immune system is best able to fight off infection when it's armed with a good night's sleep. Sleep also keeps your mind sharp, reducing the odds that you'll die in an accident. Sleepy drivers are responsible for just as many fatal car crashes as drunk drivers.

How much sleep is enough? The answer is different for everyone. Some people require as little as five hours a night, others need as much as nine. If you're groggy during the day, try to add 15 minutes of sleep each night until you no longer feel sleepy during the day.

Don't use an over-the-counter sleep remedy even if you have chronic insomnia. These often have large doses of antihistamines which might make you groggy well into the following day. Instead, get more exercise…consume less caffeine…purchase a very comfortable mattress and quality pillow…lightproof and soundproof your bedroom…and remove distractions, such as the TV and books, from the bedroom, so your mind associates the room with only sleep and sex.

Supplements such as valerian and melatonin work for some people but not for most people. Prescription sleeping pills should be used only to break cycles of insomnia. Try to avoid taking a nap during the day—this can wreak havoc with your internal clock.

●**A shared life.** A good marriage and enjoyable social life truly do help you live longer. A 48-year-old man has a 65% chance of living to age 65 if unmarried, 90% if married. For a 48-year-old woman, marriage increases the odds of reaching 65 from 80% to 90%.

Friendships, too, contribute to living longer, making us feel better about ourselves and improving our lives.

●**Fish oil (omega-3 fatty acids).** Fish oil pills are one of the few dietary supplements that actually can lengthen life. Research has confirmed that fish oil promotes heart and brain health.

Eat one to two servings of fatty fish, such as mackerel, herring or salmon, every week…or take a daily 1 gram (g) fish oil pill that contains equal amounts of *eicosapentaenoic acid* (EPA) and *docosahexaenoic acid* (DHA).

Caution: High intake of fish oil may cause excessive bleeding in some people.

Some people are worried about toxins, such as mercury, in certain fish, including tuna. For most people, the benefits of eating one or two servings of fish a week outweigh potential risks. However, pregnant women, women who may become pregnant, nursing mothers and young children may want to avoid certain fish—talk with your doctor.

●**Sunlight and vitamin D.** Studies suggest that vitamin D can help prevent breast, prostate and colon cancers, as well as arthritis. It also promotes the absorption of calcium, which is necessary for bone strength. Sunlight is the usual source of vitamin D. Spend three to five minutes in direct sunlight without sunscreen two to three times per week. (Put on sunscreen if you intend to stay in the sun longer, particularly if you're fair-skinned.)

If you live in the northern third of the US, it's impossible to get enough vitamin D from the sun between late November and the end of March, even if you spend all day outside. Multivitamins tend not to provide sufficient vitamin D, either. Take 1,000 international units (IU) per day of a vitamin D supplement during the winter.

A daily dose of sunlight also helps fight insomnia and depression, either of which could lead to a shorter life. However, vitamin D pills will not help here—you still need your three to five minutes of sun (winter sun is fine).

Erase Years from Your Age in Just 30 Minutes a Day

Michael F. Roizen, MD, chair of the division of anesthesiology, critical care management and comprehensive pain management at the Cleveland Clinic, OH. He created the RealAge concept and wrote the best-selling *RealAge: Are You As Young As You Can Be?* (Collins). He is author, with Tracy Hafen and Lawrence A. Armour, of *The RealAge Workout: Maximum Health, Minimum Work* (Collins). His Web site is *www.realage.com.*

Walking is the single best thing you can do for your health. I view it as the fountain of youth.

In my first RealAge book, I showed how aging has little to do with calendar years. A 50-year-old man could have the arteries and immune system of a 75-year-old. Someone else might be 75 but have a RealAge—measured by the risk of disease, disability or death—of a 52-year-old. Exercise is a key factor in reducing your Real-Age—and just 30 minutes of walking each day can make you healthier, more energetic and, in a real sense, younger.

HEALTH BENEFITS

Walking is easy to do, does not require any special equipment (except walking shoes) and conveys many of the same health benefits as more strenuous exercise.

Walking helps prevent fatty buildup in the arteries. When your arteries are clogged with fatty buildup, your cardiovascular system ages more quickly, and so does your whole body. Aging of the arteries brings on cardiovascular disease, the major cause of heart attacks and strokes. It also leads to loss of energy, memory loss and, in men, impotence. Walking can help keep arteries young and healthy.

Walking every day also decreases the risk of such conditions as macular degeneration (the leading cause of blindness in people over age 50) and arthritis. The long-running Framingham Heart Study found that people with arthritis who walked daily for 30 minutes and supplemented their diets with vitamins C and D and calcium were able to stop the progression of joint damage. Walking also prevented osteoarthritis in patients who didn't already have it.

Walking can even reduce the risk for some forms of cancer by as much as 50%.

GET READY

Studies show that people who walk as little as 10 minutes a day—or even just once a week—on a regular basis have less risk of dying prematurely than those who are sedentary. For optimal health gains, you should walk for at least 30 minutes daily. People who take three 10-minute walks each day have about the same health gains as those who walk for 30 minutes straight. *Helpful advice...*

•**Warm up before you walk.** Walk more slowly than usual for the first several minutes. This warm-up heats the muscles and makes them more flexible and efficient and less prone to injury. It also increases circulation in the joints.

•**Wear a watch.** Measure time rather than distance. Time is simple to count, and you can walk for 30 minutes at a comfortable pace. You don't need to follow a track or a premeasured route—and you won't try to force yourself to go a certain distance.

•**Don't miss a day.** Make 30 minutes a day of walking a priority. Things like yard work and housecleaning help, too, but they can't take the place of your daily walks.

Malls are terrific places to walk if the weather is bad, and most YMCAs have walking tracks and treadmills. If your budget permits it, buy a treadmill so you can walk any time of the day or night without leaving home.

POSTWALKING STRETCH

Once your routine has become ingrained, set aside two to three minutes to stretch after you're done walking. Stretching improves joint range of motion. Without a normal range of motion in the joints, daily activities become more difficult and the risk of musculoskeletal injury increases. Some people find that stretching also reduces soreness, though I can't find hard evidence to support that claim.

To perform any stretch, move slowly into the stretch position until you feel a gentle pulling sensation, not pain. Hold the stretch for 10 to 30 seconds *without bouncing*. Repeat each stretch two or three times.

The Fountain of Youth?

Two studies involving mice have shown that *resveratrol*, a component of red wine, can dramatically increase endurance when given in high doses...and can prolong life by offsetting the negative effects of a high-fat diet when given in moderate doses.

Caution: Resveratrol is available in health-food stores but it has not yet been studied in humans—neither the optimal dosage nor side effects have been determined.

Johan Auwerx, MD, PhD, team leader, department of physiological genetics of nuclear signaling, Institute of Genetics and Molecular and Cellular Biology, Illkirch Cedex, France.

Do More Chores and Live Longer

Older adults who regularly did vacuuming, gardening and various everyday activities burned about 600 calories more a day than sedentary adults in similar health—and were 70% less likely to die over the six-year period of a recent study.

Bottom line: At any age, more activity is better for health.

Consumer Reports on Health, 101 Truman Ave., Yonkers, New York 10703.

How Music Can Improve Your Health

Suzanne B. Hanser, EdD, chair of the music therapy department at Berklee College of Music in Boston and past president of the American Music Therapy Association and the World Federation of Music Therapy. She is a research associate at the Dana-Farber Cancer Institute, an affiliate of Harvard Medical School, also in Boston, where she investigates medical applications of music therapy.

Everyone knows the soothing effect of listening to a favorite piece of music. But until recently, there was little scientific evidence to support its effectiveness in helping to combat specific health problems.

Now: A growing body of research has found that music can affect key areas of the brain that help to regulate specific physiological functions necessary for good health. The best choice of music and the time spent listening depends on an individual's needs and preferences. *Medical conditions that can be improved by music...*

HIGH BLOOD PRESSURE

The *hypothalamus* helps control the autonomic nervous system, which regulates our breathing, heartbeat and other automatic responses in the body. It also is linked to emotional activity.

How music helps: When a person listens to music that stimulates positive memories and/or images, the activity of the hypothalamus helps slow a person's heart and respiration rates as well as blood pressure.

Scientific evidence: In a study published in the *British Journal of Health Psychology*, 75 adults performed a stressful three-minute math problem. Afterward, subjects were randomly assigned to sit in silence or listen to classical, jazz or popular music. Subjects who heard classical selections had significantly lower systolic (top number) blood pressure levels. Blood pressure did not significantly improve in people who listened to the other selections.

What to do: Observe how you respond to the different types of music. Match your state of mind to the tempo and dynamics.

Example: When you are agitated, listen to something with a strong, fast beat, then gradually switch to slower and softer music. This can reduce stress and lower blood pressure.

INSOMNIA

Although healthy adults typically fall asleep within 30 minutes, adults age 50 and older will often have more trouble falling—and staying—asleep.

How music helps: Soft, peaceful music can act as a sedative by reducing the amount of the stress-related neurotransmitter *noradrenaline* circulating in the bloodstream.

Scientific evidence: Sixty people ages 60 to 83 who reported sleep difficulties took part in a study at Tzu-Chi General Hospital in Taiwan. After just three weeks, researchers found a 35% improvement in sleep quality, length of sleep, daytime dysfunction and sleep disturbances in the subjects who listened to slow, soft music at night. The most effective types of music used in the study were piano versions of popular "oldies," New Age, harp, classical and slow jazz.

What to do: Make sure your bedroom temperature is comfortable, then lie in bed at your usual bedtime, with the lights out (light interferes with the production of the sleep hormone *melatonin*) and your eyes closed while listening to music. Experiment with different varieties of music until you discover what's relaxing for you. (Earphones are optional.) If you wake during the night, try listening to music again.

PAIN

Listening to music does not eliminate pain, but it can help distract your brain by creating a secondary stimulus that diverts your attention from the feeling of discomfort.

Scientific evidence: In a recent study published in *The Journal of Advanced Nursing*, patients experiencing chronic noncancerous back, neck or joint pain who listened to music for one hour a day for seven days reported a 20% decrease in pain, versus a 2% decrease in pain for patients given standard pain treatment. Music is not a substitute for standard treatment, but it may be used along with painkillers to maximize pain relief.

What to do: For pain reduction, it's important to identify the music that engages you—that is, it should elicit memories and/or make you want to tap your foot, sway or even dance. Singing, which requires deep breathing, or using a simple percussion instrument which does not require playing specific notes, also helps.

Make Time to Nap

William A. Anthony, PhD, director of Boston University's Center for Psychiatric Rehabilitation, and the author of *The Art of Napping* (Larson).

Winston Churchill, Leonardo da Vinci, Johannes Brahms and John F. Kennedy practiced a powerful secret to good health. Each was a napper.

Now: Marines serving in Iraq take naps to make them more alert during patrols.

According to the National Sleep Foundation, about 62% of Americans get sleepy in the afternoon at least three days a week—but our fast-paced culture discourages the habit of napping. That may be a mistake.

Our natural sleep pattern includes a significant drop in body temperature and alertness at night, as well as a similar (if less dramatic) drop at midday.

Recent research suggests that those who take 10- to 20-minute naps score better on cognitive tests. These people also have more energy, are involved in fewer accidents and, generally, are healthier—napping is believed to reduce stress, pulse rate and hypertension, improvements that promote cardiovascular health.

Naps are not a substitute for sleeping well at night. If you feel tired when you awaken in the morning, see your doctor for advice. And don't nap for too long—30 minutes or more makes people groggy when they wake up.

Best: A daily *power nap* lasting 15 or 20 minutes. That's just long enough to satisfy the body's need for rest, without interfering with nighttime sleep. Enjoy!

The Healing Power of Spices

David Winston, a Washington, NJ, registered herbalist (RH) and a founding member of the American Herbalist Guild, the only peer-reviewed organization of herbalists in the US. He is a coauthor of *Herbal Therapy and Supplements* (Lippincott).

Traditional medicine has recognized the medicinal properties of spices for thousands of years.

Now: A growing body of scientific evidence supports the use of spices to prevent—and even help treat—various diseases, such as arthritis, diabetes, cancer and Alzheimer's.*

New findings...

CAYENNE PEPPER

What it does: Lowers cholesterol...helps to prevent atherosclerosis...and decreases allergic responses. An extract from the pepper, called capsaicin, can be used in a topical cream to treat pain from arthritis, shingles, bursitis, low-back ache and neuropathy (or nerve pain). Cayenne's benefits can be attributed to all the antioxidants, flavonoids and carotenoids that it contains, all of which have anti-inflammatory effects and enhance circulation. Capsaicin depletes the nerve endings of *substance P*, a neurotransmitter that facilitates nerve transmission of pain.

Scientific evidence: One four-week study published in the *Journal of Rheumatology* found that individuals with osteoarthritis of the hands who applied capsaicin cream four times a day experienced reduced pain and tenderness.

Typical dose: Cayenne can be bought as a supplement in capsules and tincture. Take one capsule of cayenne pepper up to three times a day...or place three to eight drops of cayenne tincture in four ounces of water and drink two to four times a day. Apply a topical cream containing capsaicin to painful areas, as directed on the label. You also can season your food with powdered cayenne pepper or hot sauce.

Possible side effects: Cayenne pepper can cause gastric upset. To avoid pain and burning,

*Check with your doctor before using spices for medicinal purposes, as they can interact with prescription medication.

do not let topical capsaicin come in contact with your eyes or other mucous membranes. If you take *warfarin* (Coumadin), do not use cayenne pepper supplements.

CINNAMON

What it does: Helps prevent heart disease and type 2 diabetes.

Due to its antioxidant properties, cinnamon helps people with metabolic syndrome (a cluster of factors, including excessive abdominal fat, high blood sugar and elevated blood pressure, which increase the risk for cardiovascular disease and type 2 diabetes) use the hormone insulin in their bodies more efficiently.

Scientific evidence: A 2003 US Department of Agriculture clinical study found that consuming capsules containing 1 gram (g), 3g or 6g of cinnamon daily (about ¼ teaspoon, ¾ teaspoon or 1¼ teaspoons, respectively) for 40 days lowered blood levels of glucose and triglycerides (fats in the blood) by about 25% in adults with type 2 diabetes. It also reduced LDL "bad" cholesterol by up to 27%.

Typical dose: Use one-half to one teaspoon of powdered cinnamon daily on cereal or toast or mix into yogurt...take one capsule twice a day...or add 20 to 40 drops of tincture to one ounce of water and drink three times daily.

For tea, mix one-fourth to one-half teaspoon of powdered cinnamon with eight ounces of boiling water. Steep for 10 to 15 minutes, covered. Drink a four-ounce cup up to three times a day.

Possible side effects: Because cinnamon can affect blood glucose amounts, people with diabetes should carefully monitor their blood sugar and ask their doctors if their medication needs to be adjusted.

GINGER

What it does: Reduces the pain and swelling caused by rheumatoid arthritis and osteoarthritis ...helps to prevent the nausea and vomiting associated with motion sickness or pregnancy... enhances digestion and circulation...and eases intestinal gas.

Scientific evidence: In two clinical studies ginger relieved pain and/or swelling in 75% of arthritis patients.

Typical dose: Take one to two capsules with meals two to three times daily…or add 10 to 30 drops of the tincture to one ounce of water and drink three to four times daily.

For tea, mix one-fourth to one-half teaspoon of powdered ginger (or use a ginger tea bag) with eight ounces of boiling water. Steep for 10 to 15 minutes, covered. Drink four ounces up to three times daily.

Possible side effects: Ginger can cause a blood-thinning effect, so check with your doctor before using it if you take an anticoagulant, such as *warfarin* (Coumadin). Ginger may cause an upset stomach in people who take larger doses than those described above.

TURMERIC

What it does: Helps prevent atherosclerosis, some types of cancer and Alzheimer's disease… decreases the pain and stiffness of rheumatoid arthritis and osteoarthritis…can eliminate indigestion…and eases the symptoms of inflammatory bowel disease and of irritable bowel syndrome. The beneficial effects of turmeric (also present in curry) are due to its anti-inflammatory compounds known as *curcuminoids*, as well as the essential oils and carotenoids it contains.

Scientific evidence: In a double-blind, placebo-controlled study, 116 people with indigestion took either a 500-milligram (mg) capsule of curcumin (the substance that gives turmeric its yellow color) or a placebo four times a day. Nearly 90% of those taking curcumin experienced full or partial relief after seven days.

Typical dose: Take 250 mg to 500 mg of curcumin (standardized to 80% to 90% curcumin) three times daily…or add 40 to 60 drops of the tincture to one ounce of water and drink three to four times daily.

For tea, mix one-half teaspoon of powdered turmeric with eight ounces of boiling water and steep for 10 to 15 minutes, covered. Drink four ounces up to four times a day.

Possible side effects: Turmeric can stimulate liver function, so it should be avoided by anyone with gallstones or any other bile-duct obstruction. Preliminary studies show that curcumin may lessen the effectiveness of chemotherapy drugs, such as *doxorubicin* (Rubex) and *cyclophosphamide* (Cytoxan). If you are undergoing chemotherapy, talk to your doctor before taking curcumin.

Spice Cure for Cancer?

A powdered form of ginger kills ovarian cancer cells, according to new laboratory research. Ginger may be unique because it causes cells to die in two distinctly different ways. This discovery could aid in the development of therapies for treatment-resistant cancers.

University of Michigan Health System, Ann Arbor, *www. med.umich.edu.*

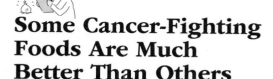

Some Cancer-Fighting Foods Are Much Better Than Others

Karen Collins, RD, a registered dietitian and nutrition adviser to the American Institute for Cancer Research (AICR) in Washington, DC. She is the author of *Planning Meals That Lower Cancer Risk* (AICR), available at college libraries, and weekly columns syndicated to more than 700 newspapers nationwide. She also maintains a private practice in Washington, DC.

Only about 10% of all cancers are due to genetics. The remaining 90% of malignancies are related to diet, weight and exercise…smoking…and/or environmental factors.

Even though most people do realize that diet can affect cancer risk, few regularly consume a variety of the foods that contain large amounts of *phytochemicals*, substances that actually can inhibit the cellular damage that leads to cancer.

Eating a combination of cancer-fighting foods is the best approach because no single food supplies all the available protective substances—vitamins, minerals, phytochemicals and fiber.

BLACK BEANS

Beans (legumes) have high levels of a cancer-fighting compound called *phytic acid*. They're also rich in fiber and *saponins*, chemical compounds that reduce the ability of cancer cells to proliferate.

The landmark Nurses' Health study found that women consuming four or more servings of legumes per week were 33% less likely to develop colon polyps than those who consumed one or fewer weekly servings. In people already diagnosed with colon polyps, those who ate more beans reduced their risk for a recurrence by 45%, compared with those who ate fewer beans.

Bonus: Beans are very high in protein. They're a good substitute for people who want to reduce their consumption of red meat—a major source of saturated fat, which can increase cancer risk.

Other cancer-fighting legumes: Small red beans, red kidney beans, pinto beans and garbanzo beans.

Helpful: If you don't want to spend the time cooking dried beans, you can get many of the same benefits by eating canned. To reduce the sodium in canned beans, empty them into a colander and rinse thoroughly with cold water.

Recommended: Eat one-half cup of beans at least four times weekly.

BLUEBERRIES

Berries are rich sources of vitamin C and other antioxidants. People who regularly eat berries have decreased risk for malignancies of the colon, bladder, esophagus and prostate. Berries also may lower the risk for lymphoma and premenopausal breast cancer.

Blueberries are an excellent choice for cancer prevention because they are among the richest sources of *antioxidants*, compounds that protect cells from free radicals that can damage cell DNA—the first step in cancer development.

Much of this nutritional power comes from *anthocyanidins*, a type of antioxidant that reduces the ability of carcinogens to damage DNA.

Bonus: Because berries are both filling and low in calories, they can be substituted for other sweet snacks to promote weight loss—which further reduces the risk for many cancers.

Other cancer-fighting berries: Blackberries, strawberries, raspberries and cranberries.

Helpful: Keep frozen berries in the freezer. They can be kept almost indefinitely without spoiling and provide virtually the same nutritional benefits as fresh berries.

Recommended: Aim for at least one half-cup serving of berries per week.

BROCCOLI

Broccoli is a cruciferous vegetable that is rich in *isothiocyanates*, a family of phytochemicals

linked to a reduced risk for colon, prostate, lung and premenopausal breast cancer. One of these phytochemicals, *sulforaphane*, reduces the ability of carcinogens to cause damage in cells, and may increase the tendency of cancer cells to self-destruct, a process called *apoptosis*.

A study published in the *Journal of the National Cancer Institute* indicates that men who consumed three or more servings per week of broccoli (raw or cooked) were 41% less likely to get prostate cancer than those who consumed less than one weekly serving.

Other cancer-fighting cruciferous vegetables: Cauliflower, brussels sprouts, cabbage and kale.

Helpful: If you don't like the strong taste (and smell) of cooked broccoli and other cruciferous vegetables, eat them raw or lightly sauté them in olive oil or canola oil for three to four minutes.

You also can microwave or steam them. (Long cooking, such as boiling for 15 minutes or more, causes the release of strong-smelling/tasting sulfur compounds.)

Recommended: Aim for three to five half-cup servings per week of cruciferous vegetables.

GARLIC

Garlic is an allium, which is a family of plants that contain *allyl sulfides*, phytochemicals not found in any other foods.

The Iowa Women's Health Study found that people with the highest intake of garlic (at least one serving per week) had a 32% lower risk of developing colon cancer than those who never ate garlic. Garlic has also been linked to a lower risk for prostate, lung, breast and skin cancers.

Bonus: Garlic can be utilized as a flavor enhancer to make healthful nutrition—vegetables, legumes, whole grains, etc.—more enjoyable… and it reduces the need for unhealthful flavorings, such as salt and butter.

Other cancer-fighting alliums: Onions (all types), leeks and chives.

Helpful: To decrease the intense taste, use cooked garlic (by sautéing or roasting it, for example) rather than raw. The flavors mellow with long cooking. Wait 10 to 15 minutes after chopping garlic before cooking, to allow the active form of the protective phytochemicals to form. The cancer-fighting properties of jarred garlic are unknown.

Recommended: Strive to eat one to three cloves of garlic per week.

WALNUTS

Walnuts provide fiber and are rich in omega-3 fatty acids, the same healthful, anti-inflammatory fats that are found in fish. Reducing inflammation in the body helps prevent cell damage that can lead to cancer.

Other cancer-fighting nuts: Almonds and hazelnuts.

Helpful: Buy packaged or bulk shelled, unsalted nuts (raw and roasted). Substituting nuts for other snacks will improve the body's ratio of omega-3 to omega-6 fatty acids—important for lowering inflammation and cancer risk.

Recommended: Eat three to five one-third-cup servings weekly.

WHOLE-GRAIN BREAD

Whole-grain bread is high in fiber. As fiber and certain starches resistant to digestion are fermented in the colon, substances are produced that block the cancer-promoting effects of bile acids. In addition, the whole grains are higher in antioxidant vitamins (including vitamin E) and phytochemicals called *phenols*, than are refined grains.

When scientists analyzed and combined the results from 40 different studies, they found that people who ate the most whole-grain bread and/or other whole grains had a 34% lower risk for cancer overall than those who consumed less.

Other whole grains that fight off cancer: Whole-wheat pasta, whole-grain breakfast cereal, brown rice, bulgur, kasha and quinoa.

Helpful: When shopping for a whole-grain bread or cereal, don't be misled by terms like multigrain, which merely means that more than one type of grain is included...and don't judge by brown color, which can result from added caramel coloring. Review the ingredients list to make sure a whole grain is listed first, such as whole wheat or whole rye. "Flour" or "wheat flour" means that the product contains refined flour made from wheat—not whole-grain flour.

Recommended: Strive for three daily servings—one-half cup of whole grains or a slice of whole-grain bread counts as one serving.

Potent Anticancer Agent: Vitamin D

Vitamin D can drive down the mortality rates from 16 types of cancer, including breast and ovarian, by up to 70%. As a possible cancer preventive, be sure to get at least 1,000 IU of vitamin D-3 (cholecalciferol—not D-2, ergocalciferol, which is less effective) in summer and 2,000 IU in winter. For most people, it is best to take 1,500 IU daily in supplement form.

William B. Grant, PhD, founding director, Sunlight, Nutrition and Health Research Center, *www.sunarc.org.*

Niacin, Naturally

Good cholesterol goes up substantially when patients having problems with cholesterol take high doses of the B vitamin niacin. When taken in its therapeutic form—*nicotinic acid*, in a dose of about 2,000 mg a day—niacin can increase HDL ("good" cholesterol) by as much as 35% and also lower LDL ("bad" cholesterol).

Caution: High niacin doses should be taken only under a doctor's supervision.

Steven Nissen, MD, chairman, department of cardiovascular medicine, Cleveland Clinic, OH, and past president, American College of Cardiology, Washington, DC.

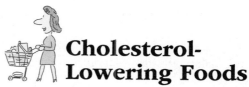

Cholesterol-Lowering Foods

In a new finding, 30% of 66 people who adhered to a diet rich in soy protein, oats, barley, margarine with plant sterols, and almonds for one year lowered their LDL "bad" cholesterol by more than 20%—the same drop seen in those who took a cholesterol-lowering statin for one month.

Reason: Soy protein reduces cholesterol production by the liver...fiber in oats and barley washes out metabolized cholesterol...plant sterols block its absorption...and almonds do all of the above.

This food combination is especially well suited for people with slightly elevated cholesterol levels.

David Jenkins, MD, PhD, professor, departments of medicine and nutritional sciences, University of Toronto, Canada.

Nuts and Seeds for Lower Cholesterol

Nuts and seeds contain cholesterol-lowering compounds.

New finding: In a study of 27 popular nuts and seeds, the levels of *phytosterols* (plant chemicals shown to lower cholesterol) were highest in wheat germ, sesame seeds, pistachios and sunflower seeds.

Helpful: Add wheat germ to cereal or yogurt...eat tahini (ground sesame seeds), an ingredient in hummus...or snack on a handful of unsalted sunflower seeds or pistachios.

Katherine M. Phillips, PhD, research scientist, department of biochemistry, Virginia Polytechnic Institute and State University, Blacksburg.

 # More Nuts

Pecans and walnuts are high in a form of vitamin E called *gamma tocopherol*...almonds are high in *alpha tocopherol*. These powerful antioxidants help reduce the risk of hardening of the arteries and heart disease. They also lower total and LDL (bad) cholesterol and raise HDL (good) cholesterol.

Best: Eat a moderate-sized handful of nuts every day.

Ella Haddad, DrPH, associate professor, department of nutrition, School of Public Health, Loma Linda University, Loma Linda, CA, and leader of a study published in Nutrition Research.

Live Longer by Meditating

Transcendental meditation (TM), a technique that produces a state of "restful alertness," has been shown to reduce stress levels and lower blood pressure.

New finding: People with hypertension (average age 72) who regularly practiced TM for 20 minutes twice daily were 30% less likely to die from heart disease over an 18-year period than those who did not practice TM.

Theory: TM lowers levels of adrenaline and cortisol, stress-related hormones, in the body.

Helpful: Practice TM for 20 minutes twice daily.

Robert H. Schneider, MD, director, Institute for Natural Medicine and Prevention, Maharashi University of Management, Maharashi Vedic City, IA.

A Little-Known Cholesterol Indicator

Pain felt in the Achilles tendon could indicate cholesterol problems. People with hereditary high cholesterol are seven times more likely to report Achilles tendon pain lasting three days or more than people without the condition.

Self-defense: If Achilles tendon pain persists, have your cholesterol tested.

Paul N. Durrington, PhD, professor, University of Manchester Division of Cardiovascular and Endocrine Science, Manchester, England.

Cherries Fight Inflammation

In a recent study, 18 healthy men and women ate 280 g of bing sweet cherries (about 50 fresh cherries) daily for 28 days. Researchers measured the levels of *C-reactive protein* (CRP), a marker of inflammation associated with diabetes and cardiovascular disease, in participants' blood during the study and for one month afterward.

Result: After one month, CRP levels dropped by 25% on average.

Theory: Cherries are rich in polyphenols that have strong antioxidant and anti-inflammatory properties.

Darshan S. Kelley, PhD, research chemist, Western Human Nutrition Research Center, US Department of Agriculture, Davis, CA.

Tomato Extract for The Heart

In a study of 54 adults with moderately high blood pressure (above 135/80), a dietary supplement derived from tomatoes reduced average systolic (top number) readings by 12 and diastolic (bottom number) readings by 6 after two to four weeks. The 250-mg capsule given daily was equivalent to eating four medium tomatoes.

Theory: Higher levels of lycopene and vitamins C and E improve function of the arterial wall, which can lower blood pressure.

Esther Paran, MD, head, hypertension unit at Soroka University Hospital, Ben-Gurion University of the Negev in Israel.

Grape Seed Extract Lowers Blood Pressure

In one recent study, 24 patients with metabolic syndrome (a cluster of heart disease risk factors, including high blood pressure, excess abdominal weight and elevated blood sugar) took a 150-mg or 300-mg capsule of grape seed extract or a placebo daily for one month.

Result: Those who took either dose of the extract experienced an average drop in systolic pressure (top number) of 12 and 8 in diastolic pressure (bottom number).

Theory: Grape seed extract boosts the production of nitric oxide, a heart-protective enzyme.

If you have prehypertension (120 to 139 systolic and 80 to 89 diastolic), ask your doctor if you should try grape seed extract.

C. Tissa Kappagoda, MD, PhD, professor of cardiovascular medicine, University of California, Davis.

Too Much Alone Time

In a recent finding, lonely people over age 50 had blood pressure readings 30 points higher than similar people who weren't lonely. This underscores the benefits of relationships with family members and friends.

Best: Maintain social connections with loved ones, and do volunteer work to stay active and involved with others.

Louise Hawkley, PhD, Chicago Center for Cognitive and Social Neuroscience, and department of psychology, University of Chicago. She is the leader of a study of 229 people, published in *Psychology and Aging*.

Best Time to Exercise to Lower Your Triglycerides

Exercise helps control triglyceride levels. Eating high-fat foods, such as whipped cream and chocolate, makes triglyceride levels spike, increasing heart disease risk.

Recent study: Triglyceride levels of all participants who ate high-fat foods rose, but the levels of people who exercised for 90 minutes before eating were 25% lower than the levels of nonexercisers.

Jason M.R. Gill, PhD, researcher, department of vascular biochemistry, University of Glasgow, Glasgow Royal Infirmary, Scotland, and leader of a triglycerides study cited in the *Journal of the American College of Cardiology*.

Nap for Heart Health

To reduce risk of death from coronary heart disease, take a midday nap.

Study: People who napped for about a half hour at least three times a week had a 37% lower risk of dying from heart attacks or other heart problems than those who did not nap. Individuals who took naps of any duration had a 34% lower risk of dying from heart disease.

Dimitrios Trichopoulos, MD, PhD, professor, department of epidemiology, Harvard School of Public Health, Boston.

Foods That May Lessen Stroke Severity

Blueberries, spinach and spirulina, a type of green algae, have high levels of antioxidants that help neutralize damaging free radicals.

Recent study: Rats that were given diets enriched with these foods for one month prior to inducing a stroke had only half as much brain damage as rats that were not fed these foods. This study suggests that including these foods—one cup of blueberries, a big spinach salad or a few teaspoons of spirulina powder—in your daily diet may lessen the severity of a stroke.

Paula C. Bickford, PhD, professor of neurosurgery at University of South Florida and James A. Haley VA Hospital, both in Tampa, and leader of the study published in *Experimental Neurology.*

The Hidden Epidemic: How to Beat Prediabetes

Sandra Woodruff, RD, a Tallahassee, FL–based licensed dietitian/nutritionist and the author of numerous books on healthful eating. She is also coauthor, with Christopher D. Saudek, MD, of *The Complete Diabetes Prevention Plan* (Avery). Her Web site is *www.eatsmarttoday.com.*

Underlying the current epidemic of type 2 diabetes is a larger epidemic—prediabetes, meaning blood sugar levels that are higher than normal but not high enough to be called diabetes. A diagnosis of prediabetes doesn't mean that you are destined for diabetes. Prediabetes can be reversed—and diabetes prevented—simply by making some basic lifestyle changes.

Almost everyone who develops type 2 diabetes has passed through the earlier phase of prediabetes. The number of Americans with prediabetes is now about 41 million. If left untreated, prediabetes almost always turns into diabetes within 10 years. Even if it's not high enough to be labeled diabetes, high blood sugar can still significantly harm your body. It can lead to obesity and damage small blood vessels, including those in your kidneys and eyes.

WHO'S AT RISK

If your fasting blood sugar level (after not eating or drinking anything but water for at least eight hours) is between 100 and 125 milligrams per deciliter (mg/dL), you already have prediabetes. Your doctor can do a simple blood test to find this figure. *You're at greater risk of prediabetes now and diabetes later if you...*

• **Are age 45 or older.** Prediabetes risk increases with age.

• **Have a family history of diabetes.**

• **Had gestational diabetes** (high blood sugar during pregnancy) or you gave birth to a baby weighing over nine pounds.

• **Are overweight, with a body mass index (BMI) of 25 or above.** (To find your BMI, divide your weight in kilograms by your height squared in meters—or check out the calculator at *www.nhlbisupport.com/bmi.*) The heavier you are, the greater your risk. If overweight, you're at greater risk if your excess weight is around your waist (in other words, you are shaped like an apple) than if it's carried in your hips and thighs (you are shaped like a pear).

• **Have low HDL** ("good") cholesterol and high triglycerides (tiny fat particles in the blood).

• **Have elevated blood pressure** (129/90 or higher).

• **Have a sedentary lifestyle.**

African-Americans, Asian-Americans and Native Americans are at the highest risk, but anyone with one or more risk factors can develop prediabetes and diabetes. The more risk factors you have, the greater the likelihood that you'll become diabetic.

STEPS TO TAKE

You *can* prevent or reverse prediabetes and keep diabetes from developing. How? With three small but consistent lifestyle changes…

•**Lose weight.** If you are overweight, losing just 5% of your body weight can make a huge difference, but even just keeping your weight steady and stopping weight gain will help. If you weigh 180 pounds, for example, you would need to lose only nine pounds to see improvement. Cutting just 100 calories a day (the equivalent of one cookie) and adding 30 minutes of walking a day, which burns about 100 calories, will lead to slow, safe, steady weight loss.

•**Eat better.** Cut back on high-calorie, low-nutrition food, such as cookies and chips.

•**Get moving.** Do moderate exercise (walking, for instance) for 30 minutes every day.

Can this plan really prevent diabetes? Yes. A major study called the Diabetes Prevention Program proved it in 2002. Overall, the study participants who followed all three steps cut their risk of diabetes by nearly 60%. Among subjects over age 60, the improvement was even greater—they cut their risk by more than 70%.

BETTER FOOD CHOICES

•**Eat only the good carbohydrates** (such as foods made from whole grains without added sugars). Take an inventory of the carbohydrates you regularly eat. If you're eating bread, make it whole grain. If you're eating sugary breakfast cereal, make it unsweetened whole grain. Instead of ordinary pasta, pick whole-wheat pasta—today there are many excellent whole-wheat and other whole-grain pastas. Instead of white rice, switch to brown. Substitute other whole grains, such as barley, for white potatoes. And, instead of cookies and snack foods, go for fresh fruit or a handful of dry-roasted nuts.

•**Get rid of bad fats.** Choose leaner meats and low-fat dairy products. Avoid the dangerous trans fats (partially hydrogenated vegetable oil) that are found in processed foods and margarine. Use healthy oils, such as canola and olive oils, when cooking or in salad dressing.

•**Enjoy dessert, but in moderation.** The first few bites of a dessert taste the best, so go ahead and have them—just don't have any beyond that. If you keep your portions small to begin with, you won't be tempted to eat more.

At home, put portions on small plates. When eating out, ask for a half portion or split an order with someone else. When making desserts yourself, cut back on the sugar and use whole-grain flours. Make an apple crumble with oatmeal, nuts and a small amount of brown sugar instead of using the standard recipe.

You can even continue to enjoy between-meal snacks. We've come to think that a snack has to come from a package and be highly processed, but snacks should be real food as often as possible—think of a snack as a small meal. Try fresh fruit, low-fat yogurt, vegetables with hummus, low-fat popcorn, baked tortilla chips with bean dip, string cheese, some salad, half a sandwich or a small bowl of soup.

THE ACTIVE INGREDIENT

Exercise is a very powerful tool for preventing diabetes. Just a half hour a day of moderate exercise acts on your body very much like an insulin-sensitizing drug. Think of exercise as your daily dose of antidiabetes medication—a medication that's free and has no side effects. Exercise makes your cells more responsive to insulin, and that helps lower your blood sugar. In addition, regular exercise helps with weight loss.

Coffee and Green Tea Cut Diabetes Risk

In a study of 17,413 adults, those who reported drinking six or more cups of green tea or at least three cups of caffeinated coffee daily were one-third less likely to develop type 2 diabetes than those who drank less than one cup of green tea or coffee a week.

Theory: Caffeine stimulates oxidation (burning) of fat.

Caution: A high caffeine intake—more than 500 mg per day—has been linked to arrhythmia (irregular heartbeat).

One eight-ounce cup of coffee contains about 100 mg of caffeine...green tea, about 35 mg. Ask your doctor how much caffeine is appropriate for you.

Hiroyasu Iso, MD, PhD, MPH, a professor of public health at Osaka University Graduate School of Medicine, Osaka, Japan.

Calcium and Vitamin D Protect Against Diabetes

In one recent finding, women who got more than 1,200 mg of calcium along with more than 800 IU of vitamin D daily had a 33% lower risk of type 2 diabetes than people who get less calcium and vitamin D.

Best: Have one to two servings of low-fat dairy, such as milk and yogurt, a day, and take a supplement containing 500 mg of calcium and a vitamin D pill containing 400 IU.

Anastassios G. Pittas, MD, assistant professor of medicine, division of endocrinology, diabetes and metabolism, Tufts–New England Medical Center, Boston, and leader of a 20-year study of 83,779 women, published in Diabetes Care.

The Truth About Glucosamine and Chondroitin

Daniel O. Clegg, MD, professor of medicine, division of rheumatology, University of Utah School of Medicine, Salt Lake City.

A widely publicized study of 1,583 people with osteoarthritis knee pain published in *The New England Journal of Medicine* indicated that the popular dietary supplements, glucosamine and chondroitin, frequently sold in combination, were in general no more effective at relieving osteoarthritis knee pain than a placebo. But in one smaller subset of patients whose arthritis was described as "moderate to severe," 79% who took these supplements reported significant reduction in pain, compared with 69% who took the arthritis drug *celecoxib* (Celebrex) and 54% who took a placebo.

Bottom line: People who have moderate to severe osteoarthritis pain who have not received adequate relief from proven methods, such as weight loss, exercise programs and analgesics, including *acetaminophen* (Tylenol), should ask their doctors about trying the supplement combination for six months.

Minty Pain Relief

Mint oil has traditionally been used to ease joint pain.

New finding: A synthetic compound similar to the active chemicals in mint blocks the transmission of pain signals. Synthetic mint oil, applied topically, might be more effective than traditional painkillers.

University of Edinburgh, Scotland, www.ed.ac.uk.

Diet for a Pain-Free Life

Harris H. McIlwain, MD, a rheumatologist and pain specialist with Tampa Medical Group, and adjunct professor at University of South Florida College of Public Health, both in Tampa. He is also coauthor, with Debra Fulghum Bruce, PhD, of Diet for a Pain-Free Life *(Marlowe).*

As many as 150 million Americans suffer with ongoing pain. This usually is caused by such problems as arthritis or injuries to the neck or back.

Being overweight and having a poor diet are crucial factors, too. Fatty tissue is an endocrine (hormone-producing) organ, just like other organs in the body. Studies indicate that patients who are overweight produce high levels of *cytokines*, C-reactive protein and other proinflammatory chemicals (substances that promote joint and tissue damage and increase pain).

Good news: Losing as little as 10 pounds can significantly reduce inflammation, pain and stiffness—regardless of the underlying cause of the discomfort. A patient who combines weight loss with a diet that includes anti-inflammatory foods (and excludes proinflammatory foods) can reduce pain by up to 90%. The effect rivals that of *ibuprofen* and similar painkillers—without gastrointestinal upset or other side effects.

PAIN-FREE DIET

The saturated fat in beef, pork, lamb and other meats is among the main causes of painful inflammation. People who eat a lot of meats (including poultry) consume *arachidonic acid*, an essential fatty acid that is converted into inflammatory chemicals in the body.

Although a vegetarian diet is ideal for reducing inflammation and promoting loss of weight (no more than 6% of all vegetarians are obese), very few Americans are willing to give up meat altogether.

Recommended: A plant-based diet that includes little (or no) meat and poultry...at least two to four weekly servings of fish...and plenty of fiber and anti-inflammatory foods. Patients who follow this diet and limit daily calories to about 1,400 can lose 10 to 25 pounds of excess weight within three months.

Helpful: It takes at least two to three weeks to establish new dietary habits. People who give up meat entirely usually find that they don't miss it after a few weeks—while those who continue to eat some meat may find the cravings harder to resist.

My favorite cookbooks: *Vegan with a Vengeance* by Isa Chandra Moskowitz (Marlowe) and *Pike Place Market Seafood Cookbook* by Braiden Rex-Johnson (Ten Speed).

Here are the best painkilling foods and beverages. *Include most of them in your diet...*

RED WINE

Red wine contains *resveratrol*, the chemical compound that blocks off the activation of the COX-2 enzyme, one of the main substances responsible for pain and inflammation. Resveratrol may be more effective than aspirin at relieving pain from osteoarthritis and other inflammatory conditions.

Other beverages made from grapes, such as white wine and grape juice, contain some resveratrol, but not as much as red wine.

Servings: No more than two glasses daily for men, and no more than one glass for women.

Alternative source of antioxidants for nondrinkers: Two or more cups of tea daily. Both green and black teas contain *epigallocatechin-3 gallate* (EGCG), a chemical that blocks the COX-2 enzyme.

BERRIES

Virtually all fruits contain significant amounts of antioxidants, which prevent free radical molecules from damaging the cell membranes and causing inflammation. Berries—particularly blueberries, cranberries, blackberries—are among the most powerful analgesic fruits because they are rich with anthocyanins, some of the most effective antioxidants. One-half cup of blueberries, for example, has more antioxidant power than five servings of green peas or broccoli.

Servings: One-half cup of berries daily, fresh or frozen.

Bonus: Berries are very high in the antioxidant vitamin C, a nutrient that builds and protects joint cartilage.

PINEAPPLE

Fresh pineapple contains the enzyme *bromelain*, which is in the stem and fruit of the pineapple and inhibits the release of inflammatory chemicals. It has been shown in some studies to decrease arthritic pain. I advise patients with sports injuries to eat pineapple because of its healing powers.

Servings: At least two half-cup servings weekly, more if you're suffering from injuries or an arthritis flare-up. Bromelain also can be taken in supplement form—200 milligrams (mg) to 300 mg, three times daily before meals.

GINGER

Ginger contains potent anti-inflammatory substances and was found in one study to reduce knee pain in 63% of patients.

Servings: One teaspoon of ginger each day. Fresh and powdered ginger are equally effective and can be added to food.

FISH

I advise patients to substitute oily fish (such as salmon, tuna and sardines) for meats. Fish has little saturated fat (the main proinflammatory nutrient in the American diet) and is high in omega-3 fatty acids. Omega-3s increase the body's production of *inhibitory prostaglandins*, substances that decrease levels of inflammatory chemicals found in the body. And this can help reduce arthritis pain.

Servings: Two to four three-ounce servings of fish weekly or 1,000 mg to 2,000 mg of fish oil (available in capsule form) daily. If you don't like fish, omega-3s also are found in flaxseed, walnuts and soy foods.

WHOLE GRAINS AND BEANS

These are among the best sources of B vitamins—especially important for people who eat a lot of processed foods, which are usually deficient in these nutrients. Studies suggest that vitamins B-1 (*thiamin*), B-6 (*pyridoxine*) and B-12 (*cyanocobalamin*) may reduce inflammation.

Other B vitamins, such as B-3 (*niacin*), also reduce inflammation and may increase natural steroid levels and reduce the risk of osteoarthritis.

Servings: Consume at least one-half cup of whole grains and/or beans daily.

Good choices: Brown rice, lentils, chickpeas, black beans and kidney beans.

Bonus: Grains and beans are high in fiber. High-fiber foods promote loss of weight by increasing a sense of fullness and maintaining optimal blood sugar levels.

Meat Eating Linked to Gout

In one study of more than 41,000 men, those who consumed the most meat (beef, poultry, pork and seafood) increased their risk for gout—a common form of inflammatory arthritis that often occurs in the joints of the feet and ankles—by 41%.

Theory: Uric acid, which causes gout, is created in the body as meat is metabolized.

Self-defense: Limit your meat intake to four to five ounces daily.

Gary Curhan, MD, ScD, physician and researcher at the Harvard School of Public Health and at Brigham and Women's Hospital, both in Boston.

Coffee Protects Your Liver...and More

The liver serves the vital function of filtering toxins from your body—and coffee helps it do this. New studies indicate that drinking coffee reduces stress on the liver, with beneficial effects that are pronounced even in moderate to heavy drinkers of alcohol, reducing risk of cirrhosis. Researchers believe that the benefit may come not from caffeine, but from the antioxidants and other beneficial compounds in coffee. In fact, coffee has more antioxidants than any other food or beverage in the American diet.

Note: Coffee may have many additional health benefits as well. Other studies indicate that drinking coffee may reduce risk for diabetes, Parkinson's disease, colon cancer, asthma, depression and even tooth decay.

Arthur L. Klatsky, MD, lead study author, division of research, department of medicine at Kaiser Permanente Medical Care Program, Oakland, CA.

A Diet for Healthy Lungs

In one study of more than 50,000 men and women, those who ate a diet high in sodium, saturated fats, meats and refined carbohydrates, such as noodles and white rice, were 43% more likely to develop bronchitis symptoms (cough with phlegm) than those who ate a more healthful diet. Chronic bronchitis will often precede or accompany chronic obstructive pulmonary disease (COPD), persistent airway obstruction.

To improve lung health: Eat more foods with lung-protecting antioxidants, such as fruits, vegetables, soy foods and whole grains.

Stephanie London, MD, senior investigator, National Institute of Environmental Sciences, Durham, NC.

New Ways to Treat Asthma— Naturally

Richard N. Firshein, DO, medical director of the Firshein Center for Comprehensive Medicine in New York City. Board-certified in family medicine and a certified medical acupuncturist, he is the author of *Reversing Asthma* (Warner), *Your Asthma-Free Child* (Avery) and *The Nutraceutical Revolution* (Riverhead).

Anyone who suffers from the wheezing, coughing and chest tightness caused by asthma knows all too well that conventional doctors typically treat these troublesome symptoms with prescription medication, such as steroids and bronchodilators (both available in inhalers and pills).

Problem: Long-term use of prescription drugs does nothing to solve the underlying causes of asthma (a disease of the lungs in which the airways become narrowed or blocked, resulting in breathing difficulties).

What's more, the research shows that asthma medications can lead to dangerous side effects, including osteoporosis (from steroids) and accelerated heart rate (from bronchodilators).

Latest development: Exciting new research has confirmed that asthma can be managed with nondrug treatments, thereby reducing—or even eliminating—the need for medication.* *Here is how it can be done...*

NUTRITIONAL SUPPLEMENTS

•**Omega-3 fatty acids.** This component of dietary fat—found abundantly in the cold-water fish, such as salmon, herring and mackerel, as well as in flaxseeds and walnuts—may act as a natural anti-inflammatory for asthma sufferers.

Scientific evidence: In a three-week study, researchers at the University of Indiana followed 20 athletes who had asthma induced by exercise (narrowing of the airways during and after vigorous exercise). Participants were given either a daily placebo capsule or fish oil capsules containing two types of omega-3 fatty acids— *eicosapentaenoic acid* (EPA) and *docosahexaenoic acid* (DHA).

*Consult your doctor before trying any nondrug therapies for asthma.

Researchers measured the participants' lung function and inflammation levels before, during and after the study. While taking fish oil capsules, the asthmatics had an 80% improvement in lung function as well as lower inflammation levels and reduced bronchodilator use. There was no improvement in participants who took the placebo.

Self-defense: Take a daily fish oil supplement, with a total of 1 gram (g) to 2 g of DHA and EPA. Benefits typically begin after a few months but may occur in as little as three weeks.

Caution: This dosage could trigger a blood-thinning effect. If you take a daily aspirin or a blood thinner, such as *warfarin* (Coumadin), be sure to consult with your physician before using fish oil supplements.

•**Magnesium.** This mineral is considered a natural bronchodilator because it slackens the muscles of the bronchial tubes that line the air passages.

Scientific evidence: In a two-month study, researchers in Brazil gave 37 asthmatic children and adolescents daily doses of either a placebo or 300 mg of magnesium. Those receiving magnesium had fewer bronchial spasms and asthma attacks, and used less asthma medication.

Self-defense: Take 250 milligrams (mg) to 500 mg of magnesium daily. Exceeding this dosage of magnesium can cause bloating, gas and diarrhea. Taking a calcium supplement (double the daily magnesium dose) can enhance absorption of both minerals. To ensure proper absorption of calcium, take no more than 500 mg of the mineral at a time.

•**Coenzyme Q10.** This powerful antioxidant helps cells manufacture energy and strengthens the cells of the lungs.

Scientific evidence: Researchers in Slovakia gave 41 adult asthmatics who took steroids either a placebo or a daily dosage of 120 mg of CoQ10. After 16 weeks, the asthma patients who took CoQ10 used fewer steroids.

Self-defense: Taking 100 mg to 120 mg of CoQ10 daily may be helpful—whether or not you take steroids.

Reliable brands of fish oil, magnesium and CoQ10: Allergy Research and Cardiovascular Research (both available on the Internet) or Emerson Ecologics (available at holistic doctors' offices).

Important: If you use both medications and nutritional supplements in treating your asthma, take them at least one hour apart to enhance the absorption of both.

ANTIOXIDANT-RICH DIET

It's an accepted fact among health scientists that oxidative stress—the increase in cell-damaging free radicals caused by factors as varied as fried food, air pollution and stress—plays a role in more than 50 diseases, from arthritis to cancer. Now, most scientists have concluded that oxidative stress also plays a role in asthma.

Scientific evidence: Scientists analyzed dietary data from nearly 69,000 women and found that those with the highest intake of antioxidant-rich vegetables, such as carrots and leafy greens, had the lowest incidence of asthma.

Self-defense: Each day, eat a variety of antioxidant-rich foods, including fruits…leafy, dark green vegetables, such as spinach and kale…as well as carrots, winter squash and other colorful vegetables rich in carotenoids (a family of protective antioxidants that includes beta-carotene). Aim for five to six one-half-cup servings daily of these vegetables and fruits…and juices made from them.

BREATHING EXERCISES

Breathing exercises have been shown to reduce the need for bronchodilators in those with asthma. However, few physicians are aware of the benefits, so most patients are not encouraged to try breathing exercises.

Scientific evidence: When researchers taught 57 asthmatics breathing techniques, which they practiced twice daily for 30 weeks, their use of short-acting bronchodilators declined by 82%.

Self-defense: To strengthen the lungs, prevent an asthma attack and/or help stop an attack in progress, try breathing exercises.

What to do: While sitting, place one hand on your stomach, with the palm open. Use this hand to feel your abdomen rising and falling as you breathe. Use the thumb of the other hand to feel for the pulse point of the wrist that is on your stomach. Let yourself relax.

Next, try to synchronize your breathing with your heart rate. Breathe in through the nose, for example inhaling every three or four beats… breathe out through the mouth, exhaling every three or four beats. Blow out through pursed lips to create a mild resistance that improves the tone and function of the diaphragm, a muscle that plays a key role in breathing. Perform for 10 to 15 minutes, twice a day—or any time you're starting to have an asthma attack.

Caution: If you are experiencing a serious asthma attack, this breathing exercise may not be effective, and you may need to use medication. But in almost all other cases, this exercise can help regulate respiration.

ACUPUNCTURE

The National Institutes of Health recognizes acupuncture as a treatment for asthma. Thousands of years of anecdotal evidence from China also confirms that acupuncture works, perhaps by balancing fundamental but unseen energy flows that affect the body.

Scientific evidence: Researchers in Beijing divided 104 asthmatics into two groups, giving one group 10 sessions of acupuncture and medications, while the second group received only medications.

Those receiving acupuncture had significantly greater improvement in their asthma symptoms and more breathing capacity. Six months later, the acupuncture group had suffered fewer asthma attacks, and had reduced their medication dosages by as much as one-third.

Self-defense: Try six to 10 initial acupuncture treatments, followed by additional treatments, if necessary.

To locate a qualified acupuncturist near you, consult either the American Association of Oriental Medicine at 866-455-7999, *www.aaom.org*…or the American Academy of Medical Acupuncture at 323-937-5514, *www.medicalacupuncture.org*.

Citrus Helps Protect Against Adult Asthma

If your asthma is aggravated by minor exercise, such as walking up stairs, increase your citrus intake and eat more fruits in general—at least four servings per day.

Study: Patients who ate a diet rich in fruits and vegetables, as evidenced by high levels of vitamin C in their blood, were less likely to have difficulty breathing because of asthma.

Nick J. Wareham, PhD, MRC Epidemiology Unit, Elsie Widdowson Laboratory, Cambridge, England.

Eating Dark Chocolate Is Good for Your Skin

Cocoa, the main ingredient in dark chocolate, improves skin's texture, thickness, blood flow and hydration. It also contains antioxidants that help protect against sun damage—although you still need sunscreen. However, since chocolate is high in fat and calories, don't eat too much!

Ulrike Heinrich, PhD, professor at the Institute for Experimental Dermatology, Universitat Witten/Herdecke in Witten, Germany.

Curry Fights Skin Cancer

In lab research of human cells, curcumin (the compound in curry that makes it yellow) was shown to interfere with the development of melanoma cells. Past studies have shown that people who eat curry in abundance have lower rates of lung, colon, prostate and breast cancers.

Theory: Curcumin curbs inflammation, a risk factor for cancer.

Self-defense: Eat a half tablespoon of curry every day.

Bharat B. Aggarwal, PhD, professor of cancer medicine, University of Texas M.D. Anderson Cancer Center, Houston.

Lower Blindness Risk

In a study of 4,170 people, those who ate the most foods rich in beta-carotene, vitamins C and E and zinc were 35% less likely to develop age-related macular degeneration (the leading cause of blindness in people over age 65) than those who ate less of these nutrients.

Theory: The antioxidants in these foods help protect against free radical damage to the retina.

Self-defense: Eat generous amounts of foods that contain the above nutrients, such as whole-grain cereal, eggs, poultry and olive oil.

Redmer van Leeuwen, MD, PhD, resident in ophthalmology, Erasmus Medical Centre, Rotterdam.

 # Better Sleep Helps Tinnitus Sufferers

Melatonin may improve symptoms of tinnitus by allowing sufferers to sleep better. About 15 million Americans have acute tinnitus, the sensation of a ringing, roaring or humming sound in one or both ears. Sleep disturbance is common among tinnitus sufferers.

Recent study: Researchers gave people with tinnitus 3 mg of melatonin every night for one month to help them sleep, then followed them for a second month when they did not take the supplement. By the end of the study, the tinnitus symptoms had been decreased by nearly 30%. Participants slept better while taking melatonin, but the improvement in their sleep and tinnitus symptoms continued through the month when they were not taking it. Patients with the worst sleep problems improved the most.

Jay F. Piccirillo, MD, associate professor, department of otolaryngology, Washington University School of Medicine, St. Louis, and leader of a study of tinnitus sufferers, published in *Otolaryngology—Head and Neck Surgery.*

Calories vs. Alzheimer's

Animal studies indicate that a low-calorie diet may reduce brain deposits of *beta-amyloid,* the protein associated with Alzheimer's disease.

The Journal of Biological Chemistry, www.jbc.org.

Marijuana for Alzheimer's?

People who smoked marijuana in the 1960s and 1970s are less likely to develop Alzheimer's disease later in life.

A new animal study suggests why: Chemicals in marijuana may reduce brain inflammation and improve memory.

Next step: To develop a marijuana-like drug without the "high."

Ohio State University, Columbus, *www.osu.edu.*

Juice It Up!

In a recent finding, people who drank three or more servings a week of fruit and/or vegetable juice had 76% lower risk of developing Alzheimer's than those who drank less (the risk reduction was greatest in people with a family history of Alzheimer's).

Probable reason: Polyphenols—antioxidants that protect brain tissue—are in fruits and vegetables. Apples, grapes and oranges have particularly high concentrations.

Qi Dai, MD, PhD, assistant professor of medicine at Vanderbilt School of Medicine, Nashville, and leader of a study of 1,836 people, published in *The American Journal of Medicine.*

Almonds May Improve Memory

In a recent study, mice with a disease similar to Alzheimer's that were fed an almond-rich diet fared better on memory tests than mice fed a diet without almonds. Almonds contain substances similar to those found in drugs used to treat Alzheimer's.

Neelima Chauhan, PhD, assistant professor of anatomy and cell biology, University of Illinois, Chicago, and leader of a study presented at the annual meeting of the Society for Neuroscience.

Exercise Reduces Risk of Dementia

In a recent finding, adults age 65 and older who exercise for 15 minutes or more at least three times a week had 30% to 40% less risk of developing dementia than seniors who did not exercise regularly.

Theory: Exercise may improve brain function by boosting blood flow to areas of the brain used for memory.

Eric B. Larson, MD, MPH, director, Center for Health Studies, Group Health Cooperative, Seattle, and leader of a study of 1,740 adults, published in the *Annals of Internal Medicine.*

Natural Remedies For Anxiety

Carolyn Chambers Clark, EdD, who is a board-certified advanced nurse practitioner, mental health specialist and faculty member in the health services doctoral program at Walden University in Minneapolis. She is the author of *Living Well with Anxiety: What Your Doctor Doesn't Tell You...That You Need to Know* (Collins).

Anxiety is a normal reaction to the stresses of everyday life. For example, everyone feels insecure or worried at times. It's also common to feel anxious regarding job interviews, public speaking and meeting new people. But approximately 40 million American adults experience anxiety that is so persistent or excessive at some point during their lives that it interferes with their ability to function.

Anxiety disorders are among the most common mental health problems in both men and women. Health effects associated with anxiety include high blood pressure, tension headache, diarrhea and fatigue.

When people suffering persistent anxiety seek out help, doctors typically prescribe antianxiety drugs, such as *alprazolam* (Xanax).

What many people do not realize: Drugs used to treat anxiety can be addictive and create severe withdrawal symptoms when patients try to stop using them. They also may be harmful to the kidneys and liver.

ARE YOU AT RISK?

Anxiety can be first learned by being around anxious parents or caregivers. And, if you have an excitable personality, which could be your natural temperament, you will be more prone to anxiety. Abuse victims and people who witness death often, such as hospital workers, soldiers and firefighters, are also prone to anxiety.

As a holistic nurse practitioner who has grappled personally with anxiety at different times during my lifetime, I've spent more than 30 years devising an effective nondrug approach to help myself and the people I treat. *Best strategies…*

REVIEW YOUR DIET

• **Caffeine** will trigger the release of the brain chemical *norepinephrine*, which increases alertness. However, caffeine also causes your body to release adrenaline—just as if you're undergoing stress.

It is best to forgo caffeine altogether. Slowly withdraw over a few days. Try adding more decaffeinated coffee to your cup and less caffeinated coffee. Remember that coffee isn't the only source of caffeine. Tea, cola, cocoa and many over-the-counter medications, such as Anacin and Excedrin, may contain caffeine.

• **Sugar** is bad news for anyone with anxiety. It's well-known that simple sugars, found in candy, cakes, cookies and ice cream, cause your body to release too much of the blood sugar–reducing hormone insulin. This imbalance leads to a huge drop in blood sugar that causes many people to feel light-headed and anxious. But *all* the simple sugars—including corn syrup, fructose and honey—may have this effect.

What your body really needs is complex carbohydrates to burn up as energy-producing fuel. Good sources include unrefined grains, found in cereal…vegetables, such as asparagus and avocados (both are rich sources of stress-reducing vitamin B)…and fresh fruit.

• **Salt** does more than raise blood pressure in some people. It causes the body to excrete potassium, which helps keep your nervous system healthy.

Read food labels to minimize your sodium intake, and avoid salting your food. Instead, use a natural salt substitute, such as tamari (available at specialty food stores), or lemon or herbs, especially basil and oregano, for seasoning.

GET THE RIGHT MINERALS

• **Calcium** acts as a natural tranquilizer. People who are calcium deficient often suffer from heart palpitations, insomnia and nervousness. To increase your dietary intake of calcium, eat more sardines, tofu, broccoli, kale, Chinese cabbage, etc.

• **Magnesium** works with calcium to relieve anxiety. People who are deficient in magnesium will often experience nervousness, irritability and weakness. Magnesium-rich foods include halibut, avocados and almonds.

Eating a diet rich in the minerals potassium (salmon, cod and apricots)…zinc (whole grains, kidney beans and chickpeas)…and phosphorus (oat bran, chicken and sunflower seeds) is also important for alleviating anxiety. To ensure adequate intake of all minerals, take a multimineral supplement.

USE GENTLE HERBS

Because herbs can be as powerful as drugs and sometimes interact with prescription medication, I recommend those with the best safety records. Tell your health-care practitioner which herbs you are taking.

• **Chamomile** is a mild relaxant. Drink a cup of chamomile tea before bed or during a "coffee break." Start with one to two cups daily. Do *not* use this herb if you're allergic to plants of the daisy family.

• **Peppermint leaf** calms the nerves. Drink one cup of peppermint leaf tea after meals to help with digestion and promote relaxation.

• **Nutmeg** promotes sleep, which often is disrupted in people with anxiety. For best results, grind up one whole nutmeg in a coffee grinder and put the powdered herb in empty capsules, which you can buy at health-food stores. Keep the capsules in the refrigerator and use within one week. As a sleep aid, take one nutmeg capsule four to five hours before bedtime. For daytime anxiety, take one capsule in the morning.

EXERCISE EVERY DAY

Exercising provides an ideal outlet for your body when you're exposed to excessive adrenaline due to stress. By triggering the release of "feel-good" chemicals known as endorphins, exercise acts as a natural tranquilizer.

Everyone knows the benefits of exercising—but few people do it daily. Thirty minutes daily is ideal. If you have difficulty scheduling this, break your activity into three 10-minute sessions or two 15-minute workouts. You don't have to go to a gym—climb up and down some nearby stairs, garden or take a brisk walk at lunchtime.

To successfully integrate physical activity into your daily life, don't do the same thing all the time—instead, mix it up. For example, try swimming…yoga…weight-lifting…team sports…and dancing. The more variety, the more likely you are to stick to an exercise program.

CREATE NEW HABITS

Anxiety can encourage people to adopt bad habits, such as drinking too much alcohol and/or smoking. Do whatever you must to halt these behaviors—go to Alcoholics Anonymous, begin a smoking-cessation program, etc. Subtle habits—ones that you might not think are harmful—also contribute to anxiety.

•**Living with negative "self-talk."** Indoctrination from as far back as childhood can make for an anxious adult.

Think back: Were you taught unhealthy beliefs, such as "Life is dangerous" or "I must be perfect"? Do your best to change these beliefs and replace them with affirmations.

Examples: "I am becoming more relaxed"…"I believe in myself"…"I can relax and breathe calmly."

By replacing negative thoughts that can cause tension with more positive ones that calm you, anxiety is reduced.

•**Not being assertive enough.** If you tend to do too much for your family members and/or friends, learn to say "no." This may be easier said than done. That's why I often recommend taking a course in assertiveness training. Phone your community college or look in your local newspaper to find a course near you.

Lack of assertiveness causes people to hold in feelings, which allows anxiety to mount. Assertiveness allows you to say what is on your mind in a constructive and respectful way, which reduces the tension associated with anxiety.

•**Accepting bad relationships.** Many times, family members and/or friends mean well but replicate old patterns that create anxiety. Speak to them about your anxiety. If they don't make changes that help relieve your discomfort, avoid these people whenever you can.

If they are binding relationships, it is important to get therapy or learn skills, such as total body relaxation or imagery, to be able to cope.

Diet and lifestyle changes should relieve some anxiety within several days. Assertiveness skills may take longer. If you don't get adequate relief, seek counseling with a mental health professional or a counselor skilled in behavioral change.

Meditation Shortcut

No time for yoga, tai chi or meditation? Simply practice deep breathing twice each day, for three to five minutes each time. This gives many of the benefits of more time-consuming approaches—decreased muscle and emotional tension plus temporarily lowered heart rate and blood pressure. Sit in a comfortable chair, feet flat on the floor, close your eyes and take five to seven seconds to breathe in. Hold the breath for another five seconds, then release it slowly.

Do not do this if it causes you to develop shortness of breath, anxiety or any other symptoms.

David L. Katz, MD, MPH, director, Prevention Research Center, Yale University, Derby, CT, and coauthor of *Stealth Health: How to Sneak Age-Defying, Disease-Fighting Habits Into Your Life Without Really Trying* (Reader's Digest).

 # Laugh Away Infection

Just thinking about something funny may help ward off infection.

New finding: In comparison to the control group, volunteers who anticipated watching a funny movie had 27% higher endorphins and 87% more of human growth hormone—both of which enhance the immune response.

Loma Linda University, CA, *www.llu.edu.*

How Exercise Helps Healing

Regular exercise speeds healing by as much as 25%.

New study: Researchers inflicted small puncture wounds on the arms of 28 sedentary people ages 55 to 77. Half followed a three-month exercise program (including jogging or walking and strength training at a moderate intensity) three times each week for one hour. The others remained inactive.

Result: Wounds healed in an average of 29 days in the exercisers, compared with 39 days in the nonexercisers.

Theory: Exercising increases circulation and also helps regulate the immune system and hormones that promote healing.

Self-defense: Aim to exercise for 60 minutes three times weekly.

Charles F. Emery, PhD, professor of psychology, Ohio State University, Columbus.

Marital Disagreements Slow Healing

In a recent finding, even low-level stress from a minor disagreement with a spouse delayed wound healing after surgery by one day. And, a major disagreement postponed healing by a full two days.

Reason: Hostility can hinder the regulation of cytokines, very important chemical messengers in the immune system. When the cytokines stay in the blood too long, they cause an increase in inflammation, which can slow healing.

Janice Kiecolt-Glaser, PhD, director, health psychology, department of psychiatry, and a member of the Institute for Behavioral Medicine Research, Ohio State University, Columbus, and lead author of a study of 42 married couples, published in the *Archives of General Psychiatry*.

Prayer vs. Health

Rebecca Shannonhouse, editor of *Bottom Line/Health*, Boardroom, Inc., 281 Tresser Blvd., Stamford, CT 06901.

It was widely publicized when a Harvard Medical School study discovered that being prayed for did not benefit patients who had undergone heart surgery—and it even seemed harmful to those who knew that prayers were being made on their behalf.

I doubt that people who pray will stop doing so as a result of this study. Nor should they.

Of 12 previous major studies on intercessory prayer (neither the patients nor doctors knew who was being prayed for), half showed positive results. Clearly, there is evidence on both sides of the issue.

Larry Dossey, MD, a mind–body expert who has spent 20 years studying the health effects of prayer, believes that there's usually no downside to praying—for yourself or for others.

When a loved one's health is threatened, some people pray for that person's recovery, but others believe it is more appropriate to ask for "Thy will be done."

As we all know, many people pray specifically to God, Jesus, Allah or another deity. But no type of religious affiliation is required to pray. In fact, many people simply believe in the life force or a cosmic consciousness.

It is well established that the act of praying produces a salutary "relaxation response" that calms the person offering the prayer.

"If you think that someone will experience anxiety at the thought of being prayed for, simply send the person love instead," says Dr. Dossey. "Rarely does a person decline being loved."

Love, caring and compassion are what prayer is about, he says. No scientific study can deny these virtues.

Cranberry Antibiotic

A traditional treatment for urinary tract infections, cranberries are now being analyzed for their ability to fight other infectious diseases.

The latest research shows that *proanthocyanidins*, compounds in cranberries, might actually change the structure of some types of bacteria, making it harder for them to attach to human cells.

Worcester Polytechnic Institute, MA, *www.wpi.edu*.

Frozen OJ Healthier Than Others

Frozen orange juice has about 25% more vitamin C than ready-to-drink juice.

Reason: At refrigerator temperatures, oxygen slowly destroys vitamin C in ready-to-drink juice. This reaction is prevented by the colder temperatures needed to store frozen juice. Once a container of any type of citrus juice is opened and exposed to air, it may lose all of the vitamin C within a month.

Carol Johnston, PhD, RD, professor and chair, department of nutrition, Arizona State University, Mesa.

Best Way to Clean Fruits and Vegetables

To get rid of pesticides and wax from fruits and vegetables—in a bowl or a basin, mix four tablespoons of table salt, four teaspoons of lemon juice and one quart of cool water. Soak fruits and vegetables for five to 10 minutes.

Exceptions: Soak leafy greens for two to three minutes…berries, one to two minutes. After soaking, rinse produce in plain cold water and dry.

Alternative: Veggie Wash. Made from 100% natural ingredients, it is available at supermarkets, health-food markets and on-line at *www.veggie-wash*.com (800-451-7006).

Joan Wilen and Lydia Wilen, authorities on folk remedies in New York City, and authors of *Bottom Line's Healing Remedies* and *Bottom Line's Household Magic* (Bottom Line Books, *www.bottomlinesecrets.com*).

Lactose Intolerant?

Lactose-intolerant people may be able to eat yogurt. Yogurt has less than half the lactose of milk.

Reason: The live cultures in yogurt secrete lactase in the intestine and stomach, which helps digest lactose (the natural sugar in dairy products that can cause gastrointestinal symptoms, such as abdominal pain, diarrhea and flatulence).

Vicki Koenig, RD, registered dietitian and nutritionist, New Paltz, NY.

The Water You Drink

Steven Patch, PhD, director, Environmental Quality Institute, University of North Carolina, Asheville.

Here are some important facts on water from a leading authority on the safety of drinking water…

•**Do not try to drink an arbitrary daily amount of liquid,** such as eight glasses of water. Urine color is a good indicator of hydration—it should be light yellow. Other beverages, such as juice, milk and soda, are treated as water by the body—even if they contain caffeine.

•**It is fine to drink tap water**—the US has some of the safest tap water in the world, and many bottled waters are just filtered tap water.

•**If your home was built prior to 1986,** have your water tested for lead contamination.

•**If your water comes from a well,** have it tested for arsenic.

•**Use a filter if your water contains contaminants** or has a taste that you dislike.

Bottled-water caution: Reusing plastic bottles that have not been sterilized could expose you to high bacteria levels. Wash bottles in hot, soapy water or clean them in a dishwasher. Store unopened bottled water in a cool, dark place to prevent damage to the plastic bottles from heat and/or light.

6

It's Personal

Natural Ways to Much Better Sex

I t's true that drugs can help with the mechanics of sex. The male who has erectile dysfunction (ED) may have better erections when taking Viagra. A woman who has low libido may benefit from testosterone cream. Medications are only a temporary solution. They don't resolve the underlying problems. Natural remedies often can.

CAUSES

Millions of men and women have impaired circulation, which can reduce the ability to have erections and diminish sexual sensation. Chronic stress dampens libido and sexual performance. Insomnia and low energy can make people too tired to enjoy sex.

Certain herbs and other natural products address these problems and have been used safely and successfully for hundreds of years. Natural treatments, taken alone or in combination, can improve all aspects of sexual energy and performance. They promote better blood flow, increase libido and make erections stronger.

Start with one supplement. Take it for a week or two. If you don't notice a difference, add a second or third supplement that works in slightly different ways.

Example: Combine ginkgo biloba (which enhances blood flow) with ginseng (which improves overall energy). Always check with your doctor before taking any supplement.

Best choices...

GINKGO BILOBA

Function: Dilates blood vessels and improves circulation to the penis or vagina and clitoris. Impaired circulation is the most common cause of ED in men. And in women, reduced blood flow can result in diminished sexual sensation and responsiveness. Ginkgo biloba is a very effective

Chris D. Meletis, ND, an associate professor of natural pharmacology at National College of Naturopathic Medicine, Portland, and a physician at Beaverton Naturopathic Medicine, Beaverton, OR. He is author of *Better Sex Naturally* (Chrysalis).

vasodilator, which means it opens (dilates) blood vessels. In one study, more than 70% of males with ED who took ginkgo improved their ability to have erections.

Anyone who is taking a selective serotonin reuptake inhibitor (SSRI) antidepressant, such as Prozac, should consider taking ginkgo. It offsets the libido-dampening side effect that often occurs in people taking these drugs.

Suggested dose: 40 milligrams (mg) three times daily. It usually takes one to three weeks to work.

Caution: Ginkgo reduces the ability of blood to clot. Do not take ginkgo if you are taking *coumadin* (Warfarin) or another blood-thinning drug. Patients taking a daily aspirin, which also inhibits clotting, should be sure to talk to their doctors before using ginkgo.

ARGININE

Function: Increases pelvic circulation…improves erections…boosts libido and clitoral sensation. Arginine is an amino acid that produces *nitric oxide*, a chemical that relaxes blood vessels and promotes better circulation.

Suggested dose: 1,000 mg to 2,000 mg twice daily. People who take arginine typically notice the effects within a few days.

Caution: Patients with heart problems who are taking *nitroglycerin* should not take arginine. The combination could result in excessive vasodilation.

Also: Don't take arginine if you get cold sores from the herpes virus or have genital herpes. Arginine promotes viral replication and can increase flare-ups.

GINSENG

Function: Helps support the adrenal glands, which produce the hormones that affect genital circulation and the ability to have an erection…modulates emotional stressors…increases overall energy and libido. Ginseng safely increases levels of testosterone, the hormone that stimulates sexual response in men and women.

Suggested dose: 10 mg twice daily. People who take ginseng usually notice an increase in energy after about one week.

Caution: Ginseng is a mild stimulant that can increase blood pressure. Do not take this

if you have been diagnosed with hypertension or heart disease.

YOHIMBE

Function: Improves libido and sexual response in women…promotes firmer erections in men.

Yohimbe is the only herb approved by the Food and Drug Administration for treating low libido and sexual dysfunction in men. It stimulates the release of *norepinephrine* from the adrenal glands, improving genital circulation and the ability to have erections. Women who take yohimbe experience greater sexual arousal.

Suggested dose: Follow directions on the label. Yohimbe works more rapidly than most natural products, so take it one to two hours before sex.

Caution: Yohimbe can trigger sharp spikes in blood pressure in some patients. It also can cause headaches and nausea. Use yohimbe only under medical supervision.

DHEA

Function: Increases sexual arousal in women…improves erections in men.

Dehydroepiandrosterone (DHEA) is a naturally occurring hormone that is converted to testosterone in the body. Testosterone and other androgens stimulate libido and sexual performance in men and women. The body's production of DHEA declines by about 1% annually after age 30, which can result in diminished sexual desire, performance and satisfaction.

Suggested dose: 5 mg daily for no more than three days a month.

Caution: Patients should take DHEA only if blood tests show that they have lower-than-normal levels. An excessive amount increases risk of side effects, such as acne, facial hair growth in women and occasionally heart palpitations. It also increases risk of tumors in the prostate gland. Men who have a history of prostate cancer should not take DHEA.

WATER

Function: Increases blood volume…improves erections in men and increases sexual responsiveness in women.

How can good old water be an aphrodisiac? Because millions of people are now chronically dehydrated—they don't drink enough water or they consume excessive amounts of caffeine, a diuretic that removes water from the body. Dehydration can result in diminished blood flow to the pelvis and genitals. Adequate hydration improves blood flow and makes it easier for men to have erections. Women who stay hydrated experience greater sexual comfort and satisfaction.

Suggested dose: Drink at minimum eight full glasses of water daily. Limit coffee and other caffeinated drinks to one or two servings daily.

Another Libido Booster

To wake up your libido, combine and drink equal parts of the tincture form of the herbs damiana and Panax ginseng. This will stimulate arousal and increase amounts of the hormone testosterone. The drink works for women and men. Consult a health-care professional knowledgeable in herbal medicine to determine if the formula is right for you and what dosage you should use.

Jane Guiltinan, ND, director, National Medicine Institute for Women's Health, Bastyr University, Seattle.

Little-Known Ways to Increase Your Sex Drive

Below are some little-known, natural ways to enhance your sex drive…

• **Sniff sugary foods.** The scents of foods such as doughnuts, licorice and banana bread have been found to stimulate libido.

• **Break a sweat.** Twenty minutes of aerobic exercise spurs significant increases in women's response to sexual stimuli. Exercising three to four days a week increases the frequency of and satisfaction from sex for men.

• **Help with housework.** Men who help in the house are seen as sexier by their partners.

• **Snuggle up.** Nonsexual contact, such as handholding, can prompt a release of *oxytocin*, which sparks arousal and increases sensitivity to touch.

AARP Magazine, 601 E St. NW, Washington, DC 20049.

 # Truth in Dating

Before meeting up with someone you have met on-line, see if he/she has a profile at Truedater.com. This free site lets users post reviews of people they've met through Web sites or on-line services. You can find out whether someone says that the person you're planning to meet is married, has children, is shorter than he claims, etc., and avoid a potentially unpleasant situation.

Better Than Sex?

Baby boomers prefer chocolate to sex. Seniors feel the same way. Both age groups said that the hardest thing to give up permanently would be reading…the second most difficult thing would be chocolate. Sex came in third for both groups.

50Plus Research, which conducts research for companies that serve the baby boomer and senior markets, San Francisco, *www.50plusresearch.com*. The firm conducted a survey of more than 500 people designed to provide an overview of boomer and senior attitudes and beliefs.

Sexual Problems Can Indicate Serious Health Conditions

In men, erectile problems can be a sign of coronary artery disease…painful ejaculation can indicate a prostate infection. In women, a deep pain during intercourse can be a symptom of a pelvic tumor or endometriosis.

For men and women, lack of desire can be a signal of depression.

Self-defense: If you have any of these symptoms, talk to your doctor.

Rosemary Basson, MD, a physician in the departments of psychiatry and obstetrics and gynecology at the British Columbia Centre for Sexual Medicine at Vancouver General Hospital, Vancouver, Canada. She is lead author of a study of the relationship between sexual dysfunction and serious medical conditions, published in *The Lancet*.

Cell Phones May Damage Sperm

In a recent finding, men who used cell phones for more than four hours a day had 25% lower sperm counts and lesser-quality sperm than men who never used a cell phone.

Possible reasons: Sperm may be damaged by electromagnetic waves from cell phones or increased temperature in the groin caused by wearing a phone on a belt or carrying it in a pocket.

Self-defense: Men should avoid excessive use of cell phones.

Ashok Agarwal, PhD, director, Reproductive Research Center, The Cleveland Clinic, and leader of a study of 361 men, presented at a recent meeting of American Society for Reproductive Medicine.

Birth Control Can Cause Migraines

In a recent study, women taking oral contraceptives containing estrogen had a 40% greater risk of suffering migraine headaches during menstruation than women who didn't take oral contraceptives.

Reason: When one is on oral contraceptives, the hormone-free week causes a steep drop in estrogen levels right before menstruation, which increases the risk of migraines.

Better for migraine sufferers on birth control: Use estrogen patches during the hormone-free week, or use the oral contraceptive Mircette, which allows for a gradual decrease in estrogen. However, women who get migraines with auras should avoid hormone birth control completely.

Karen Aegidius, MD, researcher, department of clinical neuroscience, Norwegian National Headache Center, Trondheim, and the leader of a study of 13,944 premenopausal women, published in *Neurology*.

Hormone Therapy: Benefits May Outweigh the Risks For Some Women

JoAnn Manson, MD, DrPH, chief of preventive medicine, Brigham and Women's Hospital, and professor of medicine, Harvard Medical School, both in Boston. She is also author of *Hot Flashes, Hormones & Your Health* (McGraw-Hill).

A recent study found that the rate of the most common variety of breast cancer dropped by 15% between August 2002 and December 2003—possibly because millions of women halted hormone treatment after a 2002 study showed that it increased breast cancer risk slightly.

However: Hormone treatment can improve quality of life if frequent hot flashes or night sweats make a woman unable to go about her daily activities or get a good night's sleep.

To minimize risk: Take the lowest dose possible for the shortest amount of time necessary. Women who have been on hormone therapy for several years should ask their physicians about weaning themselves off the drugs. Women just starting out should see whether they can get by on half the standard dose.

Trying to Stop Hormone Therapy?

Stopping hormone treatments suddenly after menopause results in more hot flashes within the first three months than stopping gradually. Gradual stopping—reducing the dosage by one tablet per week per month, so hormones are stopped in six months—reduces short-term hot flashes but makes them more likely after six months. Fast or slow stopping makes no difference after nine or 12 months.

It's best to work with your doctor to find the best approach.

Ronit Haimov-Kochman, MD, reproductive endocrinologist, obstetrics and gynecology department, Hadassah Hebrew University Medical Center, Jerusalem, and leader of a study of 91 postmenopausal women who had been on hormone therapy for more than eight years, published in *Menopause*.

Better Hot Flash Therapy

In a recent study, nearly 500 postmenopausal women applied an estrogen gel (Bio-E-Gel) or a placebo gel to their upper arms once a day for 12 weeks.

Result: Hot flashes were reduced in the low- (0.87 g daily), mid- (1.7 g daily) and high-dose (2.6 g daily) gel groups by 71%, 80% and 85%, respectively, compared with just 45% in the placebo group.

Bio-E-Gel increases estrogen concentrations to help reduce hot flashes, but at a dose lower than FDA-approved products.

Theory: Lower-dose estrogen could lead to fewer side effects and to less long-term risk for breast cancer.

The gel is currently undergoing FDA review.

James A. Simon, MD, clinical professor, obstetrics and gynecology at George Washington University, Washington, DC.

Menopause and Memory

In a study conducted over a five-year period, yearly follow-ups did not show a decline in memory among 803 menopausal women who took memory tests, such as repeating a list of numbers backward. It appears that menopausal changes do not cause forgetfulness.

Peter M. Meyer, PhD, associate professor and director, section of biostatistics, preventive medicine department, Rush University Medical Center, Chicago.

Vitamin D Reduces Breast Cancer Risk

In a recent study, people who got adequate exposure to the sun, which allows the body to produce vitamin D, and increased their intake of foods that contain vitamin D reduced their risk of breast cancer by 30%.

Foods that are high in vitamin D include: Milk, salmon, tuna and other oily fish.

Note: Unprotected sun exposure should be limited to 15 minutes a day for fair-skinned people.

Julia Knight, PhD, a senior investigator at Prosserman Centre for Health Research, Samuel Lunenfeld Research Institute, Mount Sinai Hospital, Toronto, and leader of a study of 576 women with breast cancer and 1,135 women without breast cancer, presented at a recent meeting of the American Association for Cancer Research.

Breast Asymmetry and Breast Cancer Risk

In a new study, researchers examined the mammograms of 252 women who later developed breast cancer and 252 women of the same age who did not develop the disease.

Result: Those who developed breast cancer had higher breast volume asymmetry (a difference in volume between left and right breasts) than other women.

Estrogen, which has been linked to breast cancer, may play a role in breast asymmetry.

Diane Scutt, PhD, director of research in the School of Health Sciences, University of Liverpool, England.

Thermography vs. Mammogram

Thermography should not be used as a substitute for mammography. In thermography, special infrared cameras are used to detect and map heat that is produced in different parts of the body. Some cancers show up as "hot spots" because new blood vessels are forming rapidly in that area.

However: The technique is not reliable. The rate of false-negatives (cancers that are undetected) and false-positives (nonmalignant areas that show up as hot spots and require further testing) is unacceptably high.

Mammography remains the most useful of the breast-cancer screening tests. The American Cancer Society recommends annual mammograms for women over age 40—and earlier or more frequently for women at increased risk.

Phil Evans, MD, FACR, professor of radiology and director of the Center for Breast Care, University of Texas Southwestern Medical Center at Dallas. He is a member of the American Cancer Society's Board of Directors.

Benign Breast Lesion Danger

Papillary lesions (benign growths in the milk-producing ducts) account for 1% to 3% of lesions sampled by core needle biopsies.

New finding: More than 20% of patients diagnosed with papillary lesions who underwent surgery or further imaging tests were found to harbor adjacent cells that increase the risk for breast cancer.

If you are diagnosed with a breast lesion: Ask your doctor what type it is and discuss whether removal is appropriate. If you have a

papillary lesion that has not been surgically removed, monitor it closely with imaging tests.

Cecilia L. Mercado, MD, assistant professor of radiology, New York University Medical Center, New York City.

Better Than a Biopsy?

Elastography, an experimental ultrasound test, measures how easily breast lumps compress and bounce back, which helps distinguish benign from malignant lumps. If larger studies confirm the test's accuracy, it could reduce the need for anxiety-producing (and costly) biopsies.

Northeastern Ohio Universities, Rootstown, www.neou. com.edu.

Osteoporosis Drug Reduces Breast Cancer

In a recent finding, *raloxifene* (Evista), a prescription drug used to treat osteoporosis in postmenopausal women, decreased the risk of invasive breast cancer by 58% in women who didn't have a family history of the disease…and by 89% in those with a family history. The drug may reduce estrogen's tumor-promoting effects.

Marc E. Lippman, MD, John G. Searle professor and chair of the department of internal medicine, University of Michigan, Ann Arbor, and leader of a raloxifene and breast cancer study, published in Clinical Cancer Research.

Better Cervical Cancer Screening

In a study including 1,305 women ages 40 to 50, researchers analyzed the results of Pap smears and testing for human papillomavirus (HPV), a common cause of cervical cancer.

Result: Twenty-one percent of the women who tested positive for HPV at the beginning of the study developed cervical cancer or precancerous cervical lesions within a 10-year period, even though the results of their Pap smears, which also had been performed at the beginning of the study, were negative.

If you're over age 40: Ask your gynecologist about having an HPV test with your PAP smear.

Susanne Krüger Kjær, MD, DMSc, professor, Danish Cancer Society, Copenhagen.

Tea Lowers Ovarian Cancer Risk

In one study of 61,057 women ages 40 to 76, subjects who drank two or more cups of tea (primarily black tea) per day were 46% less likely to develop ovarian cancer over a 17-year period, compared with the participants who didn't drink tea.

Theory: Tea contains *polyphenols*, potent antioxidants that may inhibit tumor growth.

Self-defense: Women should drink at least two cups of tea every day to receive this cancer-fighting benefit.

Susanna C. Larsson, PhD, researcher, National Institute of Environmental Medicine, Karolinska Institutet, Stockholm, Sweden.

Better Ovarian Cancer Treatment

In a recent study, researchers compared the care that gynecologic oncologists, gynecologists and general surgeons provided to 3,000 women ages 65 or older who had surgery for early-stage ovarian cancer.

Result: Patients treated by the gynecologic oncologists and gynecologists had half the mortality rate (2.1% versus 4%) of those treated by general surgeons.

Self-defense: Women diagnosed with ovarian cancer should seek treatment by a gynecologic oncologist. Contact the Society of Gynecologic Oncologists, 312-235-4060, *www.sgo.org*.

C.C. Earle, MD, associate professor of medicine, Harvard Medical School, Boston.

The Medical Tests Every Man Should Have

Richard O'Brien, MD, a clinical instructor at Temple University School of Medicine in Philadelphia, as well as an emergency physician at Moses Taylor Hospital, Scranton, PA. He is also spokesperson for the American College of Emergency Physicians, *www.acep.org*.

Many men take better care of their cars than of their own bodies' and are reluctant to go to the doctor unless they are seriously ill or injured. *The medical tests that I recommend for men...*

• **Annual prostate-specific antigen (PSA) test** starting at age 50 (and earlier for African-Americans and men who have a family history of prostate cancer).

• **Annual digital rectal exam** (or DRE) to check for enlarged prostate, starting at age 40.

• **Electrocardiogram.** Get every three or four years, starting at age 40 (earlier if there is a family history of heart disease).

• **Colonoscopy** every 10 years—or sigmoidoscopy every five years—starting at age 50 (earlier if there is a family history of colon cancer).

• **Testosterone level screening,** including blood test and lifestyle questionnaire, starting at age 40. Discuss frequency with your doctor.

• **Monthly testicle and breast self-exams** to check for potentially cancerous lumps. See your physician if you find anything suspicious. Don't just hope that a lump will go away.

Staying informed is crucial. According to the US Department of Health and Human Services, the number-one source of health information for men is women—wives, girlfriends and/or mothers. Women tend to get their information from doctors, television, the Internet and printed materials. *Bottom Line/Personal* and its sister publications, *Bottom Line/Health* and *Bottom Line Natural Healing,* can be invaluable resources. A good all-around health Web site is sponsored by the National Library of Medicine (*www.nlm. nih.gov/medlineplus*). It has a special section on men's health issues. Also check out the nonprofit Men's Health Network on the Web at *www.mens healthnetwork.org.*

The most important new research findings in men's health...

- **Taking daily aspirin,** ibuprofen or another nonsteroidal anti-inflammatory drug (NSAID) can slash in half the incidence of an enlarged prostate.

- **Low testosterone** in older men is associated with increased mortality risk. Over a four-year period, men over age 40 with low testosterone were about 70% more likely to die than men with normal levels.

- **Men with erectile dysfunction** (ED) should be watched closely for coronary artery disease (CAD). More than 90% of men with both ED and CAD reported symptoms of ED one to three years before experiencing severe chest pain.

- **About 10% of all new fathers** (compared with 14% of new mothers) suffer from postpartum depression. Male or female, anyone experiencing depression for more than two weeks should seek professional help.

Women are more accustomed to consulting with physicians, having gone to them more than males in their younger years because of pregnancy, birth control, urinary tract infections and other common conditions in women. But, men's health issues, such as prostate problems, tend to develop later in life.

Don't be shy, men. Silence can kill. And an ounce of prevention truly is worth a pound of cure when it comes to your health.

Frequent Sex Is Good for the Prostate

In one recent finding, men who ejaculated at least 21 times per month had one-third lower risk of prostate cancer than men who averaged four to seven ejaculations monthly.

Possible reason: Frequent ejaculation may remove potentially cancerous cells from the body.

It does not matter whether a man has intercourse or masturbates.

Michael Leitzmann, MD, DrPH, investigator, National Cancer Institute, Bethesda, MD.

Vitamin D and Prostate Cancer Risk

Vitamin D, which the body manufactures as a result of exposure to ultraviolet light in sunshine, has been found to *prevent* the onset and growth of prostate and other types of cancer, including breast and colon cancer. For years, scientists have known that men who live in more-northern states with less sun exposure have a higher incidence of prostate cancer than those who live in southern states. Scientists are researching how giving prostate cancer patients high-dose intravenous vitamin D may help fight existing cancers.

Self-defense: It is important for men to get regular sun exposure, especially when they are young, but to keep it to a safe level (usually 10 to 15 minutes of sunshine daily without using sunscreen) to avoid the increased risk of getting skin cancer.

Sheldon Marks, MD, adjunct assistant professor of urology, University of Arizona College of Medicine, Tucson.

Statins May Protect Against Prostate Cancer

Men with prostate cancer are almost 50% more likely to have had high cholesterol levels than men without the disease. The association is stronger for men whose high cholesterol levels were diagnosed before age 50—and for men over age 65, for whom there was an 80% greater likelihood of high cholesterol levels.

Implication: Statins (cholesterol-lowering drugs) may help lower prostate cancer risk.

Francesca Bravi, MD, epidemiologist, Istituto di Recerche Farmacolgiche Mario Negri, Milan, Italy.

Improved Prostate Health

In a 12-year study of 2,447 men ages 40 to 79, those who took a nonsteroidal anti-inflammatory drug (NSAID), such as aspirin or ibuprofen

(Advil), daily were about half as likely to develop an enlarged prostate as men who did not take an NSAID daily. The pills also cut the risk for moderate to severe urinary symptoms, such as urgency and frequency, by 35%.

Theory: NSAIDs may lessen the inflammation associated with enlarged prostate.

If you take NSAIDs, prostate health may be an added benefit. More research is needed before these drugs can be recommended for enlarged prostate alone.

Jennifer L. St. Sauver, PhD, assistant professor of epidemiology, department of epidemiology, Mayo Clinic, Rochester, MN.

Better Prostate Cancer Screening

In a study of 647 men who were tested for prostate cancer, researchers found that for those whose body mass index (BMI) was 25 or above, a lower threshold for the prostate specific antigen (PSA) density test—a measure of PSA divided by prostate volume—was necessary to accurately predict who had cancer. Researchers don't know why BMI may be linked to prostate cancer.

If you are an overweight or obese man: Ask your doctor whether you require additional screening tests for prostate cancer.

Mark Garzotto, MD, associate professor, urology, Oregon Health & Science University Cancer Institute, Portland.

Viagra Curbs Urinary Problems

An enlarged prostate is common in men who also experience erectile dysfunction (ED).

Recent finding: In a study of 370 men age 45 or older, those who took the ED drug *sildenafil* (Viagra) for 12 weeks reported improvement in symptoms associated with an enlarged prostate, such as decreased urinary flow.

Theory: The enzyme that Viagra acts on in the penis also relaxes cells in the bladder and

prostate that promote urinary flow and emptying of the bladder.

Kevin T. McVary, MD, professor of urology, Northwestern University Feinberg School of Medicine, Chicago.

 # Depression Raises Colon Cancer Risk

Women with the most symptoms of depression, including persistent sadness, lethargy, irritability, changes in appetite or sleep patterns, physical discomfort and/or difficulty concentrating, are 43% more likely to develop colon cancer than people who had the fewest symptoms, according to one study.

Possible reason: Depression has been associated with metabolic syndrome, a condition that has been linked to higher colon cancer risk.

Self-defense: Cardiovascular exercise can lift mood, and outdoor workouts can raise levels of cancer-fighting vitamin D. See a doctor if symptoms of depression remain or get worse.

Candyce Kroenke, ScD, MPH, Robert Wood Johnson Health and Society Scholar at the University of California, Berkeley and San Francisco, and leader of a study of depression and colon cancer in 82,000 women, published in the *American Journal of Epidemiology*.

A Mineral That Reduces Colon Cancer Risk

In a 17-year study of 42,000 women ages 55 to 69, those who ate more than 351 mg of magnesium a day were 23% less likely to develop colon cancer than those who ate less than 245 mg daily. The women got most of their magnesium from food. The current recommended daily magnesium intake is 400 mg.

Theory: Magnesium may decrease risk factors, such as insulin resistance and cell proliferation.

Self-defense: Women concerned about colon cancer should eat a diet that is high in magnesium. Magnesium-rich foods include artichokes, avocados, bran cereal, cashews, dark chocolate, lentils, spinach and wheat germ. Previous research has shown that fiber, antioxidants and other nutrients in foods rich in magnesium also contribute to lower colon cancer risk.

Ching-Ping Hong, senior analyst and programmer, division of epidemiology and community health, University of Minnesota, Minneapolis.

 ## Reduce Stress During Colonoscopy

In a new study, 73 patients scheduled to undergo colonoscopy received an initial dose of a sedative, like *midazolam* (Versed). About half of these patients then listened to music of their choice, via earphones, during the procedure.

Result: Those patients who listened to music required less sedation during colonoscopy than those who did not listen to music.

Theory: Music relaxes the patient, reducing the need for sedation.

If you are scheduled for a colonoscopy: Ask your doctor about listening to music of your choice during the procedure.

Benjamin Krevsky, MD, MPH, director of gastrointestinal endoscopy, Temple University Hospital, Philadelphia.

Quick Colonoscopies Are Risky

Too-quick colonoscopies can skip over precancerous growths.

Some physicians take as few as two minutes while others take 20 minutes. In a recent finding, polyps were found in more than 28% of patients when physicians took an average of six minutes or more, but in merely 12% of patients when doctors went quickly. The slower doctors found nearly four times as many polyps as doctors who perform the procedure more quickly.

Colonoscopies are the best way to detect polyps and colon cancer, which kills more than 55,000 Americans yearly. During the procedure,

a thin tube with a camera is placed in the patient's bowel to look for polyps that can become cancerous. Ask your doctor to do the procedure slowly and thoroughly.

Robert Barclay, MD, clinical assistant professor of medicine, University of Illinois College of Medicine, and partner, Rockford Gastroenterology Associates, Ltd., both are in Rockford, IL. He was leader of a study published in The New England Journal of Medicine.

Better Treatment for Sweaty Palms

A new painless and minimally invasive procedure called *percutaneous sympathectomy* is more effective than surgery or Botox injections for ending excessive palm sweating (*palmar hyperhidrosis*). The 20-minute procedure involves injecting a phenol-based medication into the upper spine in a location that interrupts the nerve signals that trigger sweating in the palms. The procedure could be available in the US soon.

Hugues Brat, MD, head of radiology department, Centre Hospitalier Hornu-Frameries, Hornu, Belgium.

New Treatment for Alcoholism

Alcoholism may be treated without intensive behavioral counseling.

Recent study: Alcoholics who took the oral medication *naltrexone* (Depade) and met for 20 minutes on nine occasions with a medical professional had clinical outcomes as good as those who had up to 20 psychotherapy sessions of 50 minutes each.

Naltrexone costs up to $5 a day.*

Mark Willenbring, MD, director of treatment and recovery research, National Institute on Alcohol Abuse and Alcoholism, Bethesda, MD, and a principal investigator of a study at 11 universities of 1,383 alcoholics, published in The Journal of the American Medical Association.

*Price subject to change.

7

Moneywise

How to Find Money You Didn't Know You Had

overnment agencies are holding on to more than $60 billion in unclaimed assets and missing money. Some of it may be yours. Life insurance policies…bank accounts…tax refunds…government benefits…savings bonds… inheritances—all of this can be lost without your knowledge.

HOW IT GETS LOST

Assets are considered abandoned when contact with the owner is lost—typically due to a name change after marriage or divorce, an unreported change of address, illegible or incomplete records, or clerical errors.

If you don't get in touch with the holder of a dormant asset promptly, you may lose out.

Banks, stockbrokers and transfer agents, utilities, employers and life insurance companies remit these unclaimed funds to the protective custody of a government trust account in a legal process known as "escheat." There it awaits your claim!

Millions of family members are not aware that they are eligible to collect unclaimed assets owed to relatives who died without leaving updated wills or detailed financial road maps for their heirs.

Important: *You* must initiate this search—the federal government and states holding unclaimed funds will likely *not* contact you.

Caution: There is no central repository or single database containing all unclaimed assets, so don't be fooled by Web sites offering paid access to one.

INSURANCE POLICIES

It's estimated that between one-quarter and one-third of all life insurance policies—amounting to hundreds of millions of dollars annually—

Mark Tofal, a consultant and consumer advocate on matters of escheat and unclaimed property, Palm Coast, FL, *www.unclaimedassets.com*. He is author of *Unclaimed Assets: Money the Government Owes You!* (NUPA).

go unclaimed upon the death of the insured. Why? Because it's generally up to family members to notify the insurance company when a policyholder dies, and many simply aren't aware that a policy exists.

What's more, many life insurance companies have "demutualized," entitling millions of current and former policyholders to receive stock and cash in addition to policy benefits. Demutualization is the process whereby mutual life insurance companies, which are owned by policyholders, convert to stock ownership. Policyholders become stockholders, and receive shares and/or cash in exchange for their ownership interest. *Examples...*

●**John Hancock**—at the time of demutualization (1999), addresses for more than 400,000 policyholders were not current.

●**MetLife**—60 million shares of stock (worth $855 million at the time of demutualization in 2000) went unclaimed.

●**Prudential**—the company was not able to find about 1.2 million policyholders entitled to compensation when it demutualized in 2000.

By law, all unclaimed policy benefits and demutualization proceeds are held in trust until claimants come forward. In 2005, trustees took custody of $22.8 billion, of which less than $1 billion has been claimed.*

Important: Act fast when making claims. Unclaimed stock from the nearly two dozen other companies that demutualized in the past decade may be sold by a government-appointed custodian. Thereafter, you won't get any dividends or stock appreciation.

For a list of demutualized insurance companies, visit the Demutualization Claims Clearinghouse site, *www.demutualization-claims.com.*

What to do: You may also be in luck if you are the heir of someone who held a policy with one of these companies. Contact the policyholder's company, and ask if you are owed money from an unclaimed policy or demutualization. With demutualization, you will most likely be directed to the company's transfer agent or the government trustee holding the compensation, if indeed it has gone unclaimed for the statutory dormant period, typically one to three years.

*Latest date for which figures are available.

SAVINGS BONDS

Contact the Bureau of Public Debt for unredeemed savings bonds. US savings bonds often go missing—they are received as gifts, put in a drawer and forgotten for decades. All US savings bonds stop earning interest at final maturity (now 30 years), and less than 1% of bondholders are notified when their bonds reach that date (only holders of Series H and Series HH bonds that pay interest by check are informed). The value of unredeemed bonds that have reached final maturity currently exceeds *$13 billion.*

Important: Be sure to use the correct form for your request...

●For bonds that are undelivered, use Form PD F 3062-4 E.

●For bonds that are destroyed, lost or stolen, use Form PD F 1048 E.

●For a missing interest check for HH bonds, use Form PD F 5235 E.

Download the form that you need at *www.treasurydirect.gov/forms.htm*, call 304-480-7711 or e-mail your request through the Web site.

LOST TAX REFUNDS

Contact the IRS at 800-829-4477. Last year, the IRS had nearly 97,000 income tax refund checks totaling $92.2 million undelivered, mainly due to unreported changes of name and/or address (typically after a move), marriage, death or divorce. In addition, each year an estimated $500 million in IRS refund checks that *are* delivered go uncashed and unpaid.

Upon request to the IRS, checks that were returned will be reissued. If no request is made, the IRS will credit the amount toward any amount due in the succeeding three years. Checks worth about $6 billion have been delivered but never cashed. A check that has been lost, voided (after one year) or destroyed can also be reissued by contacting the IRS.

Important: Generally, no refund can be issued more than three years after the due date of the return to which the refund relates. If you are the heir of a deceased taxpayer who may be owed a refund due to an overpayment made during the year of death, contact the IRS immediately—before the refund period expires.

MONEY HELD BY STATES

Last year alone, states collected $23 billion in unclaimed assets, representing everything from utility deposits, accounts in escrow and never-cashed paychecks to the contents of safe-deposit boxes. Every state (and the District of Columbia) maintains a database of unclaimed property, which may be accessed on-line. For your free links to all state unclaimed property databases, go to *www.unclaimed.com/unclaimed_property. htm.* Check every state where you and family members have had a connection—work…business…residence.

Helpful: When searching, use your maiden name, any previous married name as well as middle names and initials. Also search for names of deceased relatives.

Simple System to Organize Your Finances

Debbie Stanley, organization coach, founder and principal of Red Letter Day Professional Organizers in Clinton Township, MI, *www.rldpo.com.* She is the author of *Organize Your Personal Finances…in No Time* (Que).

Modern financial innovations like credit cards, debit cards and automatic bank deposits and withdrawals can all actually make it *harder* than ever to keep tabs on your finances. But it's possible to develop one simple system to track your spending and have better control over your records. The key is to use the system consistently. *My strategies…*

FILING

Like most people, I used to file alphabetically by category ("Credit Cards"…"Insurance"), but this was labor-intensive. Although I was unlikely to ever need most of these papers, I still had to thumb through hundreds of files to put each one away. I put off filing for months until the pile was a foot high. Also, the system relied too much on memory. I could never recall whether I put my cell-phone bills under "C" for cell phone, "S" for Sprint (my provider) or "P" for phone. And if I were to keep a separate index of names, I would need to update it each time I added a new file.

Smart alternatives…

•**File bills by month, instead of by category.** This way, filing can be done quickly. If I do need to retrieve something, it takes longer to find it than if I had filed by category, but I don't need to retrieve most bills and statements. When necessary, I can locate most bills fairly quickly by color and size.

•**Archive filed documents by the year you can discard them.** People spend far too much time organizing items they are unlikely to ever need, such as income tax records, insurance documents, utility and credit card bills, and investment statements.

My solution: Sort by the year you can throw out the files.

Example: The IRS can audit tax returns as far back as seven years in some situations, so any tax-related documents from 2007 go into a box that's marked "2015." All of the contents of this box, except the returns, get shredded and thrown out at the end of that year. (Returns and proof of filing should be kept forever in case the IRS says you forgot to file one year.)

•**File receipts for all major purchases by room,** instead of by category. I have files for purchases associated with each room of the house, including odd spaces, such as the front porch. For instance, when I buy a new television, I staple all the TV-related documents together—the manual, warranty, receipt, etc.—and place them in a file called "Family Room." I throw out TV-related documents when we throw out the TV. This system feels more natural to many people because they know where all TV-related documents are located, rather than trying to figure out if, say, the warranty should go under "TV," "Warranties" or "Electronics."

Note: This system should be intuitive. Some people keep laptop documents under "Home Office." Others file them under "Bedroom," because that's where they use their laptops.

•**Record smaller cash purchases on the backs of ATM slips** if you're trying to keep closer tabs on everyday spending. I often take out $20 or $40 to buy smaller items. I later jot down the dates and amounts, and add an arrow to the front of the slip to remind myself to look at the back when reconciling my checkbook. It is a great way to track just how you spend your petty cash. I keep my ATM slips in my wallet until I receive my month-end statement.

● **Keep a separate box or filing cabinet for special projects.** Files of special interest that accumulate paper, such as brochures, price lists and news clippings, will choke your main filing system.

Examples: "House Hunting"..."Vacation Plans"..."Car Buying."

Use words that are comfortable to you when creating folders. I file miscellaneous documents from the Internet under "Web," not "Internet."

● **Don't let a file get thicker than five inches.** At that point, it's better to subcategorize. For instance, when my "Basement" file became too thick, I added subcategories, such as "Basement/ Kid's Stuff" and "Basement/Appliances."

BILL-PAYING

● **Arrange for all your bills to arrive at the same time.** Many monthly billers, such as credit card issuers, now let you pick your own payment due date for greater convenience. Jot down the date you intend to mail each bill payment on its envelope in the space where the stamp will go.

I keep my envelopes in a small upright file on my desk. If you use financial software, program it to remind you of bill-payment due dates with a pop-up message.

If all else fails, pay bills immediately. I had a client who kept getting late fees on credit cards. Now she pays bills the day they arrive. Sure, she loses out by not leaving money in an interest-bearing account a bit longer each month, but her savings on late fees more than make up for the lost interest.

● **Make sure you and your spouse adhere to the same system.** I had clients who kept miscommunicating about purchases and over-drawing their joint checking account.

My solution: We preserved their joint checking account but also opened a new account for each spouse. Their paychecks were deposited into the main account, and bills were paid from it. Every month, the agreed-upon amount was transferred from the main account to the two individual accounts for their personal purchases and withdrawals. The checking accounts were free, so they avoided extra fees.

If you pay bills electronically: If you use a bank's on-line bill-paying service, you can still control the date the payment is sent. But if you sign up for automatic bill-paying through a vendor directly, you give the company the authority to take money from your account. Many don't remove those funds when they say they will. It could be a few days earlier, which could over-draw your bank account if you maintain a low balance.

Outrageous Fees: Shrewd Ways to Avoid Them

Greg McBride, CFA, senior financial analyst, Bankrate. com, North Palm Beach, FL, a provider of interest rate in-formation and personal finance news, articles and com-mentary, *www.bankrate.com.* He is also a frequent guest on CNN and MSNBC.

The fees *really* add up—bank fees, credit card fees, loan fees, real estate fees and car rental fees. As a consumer, you get dinged at every turn, it seems. Some of these charges may appear to be reasonable—while others are clearly outrageous. *But you can beat the system if you know how...*

BANKING AND CREDIT CARD FEES

Fees charged by banks and credit card com-panies have skyrocketed in the last several years. *Some of the worst...*

● **Doubled-up ATM fees.** When you use a machine that belongs to a bank other than the one that issued your ATM card, your bank may charge you a fee (usually $1.25 per transaction*), *and* the owner of the ATM will charge a fee, as well ($1.64 on average). It's common for banks to charge $2 or even more at ATMs in airports, hotels, sports venues and other places where they know you are under pressure to find cash.

Self-defense: Know the bank's policy regard-ing ATM fees. Use your own bank's machines or national ATMs—machines within a national sur-charge-free network, such as Alliance One (866-692-6771, *www.allianceone.coop*) and Freedom ATM Alliance (412-261-8146, *www.freedomatm. com*)—where there are usually no fees.

*Prices, rates and offers subject to change.

View the free database at my company's Web site, *www.bankrate.com*, for the best ATM fees.

• **Balance-transfer fees.** If you move your credit card balance to another card to obtain a lower interest rate, the new card company can charge you a fee.

Example: Bank of America charges 3% of the balance transferred.

Self-defense: Use a credit card company that has no fees for balance transfers and low interest rates.

Examples: Capital One (800-955-7070 or *www.capitalone.com*) has no balance-transfer fees on some cards...Wachovia (800-922-4684 or *www.wachovia.com*) exempts new customers from balance-transfer fees.

• **Credit card late and over-the-limit fees.** Your credit card company may slap on a fee for paying late or for charging beyond your credit limit, even if your payment record is otherwise perfect.

Example: Washington Mutual charges a $39 late fee to any customer with a balance of $200 or more who misses a payment deadline, and $35 to those who exceed their credit line.

Self-defense: To avoid these fees...

• Mail your credit card payment 10 days to two weeks before its due date...or if you pay on-line, a few days before it's due.

• Ask to have your payment date moved so that the bill arrives right after a paycheck.

• Contact your issuer and arrange for automatic on-line payments. Citibank, MBNA, Discover, American Express and others have on-line sign-ups to do this.

• Pay by phone at the toll-free number on the back of the credit card (there may be a charge from $5 to $15 for this service). The amount will be immediately withdrawn from your bank account and you will receive a confirmation of the transaction by mail.

What to do: Ask your issuer to waive the fee—many will do so as a courtesy to customers with good payment records.

• **Biweekly mortgage payment fees.** The "magic" of a biweekly (every two weeks) mortgage payment is that you end up making the equivalent of 13 full mortgage payments in a year rather than the usual 12, reducing the time

needed to pay down the mortgage and cutting interest payments substantially. But a biweekly payment plan from a bank often includes an up-front fee of several hundred dollars and monthly fees of about $10.

Self-defense: Instead, make extra principal payments with each one of your regular monthly mortgage payments. You'll accelerate the pay-off and decrease interest as much as you want to with no extra fees (assuming your mortgage allows this).

REAL ESTATE FEES

When selecting a home, the key is location, location, location, but at closing time, the key is fees, fees, fees...

• **Closing costs.** When shopping for a mortgage lender, consider not only the interest rate but also closing costs. By law, you will receive from the lender up front a "good faith estimate" (GFE) of closing costs. This is an itemized list of estimated costs to be paid at closing (e.g., the lender's fees, appraisal charges, title insurance premium, a partial month's interest payment).

Self-defense: Apply with three different lenders and compare their GFEs. Filling out applications takes some time, but it costs nothing to apply—and you could save thousands of dollars. Use the free search engine at Bankrate.com. Then try to get fees waived or reduced or credited toward closing costs. The lender might not budge—but it's worth asking.

Have your GFE reviewed by an attorney or other professional well before the closing. The privately run National Mortgage Complaint Center at 866-714-6466 or *www.nationalmortgage complaintcenter.com* will review it and tell you about any excessive fees.

Cost: $45.

Note: Banks should charge the buyer what they paid in appraisal, credit report and inspection fees. Often, they mark those fees up. Ask the lender to seek good deals on these items and pass along the savings to you. It may not—but it doesn't hurt to ask.

• **Title insurance.** When you obtain a new mortgage or refinance an old one, you must buy title insurance to protect against such problems as forgery of old title documents and potential interests of missing heirs. The premium is paid once and averages $800.

Self-defense: In some states, such as Texas, premiums are fixed by law. If the premium isn't fixed in your state, search under "title insurance" on the Internet or check the Yellow Pages. Call the companies to ask about their rates and coverage. If you're refinancing and have lived in the house less than 10 years, ask to get title insurance at the less expensive "reissue" rate.

More from Greg McBride, CFA...

High Interest Banking

Guaranteed high interest on bank accounts is available through EverBank (*www.everbank.com*). The bank offers its savers a "yield pledge" stating that the interest it pays on checking and money market accounts and on yield-pledge CDs will be in the top 5% among leading banks and thrifts. Current yield on money market high-yield accounts is 4.89%.*

*Rate and offer subject to change.

Electronic Banking Could Be Safest

Many people are disinclined to use on-line banking because they think it is more risky than traditional banking, but in reality just the reverse is true.

Why: Eliminating paper statements prevents the identity thieves from stealing or intercepting them. Paying bills on-line also eliminates credit card charges and paper bills that identity thieves may steal to get confidential information. And, electronic statements that are always up to date inform you of a questionable transaction more quickly than paper monthly statements.

So if you are concerned about security, on-line banking should be an attractive option.

Chris Musto, general manager of the WebExcellence division at Keynote Systems, a leader in Internet and mobile test and measurement services, San Mateo, CA, *www.keynote.com*.

Cash Is Back: Best Ways To Hold Cash Now

Deborah A. Cunningham, CFA, senior vice president of Federated Investors at 5800 Corporate Dr., Pittsburgh 15222. A director and former president of the CFA Society of Pittsburgh, she is Federated's chief investment officer of taxable money markets, with additional responsibility for the tax-exempt money market and municipal investment groups.

Just a few years ago, safe, liquid cash equivalents were yielding about 1%, or even less in some cases.

Rising tide: Since interest rates hit bottom, the Federal Reserve has lifted its key federal funds rate (the rate set for overnight lending between banks) 17 times. It's now 5.26%.*

Other short-term interest rates have escalated, too.

Result: Yields to savers are back to respectable levels.

How to sort out the choices when looking for a place to stash your cash...

BANK ACCOUNTS AND CDs

Some savers prefer bank accounts because their money is federally insured.

Bigger and better: For years, the Federal Deposit Insurance Corporation (FDIC) insured bank accounts up to $100,000 for one depositor in any one bank (you can use multiple banks to get coverage for larger amounts).

In 2006, a new rule increased the ceiling to $250,000 for IRAs and other retirement accounts. That's *in addition* to the other $100,000 of FDIC coverage.

Long or short? If you are interested in absolute liquidity (cash whenever you want it, without any penalty), one possibility is a day-to-day bank account. By shopping around (you can now shop for high yields on-line), you can find accounts with annual yields in the 4% to 4.5% range.

Even higher yields are available if you are willing to commit your money for a certain period in a certificate of deposit (CD). But, you would face a penalty for early withdrawal.

What they pay: According to *www.bankrate.com*, the average rate for a one-year CD recently

*Rates subject to change.

was nearly 5%—no better than you can get in some savings accounts. But some banks were offering up to 5.35%.

High rates: Centennial Bank of Fountain Valley, California, 5.35%...Appalachian Community Bank, 5.32%.

Five-year CDs had similar yields.

What to choose: Your choice of CDs should depend on your expectations for the rate of inflation. If inflation keeps rising, the Fed probably will resume interest rate hikes. In that scenario, you're better off in day-to-day accounts, where yields will move up...and one-year (or shorter) CDs, because they will mature relatively soon, allowing you to then reinvest the proceeds.

On the other hand, if the economy lags, the Fed may have to cut rates to spur growth. Then, you'll be glad that you locked in today's five-year CD rates.

Strategy: Diversify your bank accounts and certificates. No one really knows how the US and world economies will perform. It's possible we'll have both higher inflation and economic weakness. Therefore, you might want to hold a mix of day-to-day accounts as well as short- and long-term CDs.

MONEY MARKET FUNDS

You won't get federal insurance with money market mutual funds, but you will get easy access to your money. These funds also have a long history of preserving principal for investors.

Up and down: Yields on money market funds are reset daily, as market conditions change. This can hurt savers, as we saw back in late 2003 and early 2004, when rates plunged below 1%.

On the other hand, money market funds provide excellent protection when inflation and interest rates are rising. In 1981, after a decade of inflation, average yields reached 17%.

The current conditions: According to *www. imoneynet.com*, the average yield on a taxable money market fund recently was about 4.72%. Some firms were offering yields around 5% on their money market funds.

At the same time, the average for tax-exempt money market funds was at 3.10%, with some yields up to 3.5%.

Taxable or tax exempt? To decide which type of money market fund is best for you, just do some quick calculations.

How: Let's say that you search the Web and find a taxable money market fund paying 5.1%, among the highest yields now offered. In the top federal tax bracket of 35%, you would net around 3.3%.

If you are in a 25% federal tax bracket, you would take home more than 3.8% from that taxable fund yielding 5.1%.

Tax-free comparison: Today's highest yielding tax-free (municipal) money market funds are yielding about 3.6%. In the 35% federal tax bracket, that is equivalent to a taxable yield of 5.54%—your best choice.

In the lower brackets, you would come out ahead—perhaps far ahead—by investing in a taxable fund and paying federal income tax.

Caution: Some funds may waive a portion of their expenses but might not do that forever. Be ready to move money if your rate slips below the market average.

Federal income taxes are not the whole story. Many investors also pay state and even local income tax on interest income.

Such investors may prefer state-specific tax-exempt money market funds, which can deliver interest that's entirely tax free. Residents of California, Connecticut, Georgia, New Jersey, New York, Ohio and Pennsylvania are among those who might benefit from single-state tax-exempt money market funds.

STRETCHING FOR YIELD

Some investment options such as ultra-short-term bond funds, may offer slightly higher yields than bank accounts or money market funds.

Such funds also might have a place in a diversified portfolio. However, they are not really cash equivalents. In times of rising interest rates, investors may see the value of their shares decline.

Another option: If you are willing to invest in multiples of $25,000 or higher, consider the *auction-rate securities*. These come in both taxable and tax-exempt varieties.

Yields usually range from 25 to 50 basis points (0.25% to 0.50%) higher than yields on money market funds.

What they are: Securities offered by financial firms seeking to raise cash at short-term rates.

Although auction-rate securities have some risk (there might be a failed auction), they have provided safety for investors. There hasn't been a failed auction in 15 years.

Typically, the interest rates are reset at weekly auctions, so these securities have up-and-down yield fluctuations similar to those of money market funds. And—they can be cashed in at these weekly auctions.

You buy and sell them by calling your broker. They are automatically renewed with each weekly interest-rate reset unless you cash them in. Tax-exempt auction-rate securities are exempt from federal taxes. And, those offered by single-state tax-exempt funds are exempt from state/local tax, too.

Where to find them: Major brokerage firms offer auction-rate securities to their clients. These securities can be part of a portfolio of cash holdings designed to offer safety, yield and inflation protection.

Better Overdraft Protection

Apply for an overdraft line of credit or link your checking account to your bank credit card or to a savings account at the same bank. If a check or debit overdraws the account, the bank covers it with an overdraft line of credit loan at an annual interest rate…transfers the amount of the overdraft to the credit card…or moves money from the savings account to cover the overdraft in the checking account. Moving the balance to a credit card offers a grace period of 20 to 25 days interest-free, allowing you time to get things straightened out before you pay back the overdraft. The bank usually charges a transfer fee for both the credit card and the savings account linking, but payment is guaranteed.

Jean Ann Fox, CFA, director of consumer protection, Consumer Federation of America, Washington, DC.

A Bounced Check Can Result in a Criminal Record

The recipient of a bounced check can take legal action against you. If the collection process reaches court and the court rules against you, criminal charges remain on your record forever. However, if you make good on a bounced check immediately, the mistake remains on your credit report for only seven years.

Stephen R. Bucci, president, Money Management International Financial Education Foundation, Houston, and author of *Credit Repair Kit for Dummies* (For Dummies).

Myths About Your Bank Account and FDIC Insurance

Kathleen Nagle, chief, deposit insurance section, division of supervision and consumer protection at the Federal Deposit Insurance Corporation (FDIC), Washington, DC. For questions about FDIC insurance, phone 877-275-3342 or go to *www.fdic.gov*.

Americans depend on insurance from the Federal Deposit Insurance Corporation (FDIC) to protect their savings in the event of bank failure, but many bank customers don't understand what's covered. *Common FDIC insurance myths…*

Myth: **Any financial product sold by an FDIC-insured bank is insured by the FDIC.**

Truth: Bank deposits are covered up to certain limits. These include checking and savings accounts, CDs, the Christmas club accounts and money market deposit accounts. But, investment products, such as stocks, bonds, mutual funds, annuities and money market mutual funds, are not covered even when purchased through an insured bank. Banks need to disclose which of their products aren't covered by the FDIC.

Myth: **FDIC coverage is restricted to just $100,000 per customer.**

Truth: Your coverage generally is limited to $100,000 per bank and per ownership category—but you could have more than $100,000 in coverage at one bank if your accounts fall into multiple ownership categories.

For instance, in addition to the $100,000 coverage for individual accounts...

• **Joint accounts owned with a spouse** (or someone else) qualify for an additional $100,000 in coverage per co-owner, as long as all owners have equal withdrawal rights.

• **Individual retirement accounts** (or IRAs) held through a bank qualify for $250,000 in coverage. However, if you do have other retirement accounts at the same bank, they may all be consolidated together with your IRAs before applying this limit.

Example: A man and his wife each have $100,000 in individual accounts at a bank, another $200,000 in a joint account and $250,000 each in IRAs at the bank. All $900,000 is covered by the FDIC at that one bank.

• **Certain kinds of trust accounts** qualify for $100,000 in insurance for each "qualifying beneficiary"—meaning the trust owner's spouse, child, grandchild, parent or sibling.

• **Certain deposits held in a health savings account** (HSA) are covered. Details and limits can vary, so contact the FDIC about your situation.

• **Accounts of certain types of businesses** qualify for $100,000 in separate coverage. However, the accounts of sole proprietors are lumped in with those of their owners for the purpose of insurance.

If you divide your money among several banking companies, you can protect more. The money must be spread among different institutions, not merely different branches of the same bank.

Myth: I can increase my coverage limits by setting up joint accounts with my young children.

Truth: If your child requires your signature to withdraw money or state law doesn't allow young children to have their own bank accounts, this joint account will be lumped together with your individual accounts and the total coverage will be capped at $100,000.

Myth: I can double the amount of coverage I receive by altering my name on different accounts.

Truth: Using different names for the same person, such as Stephen A. Smith and S. Adam Smith, or changing the order of names on joint accounts will not affect the insurance coverage.

Myth: The FDIC pays pennies on the dollar, and the government can take years to refund my money.

Truth: FDIC insurance will pay 100% of the money lost up to the coverage limit and does so within days.

Are Safe-Deposit Box Contents Insured?

Nancy Dunnan, a New York City–based financial and travel adviser and the author or coauthor of 25 books, including the best seller, *How to Invest $50–$5,000* (Collins).

Unlike money in a bank account, the contents of bank safe-deposit boxes are *not* Federal Deposit Insurance Corporation (FDIC) insured. However, read your box rental contract. Some banks pay up to a certain amount if the box contents are damaged. The amount and the conditions for payment do vary widely. Also, check your homeowner's insurance policy to see whether it includes the contents of your safe-deposit boxes. If it does not, talk with your insurance carrier about purchasing separate coverage.

Regardless of your insurance situation, take pictures (or videotape) of the box contents and write up a list of the items. If you are insured, this documentation will be helpful in filing a claim.

I also recommend placing paper valuables—such as important documents, stamp collections and family photographs—in sturdy, waterproof ziplock bags or in Tupperware-type containers before storing them anywhere, including in a vault at a bank.

For the final word on what FDIC bank insurance does and does not cover, contact the FDIC at *www.fdic.gov*. Click on "Deposit Insurance." Or, call them at 877-275-3342.

More from Nancy Dunnan...

Better Credit Payments

If you pay your credit card bill on-line and send it on the day it was due, you could still be fined. Your credit card issuer may stipulate that payments processed after a *certain time*—such as 3 pm Eastern time on Monday through Friday—will be posted the next business day. Or the bill-paying service you use may not wire payments the same day you authorize them.

If your card provider has a specific deadline time, notification should be posted on its Web site—or sent to you. If you can't find mention of the deadline among the issuer's documents, call customer service and ask them to tell you where their deadline information can be found.

Don't Be Late

If the interest rate on one of your credit cards is raised because of a late payment, issuers of *all* your other cards may raise your rates. Card issuers often boost rates if you make any late payment or if your credit score drops for any reason. To get a high interest rate reduced, pay future bills on time. The exact number of on-time payments depends on the card issuer—Wachovia stipulates four on-time payments for rate reduction while some Capital One cards require 12.*

Worth trying: Call the card issuer and ask for a lower rate. If the person you talk with cannot reduce the rate, ask to speak to a supervisor. Say you will close the account if you don't get the reduction.

Scott Bilker, founder of DebtSmart.com, Barnegat, NJ, *www.debtsmart.com*, and author of *Talk Your Way Out of Credit Card Debt!* (Press One).

*Offers subject to change.

Best Way to Make Credit Card Payments

It's smart to make credit card payments on-line or by phone.

Why: If even a single payment is received late by the card company, the interest rate you are charged may skyrocket. If you are receiving a low promotional rate for transferred card balances, such as 3.99%, it may increase by 20 percentage points or more!

Trap: Even if you send a payment by mail on time, it may be delayed by the post office or in other processing—causing you to incur the higher rate through no fault of your own.

Safety: Most credit card issuers offer the option to make payments on-line or via phone. Electronic payment guarantees timely payment —and that you have proof of it.

Money, Time-Life Bldg., Rockefeller Center, New York City 10020.

For Your Teenager

Help your teenager build credit by adding his/her name to your credit card accounts. You don't have to actually give the teen a credit card. Teenagers who are added to their parents' accounts as authorized users benefit from the positive credit history even though they are not the primary account holders, and that will help them when they are seeking mortgages and other types of loans in the future.

Philip X. Tirone, mortgage broker, United Pacific Mortgage, Los Angeles, and author of *7 Steps to a 720 Credit Score* (Mortgage Capital Advisors), *www.7stepsto720.com*.

Beware of "Skip a Payment" Offers

Banks and merchants often offer to let consumers "skip" payments on a loan, or not make any payments for some months after making a purchase, as a marketing lure.

Trap: The payments are not really skipped—full interest continues to run. So, in reality, the payment is just put off with interest added until the end of the loan. Even worse, lenders often impose a fee on people who use the skipped-payment option. The result is that the consumer pays extra interest plus a fee for doing so.

Don't assume that any "skip a payment" offer is a good deal without reading the fine print.

Mary Hunt, editor, *Debt-Proof Living*, Box 2135, Paramount, CA 90723, *www.debtproofliving.com*.

Home-Equity Loans Are No Longer the Bargain They Were

William G. Brennan, CPA/PFS, CFP, Capital Management Group, LLC, 1730 Rhode Island Ave. NW, Washington, DC 20036.

Loans that use a home-equity line of credit no longer are the bargain they recently were. Their average current interest rate is now about 7.2%,* while three years ago it was about 4.6%.

Danger: The big rise in home prices is over, and prices are falling in many markets. If you borrow heavily against your home's value at current rates and its value then falls, you could lose much of your personal wealth.

Opportunity: A home-equity loan can still be used to pay down higher-rate credit card debt and other consumer borrowing.

Bonus: You can get a tax deduction for the interest on up to $100,000 of such refinancing, as long as total home mortgage debt does not exceed $1.1 million. When used this way, you aren't incurring any new debt but are reducing the interest rate on existing debt.

Caution: Be sure that you don't then start reloading charges on your freed-up consumer lines of credit.

*Rate subject to change.

Zero-Interest Loan Warning

Zero-interest loans offered by many retailers can be costly.

Problem: If you fail to repay the loan in full before the term expires, you could be socked with interest charges from the date of purchase. Even if you are only a few dollars short of the balance due, you could be hit with interest—sometimes in excess of 25% a year—on the full amount.

Study the fine print carefully before signing up for this type of loan.

Consumer Reports, 101 Truman Ave., Yonkers, NY.

A 50-Year Mortgage Option?

Some lenders now offer a 50-year mortgage option. These mortgages may be good for first-time home buyers who otherwise couldn't afford the monthly payments and any buyers who plan to stay in a home for three to seven years. A 50-year loan of $300,000 at 6.5% costs $1,691 a month, about $150 a month less than a 30-year mortgage.*

Caution: Because the payments stretch out for 20 years longer, the 50-year mortgage will cost more in interest over the life of the loan.

John Sauro, president of North Atlantic Mortgage Corporation, Stamford, CT, *www.northatlanticmortgage.com*.

*Rate and prices subject to change.

A Web Site for Home Buying and Selling

Prospective home buyers can learn about a property before looking at it. Zillow.com offers an aerial photo, map and estimated market value for most single- and multifamily homes. You also can see lists of what homes recently sold for in the area to help you price your home competitively.

write "do not copy, fax or scan" across the top and bottom.

Mark Nash, real estate writer and broker, Evanston, IL, and author of numerous books and articles on real estate, most recently, *1001 Tips for Buying and Selling a Home* (South-Western Educational).

Better Home Buying And Selling in The Current Market

The current real estate market is tricky. *Be sure to check out the following advice...*

• **Buyers need to drive a hard bargain,** starting the bidding at least 15% below a home's asking price...consider buying from a builder—many are offering substantial upgrades and low-cost mortgages.

• **Sellers should price a home right**—consult a qualified agent and visit open houses at homes like yours, then price yours accordingly. If you don't want to sell at what today's market will bring, think about renting out your home until the market for sellers improves.

Keith Gumbinger, vice president, HSH Associates, publisher of mortgage and consumer loan information, Pompton Plains, NJ, *www.hsh.com.*

Smart Tip for Sellers

Selling your home? Prevent closing delays by getting a "ready to close title guarantee." This title protection service from National Homestead (*www.nationalhomestead.com*) discovers mortgage errors, tax liens, fraudulently recorded documents, etc. It could take up to 60 days to clear problems such as this. If a problem is missed, National Homestead indemnifies the customer, ensuring that a sale goes through. Sellers can avoid legal fees, lost sales and extended delays with this service.

Cost: $295,* paid by the seller.

Note: Title insurance covers only title defects that occur before you buy the home.

David Schechner, a real estate attorney and principal at Schechner & Targan in West Orange, NJ.

*Price and offer subject to change.

ID Theft Risk for Buyers and Sellers

When buying or selling your home, protect yourself from identity thieves. Ask all parties involved if they have a *Client Identity Protection Program* already in place. Many loan processors, law firms and title and escrow companies do have these programs, which use passwords and limited access to help protect financial and personal information. Whether buying or selling, never offer your Social Security number by phone, fax or e-mail. Deliver your credit reports in person—do not fax or e-mail them. As for the IRS-required W-9 form, which will include your Social Security number,

Before You Renovate...

Some renovations can harm a home's resale. Think twice before you have these updates done...

• **Swimming pools,** except in hot-weather locations—buyers worry about upkeep, insurance and risks for small children.

• **An addition that does not enhance the home's appearance from outside.**

• **Trendy finishes for appliances or hardware**—trends change quickly.

• **A circular tub with massaging jets in the master bathroom**—busy people have little time to spend in a tub, and parents with small children prefer a conventional tub. An oversized shower is more attractive.

Consensus of real estate agents in *Money*, Time-Life Bldg., Rockefeller Center, New York City 10020.

How to Save Thousands On College Costs

Rick Darvis, president of College Funding, Inc. which trains financial professionals in college funding services, 121 N. Main St., Plentywood, MT 59254, *www.solutions forcollege.com*. He is also author of *College Solution: A Roadmap to Selecting Your Best Strategy to Fund College and Retirement Without Going Broke* (Stone People).

If you have not saved enough for a child's or a grandchild's college education, cheer up. The official tuition amounts universities post on their Web sites mean even less than the sticker prices pasted on windows of new cars. If you understand how the financial aid game is played, you can find some generous unadvertised deals at colleges and universities throughout the country.

Here are the strategies that the top college-planning specialists share with their clients...

• **Don't hesitate to apply for financial aid.** Complete financial aid forms even if you think you won't qualify for needs-based aid. A couple making $130,000 a year, for instance, may still snag a needs-based aid package if their child ends up at a pricey institution, and the income ceiling for aid can rise significantly with more than one child attending college. Besides, all the same paperwork often is necessary to qualify for tuition discounts and/or merit scholarships. Obtain a copy of the standard form, called the *Free Application for Federal Student Aid* (FAFSA), online at *www.fafsa.ed.gov* or from your school's guidance department.

• **Ask for tuition discounts.** Whether or not your family qualifies for financial aid, it pays to check for tuition discounts. The nation's private colleges and universities were offering incoming freshmen an average tuition discount of 41%, according to a 2006 CollegeBoard.com report. The price breaks may be awarded regardless of what the parents' income is.

To boost your chances, identify schools where your child's scores on standardized tests and grades put him/her in the top quarter of the applicant pool. You can compare your child's academic standing with that of students enrolled at a school by looking at student profiles posted on *www.collegeboard.com* and *www.princeton review.com* (click on "College").

• **Play on big rivalries.** Even if your child is not athletic, consider applying to schools that face off with one another on the football field or volleyball court. You will be exploiting their long-standing rivalry, not only in sports but in academics and in other extracurricular pursuits. Schools don't like losing good athletes or good students to other schools in their athletic conferences. Competing schools will learn where your child is applying because you list these colleges and universities on your financial aid form. To find out which universities are in the same athletic conference, consult the National Collegiate Athletic Association at *www.ncaa.org*.

• **Look beyond your own backyard.** The school that most wants your child could be two or three time zones away. Colleges always are looking for students from faraway states to boost the geographic diversity of their campuses. California kids, for example, are in hot demand everywhere in the US except the West.

• **Play the cheap card.** Even if your child would prefer to attend a pricey private school, be sure that he applies to at least one in-state public university. When a private university believes that it is competing with a cheaper alternative, it is more likely to kick in money to seal the deal.

• **Select a college with empty seats.** Some perfectly good colleges and universities are rejected by applicants more than others are. You can tell how often a school is spurned by asking about its enrollment yield. For instance, if a school accepts 1,000 students per year, but only 200 accept offers of admission, that's a low 20% yield. Popular schools have yields in the 50% to 60% range. Schools with more seats to fill are motivated to entice a child to attend and often are willing to negotiate tuition based on other offers that the student has received.

Your son or daughter also could apply to a school with a lower yield in hopes of receiving a fat awards package, which he can then use as leverage with schools that he really wants to attend.

•**Try negotiating.** If you're disappointed in the aid package your child receives from a college, don't give up. It is possible to negotiate a better awards package, but don't use the word "negotiate" with financial aid officers—they dislike the term. Instead say, "I would like to appeal the financial aid offer for my child." When making an appeal, send copies of awards letters from other colleges to the school your child really wants to attend.

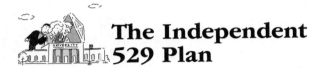

The Independent 529 Plan

The independent 529 plan has the tax benefits of other 529 college savings plans and lets participants lock in private-college tuition rates. The plan was created by a consortium of 250 private universities and colleges. If the child doesn't attend a member institution, you can roll the savings into another 529 plan or you can take a refund.

Information: 888-718-7878 or *www.indepen dent529plan.com.*

Child-Support Smarts

Ex-spouse refusing to pay you child support? Obtain a Qualified Domestic Relations Order (QDRO). It's typically utilized in a divorce to ensure that a former spouse gets a fair share of retirement assets, but a QDRO also can be used to collect child support. A lawyer or state child-support agency must determine what retirement benefits your ex-spouse is entitled to, then contact plan administrators to learn about QDRO procedures.

Information: Contact a family law attorney.

David Clayton Carrad, lawyer and president at QDRO Solutions, Inc., consultant to state child-support enforcement agencies and divorce lawyers, Augusta, GA, *www. qdrosolutions.net.*

How to Get Your Parents to Open Up About Their Finances

Dan Taylor, an attorney who specializes in elder-care issues, and president of Wealth Capital Group, a financial advisory firm in Charlotte, NC, *www.parentcaresolu tion.com.* He is author of *The Parent Care Conversation* (Penguin).

As a financial consultant, I have managed hundreds of millions of dollars for clients. But my own father, now a retired railroad foreman, never discussed his finances with me. He didn't want to burden me—and I never pressed the issue.

Then, my 74-year-old dad was found by the police wandering the streets at 4:30 in the morning, confused. He was diagnosed with Alzheimer's disease, went directly into a care facility and never returned to his old life.

I had to make wrenching choices about his living situation, his money and his possessions, for which I was totally unprepared because he and I had never spoken about such things.

Based on my personal and professional experience, here are the most common roadblocks put up by parents and other elderly loved ones when you try to discuss their futures—and the strategies to deal with them…

MONEY

Roadblock: Your parents refuse to discuss the details of their financial lives. If you press them, they say, "Don't worry about us. We're fine."

Your immediate goal: To know whether they really are financially safe and secure.

What to do…

•**Break the ice by asking for help with your own financial affairs.** Say, "Dad, I am planning to withdraw 5% a year from my portfolio when I retire. Is that realistic? How do you do it?" Asking for your parents' advice makes it easier for them to drop their guard and open up. It often leads naturally to discussions about their finances.

•**Acknowledge that they are in control.** Say to your parents, "I appreciate the fact that you've done well financially and that you can—

and should—handle all your affairs now. But if there comes a time in the future when you can't take care of your investments or other finances by yourselves, who would you want to handle them?"

• **Frame the conversation in terms of accountability.** If your parents expect you to bear any responsibility for their finances in the future, then you need to have enough information to be faithful to their wishes. Say, "Mom and Dad, if you suddenly become sick and can't handle your finances, do you expect me to step into a crisis situation blindly? If you can't open up to me, then don't make me responsible."

• **Ask your parents to go for a second opinion.** If they do open up to you and you're concerned about their financial situation, reserve direct criticism, which may make them feel inadequate. Instead, say, "I appreciate all the work you've done on this. Would you be open to talking to a professional to verify that your thinking is correct here?" I find most parents will reject a son's or daughter's financial advice, even if it is sound—but will accept an identical proposal from a qualified financial planner.

You even might offer to pay for their visit to the planner. Don't attach conditions, such as requiring them to see a planner of your choosing or letting you sit in on the session.

Helpful: If your parents seem overwhelmed with day-to-day budgeting and bill paying, consider hiring an independent party to help. The American Association of Daily Money Managers is made up of professionals trained to handle budgeting, paperwork and bill paying.

Details: $35 to $125 per hour.* 877-326-5991, *www.aadmm.com.*

POSSESSIONS

Roadblock: Your parents complain about, or don't seem to be keeping up with, the clutter in their home. But they refuse to pare down their possessions or even talk about how they would want their possessions dealt with in a crisis.

Your immediate goal: Make life more manageable for them—and for you—as they age.

After my father was hospitalized for Alzheimer's, it took me the equivalent of two full workweeks to deal with his property.

*Prices subject to change.

Example: He had hundreds of high-quality tools. I had no idea which ones he wanted to sell or give to family members or friends.

What to do…

• **Initiate a conversation about belongings** as soon as you get clues that your parents may be open to it. Typically, the signal is a comment such as, "I can never find anything in this mess," or "I would really like you to have my ring someday."

Your response: "Mom and Dad, why don't you tell me what crosses your mind when you think about what to do with all your stuff in the future?" To start the winnowing-down process, say, "If you had to move next month, what would you keep with you forever? What would you put in storage? What would you give away or sell?"

• **Address faulty solutions.** Elderly people generally offer two rationalizations to avoid dealing in a constructive way with being overloaded with belongings…

1) "We'll have a big tag sale someday."

Your response: "Sorting through a lifetime of possessions, including cherished keepsakes, is going to take a lot of energy and emotion. You'll need plenty of time to do it right."

2) "If the time comes to move, we'll have the Salvation Army take what we don't want."

Your response: "Charities no longer act as haul-away services. They've become very picky about what they will transport from your home."

• **Ask them to help take a huge weight off your shoulders.** Say, "Mom and Dad, it will be so much harder if I have to go through all your belongings in the future myself."

Rule of thumb: It's natural that your parents will want to keep everything. However, I have found that elders who are downsizing decades of clutter generally need to get rid of one-half to two-thirds of their possessions to make a serious difference in the quality of their lives.

HOUSE

Roadblock: Your parents vow that they plan to remain in their home forever. You know that this may take some real planning—if it is even possible at all.

Your immediate goal: To make sure that they can handle the responsibility of staying in their home as they age and that their living environment is safe.

What to do…

• **Acknowledge that you really want what they want.** Say, "I'd hate to have to give up my home and move to a smaller place or a care facility. In order to stay here, what changes would you be open to? For example, what would you do if it became difficult to go up and down the staircase?"

Helpful: Your local Area Agency on Aging. This organization helps older adults remain in their homes, aided by services if necessary.

Contact: National Association of Area Agencies on Aging, 202-872-0888, *www.n4a.org.*

Also: Universal Designers and Consultants offers information about adapting homes for easier living by seniors at *www.universaldesign.com.*

• **Point out realities.** It is common for parents to say, "We've got family and friends who could stop by and check on us if we ever needed it."

Your response: "Yes, you will be checked on some of the time, but there won't be visitors dropping by all the time, and visitors may not want that responsibility."

• **Accentuate the positive.** Instead of focusing on limitations, focus on new possibilities. Say, "You don't have to ever move to a smaller place, but consider how freeing an apartment would be. You wouldn't have to worry about constant upkeep." Or, "The extra money you would have after selling your house and buying an apartment would provide you with more security."

ESTATE PLANNING

Roadblock: Parents usually can be convinced to write a will, but getting them to update their estate plan as the years go by is surprisingly difficult. They say, "Our attorney is taking care of it," or "Why are you so eager to make sure our will is up to date?"

Your immediate goal: Making sure their estate plan is current, especially if there is a major tax law change or a death or change in marital status of a family member. My long experience with estate attorneys is that they tend to be short on follow-up unless the client initiates contact.

What to do…

• **Phrase the task of updating their plans in terms of making your job easier.** Say,

"Dad, I know you've done a good job planning your estate. In your view, is there anything that needs to be changed that would make my job (or insert the name of the appropriate party) as the executor easier?"

Important: If your parents are threatened or offended by your interest in their will and other estate documents, say, "I'm sorry that you've interpreted what I said as eagerness to get your money. My eagerness is to make sure that your affairs are the way you want them, regardless of the money."

Helpful: The National Academy of Elder Law Attorneys offers the latest news on legal issues affecting the elderly and can assist in locating an elder-law attorney near you. Call 520-881-4005 or visit *www.naela.com.*

Charities You Can Trust

Daniel Borochoff, president, American Institute of Philanthropy, Chicago, a charity watchdog and service that helps donors make better giving decisions, *www.charity watch.org.*

Many charities do give you a lot of bang for your buck. According to my organization—which rates more than 500 charities on the amount of their cash budget that is allocated for programs/services—about one-third of charities earned an A– rating or better and 24 of those charities got an A+.

To merit an A+, a charity must allocate at least 90% of its budget to services.

Among the 18 charities scoring A+: Animal Welfare Institute at 703-836-4300, *www.awi online.org*…American Kidney Fund at 800-638-8299, *www.kidneyfund.org*…International Medical Corps at 800-481-4462, *www.imcworldwide. org.*

Caution: Seventy-four organizations received an F for allotting 35% or less of total spending to programs. Charities with disproportionately high numbers of F ratings include those associated with firefighting, crime prevention and veterans.

One reason: Many of these charities retain outside professional fund-raisers, who keep a large portion of the donated funds.

More Web Sites That Monitor Charities

In addition to the organization mentioned in the previous article, be sure to check out the following charity-monitoring sites...

• **Better Business Bureau's Wise Giving Alliance** at *www.give.org* provides reports on compliance with both financial and government standards.

• **Charity Navigator** (*www.charitynavigator. org*) rates charities according to financial health and efficiency.

• **GuideStar** (*www.guidestar.org*) has information on 1.5 million not-for-profits and public charities.

The Wall Street Journal, 200 Liberty St., New York City 10281, *online.wsj.com.*

How to Win in Small-Claims Court

Emily Doskow, an attorney in Alameda County, CA, who has served as a judge in small-claims court. She is legal editor at Nolo Press, publisher of do-it-yourself legal guides, and editor of *Everybody's Guide to Small-Claims Court* (Nolo).

In small-claims court, you can sue an individual or a company for money owed you without having the expense of hiring a lawyer. That's the good news. The bad news is that most people have little experience with small-claims courts and tend to make mistakes that can be damaging to their cases.

Here are six common mistakes and what to do instead...

PREPARATION

Mistake 1: **Confusing "unfair" with "illegal."** Just because someone makes you angry doesn't mean that you have a legal case against him/her. *You must be able to show that...*

• **You have suffered a loss.** You can't sue your neighbor just because she leaves garbage cans out for days after the trash has been collected. You've suffered no financial loss.

• **The defendant is legally responsible for your loss.** If your car is robbed while parked in a building's garage, your suit against the building owner won't succeed unless you can show that he promised that the garage would be secure.

Mistake 2: **Being unable to explain how you calculated damages.** If you're suing for the exact amount of an unpaid debt, this is clear-cut. If your damages are more complex, you should have detailed written calculations ready for the judge. Bring receipts and appraisal estimates to establish that your dollar figures are proper.

Let's say that you paid a garage to repair your car, but the problem soon recurred.

Your calculations might indicate that you are suing for the amount it cost to have another garage redo the repair...plus the amount you paid for a tow...plus the amount you paid for a rental car while the work was being redone.

If you win your case, ask the judge to include the costs of court filing fees in the judgment.

Your state's maximum dollar limit for small-claims court suits could be as low as $1,500 or as high as $15,000. Ask the court clerk for details. Or use an on-line search engine, such as Google, to locate your state's small-claims court Web site—plug in your state name and "small-claims court" in the search window ("Connecticut small-claims court," for example).

If your damages are slightly above your state's limit, you can choose to waive the excess amount and sue for your state's small-claims limit to avoid the lawyer's bills, higher fees and more complex procedures of superior court. You may end up netting more in the end with less hassle.

Mistake 3: **Failing to properly serve the defendant.** The plaintiff must have a copy of the claim delivered to all named defendants after filing with the court clerk. Usually, for a minor fee, the court clerk can do this for the plaintiff by mailing a certified letter with a return receipt requested. Some states, including Georgia, Mississippi and Montana, do not allow service through the mail...and most states do not consider a defendant served if he refuses to sign for the letter.

A plaintiff often shows up on the trial date ready to argue his case only to learn that the defendant wasn't properly served and the suit cannot proceed. It's usually possible to re-serve papers and reschedule the court date, but that means starting the process all over again. It can take at least four weeks to set a court date after filing.

To avoid delays, phone the court clerk a few weeks after the claim was mailed to make sure that the defendant was served. If he wasn't, you might have to pay a sheriff or a private process server (typically $20 to $75*) to hand the papers to the defendant. In some states, any adult other than the plaintiff can serve the papers. Ask the court clerk for details.

Important: Each defendant you name must receive his own copy of the claim, even if the defendants are members of your family or business partners.

DURING THE PROCEEDINGS

Mistake 4: **Rambling.** Launching into an extended monologue detailing your troubled relationship with the opposing person—or making an emotional appeal to the court to correct an injustice—will only muddle your legal argument and exasperate the judge. Stick to the facts. To the best of your abilities, calmly state what happened. If you're nervous about the presentation, you can read a prepared statement. If the judge wants more information, he'll ask for it.

Helpful: Try to determine which way the judge is leaning. If he seems to be on your side, shut your mouth and let him do all the talking for you.

Mistake 5: **Being impolite to the other party.** If you let your anger at your courtroom opponent show, it could make you seem irrational. Don't interrupt this person to call him a liar, even if he is lying. Wait your turn…calmly state that much of what was just said is untrue…then do your best to prove it.

Mistake 6: **Trouble with witnesses.** If you have friends or family members appearing as witnesses, insist that they try to give an impression of impartiality, and make sure that they are there on time. Don't make the judge wait while you dash out to the car or the diner next door to get your witness. It's best to have a witness appear in person, but if that's not possible, you can bring in a sworn statement or affidavit.

*Prices subject to change.

Innocent Mistakes That Can Get You in Trouble with the Law

Joseph S. Lyles, an attorney in Greenville, SC, who has more than 20 years of experience in the personal injury field. He is the author of *How You Can Avoid Legal Land Mines: A Layman's Guide* (R.J. Communications).

Even honest, well-intentioned people occasionally run afoul of the law through bad luck or bad judgment.

ENTERING INTO A "HANDSHAKE AGREEMENT"

An oral contract is as legitimate as a written one—it's just harder to prove, which can create legal hassles.

Example: Dan entered into an oral agreement to provide various maintenance services to his neighbor in exchange for the neighbor's camping trailer. When a dispute arose regarding the maintenance chores, the neighbor called the police and reported the trailer stolen. The matter was eventually settled, but only after the police showed up on Dan's doorstep with a warrant for his arrest.

Self-defense: Even if you would rather not pay a lawyer to draw up a contract, write out and sign a statement summarizing your agreement and have it signed and dated by the other party and, preferably, witnessed.

FAILING TO REPORT A CRIME

There are many reasons people don't report crimes. The crime might appear too minor to bother the police…reporting it might expose illegal or embarrassing activities on the part of the victim…or the criminal might be a friend or relative of the victim.

Example: Susan had her wallet stolen, but she didn't bother to report the theft. There were only a few dollars in the wallet at the time, and she thought she knew who had taken it. She didn't want to get the police involved in what she considered a personal matter.

It turns out that Susan was wrong about who had stolen her wallet. Two years later, the police knocked on her door with a warrant for her arrest for writing bad checks. The thief had used her ID to open a checking account in a different county. Since the wallet had never been reported stolen, it was difficult for Susan to establish her innocence.

Self-defense: Always report a crime, no matter how minor it seems.

Even failing to report a minor auto accident can lead to problems. Sometimes the two parties agree not to call the police to avoid damaging their driving records and raising their insurance rates. But if one of these drivers changes his/her mind, he could call the police and claim that the other party fled the scene of the accident, a serious offense.

Self-defense: At a minimum, exchange all information. Carry a disposable camera to photograph the cars, driver and the surroundings. Get names and numbers of any witnesses.

IGNORING A TRAFFIC TICKET

Even honest people sometimes forget to pay traffic tickets...or incorrectly assume that they won't be held responsible for a ticket from another state.

Example: A ticket for running a red light in another state arrives in your mail. The attached letter says that a computerized camera captured the violation. You don't remember committing this violation, so you stash the ticket in your glove compartment and hope no one follows up.

Self-defense: Never ignore a ticket, even one from out of state. These days, states share ticket information.

The fine print on a traffic ticket says that the recipient must either pay the fine or appear in court for a trial. Those who fail to do so by the designated date risk a misdemeanor charge of failing to appear for trial.

In the worst-case scenario, the court could issue a warrant for your arrest and your state's department of motor vehicles could put a suspension on your license.

ALTERING A CHILD-CUSTODY AGREEMENT

When a court has made a ruling on a child-custody case, the parents do not have the right to alter the arrangement without the court's consent—even if both of the parents are in favor of the change.

Example: A father agreed to take charge of his children when their mother's job became too demanding. Both parents agreed to the new arrangement, but they didn't bother to inform the court, which had awarded the mother custody.

Later, the woman changed her mind about giving up the children, and she pressed charges against their father for violating the terms of the child-custody agreement—even though the new arrangement had been her idea. She also charged him with failing to pay court-ordered child support—although he was supporting the children.

It took a considerable amount of time and money for the father to sort out the situation.

Self-defense: Apply to a family court before making changes to any custody agreement.

ENTERING INTO A BUSINESS PARTNERSHIP

You can be found financially responsible for the misdeeds of a business partner.

If your partner runs up a big debt, you might have to pay it. If the partner engages in illegal business activities, you might share responsibility for paying fines or making restitution.

You generally can't face criminal prosecution unless you were aware of your partner's illegal actions, but it can be difficult to prove a lack of knowledge. In certain situations, you could be prosecuted even if you were completely in the dark about your partner's wrongdoing.

Example: A federal statute makes it illegal to own the equipment necessary to pirate satellite broadcasts. The way the statute is written, it could be interpreted to mean that knowledge of ownership of the equipment is not necessary to establish guilt. So, if your partner buys such equipment in the business's name, you could be guilty of a crime that you didn't know about.

Self-defense: Don't enter into a business partnership unless you're certain that your potential partner is a stickler for obeying the rules. Keep a close eye on all aspects of your partnership, even those that fall under your partner's purview. Should you later decide to leave the business, legally disband the partnership through a written agreement—do not just walk away. If you signed forms personally guaranteeing lines of credit with suppliers or lenders, cancel them by following the forms' instructions.

To avoid legal problems, set up a small business as a limited liability company.

Financial Steps After A Spouse Dies

David W. Latko, a financial planner and president of Latko Wealth Management, Ltd., Frankfurt, IL, which has $100 million in client assets, *www.davidlatko.com*. He is author of *Financial Strategies for Today's Widow* (Fireside) and *Everybody Wants Your Money* (HarperCollins).

I n addition to the emotional turmoil which comes with the death of a spouse, few people are prepared for the financial upheaval. *Financial steps to take immediately, should you experience the loss of a spouse...*

• **Obtain at least 10 to 20 certified copies of your spouse's death certificate.** You will need to present these to financial institutions and other parties. Purchase them through the funeral home or your local health department.

Cost: About $7 per certified copy.*

• **Contact your spouse's employer and/or former employer.** If your husband or wife was still working at the time of his/her death, speak to his employer's human resources and/or benefit plan administrator regarding any accrued but unpaid salary, bonuses, profit sharing, commissions, sick days, vacation time, deferred compensation and the value of any life insurance or 401(k) accounts. Also, if you had health insurance through your spouse's employer, decide if you want to continue coverage.

If your husband or wife was retired and receiving a pension, ask if you are entitled to benefits. If your spouse had a 401(k), arrange to have it rolled over into an IRA. Also, ask if you are entitled to any retiree medical coverage.

• **If your spouse had life insurance, contact the provider of the policy.** I recommend

*Price and rates subject to change.

transferring the lump sum into a money market fund until you decide how to invest the money. If the insurance was held by a trust as part of your spouse's estate plan, talk to your estate-planning attorney about what the trust language dictates.

• **Contact the Social Security Administration (SSA)** by calling 800-772-1213 or on-line at *www.ssa.gov/survivorplan/index.htm*. As a surviving spouse, you are entitled to your spouse's SSA payments or your payments (depending on your age)—whichever is greater. If you have unmarried children under age 19, they may be entitled to survivor benefits. You also can receive a onetime $255 death benefit.

• **Contact financial institutions** with which you and your spouse held joint accounts, and change the accounts to your name only.

If your spouse served in the military, you may be entitled to a military pension, death benefits and/or funeral and burial costs. Contact the US Department of Veterans Affairs (800-827-1000 or *www.cem.va.gov*). Ask to get benefits statements in writing.

• **Contact your local motor vehicle department** to cancel your spouse's license and change titles on any vehicles to your name or the name dictated by your spouse's will.

• **Inform issuers of debts held in your spouse's name and debts you held jointly** —with mortgage lenders, credit card companies, auto lenders, etc.—of your spouse's death. Ask the lenders if you or your spouse signed up for "payment protection," guaranteeing that mortgage or car payments or minimum credit card payments will continue for a certain period in the event of death. Some programs pay off the loan. The estate must pay off remaining debts. Also, cancel credit cards in your spouse's name.

• **Consult your tax adviser.** You must report any income your spouse earned in the year of his death. You can file a joint return for that year and claim the standard deduction provided you do not itemize.

Insurance Adviser

Your Legal Rights If You Become Seriously Ill

If you or someone you love is diagnosed with a serious ailment, such as cancer, heart failure or some other chronic or life-threatening disease, it's easy to become so consumed with the reality of a medical condition that you overlook important legal issues that may arise.

Most people know the importance of a will or trust, which provides for someone's estate after death, and an "advance directive" that appoints a person to make medical decisions on a patient's behalf in case the patient becomes unable to do so.

However, there are other important legal concerns for ill people—and often they are shrouded in myths that create unnecessary worry and confusion. *The most common legal myths facing patients—and the facts you need to know...*

Myth: **You will lose your health insurance if you change employers while you have a serious illness.**

Fact: The federal *Health Insurance Portability and Accountability Act* (HIPAA) allows you to move from one health plan to another without being excluded due to a preexisting medical condition, such as cancer, heart disease, etc.

Medicare, which covers Americans age 65 and older (as well as people of any age who meet Social Security disability requirements), cannot be revoked because of a serious illness. People have the option of enrolling in traditional Medicare or a Medicare Advantage plan, which is basically a medical HMO.

The same applies to people who are covered by Medicaid, the federal-state program for

Barbara Ullman Schwerin, Esq., adjunct professor of law at Loyola Law School, deputy director of community programs at the Disability Rights Legal Center as well as the founding director of the Cancer Legal Resource Center (CLRC), all in Los Angeles. The CLRC, at 866-843-2572 or *www.disabilityrightslegalcenter.org*, is a joint program of Loyola Law School and the Disability Rights Legal Center, offering information on relevant laws and resources.

low-income Americans. For more information, contact the Centers for Medicare & Medicaid at 800-633-4227 or *www.cms.gov.*

Another little-known fact: Some employers will request that a representative from their health insurance provider come to your workplace to explain coverage. This usually happens if an employer provides more than one health insurance option—or as a part of the open enrollment period when an employee can change from one plan to another. In other cases, your company's human resources department may offer guidance.

Myth: **If you are unable to work because of a serious illness, you will lose your job.**

Fact: The *Americans with Disabilities Act* (ADA) is a federal law that applies to employers with 15 or more employees. A person is protected by the ADA if he/she has a physical or mental impairment that substantially limits a major life function. To qualify, a person must be able to perform the essential functions of the job—with reasonable accommodation, if necessary (which must be provided by the employer as long as it does not create any undue hardship for the employer).

Examples: Extended periods of leave time, job restructuring and part-time work schedules.

Important: It is your choice whether to disclose your medical condition to your employer. If you do not require some type of accommodation, you are not obligated to disclose your illness. Some employees are concerned that if they tell their employers they have cancer, they will be treated differently and will face discrimination. However, you cannot claim discrimination if your employer was never told about your medical condition.

Another little-known fact: The *Family and Medical Leave Act* is a federal law that allows an employee to take up to 12 weeks of unpaid medical leave during any 12-month period without losing his job or health insurance coverage. It applies to employers with 50 or more employees, and the employee must have worked at the company for at least one year (and at least 1,250 hours in that year).

This type of leave can be tailored to the needs of your treatment.

Example: You can take all 12 weeks at once…or mornings off for radiation…or Fridays off for chemo. This leave can be used for an employee's own serious illness or that of a parent, child or spouse.

When on leave, people are usually looking for ways to cover their monthly expenses. Some states have a state disability insurance program that provides a portion of one's salary, usually for a maximum of one year.

Another option is payments under short-term or long-term disability insurance. Not every employer offers this type of insurance.

Suggestion: If your employer does not offer disability insurance, you may want to purchase it privately.

Caution: Once you are diagnosed, it may be difficult to purchase private disability insurance. Contact an insurance agent who can explore options that might be available.

Myth: **If you don't have health insurance when you're diagnosed with a serious illness, no insurer will cover you.**

Fact: Many states have a high-risk pool that covers people who can't qualify for individual insurance and don't have access to group insurance, Medicare or Medicaid. These offerings vary from state to state, and premiums may be high. Also, depending on the state where you live, there may be other options available.

Another little-known fact: Some states have additional protections. The Breast and Cervical Cancer Treatment Program, administered by the states, pays for the treatment of uninsured women with breast or cervical cancer if they meet certain requirements. Some states may have coverage for men with prostate cancer.

The specific details of coverage do vary from state to state. Check with the Department of Insurance in your state about all of the above.

Myth: **If you lose income because of a serious illness, you won't be able to pay your bills.**

Fact: The short-term disability insurance offered by some states can help. Social Security benefits might be available if you can demonstrate that you are disabled by a physical or a mental impairment that is expected to last 12 months or longer.

Social Security Disability Insurance is based on a person's work history. Supplemental Security Income is based on a person's assets and resources. For more information, contact the Social Security Administration at 800-772-1213 or *www.ssa.gov*.

Important: There is a six-month waiting period before you are eligible to receive Social Security benefits. Apply for benefits as soon as it is determined that you are going to be disabled for at least 12 months.

Another little-known fact: Many people know that it's often possible to save on health insurance by electing coverage under a spouse's health insurance plan. However, many people don't know that HIPAA protection also applies to this situation, so a preexisting medical condition cannot legally preclude you from starting health coverage under your spouse's employer-provided plan.

Also, some people may be eligible for lower utility and telephone bills, because their income has decreased.

The Disability Insurance Trap

Frank N. Darras, Esq., managing partner at the law firm of Shernoff Bidart Darras in Ontario, CA, *www.sbd-law.com*, the largest disability insurance and long-term-care law practice in the US. He has recovered more than $500 million in wrongfully denied benefits.

One out of every four Americans will miss at least 90 consecutive days of work because of an injury or sickness between the ages of 35 and 65. Disability insurance can help prevent such medical disasters from becoming financial disasters.

However, disability insurance is usually obtained through deeply flawed group policies offered by employers. Employees with such group coverage often aren't adequately protected.

In representing clients, I have seen what can go wrong with employer-sponsored disability policies. *Here's what to watch out for and how to get the best coverage...*

PROBLEMS WITH EMPLOYER PLANS

The employer-sponsored disability policies—in which all or part of the premiums are paid by the employer—generally claim to replace 60% or 70% of an employee's income when he/she is disabled beyond the typical 90- or 180-day elimination (or waiting) period. However, these promises are empty and deceptive. Insurers are allowed to reduce the benefits they pay dollar for dollar for any benefits the disabled employee receives from his state workers' compensation program...Social Security disability program...the state's disability program...and even cash settlements received for pain and suffering if the employee was injured in an accident that caused his disability.

Even worse: Any money these insurers pay out to group disability policyholders is taxed.* Beneficiaries end up with only a small fraction of what they thought they were insured for.

Other drawbacks...

•**An employer might eliminate its disability plan at any time.**

•**An employee may not be able to take this disability policy with him** if he quits or is fired.

•**If a claim is ultimately denied,** an employee in the group plan must appeal the denial in a timely manner, then sue in federal court to recover only his past-due benefits, some interest and attorney fees if the court allows. The horror of group disability litigation is that there is no trial by jury, no recovery for emotional distress and no opportunity to seek punitive damages under the *Employee Retirement Income Security Act* (ERISA). The carrier is required to pay only what it owed—in my opinion, this is like robbing a bank and returning the money years later without any penalty or jail time.

ADVANTAGES OF INDIVIDUAL COVERAGE

It is best to purchase your own individual disability coverage through an insurance agent, whether or not you are covered through your employer's group plan. You will be given the maximum benefit you're owed—tax free—even if you get other forms of compensation for your

*There are some employer plans that allow workers to pay all or part of the premiums with after-tax dollars so that payouts aren't taxed.

injury…you, not your employer, have control over the coverage…and if necessary, you can take the insurer to court, get a trial by jury and seek not only the benefits owed but also punitive damages if your state allows.

The downside is cost. A 55-year-old man in good health might spend $280 per month for a well-designed disability policy that replaces 60% of wages up to $4,000 a month after a 90-day waiting period. A 55-year-old woman might spend around $325 (women are more likely to become disabled, thus their coverage will cost more). For a 45-year-old man, the cost might be $199 a month. For a woman, it might be $281 a month.

Two ways to cut the cost of your coverage…

• **Increase your waiting period from 90 to 180 days.** This should reduce premiums by about 20% compared with a 90-day wait—but this strategy makes sense only if you can afford to live half a year without income. With a six-month waiting period, you begin to accrue payable benefits in the seventh month and would get a check at the 225th-day (seven-and-a-half-month) mark.

• **Women should ask their agents to check whether unisex policies are available.** These might cost 10% to 20% less.

MUST-HAVE FEATURES

Expect an insurer to offer coverage for up to two-thirds of your current wages, not to exceed $15,000 per month.

Three provisions that you also should insist on having…

• **"Own occupation" protection.** Without this provision, your insurer could reduce benefits by the amount you're capable of earning—even in a line of work that doesn't appeal to you.

Example: A stroke makes it impossible for a woman to continue her career as a surgeon. Without "own occupation" protection, her disability insurer might argue that she still could work as a janitor and then reduce her benefits by the $2,000 a month she could earn in that job. With "own occupation" protection, the woman receives her full benefit for as long as she can't perform surgery.

• **Noncancelable and guaranteed renewable to age 65.** With this clause in the contract, your insurance company cannot terminate your coverage until you turn 65, even if your health deteriorates. Guaranteed renewable policies also have fixed premiums.

• **Total disability and partial disability coverage.** Some individual policies provide for both total and partial disability benefits.

Example: A woman has a heart attack but still can work 20 hours per week. If her policy covers only total disability, her insurer will not owe her a dime. With total and partial coverage, she will be compensated based on the percentage of her income that she has lost.

RECOMMENDED FEATURES

• **Cost-of-living adjustments.** This feature increases your monthly benefits after disability strikes to keep pace with inflation. It's highly recommended for those younger than 40 but not vital for those over 50—inflation won't have as much time to deplete the value of their benefits. Expect a policy that provides an annual 3% to 6% increase in benefits to cost 8% to 12% more than the disability policy that doesn't provide such an increase.

• **Future increase option.** It makes sense to add on more disability coverage over the course of your career to keep up with your increasing wages. A future increase option gives you the right to buy more coverage at the initial contract rate, even if your health declines. This provision typically isn't available past age 50.

WHAT TO AVOID

• **"Except fraud" provision.** If an "except fraud" clause is written into your contract, your insurance company can attempt to take away your policy at any time by claiming that you materially misstated your medical, financial or occupational status when you applied for coverage. Insurance companies sometimes use this clause to deny benefits to honest policyholders when they find the slightest hint of an error on the application.

Better: Ask for a "two-year contestability policy" instead. After your contract has been in force for two years, the insurance company cannot contest any statements in your application.

BUYING DISABILITY COVERAGE

Ask trusted financial professionals or friends to recommend disability insurance agents…or call the top insurers to find agents in your area. Make sure an agent is licensed by your state.

There are four major individual disability insurance companies in the US...

●**Guardian** (866-425-4542 or *www.guardian life.com*)

●**Mass Mutual** (800-272-2216 or *www.mass mutual.com*)

●**Northwestern Mutual** (414-271-1444 or *www.nmfn.com*)

●**UNUM** (877-322-7222 or *www.unum.com*)

Helpful: If the agent you speak with can't get you a quote from each of these insurers, call other agents until you can compare quotes from all four companies. There's nothing wrong with checking the rates offered by smaller insurers as well, but the best deals usually come from the big four.

More from Frank Darras, Esq....

Disability Insurance Option Provides Retirement Savings

Any work-stopping disability prevents a person from contributing to a qualified retirement plan because no plan contributions can be made without having earned income. Several insurance companies have created a way for disabled individuals to make up the shortfall. If a policyholder becomes totally disabled, monthly benefits of several thousand dollars are put directly into a trust for him/her—the trust will invest the money to create a retirement income fund. One reliable disability provider is Berkshire Life (800-819-2468).

Credit Insurance Is Not Worth the Cost

Do not buy credit insurance, which typically covers up to 12 months of minimum credit card payments if you lose your job or can't work because of a temporary disability. Credit insurance is costly—89 cents per $100 balance.* The

*Rate subject to change.

money would be better spent reducing credit card balances. A disability policy, which can insure two-thirds of your income if you become disabled, is a better insurance choice.

Money, Time-Life Bldg., Rockefeller Center, New York City 10020.

Health Insurance Warning

Limited-coverage health insurance plans don't cover major expenses if you become seriously ill. These plans—sometimes called *limited-benefit plans*—are offered by many small businesses that previously provided no coverage or whose employees could not afford more expensive coverage. They can cost as little as $40 per month*—hundreds of dollars less than the cost of a typical company health plan. The plans cover many routine services, such as doctor visits and medicines, but provide little or no coverage for emergencies and hospital care—and often cap annual payouts at $10,000 or less per person.

Charles B. Inlander, a Fogelsville, PA–based consumer advocate and health-care consultant.

*Rates subject to change.

Between Jobs and Need Health Coverage?

Your cheapest health insurance option might be a short-term policy if you are between jobs. It is almost always less expensive than the federally regulated COBRA, which extends your former employer's coverage.

To compare prices: Shop at sites such as Insurance.com and eHealthInsurance.com.

Important: If you have a preexisting condition, get COBRA and then see if you can get a short-term policy. If you get one, cancel COBRA.

Bob Hurley, vice president of customer care at eHealth Insurance, a leading site for finding, comparing and buying health insurance, Mountain View, CA.

Health Insurance for College Grads

The right health insurance for students who are leaving college and who can no longer be covered under their parents' policies depends on the circumstances. Short-term coverage, which costs about $75/month* and does not cover pre-existing conditions, may be adequate for someone who is healthy and likely to find a job with benefits shortly after graduating from college. A comprehensive major medical plan with a low deductible can cost $400/month and may provide few benefits at high cost for someone who is healthy. A major medical plan with a $1,000 deductible may be a better choice for the long term, for about $200/month. But first check with the college—some schools do make inexpensive plans available for full-time students and alumni.

Robert Bland, chairman, president and CEO, Insure. com, on-line insurance brokerage, Darien, IL.

*Rates subject to change.

Answers to Your Questions on the Medicare Drug Plan

Deane Beebe, director of public affairs, Medicare Rights Center in New York City, *www.medicarerights.org*. The organization provides free information on Medicare issues to older and disabled Americans.

The new Medicare drug program—known as Part D—has resulted in much confusion about rules, benefits and costs.

Here are answers to frequently asked questions from a leading health-care advocate...

DECIDING WHETHER TO SIGN UP

• **My mother is in her 80s, in good health and does not take any medications. Does she need Part D?** Your mother may not need coverage now, but she might consider a low monthly fee plan in case she does need coverage in the future and is concerned about the penalty. For every month she puts off enrolling

after May 15, 2006 (when Part D went into effect), she will pay a penalty of 1% of the monthly premium.

For example, delaying for 15 months would mean a 15% penalty every month for the rest of her life. The typical plan charges $32 a month,* but in many states, plans may cost much less.

Note: If you enroll in Part D more than three months after your 65th birthday, when you become eligible for Medicare, you will be charged an extra 1% of the current monthly premium for every month you wait to enroll.

CUTTING COSTS

• **I prefer to fill my prescriptions on a 90-day basis. Do any Part D plans offer this option?** Certain plans do allow prescriptions for 90 days at a time, reducing copayments. Go to *www.medicare.gov*. Under "Search Tools," click on "Compare Medicare Prescription Drug Plans," then on "Find & Compare Plans."

Next, click on "Begin General Search." Once you get to Step 3, click on "Continue," then on "Continue to Plan List." Here, go to "Select Criteria to Reduce Number of Plans Shown," and click on "Plans that allow me to use mail-order pharmacies." Call to confirm.

SWITCHING PLANS

• **I have heard that an insurer can increase premiums for the following year or drop a drug from its "formulary" (list of available medications). Is this correct?** Yes. If a plan no longer seems like a good deal, you might want to switch. Each year, between November 15 and December 31, you can do so for the next year without penalty.

If your Part D provider drops a drug that you need, you can ask for an exception...appeal to the independent review board if your request is turned down...or ask for judicial review under certain circumstances.

HELP FOR LOW-INCOME PEOPLE

• **My father would like to sign up for the Medicare Part D plan, but he can't afford it. Is financial assistance available?** If his income in 2007 is below $15,315 per year ($20,535 for couples) and his assets are worth less than $11,710 ($23,410 for couples), excluding both his home and vehicle but including $1,500 per

*Prices subject to change.

person for burial and funeral expenses, he can get Part D coverage through the government's Extra Help program (new income limits will apply in 2008). If he qualifies for the full subsidy, he will have to pay $2.10 for generic drugs and $5.35 for brand-name drugs, with no premiums or deductibles. Check the Social Security Administration (800-772-1213 or *www.ssa.gov*) for additional information.

•**I work with low-income people. Pharmaceutical companies do offer programs to get these people the drugs they need, but anyone who has insurance doesn't qualify. If they sign up for Medicare Part D, their free meds will stop. What should they do?** If your clients' income and assets are low enough that they can qualify for the Extra Help program (see previous question), they should sign up for Medicare Part D. The drugs they need should be available—but check first to make sure.

Unfortunately, some people do have incomes low enough to qualify for drug companies' patient-assistance programs but not low enough to qualify for the full Extra Help subsidy. These individuals may be better off skipping Part D in order to continue to get free prescription medications through the drugmakers.

DONUT HOLE TRAP

•**Can you explain the "donut hole"?** When Part D was originally being discussed, using a "standard plan" model, the plan in 2007 would pick up a portion of expenses up to $2,400 in total drug costs, then the individual would pay 100% of expenses up to $5,451 (the so-called "donut hole"). The plan would resume picking up 95% of costs over this amount for the remainder of the year.

In the end, there was no standard plan—so when the donut hole begins, what you pay depends on the plan you select. Read the various plans' rules to find out what they provide.

No matter when your coverage gap begins, once you have $3,850 in out-of-pocket drug expenses in any calendar year—not including premiums, drugs that aren't included on the plan and drugs purchased at out-of-network pharmacies—"catastrophic coverage" kicks in and 95% of costs (not including the items that are listed above) are covered.

NURSING HOME CARE

•**My uncle is 84 and living in a nursing home. Should he sign up for Part D?** If your uncle qualifies for Medicaid assistance for his nursing home bills, then he automatically qualifies for Medicare Part D's Extra Help program.

Make sure that the plan you select includes a pharmacy that works with his nursing home. If your uncle is not getting Medicaid, he still can select a Medicare private drug plan that works with his nursing home.

CREDITABLE COVERAGE

•**I have prescription drug coverage via my wife's insurance plan at her job. I also have Original Medicare.* To obtain Part D without a penalty, do I have to sign up now or can I wait until my wife's coverage is no longer in effect?** You can wait and not pay a penalty if and when you do sign up for a Part D plan as long as your wife's coverage is "creditable"—that means it is at least as good as Medicare Part D. (Coverage purchased privately—not through an employer—also can be creditable, although Medigap drug coverage is not.) Your wife's employer should have sent her a notice stating whether the coverage is creditable. Keep a copy for your records to avoid penalties when you do sign up for Part D.

•**I go to the VA hospital for medical care and prescriptions. Is this considered creditable coverage?** Yes. (It probably isn't necessary to get a letter from the VA stating that you have coverage, but it couldn't hurt.)

MEDICARE HMOs

•**I belong to a Medicare HMO in Massachusetts. Officials there told me that they would cancel my coverage if I joined another insurer's Part D plan. There are other Part D plans more suitable for me. Can they actually cancel me if I avail myself of one of these?** Yes. If you're in a Medicare private health plan, such as an HMO or PPO, you'll lose coverage if you sign up for a stand-alone Part D plan.

Before you settle for your current provider's Part D plan, consider whether you would be better off switching to Original Medicare, which covers hospitalization and outpatient services,

*Original Medicare includes Part A coverage for hospitalization and Part B coverage for outpatient care.

and a Medigap supplemental policy to help with the deductibles and copayments that Medicare doesn't cover, plus the stand-alone Part D plan of your choice.

Important: Several insurers are promoting zero- or low-cost prescription drug plans that really are HMOs in disguise. Make sure you are signing up for a prescription drug plan only—if that's all you want.

• My father-in-law has Medicare and Tricare, the US Military's retiree health plan. Since the Tricare drug plan is comparable (actually better), do we need to sign him up for Medicare Part D? No, you don't—and since Tricare is creditable coverage, you won't face a penalty if he someday decides he does want to sign up for Part D.

HIGH-PRICED MEDICATION

• I pay $20 per month for my rheumatoid arthritis medication (Enbrel) through my employer's plan, which ends when I retire soon. My pharmacist claims the drug will cost more than $1,200 per month without insurance. I've checked the companies providing Part D coverage and cannot find any that adequately cover my drug. Any suggestions? Like many brand-name drugs, yours is in the more expensive, high-tier of the private drug plans. That probably means you'll have to pay more than you're paying now. Exactly how much more will depend on your state and the plan you choose.

Also, there may be drug plan restrictions on more expensive drugs, so you may need your doctor's assistance to obtain coverage.

DISABILITY AND MEDICARE

• I'm 64 years old and on disability, Medicare and Social Security. Can I apply for Part D now, or do I have to wait until I'm 65? If your Medicare benefits have already begun, you can sign up right away.

If you're still waiting for your Medicare benefits (for people under age 65, they don't start until two years after disability payments begin), then you can't sign up until three months before your Medicare coverage begins or in the month of your 65th birthday. The coverage begins the month you become eligible for Medicare.

BUYING DRUGS ABROAD

• I live in Wisconsin and spend my winters in Arizona. I am on several medications, which I get in Canada for a fraction of the cost I would have to pay in the US. Should I sign up for Part D or continue buying my medications in Canada? Many people have found that it's cheaper and less of a hassle to buy their prescription drugs across the border. But there's always a chance that you might one day reside in a state where cross-border trips are not as convenient…that you could require additional medications quickly…or that a medication you need might not be easily obtained in Canada.

Even if you continue buying your drugs in Canada, to play it safe, also consider signing up for a Part D plan with a very low premium.

CHOOSING A PLAN

You are under no obligation to sign up for Medicare Part D, but if you do, make sure that the plan you choose offers the drugs you need at a fair price through a pharmacy you like. Figure in premiums, deductibles and copayments.

You can compare Medicare prescription drug plans that are available in your state at the Medicare Web site, *www.medicare.gov* or by calling 800-MEDICARE.

Choose a Medigap Policy Carefully

The premium for a given level of supplemental coverage can vary greatly from one insurer to another—sometimes by as much as 50%. Timing is important, too. Make your choice during the six-month open-enrollment period (starting the first month you are covered under Medicare Part B and are 65 or older) when you cannot be denied coverage. You can do limited comparison shopping at *www.medicare.gov* or by calling 800-MEDICARE.

TheStreet.com Ratings (previously Weiss Ratings, Inc.), an insurance rating company in Jupiter, FL. For a custom report with complete price comparisons, phone 800-289-9222 or go to *www.weissratings.com/products* (click on "Shopper's Guide to Medicare Supplement Insurance").

Long-Term-Care and The Very Tricky New Medicaid Rules

Rania V. Sedhom, JD, senior manager, BDO Seidman, LLP, 330 Madison Ave., New York City 10017. Ms. Sedhom specializes in ERISA, employee benefits and retention of employees.

The new law makes it much more difficult to protect a family's wealth while having the government pay long-term nursing home costs for a family member through Medicaid. *What you need to know...*

THE TRUTH ABOUT MEDICARE

Surveys show that most people greatly underestimate their risk of needing nursing home care someday. The cost of such care already is extremely high, close to or exceeding $100,000 per year in many parts of the country and rising steadily. Over a period of years, it can consume a family's lifetime of savings and leave it deeply in debt.

Big mistake: Thinking that after the age of 65, Medicare pays for nursing home care.

Reality: Medicare pays the full cost for only 20 days of "rehabilitative" nursing home care, which must occur after a hospital stay. After that, it covers another 80 days with the patient paying the first $124 (in 2007) of daily costs (about $3,700 per month). After these 100 days, coverage ends.

WILL MEDICAID PAY?

Long-term nursing home care could be covered by Medicaid, a government program that provides health care to low-income, low-wealth individuals.

To be eligible: One must own few assets (usually less than $2,000 worth, with some exceptions noted below) and have only nominal annual income. The amount depends on where you reside—for instance, in New York you can retain income of only $692 per month. If the care recipient is married, his/her spouse generally can't have assets exceeding approximately $99,000, and can have only a modest income, with exact amounts varying by state.

Until recently, many seniors had planned to use Medicaid to cover their long-term care by transferring their personal wealth to other family members. They made gifts of assets to other family members and/or paid expenses (such as college tuition costs) for them.

Snag: The new rules make this strategy much more difficult.

TOUGH NEW RULES

To restrict the rapid growth in Medicaid costs, Congress enacted tough new eligibility rules effective in 2006, with the exact date varying by state. *Rule changes...*

• **Tougher "look-back" computation.** The look-back period has now been increased from three years to five years.

Plus, the ineligibility period that results from transfers made during the look-back period now begins only when the individual would become eligible for Medicaid benefits *but for the transfers*—that is, after his assets would have been exhausted—instead of on the earlier date when the transfers were made.

Situation: An older individual gives wealth-preserving gifts totaling $320,000 to several of his family members. Two-and-a-half years later, he needs long-term nursing home care. The cost of care in his area is $8,000 per month.

Under old law, if the individual had retained $48,000, he could use it to pay for his own care for six months. This period added to the time since the gifts were made equals three years—so he would then be eligible for Medicaid and his $320,000 of gifts would be secured.

Under new law, the five-year look-back period "catches" the $320,000 of gifts. This makes the individual ineligible for Medicaid benefits for 40 months ($320,000 divided by $8,000 per month equals 40 months).

Worse, this ineligibility period now starts only after the individual has spent down on his own care whatever wealth he's kept. He then is left with the need to finance 40 months of nursing home care on his own—while having no wealth to pay for it!

Other family members may be called on to return gifts received from the individual to pay for his care. If they have spent the funds (such as on college costs), this may not be an option.

Recommended: Know the law in your state. Medicaid laws vary greatly by state and are very complex, with many special rules and exceptions. Examine the laws of your state with a legal expert to find special rules that may help in your situation.

MORE CHANGES

Other restrictions in the new law...

•**Home ownership.** Persons with more than $500,000 of equity in a home now are ineligible for Medicaid benefits. (Individual states may increase this limit to $750,000.)

Thankfully, individuals who have a spouse, children under age 21 or adult children with disabilities living in the home are exempt from this ruling. Previously, there was no such restriction (although states might try to recover the cost of care later through a lien placed on a home or a claim made against it in probate).

•**Annuities.** When an individual who is receiving Medicaid benefits, or the spouse of such an individual, owns an annuity, the state must be the remainder beneficiary of the annuity. In this manner, the state's cost of Medicaid benefits (up to the amount provided) is repaid.

•**Spouses not receiving care.** When the spouse who receives most of a couple's income (such as from a pension) is institutionalized, applying all of that income toward Medicaid costs can result in great hardship to the other spouse (the "community spouse").

As a result, some states have enacted rules that allow shifting of assets to the community spouse free of Medicaid claims.

The new law sharply restricts such actions—increasing hardship on many community spouses in such states.

SELF-DEFENSE

To protect wealth now...

•**Purchase long-term-care insurance.** This will pay for future nursing home care. It is the safest way of providing for future care needs while protecting family wealth.

If you don't already own long-term-care insurance, consider buying it now. The earlier in life you buy, the lower the cost of the premium.

Beware of an early disability. During working years, you are more likely to be disabled, potentially requiring long-term care, than to die.

Check whether your employer provides long-term-care insurance—if it does not, purchase your own.

•**Make wealth-shifting gifts early.** For gifts to other family members to be effective at protecting family wealth, they now must be made a full five years before a need for Medicaid assistance arises.

•**Purchase items exempt from the wealth test.** Items not counted among assets when qualifying for Medicaid include clothing, jewelry, books and an auto needed for work or to travel to obtain medical care. Reduce cash balances by buying things that retain value, such as rare books and fine jewelry.

•**Purchase a single-life annuity.** This can reduce wealth by converting it to income that ends with your life (and so does not have the state as a secondary beneficiary).

•**Take out a home-equity loan.** Reduce the equity in your home to below the $500,000 (or $750,000) limit. Borrowing can be used for living expenses, to fund gifts, buy exempt assets or buy a single-life income annuity.

•**Take out a reverse mortgage.** This, too, can be used to decrease home equity—but fees are higher than the home-equity loan, and a reverse mortgage generally provides less flexibility than home-equity borrowing. Only use this strategy as a last resort.

•**Deed a home to children while retaining a life estate in it.** This gives you the right to use the home while you live while removing its value from your assets.

Snags: You expose the home to children's creditors...if future conflicts arise between you and your children, this arrangement could become uncomfortable.

•**Set up an irrevocable "Medicaid trust."** By irrevocably transferring your assets to the trust, you reduce your wealth to qualify for Medicaid. The trust administers the assets for your family as you direct, and pays you a set amount of income for life at an amount that preserves Medicaid eligibility.

Snag: The income you receive is fixed, so you must be sure it will be sufficient.

Long-Term-Care Premiums Are Now Rising

Even though long-term-care insurance policies are "guaranteed renewable"—meaning premiums cannot be increased based on your health or claims—insurers can raise them for a class of policyholders.

If you want to keep your policy: Reduce benefits to keep premiums the same. Or stop paying premiums—the insurer will pay claims any time in the future equal to the amount of premiums paid in.

If you're buying a new policy: Look for one that guarantees no premium increase for a certain period—for example, five years.

Harry S. Margolis, founder and managing attorney, Margolis & Associates, Boston, *www.elderlawanswers.com.*

A Personal-Care Contract

A personal-care contract allows a parent who suffers from a chronic illness and requires at-home care to pay a family member—such as a son or daughter—for providing care without endangering his/her eligibility for Medicaid. And in fact, the payments could accelerate Medicaid eligibility by depleting the parent's assets. The value of the services to be provided must be reasonable in relationship to the payment that's received.

To find out more, contact the Family Caregiver Alliance (800-445-8106 or *www.caregiver.org*) or the National Alliance for Caregiving (301-718-8444 or *www.caregiving.org*). Or ask a lawyer experienced in elder-care issues.

Peter J. Strauss, Esq., a lawyer specializing in elder-care issues, Epstein Becker & Green PC, New York City, and a coauthor of *The Complete Retirement Survival Guide: Everything You Need to Know to Safeguard Your Money, Your Health, and Your Independence* (Facts-on-File).

Life Insurance Smarts

Byron Udell, JD, ChFC, founder and CEO, AccuQuote.com, which provides on-line life insurance quotes and brokerage services, Wheeling, IL.

If you have loved ones who depend on you, take out a life insurance policy for eight to 10 times your annual salary. You will probably have to buy it on your own as group policies, sold through employers, are usually limited to two to three times a person's salary.

The group policies do not require a physical, which is good for people with health problems. But, healthy people might pay higher premiums than they would if they bought the policies on their own. The healthier employees pay higher rates to subsidize coverage for those who are not healthy.

There is no continuation-of-benefits rule for group life insurance. However, some plans have a provision that allows employees to continue their coverage upon leaving the company. This is subject to state availability and specific plan provisions, but if your plan has no provision to continue such benefits, you may want to buy coverage on your own.

More from Byron Udell, JD...

Is an ROP Policy for You?

Return-of-premium (ROP) term-life policies guarantee that you will get back your premiums if you live for a specified term. The policies might not be a good deal compared with buying regular term insurance and investing the extra money you would spend for the ROP—but ROP effectively forces you to save money. The longer the term, the better ROP is, because the difference between the premiums decreases over time.

Term Life Insurance Prices Have Plunged

If you bought a term life policy more than five years ago, you can probably replace it with a lower-cost policy, even though you're older.

Why: Premium costs have decreased about 50% over the past five years. Plus, insurers have become more generous in writing policies for persons who have medical conditions—such as heart disease and diabetes—that formerly made it difficult or impossible to get.

For free insurance quotes: *www.insure. com* and *www.accuquotelife.com.*

Bob Carlson, editor, *Bob Carlson's Retirement Watch,* Oxon Hill, MD, *www.retirementwatch.com.*

Most Home Owners Are Vastly Underinsured

Even if you bought your house as recently as 10 years ago, and your homeowners' insurance premiums have gone up 2% per year, the value of your house may have increased by several hundred percent. Replacement costs have greatly increased, too.

Strategy: Review your policy at least every two years, and inform your insurer of all major home improvements. Boost coverage to allow for inflation and increased valuations. Consider adding special coverage for terrorism or unusual weather. Also, discuss getting an excess liability policy with your broker.

Sam E. Beller, CLU, ChFC, Diversified Programs, Inc., 551 Fifth Ave., New York City 10176.

Home Insurance Smarts

Home insurance payouts are held by the mortgage lender when a house is destroyed by fire or another disaster. The mortgage lender pays them to the home owner as the house is being rebuilt.

Problem: If the lender doesn't release funds when the contractor insists on a payment, the home owner may have to pay out of pocket until the lender releases the money.

Self-defense: Have the contractor put in the contract a statement acknowledging that he/she will not receive money until the home owner has received it from the mortgage lender.

Also: When buying home insurance, include an ordinance or law provision. This covers the cost of upgrading your rebuilt home to meet codes that were not in effect when your original home was built.

Danny Lipford, syndicated program host of the TV program *Today's Homeowner,* regular contributor to CBS's *The Early Show* and remodeling contractor in Mobile, AL.

Don't Skip Renter's Insurance

Renter's insurance can pay for temporary housing and to replace your belongings. Policies may pay for a hotel or an apartment for up to a year if your home is uninhabitable because of fire or another disaster. Many renters don't take out policies because they feel their property has little value, but if you have rented an apartment or house for some time, you may have accumulated substantial assets. Renter's insurance also covers liability—protection if, for example, a chandelier falls and injures a guest. Rates vary by location and insurer. Be sure to shop around.

Robert Irwin, real estate investor and broker in West Lake, CA.

Filing a Homeowner's Insurance Claim?

When filing a homeowner's claim, you may be able to get back more money if you have a replacement-cost policy. Most of these policies allow insurers to hold back—for as long as six to 24 months—the difference between the cost to repair or replace a damaged item and its value before it was destroyed. Holders of these policies are entitled to the withheld funds—but they must file additional paperwork to get them. Not all insurers require the paperwork, and the type of filing varies widely. Be sure you understand your policy thoroughly—and then reread it, including the fine print, carefully after filing a claim to be sure you receive your full payout.

J.D. Howard, founder and executive director, Insurance Consumer Advocate Network, Branson West, MO, *www.ican2000.com.*

More from J.D. Howard...

Shop Around

Shop for the best car insurance rates and benefits every year. The car insurance market is extremely competitive now, with the various insurers adopting differing price and benefit strategies (such as actual cash value vs. replacement value and first accident forgiveness). This means premiums and coverages will vary greatly from company to company.

Also from J.D. Howard...

Auto Insurance Trap

A big mistake when changing auto insurers is not filing a proper cancellation form.

Trap: If you just do not pay the old policy and let it lapse, the old insurer will cancel it for nonpayment of premiums. This will go in your credit record and may cause the new insurer to raise your premium—so you wind up moving to a new insurer with a higher premium.

Insist on Payment for Actual Repair Costs

Your auto insurer may offer a cash settlement for what appears to be a minor repair.

Problem: After you accept the money, you may find that the cost to repair the damage is more than the settlement.

Self-defense: Get an estimate from an independent repair shop before accepting any offer.

David Solomon a certified master auto technician and chairman of MotorWatch, *www.motorwatch.com.*

Car Insurance Savvy

The most expensive cars to insure are usually expensive to buy and costly to repair. They often have very high horsepower and appeal to aggressive drivers.

***Cars with the highest insurance premiums from 2003 to 2005*:** Mitsubishi Lancer Evolution...Mercedes-Benz CL Class...Dodge Viper...Subaru Impreza WRX...BMW M3.

The cars with the lowest overall losses and that are the least expensive to insure are usually family-oriented vehicles that are not overly expensive to purchase or repair.

Cars with lowest insurance premiums from 2003 to 2005: Buick Terraza...Land Rover LR3...Mercury Montego...Hyundai Tucson ...Nissan Xterra.

Kim Hazelbaker, senior vice president, Highway Loss Data Institute, Arlington, VA.

*Latest period for which rates are available.

My Fender Bender Blunder

Marjory Abrams, publisher, *Bottom Line* newsletters, Boardroom Inc., 281 Tresser Blvd., Stamford, CT 06901.

Late last year, a man backed his truck into my car. No one was hurt, but my vehicle's hood was damaged. The other driver, Scott, did admit he was at fault. Fearful of going through his insurer, he offered to pay for my repairs. The estimate from the repair shop was about $500. Scott said that he would put down a deposit with the shop the next day. He didn't, and despite several phone conversations during which he promised that he would make good, he never did, and he stopped returning my calls. I'm angry at Scott—and angrier at myself for trusting him.

San Francisco attorney Joseph Matthews told me that despite my experience, people often do take care of this sort of thing by themselves—but that I should have done more to protect myself. Mr. Matthews is the author of consumer law books, including *How to Win Your Personal Injury Claim* (Nolo). *His self-defense strategies if you're in a car accident...*

• **Always report to the police and your insurer accidents that involve personal injuries or vehicular damage** that amounts to more than your state's required reporting limit—check with your insurer for the limit.

• **Obtain information regarding the other party or parties:**

• Names, addresses and phone numbers of the driver, passengers and vehicle owner if different from the driver (ask to see the insurance card and registration).

• Insurer and policy number.

• Year, make, model and license plate of the other vehicle.

• Witnesses' names and their phone numbers.

• **Document the damage** to all vehicles and their contents. Keep a disposable camera in your car for this purpose...use your cell phone to take pictures...or write detailed notes.

If the other driver prefers to bypass insurance companies, wait several days before replying.

Reason: Injuries and/or vehicle damage may not be immediately apparent. "Rear-enders" may cause back and neck problems days later.

• **Take your vehicle to a repair shop that you trust,** not one selected by the other driver or one you aren't familiar with. Once you have an estimate and you decide to settle without the insurance company, give the other party a deadline to pay you—in cash. If he/she doesn't meet your agreed-upon deadline, report the accident to your insurer. The company will then inform the Department of Motor Vehicles and settle the claim. Be sure to check with your insurance carrier on how long you have to report the accident.

Would it have been better—or, in the end, simpler—to report the accident to my own insurer? Mr. Matthews says that everyone has to make decisions like this on a case-by-case basis. My deductible is high enough that I would receive no reimbursement. And, most likely, my monthly premiums would not have gone up (as long as I could show that the accident was clearly not my fault), but the incident would go

on my record—which could cause problems if I try to switch insurers. So I'll take the loss. But, next time around, I will certainly get all of the information to ensure that the situation is adequately resolved.

Is Car Rental Insurance Worth It?

Greg McBride, CFA, senior financial analyst, Bankrate.com, North Palm Beach, FL, a provider of interest rate information and personal finance news, articles and commentary, *www.bankrate.com*. He is also a frequent guest on CNN and MSNBC.

Car rental insurance is an option in most US states and, where it's mandatory, it is included in the basic cost of renting the car. The pitch that the car rental companies use to sell collision coverage is, "If you have even the slightest damage to the rental, we're going to immediately charge your credit card for the full amount of your own insurance policy's deductible." Costs for collision damage insurance run from $10 to $35 per day,* personal effects coverage costs $3 to $6 a day and supplemental liability insurance (which can cover liability up to $1 million) is $8 to $15 a day.

Self-defense: Ask your auto insurance agent or company whether your policy covers damage to any car you are driving and includes liability coverage (which covers damage you do to someone else's property when you are driving a rental). If it does, don't buy these coverages from a car rental company. If you don't have collision insurance or don't own a car, rent your car using a credit card.

Why: All the major credit card companies offer this coverage automatically. It costs nothing extra, although specific coverage varies by card company and your credit history. Call the 800 number on the back of the card and ask to receive the terms in writing.

*Prices subject to change.

9

Tax News

The Greatest Loopholes Of All Time

With all these great tax-saving methods most everyone can uncover big money. *Here are some of the best loopholes I have encountered throughout my more than 40 years of working with taxes...*

Loophole: Convert a regular "taxable" IRA (individual retirement account) to a "nontaxable" Roth IRA in a year in which you have business losses and very little income.

Advantage: You can use the business losses to offset taxable income created by converting a traditional IRA. The money in the Roth IRA and its income will then become tax free (unless withdrawn prematurely).

Loophole: Donate appreciated long-term stock in place of cash to all your favorite charities.

When you do this, you can deduct the full fair market value of the shares and owe no capital gains tax on the stock's buildup in value since you bought it.

Example: You own 100 shares of stock, purchased 10 years ago for $15 per share. When you donate the shares, now worth $50 each, to charity, you deduct the full $5,000 fair market value—not your $1,500 cost. You also avoid paying capital gains tax on the $3,500 of appreciation in the shares.

Loophole: Shelter business or freelance income with tax-deferred retirement plans.

You can shelter income, whether from a full- or part-time job, in a retirement plan. For example, in 2007, self-employed workers (including full-time workers who run sideline businesses) can contribute up to 20% of net business income to the Keogh and simplified employee pension (SEP) plans—up to $45,000 per year. (Corporate employees can contribute up to 25%.).

Edward Mendlowitz, CPA, partner in the CPA firm of WithumSmith+Brown at 1 Spring St., New Brunswick, NJ 08901. He is also author of *The Adviser's Guide to Family Business Succession Planning* (American Institute of Certified Public Accountants).

Strategy: Business owners and self-employed workers who are older than age 45 should consider setting up a defined-benefit plan that permits larger contributions than those available in defined-contribution plans.

Caution: Defined-benefit plans can be more expensive and less flexible than defined-contribution plans. Talk to your tax adviser about the pros and cons.

Double benefit: Maximize your overall contributions by setting up a 401(k) plan as well. The maximum deduction for a 401(k) plan in 2007 is $15,500 ($20,500 if age 50 or older), and no percentage limitations apply to the contributions.

Example: You work full-time for a company but operate a sideline business. If you earn $22,000 from the business, you can contribute nearly all of this—$21,000—to retirement plans. You can put away $15,500 in a 401(k) plan, assuming you do not contribute to the company 401(k) plan, and $5,500 additional in another defined-contribution plan (25% of $22,000).

Loophole: Avoid paying alternative minimum tax (AMT) by exercising some of your incentive stock options (ISOs) each year instead of waiting until just before the expiration date to exercise all of them.

When you exercise ISOs, the difference between the fair market value of the stock and the exercise price is a "tax preference" item included in the AMT calculation if the stock is not sold in the year acquired.

Result: You may owe AMT for the year because of exercising the ISO.

Strategy: If you want to hold the stock, you can avoid the AMT by exercising small amounts of ISOs each year, just below the amount that would require you to pay the AMT.

Loophole: Replace personal debt with a home-equity loan to maximize deductible interest payments.

Interest paid on automobile loans, credit card charges, and other personal debt is not deductible, but interest paid on home-equity loans is deductible on loan amounts of $100,000 or less. You can use the proceeds from a home-equity loan for any purpose, such as paying off personal loans—and still deduct the interest—as long as you are not subject to the alternative minimum tax (AMT).

Loophole: Use your IRA, 401(k) or pension plan money to buy rental real estate.

How to do it: The property must be purchased directly by your retirement account (not in partnership with the plan participant). The plan can borrow funds, using the real estate and other plan assets as collateral, but then some of the real estate income will be taxed inside the plan.

Caution: By law, you cannot manage this property yourself. You need to hire a property manager to collect the rents and pay the mortgage, real estate taxes, utility bills, etc.

Benefits: Profits remain in the plan tax deferred. Any gains from the sale of the property are deferred until you begin taking distributions from the plan. However, those gains, like all plan distributions, are taxed at ordinary income rates, not capital gains rates.

Loophole: Operate your own business as a cash-basis S corporation.

In general, C corporations (except personal service corporations) with average annual sales for three years of more than $5 million cannot use cash accounting. Instead, they must use the accrual method of accounting, paying taxes on money not yet received. This rule does not apply to S corporations that have inventory.

Benefits: You defer tax until income is received, not when it's booked as accounts receivable.

More from Edward Mendlowitz, CPA...

Dumb Things People Do... Because Their Financial Advisers Tell Them To

It is usually worthwhile to hire an accountant or other adviser for financial advice, and most serve their clients well. Unfortunately, even these pros may give advice that isn't suitable for a particular client—or for any client. *Some traps that advisers will frequently let their clients fall into—or lead them into...*

REAL ESTATE

•**Pumping up your mortgage.** Your accountant might advise you to take out as large a mortgage as possible because the interest is tax-deductible. Even though it is deductible, mortgage interest must be paid, and payments on a large mortgage might leave you short of cash that you'll need elsewhere. You even could lose your house if you suffer a financial setback and find yourself unable to make the steep mortgage payments.

Some people take out extra mortgage money and hope to save or invest it, but the interest paid on a mortgage is usually greater than what you could earn on personal savings—a gap that can eat up most or all of the mortgage's deductibility advantage.

And it's not worth risking a big mortgage in the hope that you can use the borrowed money to earn more elsewhere.

INVESTING

• **Selling mutual fund shares improperly.** Financial advisers often fail to tell their clients that selling fund shares wisely is not as simple as buying them.

To avoid paying unnecessary taxes when you sell all of your shares in a fund, you must tally up any dividends and other fund distributions that were automatically reinvested into the fund and count this amount as part of your "basis" (your cost for tax purposes). Your mutual fund company will be able to provide you with the numbers.

Then you report your basis on your tax return, along with the amount you receive for the shares when you sell them. Including all of your reinvested distributions in your basis will help you by reducing your taxable gain or increasing your deductible loss.

Trap: If you acquired shares in the fund at different times and want to sell only some of those shares, you can specifically designate that your highest-cost shares be sold. This strategy will minimize your taxes.

How to do it: Write to your broker or the fund company (or have your adviser do so) before the sale takes place, and identify the shares that you would like to sell.

Example: "Please sell the 100 shares of ABC Fund that I bought on January 10, 2005."

Keep in mind that any gain on shares held more than one year will be taxed at no higher than 15% federally. Gains on shares held for a shorter time will be taxed at your ordinary income tax rate, up to 35% federally. If you own

both short-term-gain and long-term-gain shares, calculate the taxes you would owe in selling each, then sell the shares that result in the lowest tax paid.

• **Disposing of worthless securities without following the tax rules.** If you have invested in a company whose stock has lost all value, you can take a capital loss equal to your entire cost basis in these shares. But you must show that the company became totally worthless in the year for which you're filing a return. This may not be easy to do—and many advisers fail to tell their clients that this proof of worthlessness is necessary.

Better: Sell the securities to a sympathetic unrelated party (someone other than your spouse, sibling, parent, child or business partner) for $1, which will enable you to take a normal capital loss without having to prove that the stock became totally worthless. You will probably want to reimburse your helpful friend for any transaction costs.

Alternatively, get a letter from your broker stating that the cost of selling the securities would be greater than the proceeds you would collect. This also enables you to take a capital loss.

TAXES

• **Prepaying estimated taxes.** Some people must pay estimated taxes each quarter to their states, as well as to the IRS. The final payment for any given year is due the following January 15.

Historically, for people who itemize deductions, state estimated tax payments made in the previous December have qualified for a deduction that year on the federal tax return.

Trap: In recent years, exposure to the alternative minimum tax (AMT) has become more widespread. For people who owe the AMT, prepaying state tax can result in "wasting" a large outlay that won't be deductible.

Example: A hypothetical John Morgan, who resides in Buffalo, owes New York State a $5,000 estimated tax payment by January 15, 2008. His accountant advises him to send in a $5,000 check by December 31, 2007, to get a federal income tax deduction for 2007.

However, John winds up owing the AMT in 2007—and state tax payments aren't deductible under AMT rules. John gets no write-off for this $5,000. He would have been better off delaying the payment until 2008, when he might not owe the AMT.

Protection: Ask your accountant to consider the AMT before recommending year-end tax prepayments.

• **Taking unsupported deductions for alimony payments.** This bad advice is commonly given to divorced people by advisers.

The facts: For an alimony deduction to be valid, there needs to be a written agreement between the two parties that spells out monetary amounts and the rights and responsibilities of each party. Also, you can never deduct child-support payments—so your divorce documents should clearly delineate alimony from child support, if any.

To deduct alimony payments, you must enter on your tax return the Social Security number of the former spouse who received them. This former spouse will owe taxes on the alimony income received.

ESTATE PLANNING

• **Making unwise gifts.** In 2007, each individual can give away up to $12,000 worth of assets to any number of recipients without owing any gift tax. (For married couples, the amount that can be given away is $24,000 per recipient.) For affluent people, this can be valuable for reducing future estate taxes.

Trap: In these days of long life expectancies and soaring long-term-care costs, too many advisers don't fully evaluate whether their clients might need this money for themselves down the line. Even worse, many advisers fail to set their clients straight on a common misconception—that money given away is tax deductible. It is *not*. It is merely tax exempt for the recipient of the gift.

RETIREMENT ACCOUNTS

• **Naming the wrong IRA beneficiaries.** How valuable your hard-earned IRA assets will be after your death is highly dependent on the beneficiaries you designate now. Many advisers don't make clear the extreme importance of naming beneficiaries properly.

Common mistake: Naming your estate as the beneficiary or failing to name a beneficiary at all. This could cost your heirs the benefit of extended tax deferral. The individuals who ultimately inherit the IRA assets will, by law, have to empty the tax-deferred accounts much more rapidly than might otherwise be the case.

Better: Name one or several individuals as beneficiaries. Individual beneficiaries can stretch out required distributions (and defer paying tax on those distributions) over either their own life expectancies or the former life expectancy of the deceased IRA owner, depending on the age of the IRA owner when he/she died.

Also important: Identify contingent beneficiaries to permit your primary beneficiaries to decide whether to accept the inheritance or, if more appropriate, to let it go to another beneficiary with its tax benefits intact.

Also from Edward Mendlowitz, CPA...

Home Owner Loopholes

Owning a home creates a variety of tax-saving opportunities. *Consider all these loopholes...*

Loophole: **Real estate taxes are fully deductible,** and the mortgage interest you pay on mortgages up to $1 million, as well as the interest on home-equity loans up to $100,000, is also deductible. Real estate taxes are deductible no matter how many properties you own—but, you cannot deduct mortgage or home-equity interest for more than two residences.

The points paid for a mortgage used to buy a main residence are fully deductible in the year of the purchase. Points paid on the portion of refinanced mortgages in excess of the amount used for new improvements are amortized over the mortgage term.

Caution: When you refinance your home, you can deduct the interest only on the portion of the proceeds used to replace the original mortgage and the part used for new home improvements. Interest on refinancing proceeds used for other purposes is not deductible.

AMT pitfall: Real estate taxes and certain mortgage interest expenses are not deductible under AMT.

Strategy: Big mortgages make sense tax-wise because the interest is deductible, but make sure a big mortgage also makes sense from a financial planning viewpoint.

How to do it: Compare the after-tax cost of the mortgage interest payment to the amount you could earn if you invested the money instead.

Loophole: **When you sell a primary residence, your first $250,000 of gain is not taxed.** Up to $500,000 of the profit from the sale is tax free for couples who file a joint return and who were married at the time the residence was sold.

Requirement: You need to have owned this home and used it as your principal residence for at least two out of the five years before the sale.

In case of divorce: When a couple sells their primary residence as part of a divorce settlement, profits from the sale can be sheltered by the full $500,000 exclusion even if one spouse moved out of the house before the property was sold.

How: Make sure that the divorce/separation agreement states that the spouse who owns the house (or holds joint title) retains title and the former spouse is granted temporary possession, so each can claim the $250,000 exclusion when the home is sold.

Loophole: **Reserve the right to take the home-sale exclusion for property you have rented out.** The tax exemption for property sales is available only for residential, not commercial, properties. Under IRS rules, a "residential" property must not have generated income in at least two years of the past five years. Therefore, if you rent all or part of your primary residence, consider eliminating all rentals for three years before you plan to sell it.

Loophole: **Save estate taxes by arranging title to your residence so that each spouse owns a 50% interest** without rights of survivorship. For estate or gift tax purposes, the property would be eligible for a valuation discount, since owning a 50% interest does not provide control. And a noncontrolling interest is worth less than a controlling interest.

Loophole: **Transfer a personal residence or vacation house to a qualified personal residence trust (or QPRT).** The person who transfers the property retains the right to use it during the term of the trust, say, 10 years. Be-

cause your right to use the property reduces its value, the gift tax on the transfer into the trust is reduced. Its value is calculated according to IRS tables. The longer the trust term, the lower the value of the property for gift tax purposes.

Example: A 65-year-old transfers a house worth $500,000 to a 10-year QPRT. The taxable gift comes to about $220,000. A 15-year QPRT would equal $130,000.

Strategy 1: Although you cannot prearrange that you will be allowed to remain in the house when the term of the trust expires, you can offer the new owners a market rent lease just before the term expires.

Strategy 2: Choose a trust term that you are likely to outlive, since the house is included in your taxable estate if you die before the trust term ends. The property passes to the trust beneficiary at the end of the trust term. If the grantor dies before then, the full value of the house is included in the grantor's estate for estate tax purposes.

Caution: The beneficiary takes the same tax basis as the grantor—there is no stepped-up basis. Nor is the transfer eligible for the $12,000 annual gift tax exclusion.

Loophole: **Donate an historic or a farming easement and deduct the value of the easement as a charitable contribution.** For example, if your house is located in a landmark district or is an historically designated property, you can donate to your town a preservation easement over the facade to protect the property's appearance from alteration now and in the future, and deduct its fair market value—typically 10% to 15% of the property's total value.

Loophole: **Put property into a revocable living trust to avoid or reduce the probate process.** The trust becomes irrevocable upon your death, at which time the alternate trustee assumes control of the trust. This maneuver does not save taxes, but the assets avoid probate.

Related strategy: Transferring title to an out-of-state vacation home or second residence into an LLC can keep your estate out of probate in the state in which the property is located. Check with an attorney in the state where the property is located.

Keep Records of Home Improvements

The cost of home improvements isn't deductible. But keep records of them and add their amount to the tax cost (basis) in your home. This will reduce taxable gain on its future sale.

Key: Many people now neglect to keep such records due to the tax-free gain of up to $250,000, or $500,000 (joint), that is available on a home sale—believing that will cover all future gain.

But these tax-free amounts lose value to inflation every year, and ultimately gain may surpass them. Also, the law may change in the future.

Lawrence Berland, CPA, partner, Mahoney Cohen & Company, CPA, PC, 1065 Ave. of the Americas., New York City 10018.

The New Tax Breaks For Home-Energy Improvements

Kara Saul Rinaldi, director of policy for the Alliance to Save Energy (ASE), 1200 18 St. NW, Washington, DC 20036, a nonprofit coalition of business, government, environmental, and consumer leaders in Washington, DC, *www.ase.org*. ASE advocates energy-efficiency policies that minimize costs to society and individual consumers.

Home owners can save on energy costs, make their homes more comfortable—and more marketable—and cut down on taxes by making energy-efficiency improvements that qualify for tax breaks.

Don't wait too long. Most of the latest federal tax breaks for energy improvements apply only to improvements made in 2006 and 2007.

HELP FROM THE FEDS

The *Energy Tax Incentives Act of 2005* introduced two categories of tax credits available to home owners…

• **Energy-efficiency improvements** (qualifying doors and windows, insulation, etc.) to the building "envelope" (exterior of the home) and powering equipment.

• **Solar panels** and other systems for powering homes.

Different credit limits and other rules apply to each category.

Caution: You must reduce the tax basis of your home by the amount of any credits claimed. But basis reduction only becomes important when you sell the home and your gain exceeds the allowable home-sale exclusion ($250,000, or $500,000 on a joint return).

HOME IMPROVEMENTS

You can take a tax credit of up to $500 for making home improvements. This encompasses building envelope components that meet or exceed criteria set by the 2000 International Energy Conservation Code (manufacturers should provide this information). The credit is 10% of qualifying expenses.

Examples: Insulation systems that reduce heat loss or heat gain, exterior windows (including skylights), exterior doors and certain metal roofs that meet Energy Star requirements. (Energy Star is a government rating program that shows which items are more efficient than typical models.)

The credit is limited to the cost of materials. No more than $200 of the credit can be attributable to windows.

Heating and cooling equipment also might qualify for the credit, including 100% of qualifying expenses for…

• **Advanced natural air circulating fans** (up to $50).

• **Natural gas, propane or oil furnaces or boilers** (up to $150).

The credit can be claimed only for items added to or replaced in an existing home, not for those installed in the course of building a new home. Manufactured homes (prefab and mobile homes) do qualify. The credit cannot be used for upgrades to vacation homes—only for primary residences.

HEATING/COOLING SYSTEMS

Solar panels are nothing new—panels were popular in the late 1970s and the 1980s when the last energy crunch occurred. Currently, there are several renewable energy sources, including solar panels, that can be used to power heating and cooling systems for homes and that qualify for a tax credit through 2008. *These include…*

• **Solar water-heating systems**—a credit of 30% of expenditures up to $2,000.

• **Photovoltaic property** (solar energy generating equipment)—30% of expenditures with a maximum of $2,000.

• **Fuel cell electric generating equipment expenditures**—30% of costs with a maximum of $500 for each half kilowatt of capacity.

Exception: No credit can be claimed for systems used to heat swimming pools and hot tubs.

ADDED TAX INCENTIVE

There are very few provisions in the tax law that let you effectively multiply your tax write-offs from a single expenditure, and here is one of them—you could finance your home-energy improvements through a home loan, deduct the interest and claim a credit for the energy improvement made with the proceeds of the loan.

Deductibility: The interest may be treated as "acquisition indebtedness," producing a tax deduction if the loan is taken to make an energy expenditure that is considered to be a substantial improvement to the home. There is not much Tax Code guidance on what can be treated as a substantial improvement in terms of cost or relative to the home's value or basis. What is certain is that the expenditure must add to the home's value or prolong its useful life in order to be viewed as "substantial." If so, interest on borrowing up to $1 million is deductible.

But even if the improvement is not viewed as "substantial," the interest is still deductible on borrowing up to $100,000.

Low-interest loans: States and energy utilities may provide affordable financing to make energy improvements—a boon to home owners who cannot or prefer not to use home-equity financing. For instance, Pennsylvania's Energy Star loans carry interest as low as 5.99%.*

Note: Interest on these loans isn't deductible because the loans are not secured by the residences, a requirement for home-mortgage treatment.

STATE TAX BREAKS

States want to encourage energy conservation measure as well, and many provide tax breaks. Since 2006, more than 100 bills have been introduced at the state level to provide tax incentives for energy-saving home improvements.

*Rate subject to change.

Sales tax holiday: States may waive their sales tax on certain energy-efficient products to give home owners added incentive to upgrade their residences. For example, from October 6, 2005, through October 9, 2005, Georgia offered a sales tax holiday on various Energy Star products that cost up to $1,500—a $105 tax savings for qualified purchases up to the maximum 7% sales tax in certain areas of the state. A number of other states, including Connecticut, Illinois, Kansas, New York, Pennsylvania, Rhode Island and Vermont, are currently weighing a similar tax break. To find out if your state plans such a break, contact your state's tax, finance or revenue department. For a database of state incentives, go to *www.dsireusa.org*.

LOW-INCOME HOME OWNERS

Home owners with very modest incomes can't benefit from tax breaks (because they don't owe taxes), but still want to save money by making energy improvements to their residences. *Government programs can help...*

• **The Weatherization Assistance Program** by the Department of Energy (*www.eere.energy.gov/weatherization*) helps lower-income families (check the site for eligibility requirements) make permanent energy-saving improvements, such as foam door seals, to help cut fuel consumption.

• **States such as Colorado and Washington have similar programs** for low-income families. Check with your state's energy department.

Make Your Vacation Home Pay for Itself

Albert Ellentuck, Esq., CPA, of counsel to the law firm King & Nordlinger, LLP, 2111 Wilson Blvd., Arlington, VA 22201. Past chairman of the tax division of the American Institute of Certified Public Accountants (AICPA), he writes a column for the AICPA publication, *The Tax Adviser.*

If you own a second home used exclusively for your own getaways, the tax implications, federal and state, are fairly straightforward. You probably can deduct outlays for mortgage interest and property tax, just as you can with your primary residence. (Property tax deductions won't be deductible, though, if you are subject to the alternative minimum tax.)

Mixing business with pleasure: The rules change—and become considerably more complex—if you sometimes receive rental income from your second home.

Opportunity: Knowing how to mix rental use with personal use can result in substantial additional tax savings.

14-DAY RULE

If you rent out your vacation home occasionally, you can qualify for a prime tax break.

Loophole: You can rent out your home for up to 14 days a year and owe *no tax at all* on that income.

This can result in thousands of dollars of tax-free income if your home is near a major sports event, such as the Super Bowl or in a desirable vacation area.

Caution: It probably doesn't make sense to rent your home for just over 14 days in a year. If you do, all the income will be taxable, not just the excess from the fifteenth day on. You might pocket less after taxes than if you had rented the place out for fewer days.

14-DAY 10% RULE

Once you rent out your home for more than 14 days in a given year, it gets complicated.

Rental vs. residence: If you use your vacation home for personal purposes* for no more than the greater of (1) 14 days or (2) 10% of rental days, the home will be considered rental property. In this case, losses may be deductible.

Example: Jim Smith rents out his beach house for 100 days a year and uses it personally for 13 days. He can treat his beach house as rental property. If he uses it for 14 days, however, it is considered a residence.

Janice Jones has the beach house next to Jim's, which she rents out for 200 days a year. She can use it up to 19 days (less than 10% of 200 days) and still treat it as rental property.

Why this matters: As explained above, when you rent out a property for more than 14 days a year, the rental income is taxable. But at the same time, expenses related to that rental income can

*You must count as personal use any day that the residence is used for personal purposes by you or by a relative, even if you used it for only part of that day.

be tabulated. Such expenses might include management fees and marketing costs. You also can allocate expenses, such as insurance, repairs and depreciation to the property's rental use.

Outcome: A portion of your vacation home expenses will become business-related, which will reduce the net income you'll report from the property. You'll owe less tax on the rental income.

In some cases, business-related expenses will exceed rental income. The resulting loss will fall under the "passive-loss" rules if you can treat your vacation home as rental property.

How this works: If you have a passive loss, it can offset taxable income from unrelated passive activities. This could include other rental property you own or limited partnership income.

Even better: In addition, net passive losses might be deductible from your taxable income (the income you report on your tax return after deductions).

Required: If your adjusted gross income, or AGI, is less than $100,000 on a single or joint return, you can deduct up to $25,000 worth of net passive losses.

To deduct passive losses against your taxable income, you also have to take part in some management decisions, such as approving tenants and authorizing repairs.

Phaseout: If your AGI is between $100,000 and $150,000, you can deduct a lower amount of net passive losses.

Example: Your AGI is $145,000 this year, so you are 90% through the phaseout range. You are entitled to 10% of the maximum passive-loss deduction, thus you can deduct up to $2,500 in net passive losses (10% of $25,000).

Looking ahead: Net passive losses you can't deduct right away can be used in the future if your AGI permits a write-off at that time or if you have passive income from other sources. Otherwise, all of your deferred passive losses can offset any gains when you sell the property.

Bottom line: If you think that you'll have a passive loss from renting out a vacation home and you'll be able to deduct such a loss, keep personal use down to the level where the home is classed as rental property.

If you use the vacation home for so many personal days that it is classed as a residence rather than a rental property, no losses can be deducted.

SEVEN-DAY RULE

Yet another rule comes into play for vacation home owners.

In some areas, especially resorts, your average rental period for a vacation home may be less than seven days. If so, you face different requirements. You divide the number of days you rented by the number of your paying customers.

If your vacation home rentals average less than seven days, you may be able to avoid the passive-loss rules and deduct your losses currently, in the year that you have the loss. *To do so, you must "materially participate" in the venture by either...*

• **Devoting more than 500 hours per year** to gaining revenues from the property or...

• **Devoting more than 100 hours to this effort,** as long as this is more time than anyone else spends.

Strategy: If your vacation home rentals will average less than seven days and you expect to have net losses from this activity, consider forgoing the management company. By spending more than 100 hours per year yourself on this business, you will probably be able to deduct those losses.

What if your vacation home usage qualifies you for the seven-day rule, but you do not materially participate in running the business? You'll be subject to the passive-loss rules, without the opportunity of deducting up to $25,000 worth of net losses.

DISAPPEARING DEDUCTION

As explained, it may make sense to restrict personal use of a vacation home to qualify it as rental property so that a loss can be deducted.

Trap: A home classified as rental property is no longer a residence, so mortgage interest payments allocable to your personal use won't be deductible.

Situation: You rent out the vacation home 190 days in a year and use it for 10 days. Therefore, the vacation home is considered to be a rental property.

However, 5% of the usage (10 days out of a total of 200 days) is allocable to your personal use. Consequently, 5% of the mortgage interest you pay is not deductible.

Reasoning: That 5% cannot be allocated to your rental activities because it's attributable to personal use. Yet the home does not qualify as a residence, so that 5% is not deductible home mortgage interest, either.

Strategy: Crunch the numbers to see which will produce the best after-tax result—a deduction for home mortgage interest or passive-loss deduction.

Then, adjust your personal use to have your vacation home fall into the category that works best for you, rental property or residence.

Best: Talk with an accountant experienced in helping clients maximize the tax benefits of owning a second home.

 # Don't Miss These Surprising Medical Expense Deductions

Laurence I. Foster, CPA/PFS, tax consultant based in New York City and former partner at Eisner LLP. Mr. Foster was chairman of the Personal Financial Specialist Credential Committee at the American Institute of Certified Public Accountants (AICPA).

The IRS and courts have approved many surprising and unusual tax deductions for medical expenses. Keep all these possible opportunities in mind when planning your tax strategies or preparing your tax return.

TOPPING THE HURDLE

Medical expenses for items and services prescribed by a doctor for a specific condition are deductible, but only to the extent that their total exceeds 7.5% of adjusted gross income (AGI), and 10% of AGI if you are subject to the alternative minimum tax. *To get over this hurdle, you can deduct "big ticket" items such as...*

• **Home improvements.** When you improve your home to mitigate a diagnosed medical ailment, the cost is deductible to the extent that it exceeds any resulting increase in the value of your home.

Example: Central air-conditioning to help alleviate your respiratory condition. If you spend $12,000 putting it in, but it increases the value of your home by only $8,000, then you've got a legitimate $4,000 medical deduction. To determine how much an improvement increases the value of your home, see a real estate appraiser. *Other examples...*

• A lap swimming pool, when the swimming was prescribed by a doctor as treatment for a condition, and the individual was allergic to chemicals in the water of a public pool, and no other public pool was available.

• An attached garage, when a doctor advised the home owner to avoid cold winter air.

• An elevator for a person with a heart condition or arthritis.

An improvement to accommodate a *disability* is fully tax deductible without regard to any increase in value. *Included...*

☐ Modification or lowering of kitchen cabinets and counters.

☐ Certain bathroom modifications, including railings and support bars.

☐ Rampways into a home.

☐ Widening of doorways and halls.

☐ Grading the ground around a home to ease access to it.

Medically related improvements to a property you rent are fully deductible if you are not compensated for their cost by your landlord.

Example: On your doctor's advice, you install a bathroom on the ground floor of a house you rent to avoid having to climb stairs. Your landlord permits you to do so but does not pay any of the cost. You could deduct as a medical expense the full cost that you pay.

The operating costs, such as electricity, maintenance and repair of air-conditioners, elevators and chair lifts, and other home improvements that qualify for medical deduction also are 100% deductible.

• **Expenses paid for others.** You can deduct medical costs you pay for persons who qualify as your dependents. For tax years after December 31, 2004, the definition of a medical dependent was changed. It now includes married individuals even with their own dependents. There is no test for gross income. (See the *Working Families Tax Relief Act of 2004.*) *Examples...*

• A retired parent who doesn't live with you, when you pay more than half the parent's support —such as when this parent is residing in a nursing home.

• A person for whom you obtain a dependency exemption by filing Form 2120, *Multiple Support Agreement.* This enables a group of people who jointly support a person to obtain a dependency exemption and assign it to one among them, even when no one member of this group pays more than half of the recipient's support.

• A child after divorce, even when the dependency exemption for the child is claimed by your former spouse. *Rule:* When either divorced spouse claims a dependency exemption for a child, each spouse can deduct those medical expenses that each spouse actually pays for the child.

Note: Gifts of medical payments on behalf of anyone in any amount paid directly to healthcare providers are not subject to gift tax.

• **Travel.** If you or a dependent must travel for medical reasons, the cost of travel and lodging is deductible as a medical expense. (The cost of meals generally is not deductible.) *Examples...*

• A patient who was advised by a doctor to move to a different part of the country with an environment better for the person's medical condition found that he could claim a medical deduction for some moving costs. If you think that you have a similar situation, check with your accountant.

• Parents who sent a child to boarding school in Arizona to alleviate the child's respiratory ailment were allowed by the Tax Court to deduct the child's travel and room and board costs.

• The costs of attending a conference which presents information about a chronic disease affecting the taxpayer or a dependent are deductible.

• When one stays at a hospital or other medical facility, meal charges imposed by the facility may be deducted.

• In deducting medically related travel costs, airfares and other travel fares, including taxis, are deductible at their full cost. Driving in 2007 is deductible at 20 cents per mile, or at actual recorded out-of-pocket cost if higher, with parking and tolls also deductible.

FREQUENTLY OVERLOOKED
Don't miss deductions for the cost of...

• **Equipment used to alleviate a medical condition,** such as portable air-conditioners, humidifiers and dehumidifiers, and their operating expenses.

• **Weight-loss programs,** when prescribed as treatment for a specific medical condition, such as high blood pressure.

• **Smoking cessation programs.**

• **Cosmetic surgery** when utilized to alleviate a medical condition rather than merely improve appearance.

Example: A hair transplant surgery to improve one's appearance is not deductible. But surgery to remove skin folds that remained after a formerly obese person lost a large amount of weight is deductible as part of the treatment for obesity.

• **A wig** purchased on the advice of a physician for the mental health of a patient who lost hair due to disease.

• **Clarinet lessons,** when prescribed to alleviate a child's overbite.

• **Lamaze classes** and other childbirth preparation programs.

• **A child's special education costs,** when on a doctor's recommendation you pay extra for a teacher who is specially qualified to work with children who have learning disabilities caused by mental or physical impairments. If the child is advised to board at a school providing special education, medical expenses could include cost of tuition and room and board.

• **Psychoanalysis,** psychologist fees and psychiatric care costs.

• **Trained animals** that are used to alleviate disabilities.

Examples: Cats trained to react to sound for the deaf...guide dogs for the blind.

• **Special controls for automobiles,** such as hand controls instead of foot pedals.

• **Meals,** when special foods are prescribed by a doctor, to the extent that their cost is greater than regular foods.

• **Eyesight correction,** including contact lenses and related solutions and cleaners, eyeglasses and laser surgery for sight correction.

• **Dental treatments,** including X-rays, fillings, braces, extractions and dentures (but not teeth whitening).

• **Blood sugar test kits** and other diagnostic devices for specific maladies.

• **Hearing aids,** and special audio equipment attached to televisions, phones and other items to compensate for a hearing impairment.

• **Insurance premiums** used to cover medical care costs, including Medicare drug coverage.

Included: Insurance on contact lenses...other insurance that pays for prescription drugs.

• **Medicare Part B** (supplemental medical insurance). Premiums for it are a deductible medical expense.

• **Laboratory fees** incurred in receiving medical care or a diagnosis.

• **Acupuncture.**

For more information, check IRS Publication 502, *Medical and Dental Expenses,* available for free at *www.irs.gov.* You might have a unique medical situation that could qualify for a deduction. Check with your tax adviser.

Big College Savings Trap: Reduced Aid

Rick Darvis, president of College Funding, Inc., which trains financial professionals in college funding services, 121 N. Main St., Plentywood, MT 59254, *www.solutions forcollege.com.*

A big trap in many college savings arrangements is that they may reduce college financial aid that the child would otherwise qualify for—so the savings effectively are wasted. People who focus on cutting taxes on college savings without being aware of college financial aid formulas can walk into this trap.

Key: When savings or other assets are owned by the student, the standard federal college aid formula considers 20% of all student assets (and 50% of student income) available to pay college tuition each year—and any financial aid eligibility the student otherwise would have qualified for is reduced accordingly.

Example: Grandparents set up and fund a "college savings" account owned in a child's name that is worth $40,000 when the child goes to college. The college financial aid office deems $8,000 of the account (20% of $40,000) available to pay tuition for the first year. If without the account the child would have been eligible for financial aid, it reduces this aid by $8,000. So, if the child would otherwise have received $15,000 of aid, he now receives only $7,000.

Thus, the $8,000 withdrawn from the "college savings" account to pay tuition is met by an $8,000 increase in tuition cost—helping the child by $0. The grandparent's $8,000 savings in the account is wasted.

As this process is repeated over four years, the savings account will be nearly consumed.

In contrast: When assets are owned by the student's parents, only up to 5.6% of them are deemed available to pay college costs. If parents accumulate $40,000 in a savings account of their own, the formula deems $2,240 of this (5.6% of $40,000) available to pay tuition for their child's first year of college—and financial aid is reduced by only this much smaller amount.

THE TAX-SAVINGS TRAP

Promised tax savings lure many parents and grandparents into placing savings for college in "tax-favored" accounts that can cost far more in lost financial help than they ever save on their taxes.

Example: Gift accounts set up in children's names under the *Uniform Transfers to Minors Act* (or UTMA) have been very popular because they are taxed at the child's tax rate, which may be low or even zero. The child's rate, through 2007, only applies to children age 18 and older. Starting in 2008, the "kiddie tax" age increases making UTMA accounts unattractive for education savings.

Also, a UTMA account legally is the child's property—so a gift to one which saves several cents on the dollar in taxes may affect college financial aid at a much higher rate.

Alternative: Coverdell Education Savings Accounts and 529 plans are treated as assets of the parent for financial aid purposes—unless owned by someone other than the child's parent, such as a grandparent—and may be another option.

Before deciding on a college savings strategy, consult with a college financial aid expert about its impact on receiving tuition assistance.

Don't Overestimate The Value of the Hybrid Car Tax Credit

James Glass, tax attorney based in New York City and a contributing writer to both *Tax Hotline* and *Bottom Line/ Retirement*, newsletters published by Boardroom Inc.

Fuel-saving autos with hybrid gas-electric engines are surging in popularity—in part because of the new tax credit that could be worth as much as $3,400. But do not overestimate how much the credit is worth toward decreasing the cost of a car, or gasoline costs. *Some snags…*

• **You may not get the credit.** The tax credit isn't allowed under the alternative minimum tax (AMT). And the persons who are most likely to buy hybrids—the upper-income individuals living in urban and suburban areas paying above-average state and local taxes—are the persons who are most likely to owe AMT.

• **The credit won't cover the extra purchase cost of the car.** While the maximum possible credit is $3,400, no car actually receives one that large. In most cases, the credit is less than $2,000, and the extra cost of a hybrid over that of a comparable vehicle with a conventional engine is consistently in published comparisons significantly more than the amount of the credit.

Examples: For 2005 hybrids, the Web site Edmunds.com reported the additional purchase and five-year ownership cost of hybrids to be…

• $3,816 for the Honda Accord Hybrid versus the Honda Accord EX V-6.

• $3,429 for the Ford Escape Hybrid over the Ford Escape XLT AWD.

• **Future fuel savings probably won't cover the extra purchase cost**—even counting the tax credit. Research by consumer organizations, such as Edmunds.com and *Consumer Reports*, has shown that the gas savings of hybrid cars usually are smaller than indicated by official US government gas mileage estimates, and that most hybrid cars won't recover the extra cost of their higher purchase price through fuel savings in normal use.

Consumer Reports states in its 2006 car buying guide…

"In our analysis, only two of the six hybrids we have tested recovered their price premium in the first five years and 75,000 miles of ownership [and] that is only if buyers are able to take advantage of limited federal tax credits."

Smart buying: When aware of these potential snags, you can examine the details of a particular hybrid to see if it's an attractive purchase.

• **Tax breaks are limited.** The federal tax credit for purchasing certain hybrids expires after 2007, so act now if you had been planning on doing so.

Caution: No credit can be claimed for qualified Toyota hybrids (e.g., a Prius) purchased after September 30, 2007.

FUEL SAVING ALTERNATIVES

• **Purchasing a car with a manual** instead of automatic transmission can increase gas mileage by more than 15% while actually reducing the price of the car.

• **New diesel engines** now being introduced by leading carmakers are highly fuel efficient.

Don't Be Caught By the AMT

Thomas P. Ochsenschlager, Esq., CPA, vice president of taxation for the American Institute of Certified Public Accountants (AICPA), Washington, DC, *www.aicpa.org.*

Although the alternative minimum tax, or AMT,* originally was intended to catch wealthy tax avoiders, each year it is hitting more middle-class taxpayers with incomes of under $100,000—in some cases, well under. Even if you got hit with AMT when you filed your 2006 return, with careful planning, you can reduce your risk when you file your 2007 return. *Common triggers…*

ITEMIZED DEDUCTIONS

Many itemized deductions don't reduce your income under AMT.

Examples: State and local taxes…miscellaneous itemized deductions that exceed 2% of adjusted gross income (AGI)…home-equity

*The AMT is a parallel tax system. Each year, you calculate the taxes you owe under both regular income tax and AMT. You pay whichever amount is greater.

loan interest if the loan is not used for home improvements.

Strategy: Use charitable contributions, home mortgage interest and any large medical outlays to reduce AMT exposure. Also take advantage of tax shelters, such as 401(k) and traditional IRA contributions and health savings accounts.

CAPITAL GAINS

Even though the low 15% cap on long-term capital gains tax applies under both the AMT and the regular tax systems, taking such gains may increase your exposure to AMT because it increases your taxable income. This raises the chance that you'll lose some or all of your "AMT exemption," the amount of income that is completely sheltered from AMT liability.

In 2006, the tax exemption was $42,500 for single filers or $62,550 for joint filers. Between taxable income levels of roughly $150,000 and $300,000, an AMT exemption phased out. When this happens, the amount you would owe under AMT might exceed the amount of regular tax, which would force you to pay AMT. The 2007 exemption amounts are not yet known.

Your state may impose capital gains tax, too. State taxes aren't deductible from AMT income, so this added tax may increase the chance that you'll owe AMT.

Strategy: If possible, delay paying your state tax until a year that the AMT won't be a concern. For instance, if you do not expect to pay AMT in 2008, you usually can delay paying estimated state tax for the fourth quarter of 2007 until January 15, 2008. You could also delay taking a capital gain in a year when you expect to owe AMT.

Another approach is to spread a capital gain over more than one year—sell some appreciated stock in December 2007, for example, and some more in January 2008.

MUNICIPAL BONDS

Interest on "private activity" municipal bonds that fund nongovernmental projects, such as stadiums and shopping malls, is subject to AMT.

Strategy: Focus on municipal bonds that are not subject to AMT. Also call your fund company to make sure that your municipal bond mutual funds don't hold bonds that are subject to AMT.

INCENTIVE STOCK OPTIONS

Some employers motivate employees with incentive stock options (ISOs) instead of traditional "nonqualified" stock options. Benefit? No regular income tax is owed when ISOs are exercised, and the profits eventually will be favorably taxed as long-term capital gains if the shares are held for more than one year after the stock option is exercised.

Trap: When figuring AMT, the difference between the exercise price and the market price is counted in your income in the year that the option is exercised. Before you exercise ISOs, consult a tax adviser.

Don't Overlook Sales Taxes

Don't ignore the deduction for state and local sales taxes on your 2007 federal return. You can deduct these instead of state income taxes if doing so provides a larger tax savings.

Danger: In 2006, one in every seven taxpayers who could have benefited from claiming the deduction failed to do so.

What to do: Learn how to claim the deduction from the IRS Web site, *www.irs.gov,* and/or IRS Publication 553, *Highlights of Tax Changes.*

Gamblers and the IRS: Keep the Most and Avoid Tax Trouble

Wayne Hagendorf, an attorney and CPA with offices in Las Vegas and Los Angeles who specializes in estate planning and asset protection for business owners.

Gambling is a $50 billion business in this country, and the IRS must love it. Winnings are taxable and may be subject to withholding, and deductions for losses are restricted. *Here are some ways to make the most of both winning and losing...*

THE WINNERS

If you are lucky enough to have had a good year at the track, casino or other gambling venue, your winnings will have both a direct and an indirect impact on your taxes...

•**Direct impact.** Gambling winnings are taxable as ordinary income. This includes sweepstakes, lotteries and winnings from any illegal betting (e.g., the office football pool or on-line poker—now a $10 billion industry).

Even if you *sell* the right to collect your winnings, you get no break. The IRS says that you received ordinary income in this case—not capital gains.

Example: Suppose that you win the state lottery payable over 25 years. After you collect your first-year share, you sell the right to your 24 other payments. The amount you get from the third party is ordinary income—just as it would be had you received the payments directly from the state.

Casinos and other venues must report gambling winnings to you, and to the IRS, on Form W-2G, *Certain Gambling Winnings,* when your winnings are more than these amounts...

•$600 or more at one time if this is at least 300 times the amount wagered.

•$1,200 or more from bingo or a slot machine (regardless of the size of the wager).

•$1,500 or more from a keno game (net of the wager).

Income tax withholding: Winnings through any source are subject to mandatory withholding at the rate of 25% if they exceed $5,000 and the take is at least 300 times the amount wagered.

It is the total amount of your winnings that determines withholding. This is the case even if the purse is split between two or more winners and each winner receives less than the threshold amount for withholding.

Example: Two people buy a winning lottery ticket together for $1 and win $5,002. Withholding is required, even though each person received less than $5,000.

Caution: Watch out for increased withholding ("backup withholding"). If a winner provides a taxpayer identification number at the time of the winning, 25% will be withheld. If not, 28% will be withheld. This includes winnings from bingo, keno and slot machines.

For a noncash winning, such as an automobile, the withholding is based on the fair market value of the item. *If the fair market value exceeds $5,000, there are two ways withholding on noncash items is figured...*

• The winner pays the withholding tax to the casino, lottery authority, or other payer. The withholding rate is 25% of the value of the item minus the amount of the wager.

• The payer pays the withholding tax. The withholding rate is 33.33% of the value of the item minus the amount of the wager.

• **Indirect impact.** Gambling winnings are reported in total on your tax return. They will increase your adjusted gross income (AGI), and this can adversely affect other items on your return. *It may...*

• Increase the amount of Social Security benefits subject to tax.

• Decrease itemized deductions for medical expenses, casualty and theft losses, and miscellaneous expenses.

• Prevent a Roth IRA conversion if gambling winnings push AGI over $100,000.

RESTRICTIONS ON LOSSES

Gambling losses are deductible to the extent of winnings and only as miscellaneous itemized deductions—so you must itemize to get any tax benefit from losses. But losses are not subject to the 2%-of-AGI floor that applies to most other miscellaneous write-offs.

Professional gamblers can report losses as a business expense on Schedule C rather than as an itemized deduction on Schedule A.

The amount of deductible losses cannot exceed total winnings for the year. Thus, if you win $1,000, but lose $15,000 throughout the year, your total deduction for the year is only $1,000. The balance of your losses ($14,000) is lost forever and does not carry forward to be used in a future year.

Record keeping for losses: While winnings are reported by the casino or another payer to the IRS, it is up to you to keep track of your losses for the year. If you are a regular gambler, it is a good idea to keep a log or diary—written or electronic—tracking your betting activities. Records should show the date and type of wagering activity, the name and location of the gambling establishment, the names of other gamblers present if applicable and the amounts won and lost. Retain all losing tickets for lottery games and bets at the track.

Suggestion: If you fail to do this, you can follow the lead of a couple who used their credit card, debit card and bank statements showing cash withdrawals at a casino to help substantiate their losses (see *Traci A. Tomko*, TC Summary Opinion 2005-139).

PLANNING STRATEGIES

What can you do to make the most of your luck? *As when you receive any income windfall, it is advisable to minimize taxes through tax-planning measures that include...*

• **Charitable giving.** Decrease your taxable income by being generous to deserving causes. Note, however, that your charitable contribution deduction for the year for cash donations is limited to 50% or less of AGI.

• **AGI planning.** Keep AGI low by using salary reductions where possible—maximize contributions to your 401(k) and flexible spending account (FSA). Realize capital losses in excess of capital gains up to $3,000. Take advantage of above-the-line deductions (e.g., traditional IRA contributions).

For sizable winnings, consider using "partnerships" or trusts for family income splitting. This will allow payments to be spread among family members and, where applicable, taxed at lower rates. Change an oral partnership—a loose agreement to split winnings—to a written agreement before collecting the prize money to avoid fighting among the parties later on.

Important: While tax planning could be a prime concern after a sizable win, asset protection, such as by using an LLC (to hide your identity) or a Nevada Spendthrift Trust (which gives the trustee control of the money), should also be considered. Publicized winners, such as those who win a big state lottery, often become targets of the unscrupulous. Work only with trustworthy advisers—those you already know or for whom you have sound recommendations.

Also take into account state and local income taxes, if applicable, when planning.

The Critically Important New Rules On Gifts to Charity

Richard Vitale, CPA/PFS, chairman of Vitale Caturano and Co., 80 City Sq., Boston 02129. He is also chairman of the legislation committee and former director and vice president of the Massachusetts Society of CPAs.

If you want tax deductions for charitable contributions in 2007, you will have to be more diligent than ever before. Under new law, all cash contributions now must be substantiated, even small ones.

You can support all these deductions with a bank record, such as a canceled check. A personal log no longer is acceptable. Alternatively, you'll need a detailed receipt from the charity or nonprofit organization receiving the donation. *Details that you need to know...*

THE $250 UNDERSTANDING

Under the old rules, cash contributions of less than $250 received special treatment. (See next page for the rules on cash gifts of $250 and up, which haven't changed.)

How it worked: Previously, you could back up your claimed deduction with a canceled check or an acknowledgment letter from the charity. A personal log (a diary or memo to yourself) also was acceptable. Repeated contributions to the same charity were not aggregated.

Example: Every Sunday, you attended your church and put a $20 bill in the collection plate. You could go home and enter this donation in your diary. At year-end, if you had 50 such entries, you could claim a $1,000 charitable deduction for those donations.

New rules: As of 2007, a personal log will not be sufficient to support a charitable deduction if you are questioned. Instead, you'll need a bank record, or another form of communication from the charity showing the organization's name, the date of the donation and the amount. This may not be practical for very small contributions, though.

Strategy: Instead of donating cash to your church or other charities, give checks. Another method is to make pledges or hand over IOUs for smaller amounts, then fulfill those promises later with a check.

You also can arrange for automatic weekly church contributions from your bank account—then produce the account records if necessary.

JUST THE GOOD STUFF

A new rule that first took effect in 2006 relates to donations of used items such as clothing, housewares and furniture.

How it works: The new law states that deductions for these charitable contributions will be permitted only if the items are in "good used condition or better."

Congress reportedly was reacting to the tales of people giving away tattered underwear and threadbare socks, then claiming a tax deduction at unrealistic valuations.

Pitfall: The law does not spell out what is meant by "good used condition or better," or how such a condition can be verified.

Strategy: Assume that the intent of this provision is to confine charitable tax deductions to items that actually can be used. Don't claim deductions for torn T-shirts or broken appliances.

Do the best you can to substantiate the usability of items you donate. You might take photos of garments you're giving away, for example, before taking them to the Salvation Army.

Date those photos and keep them handy in case your deductions are ever questioned.

Loophole: The "good used condition or better" rule does not apply for those donations of any single item where the claimed value is more than $500. This claim must be supported by an appraisal from a qualified, unrelated party and must be accompanied by IRS Form 8283, *Noncash Charitable Contributions*, filed with your tax return.

Impact: If you can get an appraisal of $600 for your broken-down lawn tractor, you could write off $600.

Who can be a qualified appraiser? Essentially, someone who regularly performs appraisals of the type of property in question and understands the civil penalties that apply for intentional value overstatements.

Example: Someone who appraises household items for auctions or insurance purposes might be willing to put a value on that designer suit you're giving away because it no longer fits.

Resources: The American Society of Appraisers (703-478-2228, *www.appraisers.org*) offers a "find an appraisal expert" service, as does the International Society of Appraisers (206-241-0359, *www.isa-appraisers.org*).

PAPER PROOFS

Prior law still applies to cash contributions of $250 or more…

Required: You must get a written acknowledgment from the charity reporting the amount and date of the donation. Also, the charity must state whether any goods or services were provided to you in return.

If so, a value must be placed on those goods or services.

Example: You donate $500 to a charity, which entitles you to attend the banquet. The charity must put a value on the meal it provides. If that value is set at $100, you would get a $400 tax deduction, not $500.

Deadline: Obtain the charity's letter on or before the date you file the relevant tax return.

FROM AN IRA TO CHARITY

A section of the new *Pension Protection Act* also raises substantiation issues. This provision permits charitable IRA rollovers, which are tax-free IRA distributions to charities.

How they work: Money from an IRA can go directly to a charity. Most charities qualify, other than supporting organizations, donor-advised funds and private foundations. (Supporting organizations are the charitable entities established solely to provide operational or financial support to one or more other tax-exempt organizations, such as a specific university.)

Distributions from the IRA to the charity are excluded from taxable income. These distributions are *not* deductible.

Limits: You must be at least 70½ years old to execute a charitable IRA rollover. No more than $100,000 can be rolled over this year.

Unless the law is extended, this opportunity expires after 2007.

Benefit: Due to the interaction of various Tax Code provisions, seniors may wind up ahead by making charitable contributions from their IRA this year.

These charitable contributions count toward the IRA's required minimum distribution in 2007, as well as reduce the owner's taxable estate. In addition, taxpayers receive a state tax benefit in those states that tax required minimum distributions and do not allow for tax-deductible charitable contributions.

Substantiation: Donors must obtain written confirmation from each charity spelling out the amount and date of the contributions.

Trap: As mentioned, contributions must come directly from the IRA custodian to the charity. A charity might get a contribution from, perhaps, John Hill's IRA. But, the charity might not know which John Hill is the IRA owner and might not have the information necessary for sending the required letter.

Strategy: Take the following steps to see that the relevant information gets to each charitable recipient…

• **Write to the IRA custodian.** Formally request a charitable IRA rollover. Ask that the charity be given your name and address as the donor of record.

• **Write to each charity.** Inform each recipient that a contribution is on the way from your IRA via its custodian. Ask that the charity send you a letter at a specified address acknowledging the gift.

The Planned Giving Design Center provides sample letters for this purpose. Go to *www.pgdc. com/jfgw/item/?itemID=368499*.

Filing Taxes Early Isn't Always a Smart Move

Tax law requires that income recipients receive 1099 forms by January 31—but brokerage firms don't always have all the necessary information to prepare 1099s by then, so they may have to send out revised 1099s after January 31. Corrected forms are usually received by mid-March. If you get a corrected 1099 after you have submitted your return to the IRS, you must file an amended tax return (Form 1040X) within three years of April 15 or the extended due date, even if you don't owe more taxes or are entitled to a refund.

Bob Meighan, vice president, Turbo Tax, a tax-preparation software company, Bluffton, SC.

Five IRS Forms You Should Never File

Martin S. Kaplan, CPA, 11 Penn Plaza, New York City 10001, *www.irsmaven.com*. He is a frequent guest speaker at insurance, banking and financial-planning seminars and is author of *What the IRS Doesn't Want You to Know* (Wiley).

As long as you aren't breaking the law by doing so, don't tell the IRS things it doesn't know about you that could get you into tax trouble.

Be wary of filing these tax forms that may *seem* beneficial for you, but that aren't required.

Reason: They might cause the IRS to audit you. *IRS forms that you should never file...*

1. The owners of pass-through entities should never file IRS Form 8082, *Notice of Inconsistent Treatment or Administrative Adjustment Request*, with their tax returns.

S corporations, partnerships and trusts that distribute income to their owners report this income to the owners and to the IRS on a Schedule K-1 that categorizes the distributed income as interest, capital gain, qualified dividends, etc.

Problem: The Schedule K-1 may be mistaken, or the recipient may disagree with the entity's managers about the nature of the income (e.g., whether dividends are tax-favored "qualified" dividends or not).

If you disagree with information on a K-1 that reports income to you, you can't just recategorize the income on your tax return. Instead, the IRS says that you must file Form 8082 to tell it of the discrepancy and give an explanation of why you think the reporting is wrong.

Trap: Doing so tells the IRS that your pass-through entity may be misreporting income. It also notifies them of anything else you state in your explanation (e.g., "there is a dispute among the owners"). This essentially invites the IRS to audit not only you but the entity itself and everyone else receiving income from it. They may not appreciate that!

Better: When you receive a K-1, examine it right away. If you find a problem, address it with the manager of the entity and get a corrected K-1 *before* filing your return. Or file your return using the data on the K-1 you have, then after you receive a corrected K-1, file an amended tax return with the corrected numbers.

That way, the IRS will never find out about your entity's mistakes, internal disputes or other problems.

2. People with dubious items on their tax returns should never file IRS Form 8275, *Disclosure Statement*, with their returns.

The IRS says that you should file this form to disclose questionable or gray-area deductions or positions on your return, and provide your justification for taking them (such as citing court cases that you rely on).

Lure: The IRS says that if you do, and then your return is audited and the disclosed item is disallowed, the IRS will not add a penalty to the taxes and interest it collects. Many taxpayers find this attractive as a way of "audit-proofing" their tax returns.

Trap: Telling the IRS that you have questionable items on your return simply asks it to audit you—and, if you are selected for audit, the IRS can examine your *entire* return. It isn't limited to examining the items on the Form 8275.

If your return is audited and a deduction is challenged by the IRS, you face the exact same task in defending it whether or not you reported it on the Form 8275—only you are more likely to be audited if you have filed it.

The slight potential savings of this avoided penalty isn't worth the increased risk of incurring an audit, back taxes and interest.

3. Taxpayers being audited should never file IRS Form 872-A, *Special Consent to Extend the Time to Assess Tax*.

IRS auditors often run up against the deadline of the three-year statute of limitations on the time in which they can assess tax. When they do, they typically ask taxpayers to file this form to extend the deadline—and might threaten to disallow every questionable item on the return if the taxpayer does not comply. The taxpayer could be forced to go to Tax Court to defend these items.

Trap: Form 872-A applies to the entire return and is open-ended—it gives the IRS forever to examine your entire return.

What to do: Tell the auditor that you will sign only a limited extension applying only to specified items on the return for a limited time. This contains the audit and forces the IRS to complete it. The form to use is IRS Form 872, *Consent to Extend the Time to Assess Tax.*

You can negotiate like this because…

• Auditors are graded on the job by how they close cases—so the auditor *doesn't want* to disallow your deductions in a way that you can appeal to the Tax Court.

• You can go to the Small Case Division of Tax Court to appeal up to $50,000 of tax per tax year without using a lawyer. After filing your case, you will meet with an IRS Appeals officer and get a chance to defend your disputed deductions without going to trial at all.

4. Owners of start-up businesses should never file IRS Form 5213, *Election to Postpone Determination as to Whether the Presumption Applies that an Activity Is Engaged in for Profit.*

Most new businesses do incur start-up losses, sometimes for years. But you can deduct these losses on a personal tax return against other income if your business is a proprietorship, S corporation or partnership. This gives the business a subsidy from the government and makes the business a personal tax shelter for you.

Problem: An IRS auditor who sees the losses may conclude that you are not operating your activity with the profit motive needed to qualify it as a business. Then your losses, and all business expense deductions, will be disallowed.

But the IRS lets owners of start-up businesses file Form 5213 to put off any determination of their business's "profit motive" standing for five years after its start-up, with no risk of an audit in the meantime.

Note: There is a seven-year testing period for horse breeding, showing and racing.

Lure: The owner doesn't have to worry about an IRS audit for five years and can safely deduct

all losses in the meantime. Sounds good, but the owner assumes that after five years, there will be no problem with lack of profits or showing a profit motive.

Trap: Filing the form essentially asks the IRS to audit you after five years by saying that you expect to be running a business at a loss during that time. Moreover, in reality, many businesses fail in their first years without ever showing a profit. If your business is one of them, tipping off the IRS by filing this form may result in the IRS disallowing all of the business losses you deducted—going back the full five years, since Form 5213 extends the statute of limitations for auditing your business return to five years from the normal three.

Much better: Simply don't file the form. The IRS probably will never really notice your business—and if it does, and challenges your deductions, you can defend them as appropriate, and at worst, be at risk for only three years instead of five.

5. Business owners should never submit IRS Form SS-8, *Determination of Worker Status for Purposes of Federal Employment Taxes and Income Tax Withholding.*

One of the hottest tax dispute areas regarding businesses continues to be the categorization of workers as either employees or independent contractors.

This form asks the IRS to rule on this issue for you, on the basis of answers that you provide on a questionnaire.

Lure: You're sure that your workers are contractors and that the IRS will rule that they are, thus settling the issue in any future discussions with workers, state employment agencies, etc.

Trap: The IRS is very highly biased toward ruling workers to be employees. It may shock you by doing this with your workers—making your firm liable for back employment taxes and big benefit liabilities, and subject to state employment regulations.

What to do: Simply treat all your contractor workers as contractors, following the rules explained to you by your tax advisers. Never ask the IRS about them.

Tax Traps for Newly Married Couples

The marriage penalty—which makes a two-earner couple pay more taxes than as individuals—involves more than just tax brackets.

• **If one person has been itemizing** and the other one has taken the standard deduction, both spouses must itemize after marriage or take the standard deduction for a joint return. This can produce a lower total deduction than before the marriage.

• **If two parents with two young children apiece have claimed dependent-care credits** before marrying, they will get lower credits for the children after marriage, because the credit is a single maximum amount for the expenses of two or more children under age 13.

• **If one person had an employer-sponsored retirement plan** and the other made deductible IRA contributions, the deductibility will be phased out if the couple's combined adjusted gross income is more than $150,000.

Bob D. Scharin, JD, senior tax analyst at RIA/Thompson Tax & Accounting, a provider of advanced research, practice materials and compliance tools for tax, accounting and corporate finance professionals, New York City.

Separate, but Equal

Spouses who file separate returns must treat their deductions in the same manner. If one spouse itemizes, so must the other. This is sometimes a problem with estranged spouses.

Peter Weitsen, CPA/PFS, partner, WithumSmith+Brown, CPAs, 1 Spring St., New Brunswick, NJ 08901.

Proof of Filing

If you file by ordinary mail and the IRS says that it didn't receive your return, the legal presumption is that you didn't file and it is up to you to prove that you did. This can be very difficult even if you actually did—with the result being you incur nonfiling penalties.

But if you have a certified mail receipt, the legal presumption is that you did file and it is up to the IRS to prove that you didn't. If you did file, and kept a copy of your return, the IRS can't prove that you didn't and you will escape nonfiling penalties.

Even better: File electronically. The electronic receipt sent by the IRS proves that it actually received your return.

Lawrence Berland, CPA, partner, Mahoney Cohen & Company, CPA, PC, 1065 Ave. of the Americas., New York City 10018.

Whopping Refunds Hurt

The IRS has just announced that the average federal tax refund for 2006 returns, so far, tops $2,255—that's up 2.5% from 2005 returns. This is good news for Uncle Sam, who effectively had an interest-free loan from taxpayers of $217 billion in refund money. It is bad news for taxpayers who lost the use of that money.

Get it right this year: Review your income tax withholding and estimated tax payments for 2007 now. Adjust payments so that you come closer to breaking even when you file your return in 2008.

Greg Rosica, CPA/PFS, CFP, tax partner, Ernst & Young LLP, 100 N. Tampa St., Tampa 33602.

Where's Your Refund?

To find the status of a refund, go to *www.irs.gov* and click on "Where's My Refund?" and you will be sent to the IRS refund locator where you type in your Social Security number, filing status (married filing jointly, married filing separately, single, head of household, qualified widow/widower) and the amount of the refund that's expected rounded off to the nearest dollar. You will get information on the status of your refund and what steps you need to take, if any, other than waiting.

If you do not have access to a computer, you can go through the same process by phone at 800-829-1954.

Refunds generally take six to eight weeks if you made a paper filing...a few weeks less if you asked for direct deposit into your bank account. If you filed electronically, a typical turnaround time is about three weeks.

Nancy Dunnan, a New York City–based financial and travel adviser and the author or coauthor of 25 books, including the best seller, *How to Invest $50–$5,000* (Collins).

How to Get the Fastest Tax Refund of All

Barbara Weltman, an attorney based in Millwood, NY, and author of *J.K. Lasser's Small Business Taxes* (Wiley). She is publisher of the free monthly on-line newsletter *Big Ideas for Small Business, www.barbaraweltman.com.*

If you are owed a tax refund from the IRS for 2007, you'll want to get it as quickly as you can. *How to get the fastest refunds possible for personal taxes...*

PERSONAL REFUNDS

To get the fastest refund on your personal tax return, file electronically (e-file) on the earliest date possible and elect to have your refund sent via electronic direct deposit into a bank or investment account that you designate. Your refund will arrive within two weeks, says the IRS.

The earliest the IRS will take e-filed 2007 tax returns is January 2008.

Contrast: The IRS says that when...

• **A paper return is filed by mail and the refund is mailed back by check,** the refund can take six to eight weeks to arrive.

• **A paper return filed by mail requests a direct-deposit refund,** or an e-filed return requests a mailed refund check, the refund should take three to four weeks to arrive.

E-filing is becoming a routine for millions of Americans—76.7 million 2006 tax returns were e-filed during the 2007 tax filing season, with 22 million filed from home computers and the rest filed by tax professionals on behalf of clients.

Most taxpayers can e-file through the Free File program, a joint effort of the IRS and commercial tax-preparation firms, that provides for electronic preparation and filing of tax returns at no charge. Details about Free File for 2007 returns will be announced on the IRS Web site in January 2008.

Direct deposit: Refunds now may be sent directly not only to bank checking and savings accounts, but also to IRAs, Coverdell Education Savings Accounts, health savings accounts and Archer medical savings accounts—and every refund can be distributed among up to three of these. File Form 8888, *Direct Deposit of Refunds,* if refund deposits are to be made to more than one account.

Moreover, after you e-file your return, you can check up on the status of the refund after only seven days by using the "Where's My Refund?" utility on the IRS Web site or calling the IRS's Automated Refund Hotline at 800-829-1954. This is the fastest way to learn whether your requested refund is on its way to you—and whether there is a problem that may be slowing it down. If you file a paper return, you won't be able to verify your refund's status for four to six weeks.

To learn the details about e-filing, direct deposit and Free File, log on to the IRS Web site at *www.irs.gov,* and click on the e-File logo.

Some things are beyond your control. For instance, employers and other payers of income must provide Forms W-2 and 1099—their deadline for providing these is January 31. If you haven't received an expected form by early February, phone your employer or other payer to alert them.

More early refund strategies...

• **Start preparing your 2007 tax return now.** Pull together records and numbers to be able to complete your return as soon as possible after year-end.

• **Even better than getting a fast refund is not overpaying your taxes.** Estimate your tax position for the year now. If you think you've overpaid, you may still be able to reduce wage withholding on your last paychecks of the year. Similarly, take care not to overpay a quarterly estimated payment due for 2007 on January 15, 2008, on the basis of an earlier-in-the-year tax liability projection that has since been overtaken by events.

More from Barbara Weltman, Esq....

Is Your Tax Return Asking for an Audit?

An IRS audit. It is what taxpayers most dread as they prepare their tax returns and what 1.3 million of them faced last year—up 5% from the year before.

As the White House and Congress look for more ways to decrease the federal budget deficit, your chances of being audited are likely to grow, especially if your income tops $100,000.

Although there are no foolproof methods to avoid an audit—and many returns are chosen randomly—there are certain red flags that draw the attention of IRS computers and auditors.

Here are mistakes that could cause your return to stand out and some suggestions on how to avoid an audit...

1. Omitting or underreporting income. Employers and financial institutions sometimes report income incorrectly to taxpayers and the IRS on W-2 forms (for employees) and 1099 forms (for independent contractors).

Safest: If you do receive an incorrect W-2 or 1099, don't just substitute a different figure on your tax return. Get the mistake corrected by the source, and ask for a new W-2 or 1099.

2. Failing to fill out an alternative minimum tax (AMT) schedule. This year, more than 3.5 million individuals are forecasted to owe this tricky tax, which kicks in when tax deductions push the regular tax below a certain minimum amount. Taxpayers who live in "high tax" states, such as New York and New Jersey, are particularly vulnerable, because state and local income tax and sales tax are not deductible for AMT purposes.

Safest: Use the IRS AMT assistant, an on-line calculator at *www.irs.gov* (put "AMT Assistant" in the search window), to determine whether the AMT applies to you.

3. Messing up the math or leaving blanks. IRS computers can easily detect math mistakes and omissions.

Safest: Print out your calculations so that you can double-check them. Review all lines, as well as blanks, to make sure that you didn't leave out required information or put it in the wrong place. That includes the signature lines—remember that both spouses must sign a joint return.

Even better: File electronically. It cuts down on math errors—e-filed returns have an accuracy rate of more than 99%, compared with 80% for paper returns, because the program checks the math.

4. Claiming too many tax deductions and/or credits. The IRS is on the lookout for excessive deductions and credits.

Example: In January of 2007, the IRS said that some taxpayers were asking for too much in refunds for certain taxes they paid in the past on long-distance phone bills. Those taxes were ruled illegal, and the government offered to refund to each taxpayer a "standard" phone tax amount of $30 to $60, depending on the number of exemptions claimed on the tax return, without requiring any proof. For higher amounts, proof of what was paid in phone taxes was required. IRS commissioner Mark Everson said then that "people requesting any inflated amount would likely have their refund frozen, may have their entire tax return audited and even face criminal prosecution where warranted."

Those requesting more than the standard phone tax refund needed to have on hand the phone bills that proved what they claimed.

Safest: In general, don't claim deductions that far exceed what tax preparers say is reasonable for your income bracket, or if you do, attach an explanation. Attach copies of bills for unusually high medical expenses. Have proper documentation for donations to charity. For used clothing and household items, take pictures of the items to show that they were in good used condition.

Guidelines: There are no "standard" deduction amounts. Based on IRS statistics for 2005,* taxpayers with adjusted gross incomes (AGIs) of $50,000 to $100,000 itemized an average of $2,703 in charitable contributions and $6,144 in medical costs. Those with AGIs of $100,000 to $200,000 itemized an average of $4,057 for charity and $9,727 for medical costs.

5. Claiming losses for hobbies. Deductions for a fun activity, such as coin collecting, may be

*Latest date for which figures are available.

rejected if the activity results in losses that don't make commercial sense year after year.

Safest: Don't claim deductions for hobby expenses unless you are prepared to show that you are engaged in the activity for profit.

IRS Audits Less Deeply, But More Often

Other than a limited number of audits conducted under the National Research Program (NRP), the IRS is changing its philosophy away from collecting "every last dime" in an audit to collecting 80% of what might be available in a greater number of audits.

A top IRS official recently explained that the IRS typically can collect 80% of the tax recoverable in an audit within the first 20% of the time it would take to collect the whole amount. So it is most cost efficient for the IRS to be satisfied with the 80%, while using the time saved to conduct a larger number of audits.

Two extra benefits: (1) The less intensive audits avoid annoying taxpayers, while (2) the larger number of audits deters tax cheating due to increased risk of being audited.

Kevin M. Brown, commissioner, IRS Small Business and Self-Employed Division, 1111 Constitution Ave. NW, Washington, DC 20224.

Does Filing an Amended Return Increase Audit Risk?

An amended return that simply corrects a mistake or claims an overlooked item results in slight to no increase in audit risk.

An amendment that is very unusual or complex, or one which claims a very large refund, might increase risk of an audit. But even then, if the amendment is proper and the rest of your return is honest and in order, there is no reason to be afraid of making it. Never give the IRS money that you are legitimately entitled to claim!

Laurence I. Foster, CPA/PFS, tax consultant based in New York City, and former partner at Eisner LLP.

More from Laurence Foster, CPA/PFS...

A Reward from the IRS?

IRS informants get bigger and surer whistle-blower rewards in 2007. New tax law greatly increases rewards that can be claimed by whistle-blowers who report tax fraud to the IRS. The law was passed in late 2006 in response to reports of a $345 billion "tax gap" by which federal taxes are underpaid—more than the federal budget deficit of $248 billion for 2006.

Rules: The new law is aimed at large-dollar cases of fraud and limited to claims against taxpayers with gross annual incomes of more than $200,000 and potential indebtedness to the IRS of more than $2 million.

Rewards can range from 15% to 30% of the amount received* by the IRS when it pursues action against a taxpayer based on information brought to it by a whistle-blower. They are limited to 10% in certain cases where there has been prior public disclosure of the allegations.

Key: These rewards are mandatory. Whistle-blowers can appeal unsatisfactory awards to the Tax Court. Under prior law, rewards generally were voluntary with the IRS and couldn't be appealed—and so tended to be small and rare.

More information: *www.taxwhistleblowers. org.*

*Rates subject to change.

Inside the IRS

In the following articles Ms. X, Esq., a former IRS agent who is still well connected, reveals inside secrets from the IRS...

HOW LONG DOES THE IRS HAVE TO COME AFTER YOU IF YOU UNDERREPORTED INCOME?

The answer depends on the amount of unreported income and why it was not reported on your return.

Statute of limitations rule: Unless the IRS issues an assessment within three years from the date the tax return was filed, it is out of luck.

Exception 1: If you understated your income by more than 25% of the gross income reported on your return, the three-year limitation period is extended to six years.

Exception 2: If the IRS can prove that the understatement of income was attributable to fraud (that is, you *intended* to underreport your income—it was not a simple mistake), there is no statute of limitations and it can make an assessment at any time.

Inside information: Even in fraud cases, it is unlikely that the IRS will go back for more than six years.

DON'T BE SEDUCED BY THE IRS's "LAST CHANCE" AMNESTY OFFER

The IRS is promoting a settlement program for individuals who maintain offshore bank accounts that they have not reported on their tax returns. If you respond positively within 15 days of its offer, you must give the IRS access to every piece of information it is seeking. In return, they will not prosecute you for a tax crime.

Caution: The revenue agent may only know that you maintain an offshore bank account. He/she may not know when the money was deposited into the account or the source of that money.

Strategy: Do not respond to any questions until you have met with a tax attorney.

THE NEWEST IRS TARGETS

According to the IRS, 70% of tax returns claiming the earned income credit (EIC) are prepared by professionals. There is a significant amount of abuse as preparers pad their fees by making up numbers permitting taxpayers to get refunds for the earned income credit—for which they don't qualify.

How this increases the preparers' income: These preparers not only charge for the tax return preparation, but also receive fees from lending institutions for arranging tax refund loans at very high interest rates for their low-income clients. Fees are based on the size of the loan—and therefore on the size of the refund.

IRS approach: Certain tax preparers who have been identified by the IRS will be visited during the year and shut down if violations are detected.

PAY ATTENTION TO IRS NOTICES

It is not uncommon for the IRS to send a notice to an individual explaining that it believes that dividends, interest or stock sales occurred but were not included on the individual's income tax return. If this letter is ignored, the IRS will eventually issue a notice of deficiency and, if you can't resolve the matter within 90 days of the issuance of the notice of deficiency, you must file a petition with the US Tax Court to protect your rights. Sometimes, the items the IRS is questioning go back more than two years, so getting your hands on the records might be tough.

Suggestion: Make sure that when you respond to the IRS, you send correspondence to a specific person so that you can follow up if you don't hear from him within a reasonable period of time.

WHEN THE IRS SENDS YOU A LETTER TELLING YOU TO CALL...

Sometimes it is not in your best interest to call the IRS as soon as you receive such a letter.

Example: You owe the IRS money and you can't pay in full, but you will be able to pay the amount owed during the next 12 months. If you call the IRS, it will ask you to complete a financial statement listing all of your assets. Suppose you have a certificate of deposit or a brokerage account. The IRS will require that you break the CD or sell all the securities in the brokerage account before it agrees to enter into an installment payment arrangement with you.

Better strategy: Do not call the IRS. Instead, send in monthly payments. By the time someone from the IRS knocks on your door, or places a levy on your bank account, a good portion of the debt will have already been paid. At that point, you can generally work out a time period—about three months—to pay off the balance of your debt, without having to submit a detailed financial statement. Of course, talk to your tax adviser about your specific situation.

WHAT YOU SAY TO THE IRS WILL BE USED AGAINST YOU

The hardest job for the IRS in a criminal tax case is proving that someone had the intent to evade tax. The fact that you owe the IRS extra taxes because you neglected to report income on your tax return is not necessarily a crime. The IRS must establish that you "willfully" evaded the payment of tax. The best evidence of intent often turns out to be self-incriminating statements a taxpayer makes to IRS special agents.

Example: In response to a question as to why you didn't report certain income, you say, "Because nobody else reports this type of income, and I didn't think the IRS would single me out."

Best approach: Don't answer any questions posed by special agents—give them the name and telephone number of your attorney.

WHAT SPECIAL AGENTS WANT TO KNOW WHEN THEY CONTACT YOUR TAX PREPARER

One of the most important witnesses during a criminal case against you is the person who prepared your tax return. The preparer generally has in his possession work-paper files that contain originals and copies of financial documents and handwritten notes. An IRS special agent will summons these to obtain evidence of criminal conduct, looking for proof of intent to evade the payment of taxes by underreporting income or hiding assets.

Advice for tax preparers: Before agreeing to talk to a special agent, ask for a summons for the requested information. If the IRS issues a summons, review it with your attorney before making any statements to the IRS. You want to be certain that you have not been complicit in your client's wrongdoing.

GET A TRANSCRIPT

Always order a transcript of your account if you owe the IRS and it has assessed penalties and interest.

A transcript includes all the changes and payments to your IRS account for the year. Even the IRS admits that it makes mistakes despite the fact that a computer spits out the notices. It is possible that your account was manually adjusted by an individual at an IRS service center who input the wrong code or mistakenly charged you a penalty for late filing when you filed on time but paid late.

Strategy: Once you receive the transcript, make sure that you understand what you are reading. Either call the IRS and go over it line by line or give it to a knowledgeable tax practitioner and ask him to check it out.

BEFORE YOU MOVE ASSETS OUT OF YOUR NAME

Many taxpayers in debt to the IRS think nothing of transferring assets to another family member to "protect" those assets from the IRS.

Problems: The IRS can take the position that you have engaged in a fraudulent conveyance and file a lawsuit against the person who is now in possession of your assets. A more immediate step the IRS can take is to impose a "nominee lien" on the person to whom the assets were transferred. A nominee lien is developed by the IRS by creating a lien document, without having court approval, which is then filed with the county clerk imposing another taxpayer's liability on the transferee's real and personal property.

Before you transfer assets, speak to a knowledgeable tax professional.

IF YOUR BANK ACCOUNT IS LEVIED BY THE IRS...

Seizure of personal property in the possession of third parties (a bank, say) is accomplished by the IRS mailing Form 668-A, called *Notice of Levy*, which stipulates the amount you owe. The bank is required to remit all money in your account that has cleared and is available for withdrawal up to the amount stated on the notice of levy. The filing of a notice of levy has no effect on subsequent deposits—the IRS must file another notice of levy if it wants to take those funds.

Loophole: If the bank account is a joint account and requires two signatures to withdraw funds, then the bank is not required to honor the IRS levy. Once the IRS has your funds in its possession, it will generally not return the money unless you can prove that you will suffer a financial hardship (for example, the money is needed for rent, food or basic living expenses).

THE IRS CUTS COSTS BY RELYING ON VOLUNTEERS

One way that the IRS is seeking to reduce its overhead is in its taxpayer service function. For many years, the IRS spent considerable money staffing walk-in sites during tax season to assist low-income taxpayers in preparing their income tax returns. Today, the people who devote their time in the volunteer income tax assistance, or VITA, program fill much of the role previously assumed by paid seasonal employees.

Problem: As poor as the advice sometimes is from the IRS, at least standards were in place to monitor the advice being given by paid employees to the public. Volunteers, although well intentioned, are not subjected to formal IRS supervision, and the advice could be spotty.

According to a recently released report by the Treasury Inspector General, more than half of the tax returns prepared by the VITA program during the 2006 filing season were not accurate (statistics for the 2007 filing season are not available at press time). The Inspector General based his report on the results of a test sample of 36 tax returns. Twenty-two of the 36 were found to contain errors.

TURNING BETTING LOSSES INTO BUSINESS LOSSES

You may not have to be a full-time professional gambler to get a tax break from gambling losses. In one recent Tax Court decision (*James Castagnetta*, TC Summary Opinion 2006-24), the court ruled that an individual could deduct losses from horse race betting as business losses.

How: The taxpayer pursued the activity regularly and with continuity and operated it in a businesslike manner. He worked 40 hours per week on race analysis, created detailed computerized "speed figures" for horses, had a profit motive, actually made a profit and kept full detailed records.

Essential: For any business loss to be deductible, the taxpayer must prove a profit motive.

As long as you continue to try something new to make a profit, it is hard for the IRS to argue that you lacked a profit motive. It may be possible to sustain a tax-deductible loss from casino activity if you keep very accurate records, visit casinos on a regular basis and can establish via your records that you changed betting strategies in an effort to generate profits—even if you are not a "professional" gambler.

LEGAL FEES AND THE IRS

Simply paying a lawyer for services does not make that payment tax deductible.

Possibilities: The legal fee may be deductible in full (tax advice)…it may be capitalized as part of an investment you acquired and added to the cost of the asset (a legal fee to purchase a home)…or it may be nondeductible for personal issues such as a divorce. Before signing a legal retainer agreement, it's important to understand what portion of the fee, if any, the government will subsidize because it qualifies as a tax deduction.

Beware: Even if a legal fee is deductible, the benefit may be limited or reduced entirely if you are subject to the alternative minimum tax.

THROWING AWAY OLD TAX RECORDS

Generally, tax records should be maintained for three years after the date the return was filed.

Exception: The records relating to cost basis (stocks, mutual funds, real estate) should be held until three years after the property has been sold. Do not retain tax records longer than required, since a summons issued by the IRS could require you to produce those records. The records could be used to help strengthen the case against you (for instance, you have a 10-year pattern of overstating your charitable contributions).

Caution: If your computers contain sensitive financial information relating to old returns, consult a computer technician to ensure that deleted information can't be reconstructed.

10

Investment Wisdom

How to Get the Best Financial Advice—So You Make More Money

Anyone can call himself or herself a financial adviser or consultant—a stockbroker, an insurance agent, an accountant, even a layperson who is quick with numbers. In the past five years, the number of financial advisers has risen by almost 40% as consumers—hurt by the last bear market and intimidated by retirement planning—seek professional help.

Unfortunately, financial advisers are not required as a general rule to act solely in your best interest—a standard known as "fiduciary responsibility."

Common: A financial adviser may not recommend the best mutual fund for you, but rather the best one for you that will also pay him a commission.

Who you choose depends on your needs.

Example: Whether you want someone to draw up a financial plan or provide ongoing investment services.

DECIDING WHAT YOU NEED

To find the right money coach...

• **If you need broad financial guidance—** such as help setting up a portfolio that you will mostly oversee yourself...a plan to pay for your children's educations...a retirement plan...estate planning and tax planning—go with a fee-only planner who has a certified financial planner (CFP) designation.

Fee-only advisers do not accept commissions. CFPs are required to pass a certification exam, have at least three years of financial-planning experience, adhere to a code of ethics, attend

Donald B. Trone, president and founder of the Foundation for Fiduciary Studies, which operates in association with the University of Pittsburgh in Sewickley, PA. He is coauthor of two manuals for the financial planning industry, *Procedural Prudence* (Veale & Associates) and *The Management of Investment Decisions* (McGraw-Hill). In 2003, he was appointed by the US Secretary of Labor to represent the investment counseling industry on the ERISA Advisory Council.

continuing education courses and pledge fiduciary responsibility.

Typical cost: Onetime fee of $1,000 or more for a comprehensive plan.*

Resource: Two associations can make referrals—The Financial Planning Association (800-322-4237 or *www.fpanet.org*)…and the National Association of Personal Financial Advisors (800-366-2732 or *www.napfa.org*).

● **If you want a professional to help manage your portfolio** on an ongoing basis, look for a chartered financial analyst (CFA). CFAs undergo rigorous training in stock/bond analysis, financial accounting and portfolio management. They are required to pass a certification exam, adhere to a code of ethics and pledge fiduciary responsibility.

Important: Never give an adviser full discretion over your portfolio, no matter how trustworthy he seems. You should get at least a call or an e-mail when a trade is going to be made.

Typical cost: A fixed percentage of assets under management, from 0.5% to 2% annually for ongoing market advice and investment recommendations. For example, annual fees for an all-bond portfolio could average 0.5% of assets versus 1.5% for a mix of stocks and bonds.

Resource: For referrals to CFAs, go to *www.cfainstitute.org* or call 800-247-8132.

Important: If you have less than $300,000 in your portfolio, it can be difficult to find a financial adviser to manage it because it is not cost-effective for them.

Alternatives…

● Use a financial planner who charges hourly rates, typically $100 to $300 per hour. For referrals, contact Garrett Planning Network (866-260-8400, *www.garrettplanning.com*), a network of planners who charge by the hour. Or get recommendations from your attorney or accountant.

● Consider the new advisory services offered by large, no-load mutual fund companies. They provide low-cost individualized portfolio advice by CFPs. For example, at Fidelity (800-343-3548, *www.fidelity.com*), the counselors will manage a handpicked selection of Fidelity and non-Fidelity funds for clients who have at least $50,000 under management. Fees range from 0.25% of assets to

*Rates subject to change.

1.1%. Similar services are available from Vanguard (800-523-7731, *www.vanguard.com*) and T. Rowe Price (800-225-5132, *www.troweprice.com*).

SIZING UP CANDIDATES

● **Conduct a background check of prospective advisers and their firms.** You should work only with firms registered with the SEC. They are subject to government supervision.

Go to *www.sec.gov/index.htm*, click on "Check Out Brokers & Advisers" and on "Investment Adviser Public Disclosure." Search for the firm you want to investigate, and examine the firm's Form ADV. It contains information on the education and professional backgrounds of the firm's principals, types of clients, compensation, amount managed and disciplinary history.

You can find the same information through The National Association of Securities Dealers (800-289-9999, *www.nasdbrokercheck.com*). Any reputable adviser will make his ADV form available to you without your even having to ask.

● **Conduct a 30-minute, in-person interview with each candidate.** (You should not be charged for this.) Ask if the adviser frequently works with other financial specialists on behalf of clients and would therefore be amenable to working with your professionals. For example, if your estate plan is complex, you already may be working with an insurance agent and an estate lawyer.

Find out if the financial adviser will handle your account personally or farm out your assets to managers whom he supervises (you'll need to check the backgrounds of those managers, if that's the case)…how much time you can expect with him…and whether you can monitor your account on-line.

Ask if he will provide a comprehensive analysis of your financial situation, including specific recommendations—he should present you with a sample.

Ask about the firm's typical client, and gauge whether his/her needs are similar to yours. For instance, the firm might deal primarily with corporate executives who need help with stock options or retired people who want to maximize investment income. Ask to check actual performance figures for those clients whose goals are similar to yours.

• **Speak with at least two of the adviser's references.**

Questions to ask: Did the financial adviser educate you on complex financial issues? Did he carefully follow your directives? In particular, did he understand how aggressive/conservative a portfolio you wanted? Did the financial adviser ever make mistakes or disappoint you? What did he do about it?

• **Once you are ready to hire a firm,** get a written policy. *It should include…*

• A promise that the adviser will act as your "fiduciary."

• List of potential conflicts of interest regarding product-based commissions and a reasonable explanation of how they are addressed.

• Explanation of the fee structure, what constitutes billable work and how fee disputes will be resolved—for instance, if the stock market drops and you make a quick call asking for advice. If this is the case, any financial adviser earning an asset-based annual fee should not charge for taking your phone call.

Easy Way to Analyze a Financial Newsletter's Record

You can analyze a financial newsletter's record and quality—and the stocks and funds it recommends—using *Hulbert Interactive*, an on-line screening tool based on more than 20 years of data from *The Hulbert Financial Digest*, the newsletter that tracks investment newsletters. The screener provides consensus ratings of thousands of stocks and mutual funds based on the advice and track records of leading investment newsletters.

Annual subscription fee for Hulbert Interactive: $149, with a 30-day free trial.*

John Bajkowski, vice president and senior financial analyst at the American Association of Individual Investors (AAII), Chicago, *www.aaii.com.*

*Price and offer subject to change.

Little-Known Tax Breaks for Investors

Genevia Gee Fulbright, CPA, chief operating officer, at Fulbright & Fulbright, CPA, PA, Box 13156, Research Triangle Park, NC 27709. She's also a President's Advisory Council member of the National Association of Black Accountants and author of *Make the Leap from Mom & Pop to Good Enough to Sell* (Infinity).

Many people don't realize that the money you spend choosing and managing investments could make you eligible for tax deductions. This is the case even if your only investment is a 401(k) plan or an IRA.

How it works: If you itemize (and are not subject to the alternative minimum tax), you can take miscellaneous deductions on Schedule A of your tax return, but only if they exceed 2% of your adjusted gross income (AGI).

Example: Your AGI this year is $100,000, so your threshold for deducting miscellaneous expenses is $2,000. If these expenses add up to $2,500, you get a $500 write-off. For more information, see IRS Publication 529, *Miscellaneous Deductions.*

Keep careful track of investment expenses, along with other eligible miscellaneous deductions—including employee business expenses, education costs to improve your job skills and job-hunting outlays. This might help you to get over the 2% hurdle. The time to plan for investment-related deductions is well before year-end. *Key costs you can deduct…*

• **Publication expenses.** You can include all the money you spend on books and publications that you read for investment information. Don't forget the cost of magazines and newspapers you buy at newsstands, if you use the information in your investing pursuits.

Year-end strategy: If you are at or close to your threshold for miscellaneous deductions, be sure to pay for investment-related subscriptions (that year's subscription cost is deductible), buy investment books and so on before year-end. Those outlays are deductible.

• **Computer costs.** You can depreciate your home computer to the extent that you use it for investment research, portfolio tracking, etc. Keep a log to show how often you visit financial Web sites, such as *www.morningstar.com* and *finance. yahoo.com.*

In addition, you can deduct the cost of online services used to track your investments. For more information see IRS Publication 550, *Investment Income and Expenses.*

• **Travel expenses.** If you drive to your broker's office, you can deduct 48.5 cents per mile in 2007, as well as the costs of tolls, parking, etc.

If you own investment real estate out of town, trips to check your property may be deductible. Keep a paper trail to show that you met with your rental agent or a contractor, arranged for repairs, etc.

Caution: Be reasonable. A "property maintenance" trip to your rental condominium in Key West, Florida, in July is less likely to be challenged than one in January.

The cost of traveling to and from or attending investment seminars is not deductible.

• **Legal, accounting and advisory fees related to your investments.** If you meet with your lawyer to discuss your estate planning, for example, ask for an itemized bill showing how much of his/her fee went toward discussing the handling of your investment portfolio.

• **Safe-deposit box rental.** Store stock certificates, bonds and documents related to securities in your box to justify the deduction.

• **IRA trustees' fees,** if billed and paid separately, and service charges on dividend reinvestment plans are deductible. Trading fees and commissions within an IRA are not deductible.

How Good Is Your Broker? Beware!

Daniel R. Solin, JD, an attorney in New York City who has won judgments on behalf of investors against some of Wall Street's most prestigious brokerage firms. He is author of *Does Your Broker Owe You Money?* and *The Smartest Investment Book You'll Ever Read* (both from Perigee). His Web site is *www.smartestinvestmentbook.com.*

There are many possible danger signs that your stockbroker is not doing a great job for you. *Here's what to watch out for, and what to do if your account is mismanaged...*

RED FLAGS

• **Your portfolio is completely invested in stocks.** The safest allocation for most investors includes a mix of stocks, bonds and cash. Unless you feel comfortable taking major risks—and unless you and your broker have agreed on such a strategy—you should not be 100% in stocks.

Example: Sally placed $2 million with a full-service brokerage firm and explained that the money was for her retirement. The broker invested nearly everything in high-risk technology stocks. Over three years, her account lost $1.5 million. An arbitration panel awarded Sally only $600,000.

• **Your portfolio seems unusually volatile.** Beware when a swing in your stock portfolio's value exceeds that of the overall market, as measured by the Standard & Poor's 500 stock index.

Example: Jorge, a man in his 70s, told his broker that he wanted investments suitable for a retiree. The broker picked highly speculative stocks that were five times as volatile as the S&P 500. In 18 months, Jorge's nest egg went from $400,000 to $6,000. Luckily, arbitration awarded Jorge $550,000 in damages.

• **Account expenses seem unusually high.** The annual total you pay in commissions and margin interest (if you buy stocks using borrowed money) shouldn't exceed 3% of the total value of your portfolio. If it does, you need to earn unrealistically high returns, year after year, just to break even.

Example: Kathleen invested $380,000 with a broker at one major national brokerage firm. Over five years, her account lost $275,000. Trading commissions and interest on margin loans amounted to more than 16% of the value of her portfolio—meaning that she would have needed to earn at least that much just to break even. When Kathleen threatened the company with arbitration, it then reimbursed her for 100% of her losses.

WHAT TO DO IF YOUR ACCOUNT IS MISMANAGED

If you are not happy with your stockbroker, complaining to your brokerage firm is not necessarily the best course of action. Why? When you established your account, you almost certainly signed an agreement requiring any complaint to go to arbitration, rather than to court. If you complain to the firm, you might inadvertently make statements that will hurt you in arbitration.

Even if you have lost money based on a stockbroker's recommendations, you might not have a case against him or her. However, if any of the above warning signs are present, you might be able to bring a successful arbitration claim against your broker. Strive to recover all of your "well-managed account" losses. This phrase refers to how your portfolio should have performed if it had had reasonable fees and an appropriate asset allocation based on your age and risk tolerance.

• **If your claim is for less than $25,000,** there is a simple procedure to file for arbitration without an attorney. Contact the National Association of Securities Dealers (301-590-6500, *www.nasd.com*).

• **If your claim is for more than $25,000,** consult an attorney experienced in securities arbitration law. The Public Investors Arbitration Bar Association comprises more than 750 attorneys who represent complainants in securities arbitration proceedings. Go to *www.piaba.org* and click on "Find an Attorney" or call 888-621-7484.

Ask up front how the attorney expects to be compensated. Some work on a fee basis, but many work on a contingency basis. They take a percentage of what you win in the arbitration.

Stocks Are More Predictable Than Most People Think... How You Can Profit

Jeffrey Hirsch, editor, *Almanac Investor*, Nyack, NY, and editor in chief, *Stock Trader's Almanac 2007* (Wiley). Both of these publications are available at the Web site *www.stocktradersalmanac.com*.

Many of the old-time Wall Street sayings do ring true. That's because they reflect patterns related to seasons, taxes, political changes and even wars. By buying and selling at opportune times, you increase your odds of beating the market. *Here are the most reliable patterns...*

SELL IN MAY AND GO AWAY

The best time to sell, on average, is around May 1. From May to October, what we call the worst six months to invest, stocks tend to stagnate. Market activity slows. After paying taxes in April, people do not have much cash to invest. Then as summer approaches, traders head out of town. Vacationers prefer playing golf and tennis to buying stocks.

After Labor Day, investors begin focusing on the markets again. They get nervous about any stocks that haven't done well over the summer. Many people worry about October because several major downturns in the past have occurred then, including the Great Crash of 1929. October is when many institutions sell their losing stocks, driving down the market.

By November 1, it often pays to buy stocks again. With the holidays approaching, investors become more optimistic. Many retail stores are crowded, and sales figures show promise. Mutual funds aim to grab winners to improve their year-end returns.

THE SANTA CLAUS RALLY

One of the best periods of the year for stocks tends to include the last five trading days of December and the first two trading days of January. On average since 1950, the S&P 500 Index has gained 1.5% during this period. The Santa Claus rally also can serve as an indicator for the upcoming year. If stocks dip despite holiday euphoria, markets may be headed for trouble.

Example: At the close of 1999, the Santa Claus rally failed to materialize. The S&P 500 lost 4% over the seven-day period. The market went on to fall in 2000, losing 9.1% for the year.

THE JANUARY BAROMETER

In 1972, my father, Yale Hirsch, discovered the January barometer. If the market is up in January, most often stocks will rise for the year. This indicator has been accurate 75% of the time based on data going back to 1950.

January is important because so much happens. The Wall Street pundits issue their annual market forecasts. A new president and Congress take office then, and the president usually delivers the state of the union address in January. All this sets the tone for many investors.

January is traditionally a strong month. There's a rush of new cash into the market as investors receive year-end bonuses and make contributions to IRAs and other retirement plans.

DURING WARTIME

Wars always act as a drag on stocks. Since its inception more than a century ago, the Dow Jones Industrial Average has never reached a significant new high during a war. In wartime, with the government spending heavily, demand for goods rises and inflation increases. Rising prices erode the value of corporate earnings, hurting stock prices. Investors become pessimistic, and setbacks occur regularly, stopping rallies.

Example: As the Vietnam War escalated in 1966, the Dow attempted to pass 1,000 but failed to stay in that range until 1982, about a decade after peace was announced and the vestiges of wartime inflation began to disappear.

However, while stocks often fall after the initial shock of a war, markets rarely go into a free fall in the middle of a protracted conflict. Government spending and wartime pride help keep stocks afloat. As markets anticipate the end of the war, stocks can rally, but surprisingly, there is a letdown when peace finally appears, causing stocks to dip.

Once the current war in Iraq ends, inflation will climax, then ease up. Washington will start focusing on domestic problems, and I predict the stock market will begin a sustained bull run. After World War I and World War II, the Dow gained 500%. During the post-Vietnam bull market, from 1982 to 2000, the Dow increased by 1,400%. If the next bull market matches that pattern, we will reach a Dow Jones high of 43,000 about one decade after US soldiers depart from Iraq. Predicting when the postwar era will start is difficult, but I suspect withdrawals will occur in time for the next election.

THE PRESIDENTIAL CYCLE

The market often rises during the year before a presidential election because Washington does everything it can to boost the economy and put more money in voters' wallets.

After the inauguration, the good times usually stop. Presidents make the tough decisions early in their terms, and tax increases, cuts in government programs, etc., can send stocks tumbling. Nine of the last 14 bear markets have bottomed in the midterm year, the second year after a presidential election—1962, 1966, 1970, 1974, 1978, 1982, 1990, 1998 and 2002.

HOW TO INVEST

Devote a small portion of your tax-deferred portfolio to this seasonal timing strategy. Invest around November 1 in one low-cost exchange-traded fund, such as SPDR Trust (SPY), which tracks the Standard & Poor's 500 Index. Sell the fund around May 1, and shift to cash or a short-term bond fund. Repeat this each year.

The approach does not make money every year, but an investor who followed it since 1950 would have beaten the market. If that individual had invested $10,000 throughout the best six months—November to April—of each year beginning in 1950, he now would have $534,323. If he had invested $10,000 in May and sold in October of each year, he would have lost $272 during that period. (Figures exclude dividends.)

Another Stock Market Indicator

When inflation has stayed between 1% and 3%, the stock market has given back 13% annually on average going back to 1872. When inflation has gone above 3%, returns have averaged less than 3%.

So, where the market is concerned, what matters is how well the Federal Reserve Board does its job of containing inflation.

Ed Keon, chief investment strategist, Prudential Equity Group, One New York Plaza, New York City 10292.

The Customer Is Always Right

A portfolio of 20 to 30 companies with high customer-satisfaction ratings had a cumulative 99% return, versus a loss of 15% for the S&P

500 for the period from April 2000 through June 2006, according to recent research.

Companies with high customer satisfaction: Toyota, Apple, Yahoo!, VF Corp. For the entire list, go to *www.theacsi.org.*

Claes Fornell, PhD, director, national quality research center, professor of business administration and professor of marketing at University of Michigan's Stephen M. Ross School of Business, Ann Arbor, and lead author of a research paper, published in the *Journal of Marketing.*

Brand Names Aren't Always Best

In a recent study, portfolios of investors who bought $1,000 of each of the 20 US stocks with the most valuable global brands at the end of 2000 and held them until the end of 2006 fell by an average of 11%, versus a 49% gain for the S&P 500 Index.

Dow Theory Forecasts, 7412 Calumet Ave., Hammond, IN 46324.

Stock-Picking Secrets: From the Little Book That Beats the Market

Joel Greenblatt, the founder and managing partner of Gotham Capital, a value investing firm in New York City with $1.6 billion in assets. He is author of *The Little Book That Beats the Market* (Wiley). In 2005, he was given the prestigious Graham & Dodd, Murray, Greenwald Prize for Value Investing.

Most professional money managers can't beat the S&P 500 Index over the long term. So how can ordinary investors—who don't have research staffs or financial expertise—possibly earn market-beating returns?

Joel Greenblatt, one of the country's most successful value investors reveals how here. Over the past 20 years, his private hedge fund logged an average annual return of 40% using a low-risk system that does not depend on economic predictions.

To carry out this strategy, investors can use the free stock-screening tool at Mr. Greenblatt's Web site, *www.magicformulainvesting.com,* or other financial Web sites (see the next page).

•**Look for high-return businesses selling at low valuations.** The better companies earn high returns on investments, which might include new equipment or technology. *Screen for high-return stocks using the following measures...*

•Return on capital (pretax operating profit as a percentage of net working capital and net fixed assets) of 30% or higher. My Web site ranks 3,500 companies based on their return on capital, with the highest assigned a rank of one.

•Low stock price in relation to the company's past 12 months of earnings. To find a list of attractively priced stocks, screen for an earnings yield of 12% or more. This is the ratio of pretax operating earnings to market value plus net debt.

My Web site also ranks the 3,500 companies by earnings yield, with the highest-rated company assigned a rank of one. Then it combines this rank and the return-on-capital rank (described above), assigning the top rankings (those with the lowest numbers) to companies that have the best combination of the two factors.

For example, the company that ranked first in return on capital but 1,150th in earnings yield would receive a combined ranking of 1,151 (1 plus 1,150). A company that ranked 232nd in return on capital and 153rd in earnings yield would receive a combined ranking of 385 (232 plus 153)—a better overall ranking.

•**Narrow the field by selecting companies of a specific size** in terms of value of shares outstanding, referred to as market capitalization. Stocks of small and midsized companies, with market capitalizations of $1 billion or below, are riskier than stocks of large companies, but they offer higher returns on average. Once you have finished the screening process, invest in at least 20 of the top-ranked stocks. This eliminates virtually all of the risk of just owning one stock but keeps your portfolio to a manageable size.

•**Sell all your stocks after 12 months (unless they make the grade** for the second year in a row), and reinvest the proceeds in the new top-ranked companies. For the taxable accounts, make sure that you're eligible for the 15% federal income tax rate on capital gains by holding

177

moneymaking stocks for at least one day more than a year.

Why sell winners after only one year? I have found that for most investors, it's the simplest, most effective strategy. However, money-losing stocks should be sold a few days before one year is up so you can take the stock loss when you file your taxes.

Warning: There will be extended periods of time when your portfolio will trail the market averages, at times by double digits. That's why this strategy is intended for investors with time horizons of five years or more.

More from Joel Greenblatt...

Smart Stock-Picking Shortcuts

Here are a few easy ways to make my strategy work for you...

● **Screening.** You can use my Web site, *www. magicformulainvesting.com*, or your own favorite stock-screening site. On other sites, you might need to customize the search criteria.

Examples: Use return on assets (ROA) instead of return on capital. Set the minimum ROA for 25%. Use price-to-earnings ratio in place of earnings yield. Eliminate all utilities and financial stocks from the resulting list.

Reason: These industries use different definitions of debt and other financial measures, which make them hard to screen.

● **Trading.** Since this system generates high turnover, keep trading costs down by using a low-cost discount broker, such as *www.foliofn. com* or *www.buyandhold.com*. These firms enable you to purchase fractional shares of stock, so you do not need to invest large sums to be well diversified.

A Top Trader Shares His Secrets: "How I Turned $33,000 into $7 Million"

Michael J. Parness, chief executive officer and founder of TrendFund.com, an advisory and counseling service for active stock traders, New York City, *www.trendfund.com.* He is author of *Rule the Freakin' Markets* (St. Martin's) and *Power Trading Power Living* (Ultimate). He is frequently interviewed by *The Wall Street Journal*, CNBC, *Financial Times*, Fox News and Business Talk Radio. He conducts informational trading seminars around the country.

Eight years ago, Michael J. Parness, who at that time operated his successful sports-memorabilia business, followed a stock-broker's advice and sunk his $150,000 nest egg into a few recommended stocks. It didn't take long for his portfolio to decrease by nearly 80%. In February 1999, he opened up an on-line brokerage account and vowed to get all his money back. In just 15 months, Mr. Parness's initial balance of $33,000 had soared to $7 million.

While active trading strategies are not for the faint of heart, devoting a small amount of your portfolio to such strategies can increase profits in any market—even when stock prices overall are flat or declining. *Mr. Parness, now a professional trader and author, shares all of his favorite stock-trading techniques below...*

TAME YOUR INNER KNUCKLEHEAD

Many investors get into trouble by leaping before they look. For at least a month, try trading stocks "on paper" or open up a simulated trading account from *www.stocktrak.com/trendfund.* Once you begin to see profits, then start trading with real money.

Caution: When buying stocks, control your risk. Use a stop-loss order for each of your holdings. This is an order for your brokerage to sell the stock if it drops to a specified price that is below the current market price.

How much should you allow a stock to drop? When setting such a floor, I rely on what I call the 2% rule—no investment should lose more than 2% of the value of your entire portfolio. For example, if you have a portfolio of $100,000 and you buy 500 shares of IBM, set a stop-loss order at a price that ensures you won't lose more than $2,000 on your IBM position.

HEED MY THREE "DON'TS"

Don't invest in just one or two stocks…*don't* invest if you are not confident about a stock's prospects…*don't* buy a stock because a broker, stock analyst or TV personality pushes it—the price may jump immediately after their recommendation, and you will wind up paying a premium price.

Smarter strategy: Own at least five stocks, preferably from several sectors, based on careful research. You want to diversify so you're not crushed if one of your positions encounters bad news or is in a sector that gets pummeled.

BUY ON THE RUMOR AND SELL ON THE NEWS

The saying is a cliché, but the strategy really does make sense.

Example: When it was first rumored that Sirius Satellite Radio Inc. (SIRI) was in talks with the "shock jock" deejay Howard Stern, investors pushed the stock up from $3 to as high as $9 a share. When Stern actually began broadcasting in January 2006, the news was played out and the stock settled back to $5—it is now about $3.* Most of those who wanted to invest in the Sirius-Stern play had already done so. Many of my clients made money by selling before Stern started broadcasting.

MAKE THE TREND YOUR FRIEND

This is another cliché but still good advice—and often ignored. I've made most of my money by investing in trends or patterns that I spotted in both bull and bear markets. I look for trends that occur repeatedly in several stocks and use them to anticipate price movements in similar stocks. Trends do not last forever and are continually being replaced by new ones, so you'll need to monitor your portfolio carefully to follow this strategy.

The goal of trend trading is to capture huge profits—5% to 50% or more—within just several days or weeks.

Example: There are now a few stocks that deal in Canadian oil sands. The biggest is Suncor Energy Inc. (SU), which I have owned on and off since it was in the $30s. It is over $90 now, but the idea still is to buy stocks in the same sector that haven't quite caught up to SU's move.

*Prices subject to change.

My favorite trend play now is the booming demand for energy and health care.

KNOW WHEN TO ESCAPE

Not every stock trade will succeed. *You can reduce your chances of loss by dumping a stock when…*

• **A trend is no longer working.** In 1999 and 2000, stock splits were a major trend. You could buy a stock within two weeks of an upcoming split, and its price would go up based on the theory that after the split, more investors would buy it at the lower share price. The stock-split play stopped working from 2002 through 2005 but began working again in 2006 for such stocks as Nabors Industries Ltd. (NBR) and Netease.com, Inc. (NTES).

• **The stock's upward momentum has fizzled** or has been abruptly broken. This might happen without your stop-loss being triggered.

• **The stock is nearing $100 or $200 per share,** which is a major psychological barrier. Historically, investors have resisted pushing any stock above $100 or $200 a share.

Reason: People like to sell at prices that are round numbers, when a stock reaches $100 or $200 rather than, say, $83 or $172.

• **The stock is about to reach a resistance level**—a price that it has been unable to break through before.

Big Profits in Nanotechnology

By year 2015, nanotechnology—the science of building devices from single atoms and molecules—will be the basis for $2.6 trillion in products in chemicals and materials, equipment, electronics, energy and other sectors.

Stocks poised to profit: Intel Corp. (INTC) will repeatedly double the number of transistors on a semiconductor chip over the next 15 years. An aggressive investor might consider Headwaters Inc. (HW), an energy company developing new nanoparticles for refining oil in Canada's tar sands…and Starpharma Holdings (SPHRY.PK), an Australian company whose nanoscale device helps to prevent HIV/AIDS and detect and treat early-stage cancer.

Jack Uldrich, author of *Investing in Nanotechnology* (Adams Media) and president of The NanoVeritas Group, a technology consultancy, Minneapolis.

How to Protect Your Portfolio from the Avian Flu

You can safeguard your investments from the economic effects of Avian flu. *If the disease spreads beyond birds to other animals*, allocate more into cash—as much as 15%. *If the disease spreads among humans*, boost cash to 25%, and sell and/or avoid stocks in economically sensitive sectors, such as energy. At the same time, buy or hold tech and telecom stocks, since the flu would boost the need for electronic communications. *Finally, if the pandemic develops,* sell most of your stocks and keep only high-grade bonds—they will benefit if interest rates fall in a recession.

David Kotok, chairman and chief investment officer of Cumberland Advisors, a money management company in Vineland, NJ.

Diversify Your Portfolio While Sidestepping Capital Gains

Mark H. Leeds, Esq., shareholding partner, Greenberg Traurig, LLP, 200 Park Ave., New York City 10166. He is editor in chief of *Derivatives: Financial Products Report* (Thomson/RIA). Mr. Leeds advises his clients on financial products and strategies, including collars and variable prepaid contracts.

Investors whose net worth is concentrated largely in one asset face considerable risk. If it's a stock and the price drops, a large portion of their wealth might be lost. In recent years, there have been many cases where corporate shares—and individuals' wealth—have plunged in value.

Trap: The obvious way to reduce this risk is to sell the shares to diversify. Capital gains tax rates are at historic lows, and current laws will keep those rates in effect only through 2010. Selling and paying the tax is one option that might be considered.

However, even with today's favorable capital gains tax rates, selling highly appreciated securities can generate a sizable tax bill. In a high-tax state, the total taxes due could top 20% of the proceeds.

ON THE MARGIN

Another technique for getting cash for diversification is to borrow against the shares you own. Then you can invest the loan proceeds in a diversified portfolio.

Advantage: A loan is not a sale, so you won't trigger a tax bill.

Also, if you borrow against securities to buy other securities, the interest may be deductible. You must generate sufficient investment income to offset this interest expense, however.

Moreover, investment interest that is not currently deductible may be carried forward and deducted against future investment income.

Strategy: If you think tax rates might go up, it might be a good idea to borrow against your securities and then stockpile investment interest expense with the intention of using it against future investment income that may be taxed at a higher rate.

Disadvantage: Although borrowing against a concentrated position and reinvesting the proceeds will reduce your risk, you still stand to lose substantially if the value of your collateral drops.

Your broker might effect a margin call and liquidate one or more of your positions without even notifying you. You might be forced to come up with more cash or other collateral to avoid an involuntary sale of some assets.

OPTION PLAYS

Some of the problems involved with straight borrowing, described above, can be addressed by an *options collar.*

How it works: You buy a "put option" to protect against significant loss. The put option gives you the right to sell a certain quantity of a security to the seller of the option, at a specified price up to or at a specified date.

You also sell a "call" on the same shares to offset the cost of buying a put. A call is an option that gives the owner the right to buy a certain quantity of a security (in this case, from you) at a specified price on a certain date.

Situation: Jim Johnson spent most of his career at a public company. He holds 10,000 shares of company stock worth $1 million in a brokerage account. Those shares comprise a large portion of his net worth.

The shares now trade at $100. Jim's average basis in the shares is $10, therefore selling these shares would trigger long-term capital gains tax on $90 per share.

On a sale, he would have income of $900,000 and a tax liability of $180,000 (assuming a combined 20% federal and state tax rate).

Options: Jim might buy put (sell) options, entitling him to sell the shares at, say, $90. Such options might stay in effect for as long as three years.

Such options can be costly, so Jim also sells a call (buy) option for, say, $120 a share, allowing the purchaser to buy the shares from him at $120.

Costs: Jim might pay $20,000 for the put and receive $20,000 from the sale of the call. If so, he has created a "cashless collar"—the net cost to him is zero, except for brokerage commissions.

Vital: There's no current tax due from the sale of the call, so there's no tax drag from these transactions.

Result: This put option protects Jim from losing more than 10% of the value of his stock position. If the shares drop from $100 to $85 or $80 or even $20, he can sell for $90. At the same time, Jim limits his future upside to 20%—this loss of opportunity is the real price of the cashless collar. If the share price goes over $120, the shares will be called away from him.

Strategy: Once Jim has locked in this risk reduction strategy, he can borrow against the put option (now the minimum value that he'll receive on the company stock). The borrowed funds can be used to diversify his portfolio.

Why borrow? Because your upside is limited with a collar. You hope that the long-term return from your diversified portfolio will exceed the costs of the loan. The rate on large ($250,000-plus) margin loans now is 8.25% to 9%. In addition, if you invest in a diversified portfolio, you'll likely have losers and gainers. The losers can be sold, generating tax losses to offset the capital gains you'll recognize eventually.

Tax treatment: If there is no risk of loss or potential gain, the transaction may be immediately taxed as a sale. Assuming the facts in this example, most tax professionals would say that Jim has enough potential gain or loss to avoid an immediate tax.

FORWARD THINKING

For some investors, the collar-plus-loan approach does not go nearly far enough.

Reason: Only 50% borrowing is permitted. If Jim has $1 million worth of stock as collateral, he can borrow no more than $500,000 to diversify his portfolio. In addition, cash settlement on the collar-plus-loan can trigger adverse tax consequences.

Alternative: Another strategy could provide Jim with up to $850,000 (85%) for portfolio diversification. This can be done with a "variable prepaid forward sale."

How it works: Jim sells his shares for delivery in the future but he receives cash today. The number of shares to be delivered varies with the price of the stock. This variation, if significant enough, can defer tax until settlement.

Situation: Jim agrees to deliver some portion of his $1 million worth of stock three years from now. His brokerage firm pays $850,000 up front. *Scenarios...*

• **If the value of the stock is less than $90 in three years,** Jim will deliver all of his stock and receive no additional consideration. Delivering all of the stock would be good if the price has dropped sharply. Jim has pocketed $850,000 for shares that now may be worth less and has also deferred the tax for three years.

• **If the value of the stock is between $90 and $120,** the range used in this example, Jim will deliver stock with a current value of $1 million. He will be protected from loss and has deferred the tax.

•**If the value of the stock is greater than $120,** Jim will give up the original value of his shares—$1 million—plus an amount that equals the value in excess of $120 per share for 10,000 shares. Jim keeps any profit on the shares between $100 and $120 but forfeits all the upside over $120 a share. This loss of upside is the price Jim pays for the downside protection and for the tax deferral.

Result: This technique is similar to a collar, with limited upside and downside. But instead of the amount of cash varying, the number of shares to be delivered will vary.

Advantage: Jim has three years to do some tax planning around his anticipated long-term gain. (He has a low basis, so he'll owe capital gains tax.) During that time, he will not have to pay interest on a margin loan because no loan has been made. Jim won't have to worry about margin calls, either.

IRS issues: With Revenue Ruling 2003-7, the IRS decided that variable prepaid forward sales don't necessarily trigger current tax. However, this ruling did not address share lending by the investor.

In 2006, an IRS private ruling (Technical Advice Memorandum 200604033) held that share lending, when coupled with a variable forward sale, resulted in a constructive sale. In this instance, the taxpayer agreed to let the brokerage firm borrow these shares up front. To effect its hedge, the broker then sold the shares short, reducing its risk of a price drop.

Result: To the IRS, the entire transaction constituted a constructive sale of the securities involved, triggering capital gains tax. Accordingly, investors considering variable forward transactions should not allow the institution writing the contract to borrow the hedged shares.

Note that the embedded costs—the broker's fees and trading costs—you'll pay likely will go higher if the broker has to pay someone else to borrow shares to allow it to hedge.

Vital: For any strategy of this variety, costs such as brokers' fees and trading costs will be involved. Ask for a summary of such expenses up front so that you can see whether they are justified by the risk reduction and tax deferral you'll obtain.

In addition, complex tax issues are involved, so consult with a tax professional who is experienced in this area before entering into such transactions.

Tax-Smart Guide to Choosing Mutual Funds

Sue Stevens, CPA, CFP, CFA, director of financial planning at Morningstar, Inc., LLC, a financial information provider in Chicago at *www.morningstar.com*. Founder and president of Stevens Portfolio Design, LLC, 861 Fountain View Dr., Deerfield, IL 60015, *www.gotospd.com*, she has also been named one of the top 250 financial planners in the US by *Worth* magazine.

With mutual funds, what you see isn't what you get in many cases. And this is due to taxes. Funds publish their performance pretax. For investors, the after-tax results can be much different.

Example: During a recent 10-year period, American Century Equity Income Fund (TWEIX) had an annualized return of 12.85%.* That return placed it among the top 2% of all funds in its large-company, value-stock fund category.

DWS Dreman High Return Equity (KDHAX) fund, another in the same category, was a cut below, with a 10-year annualized return of 12.06%.

Over those 10 years, the difference in return before taxes would have been more than $2,200 for every $10,000 invested.

But after tax, according to Morningstar, Inc., the DWS Dreman fund moved in front in "tax-adjusted" terms (see below), with gains of 9.99% a year, vs. 9.16% for the American Century fund. Over those 10 years, the DWS Dreman investor would have been *ahead* by about $1,900 for each $10,000 invested, instead of lagging by $2,200.

MAKING A DIFFERENCE

These differences are by no means unusual. Some mutual funds are more tax efficient than others. Over an extended period, this can make a big after-tax difference to investors.

Crunching the numbers: To arrive at these tax-adjusted returns, Morningstar follows procedures outlined by the federal Securities and Exchange Commission (SEC). *See the following...*

*Rates subject to change.

• **All distributions of income** are assumed to be taxed at the highest federal rate that year (now 35%).

• **Distributions from short-term gains** are taxed in the same manner.

• **Distributions of long-term gains** are assumed to be taxed at the maximum rate for such gains that year (now 15%).

It's true that relatively few taxpayers are in the top federal tax bracket, which doesn't kick in until $336,550 of taxable income this year (on single or joint returns). On the other hand, the SEC formula does not include state or local income tax, which many investors must pay. Ultimately, these hypothetical tax-adjusted returns deliver a reasonable approximation of how investors actually fared and are valuable for comparisons.

LOSING FROM GAINS

Among stock funds, income from dividends now averages only around 0.3%, so they are not the main cause of tax inefficiency. Instead, capital gains distributions play a key role.

How: Stock funds generally trade their portfolios frequently during the year. Most trades result in a gain or loss for the fund.

Each year, the fund must tabulate its net gain or loss for the year. The law requires a mutual fund to distribute capital gains to shareholders if the fund sells securities for a profit that can't be offset by a loss.

Situation: ABC Mutual Fund has 10 million shares outstanding. This year, its trading activities generate a $25 million net gain.

Thus, investors will receive a $2.50-per-share distribution of capital gains. If Janice Jefferson holds 1,000 shares of ABC, her distribution will be $2,500.

If some of those gains were from stocks held for a year or less, part of the distribution will be reported as a short-term gain, taxed to shareholders at rates up to 35%.

Otherwise, the gain will qualify for favorable long-term capital gains rates, now generally 15%.

Trap: Tax will be owed on those gains, even if the distribution is reinvested in the same fund or in another security. Thus, investors may have to pay tax on "distributions" even though they haven't received any cash.

What if a fund has net losses from its trading? Such losses are not passed on to shareholders.

However, net losses are "banked" by the fund so they can be used to offset any future trading gains and thus spare investors some tax pain.

TRADE SECRETS

Mutual fund tax inefficiency is caused largely by each fund's trading patterns.

Funds that trade heavily are most likely to incur capital gains that are passed through to the investors. A fund that turns its portfolio over rapidly may generate expensive short-term gains.

What's more, buying into a fund at the wrong time can lead to high taxes, as investors learned in the 2000–2002 bear market.

What happened: The technology, media and telecommunications stocks leading the 1990s' bull market fell sharply. Funds holding those stocks sold them off to prevent further losses and also to raise cash needed to pay investors who were redeeming shares.

In many instances, those stocks were bought years earlier, at substantially lower prices, so the funds had huge capital gains on these sales.

Trap: Those gains were passed through to all investors, newcomers as well as those who had been in the funds for years.

Investors who put money into a growth fund in 2000 might have received hefty tax bills, that year and in those that followed, even while suffering sharp losses as the fund's share price fell.

DOWNSIZING DISTRIBUTIONS

To reduce your risk of lose–lose investing...

• **Evaluate a fund's history.** A fund that has consistently distributed sizable gains to investors in most years may have a management philosophy of heavy trading. Such a fund is more likely to continue to distribute taxable gains.

Before you invest, ask your broker or a fund sales representative about its distribution record.

On-line, you can go to *www.morningstar.com* and enter a fund's ticker symbol in the "Quotes" search box. Then click on "Tax Analysis" to find the fund's tax-adjusted return and "tax cost ratio." (There is no charge for this.)

Data also are available in Morningstar Mutual Funds, a binder of periodic fund profiles.

Cost: $549 per yr. for 24 issues.* But you may also find this at your local library.

*Price and offer subject to change.

Generally, if a stock fund has a tax-cost ratio (which indicates how much of its return would have been lost to tax each year) of more than 1.25, it should be held in a tax-deferred retirement account. Bond funds with tax-cost ratios of more than 2.0 also work best in a tax-deferred account.

•**Be wary of built-in gains.** Funds having a portfolio filled with highly appreciated stocks may have a potential capital gains exposure of 40% or more of assets. If those shares are sold, the gains could produce large tax bills for the investors.

Conversely, the funds that have loss carry forwards might be worth considering partly for that reason.

Example: Alger Large-Cap Growth Fund (ALGAX) recently had a potential capital gains exposure of -36%, indicating the size of its loss carry forward.

Caution: A loss carry forward should not be the primary reason to buy a fund. A fund's past performance, management expertise, and so on, are more important.

Again, information on potential gains and loss carry forwards is available from your broker, the fund company, and from Morningstar.

•**Consider tax-managed funds.** Some funds explicitly manage their portfolios to minimize investors' tax bills. They trade little and take losses to offset any trading gains.

Such funds generally have "tax-managed" in their name. Vanguard Tax-Managed Growth and Income Fund (VTGIX), for example, gets four stars (out of a possible five) from Morningstar.

•**Consider index funds.** Funds designed to track a particular index usually hold the stocks in that index. They tend to trade infrequently and thus do not incur much in the way of taxable capital gains.

So-called exchange-traded funds (ETFs) are index funds that trade like stocks. They're generally tax efficient.

Bottom line: If you hold mutual funds in a tax-deferred account, such as a 401(k) or an IRA, tax efficiency won't matter. You won't owe any tax until you withdraw money.

In a taxable account, taxes count. It's wise to evaluate a fund primarily on its management, philosophy, track record and other fundamentals —but take a hard look at its tax efficiency before you invest.

Easiest Way to Invest In Mutual Funds

Paul B. Farrell, JD, PhD, investment columnist, Dow-Jones MarketWatch, Arroyo Grande, CA. Prior to joining MarketWatch, he was executive vice president of the Financial News Network. He is author of *The Lazy Person's Guide to Investing* (Warner), *The Millionaire Code* (Wiley) and *The Millionaire Meditation*, which is available free at *www.paulbfarrell.com*.

For investors just starting out or those who have only a small amount—say, $5,000 to $10,000—to invest, the simplest approach is to use one hybrid mutual fund. Hybrid funds hold a mix of stocks and bonds and have delivered steady results in all kinds of markets. The following hybrids have long records of stellar results. *You need to choose only one...*

FOR CONSERVATIVE INVESTORS

Many of these balanced funds hold 60% of assets in stocks and 40% in bonds. They typically keep the allocation fairly steady. Big bond positions temper these funds' risk. *My favorites...*

•**Fidelity Puritan** (FPURX). 800-343-3548.

Performance: 10.66%.*

•**Oakmark Equity and Income** (OAKBX). 800-625-6275.

Performance: 12.25%.

•**Vanguard Wellington** (VWELX). 877-662-7447.

Performance: 11.32%.

FOR MORE AGGRESSIVE INVESTORS

These asset-allocation funds have more flexibility to shift holdings among asset classes, depending on market conditions. *My favorites...*

•**Fidelity Asset Manager** (FASMX). 800-343-3548.

Performance: 8.49%.

•**Vanguard Asset Allocation** (VAAPX). 877-662-7447.

Performance: 11.87%.

*Performance figures are these funds' average annualized returns for the five years ending August 9, 2007, and are subject to change.

Funds to Avoid

Avoid funds newly available to the public that are sold based on their "long-term" results. These so-called *incubator funds* are started by companies to try out an investment approach and then sold to the public after several years if the approach goes well. But by the time the fund becomes widely available, its management may have changed, fees may be higher than they were in the incubation phase and the investing style may have shifted—so the results from the incubation period may be meaningless.

Karen Dolan, fund analyst, Morningstar, Inc., Chicago.

Bond Smarts

Consider selling and repurchasing a bond if its market value is higher than its face value.

Example: Say that a 10-year $100,000 Treasury bond, issued in 2000 with a 6.5% coupon, is now worth about $105,000. After paying long-term tax on your $5,000 gain, you still come out ahead. *Reason?* Selling the bond and then buying it again creates a tax write-off for *amortization of bond premium.* This would allow $5,000 in deductions during the next five years—taken against the five years' interest of $32,500.

This approach works best for people in a high federal bracket but a low state bracket. Profits will be reduced by transaction costs.

Helpful: Go to *www.twenty-first.com*, click on "Should You Sell and Repurchase Profitable Bonds?"

Robert Gordon, president, Twenty-First Securities, brokerage and investment firm, New York City.

Emerging Market Warning

For high yields, don't look to the emerging-market bonds. Many countries have reformed their economies and have budget surpluses, but yields on emerging-market bond funds average only 5.39%,* according to Morningstar, Inc. For most investors, the spread between this yield and that of US Treasuries would need to widen to three percentage points before the sector would be worthwhile. Even then, no more than 10% of a portfolio should be in emerging-market bonds.

Alternative: T. Rowe Price Spectrum Income Fund (RPSIX), a multisector fund that periodically invests in this segment.

Mark Salzinger, publisher and editor, *The No-Load Fund Investor*, Brentwood, TN, *www.noloadfundinvestor.com*.

*Rate subject to change.

Earn Income While You Help the Community

Calvert Foundation Community Investment Notes, available in increments of $1,000, are used to fund housing, hurricane relief and other social causes. The notes do not have credit ratings, but they have a good track record. Available through brokers, they pay interest of up to 3% and have maturities of five, seven or 10 years.* That is less than investors can earn on corporate bonds used for traditional purposes or on comparable US Treasuries—but that lower rate allows the foundation to channel capital to communities in need.

Information: 800-248-0337, *www.calvertfoundation.org*.

*Rate and offer subject to change.

Tax-Exempt Bond Trap

A friend of mine was shocked to find he owed significant taxes on his "tax-exempt" municipal bonds. How can this happen?

Possible ways…

1. Only interest earned on tax-exempt bonds is tax exempt. If bonds appreciate in value and are sold at a gain, taxable capital gain results, just as from any other appreciating investment.

2. Some tax-exempt bonds pay interest that is taxable under the rules of the AMT, a tax computation that hits more taxpayers each year. These bonds generally are "private activity bonds," issued to support projects (such as sports stadiums) that benefit private parties. Check the AMT status of bonds with their issuer before investing.

3. Tax-exempt bonds are often purchased at a discount, with the amount of the discount taxable as ordinary interest income. Also, not all municipal bonds pay federally tax-exempt interest.

William G. Brennan, CPA/PFS, CFP, Capital Management Group, LLC, 1730 Rhode Island Ave. NW, Washington, DC 20036.

Tax-Smart Guide to Investing in TIPS for Inflation Protection

Lewis J. Altfest, PhD, CFA, CPA, president, L.J. Altfest & Co., Inc., a fee-only financial planning firm, 425 Park Ave., New York City 10022. He is associate professor of finance at Pace University, also in New York City, and author of *Personal Financial Planning* (McGraw-Hill).

Inflation is back in the news. Recent reports claim that prices are rising at their quickest pace in more than a decade. Stock and bond markets have been upset by these revelations.

In response, many investors have been eyeing—and buying—Treasury Inflation-Protected Securities (TIPS).

TIPS can play a useful role in your portfolio, but you must know the tax rules and consequences before you invest in them.

HOW THEY WORK

TIPS are issued by the US Treasury Department. Thus, they have the highest credit quality, with virtually no risk of default.

Loophole: As is the case with all Treasury securities, the interest is exempt from state and local income taxes.

TIPS, however, are not your father's Treasury bonds. Their nominal yield is much lower.

Example: The traditional 10-year Treasury issue now yields around 5%.* The yield for 10-year TIPS is about 2.5%.

*Rates subject to change.

Reason: When you buy that traditional Treasury, you'll receive that 5% interest, no more and no less—no matter what happens with inflation. If inflation rises, your "real" yield—the spending power of what you earn—will be diminished.

With TIPS, on the other hand, you're getting a steady "real yield." That is, you'll get the TIPS' nominal 2.5% yield plus an amount equal to the inflation rate.

Example: Say that inflation is 3% per year while you hold your TIPS. You'll wind up with a total return of 5.5% a year (3% plus 2.5%), so you would be better off with TIPS than with a 5% traditional Treasury.

The higher inflation goes, the greater the return from TIPS.

PADDING THE PRINCIPAL

The way TIPS work is not as straightforward as one might hope. For one thing, when you invest in TIPS, your *principal* is adjusted for inflation. Your interest rate, paid twice a year, is fixed, but that rate is paid on the adjusted principal.

Example: You buy $10,000 worth of 10-year TIPS in February 2007. The interest rate (the real yield) is set at 2.5%. In the first six months, inflation increases at a 4% annual rate. For half the year, that's a 2% increase.

Result: The TIPS you purchased for $10,000 now have a principal value of $10,200, including a $200 (2%) principal adjustment.

The 2.5% interest rate is applied on $10,200 worth of bonds. That would be $255, so your semiannual interest payment would be half that amount, or $127.50.

Going forward: The same process will apply every six months. The principal value will increase if inflation is positive (usually the case), and your interest payments will rise.

After 10 years, depending on inflation in the interim, you might be getting more than $350 per year in interest, and your TIPS might be redeemed for around $15,000 at maturity.

TAX TROUBLES

So far, so good. But the tax treatment of TIPS can be unattractive.

How it works: Each year, you are taxed on the total return from your TIPS. That's the inflation adjustment and the interest you receive.

However, the only cash you receive is the interest, so you're being taxed on income you haven't pocketed.

Example: In Year One, your $10,000 worth of TIPS gets a $400 inflation adjustment as well as $258 in interest. You would owe federal income tax on $658 worth of ordinary income, at rates up to 35%, although your only cash flow from the TIPS has been $258.

ADDRESSING THE SHORTFALL

How can you deal with paying tax now on income you might not receive for years to come?

Tax-deferred territory: One solution is to hold your TIPS in a tax-deferred retirement account such as an IRA. You won't owe any taxes until money is withdrawn, which might be many years from now. And you might be in a lower tax bracket then.

Trap: Withdrawals from traditional IRAs are subject to federal, state and local income tax. When holding TIPS in your IRA, or in any tax-deferred plan, you forfeit the TIPS' state and local tax exemptions.

Result: Holding TIPS in a retirement account can be a taxing experience for the residents of high-tax states and cities. This experience may be even more painful because many such taxpayers owe the alternative minimum tax (AMT), where state and local tax payments provide no federal tax deduction.

Strategy: The TIPS-in-IRA method will work best if you plan to relocate to a low-tax state in retirement. When you withdraw funds, you won't owe much, if any, state or local income tax, so the loss of the tax exemption won't be painful.

Otherwise, plan to hold your TIPS in the IRA as long as possible. Over periods of 10 years or longer, the value of deferring federal income tax is likely to outweigh the loss of the state and local tax exemptions.

Where to find them: You can buy and manage TIPS with no fees at *www.treasurydirect. gov*, the federal government's bond purchase Web site. You can view your account, track its value, transfer (to another owner), sell and redeem TIPS there.

FEELING MUTUAL

Another approach is to buy TIPS through one of the dozens of mutual funds that hold these issues. PIMCO Real Return Bond Fund (PRTNX) and Vanguard Inflation-Protected Securities Fund (VIPSX) are two that offer savvy management as well as modest costs.

When you invest in a TIPS fund, the full tax obligation from your shares (interest plus principal adjustment) is passed through to you.

Most TIPS funds also make a full distribution of interest plus the principal adjustment each year. In the above example, you might invest $10,000 in a TIPS fund and get a $658 distribution rather than collecting only $258 in interest.

Investing in TIPS through a mutual fund provides you with alternatives...

● **Hold the fund in a retirement account.** The federal income taxes can be deferred until withdrawal. This could be an especially smart choice if you expect to be in a lower tax bracket and living in a low-tax state when you retire.

● **Hold the fund in a taxable account.** You will owe the federal income tax each year but you'll avoid state and local income tax.

Option A: You can choose to reinvest all of your fund distributions. This means that you'll owe tax, without cash flow, but at least your distributions will be reinvested in more TIPS.

Option B: You can choose to receive your distributions. This will give you enough cash flow to pay the TIPS tax obligation each year.

Option B makes sense when you already are retired and tapping your investment portfolio for income. You might want to maximize cash flow each year.

Investing in a TIPS fund and taking distributions will provide you with rising cash flow and preserve your state and local tax exemptions.

Your Pot of Gold

Buying gold coins for investment purposes has become more popular as gold prices have risen—to a recent price of over $670 an ounce.* But while bullion coins track the value of gold, collector gold coins are priced according to scarcity and condition and might have much higher collector values. One-ounce coins

*Rate subject to change.

are sold at a lower premium than the fractional gold pieces of one-half ounce or less. American Eagle and Canadian Maple Leaf coins usually have slightly higher retail prices than South African Krugerrands.

Good buy: American Eagles.

Jeff C. Garrett, president of the Professional Numismatists Guild, *www.pngdealers.com*, and a rare-coin dealer in Lexington, KY. He is coauthor of *100 Greatest US Coins* (Whitman).

Investing in Real Estate?

To find the best buy among various income-producing properties, check each property's "capitalization rate." This is more important than how a house or apartment looks or its location.

How: Divide each property's annual net rent (the rent you could charge minus your expenses, such as tax, insurance and upkeep) by its fair-market value.

Example: If you can charge $2,000 a month in rent and net two-thirds of that (about $16,000 a year), and the property would cost you $250,000 to buy, the capitalization rate is 6.4%.

Other things being equal, the higher the capitalization rate, the better the investment.

Forbes, 60 Fifth Ave., New York City 10011.

 ## Flip That House?

Making big profits from reselling renovated houses seems simple on television shows, but these fix-ups can be time-consuming...and costs can easily rise a lot higher than expected. After the work is done, every day the house remains unsold cuts into the profit, which is not realized until the sale is finalized...and the property still may be hard to sell for reasons unrelated to repairs, such as location or market conditions.

Bottom line: Do a lot of research, set aside plenty of time and money, and consult real estate professionals before trying house flipping.

Scott Frank, coauthor located in Atlanta of *Buy Even Lower: The Regular People's Guide to Real Estate Riches* (Kaplan).

Wise Personal Finance Books

Lynn O'Shaughnessy, a syndicated personal finance columnist based in San Diego. Her column appears in the San Diego *Union-Tribune* and in other publications. She also is a contributor to *BusinessWeek* and the author of three investing books, including *Investing Bible* (Wiley).

Bookstores are crowded with personal finance books, many of them not worth your time. *Here are some newer books that can help you become a wiser and wealthier investor...*

•**Smart and Simple Financial Strategies for Busy People** by Jane Bryant Quinn. This is the first book the consumer maven has written since 1997. She provides sound advice on all the major personal finance topics. *Her encouraging message:* Investing doesn't have to be difficult. $26* (Simon & Schuster).

•**The Only Guide to a Winning Bond Strategy You'll Ever Need: The Way Smart Money Preserves Wealth Today** by Larry E. Swedroe & Joe H. Hempen. Surprisingly few financial books are dedicated to fixed-income investing, which makes this book even more valuable. One of the best chapters describes how to build your own bond portfolio. $25.95 (Truman Talley).

•**The Smartest Investment Book You'll Ever Read: The Simple, Stress-Free Way to Reach Your Investment Goals** by Daniel R. Solin. Dividing up your money wisely among all your investing choices is critical to success. This book explains how you can do just that. It also explains how index funds might be an investor's best bet. $19.95 (Perigee).

•**Inside the Economist's Mind: Conversations with Eminent Economists** edited by Paul A. Samuelson & William A. Barnett. This book provides an in-depth look at how some brilliant economists came up with the theories that have helped shape people's views on the economy and humanizes a topic that often is impenetrable. It's a collection of interviews with 16 prominent economists, including eight Nobel Laureates, who represent a wide variety of viewpoints. $29.95 (Blackwell).

*Prices subject to change.

11

Consumer Confidential

Consumer Rip-Offs That Can Cost You Big

T he average American consumer spends hundreds of dollars more than he or she needs to each year. Why do they do this?

Answer: Corporations use powerful marketing strategies to convince us to spend more or to buy things that we don't need at all. *The most common marketing myths now…*

Myth: Bottled water is better than tap water.

Reality: Tap water is as good as bottled water—and it may even be better. ABC News tested bottled and tap water for bacteria such as *E. coli* and found that there was no difference in purity.

Some people worry about traces of chemicals and minerals in water, such as chlorine, chromium, copper and iron. It's possible that some tap water may contain more of these than bottled water, but trace amounts usually aren't harmful and may even be helpful—that's why iron, copper and chromium are in vitamin pills.

As for taste, ABC's test showed that New York City tap water rated higher than the bottled water Evian. If you still insist upon buying bottled water, think downscale. Kmart's American Fare water finished ahead of imported waters that cost several times as much.

Myth: You can save a lot on food at discount shopping clubs.

Reality: The warehouse clubs, such as Sam's Club and Costco, offer prices as much as 20% to 30% below those of supermarkets on many items—but consumers must buy in large quantities. You'll save money only if you eat what you buy before it spoils…avoid unnecessary impulse purchases…and shop at the club often enough to justify the annual fee of about $40.*

*Rates subject to change.

John Stossel, an investigative journalist with the ABC News program *20/20* since 1981. He has won 19 Emmy awards and written several books, including *Myths, Lies and Downright Stupidity: Get Out the Shovel—Why Everything You Know Is Wrong* (Hyperion).

To make matters worse, a 2002 Cornell University study found that because warehouse club members have more food in the house, they tend to eat more, adding to their waistlines.

Myth: Discount pet food is bad for your pet.

Reality: Premium pet food costs more, but it isn't any better than cheap supermarket brands. When selecting a pet food, look for "complete" or "complete and balanced" on the label. That means it has met government standards that say essentially, "If your pet eats this food and nothing else all its life, that's okay, because this is all it needs." You can find this guarantee even on less expensive products.

Myth: Diamonds are rare, and that's why they cost so much.

Reality: South Africa's De Beers cartel controls the lion's share of the world's diamond market. By marketing heavily and restricting the supply, the company has convinced consumers that diamonds are much rarer than they actually are.

Truth is, diamonds cost much more than other gems of comparable rarity, and jewelry stores often mark up diamonds by at least 100%, guaranteeing that consumers can never resell them for anything close to what they originally paid.

Bottom line: Even the experts can't tell by the naked eye a real diamond from a well-made cubic zirconia.

Myth: Baldness cures really work.

Reality: Most hair-growth formulas will not help grow new hair. Rogaine and Propecia are the only exceptions—and even they work only for some people. According to one sampling of 20 dermatologists conducted by *20/20*, Rogaine provided noticeable hair growth for fewer than one in 10 of their patients. Propecia has shown greater promise, particularly for treating male-pattern baldness, but the new growth often is minimal—and even those gains will disappear if Propecia use is discontinued.

Myth: Roach motels and roach sprays will solve roach problems.

Reality: Roach motels effectively trap those roaches that enter the trap...and chemical roach sprays do a good job of killing roaches hit by the spray. The trouble is that the female of the most common indoor species and her offspring can produce more than 30,000 babies in a year. If you have a roach problem, these measures will hardly make a dent.

The roach baits, including Raid Roach Baits and Dial Corporation's Combat Roach Baits, are more effective. These small plastic disks contain poisons that roaches eat and carry back to their nests, wiping out whole groups at a time.

The only reason that the roach baits haven't pushed roach motels and sprays off store shelves is that sprays and motels leave at least a few dead roaches where we can view them. Roach baits tend to kill roaches while they are hidden away in their lairs. These products do much more, but they don't provide visual evidence that they're doing anything.

Helpful: Ant baits also are more effective than other ant-control techniques.

Myth: Brand-name foods usually are better quality than store brands.

Reality: Brand-name groceries typically cost 30% to 50% more than no-frills store labels. People pay this premium because they're squeamish about eating what they perceive to be lower-quality food. But in truth, there's no nutritional difference...and taste tests sponsored by ABC News indicate that many people prefer the taste of at least some store brands.

People tend to be more willing to try generic nonfood grocery items, such as soap, paper towels and garbage bags. Ironically, the quality difference between brand-name and generic products tends to be greater with these nonfood items.

Myth: Internet purchases are riskier than other credit card transactions.

Reality: Most consumers believe that shopping on-line carries great risks—but your credit card number passes through strangers' hands whether you use the card on an Internet site or in a traditional department store. A survey by the Better Business Bureau found that in 2004, the Internet was responsible for only 11.6% of the cases of identity theft for which the cause was known.

To decrease the risk of on-line identity theft, stick with large, well-known companies...shop only on Web sites that begin "https://" (as opposed to just "http://," which suggests the site doesn't have the same level of security)...use a security program to keep your computer clear of spyware…and check credit card statements for fraudulent charges.

If your credit card number is stolen, your liability is limited to $50 if you notify the credit card company within 30 days of discovering the problem.

***Myth:* Premium brand-name gas is better for your car than discount gas.**

Reality: Unless you drive a car with a high-compression, high-revving engine, high-octane gas offers absolutely no advantage over standard-octane fuel.

Exception: A higher-octane fuel might help cut down on engine knocking and pinging if you drive an older car.

Likewise, no study has ever shown that gas from a big-name chain is any better for your car than gas from a no-name mom-and-pop station. It all comes from the same refineries.

***Myth:* Funeral directors will help you arrange an inexpensive funeral.**

Reality: The average cost of a burial in the US is $6,500, more than three times what it needs to be. You should be able to bury someone for as little as $2,000…buy cremation services for as little as $400…or donate a body to science for free.

The best way to prevent overspending is to shop around before the need arises. Nonprofit memorial societies can help you explore the inexpensive burial and cremation options in your area. The Funeral Consumers Alliance's list of local memorial societies is a good place to start your research (800-765-0107, *www.funerals.org*, click on "Directory").

Area medical schools can tell you how to donate a body to science. Many programs even cremate the body when they're done and return the ashes to you for free.

Save 50% on Groceries

Reduce grocery bills by as much as 50% by comparing prices at TheGroceryGame.com. This site provides a list of products that will be on sale at your favorite supermarkets—before traditional circulars are in the mail. The store's coupon bargains also are highlighted. The service costs $10 for eight weeks.*

Susan Samtur, author and cofounder of the bimonthly magazine *Refundle Bundle* at Box 140, Centuck Station, Yonkers, NY 10710, *www.refundlebundle.com.*

*Price subject to change.

Money-Saving Tricks From the Editor of *Living on a Dime*

Tawra Kellam, editor of the free, twice-weekly e-letter *Living on a Dime, www.livingonadime.com.* Located in Wichita, KS, she is coauthor, with her mother, Jill Cooper, of *Dining on a Dime* (T&L Group).

Eight years ago, my husband and I found ourselves $22,000 in debt as a result of medical-related bills, various unexpected expenses and poor financial choices. At the time, our average annual income was about $20,000. With two kids and a disability that does not let me hold a regular job, I had to be very crafty and reprioritize. I found that self-discipline is cumulative—you get better at it over time.

Result: Within five years, we had paid off all our debt.

Our secrets…

TRIM FOOD BILLS

•**Stop eating at restaurants.** It's one of the top sources of overspending for people who have trouble saving. You easily can save $2,000 to $4,000 a year by eating at home. A family like mine could spend $72 a month just on sodas at restaurants. My family hasn't sworn off restaurants entirely. We limit them to birthdays and anniversaries, and we avoid items that pad the bill, such as appetizers, drinks and desserts.

Helpful: Come up with just 10 basic dinner menus that are tasty and easy to make. Rotate them each week. Otherwise, you wind up going to restaurants because you're tired from work and don't want to think about what to cook.

•**Buy large quantities of ingredients on sale, and freeze them.** The prices for meats that are still fresh but near their expiration dates, for example, drop by 50% to 75% at most stores, and sometimes they can be as little as 39 cents a pound, so it's smart to buy a lot. *Two essentials to have...*

•Vacuum sealer. It shrink-wraps food, keeping it fresh up to five times longer than foil or plastic wrap. *Cost:* $75 and up,* at Target and Amazon. com. *Alternative:* Zipper-sealed plastic bags and a straw. Zip the bag almost closed, then insert a straw and suck out the air. Do not use this method with raw meat or poultry.

•Energy-efficient stand-up freezer. It can cost around $400 but consumes just a few dollars of electricity per month. Available at Best Buy, Sears and major appliance stores. Avoid chest freezers—it's hard to see what's inside and easy to lose track of what you put in there.

Helpful: Use tape and a marker to label food when you put it in the freezer.

•**Annualize savings.** To help cut back on extras, I figured out what they cost per year. For instance, eliminating one bag of potato chips a week from my grocery bill saved us $104 over the course of one year. Cutting out one liter of bottled water a day saved $456 a year.

MANAGE MONEY WISELY

•**Visualize it.** My husband was the spender in our household. It was hard for him to find the discipline and awareness to save until he saw positive progress—and kept seeing it—on paper.

On the refrigerator, he posted a graph showing our progress toward our savings and debt-reduction goals. He updated this graph around once a month. Seeing our success inspired him to continue saving.

•**Take small steps.** It's unrealistic, for example, to reduce your food bill from $600 a month to $250. Instead, start by trying to spend $25 less a month, then $50 less, etc.

•**Calculate the cost in work hours.** When we were tempted to splurge, we calculated how long we would have to work to afford it. For example, my husband would like a home theater, but after calculating the cost of his friend's set-up, he figured out that he would have to work full-time for four months and put every dollar of income over that time toward the cost in order to afford it.

*Prices subject to change.

•**Play the credit card game.** The proliferation of credit cards with no interest or very low interest rates on balance transfers is a godsend to people trying to save. A key reason I was able to get out of debt was that I paid just $1,900 in interest over five years. I reduced most of my card rates from 21% to no more than 2% by transferring balances numerous times. I went from paying $100 a month in interest to $15 a month. I received most offers in the mail, or I called the card companies until I found the best deals.

Important: Zero-percent interest on your balance doesn't mean that you get six months or a year off from debt reduction. You need to maintain a steady level of payment from beginning to end.

•**Choose your money battles with your spouse.** You can't argue over every dime, or saving money becomes too stressful. We agreed that we didn't have to discuss small purchases for necessities (basic groceries, gas, etc.). I also recommend allowing some amount of personal money for each spouse to spend "no questions asked." We didn't do this in the beginning, because we were on a tight budget, but later, we allowed ourselves $25 each per month. The amount a couple chooses depends on their income and how fast they want to pay off their debt.

CUT DOWN ON CLUTTER

I have determined that being neater and more organized saved me at least $1,000 a year. You don't realize how much money you waste buying items that you already have but can't find.

Example: I threw out a lot of spoiled food simply because it went unnoticed in the back of the refrigerator.

My favorite organization strategies...

•**Schedule a family "pick-up time."** Before bed each night, I set an egg timer for 10 minutes, and each member of the family has to put away as many items as he/she can in that time.

•**Estimate how long each task will take.** You're more likely to stop the procrastinating if you time how long a chore actually takes you. People usually spend more time dreading a task than doing it.

Examples: It takes one minute to make the bed...three minutes to unload the dishwasher...five to 10 minutes to clean the bathroom...

five minutes to go through the mail and dump and file it.

- **Have rules for getting rid of stuff.** When the kids' rooms get messy, we put the things they no longer play with in a box in the garage. If the kids haven't asked about those toys for a few months, we give them away. The same goes for me—if I haven't worn an article of clothing in the last year, I give it to charity.

An Inexpensive Way To Get Books

Two Web sites let you trade your old paperback books for different ones. List the books that you have to trade, then browse for a new read. You pay only the postage on the books you send, which is usually about $2.*

Information: *www.paperbackswap.com* and *www.frugalreader.com.*

*Price and offer subject to change.

Send Packages for Less

Compare the delivery prices and the pickup options from the leading package carriers at RedRoller.com. Setting up an account and comparing pricing are free.* You can also print your own shipping labels and track the packages.

*Offer subject to change.

Energy-Saving Appliances

The lowdown on those energy-saving appliances you may be thinking of buying....

- **Front-loading washers** use less water than top loaders and are gentler on clothes and quieter—but they cost twice as much.

- **Dryers with moisture sensors** cost about the same as other dryers, but they save only about 10 cents per load*—that still can add up to $450 over the dryer's life.
- **Refrigerators with top-mounted freezers** cost less than side-by-side models and cut energy expenses by 13%, but the freezer area is smaller.

Harvey Sachs, PhD, director of buildings programs for the American Council for an Energy-Efficient Economy, Washington, DC, *www.aceee.org.*

*Rate subject to change.

Save Big on Top-Quality Clothing

Designer clothing at bargain prices can be found at The $15 Store (*15dollarstore.com*). It sells quality children's, junior and junior plus-sized clothing as well as shoes, outerwear and accessories—including hats, sunglasses, jewelry, belts and purses. Items are just $15.* Brands include XOXO, Bongo and Lulu. Free shipping for orders of $100 or more.

Recent bargain: A Romeo & Juliet Couture beaded tank (retail $108) sold for $15.

Sue Goldstein, creator of The Underground Shopper, a multimedia outlet that includes a Dallas-area call-in radio show on shopping and an Internet shopping site at *www.undergroundshopper.com.*

*Prices and offers subject to change.

Best Time to Replace Various Items

How long should you keep your toothbrush? When is it time for a new mattress? *Get the answers to these questions and more below...*

- **Disposable contact lenses can be worn for two weeks** if you take them out every night, but only one week if you sleep in them.
- **Running shoes should be replaced after 200 miles of use**—about four to five months.
- **A toothbrush lasts four months.**

• **Most unopened condoms expire in three to five years,** sooner if they contain spermicidal lubricant.

• **Mattresses typically last 10 years**—if you are uncomfortable after sleeping or notice any sagging, it is time for a replacement.

Men's Health, 33 E. Minor St., Emmaus, PA 18098.

To Get a Mattress That's Right for You...

Mary Hunt, editor, *Debt-Proof Living*, Box 2135, Paramount, CA 90723, *www.debtproofliving.com*.

When buying a mattress, to start check out the leading manufacturers' Web sites, such as *www.simmons.com* and *www.sealy.com*, to find out what's currently being offered, then...

• **Educate yourself** about features you want, such as innerspring coil count and the type of edge support, and compare mattress prices in stores by the features offered.

• **Hold out for big sales.** Department and bedding stores have them almost every month. Aim to save at least 50% off the list price.

• **Insist on a no-substitutions clause** in the sales agreement in case the bed you ordered is out of stock.

• **Pass on the pillowtop,** a layer of padding sewn permanently on the top of the mattress. This can add $100, and it may flatten before the mattress does.

• **Skip the new box spring.** If your current one is only a few years old, with no rips, warps, creaks or "give," consider using it with a new mattress.

Careful: Some mattress warranties are void unless you purchase the mattress and box spring together.

• **Look for the "comfort guarantee."** You should have anywhere from two to 12 weeks to return or exchange a bed that you don't like.

• **Ask to have your old mattress carted away for free.**

More from Mary Hunt...

Holiday Tipping Guide

Wondering what to give your newspaper boy or your hairdresser this coming holiday season? *Appropriate amounts for an annual gratuity...*

• **Postal carrier.** Cash is forbidden. Offer items worth up to $20, such as cookies or candy.

• **Newspaper delivery.** If you have daily delivery, $15 to $25...for weekend-only delivery, $5 to $15.

• **Housekeeper.** The cost of one visit—if you are happy with the service.

• **Hairdresser.** In addition to your usual tip, give 15% to 20% of your total bill for a typical visit, plus a small gift.

• **Barber.** The cost of one haircut, but not less than $10.

• **Doorman.** $25 to $100, depending on how much he helps you during the year.

Note: Service people who are especially helpful may deserve more, or you can give money plus an additional gift.

Save Big on Electronics

Save on electronics by choosing a no-name product instead of a name-brand one.

Example: With DVD players, there is little difference between a $35 one and one that sells for $200. Huge price differentials for the same product also are common for cameras and TVs.

For information on buying electronics, go to CNet.com and click on "Compare Prices."

Money, Time-Life Bldg., Rockefeller Center, New York City 10020.

When to Buy an Extended Warranty ...When Not To

James Sebastian, managing partner, Safe, LLC, a warranty consultancy firm located in Las Vegas, NV. His Web site is *www.safellc.biz.*

Product warranties for manufactured goods are growing ever shorter while manufacturers and retailers try to make money by selling extended warranties instead.

Shrewd buying: Manufacturers' extended warranties tend to be a better buy than those from retailers, both in price and by being more comprehensive.

Beyond that, for some kinds of products, buying an extended warranty is a good idea—while for others, an extended warranty simply adds to the seller's profit.

Products for which warranties actually are a worthwhile purchase...

• **Plasma TVs.** These are expensive to replace and use advanced technology prone to need repair—30% of plasma television sets need service in the first three years.

• **Laptop computers.** They are more costly, more delicate and more expensive to fix than desktop computers—and they are more likely to be dropped and damaged.

• **Wristwatches.** Standard warranties usually exclude the parts most likely to be broken, such as the face and the band. Extended warranties that do cover them often are inexpensive.

Keep your money rather than purchase extended warranties for...

• **"White goods,"** including refrigerators and washing machines. These generally are reliable, and a warranty is liable to cost as much or more than any repairs you'll actually need.

• **Desktop computers.** Most problems with these products occur early on, within the term of the original warranty.

• **Digital cameras.** So few need repairs, and those that do generally need them during the original warranty.

How to Haggle Like a Pro...Even If You Hate Haggling

Max Edison, a pawnshop owner for 10 years in Owatonna, MN, and author of several books on personal finance, including *How to Haggle: Professional Tricks for Saving Money* (Paladin).

Haggling is the secret to paying less for goods and services. Haggling isn't unseemly horse trading, it is a real form of negotiation—and it is perfectly respectable. *What you need to know to haggle successfully...*

PREPARATION PAYS

There is room for negotiation in virtually every purchase, even at large department stores, where you can get a discount if you can point out a defect in a product.

Important: Good hagglers always carefully inspect items that they're interested in.

Biggest mistake made by hagglers: Lack of preparation. A seller who is aware that you are guessing or bluffing will be unlikely to give an inch.

The most important thing that you need to know: What constitutes a fair price for what you want to buy. *When making any major purchase, it's a good idea to go to several places first to make price comparisons...*

• **For items such as appliances, electronics and jewelry,** visit several stores. Also, since prices are lower on the Internet, check on-line to see what comparable merchandise sells for—that's the price you want to beat.

• **If you are house hunting,** learn the prices paid recently for comparable houses in similar neighborhoods. To get this information, ask a real estate agent or visit your county tax office and look at sales records.

• **For automobiles,** find out how much the dealer paid for the vehicle. Edmunds (*www.edmunds.com*) is a good place to learn the invoice price of a car as well as other pricing information, including how true market value (TMV) is calculated.

Second-biggest mistake a haggler makes: Not knowing all the tricks used by salespeople.

Since you can't avoid a salesperson's negotiating ploys, your best defense is to recognize what he/she is doing. You then have a chance to use some of those tactics yourself. *Examples...*

• A car salesman says, "I'd love to make this deal with you, but my manager says no way." Counter that with, "Let me speak with the manager."

• When offering you a loan, a banker says, "You've got to take this insurance policy for death or disability for us to approve the loan." Counter that with, "I know that I don't have to have insurance for you to make the loan."

HOW TO HAGGLE

Haggling can be courteous and friendly, but it's essentially psychological warfare. *Helpful...*

• **Play hard to get.** If the seller can tell that you're in love with an item, he knows that he will be able to get top price. Pretend to be only mildly interested and don't go back too many times to look at the item.

• **If you make an offer, let it stand.** If you make an offer and it's accepted, the deal is done. If a counteroffer is made, you can then make another offer. This is how the game is played. If the seller accepts your offer and you say that you'll be back next week, you may not have a deal the next week.

• **If you and the seller can't agree on the price of an item,** ask the seller if he's got anything that he can throw in on the deal.

Examples: Ask an automobile dealer to throw in floor mats, a bicycle rack or free service for six months...with computer and stereo equipment, ask the seller for free cables and free installation...with VCR or DVD players, ask for free movies.

• **Never tip your hand.** If you are willing to pay $100 for an item, offer $80 or even $60. You never know—the other guy might take it. Even if he passes or counteroffers, he'll feel like some progress is being made.

• **Nail down early whether or not sales tax is included.** Why go through 20 minutes of haggling only to start over at sales tax time?

• **Ask for the cash price,** if you are able to pay cash for an item.

Background: Merchants lose about 2% when a credit card is used, so they may be willing to take a 2% bite if you pay cash.

• **Take advantage of a seller's weaknesses.** *Examples...*

• Politely point out any flaws in the merchandise. If the item is outdated in any way, let him know that. This works best with digital cameras, flat-screen televisions and computers, where new models are introduced seemingly every day.

• Be aware that people will be more or less willing to negotiate under different circumstances. The two main factors are time and attachment to the object. A home owner who is having a two-day garage sale knows that whatever doesn't sell is going back to the attic or to the dumpster. On the other hand, there may be an emotional attachment (this was Grandma's dresser!). If someone won't part with his stuff for a reasonable price, check elsewhere. Seasonal merchandise, such as patio furniture and fur coats, can be purchased at huge savings for buyers who can think (and haggle) months ahead.

WHO BEST TO HAGGLE WITH

You can haggle with just about every seller, but you may find the greatest success with...

• **Small-town merchants and stores that are independently owned.** Their owners are much more likely to dicker than larger outlets such as Best Buy and the Home Depot. Make sure that you talk to a decision-maker, such as the owner or at least the store manager. Many times, a mom-and-pop store will try to match their larger competitor's sale prices.

• **Jewelry stores.** These retailers have mark-ups that are usually 300% to 400% above wholesale, so they have lots of room to haggle.

• **Car dealers.** Haggling with car dealers works best when bad weather keeps other customers away...near the end of the month (when sales quotas are due)...and from August to September (when the new models are coming out).

• **Banks.** They will argue about percentage points on loans, services such as free checking and even charges from bounced checks. Always ask to have all fees waived. Go up the chain of command until you find someone who has the power to say yes.

• **Chains and discount stores** will cut prices under the right circumstances, such as buying a display model, an item with very slight damage or an air conditioner in October.

• **Individuals who place ads in the paper using the words "best offer" or "OBO"** (or best offer). These people expect a counteroffer to the price they're asking—and they're doing you the favor of saying so!

To Get the Best Price...

These free comparison-shopping sites help you find the best prices. LowerMyBills.com compares fees for services, such as cell phone plans and credit cards, insurance and car loans. Click on the category you're interested in and fill out their questionnaire. TheFind.com compares ticket prices for shows and sporting events. Enter what you're looking for into the search form on the home page.

Chris Sherman, associate editor, SearchEngineWatch. com, an industry newsletter, Boulder, CO.

Credit Card Smarts

Merchants who accept Visa and MasterCard cannot require a minimum purchase. Card companies want their cards to be used for purchases of any size. If a merchant insists on a minimum purchase amount, contact your card issuer to complain.

Greg McBride, CFA, senior financial analyst, Bankrate. com, North Palm Beach, FL.

For On-Line Credit Card Purchases...

Nervous using your credit card on-line? Sign up with "Bill Me Later" merchants (*www. bill-me-later.com*), such as Walmart.com, Overstock.com and SkyMall.

When making a purchase, you verify your billing address, date of birth and the last four digits of your Social Security number. The merchant bills you later. Bills can be paid by mail or electronic bank transfers.

Kiplinger's Personal Finance, 1729 H St. NW, Washington, DC 20006.

Avoid Sneaky Fees and Surcharges on Credit Cards, Cell Phone Plans, Airline Tickets, More

Linda Sherry, director of national priorities for Consumer Action, a nonprofit advocacy and education organization in San Francisco. To get free consumer protection reports, go to *www.consumer-action.org*.

Americans are facing a big wave of fees or surcharges for practically every service. Credit card holders recently paid more than $15 billion a year in penalty fees. Many retailers can't raise their prices because the business environment is very competitive. Instead, they cover high fees in the fine print of their contracts or simply neglect to inform you of additional costs until your bills arrive. The charges can be outrageous.

Example: A typical bank overdraft, or "insufficient funds," fee on a bounced check runs $25 to $35 (*estimated cost to the bank:* $1).*

Not only do such fees siphon hundreds of dollars a year from your wallet, they make it harder to know the true cost of purchases so that you can comparison shop for the best deals.

How to avoid being overcharged for common products and services...

ON-LINE TRAVEL

• **Penalty fees.** When you need to change an airline ticket, many airlines charge $25 to $100. Canceling a hotel reservation may trigger a fee as well. If you book through one of the travel Internet sites, such as *www.expedia.com...www. travelocity.com...www.orbitz.com*...or at *www. cheaptickets.com*, you also will be hit with their penalty charges ($100 to $150 per ticket).

*Prices, rates and offers subject to change.

Self-defense: To avoid this double penalty, book your hotel or airline directly if you think that you might have to make changes.

SHOPPING

• **Restocking fees.** Many retailers charge a fee if you purchase an item and then return it.

Amount: 10% to 20% of the cost of the original item.

Example: Electronics giant Circuit City will charge a 15% fee for returns of digital cameras, desktop PCs, notebook PCs and printers and a 25% restocking fee for home-theater equipment.

Self-defense: Ask about restocking fees. For instance, you may not have to pay if you return the merchandise unopened within 14 days.

• **Handling and/or packing charges.** Most Web sites require you to purchase a hefty dollar amount of products—say, $100 worth—to be eligible for free shipping. Some sellers on the on-line auction site eBay offer free shipping but may charge for such extras as insurance (about $2 and up depending on the item), making any shipping savings negligible.

Self-defense: Look skeptically at "free shipping" offers. Find out the total amount that you have to purchase to be eligible. If you shop on eBay, find out about additional fees. Go to *www.free-shipping.com* for a directory of sites that offer free shipping and handling (a trial membership is available).

BROKERAGES AND INVESTMENT COMPANIES

• **Account maintenance charges.** Investors with less than a certain amount in their brokerage accounts—typically $10,000 to $25,000—are charged about $25 per quarter. Investors who trade infrequently (less than three times a quarter) also might face a $10 or higher "inactivity" fee per quarter. Mutual fund firms often charge annual administrative fees of $10 to $25 for any accounts, including IRAs, that fall below a certain minimum.

Self-defense: It's best to choose brokerages that don't charge maintenance fees for most accounts, such as Etrade.com and Siebertnet.com. Also, maintain all your taxable and nontaxable accounts at the same investment firm or brokerage—your combined account total might allow you to avoid maintenance fees. Inquire about

linking accounts that are not listed under the same Social Security number. For example, if three members of your family have IRAs at the same firm and the total for your combined accounts surpasses the minimum, you all may be able to avoid fees.

OVERNIGHT MAIL

• **Remote surcharges.** The major carriers bill extra for "out-of-the-way" areas ($2.20 for Federal Express). But many of these locations are actually residential areas in cities such as San Diego, Miami Beach, Phoenix and Atlanta. To find out if a zip code is considered remote, call 800-463-3339 or 800-742-5877.

Self-defense: Whenever possible, send the package to an office instead of to a home.

Reason: UPS and FedEx apply the remote surcharge only to shipments to residences.

Or send the package by overnight mail through the US Postal Service. The rates are comparable, and remote surcharges are not levied.

CELL PHONE PLANS

• **"Federal Recovery" fees.** Wireless companies promote a low base cost without mentioning that your bill will be increased by government-mandated charges, such as the Federal E911 Fee ($1 to $3 per month*) and the Number Portability Service Charge ($1 to $3).

Some companies even tack a Regulatory Cost Recovery charge on bills to high-speed Internet customers (about $3). This fee sounds as if it is required by the law. Not true. It's just a way for companies to increase their revenues.

Self-defense: Factor in additional fees when you comparison shop for a new cell phone plan. These fees will increase the plan's base cost by 10% to 25% each month. Negotiate for reduced charges before you sign up. Cell phone companies are so competitive these days that even if they won't eliminate the charges, they may be willing to give you more minutes or throw in a better phone.

Helpful: *www.saveonphone.com/wireless.html* (Enter your zip code into the search box of their "Wireless Plan Search" box, to compare prices on wireless plans).

*Amounts vary by state.

CREDIT AND DEBIT CARDS

• **Late penalties.** Credit card companies try to trick you into paying late, such as cutting the grace period (from the time of the charge to when payment is due) from 31 days to as little as 20 days. The late penalty can range from $15 to $39.

Self-defense: You must be notified about any changes to grace periods at least 15 days before the changes take place. Federal law requires that you receive your bill at least 14 days before the due date. If it doesn't arrive on time, complain to the bank's regulator—FDIC for banks (877-275-3342) or Office of Thrift Supervision (800-842-6929) for savings and loans.

You must pay on time even if you don't receive a bill. If you can't pay in full, pay the minimum amount due immediately.

Consider Providian's Real Rewards program (800-249-1939 or *www.providian.com*). All cardholders get 500 points for paying on time for six consecutive billing cycles. Points also can be redeemed for rewards, such as gift cards at Barnes & Noble and Macy's.

• **Convenience fees.** Some merchants charge you this 3% fee on your total purchase for using a credit card.

Self-defense: Tell merchants that you prefer using your debit card and its PIN—rather than signing by hand—so you can avoid paying this charge.

GENERAL STRATEGIES

Poorly trained customer representatives often pass along misinformation. You will have a better chance when you dispute a charge if you have jotted down notes. Include the date and time of the call...full name/ID number of the phone representative...the phone number you called and the rep's extension...and what you were told.

Other smart strategies...

• **Get it in writing.** Always request that fee information you receive over the phone also be e-mailed or faxed to you.

• **Request that late fees be waived.** They often are waived, as a courtesy, the first time if you ask or if you haven't incurred any penalty fees within the past two years.

• **Skim the inserts.** Notices of higher fees and changes of terms usually are tucked into a packet of solicitations or in hard-to-read disclosure paragraphs. You don't need to read everything. Just focus on the numbers amid the legalese, and read those sections.

Choose Short-Term Cell Phone Contracts

Service providers entice new customers with free or discounted cell phones and lots of free minutes if they sign two-year contracts, but these customers pay a premium to replace lost phones and penalties if they cancel the contract. A shorter contract might mean paying more for the phone and a higher activation fee, but you won't be locked into one provider and can take advantage of other providers' lower rates.

Web sites to locate the best deals: *www.my rateplan.com...www.wirefly.com...www.saveon phone.com.*

Kiplinger's Personal Finance, 1729 H St. NW, Washington, DC 20006.

 # Be Sure You're Not Leasing Phones

Too many US households needlessly pay a monthly rental charge for phones. Most renters are older people who may have had their phones since before the breakup of the Bell telephone system in 1984. A phone that you can buy for just $20 may cost hundreds in rental fees over many years.

Self-defense: Check over your phone bill. If it shows a charge for "leased equipment," you are leasing your phone.

Chris Baker, a senior policy adviser, consumer team, AARP Public Policy Institute, 601 E St. NW, Washington, DC 20049.

Appliances Use Electricity Even When They Are Not On

TVs, stereos and microwave ovens run on low power even when they're turned off. Equipment in low-power mode may account for as much as 10% of residential energy consumption.

Amory B. Lovins, chief executive officer, Rocky Mountain Institute, nonprofit energy policy organization, Snowmass, CO, www.rmi.org.

Conserve Water and Save

You can save $200 a year by conserving water. *Here's how...*

• **Stop leaks**—check out your home's water heater, fix leaky faucets and water-supply tubing, and check outdoor systems, such as sprinklers, for leaks.

• **Replace toilets that are more than 10 years old**—the high-efficiency low-flow models, which cost about $300,* save 25 gallons per day.

• **Buy an energy-efficient washing machine** —"Energy Star" models use 50% less water.

For more tips, visit *www.h2ouse.org.*

Karl Kurka, assistant director, California Urban Water Conservation Council, Sacramento, CA.

*Price subject to change.

Are You Being Overcharged for Medical Care? How to Fight Back

Sid Kirchheimer, an investigative reporter and author of the "Scam Alert" column in AARP Bulletin. He is author of Scam Proof Your Life: 377 Smart Ways to Protect You & Your Family from Ripoffs, Bogus Deals & Other Consumer Headaches (Sterling).

Three-quarters of hospital bills have overcharges, and the average overcharge is about $1,000, according to the People's Medical Society, a nonprofit medical consumer

rights organization. Doctors, too, are handing inflated bills to patients.

Good news: It's simple to fight back.

If your health insurance completely covers hospital and doctor visits, these steps might not be necessary, though making the extra effort to eliminate overcharges can help bring down medical costs for everyone. Also, be aware that your insurance coverage might not be as comprehensive as you think—call your carrier or review the exclusions section of your policy.

DOCTORS' BILLS

To avoid paying more than you should...

• **Negotiate.** If you have no health insurance, ask your doctor for a discount. Only 13% of patients ever make this request, but when they do, the majority secure a lower price, according to a survey conducted by Harris Interactive.

Ask the doctor in person. Requests made by phone or to an office assistant rarely work.

Keep in mind that insurance companies typically pay doctors one-half to two-thirds of the amount that's billed. If you'll be paying out-of-pocket, you can offer to pay somewhere in that range when negotiating a price.

• **Get blood tests done at a lab.** When your doctor does a blood test, he/she charges you for the office visit...plus an added fee for drawing your blood...plus the amount a lab charges to run the test.

Ask the physician to waive his fees, or go directly to a lab to have the test done and pay only for the test (ask the doctor to supply any necessary paperwork).

Look in your local yellow pages under "Laboratories—Clinical, Medical, Diagnostic" or "Laboratories—Testing" for labs in your area.

• **Don't pay for the follow-up visit.** When you see a doctor about a health problem, you often have to see him again a few weeks later to confirm that your treatment was successful. Chances are, your doctor will look you over for a few seconds during this follow-up, pronounce you well—then bill you another $50 to $100 for the second appointment.

During your initial appointment, tell the doctor that you're paying out-of-pocket and ask if he'll waive or reduce the charge for the follow-up visit, assuming that it takes only a moment.

Many doctors will agree to this, particularly for regular patients.

- **Confirm that tests are necessary.** Doctors often order unnecessary medical tests out of fear that not conducting these tests might open the door for negligence lawsuits later. Unless your health insurance is picking up the entire bill, question whether recommended tests—including MRIs, CAT scans and X-rays—really are necessary. Ask your doctor what these tests will determine.

HOSPITAL OVERCHARGES

Here is how to recognize overbilling on hospital bills...

- **Ask for a daily itemized bill.** When you check into the hospital, tell the staff member who writes down your insurance information that you want an itemized bill brought to your bed every day. Hospitals are required to provide this upon request.

When you receive these daily bills, review each listing (or ask a family member to do so for you). Were you billed for two doctor visits yesterday even though you saw a doctor only once? Were you billed for tests that you don't recall getting? Are there any vague entries, such as "miscellaneous costs" or "lab fees"? Are there listings you can't understand? Tell the nurse you would like to speak with the hospital's patient advocate, then ask the advocate to explain any charge that is not clear. You might be appalled by what you are told.

Examples: Hospitals have been known to call one box of tissues a $12 "mucus recovery system" and a bag of ice cubes a $30 "thermal therapy kit."

Save the daily bills so you can reconcile them later with the final bill.

If the patient advocate will not help remove the mistakes and reduce egregious overcharges from your bill, retain an independent medical billing advocate. He will examine your bill and fight to remove any overcharges, usually for $30 to $50 per hour or 10% to 50% of the amount he saves you.*

To find a medical billing advocate: Contact Medical Billing Advocates of America (540-387-5870 or *www.billadvocates.com*)...American

*Rates subject to change.

Medical Bill Review (530-221-4759, *www.ambr.com*)...Edward R. Waxman & Associates (877-679-7224, *www.hospitalbillauditing.com*).

- **Bypass the hospital's pharmacy.** Hospitals dramatically overcharge for drugs. A patient might be billed $5 to $10 for a pill that retails for 10 cents elsewhere.

If you are taking medications on an ongoing basis and are not fully covered by insurance, bring your drugs with you to the hospital.

When you consult with your physician prior to entering the hospital, find out which drugs you're likely to be given during your stay. Ask the doctor to write you prescriptions so that you can buy these drugs at your local pharmacy in advance and avoid the hospital markup. Even if your doctor won't do this, you can bring any nonprescription pills you're told you will need, such as vitamins.

If you must get drugs through the hospital pharmacy and your insurance isn't footing the bill, ask your doctor to specify generics whenever possible. When you get your itemized daily bill, double-check that you weren't charged for brand-name drugs instead.

- **Watch for double billing.** Hospitals often bill patients twice for certain things. If your bill lists sheets and pillows, ask the hospital's patient advocate if these items are included in your daily room rate. If you're billed for the scrubs, masks and gloves worn by surgical staff, find out if these were included in your bill for operating room time.

Also double-check the times on your operating room bill. Hospitals charge from $20 to $90 for every minute you're in the operating room, so if the time you spent in surgery is padded even a little, it will add a lot to your bill. Your anesthesia records will say how long your operation really lasted.

- **Don't pay for your last day.** Hospital patients are charged the full day's room rate for the day they check in—even if they arrive at 11:59 pm. In exchange, patients are not supposed to be charged for their last day, but hospitals often try to bill for the final day anyway. Sometimes these last-day room bills are simply removed when you complain, but there are hospitals that insist the last-day charge is legitimate for patients who aren't discharged by a certain hour, often it's by noon.

During your hospitalization, ask the hospital's patient advocate whether you will be billed for your room on the final day of your stay. If the answer is, "Yes, if you're not out by a certain hour," ask your doctor on the next-to-last day of your stay to give you your final checkup and discharge okay the next morning, rather than waiting until the afternoon. If your doctor says this doesn't fit his schedule, tell the patient advocate that you shouldn't have to pay because the delay is the doctor's fault.

Save on Health Care

Negotiate health-care expenses for those procedures not covered by insurance, such as cosmetic surgery and gastric bypass.

Ask your doctor for the Current Procedural Terminology (CPT) codes on procedures he or she recommends, and use the code to look up the Medicare reimbursement rate in your area at *www.cms.hhs.gov/pfslookup/*. Offer your doctor or the facility this rate plus 10%, and agree to pay the fee immediately.

Kevin Flynn, president of Healthcare Advocates, which helps consumers negotiate health-care fees, Philadelphia.

Low-Cost Health Care

Low-cost health care is available at mini-clinics. These facilities are found in retail outlets, such as grocery chains and drugstores. They are staffed by nurse practitioners, who can write prescriptions and handle basic procedures. Clinics can save you 50% over full-service doctors.* Consider using them for minor ailments, such as bronchitis and rashes. Many of these clinics also accept insurance.

Time, 1271 Avenue of the Americas, New York City 10020.

*Rate subject to change.

Low-Cost or Even *Free* Vision Care

Jim Miller, editor of "Savvy Senior" a syndicated newspaper column, Norman, OK, www.savvysenior.org. He is also a regular guest on the NBC Today show.

Free or discounted vision care is available for people with limited incomes. *Check out these helpful resources…*

• **EyeCare America's Senior Eye-Care Program.** Coordinated by the American Academy of Ophthalmology, this program provides free medical eye care to all US citizens age 65 and older who have not seen an ophthalmologist in three or more years and who don't have coverage through an HMO or the Veterans Administration. Their program also provides a diabetes and glaucoma eye-care program.* 800-222-3937, *www.eyecareamerica.org*.

• **Knights Templar Eye Foundation.** This charitable foundation provides financial assistance for eye care to any citizen who needs surgery if they are unable to pay and don't qualify for other programs. 847-490-3838, *www.knights templar.org/ktef*. Knights Templar also cosponsors the EyeCare America program above.

• **Mission Cataract USA.** Coordinated by the Volunteer Eye Surgeons' Association, this program provides free cataract surgery to people of all ages who don't have Medicare, Medicaid or private insurance and have no other means to pay. 800-343-7265, *www.missioncataractusa.org*.

• **Vision USA.** Coordinated by the American Optometric Association (AOA), Vision USA provides free eye-care treatment to uninsured and lower-income workers and their families who have no means of obtaining care. 800-766-4466, *www.aoa.org* (at the home page, click on "AOA Public Programs").

• **New Eyes for the Needy.** This international program distributes new prescription eyeglasses to people with limited incomes. 973-376-4903, *www.neweyesfortheneedy.org*.

• **Local Lions Clubs.** This is a top referral resource for eye-care and eyeglasses programs that are available in your area. Programs and eligibility requirements vary by community. Phone your

*Offers subject to change.

local Lions Club chapter or contact Lions Clubs International, 800-747-4448, *www.lionsclubs.org.*

• **"Give the Gift of Sight" program.** Sponsored by Luxottica Retail and in partnership with Lions Clubs International, this program provides free screening and glasses to people who can't afford them. 513-765-6000, *www.givethegiftofsight. com*, or contact LensCrafters. To find a nearby store, call 800-541-5367 or visit *www.lenscrafters. com.*

Save Big on Medications

Charles B. Inlander, a Fogelsville, PA–based consumer advocate and health-care consultant. He was the founding president of the nonprofit People's Medical Society, a consumer advocacy organization credited with key improvements in the quality of US health care in the 1980s and 1990s, and is the author of 20 books, including *Take This Book to the Hospital with You: A Consumer Guide to Surviving Your Hospital Stay* (St. Martin's).

Everyone wants to save as much money as possible on medications, but some of the best ways for doing so are not well known. *My advice…*

• **Stay up to date on generic drugs.** Generic drugs are as safe and effective as brand-name medications and can sometimes be 50% to 70%* less. Unfortunately, most patients—even many physicians—are not aware when drugs become available in generic form. In the past few years, the often-used cholesterol-lowering drug Zocor (generic name *simvastatin*), the antidepressant Zoloft (*sertraline*) and the allergy-control nasal spray Flonase (*fluticason*) became available in much less expensive generic forms.

• **Shop around for generic drugs.** Pharmacies are now in a price war over generic drugs. It started in 2006 when Wal-Mart announced that it would sell 300 commonly prescribed generic drugs for $4 per 30-day supply. Other chains, including Target and Kmart, and food stores, such as Wegmans and Price Cutter, have similar programs now.

Look at the generic drugs you take to see if any are on the discount list of a store near you. These lists are available on store Web sites or

Prices, rates and offers subject to change.

you simply can call the pharmacy. If the generic medication you take is not listed, ask your doctor if you can switch to one that is. Your savings will be significant. For example, the popular generic blood pressure drug *lisinopril* costs $4 for 30 10-milligram (mg) tablets at Wal-Mart, compared with $18.99 at Drugstore.com and $30 at several community pharmacies I called. Even if you have medication insurance, the $4 price is probably lower than your current copayment.

• **Ask about older brand-name drugs.** Of course, not all drugs are available in a generic variety. More than half of all medications dispensed are brand-name drugs. But you still can save money if you ask your doctor to consider prescribing an older drug rather than one of the newer, more expensive drugs. Brand-name drugs on the market for seven or more years are often up to 40% cheaper than newer ones. Studies show that most older drugs are just as effective as new ones. It's also smart to shop around. Regardless of the drug, prices vary by up to 25% from pharmacy to pharmacy. There could even be price variations within the same chain!

• **Opt for medication insurance.** If your employer provides drug coverage, get it. It will save you up to 90% in out-of-pocket expenses. When you become eligible for Medicare, unless you have private insurance from a previous employer, sign up for one of the many Medicare drug programs available in your state.

Warning: Even if you use no drugs at the time you sign up for Medicare, get the insurance. If you do not and decide to buy the drug insurance later, you will pay a 1% penalty on your premium for every month you were not in the program. So if you wait four years to enroll, your premium will be 48% higher than if you had enrolled when you first became eligible for Medicare.

Reduce Out-of-Pocket Drug Costs

Seniors who use the comparison tool at *www. medicare.gov* can choose a Medicare Part D plan that will combine low monthly payments with low costs for the specific drugs they use. Be sure to select generics whenever possible. In one recent study, the cost of a five-drug regimen ranged from $2,692 to $3,752 out of pocket per year...compared with $622 to $1,777 for generic forms of the same medications.

Devon M. Herrick, PhD, senior fellow, National Center for Policy Analysis, Dallas, www.ncpa.org.

Heartburn Drug Savings

P rilosec OTC (over-the-counter) is as effective as expensive prescription drugs in preventing heartburn. Prilosec OTC costs only $19 to $26 a month.* Prescription heartburn drugs, such as Nexium, cost $181 to $193 per month. Even people with prescription drug plans could save if their insurers cover Prilosec OTC.

Gail Shearer, director, Best Buy Drugs, a public education project of Consumers Union, Washington, DC, www. crbestbuydrugs.org.

*Prices subject to change.

Smart Vitamin Buying

Simeon Margolis, MD, PhD, medical editor, The Johns Hopkins Medical Letter: Health After 50, University Health Publishing, 7 W. 36th St., New York City 10018.

T o get the most health benefit at the lowest cost from multivitamin supplements, check out this helpful advice...

• **Avoid buying "megadose" supplements.** They provide far more than 100% of the recommended daily allowance (RDA) for vitamins, antioxidants and minerals. Such doses provide no benefit and might prove harmful.

• **Buy a basic multisupplement.** It should provide 100% of the RDA for a large number of vitamins and minerals—a "seniors' formula" containing an extra amount of vitamin B-12 and lesser amount of iron is fine.

• **Shop by price.** Generic and store brands are just as good as higher-priced name brands, and tablets are as good as capsules.

• **Look for "USP" on the label.** This indicates that the product meets United States Pharmacopeia quality standards.

• **Avoid vitamins that contain herbs, enzymes and hormones.** The benefit of these is unproven and they could be harmful.

• **Don't pay more for unneeded features.**

Examples: All natural...timed release... stress formula...starch free...chelated (to promote absorption). They add no value.

Cut Pet-Care Costs

Woman's Day, 1633 Broadway, New York City 10019.

L ast year, owners of pets spent more than $38 billion on food, supplies, services and medical care for their 358 million pets. *To cut high pet-care costs...*

• **Leash, fence and/or supervise your dog** —dogs often sustain injuries while loose.

• **Skip fancy premium foods sold by vets,** and use name-brand pet food labeled "complete and balanced" or one that has the Association of American Feed Control Officials seal of approval.

• **Spay or neuter.** Spayed and neutered dogs have fewer health and behavioral problems.

• **Make wellness a routine.** Pet stores, humane societies and veterinary schools often offer on-site clinics that provide inoculations and wellness exams. Keep records of treatments.

• **Don't buy pet insurance.** Instead, put the amount you would have paid in premiums into a savings account for future medical bills. Or enroll your pet in a discount wellness plan, such as the one offered by Banfield, The Pet Hospital (866-277-7387, *www.banfield.net*).

• **Get a second opinion** if the estimate for a pet's medical care is for more than a few hundred dollars.

• **Shop around for medications.** Ask your vet for drug samples to get started, and then call retailers and pharmacies to compare prices.

12

Retirement Report

You May Need Less Money Than You Think For Retirement

Y ou hear it all of the time—most Americans aren't saving nearly enough money to get them through their retirement years.

But what if that warning is based on faulty assumptions? A growing number of economists and researchers say that this is often the case, even though the idea that you could save less for retirement and spend a greater amount now is heresy to the financial services industry.

Investment consultant Ty Bernicke is among the leading proponents of the view that financial firms routinely overestimate the retirement needs of their clients. Their incentive is too obvious—the more that people save, the higher the fees these firms collect.

While it's still necessary for you to save aggressively and spend conservatively, you may be better prepared for retirement than you think you are…

FAULTY ASSUMPTIONS

Most retirement planners and on-line retirement calculators assume that you will spend at an increasing rate throughout your retirement, but that's not what my clients—both married and single—end up doing.

Most of my elderly retirees spend much less than younger retirees. For instance, my clients in their 50s and 60s often travel more, go out to eat with friends often and enjoy the freedom that retirement brings. My clients in their 70s and 80s are less likely to socialize or eat at restaurants, especially because they have a difficult time driving at night. They also often have health problems and lower energy levels. These tendencies decrease food, travel, entertainment and other spending.

Ty Bernicke, CFP, a principal at Bernicke & Associates, Ltd., an investment advisory firm in Eau Claire, WI. He gained national attention for his study in the *Journal of Financial Planning*, which concluded that Americans are overestimating how much they need in retirement.

In fact, US government statistics also show a similar pattern. People ages 55 to 64 spend an average of $49,592 a year...those 65 and older spend $32,866...those 75 and older spend just $27,018. Except for health-care costs, which rise with age, that drop in spending holds true for all individual categories—including food, clothing and entertainment.

Average Annual Spending by Age Group

TYPE OF SPENDING	AGE GROUP 55-64	AGE GROUP 65 and up	SPENDING CHANGE
Housing	$15,769	$11,058	–30%
Transportation	$8,908	$5,171	–42%
Food/Alcohol	$6,656	$4,411	–34%
Health Care	$3,410	$4,193	+23%
Entertainment	$2,429	$1,593	–34%
Apparel	$1,784	$957	–46%

2005 US Bureau of Labor Statistics survey (select spending categories).*

Strategy: Sit down with your financial planner and run some scenarios based on the premise that your spending might decrease as time goes by, even when you account for inflation.

You might find that you can splurge a little bit more now on things that range from home improvements to travel to eating out—and yet still be comfortable in retirement. Or you might decide to retire earlier than first planned.

HOW TO PLAN MORE REALISTICALLY

A married couple had contributed the maximum permitted to their 401(k)s and IRAs for the past 20 years. Now they were both planning to retire at age 55 with a combined nest egg of $800,000, and Social Security payments of $12,000 each per year, which would begin when they reached age 62 and presumably increase by about 2% a year.

Traditional retirement planning calls for withdrawing 3% to 4% of your savings at first and then increasing that annually to keep up with inflation. That supposedly enables *investors* to keep their lifestyle consistent throughout retirement, but it does not reflect how people really spend as they age.

Using a traditional 30-year retirement plan, the couple expected to start out spending $60,000 a

*Latest date for which statistics are available.

year in retirement, the same as they had been spending...earn 8% per year on their nest egg ...and withdraw enough to fill in for any income needs not covered by Social Security. Using the conventional retirement calculations and assuming an average inflation rate of 3%, the couple would run out of finances by the time they reached age 85.

They weren't sure how to solve this dilemma. They would either have to keep working for several years...or boost their savings rate dramatically.

They didn't have to worry. If they could agree to spend at a declining level as they aged, in line with the US Bureau of Labor Statistic's Consumer Expenditure Survey, the couple wouldn't run out of money. Their nest egg would grow to $1.7 million in 26 years, rather than be completely depleted.

The reality: Many investors should consider withdrawing 6% of savings in the early retirement years, when they are most likely to travel and pursue hobbies. Over time, as activities decrease and expenses decline, that rate of withdrawal can be reduced.

Your housing situation also will have a big impact on your withdrawal rate. If you pay off your mortgage or downsize to a less expensive home when you retire, your expenses could immediately be lower than they were before retirement.

THE BIG EXCEPTION

In contrast to other categories, health-care expenses tend to jump as you age. *Steps to take...*

• **Budget annual increases** of at least 8% for health-care expenses. Unexpected medical bills are, by far, the biggest threat to keeping your retirement plans on track.

• **Watch the gap.** If you retire early, budget enough money to cover premiums for private health-care insurance after you retire and up to age 65, which is when you become eligible for Medicare coverage.

If you already have a health-care insurance policy and are healthy, you can probably find a cheaper one.

Example: A couple, both age 56, had obtained a policy in 1998 with premiums of $5,000 per year and a $5,000 deductible for the two of them. By 2005, they both were still in excellent health, but their premiums had nearly doubled—up to almost $10,000 with the same deductible. That's because in many states when you initially purchase insurance, you're thrown into a pool along with other people who buy insurance that same year. Over time, unhealthy people from your original pool make the policy more expensive for everyone.

By shopping around for their insurance, this couple was able to save $5,000 per year in premiums because the couple was put in with a pool of healthier insured people.

• **Plan to enroll in a Medicare supplement plan.** Medicare does not cover everything.

Examples of things that are not included: Hearing aids…dental care…emergency care during foreign travel.

There are 10 standardized supplemental Medicare plans to choose from, each varying in coverage and costs. Contact the Centers for Medicare & Medicaid Services, 800-MEDICARE, *www.medicare.gov*, for more information in your state.

Money Mistakes Seniors Are Making Now

Alexandra Armstrong, CFP, chairman of the financial planning firm, Armstrong, Fleming & Moore, Inc. at 1850 M St. NW, Washington, DC 20036, *www.afmfa.com*. She is author of *On Your Own: A Widow's Passage to Emotional and Financial Well-Being* (Armstrong, Fleming & Moore).

A young person who squanders his/her nest egg may have decades to recover. But seniors cannot afford to make big financial errors.

Common financial mistakes—and how you can avoid them…

Mistake: **Taking Social Security too soon.** Many people begin taking their Social Security when they turn 62. But the earlier you start taking benefits, the smaller your monthly check. It is usually better to postpone taking Social Security until you reach the full retirement age. That age varies—for instance, it's 65 years and 10 months for those born in 1942.

Example: If you were born in 1950 and currently earn $70,000 annually, according to the Social Security calculator from *www.ssa.gov*, you would receive monthly benefits of about $1,307 starting in 2012, when you turn 62. If you wait until age 66 (your full retirement age) in 2016, you will get $1,780 a month. You'll get $2,407 at age 70 in 2020.

Besides receiving smaller payments at 62, you run the risk of having your checks further reduced if you decide later to go back to work. That's because if you're under full retirement age and earn more than a certain threshold amount ($12,960 in 2007), you lose $1 of benefits for every $2 of earnings over this limit. But if you are above your full retirement age, your payments will not be cut—no matter how much you earn at a job.

If you wait to collect until you are age 70, you will receive the maximum monthly check. But you are taking a larger gamble on your longevity—that is, you may not live to age 70.

Calculated risk: If you wait until age 70 to start receiving Social Security payments, therefore getting the highest payments, and then live past 78, you will have received more total income from Social Security than if you had begun receiving checks at age 65 and 10 months. Nonetheless, my advice is generally to take the checks as soon as you reach full retirement age. If you don't need the money, you can invest it for a rainy day.

Mistake: **Failing to take the required minimum distributions from your retirement accounts.** When you turn 70½, you must begin taking payouts from your traditional IRAs. If you do not make withdrawals on time, the IRS can impose a penalty of 50%. This means that if you make a late $10,000 withdrawal, the government will charge you $5,000. The rule is so tough because Washington doesn't want money to stay tax sheltered indefinitely.

The IRS Web site (*www.irs.gov*) spells out correct withdrawal amounts. There, you can find your life expectancy according to IRS tables.

Example: If you're 70 now, the IRS figures you will live another 27.4 years. The government wants to spread your withdrawals evenly over your lifespan. Say you have $100,000 in your IRA. You must divide that figure by 27.4. The result is

$3,649.63—the amount you must withdraw the first year. Consult the table every year because this withdrawal figure changes as you age.

If you forget to take a withdrawal in the first year, correct your mistake and send a written notice to the IRS. The IRS is often lenient with someone who is struggling with the tables for the first time. The tax collectors may let you off with a warning about not making the same error next year.

Best: To avoid problems, contact the custodian of your IRA to have the withdrawal amount paid directly to your bank well before the end of the year—then check to make sure it happens.

Mistake: **Paying off mortgages too soon.** As they approach retirement, some people feel that they must pay off their mortgages. For peace of mind, this may be important. But if you plan to sell off other assets to accomplish this, you may do better by keeping the mortgage debt.

Example: You have a $100,000 mortgage with an interest rate of 5.75%. Because you can deduct the mortgage interest (even if you pay the alternative minimum tax), the after-tax cost of the mortgage if you are in the 25% tax bracket is about 4.3%. You could pay off the mortgage by selling $100,000 worth of investments to raise the cash.

Instead of selling your assets to pay off the mortgage, keep the money invested in a portfolio that is expected to earn more than 5.75%. That way, you can use your earnings to cover the mortgage and still have some investment income left.

Mistake: **Ignoring inflation.** Many people figure that inflation will not erode the value of their investments in a significant way. After all, the consumer price index (CPI) has historically risen at an average annual rate of only 3%, and a well-constructed investment portfolio should do much better than that over time. But over time, even small price increases whittle away at your purchasing power.

Example: Your investments earn 8% annually, while inflation runs at 3%. So, you will only have 5% left after inflation. And there is a chance that you can face above-average inflation rates. A sudden spurt in energy or health costs can wreck your budget. (Historically, people who live in big

cities on the coasts have faced inflation rates that are much higher than the long-term averages.)

For protection, emphasize the dividend-paying blue-chip stocks in your portfolio, as they tend to appreciate over time, and many increase their dividends at annual rates that are well above the long-term average increases in the CPI. Do not rely exclusively on income from fixed sources, such as bonds or pensions, which can be eaten away by inflation. If inflation is at 3% and you receive $50,000 a year from a pension or annuity, during your second year of retirement your purchasing power will have dropped to $48,500. The third year, the real value of the income will be $47,045.

Mistake: **Paying bills by check.** Many retirees insist on paying by check because they don't trust electronic systems. But the more important danger is that you will forget to pay on time—incurring penalties. That can hurt your credit rating and increase borrowing costs. *What to do…*

• **Automate deposits.** Have your Social Security checks automatically deposited into your checking account. If you are working, ask your employer to also make automatic deposits. This saves time and reduces errors. If the account is interest bearing, automatic deposits will boost your income, since payments will spend more time in your account and less time in the mail.

• **Automate payments.** Pay as many bills as possible automatically. That way, you won't miss payments—even if you take a trip overseas.

Examples: Many cable TV companies and Internet service providers permit you to charge your monthly bill automatically. Many banks and brokerages offer electronic systems that enable regular payments—such as utility bills—to be withdrawn automatically from your account.

For added efficiency, do all of your business with one bank or brokerage. There is no reason to have seven different accounts spread around town.

Mistake: **Holding stock certificates personally.** Many people insist on holding paper stock certificates in their bank safe-deposit boxes because they are afraid of losing the securities. When they need to make sales, these investors run to the bank vault, retrieve paper shares and mail them to their brokers. Investors who hold

old-fashioned paper certificates must round up individual records of dividends and transactions for each stock or bond—a time-consuming and error-prone process. This is a throwback to the Great Depression era, when many stockbrokers went bankrupt, and investors found that their securities had vanished. But all reputable brokers are members of the Securities Investor Protection Corporation (SIPC) and covered for up to $500,000 for stocks, bonds and other securities and up to $100,000 for cash. Most firms also have additional coverage.

It is now very efficient to have your broker hold on to your certificates. That way, you can sell shares immediately with a phone call or a computer key stroke. At the end of the year, the broker will send you a record of all dividends and transactions. At tax time, you have one convenient record.

How to Make Sure Your Nest Egg Lasts

William Bengen, CFP, Bengen Financial Services, Inc., 844 Singing Heights Dr., El Cajon, CA 92019. His latest book is *Conserving Client Portfolios During Retirement* (FPA Press).

A key goal for many people is determining when they'll be able to stop working and enjoy a comfortable retirement. Extended life expectancies have made this a lot harder to establish.

Another factor: How your investments are held. The more of your investing that is done in a tax-deferred account, such as a 401(k), the more you may be able to withdraw each year —making for a significant difference in your usable wealth.

BRIDGING THE GAP

To determine how much you can withdraw from retirement funds without running short of money, crunch some numbers.

Begin your retirement planning by deciding how much you would like to spend after you stop working.

A starting point: Many early retirees will spend about as much as they did during their working years. Career-related expenses will go down, but there will be more time for leisure activities, which can be expensive.

Pretax or after-tax dollars? Precise planning would focus on after-tax dollars because that's what you will be spending. For simple, back-of-the-envelope projections, though, it may be easier to use pretax dollars.

Situation: Jane Smith, who is beginning to plan for her retirement, earns $100,000 a year and invests $20,000 a year. She doesn't expect to keep investing after she retires and starts to draw down her portfolio. Therefore, her initial retirement goal is to have an $80,000 income, which will maintain her lifestyle.

Jane expects to start receiving Social Security benefits of approximately $20,000 a year as soon as she retires.

Shortfall: Jane does not expect any other type of income in retirement, so she will need to take $60,000 a year from her portfolio.

THE $60,000 QUESTION

How large a portfolio will Jane need to withdraw $60,000 per year? *Some assumptions that need to be made...*

• **Life expectancy.** Jane is in good health and her parents are still alive. Thus, Jane thinks there is a good chance that she could live for 30 years after retiring at 65.

• **Asset allocation.** The more of a portfolio that is in stocks, the higher the returns are likely to be over a long retirement. However, one has to be able to stand stock market volatility.

Recommended: Hold at least 50% in stocks to generate adequate returns. A 60/40 stocks-to-bonds allocation may be ideal.

The 4% solution: Given those assumptions, a 4% to 4.5% initial withdrawal rate is likely to allow annual inflation adjustments throughout a 30-year retirement without depleting the portfolio. (This assumes pretax earnings on average of 10.4% for stocks and 5.3% for intermediate-term government bonds, based on annualized returns from 1926 through 2005.) To be on the safe side, use a 4% rate in your planning.

Situation: Jane builds up a $1.5 million portfolio. That's enough so that a 4% first-year withdrawal will give her the $60,000 she wants.

If inflation in year one is 4%, Jane can increase her second year portfolio withdrawal by 4%, to $62,400, and so on, each year, so that her income keeps up with inflation.

Result: Assume that Jane maintains her fairly conservative portfolio split of 50/50 between stocks and bonds and follows the plan described above, with a 4% initial withdrawal increased annually by the inflation rate.

Such a strategy, implemented any time since 1925, would have kept a portfolio intact for at least 33 years. Therefore, Jane feels comfortable with a 4% withdrawal rate. If she starts with a 4.5% withdrawal, there'll still be a good chance that her portfolio will last 30 years or longer.

TAKING MORE

What if Jane decides to increase her first-year withdrawal rate to 5% instead of 4% or 4.5%?

Reasoning: The aim is to start with a $60,000 draw from the portfolio. With a 5% withdrawal, Jane needs to accumulate just $1.2 million—her $60,000 first-year withdrawal will be 5% of $1.2 million rather than the $1.5 million which was indicated above.

Caution: The smaller amount of retirement savings must earn more if Jane wants it to last for a lengthy retirement.

Strategies: Starting with a smaller portfolio and a higher draw increases your risk of running short of money, but taking that risk might make sense as long as…

●**You have plenty of exposure to stocks.** More stocks mean more volatility during your retirement but also is likely to increase portfolio accumulation over a long time period.

●**You do most or all of your retirement investing in a tax-deferred account.** The tax deferral probably will result in a larger, longer-lasting pool of funds.

TAXABLE VS. TAX DEFERRED

Since the chances of success with a 5% withdrawal rate are greater if Jane does all or nearly all of her investing in tax-deferred retirement accounts, she might invest in a 401(k) plan during her career and roll the money to an IRA when she retires.

Reason: Inside a retirement account, all investment income will be tax deferred. And, that investment income might be substantial if Jane

holds 40% to 50% of her portfolio in bonds, an allocation that may comfort retirees.

Because of the tax deferral, Jane's portfolio will grow faster in an IRA, year after year, than it would in a taxable account. Again, the higher growth may permit a higher withdrawal rate.

We can't know what the tax rates will be in 2017 or 2027 or whenever a retiree is eventually drawing down an IRA. We also don't know what the spread will be—the tax rate on long-term gains in the future versus the taxes that a retiree will pay on ordinary income after he/she stops drawing a paycheck. We do know that deferring tax results in a greater buildup inside an IRA than in a taxable account.

DRAWING DOWN

Many people will have a portfolio divided between taxable and tax-deferred accounts.

Strategy: Tap taxable accounts first so that your IRA can remain intact as long as possible. You might set a retirement goal of amassing a portfolio that's 20 times the first-year withdrawal target. Then take a 5% first-year withdrawal from your taxable account. Keep withdrawing taxable funds as long as you can.

Result: Your IRA may be larger when you start to take withdrawals, and your life expectancy will be shorter. So your portfolio may well last your lifetime, even though you started at 5%.

After you reach 70½, you'll have to take minimum required distributions from your IRA of around 3.8% the first year (for most people). So, take the minimum from your IRA, if practical, and take the balance from your taxable account, as long as it doesn't run dry.

Smart Retirement Spending

Bob Carlson, editor, *Bob Carlson's Retirement Watch*, Oxon Hill, MD, *www.retirementwatch.com*.

When you retire, you are likely to hold savings in a mix of investment accounts that are taxable, tax deferred (such as 401(k) accounts and traditional IRAs) and tax free (such as Roth IRAs). As a rule, it's best to spend down savings in your taxable accounts first.

Why: The tax-favored accounts receive more in long-term benefit from tax-free compounding. Employer plans and IRAs also receive legal protection from creditor claims, adding extra long-term security as long as you have them.

After spending down taxable accounts, spend tax-deferred ones. Save your Roth IRAs and Roth 401(k)s until last—they benefit the most from tax-free compounding, and if you die, they will be of most value to heirs because of the totally tax-free income they provide.

This general rule for retirement spending may be affected by the types of specific investments in your various accounts. Be sure to go over the details of your best spending strategy with a financial adviser.

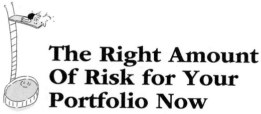

The Right Amount Of Risk for Your Portfolio Now

Frank Armstrong III, CFP, principal of Investor Solutions, Inc., a fee-only investment and money management company, 3250 Mary St., Coconut Grove, FL 33133, and the author of *Informed Investor: A Hype-Free Guide to Constructing a Sound Portfolio* (American Management Association).

More risk could mean more reward in some of life's circumstances, but not necessarily in your retirement portfolio. Thankfully, there are some simple ways to maximize returns for as little risk as possible.

RISK AND RETURNS

A significant risk most of us face is running out of money. This is also the one risk over which you have some control, by cutting spending or delaying retirement to build your savings.

Your risk of using up your money also can be controlled by how your investment portfolio is structured. As a general rule, a retiree should aim to have enough return on investment to be able to withdraw 4% of his/her nest egg a year and not be in danger of eventually using up all of the money. To do that, people often pursue

aggressive investments that claim to be able to "beat the market." That only increases the risk of losing money.

In reality, you are better off controlling your risk than chasing ways to outpace the average investment returns of the market.

Reality: Investors typically cannot beat the market because no one knows what the future holds—a stock (or fund or bond) may do better than expected or it may do worse. Unless you know better than the millions of other investors in the market, it's delusional to think that you can consistently pick winners. By trying to beat the market, or investing with those who think they can, you are taking more risk, but not necessarily getting more reward.

RISKIEST MISTAKES

Cut your risk and improve the long-term health of your portfolio by avoiding these errors…

Mistake: Buying individual stocks. I know many of my colleagues would disagree with me on this—and many individual investors, too—but, in my opinion, concentrating your money in individual stocks is taking on huge risk. For every person who struck it rich by stock picking, there are many more who loaded up on Enron or Eastern Airlines and lost everything. Stocks can do great, or they can do horribly at any given time. The risk of a blowup, while small, is too much to bear for those at or near retirement.

Mistake: Sector investing. Investing heavily in individual industries is also very risky.

Example: All dot-com stocks looked great in the late 1990s. Then the bubble burst. Today, many analysts are touting the health-care sector as the boom to come. There are two problems with that prediction—again, no one really knows what the future brings, and such a highly anticipated boom is likely to be already priced into the stocks.

Mistake: Playing it "safe" with bonds. More conservative investors think they are playing it safe by focusing on bonds, but there is risk with bonds that many people don't realize—the risk of too-low returns. Over the past 80 years, the total return of long-term government bonds was 5.5% per year, on average. Inflation averaged 3% annually during this same period. Particularly in today's low interest rate environment, bonds shouldn't be the major part of your portfolio—and that stands for inflation-pegged bonds, too. Even at the long-term yearly return of 5.5%, the return after inflation is less than retirees should be aiming for to keep their portfolios sustainable throughout their lifetimes. Plus, if interest rates rise after you buy, you may be forced to sell at a capital loss when you need the money.

***Mistake:* Investing in hedge funds and other exotic financial vehicles.** Stated simply, hedge funds and other exotic investments, such as currencies or futures, are highly risky, often generating massive losses. They aren't appropriate for retirees—or for *any* individual investor.

WHAT TO DO IN TODAY'S MARKET

Many people are concerned now with such things as how the fact that the Democrats now control Congress may affect certain sectors or whether interest rates will rise.

Best strategy: Don't worry about these or any short-term factors. Focus on profiting from the broad stock market, which provides the best returns with reasonable risk. *Here's how to do it…*

• **Diversify.** The biggest mistake many investors make is having too much invested in one stock or sector. Don't be afraid to sell and take profits—the capital gains tax is a small price to pay for eliminating significant risk from your portfolio.

• **Go global.** The best diversification is to get as much exposure to the world's stocks as possible. The foreign stock component exposes you to high-growth markets and mitigates the damage of a weak dollar. Ideally, a portfolio should have an even weighting of stocks from US and all developed foreign markets, with the smaller portion in emerging markets. A global portfolio like this returned 11% annually over the past 10 years at a risk level well below the safest individual stock, industry sector or actively managed mutual fund. Buying readily available low-cost index mutual funds or exchange-traded funds (ETFs) can get you exposure to 95% of the total world stock market for less than 0.5% per year in fees and commissions.

• **Prepare for all your income needs.** Even with the most diversified stock portfolio around, there still is the risk of a worldwide slump.

Solution: Keep bonds that mature in each of the next 10 years to ensure that you'll have some income without having to liquidate stocks at deep losses if the stock market tanks. Short-term bonds in particular (one- and two-year durations) have little inflation risk and provide decent returns. When the stock markets recover, you can use the gains in your stocks to rebalance your portfolio (that is, adjust the percentages of the different assets back to what you want them to be).

• **Know your specific situation.** Ultimately, you will need to take into account your income needs and time horizon to properly craft your investment portfolio. If needed, obtain help from someone who has a fiduciary responsibility to you, such as a National Association of Personal Financial Advisors (NAPFA) member (800-366-2732, *www.napfa.org*).

Funds for Retirement

Target-date funds are pegged to the year you will retire. The allocations of the investments in the funds are adjusted as the retirement year approaches. The investments are in funds offered by the fund group. Different groups use varying approaches.

Example: For an investor planning to retire in 2030, Vanguard currently places 80% in stock funds, but T. Rowe Price puts 90% in stock funds.

Some fund companies charge additional fees for target-date funds.

Three that offer target-date funds at no additional cost: American Century, T. Rowe Price, Vanguard.

Vern Hayden, CFP, president, Hayden Financial Group, investment advisory firm, Westport, CT, and author of *Getting an Investing Game Plan* (Wiley).

New Annuity Options

New annuity-program alternatives could be very beneficial to people who have certain medical conditions.

Example: The affordable Vanguard Lifetime Income Program (800-523-7731, *www.vanguard.com*) gives people with such conditions as heart disease, high blood pressure and diabetes the chance to qualify for a rated age—which means that for annuity purposes, they are considered older than they actually are.

This could provide these people higher income payments or enable them to pay a lower premium to generate the eventual income payments. The program also includes fixed or variable payment options.

Other companies that offer these plans: AIG Inc. (877-638-4244 or *www.aig.com*)...Genworth (888-436-9678 or *www.genworth.com*)...Allstate's Lincoln Benefit Life (800-525-9287 or *www.accessallstate.com/anon/aboutushome.aspx*).

Hersh Stern, publisher of the free on-line *Annuity Shopper Magazine*, Monroe Township, NJ, *www.annuityshopper.com*.

More from Hersh Stern...

Annuities to Avoid

It is best to avoid annuities that have inflation protection.

Example: A 65-year-old man who buys a $100,000 immediate annuity (which guarantees income for life) with a 3% per year inflation rider might receive $518 a month for the first year. Without inflation protection, the annuity would pay $687. It would take 21 years for the inflation annuity to generate more income than the regular one.

Better inflation protection: Put a portion of your portfolio into funds that focus on commodities and/or precious metals, which tend to thrive during inflationary periods.

Should You Finance Your Retirement with a Reverse Mortgage?

Barbara Stucki, PhD, project manager specializing in reverse mortgages for the National Council on the Aging, a nonprofit educational organization in Washington, DC, *www.ncoa.org*.

There has been a dramatic increase in the number of reverse mortgages—a type of loan that enables home owners to raise cash. Unlike with a standard mortgage, you don't have to pay back a single penny of a reverse mortgage as long as you live in the house.

With a reverse mortgage, you borrow against the equity in your home, often taking a line of credit or a lump-sum payment. In 2000, about 6,000 loans were originated. The number has increased to over 90,000 now.

Part of the increasing appeal can be attributed to the financial environment in general. In recent years, interest rates have been relatively low, while home prices have climbed. That has enabled home owners to borrow more against equity, while paying fairly low costs.

At the same time, the pressure to raise cash has increased, as retirement nest eggs have suffered following the tech-stock crash. In addition, attitudes about reverse mortgages have changed.

Now more middle-income home owners see reverse mortgages as a routine financial-planning tool. The mortgages are particularly valuable for people who can pay regular expenses but require help with special needs, such as home health aides, that may make it possible for the borrower to continue living in his/her own home.

HOW THE LOANS WORK

A reverse mortgage is a loan against a home. The home owner has several options for how to receive the cash (see the next page). You can receive a line of credit, a lump sum or regular payments for up to the length of time you live in the home.

About 90% of all reverse mortgages are originated under the Home Equity Conversion Mortgage (HECM) program of the US Department of Housing and Urban Development (HUD). Other loans come under programs from Fannie Mae, the government chartered mortgage company, and Financial Freedom Senior Funding Corp., a private lender. The HECM loans require paying mortgage insurance premiums, while the other lenders do not require mortgage insurance. But HECM is more popular because it enables many people to borrow bigger sums.

The amount of money that you receive depends on the value of your equity in the home and the age of the youngest borrower. Older people can borrow more because their life expectancies are shorter and there is less chance that the loan will eventually exceed the value of the home. The exact borrowable amount also depends on where you live. For a guide to how much you can borrow, go to the reverse mortgage calculator at *www.rmaarp.com.*

Example: You're age 73 and own outright a $200,000 house in Columbus, Ohio. With an HECM loan, you can get a line of credit or lump-sum advance of about $105,000.* If the house is worth $300,000, you can borrow $124,000. If you are age 70, you can only borrow $115,000.

As with any mortgage, the borrower must pay interest and the loan is secured by the house. But you need not make any payments at all until you leave the house.

Then you or your estate can sell the house and pay the principal and interest. Any appreciation belongs to the home owner or to heirs. Many home owners or their heirs elect to prepay the interest and principal—and keep the house. There are no penalties for prepayments. Throughout the process, the home owner owns the house—not the lender.

PAYMENTS TO YOU

Besides a lump sum, there are several other ways for you to take your cash from a reverse mortgage…

●**Line of credit.** You use the reverse mortgage credit line when you need it. You could spend some of the money to pay routine bills and use the rest for home repairs. You owe interest and principal only on money that is actually drawn down.

●**Monthly advances.** Under this option, the home owner in Columbus could receive monthly payments of about $735 for as long as he

*Rates and offers subject to change.

stays in the house. If the home owner dies after one year, the heirs need only pay the interest and principal of the payments already received.

●**Fixed period.** Instead of electing income for your life in the home, you can elect to receive monthly checks for a fixed period, such as five years. This could help you survive a difficult time, for example, until pension payments start or until you sell the house and move to your retirement home.

●**Combinations.** You can select more than one payment option. You might choose a lump sum of $25,000 to make repairs on the house. At the same time, you could receive monthly payments to cover living costs.

PAYING OFF MORTGAGES

About 78% of older Americans own their own homes without any debt, according to the US Department of Health and Human Services. But those with a conventional mortgage can use a reverse mortgage to pay off the debt. This relieves the pressure of meeting monthly payments and also enables the home owner to avoid foreclosure worries.

Costs: Interest rates on reverse mortgages are typically adjustable annually. The recent rate was a bit more than the interest on an average fixed-rate 30-year mortgage.

Besides the interest, an HECM borrower must pay an origination fee equal to 2% of the value of the home or $2,000, whichever is greater. In addition, there is an up-front HECM mortgage insurance fee which is equal to 2% of the value of the home.

Most of the fees can be included in the value of the loans, so the borrower does not face sizable out-of-pocket costs at the closing. Or, the fees can be paid along with the rest of the mortgage when the house is sold.

WHO SHOULD USE A REVERSE MORTGAGE

To determine whether it is worth paying the costs of a loan, meet with a financial planner to discuss all aspects of your situation. Under the rules, all borrowers must attend a counseling session with an independent expert. This process is worthwhile, because borrowers may decide that other alternatives are more attractive.

If you are in chronic bad health and may not be able to live in the house much longer, a reverse mortgage could be the wrong choice. In addition, a reverse mortgage could be unsuitable if the home is in bad shape.

In an extreme case, the property might cost more to fix up than it is worth. From your reverse mortgage, you might get a lump sum of $100,000, but have to spend $80,000 to make the house suit your needs.

Strategies to Finance Your Dream Retirement Home

Martin Shenkman, CPA and attorney who specializes in trusts and estates in New York City and Teaneck, NJ. He is also author of many books, including *The Complete Book of Trusts* (Wiley). His Web site, *www.laweasy.com*, provides sample forms and documents.

With the softening real estate market—especially in areas where many people buy second homes, such as near the shore or in the mountains—now may be a good time to shop for a home that you would like to retire to eventually. Even though prices have dropped, it may not be easy to finance the retirement home you want. The most straightforward and tax-efficient strategy is to purchase a new home with the proceeds from the sale of your current home. If your current home has been your primary residence for at least two of the previous five years, you'll be able to shield from tax $250,000 in capital gains on the sale ($500,000 if you're married).

Even though it might be a good time to buy, you might not be quite ready to move out of your home yet. *If that's the case, consider these financing alternatives...*

• **Liquidate your life insurance.** Are your children grown and living independently? Have you accumulated a big enough retirement fund to support your spouse after you have died?

If so, you may no longer need your life insurance policy. The cash from selling or surrendering the policy can be used to help pay for your

retirement home. All the money that you would otherwise use for insurance premiums can go toward upkeep, taxes and other costs associated with owning the new home.

Strategy: Ask your insurance company about your policy's cash-surrender value. That will let you know how much you would pocket if you terminated the policy. Then look into whether you would fetch a higher price by selling the policy to an outside investor. Ask your agent to obtain multiple bids. The older you are, the more the policy will be worth, especially if you have had some health problems. An investor will keep the policy in force and collect on it upon your death.

One reason *not* to get rid of life insurance is to provide liquidity in case of an estate tax obligation. However, under current law, couples with estates of up to $4 million may not be subject to much federal estate tax at all.

Consult with your tax professional to find out whether surrendering your policy or selling it will put you ahead on an after-tax basis.

• **Borrow.** Either refinance the mortgage on your existing home or take out a home-equity loan, assuming that you have enough equity to finance your second purchase and enough income to make the loan payments.

If you wish, you can eventually sell your primary residence, use the capital gains exclusion, repay the mortgage and move into your retirement home.

Caution: This strategy can greatly increase your debt, and interest on a mortgage you refinance above your old mortgage might not be deductible. Talk to a tax professional.

• **Rent.** Sell your principal residence on the stipulation that you can rent it from the new owner for a certain amount of time—say, two years. At the same time, the sale proceeds can go toward your purchase of a retirement home.

Loophole: You can enter into a sale-leaseback with a family member, such as a grown son or daughter. As long as the entire transaction is at fair market value (based on comparable prices in the area), you'll get the capital gains exclusion, while the buyer will get the tax benefits of owning rental property, such as depreciation and a property tax deduction.

FDIC Increases Protection Of Retirement Accounts

FDIC protection of retirement accounts is currently greater than its protection of all other bank deposits. The FDIC will now insure retirement accounts for up to $250,000 per depositor per bank. The higher limit applies to traditional and Roth IRAs, SEP IRAs, SIMPLE IRAs, Keogh plans—and 457 plans for state-government employees. The protection limit remains $100,000 for nonretirement accounts.

Kathleen Nagle, chief, deposit insurance section, division of supervision and consumer protection at the Federal Deposit Insurance Corporation (FDIC), Washington, DC, www.fdic.gov.

Why You Really Can't Afford a Mistake with Your IRA Now

Ed Slott, CPA, editor, Ed Slott's IRA Advisor, 100 Merrick Rd., Rockville Centre, NY 11570, www.irahelp.com. He is a nationally recognized IRA distributions expert as well as author of Parlay Your IRA into a Family Fortune (Penguin).

IRS fees for private rulings about IRA and retirement plan transactions have just become much higher. IRS private rulings often are used to obtain IRS "forgiveness" of good-faith errors, and to obtain advance IRS approval of complex or gray-area transactions that might otherwise later be questioned by an auditor.

But new IRS fee increases for private rulings now make them so expensive that many people won't want to use them. *Examples...*

● **When an IRA rollover is not completed within 60 days** due to good-faith error or factors beyond the taxpayer's control (such as a bank's mistake), a private IRS ruling approving the late rollover, to save it from taxes, formerly cost only $95.

New cost: $3,000 for a rollover of $100,000 or more*...$1,500 for a rollover of $50,000 or

Prices subject to change.

more but less than $100,000...$500 for smaller rollovers.

● **Rulings relating to technical matters—** such as the use of trusts as IRA beneficiaries, post-death distribution options for beneficiaries, late Roth IRA recharacterizations, etc.—now in general cost $9,000, up from as little as $625 for persons with income under $250,000.

When the professional fee charged by one's tax adviser for preparing a ruling request—usually several thousand dollars itself—is added to the cost of the ruling, the combined cost now may be prohibitive.

WHAT TO DO

Avoid the need for a private ruling by...

● **Using conservative IRA planning strategies** to avoid gray-area issues.

● **Taking care to avoid mistakes** that may require correction, such as by not making any IRA rollovers. You should make trustee-to-trustee transfers instead.

● **Looking up previously published private rulings** that match with your situation. Although a private ruling is officially binding only for the taxpayer it is issued to, one issued to a taxpayer in the same situation as you may be persuasive to an IRS auditor.

Private rulings are published by the leading tax reporting services, with all information that might identify the taxpayers involved removed.

More from Ed Slott, CPA...

IRA Smarts

Don't hold foreign dividend-paying stocks in an IRA.

Reason: The tax bill may be higher than it would be if they were held in a taxable account. Dividends from foreign stocks, held directly or through a mutual fund, may be subject to tax in the foreign country, and the tax usually is withheld by the IRA's custodian (the bank, broker or other institution handling the account). Unlike an owner of a taxable account, however, an IRA owner cannot claim a US foreign tax credit to offset this tax, nor may a deduction be claimed. Thus, the actual return from the foreign dividend in the IRA can be lower than you might otherwise earn.

Tax Refund Smarts

Your tax refund can be direct-deposited into an IRA under a new law. This is faster than waiting for and then depositing a paper check. Use Form 8888, *Direct Deposit of Refunds*, to tell the IRS how much to put into your IRA. Also contact your IRA custodian to say what year the deposit is for—2007 deposits can be made until April 15, 2008, while 2008 deposits can start on January 1.

Caution: Not all IRAs accept direct deposits from the IRS—check before you ask the IRS to send the money.

Beware of Investing Your IRA in Canadian Mutual Funds

Canada has begun imposing 15% withholding tax on the distributions from Canadian mutual funds to foreigners—including US IRA accounts.

Trap: Generally, US taxpayers can offset taxes paid to foreign governments against their US tax bills by using the foreign tax credit (FTC). But IRAs can't do this because they owe no US taxes—and the individual who owns such an IRA can't do it because he/she is a separate taxpayer from the IRA and, technically, does not pay the Canadian tax.

Helpful: Own Canadian mutual funds only in taxable accounts to make the FTC available for the tax.

The Kiplinger Tax Letter, 1729 H St. NW, Washington, DC 20006.

IRA Withdrawal Savvy

Take withdrawals from IRAs carefully if you are under age 59½ and using the funds to pay higher education expenses for yourself, a spouse, your child or your grandchild.

Withdrawals for this purpose will not incur a 10% tax penalty if timed correctly. The withdrawals must not exceed education expenses in the withdrawal year—so if you expect $30,000 in expenses two years in a row, make one withdrawal in each year. Otherwise, the withdrawal above that year's education costs will be subject to the 10% tax penalty. Consult with your tax adviser.

Bob D. Scharin, JD, senior tax analyst at RIA/Thompson Tax & Accounting, a provider of advanced research, practice materials and compliance tools for tax, accounting and corporate finance professionals, New York City.

When You Can Withdraw Money from Your IRA

Nancy Dunnan, a New York City–based financial and travel adviser and the author or coauthor of 25 books, including the best seller, *How to Invest $50–$5,000* (Collins).

Generally, if you withdraw from a traditional IRA before you reach age 59½, you will be hit with the 10% early withdrawal penalty on the taxable amount you are taking out. (Nondeductible contributions are not subject to the 10% penalty.)

The 10% penalty does not apply when the money is used for specific purposes that are approved by the IRS...

• **Health insurance premiums**—provided that you've been receiving unemployment for 12 consecutive weeks. If you are self-employed and have been out of work for 12 weeks, the exception also applies.

• **Expenses due to permanent disability.**

• **Uninsured medical expenses in excess of 7.5% of your adjusted gross income,** including the IRA withdrawal.

• **Qualified higher education expenses for yourself, your spouse, child or grandchild.** Among the expenses qualifying are tuition, books and supplies. If the student is enrolled at least half-time, then room and board also qualify.

• **Your first home or that of your spouse, child or grandchild**—up to $10,000 per lifetime. The money can be used not just to buy a house but also to build or rebuild one.

You can take penalty-free distributions at any age as long as they are made in a series of substantially equal periodic payments. These payments must continue at least to age 59½ or for five years—whichever comes later.

If you do make any early withdrawal that is subject to penalty, you must file IRS Form 5329, *Additional Taxes on Qualified Plans (Including IRAs) and Other Tax-Favored Accounts.*

Consult with your accountant and/or check IRS Publication 590, *Individual Retirement Arrangements* (IRAs), available at the IRS Web site (*www.irs.gov*).

More from Nancy Dunnan...

When You *Must* Start Making Regular IRA Withdrawals

You must start taking out your IRA money by April 1 of the year after the year in which you turn 70½. Your accountant can run all the numbers to determine how much you need to take out. Or, review the life-expectancy tables and other required information in IRS Publication 590, *Individual Retirement Arrangements* (IRAs), available free by calling 800-829-3676 or from *www.irs.gov*.

Tax saver: If you will still be working after age 70½, ask your accountant or financial adviser whether your income plus the required IRA withdrawals are likely to push you into a higher tax bracket. To prevent this, you might want to begin taking out money before age 70½ to reduce the impending tax bite. Doing this could reduce the value of the account and thus the required annual withdrawal.

Note: You are allowed to make withdrawals after age 59½ without a penalty.

401(k) Trap

More mutual fund companies are charging 401(k) participants for short-term trades.

Example: Vanguard recently started charging investors in many of its funds a 1% fee for selling shares within one year of buying them.

Smart: Ask any mutual fund in which your 401(k) is invested what its trading policies are.

Ted Benna, founder and president, 401(k) Association, Jersey Shore, PA, and chief operating officer, Malvern Benefits Corp., Williamsport, PA, *www.malvern401k.net.*

Rollover Alert

Be sure to give your employer 401(k) rollover instructions when you leave any job. If you do not, and you are younger than age 59½, the employer has the right to cash out your account if it has a low balance—and you may have to pay taxes on contributions and penalties to the IRS.

Good news: Employers can cash out only balances of less than $1,000. They used to be allowed to do so for balances up to $5,000.

Kaye Worden, certified financial counselor, Consumer Credit Counseling Services of Greater Fort Worth, TX.

Little-Known Tax Benefit for People With Limited Incomes

You can claim a "Retirement Savings Contribution Credit" of 10% to 50% of the amount you put in an IRA or a 401(k) or other employer-based retirement plan—up to a maximum contribution of $2,000—if you meet income limits. The lower your income, the higher the credit. For 2007, singles are eligible for at least some credit if they earn $26,000 a year or less. Heads of households must earn $39,000 or less. Married couples filing jointly must earn $52,000 or less. Ask your tax adviser for details.

Loyd J. Stegent, CPA/PFS, CFP, director, financial planning, Cornelius, Stegent & Price, LLP, Houston.

Social Security Know-How

A widow or widower can receive full Social Security benefits at age 65 or older (if born before January 2, 1940) or reduced benefits as early as age 60. Full benefits also are available earlier if a widow/widower is caring for the deceased's child who is under age 16 or disabled before turning 22.

More information: 800-772-1213 or *www. socialsecurity.gov.*

Jane Zanca, senior public affairs specialist, Social Security Administration, New York City.

Simple Steps to a Much Happier Retirement

Nancy K. Schlossberg, EdD, a counseling psychologist and professor emerita at University of Maryland, College Park. An expert in the areas of adult transitions and retirement, she is the author of *Retire Smart, Retire Happy: Finding Your True Path in Life* (American Psychological Association).

Most people look forward to retirement as a time to relax, discover new sides of themselves and enjoy life without the constraints of a job. Retirement can bring all of these pleasures, but some new retirees are shocked to find that retirement is uncomfortable and stressful.

Retirement causes dramatic changes in your daily routine and your social network. Like any transition, it goes more smoothly when you are prepared.

To create a smoother transition…

•**Think about how you enjoy contributing.** One secret to a happy retirement is feeling appreciated and depended upon. What causes are you passionate about—arts, education, politics? See how you can be more active in those areas once you retire. Begin to set the stage before you retire.

Examples: Enroll in training to become a museum docent. Apply to tutor a school-age child. Get involved in a political campaign. Sign up for a class in memoir writing.

Another way to get in touch with your true passion is to ponder any regrets. What do you wish you could do but never had time for? You can use your retirement as an opportunity to do all those things.

Examples: Learn another language…play a musical instrument…sail a boat…scuba dive.

•**Develop a support system.** Before you retire, begin to meet and network with people who can help you to achieve your dreams and cheer you on during this exciting next phase of your life.

Example: A woman who wanted to open a bed-and-breakfast began attending meetings of the B&B association in her area. She made a new circle of friends and got valuable ideas about how to get started.

•**Talk with your spouse about how your roles may change.** How much time will the two of you spend together? You probably will want to pursue shared interests (such as travel), but also consider lining up independent activities.

One recently retired couple was arguing because they were not used to being together so much, so each of them took a part-time job—the husband at a jewelry store and his wife at a flower shop. Harmony returned, and they kept their part-time jobs for several years until they got used to the transition.

Another couple decided that each of them would have a room of their own so they could comfortably retreat when one of them wanted time alone.

Roles also may shift if one spouse continues to work while the other is retired. Will the retired spouse be expected to do more around the house? Will he feel more dependent on the other for emotional support? Discuss these potential shifts before they happen, and be willing to try different ways of dealing with them.

•**Create structure** for your post-retirement day. You may love the idea of a life with a free-form schedule, but not enough structure makes some people listless and unmotivated. Instead of switching suddenly from a scheduled life to an unscheduled one, plan at least one activity a day during the first few weeks of retirement.

Examples: Exercise class, reading groups, gardening clubs. All these activities also provide social contact.

WHICH TYPE ARE YOU?

Not everyone approaches retirement the same way, but most people fall into one of four types. It may take some experimenting before you discover the path that is right for you.

• **Adventurers** will look for challenging new projects and want to develop skills that are very different from those they used on the job.

Examples: A retired government consultant enrolled in massage school and became a licensed massage therapist. A former pharmacist joined a senior baseball league.

• **Continuers** stay connected with the skills and activities they used on the job, through part-time or related volunteer work.

Example: After selling his paper company to retire, the previous owner missed the paper business. He and his wife opened a shop that sold handmade paper and gave classes in various paper crafts.

Some retirees become consultants in the fields in which they previously worked on staff.

• **Easy gliders** are comfortable with the unstructured life and content to go with the flow. They may be happiest on the golf course or playing with grandchildren.

Example: A retired TV executive enjoys being able to visit her grandchildren whenever the whim hits her.

• **Searchers** need time to find their niche. They are separating from their past but are not sure what they want for the future. They tend to explore a number of different pursuits before finding one or more that feels right.

Example: It took one man two years of trying out different volunteering organizations until he found the right spot for himself.

You're Only as Old as You Think You Are

Becca Levy, PhD, associate professor of epidemiology and psychology at Yale School of Public Health in New Haven, CT. She was the lead author of a recent study on stereotypes and aging, published in the Journal of Gerontology: Psychological Science.

Some seniors lose strength and vitality when they get older, while others remain robust. The same disparity exists when it comes to eyesight, hearing and mental faculties.

Genetics and lifestyle can play a part, but to a surprising extent, what you think about aging does as well. *Here, Yale psychologist Becca Levy, PhD, a renowned expert in stereotypes related to aging, answers some questions on this topic...*

• **How do stereotypes affect how we age?** There are numerous ways, but let's look at hearing loss as an example. Most people consider it an inevitable fact of growing older, but there's more to it than biology.

In a study conducted at Yale, we measured the hearing of more than 500 adults age 70 and older and asked them what five words or phrases first came to mind when they thought of an old person.

Three years later, the people who associated aging with stereotypes like "feeble" and "senile" had suffered significantly more hearing loss than those who had answered with positive words like "wise" and "active." In other studies, negative thoughts or beliefs about aging were linked to poorer memory as the years passed.

• **Can one's recovery from serious physical ailments, such as heart disease, also be affected?** Apparently so. In one study, we interviewed 62 heart attack patients (ages 50 to 96) about their stereotypes of aging within two weeks after their heart attacks.

Seven months later, patients who expressed more positive stereotypes had experienced better physical recoveries—as measured by tests involving balance and timed walking—than those who expressed more negative stereotypes.

• **Could a person's views on aging even affect his/her life span?** One of our studies showed just that. It involved 660 people, ages 50 to 94, who were asked questions that explored the ways they perceived their own aging.

For example, study participants, all of whom lived in Oxford, Ohio, were asked how much they concurred with such statements as "Things keep getting worse as I get older" and "I am as happy now as I was when I was younger."

Nearly 25 years later, the researchers tracked those participants who were still alive and how long the others had lived. Those who had expressed a more positive view when questioned lived a median of seven years longer, even after differences in their ages and health at that time were taken into account. It held true for both men and women who were over age 60 as well as those who were younger.

• **How do researchers explain this phenomenon?** There is no definitive explanation, but we think that several mechanisms are involved. Some are physiological and might well involve the harmful effects of stress on various systems in the body.

Another piece is likely to be behavioral—people who believe that aging means unavoidable memory decline, for example, quite possibly do not try as hard and as long to remember, and won't bother to apply strategies that could help. Similarly, people who think there's nothing that can be done about hearing loss probably aren't as quick to get medical attention if they develop hearing trouble.

In the longevity study, we found that views on aging can affect an older person's will to live—this explained, at least in part, the difference in survival. When you don't believe that the benefits of a long life will outweigh the hardships, you are less likely to follow a healthful lifestyle and seek treatments that prolong life.

• **What's the source of these stereotypes?** Negative depictions of aging can be found everywhere—from greeting cards to best-selling books to the media. We think television, in particular, has a major effect. We surveyed a group of people ages 60 to 92, who watched an average of 21 hours of television per week, and found that the more TV they watched, the more negative their beliefs were about aging.

The negative stereotyping most likely starts early—for example, wicked witches in fairy tales are gnarled and wrinkled—and sinks in deeply.

Then, as aging occurs, some individuals start applying these negative beliefs to themselves.

• **Is it possible to change these beliefs?** We've been able to show in the lab that they can change quite readily in the short term. In a recent study, we tested how fast elderly people could walk—a key measurement of frailty (a condition that includes exhaustion and weight loss as well as loss of muscle mass and strength).

Participants were randomly assigned to either a positive or negative age-stereotype group. We subliminally flashed words with positive connotations about aging, such as "wise," "alert" and "mature," to one group, and showed negative words, like "senile" and "decrepit," to the other group of subjects.

Participants in the positive stereotype group walked significantly faster and demonstrated better balance than those who were in the negative stereotype group.

To a great extent, we don't question these stereotypes because we've absorbed them so completely that we are not even conscious of them. Becoming aware of their presence in everyday life is a first step toward questioning their validity.

• **What, specifically, can we all do to help fight these stereotypes?** In the TV study, we asked participants to keep a journal describing the way that elderly people were represented. The participants were shocked to discover how often they were made the target of jokes, and that they were frequently omitted from the programming. "It is like we are nonexistent," wrote one study participant.

In your own life, make a point to pay attention to more positive examples of aging—active and effective people in politics, the arts and the community, for example. I don't mean "superstars" who are jumping out of planes at age 80. It's too easy to write them off as exceptions that have nothing to do with you. Also, spend time with elderly role models, such as relatives and residents of your community, and learn about their strengths and contributions.

• **Doesn't this promote a falsely optimistic view?** Not necessarily. It is more a matter of accepting that aging will involve a range of changes—some are positive, others are negative…some are inevitable and some are malleable. It is important to recognize the many places where a realistic attitude and positive action can make a real difference.

Great Second Careers: Have Fun Working After You "Retire"

Howard Stone, a professional life coach and founder of 2young2retire.com, an on-line community for people interested in retirement alternatives, Palm Beach Gardens, FL. He is coauthor of Too Young to Retire *(Plume).*

The concept of retirement in this country is about to fundamentally change. Waves of baby boomers will turn 60 over the coming decade and redefine this time of life. Advances in health care will keep many of us healthy and vigorous into our 90s and beyond. We will need to stay challenged to be fulfilled, and we'll have to generate income to be sure that our nest eggs last for 30-plus years.

The new "rehirement" combines work with volunteering and leisure activities. Some retirees will work for their former employers as independent contractors. Others will retrain for new careers—certification programs, such as those indicated below, will be particularly popular.

Good news for older workers: By 2010, a severe labor shortage will occur because there will be fewer younger workers.

Here, possible rehirement opportunities...

PROFESSIONAL CERTIFICATIONS

Many preretirees and retirees do want to expand their professional abilities but are reluctant to commit to a graduate degree program. A certification lets you work as an accredited professional in a specialty field. In general, the part-time training takes less than one year and costs significantly less than graduate school.

These opportunities are in growing fields and allow flexible schedules...

●**Life coach.** Help clients achieve their goals for careers, relationships, etc.

Earnings potential: $75 and up per 45-minute session, or a monthly fee of $200 and up.

More information: *www.coachfederation. org.* Certification costs $300 to $625* and requires a minimum of 200 hours of training and experience, which generally costs $5,000 to $10,000.

●**Financial gerontologist.** Counsel elderly people on how to achieve their financial goals. Course and examination requirements are lighter than those to be a certified financial planner (CFP). (You need to already have your license in a financial advisory field, such as accountancy, law or insurance.)

Earnings potential: Same rates as a certified financial planner, $100 per hour and up.

More information: The American Institute of Financial Gerontology, 888-367-8470, *www. aifg.org,* awards certification after six three-day courses, which cost about $1,250.

●**Horticulturist.** Design landscape for residential properties. Certification is by state and helps you obtain employment with a nursery or greenhouse or start your own business.

Earnings potential: $50 per hour and up.

More information: Inquire at your state's nursery and landscaping association. Links can be found at the Association of Professional Landscape Designers site, *www.apld.com/resources/ associations.asp.*

●**Family business consultant.** Help family-owned businesses function well and deal with succession planning.

Earnings potential: $100 per hour and up. Certification is available to service professionals —management consultants, psychologists, therapists, educators.

More information: The Family Firm Institute, 617-482-3045, *www.ffi.org.*

●**Hypnotherapist.** Hypnosis has become increasingly popular in the field of mental health. You'll need a graduate degree in a health discipline, such as nursing, social work or chiropractic, plus 60 hours of classroom training, which costs $1,000 to $1,500. Some states require a license in addition to certification.

Earnings potential: $75 per hour and up.

More information: The National Board for Certified Clinical Hypnotherapists, 800-449-8144, *www.natboard.com.*

*Prices subject to change.

•**Massage therapist.** In most states, you'll need just 500 hours of training to get licensed, which can cost $5,000 to $10,000.

Earnings potential: $50 to $75 per hour.

More information: The American Massage Therapy Association, 877-905-2700, *www.amta massage.org.*

•**Relocation specialist.** Manage employee transfers on behalf of large real estate brokerages and/or chambers of commerce.

Earnings potential: $50 per hour and up.

More information: Worldwide Employee Relocation Council, 888-372-2255, *www.erc.org.*

•**Yoga instructor.** Most gyms now provide classes. You need at least 200 hours of training for certification, which costs $2,000 to $2,500.

Earnings potential: Yoga instructors can charge $50 to $75 per hour.

More information: Contact your local gym or *www.yogasite.com.*

OTHER OPPORTUNITIES

The following rewarding jobs for seniors do not require professional certification…

•**Caretaker.** Care for homes, often in exotic locations, in exchange for a free room. In some cases, board, a salary and health insurance are offered as well. Jobs can last a few weeks to a year or more. Travel expenses are usually covered.

More information: The Caretaker Gazette, 830-755-2300, *www.caretaker.org.*

•**Cruise ship lecturer.** A good fit if you like to speak in public and have expertise in a popular lecture topic, such as health or money. The cruise is free for you and your spouse. Usually no cash is offered, but lecturers use these trips as a calling card to attract clients who need their advice.

More information: *www.lynnseldon.com/article312.html* for a good overview…*www.web strategies.cc/acruise.html* has an e-book on how to apply, select popular topics and make helpful connections.

•**Senior move manager.** Help the elderly and their families with the emotional and physical aspects of relocation, including selling belongings, arranging shipments and storage. Move managers often find clients through family members, attorneys, senior housing communities and real estate agents.

Earnings potential: $25 per hour and up.

More information: National Association of Senior Move Managers, 877-606-2766 or *www. nasmm.com.*

•**Virtual assistant.** Perform administrative support or business services from your home, via Internet, fax and telephone.

Earnings potential: $20 per hour and up.

More information: International Virtual Assistants Association, 888-259-2487, *www.ivaa.org*, or search for "virtual assistant" at *www.business week.com.* For current job openings, try *www. virtualassistants.com.*

BEST WEB SITES

•**On-line job sites.** Post your résumé and search for jobs at *www.seniorjobbank.com* and *www.quintcareers.com/mature_jobseekers.html.*

•**Best companies for older workers.** AARP provides its ranking of the top 50 US employers—with 50 employees or more—at *www.aarp. org/bestemployers.*

Several of the best: Mercy Health System, Volkswagen, Yale-New Haven Hospital.

Section 529 Plans Are for Seniors, Too

Although 529 college savings accounts usually are used to save for children's college costs, they can pay for *anyone's* education. If you are thinking of taking classes, even after retiring, you can save in a 529 plan for yourself.

For a list of qualifying schools, go to *www. savingforcollege.com.* Click on "529 plans," then "eligible institutions."

Benefits: Income earned in this account is tax free when used to pay qualified education expenses and contributions are tax deductible in some states. If you end up not using the savings for yourself, you can transfer the account to children or grandchildren.

More information: College Savings Plans Network, *www.collegesavings.org.*

Barbara Weltman, an attorney based in Millwood, NY, *www.barbaraweltman.com.*

Discounts for Seniors

Senior citizens can take advantage of a wide variety of great discounts. *Get started now...*

• **Log on to the site** ***www.seniordiscounts. com,*** click on "Discount Search," and enter your zip code for discounts in your area.

• **Join AARP,** which arranges discounts for insurance, travel and more for 36 million members over age 50. At *www.aarp.org,* click on "Member Discounts and Services" or call 888-687-2277.

Cost: $12.50/yr. for membership.*

• **Go to any national park and buy a $10 lifetime Senior Pass,** available for any US resident age 62 or older. It lets you and everyone in your car into national parks, forests, recreation areas and monument grounds. It never expires. (The Senior Pass replaced the Golden Age Passport in January 2007. Golden Age Passports will be exchanged for free with proof of identification—a driver's license or birth certificate.)

Jim Miller, editor of "Savvy Senior," a syndicated newspaper column, Norman, OK, *www.savvysenior.org.* He is author of *The Savvy Senior: The Ultimate Guide to Health, Family, and Finances for Senior Citizens* (Hyperion) and a regular guest on the NBC *Today* show.

*Prices and offers subject to change.

Cell Phone for Seniors

The new Jitterbug cell phone is designed for easy use by seniors who are not cell phone savvy. Its number keys are oversized, the display is in larger type and the phone is large enough for the microphone and speaker to fit next to mouth and ear as with a regular home phone. There's even a dial tone. You can dial a number by hand or by using voice commands, a programmable one-touch phone directory or

24-hour live-operator assistance. There are no complex features, such as cameras, text messaging, e-mail or video displays—and no complex operating instructions.

Service cost: From $10 a month.*

Visit *www.jitterbug.com* for more information.

*Price subject to change.

Adopt a Senior Pet

Senior animals can be wonderful companions for human seniors. They aren't overly energetic (like puppies and kittens), don't need to be housebroken and know not to scratch or chew the furniture. Moreover, it is not true that "old dogs can't learn new tricks"—Broadway animal trainer William Berloni adopts all of his performing animals from shelters and prefers the older animals, saying they are happy to accept new living patterns in exchange for obtaining "a new leash on life." And, since young animals are the most frequently adopted, you will also have the satisfaction of knowing that you may well have saved your new pet's life.

Sara Whalen, founder of Pets Alive, Middletown, NY, an animal sanctuary specializing in senior-pet adoptions, *www.petsalive.com.*

Downside of Retiring Early

Early retirement may contribute to premature death.

Recent finding: People who retire at age 55 are twice as likely to die by age 65 as those who remain working. Until recently, it was generally thought that retiring early increased longevity.

Shan P. Tsai, PhD, manager, department of epidemiology, Shell Health Services, Shell Oil Company, Houston, as well as the leader of a study of 3,500 Shell Oil retirees, published in the *British Medical Journal.*

13

Estate Planning Guide

Don't Make These Mistakes with Your Will

The number of people in the US who die without wills is estimated to be as large as 70%. And many people who do have wills have set them up improperly…allowed them to become outdated…have even forgotten exactly what they say. A poorly written will can bring turmoil and heartache to your loved ones—and cost them lots of money.

Don't make these common mistakes…

•**Not having a will.** If you die without a will, you die "intestate" and all your assets will be distributed under state law. Generally, your state's intestacy law will not produce the results you would like.

Example: Some states require that 50% of a decedent's assets go to a surviving spouse and the other 50% to the children. Even if there are no children, 50% might go to next of kin such as parents or siblings.

This may deprive your surviving spouse of needed wealth.

Caution: You might think that your assets will bypass probate (the legal process in which a court oversees the distribution of a decedent's property) if you die without a will, but that's not true. There are many ways to avoid probate (see below), but failing to execute a will is not among them.

•**Thinking your will alone is enough.** Assets that pass to heirs through your will must go through probate of your estate. Probate can be costly because of legal fees…adversarial because the will can be contested…and time consuming because a court needs to oversee the entire process.

In addition, using a will as your entire estate plan might not provide adequate opportunities for estate tax–planning.

Alexander A. Bove, Jr., Esq., partner at Bove & Langa PC, a law firm that specializes in trust and estate matters, 10 Tremont St., Boston 02108. Mr. Bove is also the author of *The Complete Book of Wills, Estates & Trusts: Third Edition* (Henry Holt).

Strategy: A will should be only one component of a comprehensive estate plan. Other components might include various trusts. Assets placed in trust during your lifetime can pass to others under the terms of the trust without going through probate.

Many types of trusts can offer estate tax reduction. A "bypass" trust, for example, may allow you to provide for a surviving spouse yet avoid estate tax on trust assets at the death of both spouses. The current federal estate tax law provides for a $2 million exemption, so anyone with $2 million–plus of assets should consider this particular strategy.

Also needed: Besides a will and trusts, other elements of an estate plan might include powers of attorney (to handle assets without going through probate), life insurance trusts (to make their proceeds estate tax free), health-care proxies and end-of-life directives.

A health-care proxy allows you to name someone who'll make decisions about your medical treatment if you become unable to make those decisions…end-of-life directives indicate whether you want to be kept alive by medical life-support systems in case of a terminal illness.

●**Creating your own will.** You can find "do-it-yourself" kits for writing your own will on-line and in bookstores. Executing your own will is promoted as a cost-saver because you'll avoid legal fees.

Reality: Your will is one of the most important documents you'll ever sign. Such a crucial document should be drafted by an experienced attorney so your heirs will avoid problems after your death. Legal fees need not be excessive—you might pay up to $3,500 for an entire estate plan, including a will.

●**Believing your will covers all of your assets.** Suppose you have a $1 million IRA, which you would like your three children to inherit. This desire may be expressed in your will, but such a bequest will be irrelevant.

An IRA will pass to a designated beneficiary, the person you name in IRA documents, no matter what it states in your will. The same is true for other retirement accounts, annuities, life insurance policies, transfer-on-death and payable-on-death accounts and assets transferred into a trust.

In addition, property that is held jointly with right of survivorship will pass to the surviving co-owner or owners. Again, a mention of such property in your will has no impact other than to incite a contest.

Bright side: All the assets described above (items going to beneficiaries, jointly held property) will not be subject to the effort and expense of probate.

Important: Make sure you review all of your beneficiary designations periodically to confirm the choices you've made.

Trap: With all IRAs and other retirement accounts, don't name your estate as beneficiary. This can result in the loss of valuable tax deferral and may even push your heirs into higher income tax brackets.

●**Not notifying your executor.** In your will you'll name your executor ("personal representative" in some states), the person who'll be responsible for handling the transfer of the assets that pass under your will.

This is a vital task, so its important to get that person's consent to serve before naming him/her. You also should name at least one backup executor in case your first choice becomes unable or unwilling to serve.

Parents of minors: It's vital to name guardians for young children in case the remaining parent is unable to fill that role. Get the guardians' consent beforehand and name backups.

●**Leaving an outdated will in place.** Once you draft a will, you can't just forget about it. Your personal situation may change—births, deaths, marriages, divorces, changes in financial status, etc., all can have an impact on your plans.

Taxes, too: Changes in federal and/or state tax law also may suggest new strategies compared with the one outlined in your current will.

Thus, revisit your will and the other elements of your estate plan after each major change in your personal circumstances and after each change in estate tax law. Even without such events, take a look at your will every few years to make sure that it still reflects your current wishes.

●**Hiding your will.** Some people hide their wills because they don't want people to find them and know what they will (or won't) inherit. Unfortunately, a hidden will might very well *stay* hidden. Your will should be kept in a place that's both safe and accessible.

The best way to make your will both private and accessible is to leave it with the friend or relative you trust the most. If there's no one you trust, name an institutional executor, such as a trust company, and let this firm hold your will.

Even if you store your will elsewhere, your executor and other loved ones need to know where you keep it. The attorney who composed your will should have a copy, as well as a note stating the location of the original.

•**Putting funeral and burial instructions in your will.** Most wills aren't read until days or weeks after death. Meanwhile, your survivors must make immediate decisions about a funeral or a memorial service. Use a separate document to spell out your final wishes and tell your executor where this letter may be found.

Don't Think Your Children Will Never Fight Over Your Will

Family heirlooms are likely to be the objects of fights—and the worst thing to do is have your will leave them among your personal items to be "divided equally" among your children.

Better: Ask all your children what items they want to receive. If there are any disputes, resolve them while you're still alive. Then have your will specifically state who gets what, with explanations of why.

Best: Give the items away while you're alive.

Elizabeth Arnold, Esq., president, Sowing Seeds, an estate planning and consulting firm, San Rafael, CA, *www.sowingseeds.com*. She is author of *Creating the Good Will* (Portfolio).

Plan Ahead

Basic steps to protect your child in the event of your disability or death…

•**Complete an "Authorization for Emergency Care of Minor Child" form**—get a free sample form at *www.laweasy.com*.

•**Sign a will and appoint a guardian** as well as several successor guardians.

•**Set up a trust** to protect your child's assets if he/she is underage.

•**Buy enough life insurance** to make sure your child will be provided for and your family will have enough resources in the event of your death or that of your spouse. The amount should cover living costs plus college tuition.

•**Write a personal letter of instruction to guide surviving family members,** guardians and your child in the future. Indicate what sorts of education and lifestyle you want your child to have. This document has no legal force, but it can be an important ethical guide.

Martin Shenkman, CPA and attorney who specializes in trusts and estates in New York City and Teaneck, NJ.

 ## Till Death Do Us Part

A long-term study of more than half a million elderly couples reports that a husband's risk for death rises 53% within a month of the death of his wife. If the husband dies first, the wife's risk of dying within a month increases 61%.

The New England Journal of Medicine, 10 Shattuck St., Boston, MA 02115, *www.nejm.org*.

How to Turn Your IRA Into a Family Fortune

Ed Slott, CPA, editor, *Ed Slott's IRA Advisor*, 100 Merrick Rd., Rockville Centre, NY 11570, *www.irahelp.com*. He is a nationally recognized IRA distributions expert as well as author of *Parlay Your IRA into a Family Fortune* (Penguin).

Your individual retirement account (IRA) can do much more than provide funds for your retirement—it can be stretched to provide millions of dollars to your children, grandchildren or other beneficiaries.

Example: An IRA balance of only $100,000 may provide more than $8 million in future distributions when left to a young child.

What you need to know…

STRETCHING AN IRA

Most IRA owners think of their IRAs as providing savings only for themselves—and their spouses, if married.

This is largely because traditional IRAs are subject to annual required minimum distributions (RMDs) that begin at age 70½ and cause the IRA's funds to be distributed over the life expectancy of its owner.

IRA owners typically believe that if they live to their full life expectancies (or longer), there will be little or nothing left in their IRAs to leave to heirs.

Surprise: The life expectancies that govern mandatory IRA distributions as given in IRS tables are not actual life expectancies. The IRS life expectancies are much longer than actual average life expectancies.

The table below indicates the life expectancies as provided by the IRS's "Uniform Lifetime Table" for IRA distributions, which is used by most IRA owners (single persons and married persons with spouses not more than 10 years younger) to determine the size of RMDs, versus actual average life expectancies as given by the National Center for Health Statistics…

Life Expectancies

Age	IRA Table Years	Actual Years
70	27.4	14.9
75	22.9	11.8
80	18.7	9.0
85	14.8	6.8
90	11.4	5.0
95	8.6	3.6
100	6.3	2.6

Key: As a result of the difference, you may be able to leave funds in an IRA for much longer than you expect.

Moreover, initial RMDs may be so small that your IRA will continue to grow in value for years after distributions begin.

Explanation: At age 70½, when RMDs start, life expectancy under the IRS table is 27.4 years.

Each year's RMD is determined by dividing the IRA balance by the number of years in life expectancy—so at age 70½, the RMD is $\frac{1}{27.4}$, or 3.6%, of the IRA's value. If your IRA earns more

than this, it will continue to grow in value in spite of the distributions.

So, if you take only minimum distributions each year from your IRA and it earns 8% annually, it will continue to grow until you reach age 88! (Under the IRS table, the RMD won't reach 8% of the IRA's value until then.)

THE STRETCH

Once a beneficiary receives an IRA, its value may resume growing at a much faster rate.

Rule: A beneficiary can take required distributions over his/her life expectancy starting in the year after the inheritance. But if the beneficiary is young, life expectancy may be 50, 60 or 70 years, or even more, making initial RMDs so small that the IRA can grow rapidly.

Example: A grandparent leaves a $100,000 balance in an IRA that earns 8% annually to a one-year-old grandchild. The child's life expectancy under the IRS single life tables used by beneficiaries is 81.6 years, so the initial RMD is only 1.2% of the IRA balance.

Under the applicable IRS life expectancy table, the RMD won't reach 8% of the IRA balance until the grandchild is 70 years old. If the child takes minimum distributions, the IRA balance will grow for 69 years—even with the child taking minimum distributions from it all that time.

In total, over the 82 years of the child's life expectancy, the IRA will pay out $8,167,629—more than $8 million from the initial $100,000.

HOW TO DO IT

Steps to make the most of your IRAs…

● **Roll over funds from other retirement accounts into IRAs.** This will let you use the "stretch IRA" strategy for as much of your retirement savings as possible.

● **Open Roth IRAs or convert traditional IRAs to Roths if eligible.** These are even better to stretch than traditional IRAs. Distributions from them are tax free and there are no required minimum distributions for the original IRA owner. (Beneficiaries must take RMDs.) This lets you save funds in them for longer periods to earn more compounding.

● **Plan retirement spending to preserve IRAs.** Build your investment portfolio for your retirement years.

Best: Plan to consume IRA funds last. This will provide more tax-favored compounding within the IRA for you, and help you leave a bigger IRA balance to heirs.

RULES FOR THE STRETCH

• **The beneficiary who takes a stretch IRA must be a named person,** not your estate.

• **Be sure the custodial agreement with your IRA trustee provides for allowing a stretch IRA**—not all do.

• **Either have separate IRAs for each beneficiary or formally "split" your IRA among them,** such as by designating a set percentage as going to each. *Traps…*

• If an IRA with multiple beneficiaries is not split up, the life expectancy of the oldest governs distributions for the others.

• If a non-person (such as a charity) is the co-beneficiary of an IRA, its life span of zero applies to all other co-beneficiaries, forcing them to take rapid distributions—and eliminating the stretch.

• **When an IRA is left to a spouse,** to use its funds to set up a stretch IRA for a child (or other beneficiary), the spouse must first convert the inherited IRA into his own IRA (only a spouse can do this), and then name the child (or other party) as beneficiary.

• **After the spouse dies,** the inherited IRA must be retitled with the deceased owner's name in it, or the IRS will deem it to be distributed and therefore taxable.

Example: "Frederic Jackson, Sr., IRA (deceased June 15, 2007) for the benefit of Sandra Jackson, beneficiary."

Important: Convince your beneficiaries of the importance of taking minimum "stretch" distributions. If they empty your IRA of money as soon as they inherit it, all the potential decades of future compounding will be lost.

Saver: A trust can be named as beneficiary of your IRA to pass through payments to an heir, assuring that only minimum RMDs are taken (unless the trustee deems there is good reason to take larger distributions) so compounding is maximized.

Many technical rules apply to trusts and IRAs generally, so consult an IRA expert.

More from Ed Slott, CPA…

How to Get Millions From $100,000

The power of compound interest over the course of time has been called "The Ninth Wonder of the World." *IRA examples…*

Facts: Steve is age 65, his wife, Deb, is 62 and their son Jeff is 27. Steve has $100,000 in a traditional IRA that earns 8%.

Steve takes RMDs from the IRA from age 70½ until he dies at 85. Deb, as his IRA beneficiary, inherits the IRA, converts it into her own IRA, names Jeff as beneficiary and takes RMDs until she dies at age 92. Jeff inherits the balance of the IRA at age 57 and takes RMDs over the 28 years of his life expectancy.

Result: The original $100,000 IRA balance pays out $1,020,366—$153,132 to Steve, $176,523 to Deb and $690,711 to Jeff.

Variation #1: The same facts, except that Steve has saved the $100,000 in his IRA when he was age 50 and Deb age 47, so 15 more years of compounding occur before distributions begin. Now the IRA pays $3,236,841—more than three times as much. Of this, $485,766 goes to Steve, $559,973 to Deb and $2,191,102 to Jeff.

Variation #2: Steve is age 50 as above, but the IRA is a Roth IRA, so there are no RMDs. Steve and Deb don't take any distributions, letting all IRA funds compound for Jeff. Jeff's distributions will total more than $11 million.

Variation #3: The IRA is a Roth from which neither Steve nor Deb take any distributions, but Deb names her newborn granddaughter, Victoria, as beneficiary (instead of Jeff).

If Steve has $100,000 in the IRA at 65, Victoria receives distributions of more than $88 million.

If Steve has $100,000 in the IRA at 50, Victoria receives more than *$281 million,* of which more than $193 million came from Steve having accumulated his savings at age 50 instead of 65.

Also from Ed Slott, CPA…

Specify IRA Beneficiaries

Get a copy of the beneficiary form for each IRA you own. Be sure you have named a primary and secondary beneficiary for each. If an IRA has multiple beneficiaries, ensure that each person's share is clearly identified with a fraction or percentage.

Also, make sure the financial institution has your beneficiary information on file and that it matches your records. Retain copies of all IRA beneficiary forms, and give copies to your attorney and financial adviser. Let all beneficiaries know where to find the beneficiary forms. Finally, review the forms annually to be sure they are correct—and update them, if necessary, in light of any new tax laws or major changes in your life, such as marriage or divorce.

How Gift Splitting Can Help Married Couples Save Lots on Taxes

Gideon Rothschild, Esq., CPA, partner in the law firm Moses & Singer LLP, 405 Lexington Ave., New York City 10174, *www.mosessinger.com*. He is also adjunct professor in estate planning and wealth preservation at New York Law School and University of Miami Law School.

After the November of 2006 election, the prospects for estate tax repeal are even more indeterminate. Therefore, it makes sense for affluent taxpayers to plan to decrease their taxable estates. Anyone who has an estate of more than $2 million, including a house and life insurance policies—or married couples with estates of more than $4 million—is vulnerable.

The core strategy is to use the annual gift tax exclusion and possibly the lifetime estate tax exemption. You'll move assets (and any future appreciation) out of your estate without paying tax.

But married couples have double exclusions and exemptions. So, a couple can elect to split gifts, which effectively doubles the amount of the tax shelter.

You can give away up to $12,000 per year to each of any number of recipients, tax free, under the annual gift tax exclusion. In the future, this exemption will periodically go to $13,000, $14,000, etc., depending on the pace of inflation.

Situation: Beth Parker has two children. She can give them a total of $24,000 in 2007 ($12,000

to each), in addition to any payments she makes directly to providers of service for medical bills or school tuition, which are themselves specifically exempt from gift tax. These $12,000 gifts will not incur gift tax. In fact, Beth won't even have to file a gift tax return.

Doubling up: Beth's husband, Dan, also can give a total of $24,000 to their two children this year. This doubles the speed of their estate tax reduction.

Catch: In this example, Dan does not have assets to give to their children but Beth does. How can they maximize their use of the gift tax exclusion?

Tactic 1: Beth can give assets to Dan or move them into a joint account. Transfers between US citizen spouses are tax free (gifts to noncitizen spouses are only tax free up to $125,000 each year). Dan can then give the assets to their two children. In this case again, no gift tax returns need to be filed.

Tactic 2: Beth may not want to transfer assets to Dan. She might find it too complicated (some assets are harder to transfer), or she simply might not want to go through all the paperwork. Instead, she can give each child up to $24,000 this year. Then Dan can elect to join in the gift. This procedure is known as gift splitting. *How it works...*

SPLITTING FOR HEIRS

When a married couple splits gifts, a gift tax return must be filed. Both spouses must consent to a 50-50 split.

Situation: Beth gives $24,000 to each of her two children this year. She files a gift tax return on which Dan consents to the use of his annual exclusions.

Therefore, Dan effectively gives $12,000 to each child this year. He uses up his annual exclusion and can make no further tax-free gifts to either child in 2007.

Required: To qualify for gift splitting...

• **Both spouses must be US citizens.**

• **Neither spouse can remarry during the year.**

• **If one gift is split,** all gifts made by either spouse to any recipient during the same year must be split.

EATING INTO THE EXEMPTION

In some cases, gifts will be larger than $12,000 per recipient in a given year. Another set of tax rules will come into play, and gift splitting can be advantageously used again.

How it works: Gifts that don't qualify for the annual gift tax exclusion may be sheltered by a lifetime $1 million gift tax exemption.

Situation: Beth's and Dan's older child, Carla, wants to buy a condo, so Beth gives her $200,000. If Beth decides against gift splitting, she can use her $12,000 exclusion and wind up over the limit by $188,000.

Assuming Beth has made no other taxable gifts, she will owe no gift tax. However, her $1 million lifetime gift tax exemption will then be reduced by $188,000, so the remaining exemption will fall to $812,000.

Estate tax effect: That $188,000 gift also reduces Beth's estate tax exemption.

Situation: Assume that Beth makes no other taxable gifts and dies when the estate tax exemption is $2 million, as it is now. Because of this $188,000 gift, Beth's estate tax exemption will be reduced to $1,812,000.

Alternative plan: If Beth and Dan split the $200,000 gift, $24,000 will be covered by the annual exclusion. The excess $176,000 will reduce their lifetime gift tax exemptions (and their eventual estate tax exemptions) by $88,000 apiece.

Result: Using gift splitting, a married couple can give away up to $2 million ($1 million per spouse) in addition to amounts sheltered by the annual exclusion. No gift tax will be due.

That $2 million worth of assets given away might grow into $3 million, $4 million or more during the couple's lifetime and thus deliver a substantial amount of estate tax shelter.

Vital: Whether or not you split gifts, be sure not to give away assets you might need for support during a long retirement.

TRUST TRAPS

Gift splitting often makes sense because it doubles the amount of assets you can transfer to younger generations without owing gift tax, for instance, in cases where one spouse owns the bulk of a couple's assets or only one spouse wants to make gifts. However, transfers to certain types of trusts shouldn't involve gift splitting.

Examples: The qualified personal residence trusts (QPRTs), grantor-retained annuity trusts (GRATs) and grantor-retained unitrusts (GRUTs).

Why this can backfire: If the grantor dies during the trust term, the trust assets are counted in the decedent's taxable estate.

Result: In this situation, the donor gets gift tax relief but not the consenting spouse.

Situation: Ed Thomas creates a GRAT and transfers assets into it. Based on interest rates in effect at that time and the trust term, the value of the transfer is placed at $500,000.

Ed and his wife, Jean, split the gift to the GRAT, effectively using up $250,000 apiece of their gift tax exemptions. When Ed dies before the trust term, the trust assets go back into his estate and the $250,000 worth of gift tax exemption that he used is restored.

Trap: Jean doesn't get any refund or any tax relief. Thus, she has used up $250,000 worth of gift and estate tax exemption and has received no benefit.

Strategy: For transfers to QPRTs, GRATs or GRUTs, don't split gifts. Funding should come from only one donor, who will be responsible for all of the gift tax. Consult a qualified adviser about your specific situation.

File a Gift Tax Return— Even When You Don't Need To

Sanford J. Schlesinger, Esq., a founding partner and head of wills and estates, Schlesinger Gannon & Lazetera LLP, 499 Park Ave., New York City 10022.

It can be smart to file a gift tax return for noncash gifts, even when it isn't legally required because the gift's value is less than the $12,000 annual exclusion.

Why: The IRS has three years to challenge a gift's valuation if it's reported on a gift tax return. But if no return is filed, the IRS has forever. It then may raise a challenge years later saying that the gift was worth more than $12,000—perhaps much more.

Let's say that you give shares in your private business to a child. Your advisers say that they aren't worth $12,000, so you don't file a gift tax return. Over the next several years, your business increases in value. At that point, an IRS auditor looks at the business's high value and thinks, "Those shares must have been worth more than $12,000 back then," and initiates a gift tax audit. This forces you to prove that the shares were worth less when the gift was made.

If a gift tax return had been filed when the gift was made, this late audit couldn't happen.

The same potential trap exists for gifts of anything that may have a subjective valuation that could be questioned later—such as interests in nontraded investments (for example, real estate or jewelry).

A late IRS challenge is especially likely to occur during an audit of the estate tax return of the gift maker—which may occur many years after a gift was made.

Living Trust Traps

Bob Carlson, editor, *Bob Carlson's Retirement Watch*, Oxon Hill, MD, *www.retirementwatch.com*.

The properly designed living trust—which is revocable while you're living but upon your death will take ownership of your assets for the benefit of named trust beneficiaries—can be a valuable estate planning device. But unscrupulous salespeople often overstate the benefits of living trusts without explaining their costs and risks. *Traps to beware of...*

● **Living trusts don't reduce estate taxes.** Property you own that goes into a revocable living trust remains part of your taxable estate.

● **Trust costs may exceed probate savings.** Assets placed in a living trust pass outside of your will and probate. This saves probate costs. But trusts have their own expenses—for organizational costs, trustee fees, investment management and more. Moreover, these costs may run annually over multiple years.

These trust costs offset savings from avoiding probate—and if you reside in a state where the probate process is relatively efficient and low cost, may exceed them.

● **Management risks.** Trusts do require management—both through a trustee, and if the trust holds assets over time, from investment advisers and/or other asset managers—and possibly also successor trustees and managers.

Poor choice of a trustee and/or other managers can be ruinous, even if the trust quickly liquidates and distributes its assets.

What to do: Don't think of a living trust as an easy way to avoid taxes or cut costs. Do consider using one if you have a specific need to control the management of assets after you die. Consult with a reputable trust expert who will examine the details of your individual situation.

Setting Up a Pet Trust to Care For Your Pets— When You Can't

Rachel Hirschfeld, Esq., 330 E. 49 St., New York City 10017. Creator of the Hirschfeld Pet Trust (*www.pettrustlawyer.com*) and chairperson of the Board of the Greater New York Chamber of Commerce, she also serves on the New York State Bar Association Special Committee on Animals and the Law.

For many people, pets are beloved family members. They offer constant and never-complaining companionship.

But there's a worry: What will happen to your pets if you become incapacitated or after your death? You certainly don't want them to be mistreated or euthanized prematurely.

You may think that your friends or relatives will care for your pets if you can't. They might—but they might not.

Strategy: Consult an attorney about setting up a trust for the benefit of your pet or pets.

LACK OF "WILL" POWER

Some people provide for pets in their wills.

Example: Kathryn Davis leaves $10,000 in her will to her niece Marina, with instructions to care for Cathy's beloved terrier, Scrappy.

Reality: Such provisions are not enforceable. Marina can pocket the money and abandon the dog without fear of legal reprisals.

The same outcome would result if Kathryn leaves $10,000 directly to Scrappy in her will. Pets are considered to be property, so they can't legally inherit anything.

MUCH BETTER WAY

Instead of relying upon your will, which won't be effective, create a trust.*

Start by contacting an attorney familiar with pet trusts and estates. You can find one by entering "pet trusts" into an Internet search engine. Or go to my Web site, The Hirschfeld Pet Trust, *www.pettrustlawyer.com*, and request a call from a pet trust expert.

Fees will vary from attorney to attorney and from area to area. Expect to spend several hundred dollars and up, depending on how much detail you want in the trust documents.

Every trust has a *trustee*—or cotrustees—who is legally responsible to care for the assets in the trust.

When trust beneficiaries can't care for themselves, as is the case with a pet trust, *guardians* (often known as *caretakers*) for the beneficiaries should be named. Oftentimes, friends or loved ones will be more than happy to agree to serve as caretakers.

Vital: While not legally required, it's a good idea to get the advance consent of a trustee or guardian before naming him/her in a legal document. Name backups in case your first choice becomes unable or unwilling to serve. Also, ask all parties involved to sign the pet trust showing their agreement.

Caution: With a pet trust, the beneficiaries can't complain if they receive poor service from the trustee. Therefore, name someone you believe to be conscientious.

Even so, you may prefer to name one person as a trustee and another as caretaker for your pet so that each party can keep an eye on the other.

Your pet trust also may designate another party as the "trust protector" to disburse funds

---

*Currently, there are 39 states and the District of Columbia that allow pet trusts. Check with your state attorney general (*www.naag.org*) or local Humane Society to find out the law in your state.

to the trustee, who then disburses funds to the caretaker.

Because some animals do outlive all caretakers and trustees, consider naming one or two not-for-profit, no-kill animal shelters as backup caretakers. Check the "Worldwide Shelter Directory" on the Hugs for Homeless Animals Web site (*www.h4ha.org*).

SOONER OR LATER

There are two strategies to follow when creating a pet trust...

• **During your lifetime.** You can arrange for the trust to become effective while you're alive.

• **At your death.** Your will can call for the creation of a pet trust.

Pros and cons: Creating a trust while you're alive means that you won't know if you'll outlive your pet, making the trust unnecessary.

Waiting until your death for the trust to go into effect will eliminate the risk of providing for a pet who has predeceased you. However, there's a chance your pet will lack care if you are unable to care for your pet.

Strategy: Create a pet trust while you are alive. Stipulate that the trust will become effective only when you are unable to care for your pet or you die.

If you set up a pet trust during your lifetime, you can transfer assets into it at any time. A trust established after your death by the person you appointed in your will to be caretaker or trustee can be funded from your estate.

Recommended: Make arrangements for the trust to be funded when necessary—at your incapacity or your death.

Funding a pet trust can be tricky. You'll want to feel comfortable that your pet is adequately provided for. However, if you fund such a trust lavishly, you may open the door to legal challenges. Other potential heirs might attempt to undo the entire arrangement, by saying that you were not of sound mind.

Always give good reasons in the trust document for the amount you transfer to a pet trust. This will substantiate your good judgment and enforce the pet trust in case of a contest.

One approach is to work with an unrelated party, such as a certified public accountant (CPA), to determine a reasonable amount to fund the pet trust.

Situation: Your CPA might determine that your total cost for caring for your pet (food, vet bills, boarding) is $1,000 per year. If you were to die or become incapacitated tomorrow, your pet might reasonably live another 10 years.

Strategy: Thus, you might fund your pet trust with at least $10,000. Add money to fund an aging pet's additional medical needs. You might also want to compensate the trustee and the caretaker. And you can leave money to hire an attorney in case your pet trust is challenged—or to pay additional costs if your pet lives with you in an assisted-living facility.

Tactic: Rely upon an insurance policy on your life for some of the trust's funding. Provide that any assets remaining at your pet's death will go to a charity, perhaps an animal shelter.

Note: Income generated by assets in the pet trust is taxable.

FINAL THOUGHTS

Trusts are very versatile. When drawing up a pet trust, you can make specific provisions for the care of these close companions.

Examples: A pet trust can include instructions requiring the caretaker to bring the pet for visits with you should you become incapacitated and your condition prevents the pet from living with you. Often, such visits can improve the pet owner's physical and mental health.

If you have more than one pet, the trust documents can stipulate they remain together, if that's your wish. Alternatively, your dog might be entrusted to someone with a big yard while your cat's guardian is another person, who is not allergic.

Day-to-day directions: You also can spell out what your pet likes to eat, which vet it has been seeing and what medications it needs. Include whatever instructions you would like in

order to ensure continuity of care for these cherished friends.

Searching for a Social Security Number?

If you're sorting out the financial affairs of a deceased loved one, it's helpful to know that you can look for the Social Security number of any deceased person for free at the Social Security Death Index (SSDI), *ssdi.rootsweb.com*.

John Featherman, a personal privacy consultant based in Philadelphia.

How Long Should Estate and Probate Records Be Kept?

The IRS generally has three years to assess an estate tax deficiency after an estate is settled and taxes are paid, unless there is fraud or the estate is underreported by more than 25%. If an estate's return has no risk of such issues, audit risk ends three years after it is filed. However, some records should be kept available to heirs indefinitely.

Examples: The value of capital assets in the estate at their owner's death for purposes of calculating the future gain or loss on them to heirs...taxes paid by the estate that could give heirs future deductions.

James E. Cheeks, tax attorney at 501 Fifth Ave., New York City 10017.

14

Travel and Adventure

Sightseeing Bargains (Free and Almost Free) In Big US Cities

A spectacular, affordable vacation can be as close as the nearest big city. That's where you can now have intriguing adventures that cost absolutely nothing or very little. We went searching for the best sightseeing bargains in four of the country's most visited cities. Assuming you find moderately priced lodgings (not difficult with a savvy travel agent or Internet travel site such as *www.hotels.com* or *www.quik book.com*) or are driving in for the day, you can have a great time without making much of a dent in your budget.

Plan to walk a bit and to cover most longer distances via public transportation, remembering that seniors 65-plus usually pay half fare and that most city transit companies sell a multiday visitor's pass good for unlimited rides. And, many

big cities, including New York, San Francisco and Chicago, offer a "CityPass," a booklet of admission tickets to the city's top attractions purchased for a substantially reduced price.

More information: 888-330-5008, *www.city pass.com.*

NEW YORK

The best bargain in town is the Staten Island Ferry that runs day and night and costs not a penny to ride from the Battery (the southernmost tip of Manhattan) across New York Harbor and back for great views of the Statue of Liberty, Brooklyn and the Verrazano Narrows Bridge.

Already downtown, walk over to the promenade that runs along the Hudson River about half a mile to the World Financial Center where you can see Ground Zero (free).

Take the subway to Chinatown (any train to Canal St., Grand St. or East Broadway stations)

Joan Rattner Heilman, an award-winning travel writer based in New York. She is author of *Unbelievably Good Deals and Great Adventures That You Absolutely Can't Get Unless You're Over 50* (McGraw-Hill).

235

for lunch, then walk on the Brooklyn Bridge as far as you like and back (no charge) for a good look at the East River and Manhattan skyline, before taking a cab to the South Street Seaport on New York's historic waterfront. Visit the shops and restaurants located on Pier 17 and the old ships docked at the Seaport Museum.

Admission: Adults, $8*...seniors age 65 and older and students with ID, $6...children ages 5 to 12, $4.

On a Wednesday (or on Saturday morning 10 am to noon), there's free admission (except for special exhibits, for which there is a charge) all day at the New York Botanical Gardens, so take the subway up to the Bronx and then, if you have the energy, hop over to the Bronx Zoo a few blocks away.

Admission: Pay whatever you wish to get in on any Wednesday. On other days, adults pay $14...seniors age 65 and older, $12...children 2 to 12, $10.

And don't forget walking tours—some charge very little and others, nothing. The tour of the United Nations costs $13 for adults and $9 for seniors. A guided walk in Grand Central Terminal costs nothing on Wednesdays and Fridays at 12:30 pm. For a free private exploration with a volunteer guide around whatever neighborhood you choose, make a reservation well in advance with Big Apple Greeter (212-669-2896, *www.big applegreeter.org*).

More information: NYC & Company, the city's tourism marketing organization, 212-484-1200, *www.nycvisit.com.*

SAN FRANCISCO

Getting around San Francisco is cheap if you use your own two feet and public transportation. Ride on the vintage streetcars of the F Line ($1.50 per adult, 50 cents for seniors and children ages 5 to 17) from the top of Market Street down to the Embarcadero, a promenade along the waterfront, and on out to Fisherman's Wharf and Pier 39 to watch the sea lions cavort in the bay and the street artists perform.

From Fisherman's Wharf you can take a ferry and audio tour to Alcatraz, once the most notorious prison in the country. A ferry tour costs

*Prices and offers subject to change.

$21.75 per adult...$20.25, age 62 and older... $13.75, children ages five through 11. Admission to Alcatraz is free.

And take a bus to the top of Twin Peaks for the view. Or ride on the famous old cable cars. They cost $5 one way and are worth every penny. Or stroll through the unique neighborhoods of the city, such as Chinatown, Haight-Ashbury, Market Street and North Beach, free on one of the many narrated tours from City Guide Walking Tours (415-557-4266, *www.sfcityguides.org*).

Many of San Francisco's museums—such as the Cable Car Museum (415-474-1887, *www.cable carmuseum.org*), where you can see how the cars work—are free, and others have open admission at least one day a month.

The San Francisco Botanical Garden, in the middle of the city, is open daily and does not charge for admission or guided tours of exhibits. The San Francisco Zoo is free of charge on the first Wednesday of the month.

More information: San Francisco Convention and Visitors Bureau, 415-391-2000, *www.only insanfrancisco.com.*

ATLANTA

You can have a fine time in this big Southern city without much money in your pocket. Hop on the Atlanta Tourist Loop bus for an exploration of downtown ($1.75), which is undergoing a renaissance. Be sure to visit the Centennial Olympic Park, the State Capitol and the downtown shopping district. Ride the free midtown trolley around the midtown area, the cultural hub of the city. Atlanta's public transportation isn't costly either—$1.75 per ride...age 65 and older, 85 cents.

Take one of the Atlanta Preservation Center's walking tours of historic places and neighborhoods, like the Sweet Auburn District, where the Martin Luther King, Jr., National Historic Site is located (404-688-3350, *www.preserveatlanta.com*).

Cost: Adults, $10...age 60 and older, $5.

Also in midtown, take the Underground Atlanta's Guided History Tour of the city's early days. You will see historic sites and landmarks, such as the Old Railroad Depot. Tours are offered on Fridays, Saturdays and Sundays (*www. underground-atlanta.com*).

Admission: $6 per person.

In baseball season, fans can get two-for-one, $8 Atlanta Braves tickets in the upper reserved sections at Turner Field for any home game on Tuesdays…or two-for-one $20 seats in the Field/Terrace Pavilion for home games on Wednesday (404-522-7630, *www.atlantabraves.com*).

For the best view of the city, take a gondola to the top of Stone Mountain, right outside of town, where you'll see the Confederate Memorial Carving and view the Appalachian Mountains (*www.stonemountainpark.com*).

Admission: $8 for a carload of people to enter the park. The gondola ride is $9 per person or free with an all-attraction pass ($24 per adult…$21 per senior…$19 per child ages 3 to 11).

Before you leave Atlanta, splurge a little and visit the newly opened Georgia Aquarium, the largest and perhaps the most spectacular aquarium in the world.

Admission: Adults, $24…age 55 and older, $20…children ages three to 12, $18.

More information: Atlanta Convention & Visitors Bureau, 800-285-2682, *www.atlanta.net*.

CHICAGO

This city is famous for the skyscrapers and other architecture, and its long, beautiful waterfront on Lake Michigan. Ride on the Loop Tour Train around the historic downtown neighborhood. A free 40-minute tour describing history and architecture departs at several times a day on Saturdays, May through September.

Make a reservation with the Chicago Greeters (312-744-8000, *www.chicagogreeter.com*), who'll match you up with a volunteer guide to take a walk around a section of the city you want to explore. The Millennium Park Greeters provide free informal walking tours of the park daily at both 10 am and 2 pm (312-742-1168). The park's attractions include gardens, classical concerts, a Frank Gehry music pavilion and the multimedia Crown Fountain, where projected video images of the faces of more than 1,000 Chicagoans purse their lips and spout water at visitors every 12 minutes.

Don't leave Chicago without taking an architectural tour because this is where the first skyscrapers were built. Many Loop walking tours are offered by the Chicago Architecture Foundation, among them "Historic Skyscrapers" and "Modern Skyscrapers" (312-922-3432 or *www.architecture.org*).

Admission: Each tour costs $15 per adult… $12 for seniors age 65 and older. A cruise along the Chicago River costs more, in case you want to splurge.

Head out to the Navy Pier, a playground on the lake, where you will find the Chicago Children's Museum (free Thursdays, 5 pm to 8 pm), live entertainment, shops, restaurants and fireworks. The nearby Hancock Observatory offers a view of the entire city from its 97th floor for a fee. But you can get off the elevator on the 96th floor and see the view for free.

More information: Chicago Office of Tourism, 877-244-2246, *www.877chicago.com*.

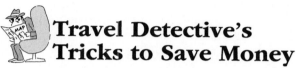

Travel Detective's Tricks to Save Money

Peter Greenberg, travel editor of NBC's *Today* show and editor of the travel Web site, *www.petergreenberg.com*. He's also author of *The Traveler's Diet: Eating Right and Staying Fit on the Road* (Villard) and *The Complete Travel Detective Bible* (Rodale).

Airline passengers used to complain a lot about the quality of onboard meals. Now, on some airlines you're charged for water. *Here's how you can still find good deals on hotels, airlines, rental cars and more…*

HOTELS

• **Call hotels at 4 pm on Sunday** to reserve a room for anytime within the next two to three weeks. You'll have a better chance of getting a low rate from a front-desk clerk who understands that an unsold room is revenue the hotel will never recoup. Don't call the hotel's 800 number—you are likely to be put through to a national reservation line. Look up the hotel's number in the city you plan to visit.

• **Request weekend rates.** At some hotels, weekend rates are one-third of regular rates. If you're staying through the week, ask that the cheaper weekend rate be extended. Make sure the room price reflects hidden charges, such as resort fees, as well as taxes.

• **Consider alternative lodging.** Many hostels have gone upscale and offer private rooms for $25 to $160 a night.* For information, contact Hostelling International USA (301-495-1240, *www.hiusa.org*).

Also: More than 70% of colleges rent dorm rooms at reasonable prices throughout popular vacation periods.

RENTAL CARS

• **Call the local rental location.** If you use a toll-free number to make a reservation, you may not get the lowest rate or the best car. Local operators can price cars to reduce a temporary surplus.

• **Avoid renting at airport lots,** which can be more expensive than in-city ones. Compare local and national rates at *www.rentalcars.com*.

Helpful: Rent on Saturday. There is a good chance cars will be available because customers requested them for the weekend but never claimed them.

CRUISES

• **Book a cruise at the last minute.** Many routes have more berths than passengers. Some travel agents and consolidators offer great last-minute packages.

Warning: Cruise lines now charge for extras that used to be included, such as onboard recreational activities. Expect to pay about two-and-a-half times the basic cruise price, so a $600 cruise actually could cost $1,500.

AIRFARES

• **Be flexible.** When calling airlines, do not provide travel dates to reservation agents upfront. Instead, ask the agent to punch into the computer every fare for the itinerary you desire within a range of dates. Ask for the cheapest fares first. If you're flexible, you may be able to cut ticket costs.

• **Buy tickets after midnight on Tuesday** in the time zone where the airline is located. Typically, airlines start fare sales late Friday, and competing airlines match the lower fares. All the matching usually stops by Monday. Airlines usually give customers who book low fares 24 hours in which to buy them. All the low fares that were booked on Monday but not purchased by

*Prices subject to change.

midnight Tuesday come back into the airline's computers at that moment.

More from Peter Greenberg...

How to Not Gain Weight on Vacation

Many people return from vacation dismayed to find that they gained several pounds. Travel guru Peter Greenberg can sympathize. Logging 400,000 miles a year, he found it impossible to eat sensibly on the road, and at one time weighed more than 280 pounds.

Then, during a TV shoot, the prime minister of Jamaica, who was watching Mr. Greenberg swim with dolphins, kidded that the dolphins were swimming with "a whale." That was the motivation he needed to lose weight.

After he consulted with personal trainers and nutritionists, Mr. Greenberg lost a lot of weight, and is determined to drop even more. *Here are some of his favorite strategies...*

DIET

• **Don't starve yourself before your trip.** Dramatically cutting back on calories will send your body into starvation mode, which means it will burn fewer calories to conserve energy.

• **Choose airport food carefully.** The best airports for healthful food, according to a survey from the Physicians Committee for Responsible Medicine, are Chicago's O'Hare, Detroit Metropolitan, San Francisco, New York's JFK, Dallas–Fort Worth and Denver.

If you have time only for fast food, try Burger King's vegetarian burger. If you skip the mayo, it has only 310 calories and seven grams of fat.

• **Drink water.** Bring several bottles on every flight. Water will keep you hydrated and also curb your appetite. Drinking bottled water also can reduce your chance of getting sick. One in six airplanes has unsafe drinking water.

• **Beware of "healthy" menus.** Just because a restaurant labels an entrée "healthy" doesn't mean it is. Ask for grilled chicken or fish with sauce on the side. Order salad with dressing on the side—then use it sparingly.

- **Pay attention to portion size.** Pick two appetizers but no entrée, or choose an entrée but skip the starters. And eat dinner before 8 pm.

- **Don't open up the hotel minibar.** Either have it removed or do not accept the key. The snacks are fattening and expensive.

- **Watch what you drink.** Cream, soda pop or a drink mixer can add several hundred calories to that of the alcohol alone. Stick with wine or light beer. Or have a mixed drink with club soda or water.

I used to drink several cans of Diet Pepsi a day, but have stopped. According to recent research, drinking two cans of diet soda a day increases your chance of becoming overweight by 55%.

Possible reason: You think it is fine to eat more food.

EXERCISE

- **Burn calories at the airport.** You won't break a sweat by sitting and reading a magazine, but you can by walking through the airport to, say, meet a connecting flight. Recently, at Miami's airport, I walked to my flight in the next terminal, which was a mile away.

- **Buy a pedometer.** With this gadget, you can monitor how many steps you're taking daily. Aim for 10,000 steps a day for weight loss.

- **Use hotel gyms.** If you expect a long layover between flights, why not work out? You may be able to buy a day pass for the gym at an airport hotel. Passes start at $10 a day.

How to Save on Group Vacations

Groople.com caters to groups that require at least five hotel rooms. It offers discounted rates for hotels, flights, trains, cruises and rental cars. General discounts range from 10% to 20%* but often can be higher depending on availability, season and event schedules. The site caters to all sizes and kinds of groups—from family and military reunions to destination weddings. Groups design their own itineraries.

*Rates subject to change.

Group Travel Trap

When you travel with others—even good friends—you might find yourself having "too much" of them as the trip goes on.

Remedy: Prearrange a few activities just for yourself.

Examples: Meeting other personal friends along the way…activities that appeal to you but not others (such as going to a special kind of museum or performance).

Also, when traveling with friends, note your differences as well as shared interests and plan to accommodate them.

Example: When a couple who are early risers travel with another who are night owls, they can agree to spend their days together from lunch through dinner and their early mornings and late nights apart. They'll all be happier.

Stacy Small, luxury travel consultant, Elite Travel International in West Palm Beach, FL, *www.elitetravelinternational.com*.

Use Frequent-Flier Miles Quickly

Some airlines are cutting back the time before frequent-flier miles expire. Delta miles will expire in two years in all inactive accounts, and US Airways miles will expire in just 18 months. The industry custom had long been three years. To keep your account active even if you are not flying much, make transactions with airline partners, such as credit cards, banks and on-line merchants. For Continental, Delta, Northwest and US Airways, you can earn miles by viewing and responding to Internet ads at *www.e-miles.com*.

Tim Winship, publisher, *The FrequentFlier Crier*, 2021 Hillhurst, Los Angeles 90027, *www.frequentflier.com*.

Into Space...

Starting in 2009, 2 million Virgin Atlantic frequent-flier miles will land you a seat on the Virgin Galactic space flight. The flight's cost will be about $200,000* without frequent-flier miles.

Information: *www.virginatlantic.com* and *www.virgingalactic.com*

*Price subject to change.

Arrive on Time

To arrive on time, fly on a Saturday. That's the day on which flights are least likely to be late. Fridays are the worst days for late arrivals. Thursdays are second-worst.

Also helpful: Travel in September, the month with the best on-time record...always fly nonstop...consider nearby alternative airports instead of larger, busier ones.

Condé Nast Traveler, 4 Times Square, New York City 10036.

Lost Luggage Protection

An estimated 30 million bags failed to arrive at their destinations on time last year.

What to do: Remove old baggage claim tags. Then attach a sturdy ID tag to your bag with your phone number, your travel agent's business address, a post office box or your business address. Do not use your home address—it may alert thieves to your absence. Include your cell phone number so that the airline can contact you if your luggage is misrouted. Put contact information on the inside of your bag in case the ID tag gets lost. Also, decorate your luggage with stickers to make it easy to identify. And, check bags at least 90 minutes before departure to ensure that they get through security in time.

Susan Foster, packing expert, Portland, OR, and author of *Smart Packing for Today's Traveler* (KSB Promotions).

Best Place to Hail a Taxi at an Airport

When taxis drop off passengers at the departure area, they often drive away without another fare. Hailing a cab that has just dropped off a passenger may enable you to negotiate a cheaper fare than you'd get at the arrival area.

MotorWatch, Box 123, Butler, MD 21023, *www.motorwatch.com*.

Does Travel Insurance Cover Airline Bankruptcies?

Travel insurance has been popular since the terrorist attacks of September 11, but many insurers modified coverage to avoid payouts to travelers if an airline files for bankruptcy.

Self-defense: Ask when buying insurance—you may have to buy from a different company or fly on a different airline to get full coverage. Airlines and other travel suppliers that are on the bankruptcy watch list can be found at *www.totaltravelinsurance.com/bankruptcyinsurance.asp* or by calling 866-226-7500.

Alex Velinov, president of Total Travel Insurance, New York City.

Smart Airline Seating

Before booking your airline flight, compare seats on-line to locate the one you want at SeatGuru.com. This Web site provides detailed seating information for 40-plus airlines, indicates "good" and "poor" seats and tells their location relative to exits, lavatories, galleys, etc. Request the seats you want when making your reservation—but realize that seating generally isn't final and may be changed until you obtain your boarding pass, so check in early to get it. Most airlines now provide on-line check-in through their Web sites up to 24 hours before flight departure time.

Kiplinger's Personal Finance, 1729 H St. NW, Washington, DC 20006.

Airfare Deals

Find airfare deals that major Web sites miss at FareCompare.com. You type in your itinerary, and the site gives the day's lowest fares plus a fare trend. If current fares are at the low end of recent trends, it is a good time to buy. If current fares are higher compared with recent ones, it may pay to wait.

If you can't wait to purchase a ticket: Go to Airfarewatchdog.com, which checks national and international databases for fare specials that other sites may overlook.

Neither of these sites sells tickets—both link you to airline Web sites and on-line agencies to do the actual booking.

Kiplinger's Personal Finance, 1729 H St. NW, Washington, DC 20006.

Buy Extra Legroom When You Fly

Some airlines sell seat upgrades for people seeking additional legroom. United charges $299 for a one-year membership* in its Economy Plus program, which offers you the chance to upgrade to seats with five inches of extra space. Northwest's Coach Choice program charges an additional $15 for coach seats with extra space, such as those in bulkheads and exit rows. US Airways' GoUpgrades program offers first-class upgrades for as little as $50. And, AirTran sells upgrades to business class for as little as $40.

Nancy Dunnan, publisher and editor of *TravelSmart,* Dobbs Ferry, NY, *www.travelsmartnewsletter.com.*

*Prices and offers subject to change.

33.

Are Duty-Free Items a Good Deal?

Duty free indicates that an item is being sold without the customs tax normally imposed by the country in which the shop is located.

Duty free applies to the merchant who sells the item to travelers—but only to take out of the country. This enables the merchant to charge you less for the item because his/her costs are lower. But there's no guarantee that a merchant will do so. Generally, items that would otherwise be subject to high duties are the best buys—perfume, liquor and tobacco products.

Best: Determine what you would like to buy ahead of time, check the price at home and then compare it with the price at the airport, port or cruise ship.

Also from Nancy Dunnan...

Does Travel Insurance Cover Bad-Weather Problems?

Most people buy travel insurance so that they will be reimbursed for plane fare or cruise costs if they have to cancel their trip—say, because of a medical emergency. To cover a snow emergency situation, you would need a policy that covers problems *during* the trip.

The airlines aren't financially responsible for weather-related delays. If you fly in regions (or during seasons) when bad weather is a higher probability, consider buying insurance that will cover your hotel room and meals should your flight be delayed or canceled.

Ask your insurance agent if he/she handles travel insurance. If not, then compare quotes for policies from *www.insuremytrip.com* (800-487-4722), a consumer-oriented Web site with information on plans from 18 different companies.

Rental car know-how from Nancy Dunnan...

Best Ways to Get a Free Upgrade

To get a car-rental upgrade, book the cheapest car available. These small and inexpensive rentals are typically the first to go, so you have the best chance of getting a free upgrade to a larger car. If you are not offered an upgrade for free, you often can get one by paying a small extra charge at the rental counter.

Slash Rental Car Costs in Half

Reduce rental-car costs by as much as 50% by booking on the Web. Bnm.com can help you track down and reserve the cheapest rental available whether you are traveling in the US or abroad. If driving a specific model is not important, you can check prices at Bnm.com or at Hotwire.com and then go to Priceline.com's car-rental section where you can bid for even steeper discounts.

Time, 1271 Avenue of the Americas, New York City 10020.

Budget Hotels Are Better Than Ever

You can have the same amenities—or better—at economy motel chains as you can at more expensive chains. They can be a good choice for business travelers, as well as for travelers on a budget.

Chains such as Days Inn, Econo Lodge, Motel 6, Red Roof Inns, Rodeway Inns, Super 8 and Travelodge are upgrading mattresses and towels. Some are offering loyalty points—redeemable at restaurants such as Denny's and Olive Garden and merchants such as Blockbuster and Home Depot. The chains usually offer breakfast but no other meals—however, low-cost restaurants are typically nearby.

And, budget chains often include amenities that more-expensive chains charge for, such as high-speed Internet access.

Maria Chevalier, vice president of global business intelligence, Advito, the consulting division of BCD Travel, Atlanta.

Bed-and-Breakfasts For Those Over 50

The Evergreen Club at *www.evergreenclub. com* offers hospitality in private homes for only $15/day* ($10 for singles) plus annual dues of $75 for a married couple or two people traveling together ($60 for singles).

Included: A stay in your host's guest room, breakfast, friendly conversation and sightseeing tips, maybe a round of golf or a game of tennis —and often, new friendships.

There are almost 2,000 B&B homestays in North America and 15 foreign countries, including city and country homes, lakeside cottages, golf course condos, farms, mountain cabins and even yachts. Members come from all walks of life, and they have varied interests and experiences—but all are eager to meet other interesting people and are over age 50.

Mary Hunt, editor, *Debt-Proof Living*, Box 2135, Paramount, CA 90723, *www.debtproofliving.com*.

*Prices subject to change.

Travel in Style

On your next European vacation, consider renting an apartment or a house rather than staying in a hotel. The Web site Rentvillas. com lists properties available for as little as three days or for months at a time. Prices are comparable—and sometimes cheaper—than hotel prices. Rentals are available from Rentvillas.com in France, Greece, Great Britain, Italy, Portugal, Spain and Turkey.

Vacation at A Lighthouse

Many lighthouses are converting into hotels and bed-and-breakfast resorts as ship navigation becomes electronic. Located along coastlines—frequently rugged ones—they often offer beautiful views and access to nature. Some lighthouses do continue to operate while hosting guests, and a few even ask the guests to help tend their beacons.

Helpful: For an on-line directory of all New England lighthouses with lodging, and a "lighthouse bookstore" that offers information about such lighthouses across the country, go to the New England Lighthouses' Internet site at *www.lighthouse.cc.*

Safer Hotel Stays for Women

Women should pick a hotel with fewer than 100 rooms, on a busy street and with active neighborhood businesses, such as restaurants and all-night food stores.

Important: A well-lit and secure parking lot. Ask for a room near the elevators, on an upper floor, away from catwalks and terraces. Use all available locks on doors. Put expensive clothing on hangers under other clothing. Lock up valuables in the room safe or hotel safe—and lock larger valuables in your suitcase.

Women's Travel Club recommendations, *www.womenstravelclub.com.*

Important Travel Vaccines

Every traveler, regardless of destination, should get vaccinated against tetanus and hepatitis A. Hepatitis A virus is found in food and water, even in the US. Get revaccinated for tetanus every 10 years.

Also: Have a *typhoid vaccination* if going to Central or South America, Africa, India, Malaysia, Indonesia, Vietnam or the Mideast. A *yellow-fever immunization* if visiting tropical South America or subequatorial Africa. The *polio booster* if you haven't been vaccinated since childhood and are going to Africa, India, Pakistan, Malaysia, Indonesia or some parts of southern China. An *influenza shot* if visiting tropical areas in the southern hemisphere, where flu occurs year-round. And, *tuberculosis testing* (PPD) should be done three to six months after travel to Central or South America, Africa, the Mideast, Eastern Europe and Russia.

Carol De Rosa, RN, executive director, Passport Health, provider of immunizations and travel consultations, Baltimore, *www.passporthealthusa.com.*

Healthier Traveling

To stay healthy while traveling, take the right supplements…

• **In addition to a multivitamin, take a probiotic** (follow the label instructions) on an empty stomach, starting three days before leaving and during the trip, to prevent diarrhea and related problems.

• **Garlic**—preferably aged garlic—reduces the risk of respiratory and digestive infections. Take two capsules per day for two days before you leave, during the trip and for two days after.

• **Melatonin**—one to three milligrams—prevents jet lag and makes sleep easier. Take it the evening you arrive, at 9 pm in the time zone you are in, and for two or three more nights.

Consult your physician prior to starting any supplements.

Mark A. Stengler, ND, associate clinical professor, National College of Naturopathic Medicine, Portland, OR, and founder and director of the La Jolla Whole Health Clinic, La Jolla, CA. He is author of the *Bottom Line/Natural Healing* newsletter. His Web site is *www.DrStengler.com.*

More from Dr. Mark Stengler…

Help for Airplane Anxiety

If you feel nervous on airplanes, try the homeopathic treatment Rescue Remedy ($10.50 for 10 ml*), available at health-food stores. This combination of flower extracts reduces anxiety without causing drowsiness and has no side effects. Put 15 drops in an eight-ounce bottle of water, and sip it before and during the flight.

*Price subject to change.

X-Rays at the Airport

Full-body scans at airports expose travelers to only one-tenth the radiation of a chest X-ray.

Current plans are to use airport X-ray machines on travelers who are selected for extra screening—beyond a standard metal detector. These travelers will be given the option of having the full-body X-ray or being patted down by a screener.

If you travel frequently: Opt for the patdown—effects of even low levels of radiation build up over a lifetime.

Everett M. Lautin, MD, FACR, a radiologist in private practice and former professor of radiology, Albert Einstein Medical College, New York City.

Water Dangers: How to Stay Safe When You Travel

Connie Lohsl, RN, BSN, a nurse manager and travel-health specialist with Passport Health, a nationwide chain of travel-health franchises that provide low-cost immunizations and other travel-related services, based in Baltimore, *www.passporthealthusa.com.*

Unprepared travelers who hope to enjoy exotic locations often spend their days in the hotel bathroom instead. Almost 40% of all travelers experience some form of stomach upset from minor to debilitating diarrhea. For people who have underlying kidney or heart problems, the dehydration from diarrhea can be life-threatening.

The Centers for Disease Control and Prevention, at *www.cdc.gov,* indicates which countries have safe drinking water. *Countries are rated by risk—high, intermediate and low...*

High risk: Africa, Mexico and Central America, South America, most of Asia and the Middle East, especially the rural areas. Hepatitis A is a concern in Russia.

Intermediate risk: South Africa, Southern and Eastern Europe.

Low risk: US, Canada, Japan, Northern Europe and Australia.

To stay safe...

• **Drink bottled water, but inspect it first.** In some countries, a container of bottled water costs $4 or more.* Unscrupulous vendors may refill empties with tap water. Always check that the factory seal is intact. Buy carbonated water, if available—it's harder to fake.

• **Wipe bottles and cans dry before drinking.** Bottled and canned beverages may be kept cold in tubs filled with ice water. Moisture on the outside may contain organisms that can get into your mouth when you drink. Of course, don't add ice cubes to beverages unless you are sure they are made from uncontaminated water.

• **Use bottled water for brushing teeth.** Also stand your toothbrush upright between using so that it isn't contaminated with water from the sink.

• **Drink bottled water on cruise ships and airplanes.** Nonbottled water could be contaminated. Coffee and tea made with boiling water should be safe.

• **Sterilize your water.** *Two ways...*

• Boiling. Put the water in a clean pot, bring it to a rolling boil, then remove it from the heat and let it cool. Transfer to a sterilized container. Boiling is the most reliable way to kill most disease-causing organisms.

• Use a water-filtration bottle. This can protect you from bacteria, protozoa and lead. Some also filter viruses, including hepatitis A. Check out the product label. Bottles are offered at my Web site, *www.passporthealthusa.com,* or at any local passport office or camping supply store. *Cost:* $40 to $100 or more.

• **Beware of swimming.** Swimming in the ocean is generally safe—few bacteria and parasites can survive in the saltwater. But lakes and other bodies of freshwater can have high levels of contamination—and some organisms pass directly through the skin.

Showering and toweling off soon after swimming will assist in removal of parasites before they have a chance to burrow through the skin. Wearing swimming shoes can protect you from parasites and puncture wounds.

Well-maintained and chemically treated swimming pools generally are safe.

*Prices subject to change.

Beach Sand Danger

Beach sand has five to 10 times more bacteria than adjacent water. Bacteria from bird droppings and human waste, such as *E. coli,* may survive longer in sand than in water because bacteria adhere to particles.

Self-defense: Wash hands after leaving the beach. Warn children not to put their hands in their mouths when digging in sand.

Walter McLeod, president of the Clean Beaches Council, Washington, DC.

Road Travel Warning

Vehicle-related accidents are a major cause of accidental deaths of US citizens abroad. Especially in developing countries, taxi and bus drivers may take far more risks than in the US—overloading vehicles, ignoring stoplights, driving recklessly on mountain roads and failing to use headlights.

Self-defense: Avoid traveling at night, especially in rural areas. Sit in the backseat, and buckle up. Don't ride in taxis that don't have seat belts in the backseat.

Road safety information: Road reports for individual countries are available from the Association for Safe International Road Travel at *asirt. org.*

Stuart R. Rose, MD, president of Travel Medicine, Inc., Northampton, MA, *www.travmed.com,* and author of *International Travel Health Guide* (Elsevier).

Much Safer Travel

Peter V. Savage, vice president and cofounder of Passport Health, a leading provider of low-cost immunizations and travel-related services to businesses and tourists, Baltimore, *www.passporthealthusa.com.* He is author of *The Safe Travel Book* (Lexington).

When you're on vacation, the last thing that you want to worry about is your safety, but it is wise to be prepared.

Below, travel author Peter V. Savage, a clandestine officer in the CIA for two decades, tells what to watch out for…

• **Contact the embassy.** Before you book a trip, call the American embassy in the country you will be visiting and ask for the Regional Security Officer (RSO). You can get the number by contacting the State Department at 888-407-4747 or *travel.state.gov.*

The RSO should be able to answer questions about disease outbreaks, high-crime areas, weather issues, where to get the best exchange rates and problems American travelers have had.

Example: Several years ago, I called the RSO in Ottawa, Canada, and asked about Montreal. The RSO told me that if I rented a sport utility vehicle (SUV) during that time, I should keep it parked in a garage. Criminals were stealing SUVs off the streets, quickly stripping them and shipping the parts to China.

• **Don't dress like an American.** I shake my head when I see Americans in foreign countries wearing clothing that announces where they're from or where they went to college. I even saw an American oilman in Venezuela wearing cowboy boots and a cowboy hat with a turkey feather. Letting others know that you're an American may lead the crooks to assume that you are a wealthy tourist worth robbing or, even worse, worth kidnapping for a ransom.

Keep all watches and jewelry—even costume jewelry that looks real—at home. If you must bring jewelry or other valuables, make sure they are insured. Also, avoid using expensive luggage. Keep cameras hidden when not in use.

• **Outsmart pickpockets.** I keep my money, passport and credit cards in a wallet that attaches to my belt and is concealed under my clothes. You can buy these at *www.austinhouse.com.*

If you wear a fanny pack, keep the pouch in front. One common trick of pickpockets is to bump into you in front and back—pickpockets typically work in teams—and quickly slice the bottom of the fanny pack and catch the valuables as they drop. Women should carry purses football fashion.

Don't bother getting traveler's checks—these days, credit cards have wider acceptance. Keep in your purse or pocket, enough cash to satisfy a mugger.

• **Prepare for medical emergencies.** Make sure you have the proper immunizations before heading out of the country. You can find a local travel medicine clinic at *www.istm.org* or at my Web site, *www.passporthealthusa.com*. Plan several months in advance—some vaccinations require multiple doses with weeklong intervals in between. If you take medication, bring extra in case you have to stay longer than planned. Before you leave, buy an emergency assistance medical and evacuation insurance policy. Providers have established medical contacts worldwide, can pay in cash on the spot and can bring you home if necessary.

Good source: www.travelguard.com.

• **Keep important information with your passport.** Write down the phone numbers of the American embassies in all the countries that you plan on visiting. Also, include your blood type and whether your blood's Rh factor is positive or negative. Make copies of your passport and keep them with you in case you lose your original. Leave copies with friends or relatives at home as well.

Travel Smart Abroad

Carry a local newspaper when on city streets abroad—especially when you go to use an ATM. The newspaper will make you look less like a vulnerable tourist. And, when using the foreign ATM, you can position the newspaper to shield your PIN from prying eyes as you type it into the keypad.

Nancy Dunnan, publisher and editor of *TravelSmart*, Dobbs Ferry, NY, *www.travelsmartnewsletter.com*.

More travel smarts...

How to Find Internet Access When Traveling

To access the Internet while traveling, use a computer that's available to the public or connect using your own laptop. If using your own laptop, you can plug in to an Internet connection or use WiFi (the wireless network that uses radiowaves to connect you to the Internet) if your computer has wireless capability, such as Bluetooth.

Free access can be found at many public libraries, in most cases, using their computers (some limit you to an hour). Also, check with the hotels where you'll be staying—many major chains, bed-and-breakfasts and hostels offer free Internet access, using their computer or your own.

Finally, consult these two resources—JiWire (*www.jiwire.com*) and AnchorFree (*www.anchorfree.com*). Both enable you to search for WiFi "hotspots" by country, state, city, zip code and category, such as cafés, libraries, marinas and airports. JiWire includes both free and paid hotspots around the world. AnchorFree, which lists only free WiFi hotspots, also has a blog so users can share tips and news.

Cheaper Calling From Abroad

When traveling in Europe and Asia, consider using prepaid phone cards, such as ZapTel (877-532-2737 or *www.zaptel.com*) or SpeedyPin MCI (800-483-3805 or *www.speedypin.com*). You first call a toll-free number, then punch in a personal identification number (PIN) and the phone number of the person you are calling. The prices range from less than 1 cent to about 54 cents a minute,* depending on the country.

Alternative: A callback service, made through an American telephone network, such as United World Telecom (561-276-7156, ext. 301 or *www.uwt4me.com*). You call up a toll-free US number and let the phone ring once, then hang up. A computer "calls" you back, you enter the number you wish to call and you benefit from US phone rates anywhere in the world.

Example: A call from the UK can cost just 8 cents per minute.

The Wall Street Journal, 200 Liberty St., New York City 10281, *online.wsj.com*.

*Prices subject to change.

Tipping When Abroad

Hotels in most countries typically charge a service fee—10% to 15% of the cost of your stay—that is distributed among the housekeepers, concierge and laundry and kitchen staff. However, most hotel service-staff members still expect individual tips. The amount varies—ask the front desk about what is customary.

Exceptions: In Australia and New Zealand, tips are not expected at hotels and service fees are rare.

Most restaurants around the world add a service fee of 10% to 15%. If there is no service fee added to your bill, a 10% to 15% tip is acceptable—up to 20% in the US and Canada.

Exceptions: In Australia and New Zealand, it is customary to tip only 5% to 10%.

Travel & Leisure, 1120 Avenue of the Americas, New York City 10036.

Foreign Taxi Tipping

Wondering how much to tip the cabbie in a foreign country? *See below...*

• **In Western Europe,** round up fares to the next euro for amounts less than 10 euros, and round up to the next euro plus one for larger amounts. For amounts more than 30 euros, round up to the next euro, then add three more as a tip.

• **In South America and Eastern Europe,** negotiate fares, including the tip, before getting in a cab.

• **In the Caribbean,** taxis have meters on some islands but not others—unmetered cabs are supposed to charge government-fixed rates, which usually are posted at airports and are included in visitor tourist guides. On in-town metered fares, tip $1 to $2...more late at night and on Sundays and holidays.

• **In Asia and the Pacific,** no tips are expected in taxis.

Travel & Leisure, 1120 Avenue of the Americas, New York City 10036.

If Your Child Is Traveling Abroad...

Roundup of college international program directors in *Better Homes and Gardens*, 1716 Locust St., Des Moines, IA 50309.

Before a student travels abroad, buy an International Student Identity Card (ISIC), which provides a 24-hour help line emergency service...basic sickness and accident travel insurance...discounts on airfares and travel services. You can apply for a card by contacting an ISIC-affiliated Student and Youth Travel Office or on-line via an ISIC member Web site. For information, go to *www.statravel.com*.

Cost for the card: $22.*

Also: Put together two folders—one to be kept at home, one for the student to take. Each folder should have his/her Social Security and credit card numbers, copies of his passport with the bar code, student visa, medical conditions and prescriptions, and contact numbers for the school if it is a school program.

Confirm that your medical insurance provides coverage—if it won't, buy supplementary insurance from an ISIC-affiliated travel office.

*Price subject to change.

Quick Ways to Learn a Foreign Language

Trying to learn a foreign language before you visit a new country? *See below...*

• **Find a language study partner** by visiting an exchange site, such as *www.mylanguageexchange.com*. Users of the site can ask members from more than 130 countries to help them practice writing and speaking on-line in voice chat rooms.

• **Download language audiobooks** onto an MP3 player to listen to while traveling.

247

Example: Through iTunes at *www.itunes. com*, you can download "In Flight Spanish" for $8.95.*

• **Listen to foreign-language news broadcasts** and other radio programs.

Example: Hear world news in French on the Internet at *www.rfi.fr.*

Newsweek, 444 Madison Ave., New York City 10022.

*Price subject to change.

Finding the Right Cruise for You

Howard Moses, president of The Cruise Authority, a travel agency based in Marietta, GA, that is focused primarily on cruise travel, *www.the-cruise-authority.com*. He has been in the cruise business for 18 years.

The most popular cruise destinations now are the Mediterranean, the Caribbean and Alaska. *Here is how to choose the perfect region for your next cruise...*

THE MEDITERRANEAN

Most cruises focus on one of two regions...

• **Western Mediterranean,** including the west coast of Italy, the French Riviera, southern Spain and Portugal and perhaps Tunisia or Gibraltar.

• **Eastern Mediterranean.** This includes the Greek isles, Turkey, Croatia and the east coast of Italy.

Mediterranean highlights: Some people fall in love with Rome and Venice. Others prefer less heralded cities, such as Lisbon, Portugal, and Split, Croatia.

When to go: The high season runs from late April through early November. The best deals and weather are in late April and May, before crowds arrive, or September and October, after they leave.

THE CARIBBEAN

There are three basic itineraries...

• **Western Caribbean** is best for those who want beaches, with an occasional visit to a historic site.

Typical ports of call: Cozumel, Mexico... Jamaica...Grand Cayman.

• **Eastern Caribbean** is best for combining sun worship with other activities, such as shopping and snorkeling.

Typical ports of call: St. Thomas...St. Martin ...San Juan, Puerto Rico.

• **Southern Caribbean** is best for those who enjoy exploring islands—the distances between the ports are short.

Typical ports of call: Curaçao...Martinique ...Antigua.

Caribbean highlights: St. Martin/St. Maarten is the smallest island to have been partitioned between two nations, France and Holland...St. Thomas features great duty-free shopping...and Grand Turk and Cozumel have exceptional diving and snorkeling.

When to go: High season is January through March. The best deals are during the first two weeks of December, when demand plummets between Thanksgiving and Christmas. April and May also are good times for deals.

ALASKA

There are two basic itineraries...

• **Inside Passage** is best for those who want to see coastal Alaska with as few hassles as possible. It departs from Vancouver and Seattle and typically gets as far north as Glacier Bay, near Juneau, before turning back south.

• **The Glacier Route** makes arranging connecting flights tricky, but it does give cruisers a chance to explore Alaska's interior before or after their cruise. The ship departs from Seattle or Vancouver. (Or it departs from Seward and ends in Seattle or Vancouver.)

Large ships provide more onboard entertainment options, but a smaller ship will get you much closer to the gorgeous coastline.

Alaskan highlights: Ships of all sizes cruise the stunning Hubbard Glacier and Glacier Bay.

When to go: Alaska's cruise season is mid-May through mid-September. Prices climb from mid-June through mid-August. Late May and early September offer the best deals. The weather will be cooler, but you'll see more wildlife.

15

Good Times

How to Get Tickets to (Almost) Anything

on't believe it when you see the "Sold Out" sign. In fact, there is hardly a game, concert, show or any other event to which tickets aren't available. *How to get them…*

●**Join a fan club.** Members often get first crack at tickets for a wide range of performances. Today, most fan clubs are Web-based.

Cost: $10 to $40 a year.* Advance ticket offers generally become available as soon as you join.

Example: The Barry Manilow International Fan Club (*www.barrymanilow.com*) offers members first access to tickets for tours. *Membership fee:* $10 per year.

Other performers, such as John Mellencamp (*www.clubcherrybomb.net*, $30 for a year), reserve a limited number of seats near the stage for fan club members. Some fan clubs also have

*Prices and offers subject to change.

phone numbers that members can call for last-minute tickets. To find a fan club, enter the performer's name and "fan club" into an Internet search engine.

●**Contact sponsors of events.** Most sporting events, including play-off games, are sponsored by major corporations that make tickets available to customers and suppliers. Individual teams often have business partners that do the same.

Examples: Business partners of the Miami Dolphins football team include DHL, Publix, Verizon and Wachovia. Major theatrical productions, including many at New York's Radio City Music Hall, also have corporate sponsors.

If you're lucky enough to know an executive of a sponsoring company, ask him/her to help you buy tickets. Or ask if your own employer does business with a sponsor that may be able to help you.

Mark Andrew Zwartynski, a former senior vice president of ticket sales and administration for the Dallas Mavericks and Indiana Pacers, and also coauthor of Two on the Aisle: How to Get Tickets to Any Event, Anytime, Anywhere (Masters).

Don't hesitate to ask for assistance. Most sponsors and their trading partners enjoy helping out.

Helpful: The names of corporate sponsors of shows, events and teams are often included in print ads for the events or on the events' Internet sites.

• **Search on-line brokers.** Not so long ago, very few companies competed with Ticketmaster (800-277-1700, *www.ticketmaster.com*). Today, there are dozens of on-line ticket brokers, including *www.stubhub.com*, *www.tickets.com*, *www.ticketsnow.com* and *www.ticketsondemand. org*. Such brokers were formerly known as "scalpers," but local and state laws have allowed them to become legitimate businesses. An Internet broker often has tickets to top events, but brokers charge hefty fees, often 10% to 20%. (Many state governments are investigating this practice.)

Important: Do business only with members of the National Association of Ticket Brokers (630-510-4594, *www.natb.org*) or the firms that are listed above.

You also can buy tickets at auction at *www. ebay.com*.

• **Phone early, phone late.** When you see an announcement that tickets will go on sale at, say, 10 am, phone an hour early and you'll often reach someone to take your order.

Don't call only the 800 number listed in ads. Call the local number, too. Local agents often have tickets when national agents don't.

Also, call on the day of the event or, better yet, show up at the box office. A few tickets may have been returned.

• **Buy a season ticket.** Most season ticket holders for sports events, theatrical productions, symphonies, etc., are offered the opportunity to buy additional tickets to postseason events and play-off games. If you don't want to buy a season ticket yourself, split the cost with a friend and take turns attending.

See New Movies for Less

Ask your human resources director whether your employer offers a corporate program with a movie theater company—you might be able to get discounted tickets. If you're self-employed, see whether your home business can get in on a corporate purchase plan by becoming a member of the National Association for the Self-Employed. You may have to buy tickets in bulk, but if you see movies frequently, you will save money.

Also: Go to the movies before 5 pm, when most theaters offer matinee tickets for up to half off the full ticket price.

ConsumerSavvyTips.org, on-line consumer advice and tips to help save money.

Insider's Guide to Playing Slot Machines

Frank Legato, a founding editor of *StrictlySlots* magazine, 8025 Black Horse Pike, Pleasantville, NJ 08232. Author of *How to Win Millions Playing Slot Machines!…Or Lose Trying* (Bonus Books), Mr. Legato is also senior editor of *Global Gaming Business* magazine, 6625 S. Valley View, Las Vegas, NV 89118.

Josephine Crawford of Galloway Township, New Jersey, didn't believe the casino employee when he told her that she had just won $10 million. But when bells kept ringing and people gathered around her, the 84-year-old former waitress soon realized that the employee at Harrah's Atlantic City was right. Her bet on the Megabucks nickel slot had paid off.

The odds are infinitesimal that you'll ever duplicate Ms. Crawford's success at the slots, but you can still have lots of fun. And who knows? You just might get as lucky as she was—especially if you know the inside tricks to playing slot machines.

Besides, playing slot machines requires little or no skill. You can play at your own pace and bet as little or as much as you want. *What you need to know…*

THE ODDS

Casinos try to take your mind off the odds. They introduce a constant stream of new slot games and offer eye-catching jackpots, such as new cars displayed on turntables in full view of the machines.

Regardless of the enticements, the majority of slot machines give an edge of 1% to 10% to the house, a term used for the owner of the machine, whether it's a casino or a convenience store in Nevada. This means that most slot players "win" back only 90 cents to 99 cents of every dollar they play.

These payback rates are calculated over the long run, which can be many thousands of games. So don't be misled when you see a player win several times during an hour's play at a particular machine. There eventually will be enough losses to bring the odds back in the house's favor. And you never know when those losses will occur.

The more it costs to play a slot, the higher the payback rate usually is. Games that cost $5 or $10, for example, might pay back 99%, while a nickel game often returns no more than 90% and penny games pay even less.

Caution: Slot games on the Internet are becoming popular.

My advice: Stay away from all Internet slots. They're illegal to play in the US, and there's no way of knowing what the payback rate is.

Also, keep in mind that even the best odds at slots aren't as good as the odds with other games, such as blackjack, that require skill, concentration and a good memory.

IMPROVING YOUR CHANCES

The best slot machine odds are in Las Vegas—but not on the city's famous Strip. Casinos on the Strip—including Bally's, the Mirage, the Stardust and the Tropicana—don't need player-friendly slots because they enjoy a steady stream of tourists. The payback on 25-cent machines at Strip casinos is 93% or 94%, and on dollar games, it's 95% or 96%.

Casinos off the Strip rely more on local residents who demand the incentive of better odds to play the slots. That's particularly true in the suburbs of Henderson and in North Las Vegas, where the payback at such casinos as Sunset Station, Fiesta Station and Green Valley Ranch is one or two percentage points higher than it is on the Strip.

In Atlantic City, the nickel slots usually have a payback rate of only 90%, while 91% or 92% is typical for quarter games and 94% for dollar slots. Casinos elsewhere in the country have similar payback rates.

Slots at most casinos pay out bonuses to players who bet two or three coins at a time.

Example: If you put one quarter in a classic Double Diamond slot and three "wild" symbols come up, you'll win 1,000 quarters. But if you bet three quarters and the same symbols line up, you will win 15,000 quarters—15 times the payback for three times the bet. Each slot machine has a written explanation of its winning combinations and prize amounts for various sizes of bets.

Today, video slots are popular, and they have the same payback rates as traditional mechanical machines, known as reel slots.

Some of the worst paybacks are at Nevada's airports and convenience stores, where the payback rate can be as low as 75%.

To find slots with the best payback rates, look at one of the gaming publications that regularly report on them. Two magazines with monthly payback reports are *CasinoPlayer* (800-969-0711 or *www.casinoplayer.com*) and *StrictlySlots* (800-969-0711 or *www.strictlyslots.com*).

In any one casino, all slots that cost the same usually have the same payback rate, regardless of the particular slot game that is featured on the machine.

Example: If you put $1 in a Blazing 7s slot machine, you'll get the same payback rate as you would by putting $1 in a machine that features Tabasco, another popular game.

Nevertheless, many players believe that some games are luckier than others, and *StrictlySlots* regularly polls players to find out which games have that reputation (see the next page). Do be aware, however, that these polls are based on anecdotal evidence, and there are no statistical data to back them up.

Biggest game in town: Progressive slots, a game where machines are connected to one another and the jackpot rises as more people play. A huge overhead meter lets players keep track of the jackpot, which has reached more than $20 million in some cases. Two of the most popular wide-area progressive slots are Quartermania and Megabucks.

While prizes continue to rise, the odds of winning them remain long—very long. Ms. Crawford, for instance, was playing the nickel Megabucks slot, where the odds of winning the jackpot are about one in 40 million.

Important: To win the top prize, you must put the maximum number of coins in the slot, usually three. If Ms. Crawford had been playing with fewer coins, she would have won a few thousand dollars instead of $10 million.

MAKE THE SLOTS MORE FUN

Set a limit on how much to wager during any one session at the machines. Then cease playing when you've reached your limit or—if luck is with you—when you've won more than the amount you started with.

This exercise in self-discipline makes sense because no matter how long you play the slots, you are likely to lose many more games than you win. By quitting when you're ahead, you'll avoid the risk of a losing streak that takes away your winnings. Remember that the odds always favor the house. If you play long enough, you're certain to lose more money than you win.

Guidelines to establish a spending limit:
At 10 spins a minute, it costs about $9 an hour to play a nickel machine with a three-coin maximum. A quarter machine would cost about $45 an hour and a dollar machine $180 an hour.

If setting a limit is hard to do, remember Ms. Crawford. On the day she won, she had set a limit of $40 for the session and was down to her last $5. But if she had gone over her limit on the previous day, she might never have played on the day she struck it rich.

More from Frank Legato...

Most Winning Slots

When *StrictlySlots* asked readers to name the reel slot games where they experienced the most success, they listed...

- **Double Diamond**
- **Red White & Blue**
- **Wheel of Fortune**
- **Triple Diamond**
- **Blazing 7s**

Video slots considered the luckiest...
- **Cleopatra**
- **Jackpot Party**
- **Reel 'Em In**
- **Wheel of Fortune**

Gamble for Free

Max Rubin (*www.maxrubin.net*), professional gambler and a member of the Blackjack Hall of Fame. A previous casino executive, Mr. Rubin is the expert analyst on CBS's *Ultimate Blackjack Tour*. He has also been featured on the Travel Channel's *The Pro's Guide to Vegas*, and is the author of *Comp City: A Guide to Free Casino Vacations* (Huntington).

Is it possible to win every time you gamble? Yes—if you play for comps, the more than $1 billion worth of favors that casinos give away every year. Even if you lose at a gaming table, you can get back more than you spend in the form of gratis drinks, meals, entertainment, etc.

Comps (short for complimentaries) occur on two levels. There are classic comps—cocktails, parking and other low-end giveaways—available to just about everyone who gambles.

Better: Premium comps—tickets to shows, limo rides and rooms and meals—are given only to qualified players. While comps are available no matter what kind of game you play, blackjack is the only game where you will get back more than you are likely to lose. People who know how to take advantage of these rewards can get the equivalent of a free vacation with little or no risk.

You do not have to be a skilled gambler to come out ahead.

Why: In blackjack, the casino wins, on average, about 2% of every dollar that's bet. This means that an average player betting $5 a hand probably loses about $5 an hour over time. If you drink two complimentary cocktails (which would normally cost at least $5 each) during that time (and don't make boneheaded playing decisions), you earn twice as much as you spend.

GET RATED TO GET COMPS

Most comps are based on a player's *rating*—a formula that predicts the casino's potential to win that gambler's money. The way comp systems are set up, a casino typically plans to give back in comps about 30% of what it expects to win.

Most casinos use the same basic formula—the average bet multiplied by the hours played multiplied by the house advantage—to determine a player's rating.

Example: A player who makes an average bet of $100 in blackjack and plays for one hour (about 60 hands) will be expected to lose $120…and will be given a rating that provides the equivalent of about $36 in comps.

Important: Request your free card for the VIP club, something every casino has, though the name may differ. It's the first step to getting rated. Once you have the card, show it to the casino supervisor (floorman) when you sit down at the blackjack table. He/she will write down your name, how many chips you bought and how much you're betting per hand on a rating ticket. When you leave, the amount that you won or lost will also be recorded. This goes to the casino's marketing department, which decides what kinds of freebies you're entitled to.

TO GET MORE

Players can manipulate their ratings by making the casino think that they're spending more money than they actually are. Suppose you are playing blackjack and the casino thinks you're betting $100 a hand 60 times an hour…when in fact you're only betting $40 a hand for about 45 hands. On average, you'll be losing about $36 an hour—but could be getting back $36 an hour in comps! *How to boost your rating…*

• **Get noticed.** The floormen are authorized to give small comps even to unrated players, and their supervisors (the pit bosses) can give comps for rooms and for more expensive restaurants. But first, you have to get their attention.

How: Buy in for a few hundred dollars when you sit down at the blackjack table. The dealer will notify the floorman, who has to OK all buy-ins over $100. When the pit boss looks your way, call him over and ask for a drink—even if you don't really want one. Ordering a drink really lets him know you're there.

Important: Make your largest bets when you see that the floorman is watching you. When he's not, bet the table minimum (to keep your overall wagering down). After you have been playing for an hour, make another large bet or two—then ask the pit boss to buy you a meal. Just say, "May I have two tickets to the buffet or coffee shop, please?"

• **Play the busiest tables.** To maximize comps while minimizing losses, play slowly. The fewer hands you play, the less money you're likely to lose. A blackjack dealer can deal up to 250 hands per hour to a single player. At a busy table, he might deal as few as 50 hands per hour.

Best: Look for a table with six other players —preferably a friendly table where people (including the dealer) are telling jokes and laughing. Delay as often as possible—but do not be obvious. Show your hand to other players and ask how they'd play it…sit out a hand now and then…and take your time when it's your turn to cut the cards. All this lets you play fewer hands, but still log plenty of gambling time—an important key to comps.

• **Coast during boss breaks.** Pit bosses take two 20- to 30-minute breaks during an eight-hour shift, and a longer break for lunch or dinner. You can pad your rating (gambling less than the bosses think) by scaling back to the table minimum while the boss's relief is on the floor, then increasing your bets when the boss returns.

This way, you could have an actual gambling average of $25 an hour, but an "official" average of $150. If you do the above once during every shift you play, you'll increase your comp rating while reducing the risk of losses.

• **Look like a loser.** Casinos like losers—and give them better ratings/comps. Even if you're a winner, you want to look like you're losing. The only way to do this is to hide chips. Casinos frown on this (it raises suspicions of cheating), but the fewer chips you have on the table after you've been gambling awhile, the more generous the bosses are likely to be with perks.

Try this: Cup your hand over a stack of chips …squeeze one or two in your palm…and casually drop them into an inside jacket pocket while pulling out a mint. A woman can drop chips into an open purse in her lap.

• **Play with a partner.** Some casinos will combine two people on a single VIP card. This allows you to buy in with more front money— one of the keys to better comps. When you play together, the floorman will credit both bets on one rating slip, giving you a higher rating and more freebies.

• **Ask for what you want.** Many people are too embarrassed to ask for a free meal, a discount on a room, a suite upgrade or other comps. When playing any game in a casino, never hesitate to ask the boss for free drinks or other amenities. If he says no, ask how much more you need to be betting to qualify for additional comps. More often, you'll be given something, even if it's not exactly what you're asking for.

Example: You ask for an unlimited coffee shop comp—you get two buffet tickets.

Important: Always be friendly—and tip often. Even if you're only handing out the occasional dollar (or chip) to the dealer, you'll stand out for your attitude, which will translate into better comps.

Strategies: Tip when the boss is watching. People who seem to be big spenders get better ratings. Or, make a bet for the dealer on your first bet. He'll be more likely to say something positive when the boss later asks about your average bet.

Casino Savvy

To get freebies and discounts at casinos, don't hop from casino to casino. If you spend your gambling budget at one casino, you're more likely to get comps. Casinos give about 25% of their gross revenue back to gamblers in this manner.

Examples: Put $1,000 into play and you could earn a free lunch at the coffee shop…put $10,000 into play and you could be awarded a free room.

But don't ask the dealer for comps. Instead, ask the floor manager who has been observing your play or a casino host.

Richard Armstrong, Washington, DC–based author of *Get Paid to Gamble: The Inside Story of Casino Complimentaries* (Slot Detector Co.). To get a free instant PDF download of his 55-page e-book, go to *www.goddoesnt shootcraps.com.*

Host a Terrific Holiday Open House: Tricks From a Party Planner

Denise Vivaldo, a party planner and consultant in Los Angeles for 20 years, and also the author of *Do It for Less! Parties* (Terrace). Her company, Food Fanatics, provides food-styling services for Hollywood television shows and movies. Go to *www.diflparties.com* or *www.foodfanatics. net* for more information.

A holiday open house is a great way to entertain without spending a lot of time and money. *Here, a longtime professional party planner reveals her secrets…*

SMART SCHEDULING

•**Opt for the third weekend of December.** This tends to be best for holiday parties—the first two weekends are usually overbooked with competing parties, and the fourth weekend falls too close to Christmas. Your holiday decorations should be up by the third weekend of the month, which means less time decorating for the party.

A late Sunday afternoon open house, maybe from 2 pm to 5 pm, will cause fewer conflicts than one on Friday or Saturday evening. Sunday night is not a wise choice, because guests will fret about getting up for work on Monday.

Schedule three to four hours for the open house—anything longer and you'll be exhausted by the end.

•**Send out invitations three weeks in advance.** Provide details about your open house on the invitation. Is dress casual or fancy? What food will be served? (You could specify, "Hors d'oeuvres and drinks" on your invitation.) Are kids welcome? Should guests skip a gift? Where should they park? If there's an important game the day of your party, your invitation should reassure sports fans that the game will be shown, perhaps in a side room. Also, ask guests to let you know in advance if they have special dietary needs so that you can adjust your menu accordingly.

Helpful: If your friends are Internet savvy, you can e-mail invitations and track responses for free at Evite.com.

FOOD

In addition to cheese and fruit plates or crudités with dip, provide at least one hearty hors d'oeuvre. Beef or chicken satay is usually a big hit at parties. Or you can opt for the traditional sliced, roasted turkey breast or ham, with rolls, mayo, Dijon mustard and other fixings for do-it-yourself sandwiches.

Hot foods are a challenge at open houses because they won't stay hot for long, but meatballs and cheese fondue (served with cubes of French bread) are two hot dishes that typically hold up well in chafing dishes. Think twice about serving other hot foods that force you to run back and forth to the oven every few minutes.

DRINK

You don't need to provide a full bar at an open house, but do have a number of drink options—not everyone likes eggnog. Provide beer, wine, sparkling water, soda and perhaps a pitcher of a popular mixed drink, such as cosmopolitans or mojitos. Cold beverages should be set out in ice-filled tubs or coolers so your guests don't have to open your refrigerator every time they're thirsty.

If some of your guests are big drinkers, ask a friend to serve as the designated driver to get inebriated guests home safely…keep the phone number of a cab company handy…or hire a pair of responsible teenagers from your neighborhood to be on call as drivers—one to drive the guest's car home, the other to follow in his/her own car for the trip back. You could be liable if a guest has an accident after drinking alcohol at your home.

TROUBLESHOOTING

• **Make sure you have enough plates and glasses.** Open houses often run short of glasses and hors d'oeuvre plates—one guest can go through four or five of each. Rent extra plates and glasses, or buy quality plastic ones.

• **Prevent used plates and glasses from piling up all over** by putting a large tray near the kitchen. Place one or two dirty dishes on it before guests arrive so they can tell that it's the busing station. You might have to clear the tray several times.

• **Do not overdo the cleaning.** Turn down the lights, and bring out the candles. (Use hurricane candle shades to reduce risk of fire.) No one will notice the floors weren't scrubbed.

• **Spread thick, clear rug-runner plastic by the door** for guests to leave wet boots and umbrellas. You might even buy a few dozen pairs of thick socks and ask your guests to leave their shoes by the door and help themselves to your holiday gift of a pair of socks.

 # When Guests Stay Too Long

Even the best of parties have to end sometime—but some guests just don't take the hint when it is time to leave. If starting to clean up and other tricks don't work, it is OK to let guests know that the party is winding down.

Tell them that you have had a nice time but that you have to get up early the next day. Or say, "I have to 'close down' in 15 minutes," which allows them to depart in a relaxed fashion.

For house guests who stay too long: Define the length of their stay from the beginning. If you haven't done that and you are ready for guests to leave, tell them, "I have enjoyed your visit, but I must return to my regular schedule." Offer a farewell breakfast as a send-off.

Peggy Post, the great-granddaughter-in-law of etiquette pioneer Emily Post and spokesperson, Emily Post Institute, Burlington, VT, *www.emilypost.com*. Her latest book is *Excuse Me, But I Was Next: How to Handle the Top 100 Manners Dilemmas* (Collins).

The Secret to Improving Your Golf Swing

Michael Yessis, PhD, professor emeritus of kinesiology at California State University in Fullerton, and president of Sports Training, Inc., a sports fitness and consulting company in Escondido, CA, *www.dryessis.com*. He is author of several books on sports training, including *Sports: Is It All B.S.? Dr. Yessis Blows the Whistle on Player Development* (Equilibrium) and *Explosive Golf: Using the Science of Kinesiology to Improve Your Swing* (McGraw-Hill).

Golf pros and golf magazines are filled with suggestions for improving one's swing, but sports fitness consultant Michael Yessis, PhD, believes some of the most common advice is wrong. He has studied the golf swing, using high-speed photography, to determine what works and what doesn't.

Here are six common myths...

Myth 1: The backswing is the key to your swing.

Reality: The backswing means less than most people believe. Golf instructors harp on the backswing simply because it is the only part of the swing that is slow enough for them to follow, but as long as your backswing is consistent, comfortable and gets you to a starting point that lets you generate power, its fine details are not a problem. Instead, focus on your down swing—that is where you will achieve both your power and accuracy.

Myth 2: Hands and arms should start your downswing.

Reality: If your hands and arms are leading your downswing, you are sacrificing a tremendous amount of power. Your downswing should begin with a forward weight shift of the hips, followed by hip rotation. Only when hip rotation is nearly concluded should the shoulder rotation even begin, starting the hands in motion. By rotating the hips before the shoulders (and arms and hands) start to move, you stretch the abdominal oblique muscles so that they can contract with greater force when your upper body does come through.

Even throughout the shoulder rotation, your hands should be following the shoulders, not driving the action. Only when shoulder rotation is virtually done should your hands and arms be powering the swing.

Bottom line: Think of your swing as a step-by-step process of transferring force from your midbody up to your shoulders and only then to your arms and hands and then onto your club.

Myth 3: You'll get more power if you drive your knee forward during your swing.

Reality: You'll get more power if you drive your hips forward and let your knee and leg naturally follow them forward as a result. The heavier the body part, the greater the power it can convey to your club head. Shifting your hips will transfer a lot more weight and power than shifting your knee.

Myth 4: Wrist break happens naturally during a good swing.

Reality: Golf instructors say it's natural because it feels natural to them. For many amateur golfers, wrist break doesn't automatically happen at the proper moment. The wrists should break as the club head nears the ball.

Myth 5: A slice is the result of an outside-inside swing.

Reality: Outside-inside swings—which loop out and then back in again—are very uncommon. If you actually did swing this way, you would be off-balance and falling backward. It's far more likely that your slice is the result of striking the ball with an open clubface—when the club head strikes the ball at an oblique angle rather than a square angle—probably because of weak wrist break or arm action.

Exercise: You can improve your wrist and arm action by improving your wrist and arm strength. Attach a 2.5- to five-pound weight to one end of a short bar, such as a dumbbell bar. Stand normally with your arms at your sides and your palms facing your legs, holding the bar in one hand with the weighted end extending behind you. Without moving your arm, turn your wrist to lift the weight (and your little finger) up toward the side of your forearm, then ease it back down and repeat.

Perform this exercise with each wrist for a few weeks, and you just might finally cure your slice.

Myth 6: The longest hitters in driving competitions stand up very straight, so you should stand up straighter, too.

Reality: Stand up straight, and you will have trouble keeping your eye on the ball, triggering frequent mishits. The competitors in driving competitions are willing to sacrifice their accuracy and consistency for distance. However, in all other circumstances, it's smarter to lean over the ball.

Helpful: Lean from the hips, not from the waist. Your drives will be longer and your back healthier if your spine is straight, in its normal, slightly arched lumbar curvature, during your swing. This might feel uncomfortable at first, but stay with it and you'll get used to it.

A Beautiful Garden In No Time!

Barbara Pleasant, contributing editor to *The Herb Companion* magazine, *www.herbcompanion.com*. She is also author of more than a dozen gardening books, including *Easy Garden Projects to Make, Build, and Grow* (Rodale). She lives in Asheville, NC, *www.barbarapleasant.com*.

A garden full of flowers and vegetables might seem like a fun idea in the spring, but by the dog days of summer, some gardeners wish they hadn't made the commitment. They are either too busy for a garden or they desire to spend sunny days relaxing, not pulling up weeds. *Here, timesaving shortcuts...*

EASY GARDEN PLANTS

Most gardeners grow the flowers they consider the most beautiful and the vegetables they consider the tastiest. But if you want your garden to be easy, figure in how much effort particular plants require. *Low-maintenance plants...*

• **Easy annuals.** Time-conscious gardeners often plant perennials reasoning that once the plants are in the ground, they'll come back every year on their own. But, well-chosen annuals are better. Easy-to-grow annuals include begonias, impatiens, marigolds and petunias.

While perennials bloom for only a month or so every season, these annuals can bloom all summer. Purchase annuals as plants rather than as seeds for faster results.

• **Tomatoes.** Tomatoes are easy to grow—just select a variety that is resistant to the diseases and insects common in your area. Call your local agricultural extension office, and ask which tomatoes it recommends.

• **Knock Out Roses.** Roses can be extremely difficult to grow, but Conard-Pyle's Knock Out Roses (*www.knockoutroses.com*) are as easy as possible. They're resistant to the diseases and insects that make most roses challenging.

Downside: They're not fragrant.

• **Native plants.** The easiest plants to grow in your garden are invariably those that grow native to your region. The Web site of the not-for-profit organization Wild Ones (877-394-9453 or *www.for-wild.org*) includes links to regional native plant societies that can help you determine which native plants might be most appropriate for your garden. The biology department at the local university also might be able to guide you.

PROVEN STRATEGIES

• **Add a thick layer of compost to your garden before you plant.** The many nutrients in compost create stronger, healthier plants that are better able to protect themselves against the diseases and insects. Obtain enough compost to cover your garden with a layer two inches thick, then mix the compost with your soil to a depth of around four inches.

Helpful: The brand that feels the softest and spongiest has the most organic material.

• **Snake a "soaker hose" through your garden,** and let it "weep" water from its tiny holes to your plants at a slow, steady pace for a few hours a day. This saves you from having to water by hand or move a sprinkler around your garden. (Bury the hose about an inch or two beneath soil if you want.) Every few days, dig your fingers into the soil to confirm that it's moist but not wet.

Helpful: It's normal for plants to look a bit wilted in the middle of a hot summer day. If they look wilted at night or in the morning, they need more water.

• **Try rollout paper mulch.** Nature does not like bare soil. As soon as you clear some land, weeds will appear and compete with your plants for water, sunlight and soil nutrients. Any type of mulch keeps moisture in and weeds out, but rollout paper mulch is probably the easiest way to apply it. Just put this paper down over your cleared garden, and cut holes for your plants.

• **Don't worry about bugs.** Some gardeners spend long hours applying insecticides or removing pests by hand. Don't bother. I find that in a battle with bugs, the bugs usually win. Fortunately, most insects are beneficial to plants, and those that do cause problems tend to harm only one plant species. Grow a wide variety of plants, and if the insects claim one or two, eliminate those plants the next year.

• **Use large pots for container gardening.** The soil in small pots dries out very fast on hot days. Large pots retain more moisture, so you won't have to water as often.

Better Digital Photos

Scott Kelby, president, National Association of Photoshop Professionals...training director, Adobe Photoshop Seminar Tour...and editor in chief, *Photoshop User* magazine, Tampa Bay, FL. He is author of *The Digital Photography Book* (Peachpit). More at *www.scottkelby.com*.

You don't need an expensive camera to take digital photos like a pro. *You just need a few tricks...*

●**Avoid using your camera's LCD screen to take your shot.** You have to hold the camera away from your face to do this, and that often leads to shaky hands and blurry shots. If your digital camera has an optical viewfinder, use that, so you can brace the camera against your face. If you must use the LCD screen, buy a camera with image stabilization (also called "vibration reduction" or "antishake").

For even greater image sharpness, use a tripod. You also can set the camera to shoot on a two-to-three-second delay, to eliminate any shake caused by pushing the shutter button.

●**Avoid shooting subjects in direct sunlight which washes out colors,** creates unflattering shadows and makes subjects squint. The best light of all will be at the very edge of a shaded area—close to, but not in, the sun.

●**Evaluate shots on your LCD screen before subjects walk away.** Digital cameras let you instantly view your pictures. Ask everyone to stay put while you make sure they all look good.

●**Set the camera to "cloudy" for outdoor shots**—even on sunny days. The cloudy setting adds richness and warmth to outdoor photos.

●**Think off-center.** Position your subject toward the left or right of the picture, not in the middle. The horizon line in a landscape should be either one-third or two-thirds of the way up, not across the dead center of the picture. Pick one-third up if the sky or backdrop is beautiful, two-thirds if the foreground is more appealing.

●**Try different angles.** Lie on the ground to take a picture of a flower from the flower's height. Take a picture of a building up its side, rather than straight on.

●**Position your subjects' eyes about one-third down from the top of the frame.** This is an old trick used to create portraits with better balance. In a close-up, that might mean losing the top of the head or some hair—which is acceptable—but avoid cutting off the chin.

●**Take all landscape photos during the "magic hours."** The most beautiful light is usually during the 30 minutes before sunset until 30 minutes after sunset...and during the 15 minutes before sunrise until 30 minutes after sunrise.

Real-Time Answers

Librarians from participating institutions nationwide offer free question-and-answer sessions on any subject 24/7 at *www.massanswers.org*. This saves a trip to the library and is helpful if your Web searches aren't finding the answers.

Real Simple, 1271 Avenue of the Americas, New York City 10020.

Greetings from the White House

The White House will send greetings signed by the president to US citizens who are celebrating their 50th wedding anniversary and beyond...80th birthday and beyond...weddings... and other types of special occasions. Requests should include the name, title (Ms., Dr., etc.) and address of the honoree(s)...the name and daytime phone number of the individual making the request...month, day and year of the special occasion...recipient's age (for birthdays) ...number of years married (for anniversaries).

Send requests at least six weeks before the event. Mail to White House, Attn.: Greetings Office, Washington, DC 20502-0039...fax them to the White House Greetings Office at 202-395-1232 ...or send them on-line through the Web site *www.whitehouse.gov/greeting* (click the second "Guidelines" under "Invitations and Greetings").

16

On the Move

Buying a Car? Avoid the Latest Dealer Rip-Offs

Some auto dealerships do sell cars at fair prices and provide good service, but some others are always thinking up ways to take advantage of car buyers. *Among the latest rip-offs...*

MANDATORY ARBITRATION AGREEMENTS

After you have agreed to all terms, the salesperson insists that you sign a "Dispute Resolution" or "Conflict Resolution" agreement. This says that if a problem develops, you will settle through arbitration, not take the dealership to court. Sounds reasonable—unless you bother to read the fine print. The agreement may stipulate that the car dealer chooses an arbiter...you pay the fee...you can't appeal the decision, but the dealership can...and you can't participate in class-action lawsuits against the dealer.

Strategy: Before you begin to negotiate, ask a salesperson if the dealership requires an arbi-

tration agreement. If so, shop elsewhere. Many dealerships that require these agreements are disreputable ones that would face frequent lawsuits without them.

SPOT DELIVERY

You have decided on a vehicle and filled out an application with the dealers's finance department. Though your loan hasn't been officially approved, you are told you can drive the car home. A few days later, the dealership calls and says that you were not approved for a loan at the interest rate discussed. Instead, you were approved for a loan at a higher rate. This means that your new car might cost you thousands more than you expected over the life of the loan.

If you try to call off the deal, the dealership claims it has already sold your trade-in model, so there is no going back. If you didn't have a trade-in to begin with, your dealership might threaten to sue you if you do not agree to the

Remar Sutton, president and cofounder of the nonprofit Consumer Task Force for Automotive Issues in Atlanta, www.autoissues.org. He is also author of Don't Get Taken Every Time (Penguin).

new terms. *You have no recourse*—buried in the fine print of the loan agreement is something called a "writ of rescission." You unknowingly agreed to pay a higher interest rate if you failed to qualify for the loan at the agreed-upon rate.

Strategy: Don't sign any application containing a writ of rescission, and don't agree to take delivery of your new vehicle until the dealership approves your loan. Better yet, get a loan from a credit union or bank. You'll probably get a better rate, and you'll certainly have fewer worries about unethical practices.

"ENVIRONMENTAL" FEES

After you have settled on a price, the salesperson or finance manager hands you a contract containing additional charges that hadn't been previously mentioned. Among them is an "environmental fee." When questioned, a salesperson might imply that it is a government charge that cannot be avoided. In truth, it is just the latest made-up fee that dealerships invented to coax a few extra dollars out of car buyers. Other common rip-offs include "protection packages," with unneeded rustproofing...fabric treatment...and overpriced extended warranties. An advertising fee may even be added on—although the cost of advertising beyond the amount included in the invoice price is the car dealership's problem, not your problem.

Strategy: Refuse to sign. If the salesperson does not back down, walk out.

"ZERO, ZERO, ZERO" DEALS

A dealership advertises what sounds like a great offer—nothing down, no interest, no payments in the first year. What the "zero, zero, zero" ads don't say is that very few buyers ever qualify for these offers. The rest must pay some interest, and once interest is added to the mix, the deals suddenly become unattractive. You pay nothing for a full year, but interest still compounds on the full purchase price. You could wind up owing more than your vehicle is worth.

Strategy: If the "zero, zero, zero" offer is what you want, get preapproved for a loan at your credit union or bank. That way, a car salesperson will be hard-pressed to show that your credit isn't strong enough to qualify for the offer that's being made.

How to Test-Drive Without the Salesperson

Do you want to test-drive a new car without the salesperson in the car? Convince him/her that you are a serious buyer. Explain why you like that specific car and what competing models you're considering. Also be prepared to show your driver's license, explain where you work and give your phone number.

If the dealership limits test-drives to one specific route with the salesperson in the car, take that drive—then, when you return, explain that you like the car and would like to drive it again alone. If considering an expensive or exotic car, visit the dealership first and expect to return another day for a test-drive.

Consensus of car salespeople and dealership managers, reported in Car and Driver.

New Car Model Woes

There typically are far more problems with reliability during the first year of a new or completely redesigned car model than there are for older models or later years of new models.

Best: Wait at least one year, preferably two, to buy a new or redesigned car model. When searching for used cars, buy models that were in production for at least two years when they were new.

To research a model: *www.edmunds.com.*
Consumer Reports, 101 Truman Ave., Yonkers, NY.

New-Car Loan vs. Home-Equity Loan

Generally speaking, the interest on a home-equity loan is lower than on car loans. Also beneficial is the fact that the home-equity loan interest is tax deductible—even for a personal-use car.

Your accountant can help you determine if you should use a home-equity or new-car loan for a new car. But first go to *www.dinkytown. net*, a site that specializes in financial calculators, such as for calculating mortgages, paying down debt, etc. Under "Auto Calculators" click on "Auto Loan vs. Home Equity Loan." The information you need to run this calculation will be the same as that required by an accountant. It includes the amount and length of the loan and the interest rate, your federal tax rate, the amount of any cash down payment, the amount you will receive if you are trading in a vehicle, the amount you still owe on any trade-in, the fee for title transfer and your state's sales tax.

Nancy Dunnan, a New York City–based financial and travel adviser and the author or coauthor of 25 books, including the best seller, *How to Invest $50–$5,000* (Collins).

Check Vehicle History Reports

Vehicle history reports for used cars, which document accident and repair records, are becoming increasingly popular among used-car buyers. They are even more important now after the widespread flooding caused by Katrina and other Gulf Coast storms damaged large numbers of cars that could be in the used-car market today. About 30% of manufacturer franchise dealers now provide history reports at no charge to potential buyers of used cars.

Jane Crane, director, automotive retail research, J.D. Power and Associates, 2625 Townsgate Rd., Westlake Village, CA 91361, *www.jdpower.com*.

Don't Get Overcharged When a Car Lease Is Up

Eric Peters, a Washington, DC–based automotive columnist and author of *Automotive Atrocities! The Cars We Love to Hate* (MBI).

Most car leases stipulate that the customer is responsible for any damage to the vehicle beyond "normal wear and tear."

When it is time for you to turn in a vehicle at the end of the lease, the lessor/dealer may charge you the full "retail" price of any repairs, even if he/she pays less than that to have them done. It may be cheaper for you to have any minor damage repaired yourself before you turn in the vehicle. *What to do...*

• **Get estimates from two or three body shops and/or detailing centers.** Get at least one estimate from a new-car dealer that sells your type of car. This will give you an idea of what the lease issuer would charge you. It's best not to check with your dealership—that alerts the lessor that your car has damage.

If an independent shop offers to fix the damage for significantly less than a dealer's price, it may be smart to go ahead and have the work done there.

• **Use a competent repair shop.** Turning in a leased auto with a shoddy repair (such as a repainted fender that doesn't match the rest of the car) is usually worse than just giving the car back without repairing it. You will have paid the repair shop and are likely to be charged by the dealer to have the car fixed properly. Check any shop you're considering with the Better Business Bureau (703-276-0100, *www.bbb.org*) and the Department of Consumer/Regulatory Affairs in your city/county (look this up in your phone book's business pages). Also, ask acquaintances for referrals.

• **Don't file a claim with your auto insurer for lease-end cosmetic work.** You may be tagged as a higher insurance risk and be subject to higher premiums.

More from Eric Peters...

When Is It Time to Dump Your Old Car?

Virtually all new cars—with the exception of a few exotics—begin to lose value as soon as they are driven off the dealer's lot. But after the initial first-year hit—when a car might lose 25% or more of its sticker price value—the depreciation slide slows. Then, typically, the vehicle's value starts to take another steep plunge after five or six years—or 50,000 to 60,000 miles—even though most modern vehicles still run reliably for another five or six years and 50,000 to 60,000 miles (or more).

Bottom line: Even though there might be nothing wrong with the vehicle, if you want to get top dollar on it as a trade-in or resale, you should be thinking about "retiring" it sometime before it reaches the five-year mark—and before it exceeds 50,000 miles.

Also from Eric Peters...

Surprising Way to Save on Gas

Fuel efficiency for diesels is comparable to that for gas-electric hybrids—and, on average, diesel cars cost less, are less technologically complex and last longer than gas-powered cars. Only a few diesel passenger vehicles are available for sale in the US—the 2008 Mercedes-Benz BLUETEC and the 2007 Jeep Grand Cherokee CRD—but more are coming soon.

Smart Ways to Save at the Pump

TravelSmart, Box 397, Dobbs Ferry, NY 10522, *www.travelsmartnewsletter.com*.

With gasoline prices soaring to more than $3 a gallon in many parts of the US, it is more important than ever to save on fuel.

Most people know not to use higher-octane fuel than their cars require and to keep their cars tuned up and tires inflated.

Here are other money-saving ideas that you might not have thought of...

- **Check the gauge.** When the tank is half empty, start looking for a gas station. This gives you time to comparison shop. Avoid interstate and highway stations—gas on major highways often costs 10 to 15 cents more per gallon than the same brand and grade in less trafficked areas. You can find the lowest gas prices in your area on the Web at *www.gaspricewatch.com* and *www.gasbuddy.com*.

- **Buy big-box gas.** Wholesale clubs sell gas at member-only pumps for 10 cents per gallon less than regular stations.* To find a station, go to the club's Web site—BJ's (*www.bjs.com*, click on "Gas & Propane"), Costco (*www.costco.com*, type "Gas Stations" in the search box).

- **Get a gas card.** The Visa card cosponsored by AAA gives you back 2% to 5% on purchases made at the pump (no annual fee, 800-551-0839, *www.aaa.com*). Pay your credit card bill in full each month so that interest costs don't wipe out the savings.

- **Don't let your car idle.** If you're going to be at a standstill for more than a minute, turn off the engine. Idling consumes up to one gallon of gas per hour. It also wastes more gas than restarting the engine.

- **Drive strategically.** Combine your errands to avoid extra trips. Use cruise control, it will cut down on gas and speeding tickets. Don't slam on the brakes or accelerate rapidly—this kind of driving lowers gas mileage by about 30%.

- **Slow down.** When you drive 75 miles per hour instead of 65, you waste about 30 cents a gallon.

- **When renting a car, choose the model that gets the best gas mileage.** The diesel versions of Volkswagen's Golf and New Beetle get about 44 miles per gallon (MPG) on the highway. The Toyota Corolla gets about 41 MPG.

To compare fuel economy among cars: *www.fueleconomy.gov*.

*Prices and offers subject to change.

Save Money at Gas Stations

Before your next fill-up, be sure to read these helpful tips...

- **Don't use your debit card.** Some gas stations require banks to automatically set aside $50 or $100 for each purchase to make sure that the customer has the funds to cover them—you may not have access to that money for up to three days.

• **Don't use gasoline credit cards.** Their annual percentage rates often are high, and many don't offer rebates on gas purchases. Check out GasPriceWatch.com and GasBuddy.com regularly to find the best gas prices in your area.

• **Don't shop at gas station convenience stores**—most inventory is vastly overpriced, although some high-volume goods, such as cigarettes, beer and coffee, could be competitively priced.

SmartMoney, 1755 Broadway, New York City 10019.

To Improve Fuel Economy…

Replacing a car's dirty air filter can improve fuel economy by up to 10%.

Carmakers' recommendation: Change the filter annually or every 12,000 miles if you tend to drive over dusty roads…every two years or 24,000 miles for normal conditions.

Car & Travel, 1415 Kellum Place, Garden City, NY 11530. Free to members of Automobile Club of America.

More Ways to Save on Gas

David Solomon, a certified master auto technician and chairman, MotorWatch, Box 123, Butler, MD 21023, *www. motorwatch.com.*

We're not done yet! Here are four more great ways to save on gas from the chairman of MotorWatch…

• **Change to 100% synthetic oil.** This will also extend your vehicle's oil change interval by 25% to 50%.

Gain in miles per gallon (MPG): 10%.

Best: Redline, 800-624-7958, *www.redlineoil. com.*

• **Use free-flowing air filters** to reduce resistance to incoming air.

MPG gain: 2%.

Best: Reusable K&N Air Filters, 800-858-3333, *www.knfilters.com.*

• **Prevent plugged fuel injectors** with a gas additive.

MPG gain: 12%.

Best: Redline SI-1.

• **Replace oxygen sensors** on pre-1996 vehicles with more than 100,000 miles.

MPG gain: 10% to 15%.

Best: Denso Oxygen Sensors, 888-800-9629, *www.densoproducts.com.*

More from David Solomon…

Don't "Top Off" Your Car's Gas Tank

Today's vehicles have an antipollution evaporative emission (EVAP) system that includes a charcoal-containing canister that absorbs gasoline fumes from a full tank. When gas runs low, the system sucks the fumes out of the canister and injects them into the fuel mix. But if the gas tank is over-filled, liquid gasoline may pour into the canister. This can destroy the charcoal, trigger a warning light on your dashboard and lead to a costly repair of your car's EVAP system.

Is Your Auto Mechanic Ripping You Off? Scams To Watch Out For

Sid Kirchheimer, an investigative reporter and author of the "Scam Alert" column in *AARP Bulletin.* He is author of *Scam-Proof Your Life: 377 Smart Ways to Protect You & Your Family from Ripoffs, Bogus Deals & Other Consumer Headaches* (Sterling).

Although most auto mechanics are honest, some are scam artists who will try to trick car owners into paying for unnecessary repairs. Such disreputable behavior is particularly common at service stations near highway exits, since most customers are only passing through. But even a local mechanic may "manufacture" a problem when you bring your car in for an inspection or some other reason.

MOST COMMON CONS

- **Loosening spark plug cables.** A garage mechanic loosens your spark plug cables, then tells you that your engine is running sluggishly and recommends a tune-up or some other pricey fix.

Solution: Before you let a mechanic service a suddenly rough-running engine, make sure your spark plug cables are all tightly connected.

- **Faking a failing alternator.** A mechanic surreptitiously splashes antifreeze on your alternator, causing it to give off smoke when the engine is hot. He/she warns you that when an alternator smokes, it needs to be replaced.

Solution: If there wasn't smoke before you pulled into the gas station, the problem might have been caused by the attendant. Try wiping down the smoking part with a moist rag to see if the smoke is eliminated.

- **Cleaning up an old part and telling you it's new.** A mechanic tells you that your car needs a new part, such as a starter or air filter. After you agree to let him do the work, he pulls out the old part, cleans it up or repaints it, then puts it back into your car and tells you it's new.

Solution: When you are handed a repair bill that includes replacement parts, insist on seeing the garage's purchase receipt from the auto-parts store. (If the work was done at a dealership where the part was in stock, there won't be a purchase receipt.)

Keep a bottle of a correction liquid, such as Wite-Out, in your glove compartment. When a mechanic tells you that a part must be replaced and the part is easily accessible, put a dot of Wite-Out on it when he isn't watching, preferably on the side or bottom so it isn't obvious. Once the repair has been done, ask for your old part back. If the part you're handed lacks your Wite-Out mark, the original part might have been used.

Also put a dot of Wite-Out on the sidewall of one tire when you bring the vehicle in for a tire rotation. If the dotted tire is still in the same position when you return, the work wasn't done.

- **"Short-sticking" the oil.** A service station attendant doesn't push the dipstick all the way in, creating the impression that your oil is low. He sells you several quarts of oil—but the oil bottles he appears to pour into your engine actually are empty.

Solution: Check the oil yourself unless you trust the garage.

- **Poking holes in radiators or tires.** A sneaky mechanic might poke radiators or tires with a screwdriver to cause leaks, then charge you to fix them.

Solution: Radiators don't often suffer small puncture holes—cracks and corrosion are more common problems. Be suspicious when a mechanic "discovers" a hole if your vehicle showed no previous signs of radiator problems.

When tires are punctured, the nail or other debris that caused the hole usually remains embedded in the rubber. If there's no nail and the tire seemed fine before you pulled into the station, you might be the victim of a scam.

Of course, the problem must be repaired. If the car is still drivable, head to another repair shop or, if you are a member of an auto club, have your car towed.

- **Spraying oil on the shock absorbers.** With a few squirts of oil on your car's shocks, a mechanic can make it appear as if they are leaking and need to be replaced.

Solution: Examine this "leaking" oil closely —if it's really from your shocks, it should look grimy and old, not clean and fresh. If you have any suspicions, don't be pressured into replacing your shocks immediately. Even if they are failing, this doesn't pose a danger—you will just have a bumpier ride. (Driving with worn shocks does somewhat increase tire wear and braking distances, however.) Wipe the suspect oil off of your shocks, and check them over the coming days. If the oil returns, you probably will need new shocks.

FINDING A MECHANIC YOU CAN TRUST

To find a trustworthy mechanic, ask friends for recommendations. Also, look up the garage recommendations in your area on the Car Talk Web site (*www.cartalk.com/content/mechx*).

Avoid shops that...

- **Have lots of municipal vehicles parked out front.** Governments often take the lowest bids, which usually don't equate to top-quality workmanship.

• **Have had the same cars sitting in front for months.** This might mean ongoing lawsuits about repair bills.

• **Have only cars of different eras or makes than yours out front.** For example, a garage that mainly works on domestic cars might not have the expertise to deal with an import.

Safest Midsized Cars In Crash Tests

The 2007 Saab 9-3 series, Audi A4 and Subaru Legacy were ranked as top safety picks in front, side and rear crash tests.

Lowest ranked: The 2007 Mitsubishi Galant, Acura TSX and Jaguar X-Type all rated *good* in front crash tests, but got the lowest scores for rear crashes. The Jaguar X-Type earned a marginal rating in side crash tests.

Adrian Lund, president, Insurance Institute for Highway Safety, Arlington, VA, *www.iihs.org/ratings*.

Are SUVs the Safer Choice for Children?

SUVs are no safer than cars for children, even though SUVs are bigger than most cars.

Recent finding: Children riding in SUVs that are involved in accidents are three times as likely as children riding in cars to sustain serious injuries due to the increased risk of SUV rollover.

Dennis Durbin, MD, pediatric emergency physician at The Children's Hospital of Philadelphia, and coauthor of a study of 3,922 children, published in *Pediatrics*. More information at *www.chop.edu/carseat*.

Air Pollution in Your Car

Air pollution inside a vehicle can be 10 times higher than outdoors.

Reason: The car's ventilation system concentrates pollution in the car.

Self-defense: Avoid roads with heavy congestion, particularly those with diesel truck traffic. Also, drive less and use public transit.

Scott Fruin, PhD, air pollution engineer, California Air Resources Board, Sacramento.

Secrets of Car Thieves

Michael Cherbonneau, co-principal investigator (with Richard T. Wright, PhD) of a research grant entitled "Auto Thieves on Auto Theft," funded by the University of Missouri Research Board. He previously took part in a study of incarcerated auto thieves while completing a masters degree from the University of Alabama–Birmingham. Mr. Cherbonneau is a doctoral student in the department of criminal justice at the University of Missouri–St. Louis.

More than 1.2 million vehicles will be stolen in the US this year alone. Most victims never come face-to-face with the criminals who drive off with their cars, but Michael Cherbonneau meets car thieves regularly. He is conducting a field-based study on how auto thieves carry out their crimes through face-to-face interviews with actual auto thieves recruited on the streets of St. Louis, Missouri. He previously assisted with one University of Alabama–Birmingham study which interviewed 54 incarcerated auto thieves.

Below, Mr. Cherbonneau tells what he has learned about how car thieves operate…which cars are at the greatest risk…and which theft-deterrent systems really work…

• **Who is the typical car thief?** The guys I have interviewed are hard-core street offenders. They all live for the here and now, spend money as quickly as they make it and consider life a perpetual party. Your car is probably safe in the daylight morning hours, between 8 am and noon, since most car thieves are still in bed.

Most of these guys are not car-theft specialists—they are hustlers and opportunists. Today they might steal cars…tomorrow sell drugs or commit robberies. But when they're in need of quick money, they consider auto theft a reliable way to get it. Compared with their other endeavors, auto theft is safe and dependable. If they mug someone or break into a home, they don't know how much they'll get or how the victim will react. When they steal a car, they can pick exactly the vehicle they want and not have to deal with the victim.

Some thieves steal cars to sell to chop shops. A chop shop strips a stolen car and sells the parts or changes the vehicle identification number and sells the entire car. But not every thief has access to chop shops—in some areas, only a few are in operation or they don't exist at all.

●How much are stolen vehicles worth? Thieves can get anywhere from $50 for a part to $3,500 for a stolen car. That might not seem like much, but thieves want to make money fast while avoiding detection, so they are willing to let cars go for "street prices." Newer cars generally fetch more than older models. Thieves also get more for cars with high-end audio systems and flashy aftermarket wheels that can be easily removed and sold. In major port cities, cars usually are stolen for export, and that can increase the thief's profits.

●Which cars are most likely to be stolen? Generally, the more popular a car is with buyers, the more popular it will be with thieves. Chop shops pay more for popular vehicles because parts removed from common cars are sure to be in demand. Stealing common cars also makes it less likely that the thief will be caught. If a gray Honda Accord or white Dodge Ram is stolen, the thief is relatively safe, because the police can't pull over every one that drives by. Also, some cars are easier to steal than others because of their ignition design. Favorites among thieves include many of the older General Motors cars and most of the new low- to mid-range Dodge, Chrysler and Pontiac models.

●How effective are the engine-immobilization security devices? These computerized security systems block the ignition or fuel flow if someone lacking the proper key tries to hot-wire the car. This "smart key" technology is a very effective theft deterrent, but many American cars—especially low-end and mid-range models—do not come with immobilizers. If I drove a car without engine-immobilization, I'd consider having it installed. Your insurance provider might even offer a discount if you do.

Be aware that thieves who can't beat an engine-immobilization system may try to steal your key. Some female thieves steal car keys from men in bars. Other thieves loiter around gas stations waiting for customers to leave their keys with their cars when they head inside to pay.

●What other automotive security devices deter thieves? No security product will make your automobile 100% theft-proof, but anything that makes it more difficult for the car thief is worthwhile…

●Alarms. Most thieves claim to be able to disable auto alarms. Even when they cannot, it is not certain that alarms are effective deterrents for vehicles parked on crowded streets—the sound of a car alarm is so common that people tend to ignore it. Still, if your car is parked in a driveway or in front of a home in a quiet area, the sound of the alarm might send some thieves running.

●The Club. The Club locks on to your steering wheel, making the vehicle impossible to operate. It can be defeated with a hacksaw, but that can be time-consuming, which increases the risk of being caught. *More information:* 800-527-3345, *www.theclub.com.*

●LoJack. LoJack is a small radio transponder hidden in your vehicle to track it when it's stolen. Many of the thieves I spoke with had never heard of LoJack, which is more likely to be on higher-end vehicles not targeted by these thieves. LoJack is of concern to thieves who target luxury cars, but these thieves know that LoJack is effective only when the victim reports the theft quickly. Many thieves simply time their crimes so the loss won't be noticed until after the car has been torn apart and the transponder smashed. For example, thieves target business parking lots in the afternoon. Car owners are back from lunch and won't notice that their cars are missing until after 5 pm. *More information:* 800-4LOJACK, *www.lojack.com.*

Based on my conversations with car thieves, I would say The Club is probably the most cost-effective deterrent, aside from engine-immobilization devices.

17

In the Home

The Biggest Remodeling Mistakes Home Owners Make

Remodeling your house can make it more comfortable, more beautiful and more profitable when the time is right to sell it. But modifying your house is tricky, and many well-intentioned projects turn into nightmares. *Successful remodeling depends on avoiding the following common pitfalls...*

Pitfall: **Neglecting basic problems.** Time and time again I see home owners who want to spend money on remodeling when just repairs are actually needed. In a way, that's understandable. Guests aren't likely to look at your newly refurbished plumbing, and a beautifully remodeled kitchen is something to show off.

However, when you put the house up for sale, prospective buyers routinely hire an inspector who will look at the plumbing. If the inspector

finds that the pipe fittings are too old and may soon need replacing, buyers may demand immediate repairs or a reduction in price.

Ignoring repairs can have more immediate consequences. A faulty roof, window or plumbing can lead to serious interior damage. Flooring and stairs that go without repairs can cause accidents.

Solution: Take care of any fundamental problems as you become aware of them. To find out about problems, hire an expert to look over the house.

A building inspector from the local government authority that enforces housing codes may be a good choice. Inspectors often do this type of work on weekends or after regular office hours. When they work on their own, they don't report problems to the local government. The problems they find, however, may be ones that you want

---

Steve Gonzalez, a residential building contractor based in Fort Lauderdale, FL. Mr. Gonzalez is a frequent radio and TV guest and author of several books, including *Before You Hire a Contractor: A Construction Guidebook for Consumers* (Consumer Press).

to tackle before considering remodeling—not just questions about windows, roofs and flooring, but also those dealing with the foundation, siding, woodwork and supporting beams.

To find an inspector, phone the city or county government and ask how to contact the appropriate department.

Cost: Less than $250,* unless your house is unusually large or far out in the country.

Alternatively, consider using a retired contractor for an analysis (those still in business might have a self-interest in offering advice). You can often find one by phoning your county or state home builders association. Almost any contractor can tell you the name of the local association.

Pitfall: **Making add-ons obvious.** Too often home owners add a room or raise a roof in a way that calls attention to itself—using different materials or a different style from the rest of the house.

This becomes important when the house goes on the market—the remodeling job will detract from "curb appeal," either lowering the value of the house or keeping it on the market longer.

Solution: Tell the contractor that you want the new bedroom or sunroom, for example, to look as though it's part of the original house—in both style and materials. Consider hiring a designer or architect to draw up specifications for the contractor. This typically costs $2,000 to $10,000, but you're likely to recoup the expense when you sell the property.

Another safeguard: Ask prospective contractors if they've done similar types of projects in your area. Then check out their remodeling jobs to make sure they meet all of your quality standards.

There's no way, of course, to know exactly how a remodeling project will affect the resale value of your house. In fact, you rarely get back as much as you spend on remodeling. *But it helps to…*

●**Ask several real estate agents for their advice.** Agents know the local market and have an interest in providing accurate information in order to get your business later on.

●**Go to the Web site of *Realtor* magazine** (*www.realtor.org/rmomag.NSF/pages/feature1 dec05?OpenDocument*). Their site shows typical

*Prices subject to change.

remodeling costs and compares them with the value they will likely add to a house.

Example: Replacing 1,250 square feet of old, low-grade siding with new, high-quality fiber-cement siding costs an average of $10,289 in the eastern part of the US, where the magazine says it typically increases the value of a house by $11,822. That's because fiber-cement siding resembles wood but is termite-resistant, durable and noncombustible.

In a more typical example, one home owner in the Midwest spends an average of $53,114 to remodel a basement with construction of a 20-by-30-foot entertainment area and a five-by-eight-foot bathroom. This major remodeling job usually adds only $38,767 to resale value.

Pitfall: **Eliminating a bedroom.** After the kids move out, it is tempting to combine two bedrooms—or a bedroom and bathroom. That's a mistake because, as a general rule, the more bedrooms and bathrooms a house has, the easier it is to sell and the more it fetches.

If you're willing to accept that drawback, go ahead and combine bedrooms. But before you do, consider an alternative, such as adding on to an existing bedroom. The cost will probably be similar, and as long as the addition is in the same style as the rest of the house, the expanded bedroom will probably make the property more desirable.

Two potential disadvantages: When you add on to an existing bedroom, you'll decrease the size of your yard. And, you may boost your property taxes because you've added square footage. Check with the local tax office that assesses property values.

Pitfall: **Going with a fad.** Dark kitchens are the rage—dark flooring, dark stone countertops, dark wood cabinets and dark-colored appliances to match. In most parts of the country, all these can easily cost more than $80,000 for a 10-by-20-foot kitchen—much more, in fact, if remodeling includes top-grade granite countertops.

However, dark kitchens may be passé in a few years and depress the resale value of a house. A more immediate concern could be safety unless a home owner also installs additional lighting in a dark kitchen.

You don't have to avoid fads. Just be aware of the potential drawbacks before you start any remodeling project. If you do have doubts, wait awhile and see whether it's merely a fad or a long-term trend.

Example: Not long ago, fireplaces seemed to be a fad in South Florida, where they're rarely needed. But since then, fireplaces have become a common feature in Florida houses. They might not be necessary, but they add a coziness that home owners are likely to want for many years to come.

Pitfall: **Overpersonalizing.** While fads are one trap, turning your house into a personal design statement can be another. We all like our homes to reflect our individual personalities, but it's easy to go too far.

Examples: Building a wine cellar or turning a bedroom into a library.

If you'll actually enjoy features like this—and as long as you understand that they limit the market for your house—go ahead and add them to your home.

Better: Install personalized features in a way that lets future owners convert them back to a more conventional use. Instead of putting built-in shelving into a library, for instance, consider stand-alone cabinets that would be easy to remove if a buyer wanted to convert the room back to a bedroom.

When Looking for A Repairman…

Money, Time-Life Bldg., Rockefeller Center, New York City 10020.

To get a reasonable price from a repairman, be sure to follow the helpful tips outlined below…

• **Ask a friend for a referral**—a company is less likely to overcharge the friend of a good customer.

• **During your initial phone call, explain what's broken**—this helps to narrow the scope of the repair.

• **Tell the repairman if there has been a history of problems** with this appliance.

• **Ask if you can try to fix it yourself**—sometimes a repair person will tell you how to make the repair, particularly if he/she is busy.

• **Ask about the company's rates and if there is a minimum charge**—most companies have a base charge of $50 to $100, plus an hourly rate.

• **Offer to e-mail a photo of the problem**—this may save you the cost of a visit if the repairman is the wrong person for the job.

• **Offer to buy the supplies yourself**—you could save yourself the 20% markup and the hourly rate for shopping time.

How to Keep Water from Destroying Your Home

Bill Keith, a 25-year remodeling veteran in St. John, IN, and host of *The Home Tips Show* on Chicago-based PBS TV and radio stations, *www.billkeith.com.* Mr. Keith is also president of Sunrise Solar Inc., and was named an "Energy Patriot" for his solar-powered attic fans.

Your roof begins to leak during a rainstorm…a pipe bursts in your wall and dumps an inch of water on the kitchen floor…the washing machine hose cracks and soaks the carpeting in your basement.

Flooding doesn't have to come from headline-making hurricanes to cause expensive damage in your home. *Six steps to take…*

STOP THE SOURCE

If water is coming from a pipe or hose, shut off the main water valve to the house. To find it, look near the furnace or water heater. If you can't do it yourself, call a plumber. It is best to find out *before* an emergency how to shut off the water. Ask your plumber.

If water is coming through the roof, get into the attic and, as a temporary solution, lay down heavy (4-mil) plastic sheeting and set buckets to catch the water. Keep some sheeting on hand, just in case. Or call a roofing company to tack a waterproof tarp over the outside.

Smart: You can bill your insurance company for any work you do yourself to stop or repair damage from flooding, including the costs of parts and labor.

Home insurers don't like to publicize this fact, and they may not let you bill more than $10 to $15 per hour—but charging for your efforts can help pay off some of your deductible.

CONTACT YOUR INSURANCE AGENT

Ask for phone numbers of emergency plumbers (if you haven't called one), roofers and/or specialists in drywall who are preapproved by your insurer. Many insurers have a preferred contractor program to control their costs.

Also, ask how to best document the damages for insurance claims...how soon an adjuster will be sent to your home...and what kind of rental equipment will be covered.

Example: Most insurers will cover rentals of fans or steam cleaners that reduce the damage.

Important: If the flood involves contaminated water, such as from a sewer or storm drain, it may be more dangerous than household water. Ask your agent to recommend a specialist.

PUMP OUT STANDING WATER WITHIN THE FIRST 12 HOURS

After that, damage becomes much more significant. Before attempting to pump out water, have an electrician inspect the area for electrical shock hazard. Then turn off the main circuit breaker and unplug electrical appliances, such as refrigerators, floor lamps and water heaters. Wear rubber gloves and boots.

Important: Don't plug in appliances that were submerged until you dry them out and have them checked by an appliance repair person. This service is usually covered by your insurer.

Place a submersible pump in the middle of the flooded area with enough hose to carry the water outside. Sump pump kits are available at home-improvement stores for about $100,* or you can rent one for less than $50 a day. For more information on pumping out floodwater, go to *www.sump-pump-info.com.*

REMOVE/CLEAN SOAKED MATERIAL

• **Carpeting.** If the carpet is just damp, not soaked, rent a commercial blower (for around $20 per day), and position it so it blows air underneath the carpet. To reach under the carpet, simply grab one corner of it with a pair of pliers and pull. The carpet should pull away from the tack strip on the floor very easily.

*Prices subject to change.

If the carpet is soaked, first remove the water with a wet/dry shop vac or a commercial carpet cleaner.

Cost to rent: About $20 to $50 per day.

After the water has been sucked out, lift a corner of the carpet and blow air underneath. Once the carpet is dry to the touch, hire a professional carpet layer to restretch the loose corner.

Cost: About $100.

Reality check: If the carpet was soaked with water from your water pipes (clean water), then it can be saved. If the water came from an outside source, such as rain or a sewer backup, the carpet needs to be removed and thrown away.

• **Furniture.** Dry it off with towels or cotton rags. If white spots or a cloudy film develops on wood furniture, rub the surface with a damp cloth dipped in turpentine or camphorated oil—be sure to test an inconspicuous area first. Wipe dry, and polish with furniture polish.

For fabrics, rent a carpet shampooer with an upholstery attachment (about $25 per day) and use it to dry the fabric. Or have a restoration contractor do it.

• **Books.** I have never seen a book fully recover once it's soaked. However, for books you don't want to part with, such as school yearbooks, try the techniques described below.

Stand the book up with as many pages as possible separated. Sprinkle cornstarch between the pages to absorb moisture. When the book is partially dry, pile it between other books and press them together to prevent the pages from crumpling. To prevent mildew, alternate between drying and pressing at least once every hour until completely dry. Use a fan to hasten drying.

DRY OUT THE WALLS AND FLOORS

Rent floor-blower fans, and buy a dehumidifier for about $120 (depending on the size of the room). Blowers are needed for the initial drying...and a dehumidifier for long-term moisture control. Both of these products are available at home-improvement stores.

Turn on your heating system to speed up drying time.

Caution: If your oil tank and burner were submerged, have them inspected before using.

If slats on your wood floors buckle after a few weeks of drying, have them professionally sanded and refinished to smooth out the buckles. Otherwise, you'll need to replace all of the flooring.

If you haven't gotten rid of all the moisture, there's a chance that mold and mildew will form, most commonly seen as black spots on walls.

What to do: Scrub with a household detergent solution, then wipe with chlorine bleach (one-half cup per gallon of water). To clean mildewed woodwork and floors, scrub with a mild alkaline solution, such as washing soda or trisodium phosphate (four to six tablespoons per gallon of water), available at home-improvement and grocery stores.

Caution: Never mix bleach and ammonia-based cleaners. Toxic fumes can result.

EXAMINE THE STRUCTURE FOR WATER DAMAGE

If you have not already identified it, look for the source of the flood and any hidden damage it caused. If water entered the basement, check the foundation and areas around the basement windows for cracking. If rainwater was coming in through the roof, look for loose or worn-out flashing—the metal used to waterproof the areas where chimneys and vent pipes meet the roof. Also, look for clogged downspouts or eaves as well as deterioration. Any wood or composition shingles on southern exposures deteriorate first.

To find holes, check for a drip trail or a spot of light coming through in the attic. Stick a wire through the hole to mark the spot on the outside for your roofer.

Dishwasher Tip

For a cleaner dishwasher, first remove bits of food from the drain. Run the empty washer, and stop the cycle when the bottom is full of water. Add two cups of vinegar to the water, and let sit for 30 minutes to remove hard-water buildup. Scrub walls with a sturdy brush, and let the cycle finish.

Good Housekeeping at 300 W. 57 St., New York City 10019.

The Best Way to Get Rid of Ice

Ice should be melted, not chopped, to prevent damage to concrete and asphalt. Use a shovel to remove loose snow or large ice chunks. Apply a melting agent to the ice-coated surface. Rock salt and calcium chloride are low-cost but corrosive to asphalt and concrete, as well as damaging to plants.

Alternative: The environment-friendly liquid deicer Storm Team Ice Melt Plus Liquid (800-474-7294 or *www.interstateproducts.com*).

Cost: $99.75/five-gallon pail* (one gallon covers 500 to 1,200 square feet).

Stephen Elder, home inspector, Pittsboro, NC.
*Price subject to change.

Electrical Outlet Warning

Outlets with ground fault circuit interrupters (GFCIs) may need to be replaced if they are 10 or more years old. GFCIs, the outlets with "test" and "reset" buttons, are designed to prevent electrocution. The circuitry in older GFCIs may no longer provide protection.

Solution: Most hardware stores carry GFCI testers, which will tell you if an outlet needs to be replaced.

Cost for a tester: About $10.*

The Family Handyman, 2915 Commers Dr., Eagan, MN 55121.
*Price subject to change.

Mop the Floors Without Lifting a Finger

The robotic *Scooba* cleans tile, linoleum and sealed hardwood floors. The small, round machine sweeps loose debris, sprays a cleaning solution onto the floor, scrubs the surface with a brush and then uses a "squeegee-vac" to suck up dirty water. Scooba maneuvers around chairs and tables and has sensors that prevent it from falling down stairs or accidentally mopping carpet. It costs $300 to $500.*

Information: 800-727-9077, *www.irobot.com.*

*Prices subject to change.

Five Top Home Stylists Share Favorite Tricks

Ann Farrow, founder, homeStyle, a home-staging company that serves the Greater Bay Area, San Francisco, CA, *www.homestylestaging.com.*

Daniel Lagemann, president, Scrub Systems, a service co-op comprised of more than 30 owner-operated home-staging and cleaning services, Maplewood, NJ, *www.scrub systems.com.*

Barb Schwarz, CEO for StagedHomes.com, a training company for home stagers with offices in Concord, CA…Chicago…and Seattle. She is founder of the International Association of Home Staging Professionals (*www.iahsp.com*) and author of *Home Staging: The Winning Way to Sell Your House for More Money* (Wiley).

Aileen Sideris, president, Showcased Interiors, a home-staging and design firm in Manchester, NH.

Bette Vos, president of Showtime! Staging and Organizing in Rowell, TX, outside Dallas. She is an accredited staging professional course trainer.

Home "stagers" are called in to spruce up houses that are about to go on the market. Often just a few simple changes can make a home more appealing, leaving the sellers wondering why they did not make those changes years before.

Below, some of the country's top professional home stagers share their favorite tricks for helping houses sell—tricks that also work wonders for home owners who aren't planning on going anywhere…

WALLS AND FLOORS
Aileen Sideris

•**Paint it sage.** Home stagers usually paint walls neutral colors, such as white or beige, but if these tones bore you, consider a subdued shade of green. It's just as soothing and universally inoffensive as beige, yet still fresh and different. Stick with soft natural greens, such as sage or moss—not bright lime or chartreuse. In particular, I like

Benjamin Moore's "Old Prairie" (very soft green) and "Camouflage" (moss green).

Ann Farrow

•**Use the same accent paint.** Paint all your baseboards, door frames and window casings the same color. Even if the color scheme for your walls and furnishings is varied, using the same accent paint throughout the house will give it a pulled-together feel. A great universal trim color is Kelly-Moore's "Swiss Coffee," a shade of white that goes with virtually everything.

Daniel Lagemann

•**Feather-sand floors.** Wood floors become scuffed and dull over the years. Newly finished floors make rooms feel bright and fresh, but rather than spending $400 to $500 per room* to have your floors completely sanded down and refinished, pay $200 to $300 for feather-sanding, a very light sanding technique that removes minor surface scratches. It makes floors shine but creates less dust, so it is easier to live in the house while the work is being done.

FURNITURE
Ann Farrow

•**Group it.** Most people push furniture in a room back against the walls. In larger spaces, this does not look very attractive and isn't very functional—you can't comfortably converse with someone who is 20 feet away. Instead, group furniture around one focal point, such as a fireplace, large window or built-in bookcase.

•**Angle it.** Consider turning a small sofa at an angle so it cuts off a corner. Put an uplight in the triangle behind the sofa so there's no dark corner. (Small canister uplights that sit on the floor are available for around $10 apiece at hardware and home-goods stores.) You also can put a bookcase, armoire or other piece of significant furniture at an angle.

Bette Vos

•**Shrink it.** Make your dining room feel larger by taking the leaf out of the table and moving two of the six dining chairs out of sight. Give the illusion of more space by taking everything out of a guest bedroom except the bed, one chair and a small dresser. If your living room is not

*Prices subject to change.

very big, replace your full-sized couch with a love seat and suddenly the space will feel more spacious.

Aileen Sideris

• **Go with the flow.** You shouldn't encounter the back of a couch when you enter a room—this blocks off the flow of traffic and makes the room seem smaller and less inviting. Furniture also shouldn't block the view of focal points, such as fireplaces or bay windows.

MORE TRICKS
Daniel Lagemann

• **Recaulk.** Moldy caulking around your tub or sink is all it takes for a bathroom to appear dingy. Scrubbing won't do it. Recaulk using a mildew-proof caulk as soon as discoloration occurs. A six-ounce tube costs less than $5.

Bette Vos

• **Box the clutter.** Decorative boxes keep the clutter under control without fuss. You can purchase ready-made plastic, canvas and rattan ones at stores such as Wal-Mart, Target, etc. Put the boxes wherever clutter tends to congregate in your home, and cleanup becomes a snap—just toss the clutter into the box.

Barb Schwarz

• **Bring the outside in.** Leafy branches and other greenery brought in from the yard add the refreshing feel of nature to any room—even the bathroom—and create flow from outside to inside. Cut a few tall branches, and stand them in an attractive container in a corner. Add an uplight behind them for a dramatic look.

• **Be creative.** Take items not meant to be decorative and use them as part of your decor.

Examples: Sports equipment such as fishing poles, golf clubs, ski poles and hockey sticks make great curtain rods in a den, family room or teen's bedroom. Or try using copper plumbing pipes as curtain rods.

Cleaning Out Your Closet? Where to Donate Unwanted Items

Daniel Borochoff, president, American Institute of Philanthropy, Chicago, a charity watchdog and service that helps donors make better giving decisions, *www.charitywatch.org.*

Most people know that they can donate unwanted items to Goodwill and Salvation Army, but there are other charities that make use of specific items, such as…

• **Children's and teen's books.** Reader To Reader (413-256-8595, *www.readertoreader.org*) gives them to schools.

• **Prescription eyeglasses.** Give the Gift of Sight (513-765-6000 or *www.givethegiftofsight.com*) sends used glasses to developing countries. Drop them at LensCrafters, Pearle Vision, Sears Optical, Target Optical, BJ's Optical, Sunglass Hut or Lions Club.

• **Cell phones and rechargeable batteries.** Call2Recycle (877-273-2925, *www.rbrc.org/call2recycle*) refurbishes and resells them, and part of the proceeds goes to the Boys and Girls Clubs of America and the National Center for Missing and Exploited Children.

Drop-off sites: Best Buy, Circuit City, Lowe's, Sears and Target.

• **Coats.** One Warm Coat (877-663-9276, *www.onewarmcoat.org*) distributes outerwear.

• **Musical instruments.** Hungry for Music (202-479-2810 or *www.hungryformusic.org*) distributes used musical instruments to underprivileged children.

• **Computers.** National Cristina Foundation (203-863-9100, *www.cristina.org*) gives laptops, desktops and printers to nonprofit agencies.

• **Business clothing.** Career Gear (212-577-6190, *www.careergear.org*) provides clothing for job interviews to low-income men, and Dress for Success (212-532-1922, *www.dressforsuccess.org*) does the same for women.

• **Gowns and shoes.** Fairy Godmothers Inc. (215-675-9391, *www.fairygodmothersinc.com*) distributes dresses and accessories to needy high school girls for their proms.

Relocation Know-How

If you're planning a relocation for retirement or due to another life change, keep these tips in mind...

• **Sell first, buy later.** Rent a furnished apartment, and put your belongings in storage. This gives you time to hold out for a better price on the old house and shop for a new one.

• **Research the new area.** Talk to local residents, and check out neighborhoods.

• **Get details about public schools nationwide** at *www.schooltree.org*.

• **Use a national bank,** so you don't have to close old accounts and open new ones.

• **Get change-of-address forms in on time** so that you can stay up to date on bills.

• **Sign up for a cell phone plan with unlimited in-network calling** so that any family members who must stay behind to take care of unfinished business can be in contact without incurring high phone bills.

Money, Time-Life Bldg., Rockefeller Center, New York City 10020.

Aphid Deterrent

Aphids—also called plant lice—can damage garden plants. To keep them at bay, spray plants with a homemade citrus mixture.

To make it, combine one tablespoon of freshly grated citrus rind, such as orange, lemon or grapefruit, with one pint of boiling water. Let the mixture steep overnight, then strain through a coffee filter into a spray bottle. Add three drops of dishwashing liquid to the bottle.

Aphids are repelled by the scent of the citrus rind, and the soap helps the mixture adhere to the plants. Spray every five to seven days until aphids are gone.

Christine Bucks, editor, *Great Garden Fix-Its: Organic Remedies for Everything from Aphids to Weeds* (Rodale).

Dangers in Your Own Backyard

Richard O'Brien, MD, a clinical instructor at Temple University School of Medicine in Philadelphia, as well as an emergency physician at Moses Taylor Hospital, Scranton, PA. He is also spokesperson for the American College of Emergency Physicians, *www.acep.org*.

The combination of warmer weather and outdoor activities sends millions of Americans to emergency rooms each summer. Most of their injuries could have been prevented. *Here, an emergency room physician reveals the biggest dangers and how to avoid them...*

LAWN MOWERS

The lawn mower is probably the most dangerous tool around your house. A nine-year study published in the *Annals of Emergency Medicine* reports an annual average of 74,000 emergency room visits due to lawn mower injuries. Most injuries are caused by debris flying into the bodies or eyes of lawn mower operators and bystanders. About one-third of lawn mower–related hospitalizations are due to injuries from the blades, including the loss of toes and/or fingers.

Self-defense: Remove twigs, sticks and rocks before mowing. Keep bystanders, especially children, away from the mower. Wear shoes—not sandals—long pants and safety goggles while mowing. Don't depend on glasses or sunglasses to protect eyes—debris can enter at the sides.

Also, wear hearing protection (ear plugs, ear mufflers, etc.). Don't use an iPod or similar portable music device—you really have to crank up the volume to hear the music, which can result in permanent hearing damage.

ELECTRIC HEDGE TRIMMERS

I see at least one patient a month who has been hurt by a hedge trimmer. It can cut off a finger instantly or cause a nasty injury—crushing tissue and bone—that is very difficult to repair.

Self-defense: Wear heavy leather or canvas gloves, sturdy shoes and long pants when using a trimmer. Don't overreach—you may lose your balance. Turn off the trimmer and unplug it before trying to clear it of stuck debris.

GARAGE DOORS

Some manual and electric garage doors have large, heavy springs on each side. A spring that suddenly loosens can hit your head with the force of a swinging baseball bat. A spring also can take off a finger.

Self-defense: Never attempt to repair or replace a garage door yourself. Hire an experienced professional to do it.

TICK BITES

Lyme disease gets most of the headlines, but ticks carry many other diseases, including ehrlichiosis and Rocky Mountain spotted fever, both bacterial infections that can cause fatigue, fever, severe muscle pain and headaches, and also can be life-threatening.

Self-defense: Removing the tick from your skin within 12 to 24 hours almost guarantees that you won't get sick. Grip the tick close to the skin with tweezers and pull it out. If part of the tick remains in the skin, try your best to remove it. If you're not able to remove it all, see a doctor. Wash the area well, and apply an antibiotic ointment to prevent infection.

If you're spending time in grassy or wooded areas, you can prevent most tick bites by using an insect repellent that contains DEET. Apply the repellent to exposed skin and clothing. A non-DEET repellent, Picaridin, is helpful for people whose skin is sensitive to DEET. Also, always wear closed shoes rather than sandals, tuck long pants into socks and wear a long-sleeved shirt, tucked in.

POISON IVY, OAK AND SUMAC

All of these plants contain *urushiol*, an oily substance that can cause an itchy rash in people who are sensitive to it. (To view the plants so you can recognize them, go to *www.poisonivy.aesir.com*.) As little as one-billionth of a gram of urushiol can cause the rash—so even brushing against one of these plants is a problem. The oil also can get on tools, gloves and clothing and stays active indefinitely, so it must be washed off.

Self-defense: If your skin comes into contact with one of the "poisons," wash the area immediately with soap and water. If you're outside and don't have access to soap or water, splash the area with any liquid—soda, beer, etc. If a rash develops, apply *hydrocortisone* ointment, available at drugstores. If the rash worsens, see a doctor.

CYCLING

Each year, bicycle accidents result in more than half a million visits to emergency rooms. More than 800 bicyclists die every year, many from head injuries.

Self-defense: Always wear a helmet, even if you (or your children) are riding close to home. Studies indicate that helmets are up to 85% effective in avoiding head injuries. Helmets with visors are helpful for preventing facial lacerations. Be sure that the helmet fits properly and is buckled snugly.

Warning: Most cycling fatalities occur between 6 pm and 9 pm, when visibility is diminished. Always wear reflective clothing.

SWIMMING

Drowning is one of the leading causes of accidental death in the US.

Reasons: People overestimate their swimming ability…panic in deep water or fast currents…or consume large amounts of alcohol before entering the water.

Self-defense: Enter unfamiliar water feet-first to prevent head and neck injuries. Do not depend on flotation devices, they can fail and sink. Never drink alcohol before or while swimming.

Danger for women: The bacteria that cause urinary tract infections thrive in moist environments. Women who sit around in wet swimsuits give these organisms an opportunity to proliferate and migrate into the urethra—and possibly up into the kidneys, resulting in a potentially life-threatening infection. Change into dry clothing after swimming. Also, drink lots of water—it increases urination, which flushes out bacteria.

Backyard Trampolines Are Dangerous

More than 88,000 people visited emergency rooms each year from 2000 to 2005* with trampoline-related injuries that included cuts and

*Latest period for which figures are available.

bruises, broken limbs and spinal cord injuries. Some injuries even resulted in death.

To decrease risk: Only one person should use the trampoline at a time. Jump only in the center, and don't attempt flips or other stunts. Put shock-absorbing safety material below and around the trampoline, and cover the steel frame and springs with a safety pad. Don't allow anyone under the age of six to use a trampoline.

Gary Smith, MD, DrPh, FAAP, chairperson of the American Academy of Pediatrics' Committee on Injury, Violence and Poison Prevention, Columbus, OH.

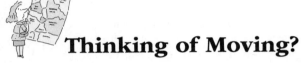

Thinking of Moving?

The best place to raise a family in the US is Louisville, Colorado.

Other top 10 locations: Gaithersburg, Maryland...Roswell, Georgia...Lakeville, Minnesota... Flower Mound, Texas...Fort Collins, Colorado... Cary, North Carolina...Sugar Land, Texas...Columbia, Maryland...and Noblesville, Indiana.

Cities were evaluated on a variety of factors, including education, housing and employment opportunities...climate...and community feel.

Bert Sperling and Peter Sander, authors of *Best Places to Raise Your Family: The Top 100 Affordable Communities in the US* (Frommer's).

How to Choose the Best Real Estate Agent

Pam O'Connor, CEO, Leading Real Estate Companies of the World, a network of more than 650 firms, Chicago, *www.leadingre.com.*

When selecting your real estate agent, look for someone who has at least three years' experience in your market and who averages a minimum of 12 transactions each year—the more, the better. Avoid the high-profile agents, such as ones you see advertised on the large billboards—you'll likely spend a lot of time talking to their assistants. Ask for client references.

Also, pick someone with good pricing skills—ask for a list of homes the agent has listed and sold in the past year, with both listing and final sales price for each. Commissions are negotiable, but don't opt for a less experienced associate whose fee may be lower—you may not get top dollar for your home.

Note: Look at agents' listing companies, too. The best have helpful Web sites and other resources, such as good promotional advertising, a strong base of other agents who will add to your home's listing exposure, and one-stop convenience for procuring mortgages, titles, etc.

Home Owners' Rights: What We All Can Learn From Real-Life Disputes

Mark Warda, lawyer and president of Land Trust Service Corporation in Lake Wales, FL, an organization that holds property in trust, *www.floridalandtrust.com.* He is also the author of *Homeowner's Rights: A Legal Guide to Your Neighborhood* (Sphinx).

Many real estate laws are meant to prevent a bad neighbor from interfering with the quality of life of people who live nearby, but sometimes these well-meaning laws are excessively restrictive or confusing.

Here's a quick look at some landmark legal decisions and what they tell us about our rights as home owners...*

● **A great view is a bonus, not a right.** While some towns have specific "view protection ordinances," these are the exception, not the rule.

Landmark case: A couple bought a home on the western slope of Capitol Hill in Seattle in 1989 because they loved their view. Soon after, multistory condominium buildings were erected on a hill just below them, blocking their view. The couple sued, but the court ruled that because the buildings violated no zoning laws, the couple had no legal right to their view.

What to do: Unless zoning or building rules are violated, your neighbor—or a real estate

*The property laws vary from state to state. Zoning restrictions and restrictive covenants are even more localized. Consult your town's zoning officials or an attorney for more details about laws in your area.

developer—is free to block your view and even your sunlight. Keep this in mind if you're thinking of buying a property because of the view.

Exception: If a neighbor erects a "spite fence" for no reason other than to block your view, a court might order it shortened or removed.

• **You can't always decide who lives in your home.** Single-family zoning ordinances remain common.

Landmark case: In 1974, the Supreme Court ruled that a home owner in Belle Terre, New York, didn't have the right to rent his house to six students. The home was in an area zoned for single-family dwellings. In another case two years later, the court clarified that an extended family, including grandparents and cousins, can be considered a single family.

What to do: Check whether your neighborhood has a single-family ordinance or any similar restriction. If it does, you could be breaking the law if you have a nonrelative live with you. (Contemporary zoning rules typically do allow unmarried couples to live together.) Still, it's unlikely that anyone will try to stop you unless this new resident's behavior is disruptive.

• **Trees are legal land mines.** Neighbors often feud over trees.

Landmark case: In this 1994 case, a California man hired a contractor to dig a three-foot trench—to remove the roots of his neighbor's 40-year-old Monterey pine—because the roots had grown across the property line and cracked the man's sidewalk. The tree died as a result of the root loss, and the neighbor had to pay to have the tree removed. The neighbor sued, but the court ruled that property owners have a right to cut roots or trim branches that encroach on their property.

What to do: As a rule of thumb, if a tree's trunk is on your property, you own the tree and are responsible for it. (You also are entitled to any fruit produced by the tree, even if it's on a branch that overhangs your neighbor's yard. Laws are often unclear about fallen fruit.) However, in most states, if your tree is causing imminent danger to a neighbor's life or property, the neighbor has the right to trim branches or roots as far back as the property line. In certain states—Hawaii, Indiana, Kansas, Michigan,

New Mexico, New York, Ohio, Oklahoma and Tennessee—a neighbor even can insist that you pay the bill for trimming the tree that's causing problems. Tree laws vary by state and can be surprisingly complex, so it's often wise to consult an attorney.

• **You have the right to peace and quiet.** Some towns have laws prohibiting noise above certain decibel levels, or restrictions against specific noises, such as unnecessary car horn use.

Landmark case: In the 1940s, a woman in Brookline, Pennsylvania, put a marimba (a type of xylophone) on her porch and played loudly for long stretches and at odd hours. She sometimes played songs meant to poke fun at her neighbors, such as "Jingle Bells," whenever she spotted a large man who reminded her of Santa Claus. Eventually, the woman was charged with creating a nuisance. The court ruled that while the woman had a right to play her marimba, the way in which she was playing it did indeed constitute an illegal nuisance. The judge limited the number of hours and time of day the woman could play her instrument and prohibited intentionally annoying songs.

What to do: Follow the prevalent rule that you're creating an illegal nuisance if a noise (or bright light or strong odor) is unreasonable to a person of ordinary sensibilities. A judge or jury must decide case by case who has overstepped the line. Noises that are reasonable during the day might not be considered reasonable at night, and noises that are reasonable in a business district might not be considered reasonable in a purely residential neighborhood. However, you are not required to be sensitive to a neighbor's special needs.

Example: Your neighbor can't force you to stop mowing your lawn in the afternoon simply because he works nights and sleeps during the day. Of course, the neighborly thing to do would be to delay mowing anyway.

• **Your home-based business is your town's business.** Home businesses have become very common, but they often are prohibited under zoning laws.

Landmark case: In 1959, the New Hampshire Supreme Court ruled that a roofing contractor could not run his business from his home

—making phone calls and sending letters—because it was in an area zoned residential.

What to do: Check your local zoning ordinances. Some prohibit only loud or otherwise disruptive business activities, but if your town is more restrictive, you might be breaking the law if you conduct any business from your home—even selling items through eBay.

If your home-based business comes under scrutiny, ask your town council to change the rules to permit nondisruptive home businesses. Argue that home businesses have become common—the law no longer reflects today's reality. Point out that home businesses can deter crime because it means more people are home during the day.

For a Smarter Child...

Children do better on developmental tests, including IQ tests, if their mothers ate more fish while they were pregnant. Children whose mothers limited fish to 12 ounces or less a week during pregnancy—as the Food and Drug Administration (FDA) now recommends—do slightly less well on these tests than the children whose mothers ate more fish. The FDA restriction is designed to reduce exposure to mercury, which may harm brain development.

Theory: The good done by the omega-3s in fish outweighs the possible problems caused by mercury.

What to do: Ask your doctor how much fish is best for you.

Gary J. Myers, MD, professor of neurology and pediatrics, department of neurology, University of Rochester, Rochester, NY. His editorial on an analysis of fish consumption among nearly 12,000 pregnant British women whose children were tracked through age eight was published in *The Lancet*.

Need a Babysitter?

The Web sites SitterCity.com and BabySitters.com offer profiles for thousands of sitters,

sorted by location. Parents pay a fee to contact a sitter—sitters can list themselves for free.

Caution: Don't make a decision based solely on a profile. Contact at least two of a sitter's references...interview the sitter...arrange a tryout while you are in the house...and consider doing a background check if the babysitter is over the age of 18.

Sue Shellenbarger, work and family columnist for *The Wall Street Journal*.

Happier Kids

Give children specific affirmations, not general ones.

Example: If a child hits a home run that wins a baseball game, don't simply say, "Good game." Encourage self-esteem and team spirit by saying, "What a great hit! You won the game for your team—and everyone played so well."

The more specific an affirmation is, the more your child will know you are praising his/her individual accomplishments—and the more meaningful the praise will be.

Jean Tracy, MSS, parenting expert, Edmonds, WA... founder of the Kidsdiscuss.com parenting Internet site... and author of *Character Building—Family Meeting Diary* (Kidsdiscuss.com).

Help Your Kids Get Organized

To help a child get more organized, follow this helpful advice...

• **Create checklists** that he/she can use on his own.

• **Break down bigger tasks into smaller ones.**

• **Prioritize all assignments**—the hardest or most time-consuming one should be done first.

• **Establish routines,** such as doing homework at the same time every day.

• **Put up a wall calendar,** and write appointments and due dates on it.

• **Prepare for the next day by laying out your child's homework,** textbooks and clothing the night before.

Armin A. Brott, the host of *Positive Parenting*, a weekly radio program in the San Francisco Bay Area, and the author of six books about fatherhood, including *Father for Life—A Journey of Joy, Challenge, and Change* (Abbeville). His Web site is *www.mrdad.com*.

Keep Track of Your Kids

A cell-phone GPS tracker lets parents locate children anytime. The phone contains a chip and software that allow a parent to log on to a computer and monitor the child's whereabouts. The tracking product—CAT*TRAX*—works with Java-equipped Nextel phones that have GPS. It costs $20 per month* for tracking.

More information: CATS Communication, 877-229-CATS (2287), *www.cattrax.us*.

*Price subject to change.

Abduction Protection

To protect children against abduction, check sex offender registries and public databases (type "sex offender registry" into any search engine, such as Google.com, for access to national and state registries). If children walk to and from school, identify the safe places along the route where they can go if they need help. Also, teach kids to run from danger and to loudly resist anyone who attempts to grab them. Children should yell, kick, scream and make every effort to get away. If followed by a vehicle, they should run in the opposite direction and tell a trusted adult.

Recommendations from the National Center for Missing & Exploited Children, Alexandria, VA. For more information, call 800-843-5678 or visit *www.missingkids.com*.

Getting Glasses?

Melvin Schrier, OD, vision consultant and retired optometrist, Rancho Palos Verdes, CA.

Distance glasses can worsen nearsightedness (myopia) in children. They are prescribed routinely by some doctors when children start to become nearsighted.

Some children can become nearsighted because they spend excessive time on computers or playing video games. That can bring on eyestrain and focusing problems. Most nearsightedness, however, is genetic. Physicians will often prescribe distance lenses to clear the blur, but the lenses may aggravate the problem by bringing everything closer, forcing the child's vision to refocus and strain. This may lead to a need for stronger lenses every year or two.

If other visual tests show that the eyes are under stress, children should be given nearpoint, or "plus," lenses for reading, using the computer and playing video games. Reading lenses tend to push things farther away, allowing the focusing muscles to relax.

Also: Don't be afraid of bifocals for children if your optometrist recommends them—they can play a big part in limiting myopic changes.

A Vaccine for All Kids

A childhood vaccine for bacterial pneumonia, among other invasive pneumococcal diseases, such as meningitis, is now recommended for all children in the US. The vaccine—Prevnar—has been shown to reduce the incidence of pneumococcal illnesses in adults as well.

Keith P. Klugman, MD, PhD, William H. Foege Chair, Rollins School of Public Health, Emory University, Atlanta, and the leader of a study of more than 37,000 children in Soweto, South Africa, published in *Nature Medicine*.

New ADHD Patch

The Daytrana patch, which is worn for nine hours every day by children with attention deficit-hyperactivity disorder (ADHD), contains *methylphenidate*—the same stimulant found in Ritalin. The patch is recommended for children ages six to 12 who have ADHD and may provide an alternative for those children who have trouble swallowing pills. It can be removed immediately if it causes side effects, such as nausea or irritability. Ask your child's pediatrician for more information.

Thomas Laughren, MD, director, psychiatry products, Food and Drug Administration, Washington, DC.

Rethink Sports Drinks If Your Child Is Ill

Sports drinks, including Gatorade, do not replace the nutrients and minerals lost when you or your child has diarrhea.

Better: Drink an electrolyte rehydration solution, such as CeraLyte or Pedialyte.

Centers for Disease Control and Prevention, Atlanta, *www.cdc.gov*.

Teens Feel Less Empathy Than Adults

In one recent finding, when asked how they would react in certain situations, adults used more of the front of the brain, associated with empathy, and teens used more of the back of the brain, which doesn't take into account other people's feelings.

Sarah-Jayne Blakemore, PhD, research fellow, Institute of Cognitive Neuroscience, University College London, and also leader of a study of 30 people, presented at the British Association for the Advancement of Science Festival in 2006.

College Tours Without Leaving Home

Collegiate Choice offers DVD tours of more than 350 colleges in the US, Canada and Europe. The DVDs are recordings of student tours, not promotional videos, so you see a more intimate glimpse of the campus. This lets you pre-screen colleges and save on airfare, hotel costs, etc. Each tour runs between one and two hours. $15 for each school.*

Information: Collegiate Choice at 201-871-0098 or *www.collegiatechoice.com*.

*Price subject to change.

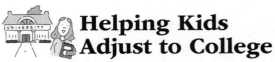

Helping Kids Adjust to College

Laura S. Kastner, PhD, a clinical associate professor of psychiatry and behavioral sciences at University of Washington, Seattle. She writes and lectures widely on adolescence and family behavior, and is coauthor, with Jennifer Wyatt, PhD, of *The Launching Years: Strategies for Parenting from Senior Year to College Life* (Three Rivers).

Most freshmen entering college experience tremendous anxiety. The signs of "launch anxiety" typically start during the senior year in high school, when teenagers drag their feet on college applications, neglect their schoolwork and appear increasingly rude or disrespectful.

Once they leave their homes, many students become overwhelmed by the new freedom and responsibilities.

Common problems: Procrastinating on their school assignments, experimenting with drugs or alcohol, having difficulty making friends and feeling lonely or depressed.

To help kids adjust…

•**Discuss phone/e-mail communication.** Regular contact will help you to stay in touch with your child and help him/her get through the adjustment period. At least once a week is the minimum. You could discuss ahead of time whether it's better "just to check in" or to call or write on a particular day. *Don't call every day.* Children need to feel that they have the freedom to live their own lives.

• **Anticipate the "dump call."** The first two weeks away from home are the hardest. Students may call and say they just can't stand it—they're lonely, can't keep up with the work and want to come home.

Do not overreact. The "dump call" is usually just a way for students to vent their feelings. They don't need to be rescued. They're usually just having a bad moment and may not even remember the conversation later.

Red flag: If your child sounds seriously unhappy day after day, can't stop crying or seems increasingly withdrawn, there is a bigger problem. Take these signs of depression seriously. Freshmen account for 40% of all undergraduate suicides. Encourage him to see a campus counselor immediately—and don't hesitate to hop a plane and check on things yourself.

• **Don't micromanage.** A big part of the college experience is learning responsibility—managing class work, getting to bed at a reasonable hour, dealing with difficult professors, etc. Many parents, accustomed to taking care of everything when their children were young, have a hard time letting go. They want to solve every problem. Some even call their children's roommates to "settle" disputes between the students.

Kids need to learn to handle these things on their own. When your child calls to complain about a problem, do be empathetic but let him know you have confidence in his abilities. Say something like, "I know that can be difficult, but I've seen how good you are at handling these kinds of things."

Exception: There may be times when your child needs adult intervention—because of sexual harassment, for example, or something else that threatens his personal safety. Don't hesitate to get involved—by calling the dean of student affairs, for example—if it's clear that a problem requires your attention.

• **Help your child find a social niche.** Loneliness is among the main challenges freshmen face. Before your child leaves for school, suggest that he get involved in activities and clubs.

Planned activities can help him quickly meet like-minded people he can have fun with.

• **Talk about drug and alcohol use.** Some schools have reputations for hard-core partying—and use of alcohol and drugs is common just about everywhere. You can't control whether your child drinks or takes drugs while away from home, but you can discuss some of the risks, including sexual assault.

Helpful: Rather than lecturing your child to "just say no," encourage safety. You might suggest that your daughter, for example, always go out with friends rather than alone.

• **Be flexible.** About 60% of undergraduates take longer than four years to graduate. Taking time off is not only legitimate, it also may be something to encourage. Travel, work or volunteering, or a combination of these, can help kids get the most out of college.

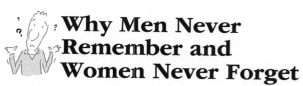

Why Men Never Remember and Women Never Forget

Marianne Legato, MD, FACP, a physician and professor of clinical medicine at Columbia University and founder of Columbia's Partnership for Gender-Specific Medicine, New York City. She is author of several books, including *Why Men Never Remember and Women Never Forget* (Rodale).

N either men nor women can claim that their brains are "better." Even though men's brains are 10% larger on average, women's brains have more elaborate connections that make them more efficient. Male and female brains unquestionably are different, in terms of both structure and chemistry, and that can trigger problems when we try to communicate with one another.

Most of us speak to our spouses just as we would speak to members of our own sex—then wonder why they don't seem to understand.

Here's how to communicate more effectively with the opposite sex...

NONVERBAL CUES

The female brain is good at decoding nonverbal signals, including facial expressions and tone of voice, perhaps because mothers must understand the needs of children too young to speak. When women send nonverbal signals to men, women are often dismayed to find that these signals are ignored.

Women do not realize that the typical male brain is not very skilled at interpreting nonverbal communications. And, men are particularly bad at identifying signs of sadness in women—though men are pretty good at spotting signs of anger and aggression.

Women: Tell him verbally when something is bothering you. A sad expression or the silent treatment won't get you anywhere. It's not that he is ignoring your feelings—he is just unaware of them.

If a man asks you what he can do to make you feel better, tell him. If you say "nothing," he'll assume that you mean nothing and he'll do nothing. He isn't trying to hurt you—men's brains just work in a more linear, literal manner. Because men often like to be left alone when they're upset, he might conclude that he is doing you a favor by giving you some space.

Men: Search for the clues beyond her words when she seems unusually quiet or terse. She might be sending signals that you're not picking up. If you can't figure out the signals and she won't tell you what she needs, remind her that you really want to help, but it's hard for you to pick up her nonverbal cues.

LISTENING

The female brain seems to be better at listening than the male brain—women have more nerve cells in the areas known to process language and put a larger percentage of their brains to work when they hear someone speak.

The more elaborate wiring of the female brain also makes women better multitaskers than men. Evolution likely made women this way so that mothers could keep an eye on the children and still get other things done. Evolution shaped the male brain to focus on one very difficult task at a time. Tiger hunts were more successful when the hunters focused on the tiger.

Add men's inferior listening ability to their superior focus, and the result is a phenomenon most wives know well. Tell a man something important while he's watching a ball game, and he might not remember a word of it. He is not

purposely ignoring you—his brain simply isn't wired to hear what you said.

Women: Put him on alert that what you are about to say is important. If it's particularly vital information, begin with a gentle, "I need you to look me in the eyes." If there are too many distractions in your present location, ask him to go with you for a walk or out to a quiet restaurant.

Men: Don't be insulted if she doesn't stop what she is doing when you want to talk to her. Chances are that she can pay attention to you even if she is occupied. If you want her undivided attention, ask for it.

PROBLEM SOLVING

The structure of the male brain makes men straight-ahead thinkers—when they see a problem, their instinct is to try to solve it.

Women are more likely to ruminate over a decision. They will verbalize a problem and talk though all of the implications and issues before they proceed. When women try to talk through their problems with men, they're often dismayed and insulted that the men try to tell them what to do. This confuses the men, who thought they were being asked for a solution.

Women: Tell a man the specific type of response you want before you share a problem. Are you asking the man for a solution, or do you just want to talk through the issue so it's clear in your mind? If you don't specifically tell him that it's the latter, he'll assume it's the former. If he tries to solve your problem anyway, understand that this is just how his brain responds.

As for how to respond to a man's problems, this rarely comes up. Men tend not to share their problems with anyone.

Men: Understand that women like to verbalize their thinking and don't always want you to solve their problems. Instead, wait for a question before providing an answer. Ask what you can do to help rather than assume you know. And if your wife starts crying, hold her quietly. Don't tell her she's being too emotional.

DIFFERENT INTERESTS

Women tend to expect their male partners to be interested in every subject they wish to discuss. That isn't fair. A woman wouldn't expect her female friends to chat about a subject that she knows bores them.

Women: Customize the conversation to your partner's interests. (Men should do this, too, but because men talk less, it isn't as often an issue.) Find other conversation partners for topics that don't interest him.

Men: Encourage your partner to spend time with female friends so there's another outlet for the conversations that don't interest you. Don't get upset if she's busy with friends.

BETTER ARGUMENTS

During an argument, women are more likely to bring up previous events. Estrogen increases the amount of *cortisol*, a memory-boosting hormone, that is released during stressful moments. Because a female brain has more estrogen, the memories of old fights remain fresher in a woman's mind. The male brain finds it easier to forget emotional situations and move on. Maybe forgetting a close call on the tiger hunt made it easier for men of the past to continue to hunt.

Women: Use simple, declarative sentences, and state what you want in outline form when imparting important information to men. Leave out anecdotes and unnecessary adjectives. Take advantage of your ability to read his emotions to spot the signs of boredom. When you see them, sum up your argument with a closing statement and end the conversation. Try not to rehash old arguments.

Men: Try to keep a woman focused on the point under discussion. If during an argument she brings up a fight you had five years ago, tell her, "We've discussed that already and it isn't going to help to go over it again. Let's focus on the current problem."

Stay in Touch

A "family blog" is a private Web site that any family member can use to post written messages, pictures, video and sounds at any time for all others to enjoy. It's password protected to bar unauthorized visitors.

Simplest: Use the free Blogger utility provided by Google at *www.blogger.com*—there's no charge for the Web site.

Other ways: E-mail can be used to send pictures, video and sounds as well as text messages. Instant messaging can let family members "chat" in real time.

All of these can keep family members in close contact even when they are located on different continents.

Patricia Robison, president, Computing Independence, Box 2031, New York City 10011.

Filial Responsibility

A recent court decision in California, one of 30 states that have such laws, affirmed the legal obligation of adult children to support indigent parents to the extent that they are able to.

Court ruling: Filial responsibility laws are akin to those imposed on parents with respect to minor children, and neglect of an indigent parent is punishable as a misdemeanor.

Sanford J. Schlesinger, Esq., a founding partner and head of wills and estates, Schlesinger Gannon & Lazetera LLP, 499 Park Ave., New York City 10022.

Keep an Eye on Elderly Family from Afar

Jim Miller, editor of "Savvy Senior," a syndicated newspaper column, Norman, OK, *www.savvysenior.org*. He is also a regular guest on the NBC *Today* show.

Many new technologies have been developed to help adults ensure that their older loved ones are safe...

HOME MONITORING

A basic form of this system—the personal emergency response system (PERS)—has been around for years. With a PERS, a person wears a device (panic button) that sends out a call for help if needed. The problem is that many who have such a device don't wear it or aren't alert enough to hit the button if they fall or get ill.

High-tech home-monitoring systems (which do still offer the panic-button feature) require no input from the person being cared for. They all work through wireless motion sensors installed throughout the senior's home and collect information on the activities of everyday living, such as getting out of bed, using the bathroom, eating and taking medicine. The system establishes the person's routines so it can detect when there are changes to those patterns, such as a person failing to leave the bedroom in the morning. Alerts are sent to the caregiver via phone or by e-mail. Family members also can check on their loved one's patterns via the system's secure Web site. *Companies that offer this product...*

• **QuietCare.** A leader in the industry and the first to offer this service.

Cost: From less than $200,* plus about $90 a month for monitoring (varies by area). 877-822-2468, *www.quietcare.com.*

• **Healthsense.** Provides a more comprehensive monitoring system that allows you to keep a watch on just about everything. With a variety of sensors, you can monitor such things as sleep patterns, use of the shower and toilet, whether the stove has been left on, when your loved one has left the house, etc.

Cost: $1,000, plus $90 for monthly monitoring, though prices vary depending on tier of service and size of the home. 800-576-1779, *www.health sense.com.*

• **GrandCare Systems.** In addition to monitoring, this system offers a small computer that connects to the Internet and plugs into the TV, allowing family members to share pictures, e-mail and more on a dedicated TV channel.

Cost: For prices phone 262-338-6147 or visit *www.grandcare.com.*

MEDICATION MANAGEMENT

Remembering to take medications is a challenge for many seniors. The MD.2 program can help organize medications and dispense them on schedule. It also provides multiple reminders to take the medication. Caregivers are alerted if necessary. Monitoring can be done on the Web.

Cost: $899, plus a $25 monthly monitoring fee, or it can be rented for less than $100 per month, but the cost will vary by distributor. 877-563-2632, *www.imd2.com.*

*Prices subject to change.

Helpful: www.epill.com offers a large line of medication-reminder products. 800-549-0095.

VIDEO CHAT SERVICE

An on-line video chat service allows you to speak to and see each other. It is easy to set up, though both parties need a computer, Webcam and high-speed or broadband Internet connection. Try Windows Live Messenger (*get.live.com*) and SightSpeed (*www.sightspeed.com*).

The all-in-one videophones (*www.packet8.net* and *www.ojoservices.com*) also offer this service.

Cost: About $200 per phone, plus $25 to $50 per month.

Caregiver Support

Caregiver support groups supplement family visits to seriously ill patients. Group members may be especially helpful if loved ones do not live near the patient. Information is available at the Family Caregiver Alliance (800-445-8106, *www.caregiver.org*), National Family Caregivers Association (800-896-3650, *www.nfcacares.org*), Share (866-891-2392, *www.sharecancersupport. org*) and CancerCare (800-813-4673, *www.cancer care.org*).

Sheila Warnock, founder and president, ShareTheCaregiving, Inc., which promotes group caregiving, New York City, and coauthor of *Share the Care* (Fireside).

 # High-Tech Pet ID

If you lose your pet, these high-tech methods increase the odds of getting it back safe...

• **Pet*iD Short Cut Home tag** includes a Web address, a pet's personal ID number and a 24-hour, manned toll-free number.

Cost: $25 for first three years of service,* $10 for each additional three years thereafter (800-836-7383, *www.petid.com*).

• **Dog E-Tag** is a digital collar device that stores up to 40 lines of information.

Cost: $45 at Petco, *www.petco.com.*

Prevention, 33 E. Minor St., Emmaus, PA 18098.

*Prices subject to change.

18

Winning Ways

A New Twist on the Power of Positive Thinking

When an Australian production company released *The Secret*—a documentary created by Rhonda Byrne, a former television producer, about the "law of attraction"—it soon became a self-help sensation. According to this theory, people can make their own realities through their thoughts.

Millions of DVDs and books based on it have been sold. Oprah Winfrey devoted two broadcasts to *The Secret*, telling her audience that she had been living her whole life according to the law of attraction, without even knowing it.

We asked one of the self-help gurus featured in the documentary, who has written his own book on the law of attraction, to tell us more about what this concept is and how we can make it work for us…

UNDERSTANDING THE LAW

The idea that we attract things to ourselves with our thoughts might seem controversial, but at a certain level, it's just common sense.

Is there any doubt that people who have positive thoughts about their careers are more likely to attract promotions and raises than those who think of their work as an unpleasant chore? Or that people who have upbeat, positive attitudes about their fellow man are more likely to attract friends than those who think everyone is against them? Medical science has shown that patients who think they will recover are more likely to do so. Our thoughts and attitudes unquestionably affect our world.

The law of attraction takes this a step further. Our thoughts shape every aspect of our existence. It isn't our boss, our family, bad luck or the economy that is holding us back—it is our

Joe Vitale, PhD, president of Hypnotic Marketing, Inc., a marketing consulting firm based outside Austin, TX. He is the author of more than 20 books, including *The Attractor Factor: 5 Easy Steps for Creating Wealth (Or Anything Else) from the Inside Out* (Wiley). You can subscribe to his free e-letter at *www.mrfire.com*.

own thoughts. The idea is to awaken and take conscious control—choose what we want to be or have. It's up to us to make things right.

ONE WAY IT WORKED FOR ME

I always wanted to have an audio program in the well-known Nightingale-Conant catalog of self-help audiotapes. Its roster of greats includes Tony Robbins, Deepak Chopra, Brian Tracy and Wayne Dyer. Despite the fact that I always sent the editors of Nightingale-Conant my new books as soon as they were published, I couldn't interest them in my work.

But I didn't give up. I simply held on to the dream, picturing my work in the catalog and trusting that something would give sooner or later. In the meantime, I kept writing books that I hoped would inspire and help people. One day, a man began sending me e-mails related to my book *There's a Customer Born Every Minute* (AMACOM), based on P.T. Barnum's life. I answered all his questions, glad to help.

Eventually he sent me an e-mail which said, "If you ever want your material considered by Nightingale-Conant, let me know. I'm their marketing project manager."

I immediately sent him my books, which he loved. He then proceeded to convince others at the catalog company to include my work. It did take nearly 11 months, but Nightingale-Conant now carries my audiotape *The Power of Outrageous Marketing*, and it is a best seller for them.

This story illustrates many lessons. One is the power of the Internet—my contact found me at my Web site. Another is that I was willing to be helpful to someone who wrote to me out of the blue—if I had ignored his e-mail, I never would have found out where he worked. Still another is the importance of having someone believe in you. But certainly one key lesson is the true magic of the power of a dream.

THE FIVE STEPS

• **Step 1.** Know what you want. It is easy to become fixated on the pain of a bad back…the mental strain of a mountain of bills…or the frustration of a go-nowhere job or challenging relationship. But our bitterness about our problems only attracts more problems to us.

Replace negative thoughts about your problems with positive thoughts about the way you would like things to be, and you'll draw those things to you instead. "I'm fed up with these interruptions" becomes "I want a quiet, peaceful place where I can read a book." "My feet are killing me" becomes "My foot pain will go away soon, and I will be just as mobile as ever." "My marriage is failing" becomes "I have a wonderful spouse whom I love, and I'm going to make this work."

• **Step 2.** Think big. Decide what your goal is. What would make your heart sing? What would you do if you knew you could not fail? What would you want if you could have anything?

Most people feel bound by the limits of what they consider feasible for their lives. They hope to get through a difficult day…or to find enough money to pay the bills. They don't dare hope for a truly fabulous, life-changing day…or to make enough money to put them on easy street. But even your biggest dreams are not big to the universe. There are trillions of dollars worth of wealth floating around the world—who's to say you can't be a millionaire? Set aside the constraints, and think about what you would want if you could have anything at all.

Write your goal on a card, and put it in your pocket or purse. By doing so, you will unconsciously remind yourself of your intention. Your own mind will then nudge you in the direction of making your goal a reality.

• **Step 3.** Clear all negative or limiting beliefs. It's crucial to rid ourselves of any negative beliefs we have about ourselves. Common examples include variations of "I'm not good enough"…"If it hasn't happened yet, it never will"…"Somebody (or something) always will stand in the way of my success"…and "If I get my hopes up, I'll only get hurt."

Example: If your weight-loss attempts always fail, the reason could be a negative self-belief. You might believe that since your parents were overweight, you are destined to be overweight, too…or that the failure of your earlier weight-loss attempts is proof that you're incapable of sticking to a diet. You might believe that looking better will change who you are…damage your relationships with your friends…or inspire new romantic relationships that will end in heartache.

Once you find a negative belief, confront it. Clear it from your mind, and replace it with a positive thought, one based on the idea that you are capable and worthy of achieving your goal.

• Step 4. Feel what it would be like to have, do or be what you want. Just imagine that you already have what you want. If you are a salesperson and your goal is to make $200,000 in sales commissions this year, think about how you would feel if you achieved that. Pretend you are a movie director, and write a script for what you want to experience. Really get into it as you write it. Feel it. Sense it.

Instead of writing, "I want a customer to call me with a big order," write, "A brand-new customer just phoned and ordered $100,000 from me. I feel fantastic! I'm still smiling about it. The customer was so pleased."

Visualizing your goals and desires can set the process in motion, drawing close to you people and things that help you get what you want.

• Step 5. Let go as you act on your intuitive impulses and allow the results to manifest. Once you start thinking, "I'm going to be a millionaire," then ideas, contacts and opportunities capable of making you a million dollars will be pulled toward you. You will notice a societal need that you could fill by starting a company…or see the perfect way to promote the skills or ideas you already have…or realize that the person you just met could help put your career on the fast track.

Once you start thinking, "My spouse (or boss) will treat me wonderfully," you'll begin to see ways to give your spouse (or boss) what he/she wants from you. When you learn to give these people what they want, they will start to treat you wonderfully.

How to Win Anyone Over with Charm

Brian Tracy, chairman and CEO of Brian Tracy International, a leadership and success consulting company, Solana Beach, CA, and president of Brian Tracy University, a private on-line university for sales and entrepreneurship, *www.briantracy.com.* He is also a coauthor of *The Power of Charm: How to Win Anyone Over in Any Situation* (Amacom).

Charming people are generally more successful than their less charming counterparts. And, in fact, charm is the single most important quality you can possess if you want to be a leader. But what is it that charming people do differently from everyone else? They are not necessarily wittier or better-looking or more sophisticated. All charming people simply have taught themselves a few interpersonal skills—skills that anyone can master.

Surprisingly, the point of these interpersonal skills isn't primarily to make us seem more appealing to others—it is to make the individuals we interact with seem more appealing to themselves. People are attracted to any person who increases their self-esteem. They are inclined to help him/her and predisposed to believe what he has to say—even if they do not completely understand why.

To be more charming…

• Greet everyone you meet as if he were very special. Do this with strangers and longtime acquaintances alike. If you cannot muster the necessary enthusiasm naturally, tell yourself that each person you meet is a dear childhood friend whom you haven't seen in decades. Act as though you are absolutely thrilled to have this old friend back in your life.

It can be particularly difficult to smile and seem thrilled to meet people when you are nervous. If a situation fills you with anxiety, mentally rehearse being warm and genial.

Example: Before a job interview, imagine that you are smart and charming and that everything goes very well.

• Be free with a "thank you." Thank everyone for every reason you can find. Thank your spouse for listening to your problems, even when your spouse is the problem. Thank your employees for their work, even when they are just doing their jobs. Thank the maitre d' for trying to find you a table, even if it was he who lost your reservation in the first place.

A heartfelt "thank you" lets people know that we appreciate what they've done, which boosts their faith in their own importance and competence. They feel better about themselves and are drawn to us for making them feel that way.

Saying "thank you" inflates our self-esteem, too, because it reminds us of our ability to help others. The higher our self-esteem climbs, the more comfortable we are around others and the more charming we become.

Helpful: Before visiting a foreign country, learn to say "thank you," "you are welcome," "please" and "good morning" in the language.

• **Pay attention.** Listen to people as if you are hanging on every word. And, lean forward slightly, nod every minute or two, focus on the speaker's eyes, occasionally "flicking" your gaze from one of his eyes to the other. There is no such thing as too intense a gaze when you are listening—imagine that your eyes are sunlamps and your goal is to give the speaker's eyes a tan. When people feel listened to, they feel happier and will tend to associate you with those happy feelings.

The longer you can keep a conversation partner speaking on subjects that interest him, the more charming he'll consider you. If you don't know what topics are of interest to this person, inquire about his family or ask, "What sort of work do you do?" Be sure you use the phrase "sort of work." The vagueness lets people who are currently unemployed discuss their fields in general rather than admit that they're out of a job. Follow this up with "How did you get into that line?"

At some point, the person will pause to make sure you are still listening. Prompt him with an encouraging question, such as "What did you do then?"

• **Praise people's efforts.** Humans have an unquenchable need to be reassured that they are worthy of praise. If you feed this need in people, they will repeat whatever behavior earned them your praise, hoping that they will get more. Almost like addicts, they will return to you for a praise fix again and again.

Some people will try to downplay your praise, claiming that their efforts were nothing special. Don't let them stop you. People who aren't good at accepting praise still love to receive it.

• **Find something to admire.** Compliment something about everyone you meet. Your compliments need not be about big things—sometimes we score more points by noticing the little things that everyone else tends to overlook.

It is sometimes tricky to compliment people we have just met, since we don't know much about them yet. Consider complimenting something they are wearing.

Example: The famously charming former president Bill Clinton often would say in receiving lines, "I like your tie."

Great Conversation Starters

Dorothy Leeds, communication expert, *www.dorothyleeds.com*, and author of *The 7 Powers of Questions* (Perigee) and *Smart Questions: The Essential Strategy for Successful Managers* (Berkley).

W hether in business or social settings, asking the right questions is key to getting people to open up.

Many people do have a difficult time making conversation, particularly with strangers. When I am counseling clients, open-ended questions are crucial for eliciting important information, promoting critical thinking and leading to genuine connections. (Closed-ended questions are those that can be answered with just a word or two.) The average person asks 39 closed-ended questions for every one open-ended question.

Here are some common conversation starters that typically go nowhere—and alternatives that are more likely to open up a discussion…

• **"Isn't the temperature ghastly?"**

Better: "It's been so hot lately that I'm thinking of putting in central air-conditioning. How do you cool your home?"

• **"Have you seen the latest Tom Cruise movie?"**

Better: "I'm thinking of going to the movies this weekend. What have you seen lately that you liked—or hated?" A conversationally challenged person might just give you the name of the movie—but follow-up questions are easy. ("What did you like about it?")

Here are my tricks for starting conversations in situations where many people blunder…

On an airplane: I introduce myself to seatmates, ask whether they are heading home or going on a trip and take the conversation from there. (I also will ask whether they would prefer to talk or to stay quiet, adding something like "which is fine with me.")

At a party: I might first ask how a guest knows the host and follow it up with a more creative question. For example, at a graduation party (or other milestone event), "Tell me about the best gift you ever received." On New Year's Eve, "What's your most outrageous fantasy for the New Year?"

Conducting a job interview: "What were the tasks you most enjoyed on your last job and why? What were the tasks you least enjoyed and why was this the case?"

Even well-phrased questions will not get people to open up if your body language communicates that you don't truly want a conversation. *Dos and don'ts...*

- **Don't cross your arms.** That posture suggests that you don't really want to talk.

- **Don't be a "space invader."** Most people are comfortable with a one-and-a-half- to two-foot distance from new acquaintances. A very funny episode of the *Seinfeld* TV series involved a character who kept leaning in until he was about six inches away from the person to whom he was speaking, which made that person very uncomfortable.

- **Do use a gracious tone.** Don't ask questions in a terse, combative or interrogative way.

- **Do give your full attention.** Shifting eyes make people think that you are not interested. Do not stare, but try to maintain plenty of eye contact.

The person who asks questions automatically controls the conversation, so beware of monopolizing. Managers interviewing job candidates say that they spend 70% of the interview time listening—but research shows that they actually talk 70% of the time.

How to Get People To Do What They Don't Want To

To get someone to do something you think they do not want to do, say: "I know you don't want to do this, but..." People are 29%

more likely to grant a favor when the person asking for it uses this phrase.

Reason: Showing that you understand that someone is reluctant empowers him/her to feel that he has a choice—and to decide it might not be so bad to grant your request.

Eric Knowles, professor of psychology at the University of Arkansas, Fayetteville...chief scientist at Omegachange. com...and co-editor of *Resistance and Persuasion* (LEA).

Two Top Executives Reveal Their Success Secret: Being Nice

Robin Koval, president, and Linda Kaplan Thaler, CEO and chief creative officer, The Kaplan Thaler Group, Ltd., a New York City advertising agency responsible for such successful ad campaigns as the award-winning Aflac duck. They are the coauthors of *The Power of Nice: How to Conquer the Business World with Kindness* (Currency).

Nice has an image problem. Nice people often are considered to be wimpy and naïve—and not particularly successful. We're told that nice guys finish last. In reality, nice wields amazing power. *Here's how...*

- **Nice people live longer.** People who volunteer their time typically outlive nonvolunteers, according to a study conducted by researchers at the University of Michigan.

- **Nice people are more productive workers and more effective bosses.** Each 2% increase in the cheerfulness of any organization's employees can lead to a 1% revenue increase, according to research from psychologist Daniel Goleman, PhD, co-chairman of Rutgers University's Consortium for Research on Emotional Intelligence in Organizations.

- **Nice people have better love lives.** Low-key, congenial people are 50% less likely to divorce than the population as a whole, according to a University of Toronto study.

- **Nice people stay out of court.** Doctors who spend more time positively interacting with their patients are less likely to be sued, according to health-care researchers.

HOW TO BE NICER

- **Make small gestures of kindness** to those often treated poorly. The worse the treatment someone tends to receive, the more he/she will appreciate even the smallest kindness.

  Example: An airline passenger offered a cookie to a harried flight attendant—and was rewarded with an upgrade to first class.

- **Share credit.** Turn your victories into triumphs for your colleagues. Not only is this a nice gesture, it creates a group of people who have an interest in seeing your ideas succeed.

- **Be free with compliments.** People worry that frequent compliments make them appear phony or smarmy, but they rarely do if given sincerely.

- **Help your rivals.** A rival need not be an enemy. Today's competitor might be tomorrow's ally.

  Example: Magician Tony Hassini shared blueprints for some illusions he was not using with a promising young magician. That young magician, Doug Henning, went on to tremendous success and ended up hiring Hassini to help with his Broadway show.

- **Give people a little more than they expect.** Small, unanticipated gestures convey the message that you really care.

  Example: The service department at one Lexus dealership in California places chocolate candies in vehicle cup holders when customers retrieve their cars. Business has climbed 20% since this policy began.

- **Show vulnerability.** Admit that you're new at something and even a little scared. Your admission of weakness makes those around you feel better about their own insecurities. It also could win them to your side, because people generally root for beginners and underdogs.

- **Make connections for others.** When you meet someone new, ask yourself if someone you already know would benefit from making his acquaintance. Then make the introduction.

- **Repair lapses in niceness.** We all have days when we speak rudely or treat someone poorly. Acknowledge your mistake. And do so promptly—the longer you wait, the more the hurt grows.

Lay on the Guilt

The fear-and-guilt combination provides the best motivation for improving behavior. Researchers claim that this combination is much more effective than a hopeful or positive message at changing behavior.

Example: The message of "Smoking pot may not kill you but it will kill your mother" proved much more effective than positive and educational messages when deterring drug use among teenagers.

Conclusion: Making someone feel hopeful, good or informed is much less important for changing behavior than making a person feel accountable.

Kirsten A. Passyn, PhD, assistant professor of marketing, Salisbury University, Salisbury, MD, and Mita Sujan, PhD, Woldenburg professor of marketing, Tulane University, New Orleans.

Rational Responses To Irrational Verbal Attacks

If someone verbally attacks you, stay calm and try these strategies...

- **Ask the person what he/she is upset about.** This shows that you want to communicate, not argue—and it puts the responsibility back on him.

- **Concede one kernel of truth,** if there is one, but deny the generalization.

  Example: If your sister-in-law calls you a screwup, admit to one specific error but say that it does not represent everything you do.

- **Take a stab at what you think the person is feeling:** "You sound angry right now. I'm sorry you feel that way." Do not blame.

- **Resist the urge to win.** Instead, listen and ask questions, which will ultimately help the other person independently arrive at a workable solution.

Nando Pelusi, PhD, psychologist in private practice, New York City.

"What Did You Say?"

Women who claim that men do not listen might have a point. A woman's voice is more complex than the male voice. Men hear a woman's voice more clearly than a man's, but they require additional brain activity to process the sounds. The male brain may tire from the extra effort.

American Family Physician, American Academy of Family Physicians, 11400 Tomahawk Creek Pkwy., Leawood, KS 66211, *www.aafp.org*.

The Right Way To Handle Difficult Conversations

Barbara Pachter, president, Pachter & Associates, workplace communication consultants in Cherry Hill, NJ. She is the author of several books, including *New Rules @ Work: 79 Etiquette Tips, Tools, and Techniques to Get Ahead and Stay Ahead* (Prentice Hall).

It is not fun to confront a neighbor about his barking dog…inform a coworker that he has bad breath…or tell a friend her behavior is inappropriate—but sometimes something must be said. *Here's how best to say it…*

• **Ask permission before you stick your nose in.** You think a close friend needs to rethink his comb-over, but you are unsure how he'll react if you suggest it. The odds that he'll respond favorably improve dramatically if you first get his go-ahead to raise a difficult subject.

Example: "There's something I have been thinking about. I don't know if it's really my business to bring it up, but if it were me, I'd want someone to say something. Is it okay if I raise a sticky subject?"

• **Pick a calm moment.** Say your neighbor doesn't mow his grass for weeks at a time. You have been stewing over the situation all day and decide to confront him when he gets home from work. However, people tend to be tightly wound when they first get home, making a tricky conversation that much more challenging. It is better to wait until he is relaxed. People tend to be calmer on weekends than on weekdays…after an hour or more at home than immediately after fighting traffic…and soon after a meal than when hungry. In the workplace, people are calmest when they are not facing deadlines.

If you're worked up over the problem—or even about an unrelated problem—postpone the conversation until you're calm, too.

• **Act as though it is no big deal.** A coworker has food on her face at an important lunch meeting. Minimize her embarrassment by sharing this information without judgment or embarrassment on your part. When the messenger seems embarrassed, the message inevitably seems more embarrassing. Simply describe the situation—"Mary, you have a little piece of broccoli on your cheek."

If this person still seems embarrassed, add, "Don't worry, it happens to everyone"…or "I don't think anyone noticed but me."

Whenever possible, tell the person in private. If there's no way to escape the crowd, whisper or write a note to keep things confidential.

• **Don't just raise a problem—**also propose a solution. Your natural inclination when you share difficult information might be to blurt out the problem and escape the conversation as soon as possible, but this might leave the other party feeling confused or angry. After saying there's a problem, mention a potential solution (unless it's obvious), then check that everything is still okay between you and this person. By ending with a question, you help to turn a confrontation into a conversation.

Example: "Jack, your dog's been doing his business on my lawn and digging up my wife's garden. Could you tie your dog up when you put him out back or just keep an eye on him? Would that be okay with you?"

• **Assume the best.** A neighbor's loud music has been keeping you awake every night for a week. You feel like telling the jerk what you think of him. Instead, enter the conversation under the assumption that this person is unaware of the problem and would genuinely want to know. If people sense our dislike for them, they're less likely to change their behavior for us.

• **Mix the good with the bad.** The text in a coworker's slide presentation is so small that no one can read it. Share this problem, but include good news.

Example: "I loved your presentation. You really covered all of the facts. One thing—you might consider using a larger font next time. It was hard to read from the back of the room."

• **Keep it focused.** You finally get up the nerve to confront a relative about something that has been bothering you…then you mention a few other problems as well. Better to discuss only one tough issue per conversation. Presenting a list of quibbles might make the other person feel as if you're piling on bad news—and the secondary issues could detract from your main point.

• **If someone confronts *you*, respond with grace, not anger.** Let's say a neighbor asks you to replace your rusty old mailbox. Even if you don't think this is any of his business, say something positive, such as, "Thank you for letting me know. I'll think about that." If you decide you want to keep the mailbox, you may want to explain why—"It's been in my family for years."

• **Know how to duck a difficult conversation.** When a problem is likely to resolve itself if we do nothing…the time isn't right for confrontation…or you want to avoid an issue…

• Suddenly "remember" a previous responsibility and excuse yourself.

• Say, "Oh, I just remembered, I wanted to ask you about…" then raise a completely different matter.

• Answer a difficult question posed to you with "Well, what do you think?"

• Dodge the issue when asked your opinion about something you dislike with "I bet everyone will love it."

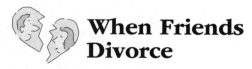

When Friends Divorce

If close friends are divorcing, be sure you handle the situation appropriately…

• **Tell them separately that you care about them,** and express your willingness to talk with them about anything except the other person, the marriage or a new love. Make it clear that you are saying the same thing to both spouses.

• **Invite both of them to parties.** Tell each one that the other may be coming, and let the two of them work it out.

Common solution: Attending in shifts. One arrives early and leaves early, while the other arrives late.

• **Do not introduce either one to any potential dates** until after the divorce is final or, better yet, don't do it at all. It may look as if you are favoring one over the other.

Joy Browne, PhD, clinical psychologist in New York City, host of a syndicated call-in radio show and author of several books, including Dating Disasters and How to Avoid Them *(Hay House).*

How to Help Someone Who Is Mourning

When a friend is in mourning, don't ask if he or she needs help—he may be unable to focus on what he requires. Just assume that nothing has been done. Help with errands, dog walking, laundry, baby care, housecleaning and even bring in a meal. People in mourning may be overwhelmed. Anything you do for them will be appreciated.

Rabbi Aryeh Markman, executive director, Aish HaTorah Los Angeles, part of a worldwide network of Jewish educational centers with programs offered in 200 cities, www.aish.com.

Anxiety Helper

Nervous about a stressful situation, such as public speaking? Have sexual intercourse the night before.

Recent finding: Participants who engaged in intercourse before stressful events had lower blood pressure levels and felt less stressed the next day than those who abstained from sexual intercourse.

Stuart Brody, PhD, full professor of psychology, University of Paisley, Scotland, and the leader of a study of 50 people, published in Biological Psychology.

Surprising Ways to Fight Fatigue! Boost Mood! More!

Pierce J. Howard, PhD, a leading cognitive science researcher and cofounder and director of research at the Center for Applied Cognitive Studies in Charlotte, NC. He is adjunct professor of organizational psychology at University of North Carolina, Chapel Hill, and author of *The Owner's Manual for the Brain* (Bard).

Though many of the brain's inner workings remain mysterious, scientists make new discoveries about this powerful organ almost weekly. Recent brain research has revealed ways to significantly improve memory and mental ability along with practical ways to prevent stroke and other brain diseases, including Alzheimer's.

Highlights…

BOOST PERFORMANCE WITH STRESS

Scientists used to view stress as a detriment to mental performance. They advised people who were trying to improve learning and memory skills to minimize stress—with regular meditation, yoga, etc.

New finding: People learn more efficiently when they maintain an optimal level of stress. A principle called the Yerkes–Dodson Law has shown that a certain amount of stress (arousal) motivates people to try harder.

Balance is the key. Individuals experiencing very little stress—when taking an exam or writing a paper, for example—tend to make errors of *omission*, such as forgetting to complete all the answers. People who experience too much stress make errors of *commission*, such as hitting the wrong computer keys.

What to do: If you find you're making more errors than usual in completing a task, you're probably experiencing too much stress. If you're bored, your stress levels are too low. For optimal mental performance, it is best to be in between these two extremes.

How to achieve stress balance: Too much stress is typically caused by one of two factors—having too few personal resources in a demanding situation or feeling that you have no good options.

In the first case, increase your resources (practice, learn new skills, find helpers) or decrease the demands made on you (change to a less demanding task, simplify the task in some way).

In the second case, talk with your associates or with a counselor or doctor to identify ways to gain more control over the situation.

Too little stress is caused by having too many resources in a situation that is not very demanding—you are overqualified for the task at hand. Address this by handicapping or otherwise limiting yourself.

Example: When my daughter was younger and I played tennis with her, I would hit to her singles court, while she hit to my doubles lanes, so that the tennis became more interesting for me. Or you could increase the level of difficulty or complexity of what you are doing. For example, if you are bored writing something, try doing it without using the verb "to be."

REDUCE STROKE RISK WITH CHOCOLATE

People who consume moderate amounts of chocolate have better brain circulation and can reduce their risk for stroke. Cocoa beans—the primary ingredient in chocolate—contain natural antioxidants known as cocoa flavonoids. The flavonoids in chocolate are more powerful than vitamin C at restricting fatty deposits (or plaque) in arteries in the brain and heart. A buildup of plaque can impair mental performance and are the main cause of strokes.

Chemical compounds in chocolate also increase the levels of *nitric oxide*, a critical compound in the blood that relaxes the inner walls of blood vessels and promotes enhanced blood flow and lower blood pressure. A study of 470 healthy men in the Netherlands found that those who ate the most cocoa beans—in the form of chocolate bars, pudding, hot cocoa, etc.—had lower blood pressure and half the risk of dying during the study period than those who ate the least cocoa bean products.

What to do: Have one to two cups of cocoa or two small squares of a bar of chocolate daily. The darker the chocolate, the better. According to the ORAC scale—a measure of the antioxidant levels in foods—dark chocolate has double the amount of antioxidants of milk chocolate.

FIGHT AFTERNOON FATIGUE

Nearly everyone gets sleepy after lunch. You can prevent this afternoon slump by eating protein first during lunch, then carbohydrates. The protein will trigger an energy-promoting amino acid in the brain.

Foods that are high in the complex carbohydrates, including whole-grain bread, fruits and vegetables, are good for you, but they contain an abundance of the amino acid *L-tryptophan*, which helps promote relaxation and sleepiness. High-protein foods, such as meats and fish, contain *L-tyrosine*, which makes you more alert and less likely to feel tired. Your energy level after lunch will depend on which of these amino acids reaches your brain first.

What to do: Start your meal with a bite or two of protein. This will enable the L-tyrosine to reach the brain before the L-tryptophan. But don't just eat protein—carbohydrates are your body's main source of fuel.

GET HAPPY WITH OMEGA-3s

In countries such as Norway and Japan, where people eat the most fish—the best source for omega-3 fatty acids—the incidence of depression and suicide is much lower than in countries where people eat less. Omega-3s can help prevent and treat a variety of disorders, including bipolar disorder and attention deficit hyperactivity disorder (ADHD).

Unfortunately, Americans get excess amounts of another fatty acid group, the omega-6s, found mainly in meats, cooking oils and soybeans. In the last century, the ratio of omega-6s to omega-3s has soared, increasing the risk of mood disorders, including depression.

What to do: Eat three to four fish servings weekly to get more omega-3s. (Avoid fish high in mercury, such as shark, swordfish, tilefish and king mackerel, as well as large tuna, such as albacore, yellowfin, bigeye and bluefin.) Or you can eat nuts if you prefer. Ten to 15 walnut halves or 15 to 20 pecan halves provide the recommended daily amount of omega-3s.

REST—BUT DON'T NAP

The inventor Thomas Edison was famous for getting by on only two to four hours of sleep a night. When he was working on a particularly difficult problem, he would rest for five to 10 minutes. In the brief period between wakefulness and sleep, he often would experience an "A-ha!" moment and find the solution to his problem.

Scientists have noticed that when the brain enters into the "alpha state"—characterized by brain waves that are slower than the beta waves of wakefulness—people often develop insights, along with more focus and energy.

What to do: Close your eyes and let your mind relax for five to 10 minutes. Resting in this fashion is not sleeping. People who slip into a true sleep are groggy and less alert when they wake up.

 # Get More Done in Less Time

Susan Martin, founder of Business Sanity, a coaching and consulting firm that helps business owners and independent professionals increase profits, avoid burnout and run their businesses and lives more effectively, Brooklyn, NY, *www.business-sanity.com*.

Do you have trouble getting things done? Often miss deadlines? Or show up late for most appointments? If yes, your time-management skills need improvement now.

Five simple steps that can help…

• **Identify time wasters.** Most people who struggle with management of time tend to get caught up in activities that waste time, such as surfing the Internet or making long phone calls. Pinpoint these habits, and post a list to remind yourself not to do them.

• **Trim your to-dos.** Many of us have to-do lists that are full of tasks that don't really help us reach our goals and thus aren't priorities. Review your list, and decide what really needs to be done.

• **Value your time.** Many people misjudge how much they can accomplish and think they can do everything themselves, which makes it impossible to manage time. Be sure you're doing things that can be done only by you. Try to delegate or outsource everything else to family members, colleagues and people you hire, such as gardeners and cleaning people.

- **Get more real.** Probably the biggest time-management trap is underestimating how much time things really take. Estimate how long you think a task will take and then double or triple the amount of time until you're better able to accurately judge how much time is needed.

- **Set up an appointment with yourself.** Schedule focused work periods to accomplish specific tasks. During these periods, have voice-mail pick up your phone, turn off the Internet and e-mail, and tell others that you will not be available during that time.

Hidden Benefits Of Being Messy

David H. Freedman, a business and science journalist located in Needham, MA, who has written books on the management principles of the US Marine Corps and the structure of modern computers. He is also coauthor, with Eric Abrahamson, of *A Perfect Mess: The Hidden Benefits of Disorder* (Little, Brown).

Society isn't kind to messy people. Parents punish children who won't clean up their rooms, and bosses question the competence of employees who have unkempt desks. But is messy really so bad?

The professional organizers claim that clutter costs us hours each day by making it harder to find things. Our surveys, however, suggest that messy people spend only nine minutes per day, on average, trying to find things in their homes and another nine minutes trying to find things in their offices. Most messy people can locate what they need fairly quickly—they just look where they last had the item. When a mess has been cleaned, it often takes longer to remember where the item has been stored.

Some experts believe we need schedules and plans to stay headed in the right direction, but people with plans often stick to those plans long after it should have been obvious that their plans were not working. Disorganized people usually are better at rolling with the punches and seizing serendipitous opportunities.

Example: The Scottish biologist Alexander Fleming discovered penicillin when samples he had carelessly left exposed in his mess of an office were contaminated while he was away on vacation.

For many people, a certain amount of messiness can be beneficial...

MESSY HOUSE

What does a tidy home actually do for you? It will not make you more productive—the hours spent cleaning will not save you much, if any, time finding things later. It will not make you healthier—if anything, exposure to the chemicals in household cleaners tends to be worse for our health than living in a cluttered home, unless the mess is extreme and dust and mold accumulate. Finally, a tidy home probably will not make you happier—perhaps you feel better when your house is neat, but if your family does not share this passion for spotlessness, your demands for cleanliness are likely to lead to arguments and unhappiness. *What to do...*

- **Allow certain sections of the house to be messy.** Let your messy spouse have a disorganized den...permit projects to pile up on the otherwise unused dining room table...don't worry if the kids' rooms are a mess.

- **Permit mess cycles.** Don't try to keep the home spotless all the time. Let the mess build, and pick up every few weeks or when guests are coming.

CLUTTERED DESK

Neat people tend to equate messy desks with inefficiency, but for a naturally messy person, a messy desk might be the most efficient arrangement for him or her.

Helpful: Messes don't look as messy when they're arranged in stacks. Things will be easy to find because they will be piled close to where they were last used, and stacking is quicker than organizing and filing. It doesn't take substantially longer to dig through a pile of papers on a desk to find an item than it does to sort through a filing cabinet trying to remember where the item was filed.

UNTIDY YARD

Tending to a lawn absorbs hours of our time, wastes hundreds of gallons of water and often involves drenching your yard in pesticides. We all would be better off if "neat" lawns were replaced with "messy" fields of native plants.

You can make a naturally landscaped lawn more palatable to fussy neighbors by placing a border of neat grass around the edges. Also, explain to your neighbors what you're doing and why. You might even get them thinking about their own lawns.

How to Find Lost Objects—Fast

Michael Solomon, a writer residing in Baltimore, MD, *www.professorsolomon.com.* He refers to himself as a "find-ologist" and is the author of five books, including *How to Find Lost Objects* (Penguin).

One of life's persistent aggravations is misplacing everyday objects, such as keys, cell phones and reading glasses. You wind up wasting time ransacking the house in a frenzied search. Michael Solomon has studied how things get lost and how best to find them. *His strategies...*

• **Identify the Eureka Zone.** The majority of lost objects tend to travel no more than 18 inches from their last known locations. I call this the Eureka Zone.

Examples: A pencil that has rolled beneath the computer. Eyeglasses under a newspaper.

Whenever I lose something, I explore the Eureka Zone meticulously.

• **"Lose" another object.** If you happen to drop and lose sight of an object that has one or more identical counterparts (such as a screw or an earring), try purposely dropping a second one and watching where it goes. This gives you an estimated radius for how far the first object might have rolled or bounced.

• **Make sure you are not staring right at it.** When you're feeling rushed and agitated, your vision literally narrows. This is why your spouse or a friend often finds the lost object as soon as he/she joins in the search. You can improve your focus by taking a few deep breaths and repeating to yourself the name of the lost object over and over—"car keys, car keys, car

keys"—which can prevent you from becoming distracted from the task at hand. Also, the object may look different than you imagine.

Example: My friend couldn't find a hardcover book that he needed. We searched his apartment in vain until I grew suspicious of his description and began to examine the paperbacks on his bookshelf. There was the book, a paperback, in plain sight.

• **Check whether you've substituted one routine motion for another.** Instead of being where it's supposed to be, your object may be where something else is supposed to be. This often happens in the kitchen.

Example: You normally keep scissors in a jar on the kitchen counter, but you mindlessly returned them to the tool drawer.

It's also a problem when filing items.

Example: You file your Bruce Springsteen CD under "B," instead of "S."

• **See if the object has been borrowed.** Is it something that your spouse or your coworkers may have used since the last time you saw it? Remember to ask before you drive yourself crazy looking for something.

Six Simple Steps to Better Mental Fitness

Sandra Cusack, PhD, Guttmann-Gee Research Fellow in Educational Gerontology at the Gerontology Research Centre at Simon Fraser University in Vancouver, Canada. She is coauthor, with Wendy Thompson, of *Mental Fitness for Life* (Bull).

Most people, including many doctors, do believe that memory and cognitive abilities inevitably decline at middle age—even though there's virtually no scientific proof to support this belief.

What most people do not realize: Even though some brain cells (neurons) die with age, the brain retains the ability to form new neurons and connections between neurons. In fact, the number of nerve endings (dendrites) in the part of the brain that processes information *increases* between ages 50 and 80.

Imaging tests allow us to see changes in brain physiology that occur in response to brain exercises and new learning. Age-related diseases, such as dementia—and even some medications—can lead to memory loss and reduced mental function, but these problems are not an inevitable part of aging.*

CREATING A "BRAIN WORKOUT"

People who exercise their minds frequently and develop positive psychological traits, such as optimism and self-confidence, can literally "rewire" their brains (that is, new neurons can be formed, and existing neurons can form new connections). *Here's how...*

• **Step 1.** Set goals. Goals create a sense of purpose and promote feelings of self-worth. Goals that are especially meaningful or that require a good deal of effort and concentration, such as raising money for charity or researching your genealogy, are believed to promote brain health.

Goals are particularly important for the older adults who have a tendency to stop challenging themselves mentally in the assumption that their cognitive abilities decline with age. Any goal that improves overall health, such as losing weight or reducing stress, contributes to brain health.

Helpful steps...

• Write down 10 things that you want to do before you die. *Examples:* Short-term goal—lose 10 pounds in the next three months...long-term goal—become a part-time teacher. Choose goals that stretch your abilities but aren't impossible.

• Write down all the advantages of reaching your goals. *Examples:* "I'll be healthier and look better if I lose weight," and "It makes me happy to help people learn."

• Make your goals measurable. Suppose your goal is to complete a university degree that was abandoned years ago. Measurable goals might include applying for admission to the local college and enrolling in courses that are challenging.

• Set deadlines. Choose a date for each goal, and identify key steps along the way.

• **Step 2.** Be a power thinker. Because many older adults have negative perceptions of their mental abilities, they often say things like, "I can't remember your name because my memory isn't as good as it once was." Such statements indicate a willingness to accept the status quo and often lead to a self-fulfilling prophecy.

Better: Think—and phrase things—positively. Tell yourself, "I don't want to forget names, so I'm going to take the necessary steps to retain my memory."

• **Step 3.** Cultivate creativity. We used to believe that creativity declined with age. But some people reach their prime later in life.

Examples: Goethe finished writing Faust at age 83...Grandma Moses began painting in her 70s.

There are many ways to be creative. Humor is a form of creativity. So is keeping a journal, cooking or rearranging furniture in a room. Every activity is creative if you put your personal stamp on it.

Creative people are natural problem-solvers. Studies indicate that they engage both sides of their brains and reap the rewards of cognitive effort—including better memory and more efficient processing of information.

• **Step 4.** Develop a positive mental attitude. In the 1960s, Mayo Clinic researchers classified 839 patients as either optimists or pessimists, depending on the number of positive words that appeared in written statements they provided. Thirty years later, many more of the optimists were still alive, having lived an average of six years longer than the pessimists. Optimism, the hallmark of having a positive mental attitude, appears to have powerful effects on mental health, which may help protect cognitive abilities.

• **Step 5.** Perform memory-boosting exercises. Memory is like a muscle—the more you use it, the stronger it gets. Brain stimulation caused by learning new, challenging material triggers an increase in the number of dendrites as well as synapses (connections between dendrites).

Helpful: Create a "brain workout" schedule.

Example: *Sunday*—Read a classic book... visit an art museum. *Monday*—Listen to tapes or CDs to learn a foreign language. *Tuesday*—Do a crossword puzzle...attend a meditation class. *Wednesday*—Play bridge...write in your journal. *Thursday*—Take an art class. *Friday*—Volunteer as a tour guide at an art gallery. *Saturday*—Host a dinner party...try out a new recipe.

*Caution: If you have experienced a sudden memory decline, consult a physician. You may need to be evaluated for a memory disorder.

Also helpful: Learn one new word a day. Write it down and repeat the definition a few times. The next day, write down another word and review the one from the day before. Review all seven words at the week's end. Doing this daily will increase your vocabulary as well as your ability to retain new information of all kinds. To receive a free word-a-day e-mail, go to *www.wordsmith.org.*

Or for free Sudoku puzzles, the very popular number-logic game, try *www.free-sudokus.com.* Nintendo's "Brain Age," which has both math and logic activities, and similar video games also give your mind a good workout.

•**Step 6.** Speak your mind. People who assert themselves—by being active in their communities, meeting new people or simply feeling free to say what they're thinking—develop a tremendous amount of self-confidence. Believing that your thoughts matter will encourage you to think clearly, critically and creatively. It's also a great way to engage the world and keep your mind active.

Important: Take every opportunity to speak your mind. Join in casual discussions with your family and friends—everyone has something to contribute. Talk to people when you're waiting in line at the post office or grocery store—and, just as important, listen to what they have to say. As we hear different points of view, we develop mental flexibility and an open-mindedness. You can practice this skill one-on-one, or in groups, such as book clubs or adult-education classes.

ARE YOU MENTALLY FIT?

Rate yourself on a scale of 1 to 10 (10 being the highest rating).

1. Confidence in your mental abilities
2. Setting and achieving goals
3. Willingness to take risks
4. Optimism
5. Creativity
6. Mental flexibility
7. Ability to learn new things
8. Memory
9. Ability to express opinions clearly
10. Overall mental fitness.

Add up your score…

Less than 40: Poor. Get started on this program right away!

40-54: Fair. You could significantly improve your brain health with this program.

55-69: Good. You stand to gain from this program.

70-84: Very good. You're well on your way to a rich and fulfilling life, but you could be doing better.

85-100: Excellent. You are an inspiration to others—keep it up!

Stress Kills Brain Cells: How to Protect Yourself

Richard O'Connor, PhD, a psychotherapist who has offices in both Canaan, CT, and New York City. He is the author of *Undoing Perpetual Stress: The Missing Connection Between Depression, Anxiety, and 21st Century Illness* (Berkley), *Undoing Depression: What Therapy Doesn't Teach You and Medication Can't Give You* (Berkley) and *Active Treatment of Depression* (Norton).

Everyone knows that stress can contribute to weight gain, diabetes and many other ailments, but few people realize just how harmful stress can be for your brain.

Latest development: Although chronic stress has long been known to trigger the release of excessive amounts of stress hormones, such as *cortisol* and *adrenaline,* new studies show that both hormones actually kill brain cells and interfere with the production of new ones.

Fortunately, new research on the brain suggests that there may be ways to minimize, slow down and perhaps even reverse this damage. Here, Richard O'Connor, PhD, a renowned psychotherapist who has extensively researched the harmful effects of stress, gives his advice on the most effective brain-protection strategies.

•**Why has stress become such a serious health threat in recent years?** It's a long-term historical trend that involves culture and economics. Before the Industrial Revolution (in the late 18th century), people tended to awaken in the morning when it became light and to go to bed when it turned dark. They also had a great deal of leisure time. That has been changing—and just in the past 25 years, has changed dramatically. We are working 25% longer and harder to attain the same standard of living we did a quarter of a century ago. In fact, Americans now work as many hours as anyone in the world, including the Japanese, who are known for working incredibly long hours.

• Doesn't a reasonable amount of stress make people more productive? Yes, people are more productive when their work provides enough of a challenge to help them grow. But when the work is too difficult or the hours are too long, or our home life provides no relief, then stress becomes chronic. Research has consistently shown that chronic stress disrupts the functions of the immune, endocrine and digestive systems. This can result in a variety of health problems, such as asthma, heart disease and immune system deficiencies.

During the prior 15 years, advances in technology have given scientists an opportunity to examine the human brain in great detail. For example, imaging studies have allowed researchers to visualize the significant loss of gray matter (the brain's information processing center) that can result from years of stress-related conditions, such as depression and anxiety. Unfortunately, no one knows for sure whether these effects are permanent.

• Are most people aware of the degree to which they are suffering from stress? By no means. We have an interest in denying the effects of stress. Our society admires people who show grace under pressure, and we all want to believe we can handle whatever life dishes out.

• Given the nature of our lives today, is it really possible to avoid stress? Yes, absolutely. The first step is to believe that you have some degree of control over your own life. Many people feel out of control—as if events are driving them rather than the other way around. Many people think that they must work 60 hours a week, but that is simply not so. If your job requires long, stressful hours, consider changing professions or finding a job in your profession that has shorter hours.

The stakes are high. People who can't reduce chronic stress live shorter lives, suffer more illness and disability, have less satisfying relationships and often are plagued by anxiety and/or depression.

• What if it's not practical to make such a drastic change? Changing our thought patterns helps. This can allow us to prevent and even reverse some of the adverse changes, such as loss of gray matter, that occur in our brain's neural circuitry as a result of long-term stress. Meditation is an effective stress-reducing strategy. Research has shown that people who spend just 20 minutes a day focusing on their breath or on calming thoughts achieve such benefits as lower blood pressure, less anxiety and reduced chronic pain.

• What can be done in addition to meditation? As we all know, exercise can serve as an excellent stress fighter. However, few people appreciate the importance of intimate communication. When we feel like we have a partner or are part of a group, we feel safer and more secure. As a result, the stress-hormone cascade is reduced. Feeling that we have a purpose in life—having a child or pet to care for, a cause that's meaningful to us, people who need us— these are good stress fighters.

In one landmark study, residents of a nursing home were split into two groups. Half of the residents were told that they were responsible for taking care of a plant. The other half were told not to worry about the plant. After one year, those who were caring for a plant were healthier and had fewer illnesses. They also lived longer.

• How can we improve the way we communicate with others? Communication always occurs on two levels. It's not only about the content of what's being said, but also the nature of the relationship between the people. Content communication is usually conveyed through words… relationship communication comes through tone, face and body language. It's perfectly possible to say the words "I love you" but contradict the words through a dismissive tone or a frown. Content communication should be consistent with relationship communication.

• What if these strategies are not effective? For some people, self-help practices are not enough. Some of the newer antidepressants, such as selective serotonin reuptake inhibitors (SSRIs), seem to reverse stress-related brain damage and help people regain the ability to grow new brain cells.

We have evidence that psychotherapy can do the same thing. Cognitive behavior therapy, which trains patients to see how their psychological problems are the result of faulty thought patterns, has been around for more than 40 years—and it works to fight the effects of stress. To find a cognitive behavior therapist in your area, consult the Academy of Cognitive Therapy, *www.academyofct.org*, 610-664-1273.

Computer Games To Keep Your Mind Sharp

Domenic Greco, PhD, a psychologist located in San Marcos, CA, who studies the effect of games on the people who play them. He has adapted his video game neurofeedback technology for NASA. This same technology, the S.M.A.R.T. BrainGames Technology, is the basis for all his company's consumer products, which let video game players monitor their brain waves as they play. *Information:* CyberLearning Technology (*www.smartbraingames.com*).

Don't scoff at the games kids play on computers. More and more adults are discovering that on-line games help keep their minds sharp and allow them to socialize via the Internet with people all over the world.

On-line games are by no means all fast-action electronic versions of what you once might have played at penny arcades. The Internet also gives you access to dozens of traditional games, including bridge, canasta, mah jong, hearts, dominoes, chess and backgammon. You play these and other games against a computer or against real competitors.

GOOD FOR THE BRAIN

If you have any doubt that computer games are good for the brain, your skepticism might be allayed by the experience of James Rosser, Jr., MD. He's the director of the Advanced Medical Technology Institute at Beth Israel Medical Center in New York City—and he asked his staff of surgeons to periodically play video games.

Dr. Rosser recently discovered that the surgeons who played games three hours a week performed their medical tasks faster and more accurately than those who did not. Dr. Rosser's findings aren't unique. Experiments at my own company, CyberLearning Technology, show that people who regularly play video games have an easier time learning new tasks.

For older people, on-line games have another benefit. They can introduce you to activities you'll enjoy with younger family members.

GETTING STARTED

For an overview of available on-line games, visit one of the major sites, called portals, that have links to hundreds of games. Some of the bigger game portals include *http://games.yahoo.com/games/front…http://games.aol.com…*and *http://zone.msn.com*. To find other game sites, enter "on-line games" into Google or another search engine.

At least one portal, *www.aboutseniors.com.au/ComputerGames.html*, gives links to games traditionally popular with seniors, including bingo, solitaire, cribbage and canasta.

Before you can play, you may have to register by submitting your e-mail address and choosing a password. Most sites are free, and those that charge usually have fees of less than $100 a year.

Caution: Do not register unless a site states that it will not share your e-mail address. Also, some on-line games require you to download software that enables you to play the game on your computer. Before you do, make sure your computer has a security program that screens downloads for viruses and other unwanted bits of computer code.

Game sites usually permit you to play with people you know, who must also register, or with anonymous opponents chosen by the site on the basis of the skill level that you select.

CHOOSING A GAME

●**Backgammon.** "It's Your Turn" at *www.itsyourturn.com* has classic backgammon as well as several variations that you and a friend can sign up for and play for free. As in all backgammon games, winning requires you to remember complex numerical combinations and to vary your strategy as your opponent moves.

●**Battleships.** "Battleships–General Quarters II" at *www.battleships.f-active.com* is a favorite free site for young people and is now attracting a multigenerational crowd. Each of two players is in command of a fleet of five ships, and the object is to eliminate your opponent's fleet before the opponent destroys yours. The game is tricky, requiring physical coordination to work the mouse as well as quick decisions.

• **Bridge.** "OKbridge" at *www.okbridge.com* has been sanctioned by the American Contract Bridge League. It is the oldest and largest on-line bridge club, with members from 100 countries. Unlike most other games, bridge is played with a partner, a feature that can hone your skill in communications and patience.

Cost: $99 a year after a free seven-day trial.*

• **Chess.** "Free Internet Chess Server" at *www. freechess.org* allows you to play—free of charge —against its computer or a real person.

• **Crossword puzzles.** "Best Crosswords" at *www.bestcrosswords.com* offers seven new puzzles a day. Solvers have the option of submitting their results so they can track their improvement and also compete against others. Like most other word puzzles, crosswords build vocabulary and remind you of words you may have forgotten.

• **Dominoes.** "GameDesire," at *www.game desire.com* has a classic domino game with 28 "bones," or pieces. Play is free.

• **Mah jong.** "GameHouse," *www.gamehouse. com/onlinegames* lets Internet users play a variety of solitaire mah jong games for free.

*Price and offer subject to change.

Lucky Seven Works

Because the average person's brain can store up to seven chunks of information at a time, the best way to remember something is to break it down into groups of seven or less.

Examples: To remember a phone number with area code, separate the number into two pieces—the area code and the seven-digit number. To remember a poem, focus on the first seven words—then, after you memorize them, the next seven, and so on.

Women's Health Letter, 7100 Peachtree Dunwoody Rd., Atlanta 39328.

Memory Blocked?

If a word is on the tip of your tongue, but you just can't recall it, try gesturing. Physical movement can sometimes unlock a temporary memory block. If possible, move your hands in a shape related to the word.

Example: When trying to remember a type of bird, shape your hands like wings.

Elena Nicoladis, PhD, assistant professor of psychology, University of Alberta, Edmonton, Canada.

Green Tea Boosts Brain Power

In a recent Japanese study of cognitive function in subjects age 70 or older, participants who drank two or more cups of green tea per day had a 54% lower prevalence of cognitive decline—measured via memory, attention and language-use tests—than those who drank three cups or less weekly.

Theory: Antioxidants in green tea may reduce the buildup of a type of plaque in the brain that is responsible for memory loss in Alzheimer's disease.

Self-defense: Consume two or more cups of green tea daily to help promote brain health.

Shinichi Kuriyama, MD, PhD, associate professor of epidemiology, Tohoku University Graduate School of Medicine, Sendai, Japan.

Memorize While You Sleep

To memorize speeches and other material, review them before going to bed.

Reason: Most of memory consolidation happens during sleep, so what you read immediately before going to bed is more likely to be encoded in your long-term memory, making it easier to recall when you need it.

Candi Heimgartner, MS, instructor, department of biological sciences, University of Idaho, Moscow.

Get Your Sleep

Not getting enough sleep affects mental processes as much as not sleeping at all.

Recent study: The response times and memorization abilities of people who slept six hours or less a night for two weeks were no better than those of people who stayed awake for one to two days.

Most people need seven to eight hours of sleep a night.

David F. Dinges, PhD, professor of psychology, department of psychiatry, and chief of the division of sleep and chronobiology, University of Pennsylvania School of Medicine, Philadelphia, and principal investigator for a study published in *Sleep*.

Beat "Sleep Inertia"

On first waking in the morning, mental performance is as poor as if one had stayed awake all night. So, don't schedule challenging mental tasks for soon after waking—allow time to wake up first (by showering, reading the paper, etc.). Some people have found that they become alert more quickly by leaving the bedroom curtains open or having an alarm clock that turns on the lights. However, the one scientifically proven strategy for becoming alert quickly in the morning—you may have guessed it—is taking caffeine.

Hans van Dongen, PhD, associate research professor, Sleep and Performance Research Center at Washington State University, Spokane.

Bonus Cell Phone Uses

Cell phones can have other uses besides just making phone calls. *See the following list...*

- **Flashlight.** The display light can help you find a keyhole or locate something that fell under a car seat in the dark.
- **Photographic memory.** Use the camera in the cell phone to take a picture of where you parked in an airport parking lot, or of anything else you need to remember.
- **Clock.** Your cell phone will tell you the time and date, and many have an alarm clock.
- **Portable address book.** Keep names and full contact information in it.
- **Media player.** Many phones can download and play music and videos.
- **Calculator and computer.** Cell phones can function as calculators, provide Internet access and have general computer functions.

James Glass, a tax attorney based in New York City and a contributing writer to both *Tax Hotline* and *Bottom Line/ Retirement*, newsletters published by Boardroom Inc. He also writes about information technology for major consulting firms.

 # Say Cheese!

To look better in photographs, check out the following helpful tips...

- **Chat with the photographer about some subjects of mutual interest**—you will appear more relaxed if your mind is focused on something other than the picture.

- **If you have a double chin,** pay attention to camera position. The lens should be at your eye level or above. If it is not, bend your knees for the photo or sit in a chair so that you are looking up. Also, project your chin out an inch more than normal—this feels awkward but makes the picture look better.

- **If your eyes are often closed in photos,** close them before the photo is taken, have the photographer count to three, and open your eyes when he/she says "three."

Real Simple, 1271 Avenue of the Americas, New York City 10020.

19

Business and Career Coach

How to Ace a Job Interview Even When You're Over 50

As you grow older, you need to alter your job interview tactics. Once you learn the strategy, it is as easy to ace an interview when you are over 50 as it was when you were in your 20s.

First move: Weed out the losers—the companies that probably won't hire you because of your age.

You might persuade a biased company to hire you, but you can greatly improve your job prospects by concentrating on businesses that welcome the older applicant. The best way to find them is to be up front about age on your résumé. Most companies with an age bias won't even schedule an interview.

Too often, however, older applicants try to hide their age by omitting dates, especially those of college graduation and/or early jobs.

My advice: Put the dates in, and don't worry. The companies that call you back to schedule an interview are usually those that know the value of older employees.

LAYING THE GROUNDWORK

Your résumé is likely to be the interviewer's only information source before talking with you in person. That is why it pays to research the company and tailor your résumé accordingly. The object is for the person who schedules interviews to read your résumé and say something like: "Here's a perfect candidate! I'll schedule an interview immediately."

Visit the company's Web site and download brochures and the annual report, or phone and ask the firm to send them to you. If possible, talk with someone you know who has worked for the business, and also look for information

---

Todd Bermont, president of Ten Step Corporation, a Chicago-based company that counsels job seekers. He's also a business development manager at Lee Technologies, a computer security provider for corporations and other large organizations. His latest book is *10 Insider Secrets to a Winning Job Search* (Career).

on the company in magazines, newspapers and on the Internet (using Google or another search engine). Also check the AARP Web site of the best companies to work for at *www.aarp.org*.

What to look for: Information about the company's goals and what it values—technology, customer relations, growth in certain geographical areas, etc. With all this information in hand, you can write a résumé so it shows that you possess the skills a company values.

Examples: If applying for a job at a retail chain which values customer relations, mention how your experience in this area benefited previous employers. Or if a company is targeting the Hispanic market, tell how a previous employer profited from your knowledge of Spanish.

Keep your résumé to one page—many human resources (HR) managers do not read the second page. If you require a second page, list several major accomplishments near the top of the first page.

Examples: Saving your employer a large sum of money or making a crucial sale.

Explain all these and other achievements at greater length later on in the résumé. It's unlikely that résumés of competing job candidates—particularly younger ones—will start with a list of attention-grabbing accomplishments.

When you find an opening at a company you would like to work for, phone the HR department and ask about the position.

Helpful question: "What are some characteristics of people who have succeeded on your team at work?"

Most companies designate a person in the HR department to answer questions about specific job openings. But even if you reach a low-ranking assistant, it pays to ask, "What kind of person is your boss looking for?" You'll often pick up facts about the job that other candidates don't know and that will be useful in the interview.

Examples: The position requires traveling, computer skills aren't important or the company would consider a part-time employee.

GETTING PSYCHED

Hiring managers—the people who determine whether to employ an applicant—rarely admit it, but the first minutes of an interview are crucial. It is then that they decide whether to consider the candidate seriously or just get the interview over with as quickly as possible.

With that in mind, it pays to prepare to make a great first impression for the interview…

• **Wear standard business attire**—even if most employees dress informally. That means a dark suit and tie for men and a professional business suit for women. Above all, don't make the mistake of wearing an outfit that, in your mind, will make you look younger. They usually have the opposite effect.

• **Wear your hair in a traditional style—** nothing unusual.

• **Practice in front of the mirror.** Do this several times during the days before an interview. Smile and say to yourself, "I'm great!" It sounds corny, but the technique actually works. It shows you how much better you look with a smile on your face and lets you practice the smile so that it comes naturally when you walk in for the interview.

• **Practice shaking hands firmly** and looking the other person in the eye when you speak. That's what to do at the beginning of an interview. The gestures should also come naturally.

• **Visualize the interviewer** extending a hand and offering you a job. Doing that puts you in a positive frame of mind that you'll automatically telegraph with body language during the interview.

PLAYING YOUR ACES

Get the edge on other job candidates by asking questions that let you talk about ways in which the company will benefit by hiring you. *Examples…*

• **What are the characteristics of your ideal candidate?** Many interviewers will be delighted by the question, and the answer gives you an opening to point out how many of the characteristics you have.

If the interviewer mentions any qualification you lack, it may turn out that the company can help you with it—learning a computer program, for example. Immediately stress the point that someone with your accomplishments couldn't have succeeded without a willingness to learn and adapt to change.

• **What projects or challenges are involved with this job?** The answer gives you another opportunity to relate your skills to the work that will be expected of you.

•**What accomplishments will I have to make in order to get a perfect score on my yearly performance review?** This works because it assumes you're already hired and shows a positive attitude. And again, use the answer to talk about your qualifications and skills.

It's best to keep your statements short and to let the interviewer do most of the talking. If the interviewer fidgets, avoids eye contact or crosses his/her arms, you're talking too much.

The interviewer is interested in what you are saying if he smiles, nods frequently or moves forward in his chair. But even then, don't drag out your answers. If there's any doubt, ask the interviewer if you've given enough information.

Don't ask about salary or benefits (unless the interviewer brings up the subject). If you need information, ask HR after the interview. If you have problems with the compensation package, wait until you get an offer and then negotiate.

More from Todd Bermont...

When Discrimination Starts

The federal *Age Discrimination in Employment Act* of 1967 (ADEA) makes it illegal to put an employee or job seeker at a disadvantage because he/she is over age 40. Some state laws set the threshold as low as 21. Vulnerability to discrimination usually increases when an employee reaches the age of 50.

Discrimination is illegal in all but a few situations where the job requires a person of a certain age, such as a movie role for a teenager.

More information: Access the US Department of Labor Web site at *www.dol.gov* and click on "Workers."

Spot a Bad Boss During Your Interview

If you see these common warning signs during a job interview, beware...

•**Someone who is easily distracted** during the interview and doesn't seem to pay much attention to you.

•**Barely makes eye contact** and/or offers shallow answers to your questions.

•**Seems to be an egomaniac,** talking mainly about his/her accomplishments.

Beverly Kaye, founder and CEO of Career Systems International in Sherman Oaks, CA, and coauthor of *Love It, Don't Leave It: 26 Ways to Get What You Want at Work* (Berrett-Koehler).

Increase Your Chances Of Getting the Job

The contestants who perform later in competitions are rated more positively by judges than those who perform earlier. Known as the "serial position effect," this can be applied to daily life.

Example: When scheduling a job interview, ask to be one of the last candidates seen to increase your chances of getting the job.

Wändi Bruine de Bruin, PhD, research faculty, department of social and decision sciences, Carnegie Mellon University, Pittsburgh, and leader of a study involving singing and ice-skating contests, published in *Acta Psychologica*.

If Another Company Wants You...

If you get a job offer from another company, negotiate a counteroffer with your current employer only if you are seriously thinking of leaving the company. Be direct about what would convince you to stay, such as a raise, a different work assignment or a promotion.

If you accept your current company's counteroffer: Be prepared to work harder and demonstrate your loyalty—your employer will expect to see results.

Steve Gross, worldwide partner at Mercer Human Resource Consulting, Philadelphia.

Don't Accept the Wrong Job

During your interview, find out what hours are expected...whether anyone has been promoted out of the job...and why the position is open.

If a new job is not what you expected: Speak up. Tell the boss what is wrong and ask for changes.

Example: If you are overloaded, ask him/her to help you set priorities.

Maria Marsala, a business coach in Poulsbo, WA, *www.elevatingyourbusiness.com.*

Career Smarts

It is better to work for a bad boss at a good company than to work for a good boss at a bad company.

Reasons: Leaders at the good company will eventually identify and get rid of a bad boss, and you may be rewarded for staying. And the experience you get at a good company will look better on a résumé.

BusinessWeek, 1221 Avenue of the Americas, New York City 10020.

Genuine Work-at-Home Opportunity

Companies such as J. Crew and Sears are outsourcing call centers to people who work at their homes in the US, rather than overseas. The number of home-based call center agents has tripled since the year 2000 to 672,000 workers in the US and Canada. Pay is typically between $25,000 and $40,000 a year,* and the jobs usually do not include benefits. Legitimate jobs are

*Rates subject to change.

available through established outsourcing firms, such as West Corporation, LiveOps, Alpine Access and Working Solutions.

Caution: Ignore work-at-home offers on the Web—they are almost always scams.

The Wall Street Journal, 200 Liberty St., New York City 10281, *online.wsj.com.*

Snakes in Suits: Dealing With Psychopaths in The Workplace

Paul Babiak, PhD, industrial and organizational psychologist and president of HRBackOffice, an executive coaching and consulting firm, Dutchess County, NY. He is coauthor, with Robert D. Hare, PhD, of *Snakes in Suits: When Psychopaths Go to Work* (ReganBooks).

In a study of high-performing businesspeople, as many as one of every 30 was found to be a psychopath, a figure several times higher than that of the general population. A psychopath has no conscience and no ability to develop one. We think of a psychopath as a serial killer, but in reality, many psychopaths just desire money or power. They think nothing of ruining someone else's career if it helps them get ahead.

Example: Frank had a great relationship with his company's CEO until Dave, a recently hired psychopath in his department, started telling the CEO that Frank was criticizing the CEO's leadership behind his back. The CEO believed Dave's lies, fired Frank and gave Dave his job.

IDENTIFYING A PSYCHOPATH

When we first meet psychopaths, we might sense that something is not quite right, even if they seem friendly. This vague sense of unease could be the primitive part of our brain warning us that we're in the presence of a predator. If at some level you feel there is something wrong with a new coworker, keep an eye out for lies and more subtle deceptions. *Psychopaths will...*

• **Find reasons to blame others** whenever anything goes wrong.

• **Take credit for others' work.**

• **Spread damaging rumors,** and attempt to break down existing friendships.

• **Quickly deduce coworkers' weaknesses** and exploit them.

Example: A psychopath discovered that Bob's shy nature made him petrified of giving presentations. He told Bob that he was afraid of speaking up in public, as well—to get Bob's friendship—then maneuvered Bob into a situation where Bob needed to lead a presentation. When Bob floundered, the psychopath rushed to the rescue, making himself look like the hero at Bob's expense.

HELP FOR VICTIMS

If you feel a workplace psychopath is trying to turn your bosses and colleagues against you, try to maintain a positive, friendly relationship with everyone. The more all your coworkers like you, the less likely they are to accept the psychopath's accusations.

Do not complain or make negative statements about the psychopath or anyone else in the office—this only supports a psychopath's attempts to paint you as the real troublemaker. And never call anyone a psychopath, either to his/her face or to others. This makes you seem paranoid and gives the psychopath an opportunity to accuse you of slander.

Should a psychopath tell you that someone else in the office does not like you or has it in for you, speak with this person directly and ask if it's true. Also ask the coworker whether the psychopath has told him the same thing about you. A psychopath's lies can be exposed when coworkers maintain open communications.

If you feel the psychopath is trying to ruin your career, keep careful records of all your interactions with him in a day planner. If your diligence or loyalty is questioned, you can establish what has and has not transpired.

If a psychopathic boss instructs you to do something that you consider unwise, send an "e-mail of understanding" to the boss summarizing the orders you have been given and keep a copy for yourself. This way, you will have written proof that you were following instructions if the psychopathic boss later tries to blame you for the decision.

Dealing with Difficult People at Work

To get along with a self-centered coworker, try these tips…

• **Butter him/her up.** Compliment him into not being so difficult.

• **Let him be the center of attention.** Self-absorbed coworkers tend to be below-average performers, but they may do more than their share of the work when they can show off.

• **Keep your sense of humor.** Self-centered workers can be a pain, but if you keep a sense of humor, they can begin to seem entertaining.

Psychology Today, 115 E. 23 St., New York City 10010.

The Fine Art of Compromise

Sonya Hamlin, president of Sonya Hamlin Communications, New York City, a firm helping corporate executives, trial lawyers and business school students to communicate effectively. She is the author of *How to Talk So People Listen: Connecting in Today's Workplace* (HarperCollins) and *What Makes Juries Listen Today* (West).

The secret for successfully handling a difficult situation is thinking through not only your goals and needs but also the other person's goals and needs. How can both of you come out with some "wins" instead of ending with "I win, you lose"? *Helpful…*

• **Begin with a question to engage the other person** in arriving at a solution rather than giving the solution yourself.

Example: "We are having a problem getting reports out on time. What's needed to turn this around? Can you help us?" Sincerely asked questions help keep situations from becoming accusatory and adversarial.

• **Use the word "I" instead of "you."** "I must not have explained that well," rather than, "You got this all wrong." This helps others save face, which enables them to hear you and change what's wrong.

● **Look down rather than making eye contact with the other person.** Do this when presenting a problem that needs solving. This helps him/her get over his embarrassment and focus on the subject. Avoiding eye contact makes the problem objective, not personal. Continue your eye contact after you have outlined the complete problem.

● **Edit what you say.** Some people provide so many details when they talk that the main points get lost. Simply refer to what the other person already knows, then add your point of view about the situation.

● **Ask another question if the person appears to have stopped listening** to what you are saying. The secret to giving and getting information is dialogue, not monologue.

One Simple Habit That Leads to Big Success

Michael Masterson, publisher of *Early to Rise* (*www. earlytorise.com*), a free e-letter providing tips on wealth-building and career success, Delray Beach, FL. He is the author of several books, including *Seven Years to Seven Figures* (Wiley).

I n the past 30 years, I have started dozens of moneymaking businesses, including two that grew to more than $100 million in revenues. The single habit that has been invaluable to my success is getting to work one hour earlier than everyone else.

EARLY TO RISE

"Early to rise" is not an absolute mandate for success (Thomas Edison was a night owl), but most successful people I know get to work before their colleagues. Getting to work early provides you with quiet time that can be profitably spent before the rest of the world starts working. Arriving early also sends a strong message to colleagues and bosses that you are on top of your game. Early birds are viewed as energetic, organized and ambitious. People who arrive late and leave late look as if they're not in control.

Arriving early will have a significant and enduring effect on your career only if you use that extra hour to accomplish something important. *Here's how to make the most of it...*

DON'T PLAN YOUR DAY IN THE MORNING

Over the years, I have found it much more effective to plan my next day's tasks at the end of each day. That way, I can begin the next day by focusing on something important.

When planning each day, ask yourself, "Of all the things I must do tomorrow, which are the three or four that will best help me achieve my most important long-term goals?" Don't allow yourself to say, "Everything is very important," because everything isn't. I limit my selection to three or four tasks and then highlight them in my daily planner. Finally, I choose one task to attack first thing the next morning.

FOCUS ON GOALS

When I arrive at work—generally between 6:30 and 7:00 am—I close my door (to prevent interruptions) and get to work on my most important goal. I know that focusing on what is important will have a profoundly positive effect on my future.

One hour a day, subtracting weekends and a two-week vacation, is about 250 hours a year. It's possible to accomplish many career-changing objectives in that time. *Sample goals...*

● **A great new product idea you want to develop.**

● **The clever marketing plan you want to test out.**

● **Networking activities that you want to engage in.**

● **The financing proposal you have been meaning to create**.

HOW I SPENT MY HOUR

The first thing I did when I started getting to work early was write a book about wealth, which I had been meaning to write for 10 years. At 500 words a day—a comfortable pace for me, since I was writing about something I was so familiar with—I wrote a 60,000-word book (288 pages) in just over six months. That book went on to become a best seller, and it encouraged me to write three more books over the next several years.

AVOID DISTRACTIONS

Don't listen to the radio or make any unnecessary phone calls.

Do not even open your e-mail. If you spend the extra hour in the morning responding to e-mails, you'll end up wasting time and energy on insignificant matters, including things that you probably shouldn't get involved in.

Job Stress Increases Diabetes Risk

Workers who were identified as suffering a high level of burnout related to job stress were 84% more likely to develop type 2 diabetes than those with low levels of burnout in part because stress inhibits the body's ability to process glucose.

This study suggests that work burnout could have the same negative effects as other risk factors, such as smoking and obesity.

Samuel Melamed, PhD, professor, department of epidemiology and preventive medicine, Tel Aviv University Sackler School of Medicine, Israel, and leader of a study of 677 people, published in *Psychosomatic Medicine*.

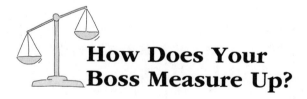

How Does Your Boss Measure Up?

Two-fifths of bosses do not keep promises and this increases job tension and reduces workers' loyalty.

Other findings: 37% of employees say their supervisors fail to give credit when it's due…27% say supervisors bad-mouth them…23% say supervisors blame others for their mistakes.

Wayne Hochwarter, PhD, associate professor of management, College of Business, Florida State University in Tallahassee, and leader of a survey that asked more than 700 people how their supervisors treat them, published in *The Leadership Quarterly*.

A Better Relationship With Your Boss

After you are warned or suspended for an infraction at work, use the *three-contact rule* to develop a more harmonious relationship with your boss. Pick three reasons to ask for your supervisor's advice each week for at least three weeks. Choose a safe subject on which you will have no problem following whatever direction he/she gives. Ask the supervisor's opinion, be receptive to it, follow the advice—and be sure to let him know later that you appreciated the advice and followed it.

By doing this, you should convince the supervisor that he can work with you, despite the earlier disciplinary action.

Richard C. Busse, Esq., senior partner, Busse & Hunt, plaintiff's employment law firm, Portland, OR, and author of *Fired, Laid-Off or Forced Out* (Sphinx).

In Meetings

To stand out in meetings, use assertive language. Do not ask to ask a question. Also, make sure everyone can hear you, and look at others as you speak, not at your notes. Finally, support people with whom you agree—to show you are a team player.

Barbara Pachter, president, Pachter & Associates, workplace communication consultants, Cherry Hill, NJ.

Keep Meetings Under Control

If you are the one in charge and one of the participants is talking too much or causing the meeting to be sidetracked, break in when there is a pause, compliment the speaker and thank him/her for his contribution, and then move the meeting along with a transitional phrase.

Examples: "Let's put it aside for now"... "Let's talk more about this at our next meeting"... "Let's stick to the agenda so we can finish up on time."

If you are not running the meeting, it may not be appropriate to try and move things along—except maybe by introducing a more relevant topic if things go very far off track.

Peggy Post, the great-granddaughter-in-law of etiquette pioneer Emily Post and spokesperson, Emily Post Institute, Burlington, VT, www.emilypost.com. Her latest book is Excuse Me, But I Was Next...How to Handle the Top 100 Manners Dilemmas (Collins).

Planning a Presentation?

Before your speech, ask colleagues to raise specific questions to break the ice during the question-and-answer session. This ensures that the discussion goes in a constructive direction—and encourages other attendees to participate during your presentation.

Mark Goulston, MD, corporate consultant and assistant clinical professor of psychiatry, University of California, Santa Monica, and author of Get Out of Your Own Way at Work (Putnam).

Free Teleconferencing

Set up a free teleconference at *www.freeconfer ence.com*. Participants pay what they regularly would for a long-distance call, and conference calls take place on regular phone lines. All participants call the same dial-in number. Up to 150 participants can take part, and the call can last up to three hours.

Google Helps Out

If your computer is experiencing a problem, just type the error message or explanation of the problem into Google.com. You'll bring up a list of sites that could help. It may take some digging to locate a fix for your problem, but it's a good first step before calling technical support (or while on hold with technical support). You also can try this for household or other problems—just type your question into Google.

David Boyer, research editor and resident computer guru, Bottom Line/Personal, Boardroom Inc., 281 Tresser Blvd., Stamford, CT 06901

Checks Can Be Deposited via The Internet

Desktop Deposit, a new service from Wells Fargo Bank, allows businesses to log on to the bank's Web site, scan checks, type in the amounts of each check and deposit them. Scanners can be purchased or leased from the bank.

This service is available only for commercial electronic office and other business accounts. BankServ also offers this type of service.

BusinessWeek, 1221 Avenue of the Americas, New York City 10020.

Employers: Now You Can Legally Use E-Mail To Send Official Notices to Employees

Peter A. Michaelson, CPA, tax partner, Eisner LLP, 750 Third Ave., New York City 10017. Mr. Michaelson specializes in tax advice for high-net-worth individuals.

E-mail in the workplace is no longer only for mundane or task-related communications. It now can also be used legally for a number of personnel-related exchanges between an employer and employee. E-mail, instant messaging and other forms of electronic media are accepted by the IRS just the same as their hard-copy versions, as long as they meet the same standards.

Advantage: It saves time and is cost efficient.

BENEFIT PLANS

Starting January 1, 2007, on-line correspondence can be used to inform employees, plan participants and beneficiaries about all notices, elections or other communications that relate to their qualified retirement plans and fringe benefit plans. *Examples of employee actions…*

• **To make elective deferrals under 401(k) plans** and savings incentive match plans for employees of small employers (SIMPLEs).

• **To elect out of automatic enrollment in 401(k) plans** (or to choose a lower contribution percentage than the default elective deferral amount).

• **To select benefit options under a cafeteria plan.**

ELECTRONIC COMMUNICATION REQUIREMENTS

Under recent final IRS regulations, the standards for electronic communication between an employer and an employee are no less stringent than for traditional communication modes. The communication must satisfy the same timing requirements as other modes. It must also provide information that is no less understandable than a written paper document.

The notice must alert the employee or other recipient to the significance of the transmittal… identify the subject matter in the subject line of an e-mail message…and include all instructions to access the notice, if needed.

Important: Before any electronic notice can be sent, the employer must obtain employee consent to receive notices and other communications electronically. This consent can be obtained electronically or via a written document.

Employees must be given the opportunity to receive communications by paper and cannot be forced to accept electronic transmittals.

Special rules for plan participant elections: The electronic medium that a participant can use to make an election must be one that the person can access and which is reasonably designed to preclude anyone else from making the election. The system must give the participant an opportunity to review, confirm, modify or rescind the terms of an election before it becomes effective and must send a confirmation of the effect of the election—electronically or by a paper document.

On-line notary: Where a participant's election must be witnessed by a plan representative or notary public, as in the case of spousal consent to waive a joint and survivor annuity, the participant's or other beneficiary's on-line signature must be witnessed in the physical presence of the plan representative or notary public.

If technology changes, in the future it could be possible to obtain all the required witnessing without having a physical presence. When this happens, the IRS will provide further guidance on the matter.

W-2s AND OTHER TAX FORMS

Employers can send employees' W-2 forms electronically, instead of preparing paper forms. For employers, this saves time and reduces the preparation burden. They also gain a later filing deadline. Electronic filers have until March 31, 2008, rather than the normal February 29, 2008 deadline, to file copies of their W-2 forms with the Social Security Administration (SSA).

Caution: Filing electronically with the SSA does not give the employer more time to furnish W-2 forms to staff. A January 31, 2008, deadline still applies to this employer responsibility.

Employers preparing up to 20 W-2 forms can do so directly through the SSA Web site (*www. socialsecurity.gov/employer/how.htm*). No special software is required. These forms can be printed out for a paper delivery to employees or sent to them electronically. Larger employers can create files according to SSA specifications and upload the information electronically to the SSA.

When employers file the forms with the SSA, they receive an immediate receipt for proof of filing.

To send employees their W-2 forms electronically, all seven of the following conditions must be met…

• **Employees must be informed that they can receive a paper W-2** if they do not consent to electronic receipt.

• **Employees must be told the scope and duration of the consent** (e.g., for the year or indefinitely until consent is withdrawn).

• **Employees must be informed about the procedures to obtain a paper copy of any W-2 form.**

• **Employees must be told how to withdraw consent.**

• **Employees must be informed about the conditions under which W-2 forms will no longer be issued electronically,** such as following termination of employment.

• **Employees must be advised about how to update their contact information** (e.g., a change of address).

• **Employees must be notified of changes to employer contact information** (e.g., a new employer name, address and phone number following a merger).

OTHER TAX FORMS

Employers can set up electronic systems to receive any of the following tax forms from their employees…

• **Form W-4,** *Employee's Withholding Allowance Certificate.*

• **Form W-4P,** *Withholding Certificate for Pension or Annuity Payments.*

• **Form W-4S,** *Request for Federal Income Tax Withholding from Sick Pay.*

• **Form W-4V,** *Voluntary Withholding Request.*

• **Form W-5,** *Earned Income Credit Advance Payment Certificate.*

The electronic system must ensure that the information received by the company is the information actually sent by the employee or other payee (i.e., make certain of the system's integrity). The information sent electronically must mirror what would otherwise be included on a paper form. It must include an electronic signature, and if requested by the IRS, a paper copy must be sent to them along with a statement that to the best of the company's knowledge, the information was submitted by the employee or other payee.

Note: The same record-keeping requirements apply to electronically sent forms as to paper forms. Most employment-related forms must be retained for at least four years.

Verify SSNs On-Line

Employees' Social Security numbers (or SSNs) now can be verified on-line. Employers can submit up to 10 names and SSNs at a time for immediate verification—an ideal option for new hires—or upload a file of up to 250,000 names and SSNs to receive verification of them the next business day. Verification ensures the accuracy of information submitted by new hires and prevents problems in processing payroll and tax information later. Access the Social Security Administration Web site at *www.ssa.gov/employer/ssnv.htm* for more information.

How to Use Your IRA Money to Start a Business

Robert S. Keebler, CPA, MST, partner, Virchow, Krause & Co., LLP, a leading regional CPA and consulting firm, 1400 Lombardi Ave., Green Bay, WI 54304. Mr. Keebler is author of *A CPA's Guide to Making the Most of the New IRA* (American Institute of Certified Public Accountants).

IRA owners may want to shoot for higher returns than the stock and bond markets are likely to produce. You can, for instance, invest in an oil well your neighbor is drilling. If he strikes oil and the price goes to $100 a barrel, your return could be huge.

Getting real: What if you want to use your IRA to finance your own oil well? Or your own restaurant, Internet search company or some other venture? You might get higher returns from your own business than from an investment portfolio. And inside your IRA, taxes can be deferred.

Financing a business with IRA money: After going through whatever procedure you would use to finance a start-up company, use money in your IRA—by forming a corporation and issuing shares to your IRA—instead of money in your bank account.

Caution: When you use your IRA to back your own company, you have to contend with

IRS rules on self-dealing (a transaction between an IRA owner and a business venture that the IRA owner controls), which is prohibited. A misstep could terminate your IRA and trigger the deferred income tax, plus interest and penalties.

Strategy: Some court decisions have shown that it's better to use your IRA to finance a start-up company than a company that is already in existence.

THE SWANSON CASE

A case decided by the Tax Court in 1996 (*Swanson*, 106 TC 76) indicated that new companies' shares can be held in IRAs.

Background: The taxpayer formed a corporation, which issued shares to his IRA. A start-up business may have a very low value, so the shares need not be expensive at start-up. Over the next few years, this corporation paid nearly $600,000 in dividends to the IRA.

Loophole: All of the tax on those payments was deferred inside of the IRA.

Note: Federal law prohibits using retirement funds for certain types of transactions. The person or people in control of those funds cannot make deals with themselves using plan money. Although these rules were created to protect employees in employer-sponsored plans, they have been extended to IRAs.

Ruling: In its opinion, the Tax Court wrote that starting up a company is not considered a transaction—so it can't be a "prohibited transaction" under the Tax Code.

Similarly, forming a new business and using IRA money to buy shares in that business is not self-dealing.

Trap: *After* you form a company, the company becomes a "disqualified person" relative to your IRA, so the prohibited transaction rules will apply.

From that moment on, any sales, exchanges, leases or loans between the business and the IRA would not be allowed. Such business transactions are prohibited between people in control of retirement plans and other ventures they control.

THE ROLLINS CASE

The IRS continues to pursue the issues of self-dealing and prohibited transactions. In *Rollins* (TC Memo 2004-260), the taxpayer lost in Tax Court.

Why this matters: Although this case involved a profit-sharing plan, the principles also apply to IRAs.

Background: An accountant's firm sponsored a retirement plan, which loaned money to three business ventures. In each situation, the accountant held the largest interest in the borrowing business.

Ruling: The Tax Court said that any use of a plan's assets or income for the plan sponsor's benefit is a prohibited transaction. Here, the accountant derived benefits because his ventures were able to secure financing without having to deal with independent lenders. The principles of the Rollins case illustrate the Tax Court's approach to prohibited transactions, the same approach it takes to transactions involving IRAs.

REDUCING THE RISK

As indicated, giving your IRA direct ownership of a new venture is a better way to proceed, rather than having your IRA make loans to a business you control. *Other strategies to consider...*

• **Ask before you leap.** For any transaction that might be considered self-dealing, it's safest to get a Prohibited Transaction Exemption ruling from the US Department of Labor. If it's approved, your arrangement will be upheld.

Cost: Getting a ruling will cost from $7,500 to $25,000,* depending on the complexity of the issues involved.

Questions or requests for advice about an exemption or application should be put in writing and directed to the US Department of Labor, Employee Benefits Security Administration, Office of Exemption Determinations, 200 Constitution Ave. NW, Suite N-5649, Washington, DC 20210.

• **Divide your IRA.** You can split your IRA into two accounts and use one to finance your start-up venture. That would preserve the other IRA, no matter what ends up happening with your new business.

Situation: You have $1 million in your IRA and you want to invest $100,000 in a new company. The only place where you easily can find $100,000 is in your IRA.

*Rates subject to change.

In this situation, you could split your IRA into two IRAs, moving $100,000 into a new IRA account. That $100,000 IRA could be used to finance the start-up business.

To finance a start-up business: After creating the business, use IRA money to buy shares in the business. Then use that money for the expenses of the business.

If IRA One owns the business and the business has debt, that IRA could be tapped for repayment of debt. But, IRA Two would not be exposed.

Advantage: If the business goes under or if you didn't obtain a prior ruling and you lose a challenge by the IRS, only the $100,000 IRA is at risk. The other $900,000 IRA will be protected.

Strategy: The precaution of splitting up your IRA into two accounts makes sense even if your IRA invests in the business when the new business is created.

OUT OF CONTROL

Using your IRA to back a new business will be on solid ground, backed by the Tax Court decision in the Swanson case, if the business pays dividends to your IRA. But what about having other types of income, such as sales or leasing proceeds, flow through to your IRA?

If you control the company, it may be considered a "disqualified person" in relation to your IRA, thus having your IRA collect money from sales or leases or loans can be prohibited.

Tactic: If you do not control the company, it won't be a "disqualified person" where your IRA is concerned. Therefore, you may want to bring in other investors alongside your IRA.

Situation: You retire and move to a beach resort. You use your IRA to help with financing the purchase of a marina, which will rent boats for fishing, sightseeing, etc.

In addition to the IRA, several other investors participate in the venture so that your IRA does not control the business. The marina is leased to a third party, which operates the marina.

Result: Your IRA will be able to share in the leasing revenues in the scenario above.

What if you want to work for this new business and draw a salary? The law here is unclear, but that sort of arrangement probably won't fly if your IRA controls the business.

Even if your IRA does not control the business, there is no certainty you can be paid to manage it without risking a possible violation of the prohibited transaction rules. This, in turn, could disqualify your IRA and cost you taxes, interest and penalties.

Strategy: Instead of drawing a salary, structure the business to maximize dividends that can be paid to the IRA as owner or part owner of the business.

Turn a Hobby Into a Business

If you have a passion for antique collecting, photography or any other pastime, consider turning your hobby into a business to earn extra income and valuable tax breaks. The new small-business CD-ROM package from the Federal Reserve tells how, including how to check the feasibility of a business idea and develop a business plan...the legal and accounting steps to starting a business...and all the tax forms, instructions and publications you will need.

The cost is $1.* To order, go to *www.pueblo.gsa.gov* or call 888-878-3256 and ask for the "Small Business Resource Guide."

*Price subject to change.

Best and Worst States For Business, Tax-Wise

A new study ranks all states in the US by the burden that their taxation systems impose on business.

The 2007 "State Business Tax Climate Index" considers not only the amount of tax imposed by each state's tax system, but also the complexity of tax rules, number of different kinds of taxes imposed, amount of "loopholes," preferences that favor some kinds of businesses over others and other tax-system factors. *Findings...*

Best States	Worst States
1. Wyoming	50. Rhode Island
2. South Dakota	49. Ohio
3. Alaska	48. New Jersey
4. Nevada	47. New York
5. Florida	46. Vermont
6. Texas	45. California
7. New Hampshire	44. Nebraska
8. Montana	43. Iowa
9. Delaware	42. Maine
10. Oregon	41. Minnesota

More: The full report is available on the Web site of the Tax Foundation, at *www.tax founda tion.org/sbtci.html.*

Seven Steps to Starting Up Your Own Small Business

Martin S. Kaplan, CPA, 11 Penn Plaza, New York City 10001, *www.irsmaven.com.* He is a frequent guest speaker at insurance, banking and financial-planning seminars and is author of *What the IRS Doesn't Want You to Know* (Wiley).

S tarting a new small business of your own —even as only a sideline—can give you valuable tax savings right away and tax-sheltered income in the future as your business matures and becomes profitable.

Seven wise steps to take…

1. Deduct costs incurred before starting your business. Before you start a business, you may incur costs for items such as market research, consultations with experts and initial supplies. These costs are usually not deductible as business expenses because you are not operating your business yet when you incur them.

Saver: Up to $5,000 of such expenses now can be deducted on your business's first tax return (a tax law change created by the *American Jobs Creation Act of 2004*). Amounts in excess of $5,000 can be deducted over a 180-month period after you start operating your business. The $5,000 deduction applies only if start-up costs do not exceed $50,000.

What to do: While you are exploring the possibility of starting a business, keep a record of all your related expenses. Then, if you do start the business, you will be able to deduct them.

2. Choose a "pass-through" form of organization. This allows you to deduct business expenses and start-up losses on your personal tax return.

Options: Proprietorship, partnership, limited partnership (LP), limited liability company (LLC) and S corporation.

If you will be the sole owner of your business, the better option at first probably will be the simplest—a proprietorship, with its income reported on Schedule C of your personal tax return. Any other choice will incur legal organization costs and extra tax-reporting requirements and may prematurely commit you to one form of organization for the future.

Example: After your business grows and evolves, it may become clear that one kind of entity will provide advantages over another—but which kind might not be apparent in advance. If you make a wrong choice at the start, it will be costly and difficult to switch later. But if you start as a proprietorship, you can easily convert to any of the other options later.

Strategy: The main reason for organizing a new small business as an S corporation, LP or LLC usually is not tax related. Rather, it is to protect the owner against personal liability should someone sue the business.

So ask yourself, "What are my chances of being sued?" Usually the risk is slight and can be protected against by increasing liability insurance to a minimum of $500,000 plus umbrella liability coverage of about $5 million. These coverages are not that expensive and are adequate for most businesses. If you think that the risk of a lawsuit is too great—such as if you sell a product that might cause injury or your business is in the medical or health field—consult a local legal expert. He/she will provide guidance.

3. Protect the loss deductions—your "start-up subsidy" from the IRS. Most new businesses do lose money at first. But when one is organized as a proprietorship or other pass-through entity, its losses are deductible on its owner's personal tax return against other income—such as wages and investment income.

This effectively is a tax subsidy that the IRS provides to help pay your initial costs. If losses run more than one year, you can continue to deduct them.

Important: To deduct such losses, you must show that you operate the business with a profit motive. *It's especially important if the business...*

- **Incurs losses for several years in a row,** and/or...
- **Is an activity you enjoy,** such as a former hobby converted into a business.

To show a profit motive, you need not ever actually make a profit, but you must operate in a "businesslike" manner.

How: Obtain all necessary business licenses, keep good books and records, keep segregated business bank accounts and credit cards, advertise, consult with experts and draw up a formal business plan that you update in light of changing business results.

4. Set up a home office. This is a perfectly legitimate way to convert previously nondeductible personal expenses into deductible business expenses.

Examples: Insurance, maintenance and repair costs attributable to the part of your home that is used as an office, plus either depreciation or a portion of your rent. You can also depreciate furniture located in your office even if you have already owned it for years.

A home office also makes it much easier to get full deductions for items located in it that are subject to deduction restrictions otherwise, such as personal computers and extra telephone lines. (The basic charges of the first home telephone line are not deductible.)

To qualify as a home office, part of your home must be used exclusively for business, and be either...

- **The primary place where you conduct your business,** or...
- **Necessary for record keeping** when you conduct your business elsewhere (such as making sales on the road) and have no other office for this purpose.

Part of a room may qualify as a home office (such as space set up with a desk, business cabinets, etc.).

Don't worry about a home-office deduction increasing audit risk—it creates no more audit risk than any other deduction, provided it is not excessive.

Even if your deduction is very large (such as if you use much of your home to store business inventory), you can protect it by documenting your use of the office with photographs that you keep filed with your tax records.

5. Deduct business equipment. For 2007, up to $125,000 of new business equipment can be deducted immediately, instead of over a period of years through depreciation, by using "Section 179 expensing."

Eligible items can include computers and other electronic equipment, furniture and even up to $25,000 of the cost of a sport-utility vehicle weighing more than 6,000 pounds.

Opportunity: If your Section 179 deduction exceeds the income from your new business, you can claim it against income from other businesses you were active in, plus wages you may have earned as an employee. So the purchase is a legal tax shelter that boosts cash flow.

Example: You buy new and used equipment for a sideline business on credit and place it in service just prior to year-end. You can deduct the full cost of the equipment against your salary income to receive a speedy cash tax refund, even though you haven't paid cash for the equipment yet.

6. Employ family members. When you employ a low-tax-bracket family member, you can deduct the salary at your high-tax-bracket rate while it is taxed at the recipient's lower rate—cutting the overall family tax bill. If you are a sole proprietor, no Social Security tax or Medicare tax is owed on wages paid to your child under age 18.

The Tax Court has permitted deductions for salaries paid to children as young as seven years old who performed work such as cleanup tasks and taking messages, when the pay was reasonable for the work done.

7. Set up tax-favored benefits. Your business's income can be legally tax sheltered through benefits. *Examples...*

- **A "solo 401(k)"** allows a sole proprietor to deduct in 2007 the first $15,500 of business income ($20,500 if age 50 or over) *plus* 20% of total self-employment income. So, if a proprietor age 50 or older has $25,625 of income from a sideline business, he can deduct *all* of it by placing it in the 401(k) ($20,500 + 20% of $25,625 = $25,625). This assumes that you're not covered by a 401(k) at your main job.

•**A proprietor cannot be covered by an employee benefit plan.** But a medical reimbursement plan can enable the proprietor who employs his spouse to deduct as a business expense payments for medical costs and insurance premiums. The plan can provide coverage for employees' spouses (which would include the proprietor) and dependents.

More from Martin Kaplan, CPA...

Resources for Starting A Small Business

For help in various areas important to small businesses, check out the following...

•**Tax help.** Visit *www.irs.gov/businesses/small* for tax resources and links to federal and state agencies dealing with employee issues.

•**Legal and business plans.** The site *www. allbusiness.com* covers business financing, law, technology and other issues. It also features expert advice, on-line tools and helpful downloadable forms.

•**Loans and assistance.** Visit *www.sba.gov* for advice on starting, expanding and financing your business, including SBA applications and assistance programs.

Also from Martin Kaplan, CPA...

Today's Hottest Audit Red Flags: How Your Business Can Avoid Them

Audit rates are rising again—after several years at record low levels—as the IRS increases its enforcement efforts to close up the estimated $345 billion "tax gap," the difference between what taxpayers really owe and what they voluntarily pay.

Moreover, business audit rates have increased at a faster rate than the audit rates for personal tax returns.

Here are the top IRS audit targets that owners of small businesses should be aware of—and what to do about them...

•**Sole proprietors.** The IRS believes that, in aggregate, sole proprietors underpay their taxes more than any other type of business—by $68 billion, compared with only $30 billion for all large corporations, in 2001, the year of the most recent "tax gap" computation.

As a result, the IRS is focusing its audit efforts on individual tax returns that report business proprietorship income on Schedule C.

In 2005, the audit rate for all personal tax returns was only 0.93% (up from 0.65% in 2003). The face-to-face audit rate, which excludes "correspondence audits" conducted by mail, was a very low 0.19% (barely up from 0.16% in 2003).

However, audit rates for personal returns that include a Schedule C are much higher and have increased sharply over the last two years.

The following table examines the 2005 audit rates and their change since 2003...*

PERSONAL RETURNS INCLUDING SCHEDULE C—CHANGE FROM 2003

Gross Business Receipts	Total Audit Rate	Face-to-Face Audit Rate
<$25K	3.68% (+23%)	0.55% (+12%)
$25K to <100K	2.21% (+66%)	1.06% (+71%)
$100K+	3.65% (+149%)	2.00% (+82%)

This fast rise in audit risk for proprietorships can be expected to continue in coming years as the IRS cracks down on what it deems the number one area of tax noncompliance.

Alternative: Businesses organized as "pass-through entities" (S corporations, partnerships and limited liability companies) have a much lower audit risk. In 2005, only 0.31% of their returns were examined—a rate about 90% lower than the average for proprietorships—and only 0.28% incurred face-to-face audits.

Strategy: Proprietors usually decide to organize their businesses as "pass-through entities" to obtain legal protections under state law, but should be aware of the chance to reduce audit risk as well. For more information, see the following article on page 319.

•**Businesses for which "audit guides" exist.** The IRS compiles "audit technique guides"

*Latest period for which figures are available.

that its tax examiners follow when conducting audits of particular kinds of businesses. These guides are available to taxpayers on the IRS Internet site (*www.irs.gov*).

Any type of business for which the IRS has prepared such a guide should consider itself an "audit target"—at more risk of audit than other businesses generally.

Audit technique guides are written by teams of IRS experts who study a particular industry, learn the details of how it operates and the most common means of tax avoidance used within it. They then put the knowledge they gain into the guides for use by IRS tax examiners.

Just the simple fact that the IRS invests the resources necessary to compose such a guide shows that the business types are heightened audit targets. Most are cash-intensive businesses—the kind in which the IRS knows it is easy to divert cash and underreport income.

Examples: Automobile dealerships and repair shops, construction, law, retailing.

Benefit: If there is an audit guide for your business, you can obtain it, learn the audit risks faced by the business before it files its return, then take steps to reduce the risk in advance.

About 40 audit guides, many of which relate to specific kinds of businesses, are available free in the "Businesses" section of the IRS Web site.

●**Noncash compensation for top executives.** In a recent study of a sampling of executive compensation packages, the IRS found what it considered to be many abuses. As a result, it has initiated a special examination program for top executive compensation packages.

No fewer than seven compensation-related audit technique guides have been compiled by the IRS on subjects such as stock options, deferred compensation, stock-based compensation, salary deduction limits, fringe benefits, golden parachutes, and split-dollar life insurance.

For details, enter "Corporate Executive Compliance" in the search box at the IRS Web site.

●**Owner/CEO salary amounts.** When a privately owned corporation's owner is also its top executive, the IRS is likely to examine whether the salary paid to the owner/CEO is too much or too little. *If the business is…*

●A regular corporation, the IRS will object if salary is too high, saying that the company is deducting through salary payments what should be a distribution of profits through their nondeductible dividends.

●An S corporation, the IRS will object if salary is too low—saying that the company is trying to avoid paying employment taxes on the owner's wages, since profits that are increased by a low wage payment are taxed to the owner without being subject to employment tax.

Self-defense: Take care to pay a wage that is "reasonable" by being in the range that comparable businesses pay for comparable work.

●**Independent contractors.** This is a perennial hot audit target for businesses—the IRS always is on alert to the fact that workers who are actually employees not be treated as independent contractors so as to avoid paying employment taxes on their wages.

To learn how the IRS determines worker status, go to its Web page on the subject by entering "Independent Contractors vs. Employees" in the search box at the IRS Web site.

●**Large cash payments.** Payments of cash in excess of $10,000 received by a business must be reported to the IRS on Form 8300, *Report of Cash Payment Over $10,000 Received in a Trade or Business*. The reporting obligation also exists for a series of related payments that total more than $10,000—so reporting can't be avoided by receiving payments in installments or otherwise breaking a payment into smaller amounts.

Violating the reporting requirement can lead to severe penalties—and even criminal charges.

●**Autos, meals and entertainment.** A business should consider a thorough examination of its records for auto expenses, meals and entertainment an "automatic" in any audit.

Why: The Tax Code specifies the exact records that *must* be kept to deduct these items or the deduction is disallowed, even if the expense was actually incurred and perfectly legitimate.

This makes these items different from other business expenses that may be deductible even without records specifically documenting them if it is clear from larger circumstances that they must have been incurred.

IRS auditors know that owners of small businesses frequently are poor record keepers, thus

318

examining the records for these items provides easy pickings in disallowed deductions.

Self-defense: Have the business's tax adviser implement a record-keeping system for these items, and have employees use it to protect tax deductions.

More audit advice from Martin Kaplan, CPA...

Why Pass-Through Entities Face Much Lower Audit Risk

Organizing a business as a pass-through entity (S corporation, partnership or limited liability company taxed as a partnership) rather than a proprietorship can lower its audit risk in two ways.

First, pass-through entities have a much lower audit rate than proprietorships in general.

In addition, some reporting items that can act as audit red flags on a proprietorship's Schedule C do not exist in a pass-through entity's tax filings.

Example: The home-office tax deduction is considered by many to be an audit red flag on an individual's tax return. It is claimed by attaching IRS Form 8829 to the Schedule C—thus "announcing" the deduction to the IRS and breaking out its component elements (the size of the office relative to the size of the home, amounts that are deducted for utilities and maintenance, etc.).

Contrast: If the same business is organized as a one-owner S corporation, the owner can have the same office and deduct the same costs—but won't deduct them directly on his/her personal return, and won't file Form 8829.

Instead, because he is an employee of the corporation, he will obtain reimbursement for his office expenses from the corporation. When the documentation requirements of an "accountable plan" are met, the reimbursement is tax free to the owner and deductible by the corporation.

Advantages: Your reimbursement cost will decrease the corporation's income (or increase its loss)—and, since its income is taxed to its owner, this reduction "passes through" to him and effectively provides the deduction on his personal return indirectly.

Meanwhile, no specific "home-office deduction" is claimed anywhere—so the audit red flag does not exist.

How to Audit-Proof Your Schedule C

Barbara Weltman, an attorney based in Millwood, NY, and author of J.K. Lasser's Small Business Taxes *(Wiley). She is publisher of the free monthly on-line newsletter* Big Ideas for Small Business, www.barbaraweltman.com.

In December 2006, then IRS Commissioner Mark Everson indicated that the IRS plans to conduct more audits on individuals with sole proprietorships (those filing Schedule C, *Profit or Loss from Business). More?* IRS audit statistics *already* reveal that Schedule C filers are audited at a higher rate than all other businesses. The IRS believes that a sizable portion of the "tax gap" (the spread between what the government actually collects and what it thinks it should collect) is attributable to unreported income by self-employed individuals.

As Schedule C filers complete their 2007 income tax returns, they should try to keep audit-proofing strategies in mind.

Can anyone actually audit-proof a tax return? There are no surefire measures, but there are steps you can take to reduce the risk of an audit. And you can protect yourself if you're selected for review. *Most productive...*

• **File completed forms and schedules.** This may seem obvious—but you would be amazed at how often Schedule C filers simply leave out information. Answer all questions and complete all required lines on the return. IRS computers are very good at detecting omissions.

Example: Be sure to answer the questions on lines F, G and H—indicate your accounting method, tell whether you materially participated in the operation of the business and say whether you acquired or started the business in 2007.

If you claim a deduction for vehicle use, be sure to complete Part IV of Schedule C related to information about the vehicle.

• **Don't round off numbers.** Use numbers that accurately reflect your records (e.g., $4,299 rather than $4,300). Exact numbers imply good record keeping, while round figures imply that you are estimating.

• **Report all income in the year required.** This isn't always straightforward.

Example: You are on the cash basis of accounting, meaning that you are required to report income in the year you receive it. Early in 2008, you receive a check for $1,000 dated and mailed in 2007. This income will show up on a 1099 for 2007, but you should report it on your 2008 tax return.

Trap: Simply omitting the income from your 2007 return would trigger scrutiny of that return. IRS computers can easily pick out mismatched reporting amounts.

To properly report this income on Schedule C of your 2007 return: Enter the 1099 amount ($1,000) and then subtract $1,000. Attach an explanation for the adjustment, such as "I'm a cash basis taxpayer and didn't receive this check till January 4, 2008."

In 2008, simply report the income. You don't have to have a 1099 to report income.

• **Do not be afraid to take a home-office deduction.** Businesses that are operated from the owner's home are most likely not more vulnerable to audit because a home-office deduction is claimed—as some do fear. If the business qualifies for the home-office tax deduction (the home is used as the principal place of business and meets other requirements), there is no reason to forgo this write-off. There is no proof that this deduction is an audit red flag.

RECORD KEEPING

Even proprietors who take every precaution to keep a low profile may find their returns selected for review. To withstand an IRS examination. you'll need accurate and complete records to back up all positions on your return.

Pay special attention to all record keeping for travel and entertainment costs. These expenses are frequent targets for audit, so be prepared to meet high IRS record-keeping standards. *Be prepared to provide...*

• **Written documentation.** A diary, logbook or expense account statement showing the date of the expense, the reason for it and other required information.

• **Receipts.** A credit card statement, invoice or other statement showing the amount of the expense.

Review travel and entertainment substantiation requirements in IRS Publication 463, *Travel,*

Entertainment, Gift, and Car Expenses, which is available at *www.irs.gov.*

EXPENSES AND LOSSES

It is not always a good idea for a business to claim every single deduction—for instance, where the deduction is valid but you lack documentation, or where the law is unclear about whether the deduction is allowed.

IRS audit models may say that a business in a certain industry with a certain amount of income should have a deduction of no more than a set amount for, say, advertising.

So, even though your business may be entitled to a higher amount, the best way to avoid the time, expense, and aggravation of an audit may be to claim a smaller write-off. Unfortunately, the IRS does not disclose what numbers trigger an audit, so it's best is to keep deductions reasonable in proportion to reported income. The IRS has available on its Web site more than four dozen audit guides for businesses. Check the one for your type of business, if available.

If 2007 was not a profitable year and Schedule C shows a loss, be prepared to withstand an IRS challenge that the activity is a hobby and your losses are not deductible—especially if there are losses year after year. You must prove that you have a reasonable expectation of making a profit and demonstrate this by various factors, including maintenance of good books and records for the business. Profit motive generally is assumed if a profit is shown in three out of the last five years, but having more frequent losses can be overcome by mustering favorable profit-motive factors.

Note: If the IRS does not believe that you do have a profit motive, income must still be reported (it will be added to Form 1040 as "other income"), but deductions will be limited to the amount of income and will only be allowed as miscellaneous itemized deductions on Schedule A (i.e., only to the extent that they exceed 2% of adjusted gross income).

OBTAIN A FILING EXTENSION

Although there are no statistics to prove it, it is believed by some that the IRS selects most tax returns to be audited from the first returns filed so that the later you file, the less likely you are to be selected for audit. Tax practitioners have long believed that the closer a return is filed to the extended due date without being late, the lower the chances of being audited. Certainly, there is nothing to be lost by filing at this time.

Schedule C filers can obtain an automatic six-month filing extension to October 15, 2008. This means requesting the extension no later than April 15, 2008 (April 16 for those filing in Andover, Massachusetts).

Note: Requesting the extension doesn't give more time to pay the tax, so pay what you believe you owe to avoid underpayment penalties and interest.

CHANGE YOUR FILING STATUS

Going forward, you can remove yourself from the pool of Schedule C filers by changing your form of entity. Even if you are the only owner of the business, you can incorporate it. This gives you the option to be a C (regular) corporation, filing Form 1120, *US Corporation Income Tax Return*, or an S corporation, filing Form 1120S, *US Income Tax Return for an S Corporation*. For example, if you incorporate on March 3, 2008, you have until June 16, 2008, to elect S corporation status for 2008. See instructions to Form 2553, *Election by a Small Business Corporation*, for more details.

Caution: Audit exposure is only one factor that should be used in determining which entity type to use. Payroll taxes, state tax treatment and additional accounting costs are other factors to consider. Review your choice of entity with a tax adviser before making any change.

CONSIDER RELOCATION

The chances of being audited vary greatly with the state in which you live because of IRS staffing differences from state to state. Taxpayers in some locations have higher audit rates than others (see *www.irs.gov/taxstats/indtaxstats/article/0,,id=96947,00.html*). While relocating may be a drastic measure to take, your particular business situation may warrant it.

Small Business Alert

These days, owners of small businesses are landing in jail for filing bogus payroll tax returns that indicate smaller salaries. Restaurant owners, in particular, seem to be a good target for IRS investigators. These businesses tend to have at least some employees who are on the books for some portion of their salaries, with the balance of their compensation paid in cash.

Defense: There is not much of a defense that can be mounted if the IRS can put together five or six employees who will testify that they were paid in cash—even though the employees will admit that they did not report the cash on their own income tax returns.

Best bet: Clean up your act now. The payroll taxes saved by paying employees with cash is not worth the legal expenses and potential time in prison.

Ms. X, Esq., a former agent with the IRS who is still well connected.

Service Business Loopholes

Edward Mendlowitz, CPA, partner in the CPA firm of WithumSmith+Brown at 1 Spring St., New Brunswick, NJ 08901. He is also author of *The Adviser's Guide to Family Business Succession Planning* (American Institute of Certified Public Accountants).

Owners of small consulting or other service businesses can drastically reduce the taxes on their business income using these strategies...

Loophole: **Set up a corporation to use the cash method of accounting.**

How it works: In general, most corporations must use the accrual method of accounting and report income when the company books its accounts receivable. In contrast, certain small businesses can use the cash method, which means that they don't have to report taxable income until payments actually are received.

Who is eligible: A qualifying corporation is defined as one with annual gross revenues of $10 million or less.

Opportunity: Personal service corporations —C corporations that offer personal services performed by owner/employees—can use cash basis accounting regardless of their sales volume.

Examples: Both business and computer consultants.

Caution: Income from professional service corporations (lawyers, doctors, computer consultants) accounted for on the cash basis is taxed at a flat 35% rate—these companies cannot use lower graduated corporate tax rates.

Loophole: Certain small service businesses with inventory are permitted to use the cash method.

In general, businesses with inventory must use the accrual method.

Exception: Small service businesses (annual revenues under $10 million) that sell products related to the business they do can report their income on the cash basis.

Examples: Plumbers or electricians who sell incidental plumbing or electrical materials.

Also eligible: Certain manufacturers, wholesalers, retailers, and other specialized businesses that are principally service businesses or do certain kinds of custom manufacturing where gross receipts don't exceed $1 million.

Loophole: Minimize Social Security taxes by operating as an S corporation.

Operating as a sole proprietorship, partnership or LLC, or as another unincorporated entity means that the business's entire income up to $97,500 (in 2007) is subject to Medicare taxes and Social Security taxes. In contrast, profits and dividend distributions of S corporations are not subject to these taxes.

Strategy: Salaries given to employee/shareholders of S corporations are subject to Medicare taxes and Social Security taxes. Therefore, owners of S corporations should minimize their salary payments and leave more money in the form of corporate profits, which then can be distributed as tax-free dividends.

Caution: The IRS requires that employees receive a "reasonable" salary for their work. Also, there could be state corporate income taxes on the profits.

Loophole: Shelter business income with tax-deferred retirement plans.

Owners of consulting or other service businesses could contribute up to $45,000 for 2007 based upon the type of plan. Retirement plans offer some of the best opportunities for tax savings, so plan ahead to make the most of them. *To maximize tax-deferred income...*

• **With a defined-contribution plan, such as a 401(k) plan, you can shelter up to 25% of salary** compensation provided the business is incorporated.

• **People with unincorporated businesses can contribute up to 20% of net business income to Keogh** (reduced by 50% of self-employment tax) and simplified employee pension (SEP) plans.

• **People who are older than age 45 have less time to build up retirement plans.** They might consider starting up defined-benefit plans that would allow plan deductions to exceed the $45,000 limitation. In some instances, contributions can exceed $100,000. Check with an actuary.

Loophole: Maximize your overall retirement plan contributions by setting up the 401(k) plan in addition to other types of plans.

The maximum 2007 contribution for a 401(k) is $15,500, and no percentage limitations apply.

Example: If you earn $20,000 from an unincorporated sideline business, you can contribute nearly all of it—$19,500—to retirement plans. That is $4,000 to a defined-contribution plan (20% of $20,000) and another $15,500 to a 401(k).

Older worker strategy: If you are age 50 or older, you can contribute another $5,000 to a 401(k) as a "catch-up" contribution regardless of the overall limits for your other plans.

Loophole: Medical insurance is deductible in full for owners who work in their businesses.

The deduction is allowable on page one of your individual income tax return as an adjustment to income and is not subject to the overall medical expense limitation—7.5% of adjusted gross income.

Loophole: Pay your children a salary for services they perform.

Children under age 18 working in their parent's unincorporated business do not need to contribute to Social Security or to pay Medicare taxes. As long as the compensation received by a child is reasonable for the work he/she does, these payments will be deductible by the business. The child will not owe taxes on the first $5,350 of earnings for 2007.

A Home-Equity Loan to Pay Business Expenses

If you use a home-equity loan to pay business expenses, you can deduct the interest on it as business interest instead of mortgage interest, provided that you can trace the loan proceeds directly to a business use.

Doing this provides you several advantages. *See below...*

• **Business interest is deductible on an unlimited amount of home-equity borrowing.** In addition, you can deduct *mortgage interest* on up to $100,000 of home-equity borrowing.

• **The business interest tax deduction is allowed under the AMT,** but the home-equity mortgage interest deduction isn't, to the extent that it is not used to buy, build or substantially improve your home.

• **Business interest expense reduces income from a proprietorship and thus self-employment taxes**—and also reduces adjusted gross income (AGI), increasing other deductions with AGI-related restrictions. Mortgage interest does not.

Peter Weitsen, CPA/PFS, partner, WithumSmith+Brown, CPAs, 1 Spring St., New Brunswick, NJ 08901.

Get Your Graduate Degree On-Line from A Top University

Thomas Nixon, Fresno, CA–based coauthor of *Bears' Guide to Earning Degrees by Distance Learning* (16th ed., Ten Speed). He is founder of CollegeoftheWeek.com, an e-mail service showcasing schools, and featured columnist for About.com's Adult Education Web site (*adulted. about.com/cs/finishhighschool/a/tnixon.htm*), which covers on-line educational programs.

Only a handful of universities provided graduate degrees via the Internet just five years ago. Today, on-line graduate school programs number well into the hundreds and include some of the world's best universities. On-line courses are attractive for would-be grad students who don't want to leave careers, families and homes to return to campus.

HOW ON-LINE PROGRAMS WORK

It is generally more difficult to get into programs at traditional schools than ones specializing in distance learning. However, the entrance requirements are similar to those of on-site programs—strong college transcripts and scores on tests, such as GMATs and GREs. Many master's programs are moving away from requiring essays and references.

On-line courses are as academically rigorous as those taken on campus. On-line grad students typically "attend" classes by watching a video feed over the Internet, either in real time or by accessing a stored file. Exams are sometimes administered at a high school or college in your area. (Of course, you do have to leave home for these.)

The degrees earned are the same ones awarded to students who attend in person. No difference is noted on the diploma or anywhere else.

Important: Choose a school that is accredited by one or more of the agencies listed on the Web site of the Council for Higher Education Accreditation (at *www.chea.org*, click on "Databases and Directories," then on "CHEA Recognized Accrediting Organizations"). To view a list of legitimate, accredited on-line graduate programs, go to *www.degreeinfo.com*.

On-line degrees will typically cost the same amount per credit as on-campus programs, but on-line students save on room, board and travel, and expand their options to include distant universities that may offer quality educations for far less than local schools.

The big downside is the absence of college atmosphere—networking and studying with other students, attending lectures by guest speakers and chatting with professors. Some on-line programs try to replicate these experiences through on-line access to professors and classmates or by organizing groups of students who can meet in person.

MBA PROGRAMS

• **Duke University Fuqua School of Business–Cross Continent Program.** Fuqua's program is not 100% on-line—students spend nine weeks on campus during the two-year program (919-660-7804, *www.fuqua.duke.edu*).

• **Indiana University Kelley School of Business** consistently ranks among the 20 best MBA programs in the US (877-785-4713, *www.kd.iu.edu*).

• **Penn State University MBA Program,** a well-designed on-line program from the well-known university in Pennsylvania (800-252-3592, *www.worldcampus.psu.edu*).

• **Edinburgh Business School.** Though the school is based in Scotland, MBAs from Edinburgh are well-respected by American employers. If you have extensive work experience, you might not even need a bachelor's degree to attend. Tuition for the entire program is less than $15,000* (011-44-131-451-3090, *www.ebsmba.com*).

Note: British schools are not accredited by US accreditation agencies. Instead, they receive a "Royal Charter."

ENGINEERING AND COMPUTER SCIENCE PROGRAMS

• **Carnegie Mellon School of Computer Science, Distance Education.** Software engineering and information technology graduate degrees (412-268-5067, *www.distance.cmu.edu*).

• **Rochester Institute of Technology On-line.** Highly regarded RIT offers a wide range of on-line graduate degrees, including information technology, software development and telecommunications engineering (800-225-5748, *www.distancelearning.rit.edu*).

• **Stanford Center for Professional Development** offers electrical and mechanical engineering, management science and computer science degrees (650-725-3000, *scpd.stanford.edu*).

*Rate subject to change.

MASTERS OF EDUCATION

• **Drexel University e-Learning Program** provides an on-line MS in higher education and other programs (877-215-0009, *www.drexel.com/online-degrees/masterdegrees.aspx*).

• **University of Illinois, Urbana-Champaign,** offers an on-line MS in curriculum, technology and education reform (217-244-3315, *cter.ed.uiuc.edu*).

MASTERS OF SOCIAL WORK PROGRAMS

• **Florida State University MSW Program** was among the first MSWs to be offered on-line (800-378-9550. *ssw.fsu.edu/index.php?clicklink-online-offcampus*).

• **University of North Dakota MSW Program** combines lectures and discussion. It also includes a fieldwork component (877-450-1842, *www.conted.und.edu/ddp/msw/index.html*).

Is It Important to Go to An Ivy League School?

Only seven CEOs from the top 50 Fortune 500 companies graduated from Ivy League schools.

Also: College students who were accepted at top schools but attended the less selective ones earned just as much 20 years later as their peers who attended highly selective colleges.

The Quarterly Journal of Economics, Harvard University, 1875 Cambridge St., Cambridge, MA 02138.

20

Safety Alert

A Police Detective Reveals Very Clever Ways To Hide Your Valuables

Most burglars like to get in and out of a house quickly. They will focus on closets and drawers and under the mattresses. Their favorite targets include cash, jewelry, checkbooks and credit cards, handguns, cameras and laptop computers.

The safest place to keep valuables is in a safe-deposit box or a safe built into the wall or the floor of your home. If you decide to use another location, let a trusted relative know about your hiding spot or put a note in your safe-deposit box describing the location. Otherwise, the valuables could be lost if you pass away or forget where they're hidden.

If there are young children in your house, make sure your hiding place isn't somewhere that they're likely to discover.

SIMPLE HIDING PLACES

Here are simple hiding spots for small items, such as cash, jewelry and rare coins...

• **Dry goods jar.** Seal your valuables in small plastic bags, then bury them in a large jar of rice or flour. Store near the back of a kitchen cupboard.

• **Frozen with vegetables.** Defrost a package of frozen vegetables, put your valuables in a small plastic bag and put the bag in the package. Glue the package shut and refreeze. Even if a thief did look in your freezer, he wouldn't take the time to defrost your peas. This is appropriate only for items that won't be damaged by being in the freezer and that are used infrequently, because it will take some time for the valuables to thaw out.

• **Tennis ball.** Cut a small slit in a tennis ball, squeeze the ball to open the slit and insert your

Detective Sergeant **Kevin Coffey**, who has 26 years of experience at a major US police department. He is founder of Corporate Travel Safety, LLC, which provides security products and seminars, Calabasas, CA, and on the Internet at *www.corporatetravelsafety.com*.

valuables. Put the ball back in its canister with two normal tennis balls. Make sure the canister doesn't rattle when moved, or you might tip off an alert thief.

• **Foam couch cushion.** Unzip a foam couch cushion, cut a slit into the foam, insert valuables and rezip. This is appropriate only for durable and flexible valuables, such as cash.

• **Diversion safe.** This is a small container that looks exactly like an ordinary household item, such as a can of brand-name soda or shaving cream. My favorite diversion safe is a book, which can be kept with other books on a shelf. To find products, click on "Travel Safes" in the travel products section of my Web site, *www. corporatetravelsafety.com/catalog.*

DO-IT-YOURSELF "SAFES"

These hiding spots will take a bit more time and effort to construct. They might be worth the trouble if you have basic carpentry skills and you keep a significant amount of valuables in your home. Some are best for small items, such as jewelry. Others can hide larger items, such as a laptop computer.

• **Posts of a poster bed.** The tops of the bedposts usually unscrew. Take the tops off, drill down into the wood posts to create hiding spaces for valuables (be careful not to drill into the grooves where the top screws in).

• **Fake pipe, vent or electrical outlet.** Add an unnecessary pipe or duct among the real pipes and ducts in your attic, basement, laundry room or kitchen, and store valuables inside. This pipe or duct should look as if it is part of the home's plumbing or heating, ventilation and air-conditioning (HVAC) system.

Or use a phony electrical outlet or vent to provide access to valuables hidden in the wall. The fake outlet or vent should match both the color and style of the real outlets or vents that are in your home.

Caution: Remove these valuables before you have your plumbing, HVAC or electrical system serviced.

• **Below a bookcase.** The lowest shelf of a wooden bookcase often is a few inches above the floor. You can turn the space below into a hiding area big enough for even your laptop

computer simply by cutting a secret door into the wood facing.

HOTEL ROOMS

Your best security options are the front-desk safe and the safe in your room. If these are not available, there's often room to hide things beneath the lowest dresser drawer. Pull the bottom drawer out completely and stash your valuables below, or put them behind the television in the armoire.

Another possibility is to bring along a diversion safe that looks like a personal-care product, such as shaving cream or hair spray.

Or lock valuables inside luggage. Locks can be pried open with screwdrivers, but few hotel thieves carry screwdrivers. There also are portable safes and steel briefcases on the market.

CARS

Valuables left in parked cars are at risk no matter how well they are concealed. When this must be done, the safest spot is in the trunk, under or behind the spare tire.

Stow all valuables in your trunk before you arrive at your destination. Otherwise a criminal could see you put something in the trunk, then break in when you walk away.

More from Detective Sergeant Kevin Coffey...

Stop Theft While Traveling

When traveling be aware that thieves just love carry-on bags (other people's, that is). Why? That is where travelers keep their valuables. Always rest your luggage in front of you—never to your side, in back of you or in a cart.

Also, be cautious when strangers strike up unprovoked conversations. Often, an accomplice may be waiting for you to be distracted. The best crooks are superb actors and will stage entirely believable fistfights or other dramas. While you're busy helping the "victim," someone else steals your wallet.

Be especially alert when strangers seem to require your help or offer to help you. Safeguard your property before you offer assistance—or bring the situation to the attention of a police officer or security guard.

Thieves have been known to squirt their targets with mayonnaise and then tell them that they are covered with bird poop or some other objectionable substance. The crook is kind enough to help wash the stuff off—while the accomplice does his work.

For other thief-thwarting strategies, log on to *www.kevincoffey.com* and click "Safety Tips."

Also from Detective Sergeant Kevin Coffey...

Hotel Identity Theft Scam

Don't give credit card information over the phone to the front desk when staying at a hotel.

Scam: An identity thief calls a hotel, asking for a guest with a common name. He/she is then connected to the guest's room and pretends to be calling from the front desk. He says there's a problem with the credit card and asks the guest to verify the account number, expiration date and security code. The scammer then sells the information or uses it to run up charges on your credit card.

Burglars Are as Smart as You Are

It's very difficult to find a place to hide a key or item of value that a professional burglar won't think of and find. From keys under the doormat to fake food cans, hollow "rocks," hidden drawers and hollowed-out wall spaces, professional burglars know most of the tricks.

Best defense: Invest in a personal safe made of fireproof, heavy-duty steel that can be bolted in place, and keep your most valuable items in it.

Also: The safest place for a spare key to your home is in the possession of a trusted neighbor —one who will also check your house while you're away.

Jean F. O'Neill, director, research and evaluation, National Crime Prevention Council, Washington, DC, *www.ncpc.org*.

Smart Crime Protection

Captain Robert Snow, commander of the Indianapolis Police Department's organized crime branch. He is also the author of *The Complete Guide to Personal and Home Safety* (Da Capo).

It's time for all of us to theft-proof our lives as much as we can. *Check out this advice for the home from a personal safety expert...*

• **Watch your back door.** Although many homes do have sturdy front doors, other doors often are not made of solid material and may shatter easily. (That's why police SWAT teams typically try the back door first when they need to break into a building.) Avoid doors with windows. Outside doors should be made of metal or solid wood. Sliding glass doors should have bar locks (metal bars that prevent anyone from sliding open the door).

• **Watch your windows, too.** The ubiquitous turn locks are no good for windows. They can be opened easily from the outside using only a butter knife. Get locks that require pressing a button to lock into rails on both sides (you can add these to existing windows)—or drill a hole in the window casing and insert a dowel so that the window can't be opened.

• **Consider replacing basement windows** —prime targets for thieves—with glass bricks, which are hard to break.

• **Install bright lights with motion detectors outdoors.** Beware of solar-powered lights, they may not illuminate when you need them.

There are plenty of precautions to take when you're away from home as well. Did you know that 30% of vehicle thefts involve keys left in the car—either accidentally or when running into a store for a quick errand? Car thieves also do quite well at beaches, pilfering purses or lost car keys from lounge chairs and using these keys' panic alarms to locate vehicles in the parking lot.

Cell Phone Smarts

If your cell phone is stolen, you pay for all calls that are made until you report the theft.

Example: One woman was stuck with a $26,000 bill when her phone was stolen while she was on vacation—the thief made a week's worth of international calls.

To decrease risk: Program a password into your phone so that only you can use it (check your owner's manual for instructions or call your phone service provider). Put a hold on your account when you notice the phone is missing, even if you think it's simply misplaced.

David Wood, founder of DialingforDeals.com, which offers tactics for saving money on phone bills and avoiding telephone scams, Desloge, MO.

Smoke Alarm Warning

Standard US smoke alarms do not have the most effective signal to awaken older adults. Because many people age 65 and older have problems hearing high-pitched sounds, they are more likely to awaken to a mixed-frequency signal (500 to 2500 Hz), such as those found in some smoke alarms for the hearing impaired, rather than the more common high-pitched alarms.

Strategy: Use an interconnected system that includes an alarm in each bedroom to increase the chance of being awakened in case of fire.

Dorothy Bruck, PhD, associate professor, Victoria University, Melbourne, Australia.

Cell Phone Dangers

Rebecca Shannonhouse, editor of Bottom Line/Health, Boardroom Inc., 281 Tresser Blvd., Stamford, CT 06901.

There are now more than 208 million cell phone users in the US—and researchers are beginning to identify some of the associated risks.

While studies have shown that there appears to be no increase in the risk for brain cancer among cell phone users, these devices may not be safe in all circumstances.

Driving and talking on a cell phone is dangerous—even if you're using a "hands-free" model. A new study indicates that motorists who talk on any type of cell phone show the same kind and

degree of impairment—such as slowed reaction times—as drunken drivers.

Individuals engaged in cell phone conversations experience "inattention blindness"—even though they're looking at the road and traffic, their ability to process information drops by as much as 50%, explains Frank Drews, PhD, professor of psychology at the University of Utah in Salt Lake City and coauthor of the study.

Some people do argue that other distractions, such as putting on makeup or talking to a passenger, are equally risky, but Dr. Drews doesn't buy this. "I have never seen a driver putting on makeup in the car—but at least every fourth or fifth driver is on a cell phone."

Meanwhile, in London, a 15-year-old girl recently suffered severe injuries after being struck by lightning while talking on her cell phone. People struck by lightning are often not critically injured, but holding a cell phone to the ear during a storm can provide a conduit that allows electricity—more than 100 million volts, in some cases—to flow into the body.

It pays to stop and think before picking up a cell phone.

Remember to Replace Supplies

Emergency food supplies should be replaced periodically. Mark on each container the date the item was bought.

- **Within six months,** you need to replace boxed powdered milk, dried fruit, crackers and instant potatoes.

- **Within a year,** replace canned meat and fish and vegetable soups…canned fruits, fruit juices and vegetables…cereal, peanut butter, jelly, baking powder and vitamin C.

Items that can be stored indefinitely (in airtight containers): Flour, vegetable oils, instant coffee, tea, salt, white rice, bouillon and dry pasta.

USA Today, 7950 Jones Branch Drive, McClean, VA 22108, www.usatoday.com.

In Case of Emergency...

Identify emergency contact numbers on your cell phone using the acronym "ICE," which stands for "in case of emergency." Emergency workers check cell phones and PDAs for the acronym so they can contact your loved ones. For multiple emergency contacts, identify with numbers the order in which these individuals should be contacted.

Examples: ICE-1-My wife, ICE-2-My son.

More information: ICE Contact USA, 877-564-6423, *www.icecontactusa.com.*

Emergency Life for Your Cell Phone

Charge 2 Go is a reusable emergency phone charger that is powered by one AA battery. Add a battery and plug the adaptor into your phone. Adaptors are available for most phone models. A two-hour charge provides up to three hours of talk time and 90 hours of standby time. Available in plastic or aluminum casing in black, blue, red or silver.

Cost: $25.*

More information: Charge 2 Go, 800-248-4694, *www.chargetogo.com.*

*Price subject to change.

Scammers Seek Ways to Profit from Our Natural Desire to Cut Taxes

James Glass, a tax attorney based in New York City and a contributing writer to both *Tax Hotline* and *Bottom Line/ Retirement*, newsletters published by Boardroom Inc.

The 10 most common tax scams today, as identified by the IRS, are outlined below. *Take precautions now...*

●**Phishing.** The hottest tax scam now, it involves bogus e-mail messages purportedly from the IRS that deceive victims into revealing confidential information—such as Social Security and bank account numbers. The con artists then use this information to commit ID theft.

How it works: An e-mail message says that there is some reason for the recipient to contact the IRS—such as to expedite a tax refund or to clear up a tax account problem. The message includes a link for the recipient to click to go to the IRS Web site, but the link actually goes to a counterfeit Web page that only looks like it is part of the IRS Web site. The Web page then prompts the individual to enter confidential information that is supposedly needed to resolve the problem.

Danger: The IRS notes that more than 100 different variations on this scam have appeared since November 2005, and that new ones are appearing all the time.

Self-defense: Know that the IRS never sends out unsolicited e-mails that discuss confidential tax matters or seek personal information—so if you do receive this type of e-mail, you know it is bogus.

●**Misuse of trusts.** For years, unscrupulous promoters have falsely sold trusts as tax-avoidance devices—and they continue to do so.

Sometimes the promoters say that by paying wage or investment income into a trust, an individual escapes the duty to pay income tax on it. Other scammers claim that by putting your home and other assets into a trust you own or control, you become able to deduct payments made to the trust for use of the house or assets. The scammer can claim anything that might be believed by a victim.

Reality: Trusts can serve many good, legal purposes, but tax evasion is not one of them. Generally, income earned in a trust continues to be taxable to you if you continue to control and use the trust assets. If you truly give away the assets within the trust, the income earned on them will be taxed to the trust itself or its owner—so tax payments will remain due.

It's true that there are particular types of trusts approved by the Tax Code and IRS that can reduce taxes under specific circumstances.

Self-defense: If you think you are obtaining one of these legitimate trusts, have it reviewed by an independent expert, such as a tax lawyer or CPA. Don't rely on the word of the person selling it.

• **Dubious credit-counseling agencies.** The IRS warns that many credit-counseling agencies that advertise being "tax exempt" and "nonprofit" charge debtors large fees while doing little or nothing to help them reduce their debts. The IRS is now reviewing and revoking the tax-exempt status of many of these.

Self-defense: Before going to a credit-counseling agency, ask for referrals from friends or your lawyer, accountant or other professional adviser who may have direct knowledge of a legitimate agency, and check its status with the Better Business Bureau.

• **Abuse of charities.** The IRS says that it is detecting growing abuse of charities by persons who set them up and then pay themselves very high "fees" for managing them, and/or use the funds in them for their own personal purposes. They rely on the goodwill of donors, and the fact that charities pay no taxes and, thus, generally receive little audit scrutiny, to escape detection. But the IRS says that it is now increasing audit examinations of suspicious charities.

Self-defense: Before donating to an unfamiliar charity...

• Obtain its IRS Form 990, *Return of Organization Exempt From Income Tax.* This tax return details how its funds are spent. Form 990s are available at *www.guidestar.org*, which has data on 1.5 million nonprofits.

• Check a charity's behavior against the recommended standards set by the Better Business Bureau's Wise Giving Alliance by checking its free evaluative reports on national charities at *www.give.org*.

• **Asset-hiding offshore transactions.** Many people move funds into foreign banks, brokerage accounts, trusts and/or investments (such as annuities) believing that after they move funds abroad, they are not required to report income earned on them—or can get away with not doing so.

Reality: US citizens are liable for income tax on all their income worldwide, and are required to report such income on their tax returns, no matter where it is earned or received. The IRS has initiated new enforcement efforts that have proven effective at finding funds in foreign accounts, such as by examining the records of US credit card companies to find cards drawing on funds abroad.

Self-defense: Always report all income from all sources.

• **Frivolous legal arguments.** There are always tax protestors arguing—and selling books and materials "proving"—false legal claims.

Examples: The 16th Amendment, which authorizes the income tax, was never properly ratified...the duty to file a tax return violates the Fifth Amendment right against self-incrimination or Fourth Amendment right against unreasonable search and seizure...the payment of taxes legally is "voluntary"...and so on.

In fact, people who act on such claims risk winding up with back tax bills, interest and expensive penalties.

Self-defense: Don't waste your money or time, or risk your wealth, on any of these materials.

• **Employment tax evasion.** Here employees instruct the employers to not withhold tax from wages, falsely claiming that they don't owe the tax, or claim greatly excessive tax-free "reimbursements" for medical expenses, business driving and other items.

Warning: During fiscal 2005, more than 50 individuals were sentenced to prison for employment tax evasion, for an average of 30 months. Employers can be held liable as well.

Self-defense: File a correctly filled out Form W-4 with your employer.

• **Return preparer fraud.** Unscrupulous tax return preparers seek business from potential clients by promising tax refunds to them even before reviewing their particular tax situations. This should be a big red flag to the potential client. But individuals who are eager to cut their taxes may believe such claims—or at least believe that if they themselves don't prepare the return, they won't be liable for false statements on it.

Warning: You are responsible for what's reported on your own tax return, no matter who prepares it. This means not only for paying the taxes, but also for penalties and potential fraud charges.

Self-defense: If the promises of your preparer sound too good to be true, they most likely are. It may be time to change to a "safe" preparer.

• **Zero wage "corrected" returns.** In this relatively new scam, the taxpayer files a substitute Form W-2 or "corrected" 1099 to reduce amounts reported as wages or business payments on an original W-2 or 1099.

The "corrected" income numbers may be reduced to zero—and often this is all reported on an amended tax return, Form 1040X, in the hope that the IRS will accept the amended return without referring to the data on the original return.

The IRS warns it is on to this scam and is checking such amended forms and filings.

Self-defense: File an amended return only if you have a legitimate correction to make.

• **The "no gain" deduction.** Here, filers attempt to eliminate their adjusted gross income (AGI) by deducting it on Schedule A. The filer lists his AGI under "Other Miscellaneous Deductions" and attaches a statement to the return that refers to court documents and includes the words "No Gain Realized."

Self-defense: Although it's increasingly common, this scam is based on yet another false legal argument and is easily identified and flagged by IRS computers that check tax returns for unusually large deductions—so don't even think about trying it.

More from James Glass, Esq....

What to Do If You See a Scam

If you think that you've seen any of the scams described in the article above, here's how to report it...

• **Phishing.** Forward the full text of all suspect e-mails to *phishing@irs.gov*, a special address set up by the IRS.

• **Tax fraud.** Report tax fraud on IRS Form 3949 A, *Information Referral*, available at *www.irs.gov* or by calling 800-829-3676. Fill it out and mail it to Internal Revenue Service, Fresno, California 93888. You can do so anonymously.

• **Abusive tax shelters.** The IRS has special forms and addresses for reporting abusive tax shelters, their promoters and salespeople and unscrupulous tax professionals. You can find all this information at *www.irs.gov* by typing "Reporting Abusive Shelters" in the search box.

Social Security Administration Warns Against Scam E-Mails

One e-mail with the subject line "Cost-of-Living for 2007 update" gives information about the 3.3% inflation adjustment to benefits for 2007, then directs the recipient to a counterfeit Social Security Administration (SSA) Web page to enter information to "update" his/her account. Any information entered is used by the scammer to commit identity theft. The SSA urges recipients to report such scam e-mails by calling 800-269-0271, or on-line at *www.socialsecurity. gov/oig*.

Alert: The IRS says that many such bogus e-mails have been sent out in its name as well, so expect more invoking of the SSA and other government agencies. Be wary of all such unsolicited e-mails.

More E-Mail Scams

Bob Hopper, manager of the computer crimes section, National White Collar Crime Center, *www.nw3c.org*. The center is a congressionally funded nonprofit corporation that helps law-enforcement agencies combat crimes, particularly those in high-tech areas.

Think you'll never fall for an e-mail scam? You're just the kind of person the scammers are looking for. E-mail scammers are not necessarily very clever. But they have learned to send out millions of bogus messages and hope that just a few recipients will fall for their traps.

They're never disappointed. And the victims are usually people who let down their guard because they think they could never be caught in a scam.

At best, you might suffer the temporary inconvenience of having your e-mail account hijacked. At worst, your identity could be stolen, leading to a financial loss and a lot of inconvenience.

Good news: You don't have to go to extraordinary lengths to avoid scams. But you do need to be vigilant and take some relatively simple steps to cut the chances of being scammed to nearly zero. *What you should know…*

THE BAIT

How do scammers mislead even the wary?

One particularly successful scam starts with an e-mail that purports to be from a bank, credit card company or PayPal, the payment system used by many Internet marketers, or even from your own Internet service provider (ISP). The e-mail looks authentic and even displays a credible replica of the company's logo.

The message might say, for instance, that your credit card was inadvertently charged $127.83, but it assures you that the error can be corrected. All you have to do is send certain information to a certain e-mail address. This information includes confirmation of your credit card number, your Social Security number, street address and telephone number.

In reality, the e-mail is from a scam artist who uses your information to buy products with your credit card or to apply for credit in your name—in other words, to steal your identity. In a short time, you can wind up with thousands of dollars of debt and a severely damaged credit record.

MORE E-MAIL SCAMS

•**Premium rate phone calls.** You receive an e-mail that gives you a seemingly plausible reason to make a phone call—to collect a prize that you've won or to help a relative who's trying to get in touch with you.

But the number you're asked to phone is one that bills the caller several dollars a minute, as numbers for horoscope readings and gambling tips legitimately do. In this case, the person you phone runs up the bill by getting you to stay on the line for as long as possible.

In the US, these "premium rate" numbers are easy to identify because they usually have a 900 or 976 prefix.

Trap: A call may be surreptitiously forwarded to such a number, and you'll never know

until you get the bill. Or you may be asked to phone overseas, where premium rate numbers can have many other prefixes.

•**Cheap prescription drugs can seem irresistible.** Scammers know this when they send e-mail that purports to be from a pharmacy that sells at a deep discount. To take advantage of the prices, you're asked to supply your address and credit card information. You never see the drugs—just huge charges to your credit card.

•**Work-at-home scams.** Want to make easy money by working in your home? In one popular scam, you get an e-mail that promises quick profits if you assent to receive retail goods at your home, repackage them and send them on to other addresses.

Scammers say they need this service to make sure the products are not damaged. In fact, the goods have usually been bought with fraudulent credit cards. The scam artist avoids detection by having them sent to your address, but needs your help in sending them on to him/her.

EFFECTIVE PROTECTION

•**Never open e-mail from an unknown source.** Even though the sender might not be trying to scam you, the message could contain computer codes that can mean big trouble for your machine.

In reality, however, most people do occasionally open unsolicited e-mail, especially if it appears to come from a legitimate source, such as a well-known company.

•**Always independently check with the company before responding to its e-mail.** Use Google or another search engine—not a phone number or Web address in the e-mail—to find the company's contact information. If it's a nationally known firm, phone and find out if it was actually the source of the e-mail. Or if you've previously received statements from the company, use contact information contained in that correspondence.

If it's a company that you don't know, contact the Better Business Bureau in the company's purported hometown to make sure that it has a clean record before dealing with it.

Similarly, check out any company that says it provides a way to earn money at home.

•**Don't give out your personal information**—phone number, address, etc.—to a company or person whom you don't know.

Also: When an e-mail asks for your password, assume it's a scam and delete the mail. The only parties who should know the password are you—and perhaps family members—and your Internet service provider. ISPs never ask because they already know.

•**Install security software** which protects your computer from e-mails that might contain viruses, spyware and other harmful programs sometimes referred to as "malware."

Most ISPs provide some degree of protection, which you can reinforce by installing your own security products from companies that include McAfee (866-622-3911, *www.mcafee.com*) and Symantec (408-517-8000, *www.symantec.com*).

Don't, however, be lulled into a false sense of security by thinking that even the best products will protect you from all harmful programs or from e-mail sent by scammers. Stay alert, and take the protective steps just mentioned.

•**Cut down on spam.** Sooner or later, nearly all e-mail addresses fall into the hands of spammers. To cut down on the amount of spam you get, change your e-mail address once or twice a year. That might seem inconvenient, but you can make this procedure less troublesome by e-mailing your friends and frequent correspondents whenever you change addresses.

Alternative: For family members and close friends, use an e-mail address that you rarely change. For all others, use one that you change periodically.

•**Change passwords twice a year.** This will reduce the chance that your passwords will fall into the wrong hands.

If, despite these steps, you fall victim to an e-mail scam, contact the Internet Crime Complaint Center at *www.ic3.gov*. The organization, a partnership between the FBI and the National White Collar Crime Center, channels complaints to the appropriate law-enforcement agencies. Also contact your ISP, which can take legal action against scammers.

Sadly, however, it's highly unlikely that you'll ever recover any money you lose.

Reason: E-mail scams are usually short-lived, and the perpetrators quickly move on. Nevertheless, reporting the crime is important because it

helps reduce the number of fraudulent e-mails that you and others receive.

How to Remove Personal Info From the Web

John Featherman, a personal privacy consultant based in Philadelphia.

The risks for identity theft are only getting worse. More local governments are making their records available on the Internet—so it is even easier to steal someone's identity—and data-harvesting companies are increasingly defending their rights.

It's smart to find out what information there is about you (and your loved ones) on the Internet. Each month, check in search engines such as Google.com, Whitepages.com, A9.com, Live.com, Yahoo.com, PrivateEye.com and Zabasearch.com. Search for variations of each person's name, and type the name in quotation marks ("Charlie Smith," "Charles G. Smith," etc.).

Even better: Set up a Google Alert (at *www.google.com/alerts*), which will inform you whenever the "crawler" finds old or new pages with your name. You can choose to be updated weekly, daily or as soon as a page is found. (It's best to get the information when it is found.)

To remove your personal information from the Web…

•**If you have your own Internet site**—for friends or for business clients—you can create a block against most search engines. For example, type "Removing information from Google" into Google Search, and click on "Websearch Help Center" for directions.

•**If your information appears on a public site**—say, in a phone directory—check whether the site has a mechanism for opting out. If not, contact the site and request that your information be removed.

Some local governments are reviewing their on-line documents so that Social Security numbers and other sensitive information can be edited out, but it is up to individuals to make sure this is done. If you find information that you want removed, ask the agency in writing to do so.

If any kind of fraud or illegal business practice is involved, the quickest way to get action is to contact the National Association of Attorneys General (202-326-6000, *www.naag.org/ag/ful_ag_table.php*)...the Federal Trade Commission (877-FTC-HELP, *www.ftc.gov*)...the Federal Communications Commission (*www.fcc.gov*)...and/or the consumer protection office for your specific state (*consumeraction.gov/state.shtml*).

Most job-search and dating services allow users to remove résumés and personal "portraits," but this doesn't mean that they will disappear from the Internet—other Web sites could have made the information accessible. Similarly, you can delete all or part of your own blog, but material from it still may be floating around, and you can't remove postings you have put on others' sites. People have been fired from jobs due to personal postings, particularly on social networking sites.

Of course, the safest thing is to not post personal information in the first place—but if you are going to do so, check privacy policies carefully...and post cautiously.

More from John Featherman...

ID Theft Protection

Most people know that it is risky to give out your Social Security number, but what do you do when it's required, such as when you are signing up for a new phone or insurance? New laws restricting access to Social Security numbers (SSNs) are likely, but they have not yet been put into effect. Since the passing of the *Patriot Act*, the government has required SSNs for more purposes, but the agencies are supposed to disclose whether it is required or only requested. Private companies can refuse to open an account or provide a service if you don't provide your SSN.

If you need the service but are worried about identity theft, offer to provide your SSN if you get a written statement that it is to be used only as an identifier. You may have to ask for a manager. If the company refuses, you have to decide whether you want the service enough to provide your SSN.

To Prevent Credit Card Fraud...

Audri Lanford, PhD, cofounder and codirector of Scam Busters.org, Boone, NC, a Web site that reports on scams and cons.

There are some simple things you can do to prevent credit card fraud. *See below for eight practical tips...*

• **Do not give out your account number on the phone** unless you originate the call.

• **Never provide your card number to a Web site that is not secure**—look for "https" in the site address and a padlock icon on the page.

• **Sign new credit cards as soon as you get them.**

• **Shred unwanted card applications.**

• **When using your card in public, shield it with your hand** so that people nearby cannot copy the number or use a cell phone or camera to capture it.

• **Carry only cards you really need.** Keep less-used ones securely at home.

• **Open bills promptly, and review each one for any charges you do not recognize.** Report any unrecognized charges immediately.

• **Don't respond to spam solicitations (unsolicited or junk e-mail) for credit cards,** and never send your credit card number via e-mail.

Don't Apply for Store Credit Cards in the Store

An application for credit includes your name, address, Social Security number and other information that makes you vulnerable to identity theft. You do not know the person in the store who takes the application, and you do not know who else will have access to it.

Self-defense: If you want a store credit card, apply for it on-line or mail an application to the credit department.

Curtis Arnold, president and founder, CardRatings.com, North Little Rock, AR.

Self-Defense Against ID Theft Ploy

A favorite ploy of identity thieves is obtaining instant credit in your name. A thief can walk into a store, pick out a big-ticket item and have a credit account approved in seconds, using your Social Security number and address.

Self-defense: Never carry your Social Security card. If you must carry a Medicare ID card, photocopy it and snip off the last four digits of your Social Security number (which is used as your Medicare ID number).

Also make sure the security software on your home computer is up-to-date. And, check your credit report at least once a year. You can get one free report per year from each of the three credit bureaus—Equifax, TransUnion and Experian. To request your report call 877-322-8228 or go to *www.annualcreditreport.com.*

Jay Foley, codirector of Identity Theft Resource Center in San Diego, *www.idtheftcenter.org.*

Smarter On-Line Shopping

When shopping on-line, paying with a credit card is safer than debiting your account or paying by check.

Reason: When you discover any charge that seems incorrect, you can dispute it—you have 60 days from the date of billing to do this. The credit card company will not pay the merchant until the dispute is resolved.

Also: Your maximum liability on a credit card that is stolen is only $50, and credit card companies often waive that.

Contrast: When you use a PayPal account to pay a merchant, unless you tell PayPal to use your credit card, funds are debited from your checking account immediately.

Mari J. Frank, Esq., a lawyer and privacy and identity theft expert in Laguna Niguel, CA, *www.identitytheft.org.* She is author of *Safeguard Your Identity* (Porpoise).

Check-Clearing Scam

Susan Grant, director, National Fraud Information Center, Washington, DC, *www.fraud.org.*

A check that you deposit can bounce after your bank reports that it has "cleared" into your account.

How: Federal law requires that your bank credit your account with the amount of any check you deposit within five days of the deposit. The funds will appear to be in your account—a teller may even tell you that the check has cleared.

But it can take more than five days for your bank to learn that a check you deposited is no good. In that case, you must pay the bank back.

Scam: A scam artist writes a large check to a victim, who sees the check's amount credited to his/her account after five days, and thinks that the check is good. The con artist then convinces the victim to wire a smaller amount *back* to him.

Typical example: The scammer gives a check that is larger than the agreed-upon amount to pay for an item and says the extra amount is to cover additional expenses. (In the case of one seller/victim, who sold his classic car to someone overseas, the extra was to cover shipping.) The scammer then asks the victim to wire the excess money to either him or another party after the check clears.

Trap: Once the scammer has your money, he disappears. His check then bounces. You owe the full amount of the check—plus you have lost the money the scammer tricked you into wiring.

Self-defense: Be skeptical of any large check written to you by a stranger. If a stranger gives you a check and asks you to wire some of the money anywhere for any reason, be suspicious and call the whole deal off.

Check Fraud Protection

Protect yourself against this common check fraud scam.

How it works: A thief steals from your mailbox a check you have written, washes off your writing with a common household cleaner, then fills in the now blank check.

Protection: Use a Uni-Ball 207 pen to write checks. It uses a pigment that bleeds into the paper so it can't be washed out by chemicals.

Frank Abagnale, president of Abagnale and Associates, secure-technology consultants in Washington, DC, *www.abagnale.com.*

On-Line Banking Danger

Remote Access Trojans (RATs) are hidden programs that are downloaded to unsuspecting users' computers. RATs do nothing until a user types in the Web address of any on-line bank. Then the programs copy every subsequent keystroke and send the information to cyberthieves, giving them a way to access the user's account. Banks are working on security measures to authenticate consumers, such as interrupting access with personal questions for which the customer supplied answers beforehand.

Dan Clements, CEO, CardCops.com, a Web site that monitors on-line fraud, Malibu, CA.

Rare Coins Can Be Fool's Gold

Don't be fooled by the advertisements to buy "rare" gold coins. They often are not rare.

Example: A one-tenth–ounce gold coin (with a $5 face value) offered for $71, plus $31 for shipping, handling and insurance. Although the premium to the price of gold might be acceptable (with gold at over $670* an ounce, the actual gold value of the coin is about $64), the shipping charges can be exorbitant. And there's very little chance that there will be any collectible value above the value of the gold.

Chuck Whitlock, an expert on white-collar crime, con artists and scams, Vancouver, WA, *www.chuckwhitlock.com* and author of *Mediscams* (St. Martin's).

*Price subject to change.

More from Chuck Whitlock...

Not All 800 Numbers Are Legitimate

Scammers will frequently use call forwarding to send a phone call made to an 800 line to the 900 line at a different telephone company. The moment the phone call is connected, you start being charged as much as $25 per minute. Because this forwarding is done electronically and automatically, the phone companies don't know what is happening until the victims call to complain about the excessive charges on their phone bills.

The criminals using this scam generally keep the forwarding in place for only a month or two, then move on to different phone numbers—but in just that short time, they are able to take in many thousands of dollars.

Self-defense: Call your phone company if you think that you have been scammed. Phone companies are not required to credit customers for these illicit charges, but they often will to avoid any bad publicity.

Beware of Internet Romance Scams

On-line romance swindles have become so common that an entire Yahoo users group is dedicated to them (*http://groups.yahoo.com/groups/romancescams*). The scams use phony postings at dating sites to ask for money. The postings usually involve claims of being stranded in an overseas country, such as Nigeria, and having difficulty cashing paychecks. Scammers have a few chats with targets, claim to be falling in love, then ask for favors involving money.

Self-defense: Beware of anyone who seems too good to be true...claims to be in trouble overseas...or says "I love you" after a brief on-line acquaintance.

Index